Vegan
Everyday

500 Delicious Recipes

Douglas McNish

Robert
ROSE

For complete cataloguing information, see page 576.

Disclaimer

The recipes in this book have been carefully tested by our kitchen and our tasters. To the best of our knowledge, they are safe and nutritious for ordinary use and users. For those people with food or other allergies, or who have special food requirements or health issues, please read the suggested contents of each recipe carefully and determine whether or not they may create a problem for you. All recipes are used at the risk of the consumer.

We cannot be responsible for any hazards, loss or damage that may occur as a result of any recipe use.

For those with special needs, allergies, requirements or health problems, in the event of any doubt, please contact your medical adviser prior to the use of any recipe.

Design and Production: Kevin Cockburn/PageWave Graphics Inc.
Senior Editor: Judith Finlayson
Recipe Editor: Tracy Bordian
Copy Editor: Gillian Watts
Recipe Tester: Audrey Wilson
Proofreader: Gillian Watts
Indexer: Gillian Watts
Food Photography: Colin Erricson
Associate Photographer: Matt Johannsson
Food Styling: Michael Elliott
Prop Styling: Charlene Erricson

Additional fruit and vegetable market photos: © iStockphoto.com/acceptfoto

Cover image: Roasted Cauliflower and Chickpea Tacos (page 196)

The publisher gratefully acknowledges the financial support of our publishing program by the Government of Canada through the Canada Book Fund.

Published by Robert Rose Inc.
120 Eglinton Avenue East, Suite 800, Toronto, Ontario, Canada M4P 1E2
Tel: (416) 322-6552 Fax: (416) 322-6936
www.robertrose.ca

Printed and bound in Canada

1 2 3 4 5 6 7 8 9 MI 23 22 21 20 19 18 17 16 15

Contents

Acknowledgments

Writing a cookbook is no small feat, and by no means is it a one-person show. From start to finish many people are involved, each playing an important role in the process and each lending his or her expertise to take it from concept to bookshelf. I would like to offer my thanks to the following people.

To my mom, who passed away as I began work on this book. I will always remember making gnocchi with you when I was little. May your spirit live on through what you taught me, and may your inspiration that encouraged me to follow my dreams to become a chef shine through in these pages.

To my wife, Candice, for your constant support, for believing in me, for always being my cheerleader and for your ability to see the good in everything. I do not know where I would be without you. I am truly blessed to call you not only my wife but also my best friend.

To my friend Lisa Borden, who reminds us all "If you think you are too small to make a difference, try sleeping with a mosquito." Thank you for believing in me, and thank you for treating me like family. Since the day you walked through the doors at Raw Aura, my life has changed for the better. I can't thank you enough.

To Mika, the bean.

To Bob Dees, for believing in this book and for your constant business support.

To Judith Finlayson, for your expert eye, immense knowledge of classical cooking, skilled editing and countless hours of work on this book. Without you this would not have been possible. For this I thank you.

To Tracy Bordian, for your expertise and insight day in and day out. It has been a pleasure to work with you again. I truly believe that my recipes are enhanced by your dedication and tireless hard work.

To Gillian Watts, for having the editorial eyes of a hawk.

To Kevin Cockburn and everyone at PageWave Graphics, for the hours and hours of work that it takes to bring this all together.

To my staff. Thank you for your hard work and dedication. A business is difficult to run, and I would not be able to do this without you.

Last but not least, to everyone who supports what I do — thank you. I would not be where I am without you. If you have ever purchased a meal I have cooked, come to one of my classes or supported me in any other way, this book is for you.

Introduction

Today the vegan lifestyle is widely celebrated. Learning about it is as easy as turning on the television or flipping through your favorite magazine, and vegan cookbooks make regular appearances on the bestseller lists. But more than 10 years ago, when I started down the path of organic vegan cuisine, the world was a different place. Many people had never even heard the word *vegan*. Not surprisingly, there were very few vegan cookbooks on the market. As a chef I found it very difficult to hone my craft in vegan cuisine, because so few resources were available. So instead of consulting other sources, I worked at deconstructing recipes I had already mastered, using plant-based ingredients to achieve similar results. Not every experiment was a success, but through trial and error I was able to move along and expand my recipe repertoire.

As a classically trained chef, my job is to create fabulous flavors, textures and colors. As a vegan, I use my skill set to determine the best way to make my recipes taste just as good as — if not better than — their traditional counterparts. When I develop a new recipe, I like to think of the process as one part alchemy, one part knowledge and one part learning from my mistakes. I begin every recipe with an idea of its ultimate taste, texture and mouthfeel. In other words, I pretty much envision the final product and work backward to recreate it.

The recipes I have included in this book showcase an incredibly wide selection of dishes that use whole, plant-based ingredients — dishes that will appeal to both you and your family and quickly become favorites. It is my hope that this book will be the only cookbook you reach for when you want to prepare organic, gluten-free, vegan meals.

One of the reasons I work so hard to create delicious, nutritious recipes is that, these days, a great deal of vegan food on the market is simply not healthy. It is loaded with salt and preservatives, refined grains and starches and unhealthy sugars and fats. I have experienced this myself. At an early stage of my career, while working as a chef in a vegan café, I gained 40 pounds because of poor vegan food choices. Vegan food is like any other type of food: there is both good and bad. Always read the labels and make sure you understand what you are eating. Choose whole, unprocessed foods — fruits and vegetables, nuts and seeds, grains and legumes — all of which are nutrient-dense.

Once you learn some basic cooking techniques and become familiar with the ingredients you should keep in your pantry (see page 6), making my recipes is as easy as preparing their traditional counterparts.

Whether you are a committed vegan or simply looking to introduce more plant-based foods into your diet, I want you to have fun with the recipes in this book. I encourage you to try out my techniques and recipes using your own ingredients. With a little practice and an understanding of basic cooking, you can be a chef in your own home.

From my kitchen to yours,
Chef Doug McNish

The Vegan Gluten-Free Pantry

Stocking Your Pantry

Having a well-stocked pantry allows you to produce delicious and healthy meals in no time. In this section, I have included information on the basic pantry items used to make the recipes in this book.

Always choose local, organic and, whenever possible, fresh ingredients. Organic produce is preferable because it reduces your exposure to pesticides. When purchasing corn and soy products, always buy organic to avoid genetically modified organisms (GMOs); most of the soy and corn grown in North America is genetically modified. Farmers' markets, independent grocers and health food stores with a focus on ethical and fair trade products are your best bets for making informed purchases. If you do your shopping at larger supermarkets, check their product sourcing.

Using Whole Foods

While I strive to use only whole foods in my cooking, I occasionally must use refined products in order to recreate a desired mouthfeel or texture. Ingredients such as white rice flour or potato, tapioca or arrowroot starch are often necessary in order to create the best end result. White rice flour, for example, has a very fine texture because the bran has been removed from the grain before it is processed into flour. Using this refined product rather than whole-grain brown rice flour can sometimes mean the difference between a very smooth texture and one that is unacceptable. Not only do starches aid in producing acceptable textures, in many cases they also help to bind other ingredients together.

Vegan gluten-free baking has come a long way in the past few years, but for

---

Spices and Herbs

Spices

- allspice
- bay leaf
- berbere
- black peppercorns
- black salt (kala namak)
- caraway seeds
- cardamom, whole and ground
- cayenne pepper
- chiles, dried
- chili powder
- Chinese five-spice powder
- chipotle powder
- cinnamon, sticks and ground
- cloves, ground

- coriander seeds, whole or ground
- cumin, whole or ground
- curry powder
- fennel seeds, whole or ground
- fenugreek seeds
- garlic powder
- ginger, ground
- hot pepper flakes
- nutmeg, whole and ground
- onion powder
- paprika, sweet, hot and smoked
- saffron
- salt, fine sea
- turmeric, ground

- vanilla bean powder
- vanilla pods, whole
- vanilla extract, alcohol-free

Herbs (Fresh and Dried)

- basil
- bay leaves
- chives
- cilantro
- dill
- makrut (kaffir) lime leaf
- oregano
- parsley
- rosemary
- sage
- thyme

Vanilla

Unless whole vanilla bean is specified, most of the recipes in this book can be made using either alcohol-free organic vanilla extract or organic vanilla powder, which is made from dried, ground vanilla beans. Both can be found in well-stocked health food stores or online. Using vanilla bean powder will produce a better final flavor in some recipes, but it will not affect texture, so using extract is perfectly acceptable.

Vanilla extract		Vanilla powder
1/2 tsp (2 mL)	=	1/4 tsp (1 mL)
1 tsp (5 mL)	=	1/2 tsp (2 mL)

the moment, some recipes do require the use of refined products. I have, however, kept their use to a bare minimum.

Seasonings

apple cider vinegar, raw (unpasteurized)
Unpasteurized apple cider vinegar contains the "mother," the active healthy bacteria from the fermentation process. You can see it floating at the bottom of the bottle. It is said to be detoxifying and great for digestion.

balsamic vinegar
Some vinegars may be clarified using animal components such as gelatin. If you have concerns, ask your purveyor.

brown rice vinegar
Brown rice vinegar is available in most well-stocked supermarkets and natural food stores. It has a milder, more mellow flavor than traditional white rice vinegar.

dry mustard
Dry mustard is great for spice rubs and spice blends and, in a pinch, can be used in many soup or stew recipes where Dijon mustard is called for. It is available in most well-stocked supermarkets.

hoisin sauce
If you are following a gluten-free diet, be sure to look for gluten-free hoisin sauce. It is available online and at specialty retailers.

hot sauce
If you are following a gluten-free diet, look for hot sauces labeled as such. They are available in most well-stocked supermarkets and natural food stores.

mirin
Mirin is a sweet Japanese cooking wine that is low in alcohol. The sugars are naturally fermented and the flavor is complex, which makes it great for seasoning Japanese dishes.

miso (brown rice miso, yellow miso, chickpea miso)
Many forms of miso contain gluten (in ingredients such as barley). If you are following a gluten-free diet, look for gluten-free miso pastes. They are available in most well-stocked supermarkets and natural food stores.

nutritional yeast
Nutritional yeast adds a deep, rich, cheesy flavor to many foods and can be used as a seasoning on popcorn, rice, quinoa or even vegetables, to name a few things. It is usually grown on beet molasses and then pasteurized, rendering it inactive. Look for brands that are fortified with B vitamins, as they are nutritionally beneficial.

red wine vinegar

Red wine vinegar has a wonderful full-bodied flavor that works well in marinades and salad dressings. Use it in recipes that contain stronger herbs such as rosemary and oregano.

rice wine vinegar

Rice wine vinegar is made from Japanese rice wine. It is higher in alcohol and lower in sugar than brown rice vinegar, making it good for marinades, sauces and sushi applications.

tamari, wheat-free

Wheat-free tamari is full-bodied, rich and flavorful. It helps to add umami (a savory taste) and great mouthfeel to many dishes. Substitute an equal amount of gluten-free soy sauce, but be warned: gluten-free soy sauce does not have the same rich flavor as tamari. Look for tamari in most well-stocked supermarkets and natural food stores.

toasted sesame oil

Toasted sesame oil is an Asian condiment used to season foods such as sushi and sauces. Be sure to look for oil from toasted sesame seeds, as the regular kind does not have the same sesame flavor.

white wine vinegar

White wine vinegar has a mild, pleasant flavor that's great for dressings, dips and sauces. Red wine vinegar is generally suggested for more robust dishes, while white wine vinegar is for milder applications such as light vinaigrettes. It is available in most well-stocked supermarkets.

Sweeteners

agave nectar, raw

Agave nectar is the syrup that is produced from the center (also called the piña) of a cactus native to New Mexico. Be sure to use organic raw (not processed) agave nectar. It is a 100% natural (non-GMO) sweetener that contains naturally occurring fructose and is low on the glycemic scale, which means that it releases glucose slowly, providing sustained energy. I use high-quality ethically sourced raw agave nectar because it does not spike blood sugar levels. It also provides a wonderful texture for many recipes.

Based on my research, I am convinced that organic raw agave nectar is a healthy, wholesome ingredient. However, there is a lot of controversy surrounding agave nectar. I suspect it is based on the processed versions. If using agave nectar concerns you, try substituting an equal amount of organic coconut nectar or pure maple syrup. Keep in mind that coconut nectar has a thicker, more viscous texture than agave nectar, and maple syrup has a high water content, which makes it thinner.

cane sugar, raw

Raw cane sugar is produced from the first pressing of sugar cane and contains some of the natural molasses (and therefore some trace minerals). Raw cane sugar may also be labeled as "turbinado sugar." It has a deeper, darker flavor than traditional refined brown sugar.

coconut sugar

Coconut sugar is a natural sweetener made from the sap of cut flower buds of the coconut palm. It is said to be very low on the glycemic scale (which means it won't spike blood sugar levels), and it contains some trace minerals. Coconut sugar tastes like light brown sugar and can be substituted in equal measure for cane sugar in most recipes. It is available in most well-stocked supermarkets and natural food stores.

maple syrup, pure

Pure maple syrup is made from the sap of maple trees. The sap is slowly boiled to evaporate the water and concentrate the sap, resulting in a sweet syrup that contains many trace minerals and has a wonderful, complex flavor. It's delicious in sauces, baked goods and desserts.

molasses (light/fancy, dark and blackstrap)

Molasses is the by-product remaining after sugar — derived either from cane or beet — has been processed. It is thick and rich, and great for use in various baking applications, sauces (such as barbecue) and some baked goods. Blackstrap molasses is a particularly good choice if you are following a vegan diet, as it contains high levels of B vitamins.

Oils

grapeseed oil

This high-heat, neutral-flavored cooking oil works well for frying and sautéing. Not only does it not impart flavor into food, it also remains stable and does not begin to smoke when heated to high temperatures. Look for brands that are organic and free from chemical extraction processes.

hemp seed oil, cold-pressed

This dark, rich raw oil is extracted from hemp seeds and is high in omega fatty acids. It has a very low smoke point, and because heat will damage the heart-healthy omegas, it should be used only for cold applications and not for cooking.

olive oil, extra virgin

Extra virgin olive oil is a wonderful fat used in dressings, dips, sauces and other cold applications. It has a moderate smoke point, but I prefer not to use it for cooking because I'm concerned that too much heat will damage the heart-healthy fats. It's also a bit pricey, so I save it for cold applications.

Coconut Products

coconut butter

Coconut butter is a blend of the meat and oil from raw coconut. It is thick and rich, and great to use in spreads, dips, sauces and desserts. It is available in most well-stocked supermarkets and natural food stores.

coconut cream

Coconut cream is similar to coconut milk except that it is lower in water content and higher in fat. It is great for use in sauces, dips, desserts, ice creams and more. Look for it in well-stocked supermarkets, Indian markets and natural food stores.

coconut milk

Coconut milk is made by grating the tough flesh from a brown coconut. It is then strained and generally canned for commercial use. It is great to use in sauces, dips, soups, stews and curries.

coconut oil (virgin and refined)

Virgin coconut oil is the oil that comes from the first cold pressing of a coconut. It is full of healthy fats. It tastes mildly of coconut, so keep that in mind when cooking with it. Refined coconut oil is made from subsequent pressings of the same coconut and does not have a coconut flavor. Since the coconuts have been pressed previously, most of the healthy fats have already been removed.

coconut, unsweetened shredded unsulfured

Shredded coconut is a wonderful addition to desserts and salads, can be used as a coating when breading foods or can even be sprinkled on cereals. Look for unsulfured coconut to ensure that you are avoiding preservatives. Sulfur dioxide can cause severe headaches (among other effects) when consumed by some people.

Nuts and Nut Butters (Raw)

Whole raw nuts are wonderful sources of energy. I keep them in my pantry to toss with salads, blend into sauces and dressings, or enjoy as a snack on their own. While most people tend to be concerned about the calories and fat found in nuts, many studies have shown them to be very beneficial and heart-healthy.

I also keep a jar of organic peanut butter and one of almond butter in my pantry for energy in a flash. I like to add nut butters to smoothies, use them as a dip with fresh vegetables such as carrots and celery, or spread them on crackers.

Seeds and Seed Butters (Raw)

Like nuts, whole raw seeds are wonderful sources of energy that can be used in similar ways. They are very nutrient-dense.

I always keep a jar of tahini on hand. You can add it to the blender with a few other ingredients and whip up a sauce in no time. Pumpkinseed butter is great for spreading on your favorite gluten-free bread or crackers or blending into smoothies.

- chia seeds, white or black
- flax seeds, golden or brown
- hemp seeds, shelled
- pumpkinseed butter
- pumpkin seeds
- sesame seeds, white and black
- sunflower seeds
- tahini

Soy Products

edamame

Edamame are young soybeans that can be purchased either shelled or with the shell on. They are great on their own or as a snack or can be tossed with your favorite stir-fry or salad for an added kick of protein.

silken tofu (firm, medium, soft)

Silken tofu is usually purchased in an aseptic box that is shelf-stable. It is often blended and used in recipes for sauces, dips or creamy desserts. It also works in baked applications. Do not stir-fry silken tofu; it will fall apart in the pan while cooking.

tempeh, frozen (unpasteurized)

I like to use frozen unpasteurized tempeh in my recipes because it has a stringy, meaty texture and contains living bacteria that are beneficial for the gut. Use tempeh anywhere you would use beans or meat in traditional recipes. It is great in stir-fries and pasta dishes and can be ground and used as a sandwich filling, among other uses. If frozen unpasteurized tempeh is not available, you may substitute regular refrigerated tempeh.

tofu (firm, medium, soft)

Tofu is made by combining soy milk with an acid such as lemon juice so it coagulates. It comes in various textures, and each has various applications. I use firm tofu for stir-fries, and medium or soft tofu for baked or stewed applications.

Grains/Pseudo-grains

amaranth

Technically a seed (like quinoa), amaranth is high in protein and naturally gluten-free. Use amaranth in soups, stews, puddings and cookies or as a substitute for rice.

buckwheat

A high-protein pseudo-grain (actually a seed, not a grain), buckwheat is a member of the rhubarb family. It is high in protein and B vitamins and is naturally gluten-free. It is great in cereals, puddings, desserts and more.

millet

Millet is a small, yellow, naturally gluten-free grain that resembles cornmeal. In some markets it can actually be white, yellow or red. It is an ancient grain that is great in cereals, soups and stews or used as a substitution for rice in many dishes. It is naturally high in B vitamins, calcium and iron. It is also naturally gluten-free.

oats (quick-cooking rolled oats and large-flake [old-fashioned] rolled oats)

Look for oats in the packaged and bulk sections of supermarkets. Quick-cooking rolled oats are oat groats that have been lightly roasted, steamed, cut in half and then pressed to make them cook more quickly. Large-flake oats have been pressed even flatter for quick cooking. All types of oats are perfect in cereals, breads and energy bars. Generally, the larger the oats, the more nutritionally dense they will be.

quinoa

Quinoa resembles little seeds and is available in the packaged and bulk sections of supermarkets. Quinoa comes in three colors — white, red and black — but is most readily available in white. All three types can be used in soups, stir-fries, stews, chilis and virtually anywhere rice is used. White quinoa is softer and fluffier when cooked (as opposed to red and black quinoa), so it's a better substitute for rice. Red and black quinoa are denser in texture and nutty in flavor; they are great in salads and stuffings. Quinoa is a complete protein and naturally gluten-free.

teff

Teff is a nutrient-dense gluten-free grain that is the size of a poppy seed. It is great in soups and stews and pairs well with other grains such as rice or quinoa. It can also be used in place of cornmeal in some recipes.

wild rice

Wild rice is actually a nutrient-dense grass that can be cooked and added to soups, stews, stuffings and salads or used in place of regular white or brown rice. Look for it in the bulk section of your local supermarket.

Corn

cornmeal, stone-ground (fine, medium, coarse)

Cornmeal is made from ground and dried pieces of corn. It is available in both the packaged and bulk sections of supermarkets. Always look for organic corn products to avoid GMOs. Cornmeal is used to make creamy polenta when cooked with a liquid (most commonly water); it also makes a crisp gluten-free breading for your favorite foods.

corn tortillas, organic gluten-free

Available at most well-stocked supermarkets and natural food stores, corn tortillas make a quick and convenient meal when wrapped around your favorite filling. You can also toast them and dip the crispy pieces in your favorite sauce or dip. They are most commonly available in the 6-inch (15 cm) size. Always look for organic corn products to avoid GMOs.

Rice

black rice

Black rice is deep black in color and is very nutritionally dense. The non-sticky varieties make a great addition to sushi or you can substitute them anywhere traditional rice would be used, such as stir-fries or salads.

brown rice (short-grain and long-grain)

These small, nutrient-dense brownish beige grains can be found in both the packaged and bulk sections of supermarkets and natural food stores. Brown rice has many applications; try it in sushi, soups, stews, salads or on its own as a side dish with lunch or dinner. Short-grain brown rice has a higher starch content, so it cooks up a little more plumply than long-grain rice. Long-grain rice is a bit fluffier when cooked.

jasmine rice, brown

Brown jasmine rice resembles traditional long-grain rice in appearance and is readily available in most well-stocked supermarkets. This rice is perfectly suited for Indian or Thai dishes because of its natural aromatic flavor (it is sometimes also called "fragrant rice"). It can be used in soups, salads, stews or curries.

jasmine rice, white

White jasmine rice resembles white long-grain rice and can be found in both the packaged and bulk sections of supermarkets. It is a little softer than brown jasmine rice because it has had the outer bran removed in processing. This rice is perfectly suited for Indian or Thai dishes because of its natural aromatic flavor (it's also sometimes called "fragrant rice"). White jasmine rice has a soft, fluffy texture when cooked.

red rice

Red rice is a small reddish brown grain available in most well-stocked supermarkets and natural food stores. Some of the common varieties are Bhutanese, Camargue and Thai red rice. It has a mild, nutty taste that is perfect for dishes with more robust flavors. Try using it in curries, soups, stews and salads. Even though some red rice may be labeled as glutinous, it is naturally gluten-free ("glutinous" refers to its starch content).

brown rice pasta, dried gluten-free

Dried brown rice pasta is convenient to have on hand so you can whip up meals in a pinch (toss with sauce and a protein and enjoy). Gluten-free brown rice pasta available in many shapes and sizes (lasagna, fusilli, macaroni, spaghetti, fettuccini, linguine). Always cook gluten-free pasta in a lot of rapidly boiling water.

brown rice Asian-style noodles

Brown rice noodles are generally an opaque white color. You can find them with the pasta in well-stocked supermarkets. They are perfect in stir-fries, soups and salads. They are commonly used in Thai cuisine but are easily adapted to other styles such as Chinese, Japanese and Mediterranean.

brown rice tortillas, gluten-free

These wraps are generally white in color and readily available in $8\frac{1}{2}$-inch to 10-inch (20 to 25 cm) sizes. They are generally sold frozen since they contain no preservatives (bring to room temperature before using). They are great for making burritos, wraps, quesadillas and more. It is good practice to toast these a little bit to help make them pliable before wrapping.

Gluten-Free Flours

Keep a supply of basic gluten-free flours in your pantry. Brown rice, sorghum and white rice flours are very common, but white rice flour is refined, so I try to limit its use. Tapioca and arrowroot starch, although refined, are commonly used in order to achieve good results. Other flours such as quinoa, millet, buckwheat and chickpea flours (all of which are excellent because they are whole foods) can be used for specific purposes.

Making Your Own Flour

If you are lucky enough to have a high-powered blender, you can grind your own grains to make flour. Just blend 1 to 2 cups (250 to 500 mL) of grain at high speed until flour-like in consistency (be careful not to blend too much at a time or the blender may overheat). You can also make flour using a grain mill, which can be found in most restaurant supply stores or kitchenware stores and usually comes with instructions on how to grind your own flours.

Know Your Flour

Gluten-free flours can vary drastically in texture from brand to brand. This has to do with the various grinds of the flours. Some brands have been ground very finely, so they resemble the texture of fine pastry flour, while others have a very coarse grind. The grind will have a major impact on the outcome of the recipes.

Coarsely ground flours will produce results that have a grittier texture. In addition, the recipes may not hold together as well as those made with a finer grind. That's why more finely ground flours are optimal for use in my recipes (unless otherwise noted). Finely ground flours will absorb the liquids and

fats in the recipes and hold together as needed. If you have questions about the grinds of your flours, it is best to speak directly with the company selling the flours or with your local purveyor.

Using Gluten-Free Flours

When working with gluten-free flours, it is particularly important to aerate them before measuring: place the flour in a bowl and whisk. This prevents lumps, which are likely to form from sitting. Scoop out the desired amount using a dry measure, and use a kitchen knife to level it off. Adding a bit of air helps to ensure lightness in the end result.

In general, vegan, gluten-free recipes will never be identical to their traditional wheat flour counterparts. This is particularly true of those that use whole-food ingredients. Items such as pancakes, waffles and breads that contain nutritious gluten-free flours will almost always seem denser than their traditional versions. This is due in part to the lack of gluten. Gluten is a protein that helps to bind ingredients together and also provides a chewy texture.

blanched almond flour

Blanched almond flour is made using raw almonds that are pasteurized, have their skins removed and then are finely ground. It's used in recipes that require very finely ground flour or where a delicate texture is needed, such as shortbreads or cakes.

brown rice flour
Brown rice flour is made from ground brown rice and is perfect in cakes and pastries or for use as a breading.

buckwheat flour
Made from ground buckwheat groats, buckwheat flour is perfect for making pancakes, muffins, cookies and other baked goods.

chickpea flour
Naturally high in protein, chickpea flour yields a dense texture. It can be used as a binder to replace eggs in some recipes. Be aware that using too much chickpea flour can impart a mildly bitter flavor to products.

quinoa flour
Quinoa flour makes a great crispy coating for fried or deep-fried foods. It can also be used in baked goods such as cookies, muffins and cakes.

sorghum flour
Sorghum is commonly used in gluten-free flour blends for baked goods, cakes and pastries. To avoid any grittiness in your final product, be sure to choose finely ground sorghum.

tapioca starch
Tapioca starch (also called tapioca flour) is commonly used in gluten-free flour blends, baked goods, cakes and pastries. It provides a chewy texture in baked goods, adds crispness to pastries and can be used as a thickener in sauces and other recipes. It can also replace cornstarch.

white rice flour
Similar to brown rice flour but made from white rice, which is refined, this flour yields a smooth, less gritty result in baked goods such as cakes, pastries, pancakes and doughs.

Starches and Other Thickeners

agar (powder and flakes)
Agar is a clear seaweed (also referred to as "kanten") that is native to Asia. It is often used as a vegetarian gelling agent (in place of animal-derived gelatin) in sauces, desserts and other recipes. Agar flakes and agar powder are usually interchangeable in recipes, but do follow the manufacturer's instructions on the packaging. As a rule of thumb, agar flakes are more readily available than agar powder. If a recipe calls for agar powder and all you have is flakes, double the amount of flakes. For example, if a recipe calls for 1 tsp (5 mL) powder, you would substitute 2 tsp (10 mL) flakes. Some exceptions may apply, so read each recipe well before trying.

arrowroot starch
Arrowroot starch is a finely ground powder derived from various types of tropical South American plants. It is available in most well-stocked supermarkets and natural food stores. It is a common ingredient in gluten-free baking, used to help bind and hold together other gluten-free flours.

cornstarch
Cornstarch is a finely ground starch derived from corn. Always purchase organic cornstarch to avoid GMOs. Cornstarch is used as a thickener; it can be whisked with cold water to help thicken and bind sauces (this is commonly referred to as a "slurry"). If following a gluten-free diet, look for brands labeled gluten-free — many brands have been processed in the same facility as products containing gluten.

xanthan gum
Xanthan gum is a finely ground white powder made from the fermented sugars most commonly found in corn. For this reason, look for xanthan gum that is organic or, at the very least, verified non-GMO. It is used as a thickener and binder in gluten-free baking, as well as a stabilizer in desserts, sauces and dips. A little goes a long way (too much can make foods quite gummy), so be sure to follow the recipe and use only what you need.

Baking
baking powder, gluten-free
Baking powder is a fine powder made from a carbonate (baking soda), a weak acid (cream of tartar) and a moisture-absorbing agent. It is usually used in baking recipes to help leaven where yeast is not used. It works by releasing carbon dioxide, which helps to create air pockets and make the dough rise. Many baking powders are not gluten-free (they can contain wheat flour), so ask your purveyor if you have any questions.

baking soda
A common leavening agent used in baked goods, baking soda is a finely ground white powder that is available in well-stocked supermarkets. Baking soda begins to release carbon dioxide into a batter as soon as it comes into contact with something acidic and a liquid. Recipes that call for baking soda must be mixed after the soda has been added.

cacao nibs, raw
Raw cacao nibs are small brown pieces of the whole cacao bean. They are the pieces that fall off the bean when making cacao powder, after it has been roasted, processed and split. The nibs look like small chocolate chips but are much more bitter in flavor

because they contain no added sugars. Look for them in the bulk section of well-stocked supermarkets and natural food stores.

cacao powder, raw
Raw cacao powder is made by milling whole raw cacao beans at low temperatures. It has been defatted of much of the cacao butter (the fat found in chocolate and cacao beans), making it powder-like in consistency. When a recipe calls for raw cacao powder, an equal amount of cocoa powder can be substituted, but be aware that the flavor will not be as deep and rich.

chocolate chips, non-dairy
You can find non-dairy chocolate chips in the packaged and bulk sections of well-stocked supermarkets and natural food stores. Look for chocolate chips that have no dairy products added and, if you are following a gluten-free diet, that are certified gluten-free. They are a delicious addition to baked recipes such as cookies or muffins.

maca root powder
Maca is a root vegetable native to the region of the Andes Mountains in South America. It is light beige in color and has a malty, almost burnt caramel flavor. It is great in desserts, sauces and smoothies. Look for it in well-stocked supermarkets and natural food stores.

Legumes
Legumes are a significant component of the vegan diet. Purchasing dried legumes in bulk can save you money. It also allows you to cook the exact amount you need at one time. If using canned legumes, choose products packaged in BPA-free cans and with no sodium added. Be sure to rinse them under cold running water and drain well before using.

Legumes I like to use include:

- adzuki beans
- black beans
- cannellini beans
- chickpeas
- kidney beans
- lentils, green and red
- lupini beans
- mung beans
- navy beans
- pinto beans

Other Ingredients

- arame
- Dijon mustard
- dulse flakes
- mayonnaise, vegan
- non-dairy butter or margarine, unsalted
- spirulina powder
- sun-dried tomatoes
- tomato paste
- tomato purée
- tomatoes, canned (whole, diced)
- vegetable stock

Basic Equipment

You may already have most of the basics required to make the recipes in this book. If you are new to a vegan diet, you can make most of the recipes with the kitchen tools noted below. Once you become accustomed to this way of eating, I recommend that you consider investing in a juicer because fresh juices are so nutrient-dense. A high-powered blender, although expensive, is a wonderful machine that allows you to make a smooth purée of any nut, seed, vegetable or fruit, among other uses.

- baking dishes
- baking sheets
- blender
- chef's knife
- cutting board
- fine-mesh sieve
- food processor
- mixing bowls
- nut-milk bag
- paring knife
- tongs
- vegetable peeler

Breakfasts

Lemon Vanilla Cashew Yogurt

Enjoy this creamy "yogurt" for breakfast with fresh strawberries, blueberries or raspberries. Sprinkle with some chia and hemp seeds for added protein.

**MAKES
3 CUPS (750 ML)**

Tips

If you have a high-powered blender, use it for this recipe. If using a standard blender, you may need to blend a little longer to achieve a smooth texture.

To soak the cashews: Place in a bowl with 4 cups (1 L) water. Set aside for 8 hours. Drain.

● **Blender**

2 cups	raw cashews, soaked (see Tips, left)	500 mL
1 cup	water	250 mL
1½ tsp	finely grated lemon zest	7 mL
½ cup	freshly squeezed lemon juice	125 mL
¼ tsp	organic vanilla powder (see Tips, page 20) or ½ tsp (2 mL) alcohol-free organic vanilla extract	1 mL

1. In blender, combine cashews, water, lemon zest, lemon juice and vanilla. Blend at high speed until smooth and creamy, stopping the motor to scrape down sides of blender jar as necessary. Serve immediately or transfer to an airtight container and refrigerate for up to 1 week.

Amaranth Oatmeal

This recipe is a creamy alternative to traditional oatmeal. Amaranth also provides a complete protein. Served piping hot, it's perfect for cool mornings.

MAKES 4 SERVINGS

Tips

Amaranth is an ancient grain that is available in most well-stocked supermarkets and natural food stores.

For additional nutrition, top your bowl of cereal with nuts and seeds, such as raw cashews, almonds, sunflower seeds, hemp seeds or chia seeds.

3½ cups	water	875 mL
1 cup	amaranth, rinsed and drained (see Tips, left)	250 mL
⅓ cup	pure maple syrup (see page 9) or ¼ cup (60 mL) raw agave nectar	75 mL
½ tsp	ground cinnamon	2 mL
Pinch	fine sea salt	Pinch

1. In a saucepan, combine water, amaranth, maple syrup, cinnamon and salt; bring to a boil. Cover, reduce heat to low and cook for 30 minutes or until amaranth is tender and porridge-like and all the liquid has been absorbed. Serve immediately.

Steel-Cut Oats Bowl

This is a simple way to prepare a quick, filling, yet nourishing breakfast bowl. Grinding the steel-cut oats means you can cook them in far less time than they normally require.

MAKES 4 TO 6 SERVINGS

Tips

If you don't have a high-powered blender, use a clean coffee grinder for grinding the oats. You will need to grind them in 4 batches of ¼ cup (60 mL) each.

To make this dish even creamier, substitute an equal amount of your favorite non-dairy milk (such as Almond Milk, page 61) for the water.

Hemp seeds are considered a complete protein, meaning that they contain all eight essential amino acids. One tablespoon (15 mL) raw shelled hemp seeds provides up to 5 grams of protein and appreciable amounts of vitamins B_1 (thiamine) and B_6 (pyridoxine), folate, phosphorus, magnesium, zinc and manganese. Two tablespoons (30 mL) hemp seeds meet your daily requirement for omega-3 essential fatty acids.

High-powered blender (see Tips, left)

1 cup	gluten-free steel-cut oats	250 mL
3 cups	boiling water (see Tips, left)	750 mL
3 tbsp	pure maple syrup	45 mL
¼ tsp	organic vanilla powder (see Tips, page 20) or ½ tsp (2 mL) alcohol-free organic vanilla extract	1 mL
½ cup	blueberries	125 mL
2 tbsp	raw shelled hemp seeds (see Tips, left)	30 mL
1 tbsp	chia seeds	15 mL
1 tbsp	goji berries	15 mL

1. Place oats in blender and blend at high speed until flour-like in consistency. Transfer to a bowl.
2. Pour boiling water over ground oats and whisk until smooth. Stir in maple syrup, vanilla and blueberries.
3. Transfer mixture to a serving bowl. Top with hemp seeds, chia seeds and goji berries. Serve immediately or transfer to an airtight container for up to 5 days.

Slow-Cooked Apple Cinnamon Oatmeal

Make this sweet, hearty oatmeal before you go to bed. Let it cook overnight so you can wake up to the comforting aromas of apples and cinnamon.

MAKES 4 SERVINGS

Tips

Coconut cream is higher in fat than coconut milk. It can be found in most well-stocked supermarkets or natural food stores. If you can't find it, substitute an equal quantity of canned coconut milk (not coconut milk beverage) in this recipe.

Organic vanilla powder can be found in most well-stocked supermarkets and natural food stores. It is made from dried and ground whole vanilla beans and will add a lot of flavor to your dishes. You can substitute ½ tsp (2 mL) alcohol-free organic vanilla extract in this recipe.

Use a fine-tooth grater, such as the kind made by Microplane, to grate the nutmeg.

Do not lift the lid of your slow cooker while cooking. Heat will escape and you will need to add 20 to 30 minutes of cooking time to your recipe.

- **Medium (about 4 quart) slow cooker**

2 cups	chopped apples	500 mL
2 cups	chopped bananas (about 2 large)	500 mL
1	can (14 oz/400 mL) full-fat coconut cream (see Tips, left)	1
2 cups	Almond Milk (page 61)	500 mL
1 cup	gluten-free steel-cut oats	250 mL
3 tbsp	organic coconut sugar	45 mL
1 tbsp	pure maple syrup	15 mL
½ tsp	ground cinnamon	2 mL
¼ tsp	organic vanilla powder (see Tips, left)	1 mL
⅛ tsp	freshly grated nutmeg (see Tips, left)	0.5 mL
3 tbsp	Whipped Non-dairy Butter (page 554), cut into cubes (optional)	45 mL

1. In slow cooker stoneware, combine apples, bananas, coconut cream, almond milk, oats, coconut sugar, maple syrup, cinnamon, vanilla and nutmeg. Cover and cook on Low for 8 hours.

2. Using a wooden spoon, stir oatmeal, scraping up any brown bits from bottom of stoneware. Stir in non-dairy butter (if using). Serve immediately or transfer to an airtight container and refrigerate for up to 5 days.

Açai Superfood Bowl

This breakfast bowl is perfect for beginning your day.

MAKES 2 SERVINGS

Tips

Using frozen berries helps make the mixture thick and rich. You can substitute an equal quantity of frozen strawberries or raspberries for the blueberries.

Açai powder is available in well-stocked supermarkets, natural food stores and online specialty stores.

● **Blender**

1 cup	freshly squeezed orange juice	250 mL
½ cup	frozen blueberries (see Tips, left)	125 mL
¼ cup	chia seeds	60 mL
2 tbsp	freeze-dried açai powder	30 mL
¼ tsp	alcohol-free organic vanilla extract (see page 7)	1 mL
½ cup	chopped mango	125 mL
¼ cup	each chopped apple, raspberries and hulled strawberries	60 mL
2 tbsp	raw shelled hemp seeds	30 mL
2 tbsp	raw cashews	30 mL

1. In blender, at high speed, blend juice, berries, chia, açai powder and vanilla until smooth. Transfer to a serving bowl. Top with remaining ingredients. Serve immediately.

Quinoa Maple Berry Porridge

Maple syrup and fresh berries make this a sure-fire hit.

MAKES 4 SERVINGS

Tip

I like to use Almond Milk (page 61) for this recipe, but any higher-fat non-dairy milk, such as Cashew Milk (page 61) or Coconut Milk (page 62), will work too.

3 cups	non-dairy milk (see Tip, left)	750 mL
1 cup	white quinoa, rinsed and drained	250 mL
1 cup	each blueberries, raspberries, and hulled strawberries, divided	250 mL
¼ cup	pure maple syrup	60 mL
½ tsp	ground cinnamon	2 mL
½ tsp	alcohol-free organic vanilla extract	2 mL
¼ cup	raw shelled hemp seeds	60 mL
¼ cup	raw cashews	60 mL

1. In a saucepan, combine milk, quinoa, ½ cup (125 mL) each of the berries, maple syrup, cinnamon and vanilla; bring to a boil. Reduce heat and simmer, stirring occasionally, until most of the liquid has been absorbed, 18 to 20 minutes. Divide mixture among four serving bowls. Top each with 2 tbsp (15 mL) of each of the berries and 1 tbsp (15 mL) of the hemp seeds and cashews. Serve immediately.

Roasted Peach Chia Seed Pudding

This delicious breakfast is best made with ripe fresh peaches during the height of summer. To make a complete meal, serve with a glass of Matcha Me Green Juice (page 41).

MAKES 2 SERVINGS

Tips

I like to use Almond Milk or Cashew Milk (page 61) for this recipe, but any type of non-dairy milk works well.

Be sure to use raw (not processed) agave nectar. It is a 100% natural (non-GMO) sweetener that contains naturally occurring fructose and is low on the glycemic scale, which means that it releases glucose slowly, providing sustained energy.

If you cannot find organic vanilla powder, substitute ½ tsp (2 mL) alcohol-free organic vanilla extract.

To slice peaches, run a paring knife around the middle of the fruit through to the stone. Using your hands, twist the peach into two halves. Slice the half without the stone into the desired number of pieces. For the other half, use your knife to loosen and remove the stone before slicing.

- Preheat oven to 500°F (260°C)
- Rimmed baking sheet, lined with parchment paper

1½ cups	non-dairy milk (see Tips, left)	375 mL
⅓ cup	chia seeds	75 mL
3 tbsp	raw agave nectar, divided (see Tips, left)	45 mL
¼ tsp	organic vanilla powder (see Tips, left)	1 mL
2	peaches, pitted and sliced (see Tips, left)	2
1 tbsp	melted coconut oil	15 mL
½ tsp	ground cinnamon	2 mL

1. In a bowl, whisk together milk, chia seeds, 2 tbsp (30 mL) agave nectar and vanilla. Cover and set aside for 15 minutes so chia seeds can absorb liquid and swell.

2. Meanwhile, in a bowl, toss peaches with coconut oil, remaining 1 tbsp (15 mL) agave nectar and cinnamon, until well coated. Spread evenly on prepared baking sheet and roast in preheated oven for 15 minutes or until peaches are tender and slightly browned. Remove from oven and transfer roasted peaches to a serving bowl.

3. Pour prepared chia mixture over peaches. Serve immediately or cover and refrigerate for up to 2 days.

Buckwheat Coconut Pancakes

The blend of three clean, gluten-free flours in this recipe yields soft, moist pancakes. I love to serve these with a big dollop of Whipped Non-dairy Butter (page 554) and a drizzle of warm maple syrup.

MAKES 8 PANCAKES

Tips

To soak the cashews: Place in a bowl with 2 cups (500 mL) water. Set aside for 30 minutes. Drain.

For richer pancakes, substitute an equal amount of Almond Milk or Cashew Milk (page 61) for the water.

When working with any flour, particularly those that are gluten-free, whisk before measuring. This aerates the flour and ensures more accurate measuring. Be sure to use a dry measure (not a glass measuring cup) and to level off with the side of a knife.

The texture of my pancake batters is very thick — often closer to cookie dough than batter. However, they soften in cooking. If you find the batter too thick, add more water, 1 tbsp (15 mL) at a time, until you reach the desired consistency.

Because gluten-free flours vary so much among brands, it is hard to be precise about the quantity of liquid required in any recipe.

Blender

1 cup	buckwheat flour	250 mL
½ cup	brown rice flour	125 mL
¼ cup	coconut flour	60 mL
1½ tsp	baking soda	7 mL
¼ tsp	ground cinnamon	1 mL
⅛ tsp	fine sea salt	0.5 mL
1¼ cups	(approx.) water (see Tips, left)	300 mL
½ cup	raw cashews, soaked (see Tips, left)	125 mL
½ cup	chopped banana (about 1 small)	125 mL
¼ cup	melted coconut oil	60 mL
2 tbsp	raw agave nectar (see Tips, page 22)	30 mL
¼ tsp	organic vanilla powder or ½ tsp (2 mL) alcohol-free organic vanilla extract	1 mL

1. In a bowl, whisk together buckwheat flour, brown rice flour, coconut flour, baking soda, cinnamon and salt. Set aside.

2. In blender, combine water, soaked cashews, banana, coconut oil, agave nectar and vanilla. Blend at high speed until smooth. Add cashew mixture to flour mixture and mix until well combined and no lumps remain, adding more water if necessary. (Batter should be thick.)

3. Heat a nonstick skillet over medium heat. Drop batter into pan, using about ¼ cup (60 mL) batter for each pancake. Cook for about 4 minutes, depending on the thickness of your batter, until golden brown on the bottom and bubbles form on the top. Flip and cook for about 2 minutes more, or until golden brown on other side and cooked through. Transfer to a plate and set aside, keeping warm. Repeat with the remaining batter.

Coconut-Crusted French Toast

This recipe is a wonderfully sweet dairy-, egg- and sugar-free alternative to traditional French toast. I like to serve it with warm maple syrup and fresh berries.

MAKES 4 SERVINGS

Tips

Choose medium-shred unsweetened coconut for this recipe — it sticks to the bread easily.

I like to use gluten-free bread made without preservatives and added starches.

Most good-quality gluten-free bread needs to be stored in the freezer until used. To defrost, place slices in a shallow pan and set aside in a warm place for 1 hour.

The French toast can also be baked. Preheat oven to 400°F (200°C) and line a baking sheet with parchment paper. In Step 4, transfer prepared bread to baking sheet and cook in oven for 12 to 15 minutes, or until golden brown and crunchy, flipping halfway through the cooking time. Serve immediately.

• Blender

2 cups	Almond Milk (page 61)	500 mL
1 cup	chopped bananas (about 2 small)	250 mL
¾ cup	brown rice flour, divided	175 mL
1 tbsp	melted coconut oil	15 mL
¾ tsp	ground cinnamon, divided	3 mL
¼ tsp	organic vanilla powder (see Tips, page 26) or ½ tsp (2 mL) alcohol-free organic vanilla extract	1 mL
1 cup	unsweetened dried shredded coconut (see Tips, left)	250 mL
Pinch	fine sea salt	Pinch
8	slices gluten-free bread (see Tips, left)	8
¼ cup	grapeseed oil, divided	60 mL

1. In blender, combine almond milk, banana, ¼ cup (60 mL) brown rice flour, coconut oil, ½ tsp (2 mL) cinnamon and vanilla. Blend at high speed until smooth. Transfer to a shallow container and set aside.

2. In a bowl, toss together coconut, remaining ½ cup (125 mL) brown rice flour, remaining ¼ tsp (1 mL) cinnamon and salt.

3. Dip each slice of bread in milk mixture, coating both sides, and then dredge in coconut mixture until evenly coated. Transfer to a tray.

4. In a large skillet over medium-high heat, heat 1 tbsp (15 mL) grapeseed oil (see Tips, left). Working in batches, cook prepared bread until golden brown on the bottom, 3 to 5 minutes, adding more oil as necessary. Flip and cook other side for 2 to 3 minutes, until golden brown and cooked through. Serve immediately.

Chocolate Hazelnut Waffles

These light and fluffy waffles are a staple on my brunch menu.

MAKES 4 TO 6 WAFFLES

Tips

Potato starch is different from potato flour — be sure to use potato starch in this recipe.

Coconut flour is available in most well-stocked supermarkets and natural food stores.

Substitute 3 tbsp (45 mL) cocoa powder for the raw cacao powder.

Because gluten-free flours vary among brands, it is difficult to be precise about the quantity of liquids in any recipe. For this recipe you want the batter to be thick but almost pourable. If it is too thick, add almond milk, 2 tbsp (30 mL) at a time. When in doubt, preheat the waffle iron and test a small amount of batter.

To make blueberry waffles: Omit cacao powder and hazelnuts. Add 1 cup (250 mL) frozen blueberries to blender in Step 3.

- **Blender**
- **Preheated waffle iron**

2 tbsp	ground raw flax seeds	30 mL
¼ cup	hot water	60 mL
1 cup	white rice flour	250 mL
¾ cup	brown rice flour	175 mL
¼ cup	potato starch (see Tips, left)	60 mL
2 tbsp	each almond, coconut and tapioca flour	30 mL
2 tbsp	raw cacao powder (see Tips, left)	30 mL
2 tbsp	organic coconut sugar	30 mL
1 tsp	gluten-free baking powder	5 mL
¼ tsp	organic vanilla powder (see Tips, page 26)	1 mL
¼ tsp	fine sea salt	1 mL
½ cup	chopped raw hazelnuts	125 mL
1½ cups	Almond Milk (page 61)	375 mL
1 tsp	raw apple cider vinegar	5 mL
2 tbsp	melted coconut oil	30 mL
2 tbsp	raw agave nectar (see Tips, page 27)	30 mL
1 tsp	finely grated lemon zest	5 mL
2 tbsp	freshly squeezed lemon juice	30 mL

1. In a bowl, whisk together flax seeds and hot water. Cover and set aside for 10 minutes.

2. In another bowl, whisk together white rice flour, brown rice flour, potato starch, almond flour, coconut flour, tapioca flour, cacao powder, coconut sugar, baking powder, vanilla and salt. Add hazelnuts and stir just until combined.

3. In blender, combine almond milk, vinegar, coconut oil, agave nectar, lemon zest and lemon juice. Blend at high speed until smooth. Add to flour mixture with flaxseed mixture and whisk until no lumps remain.

4. Drop about ¼ cup (60 mL) batter onto lightly oiled preheated waffle iron. Close iron and cook following manufacturer's instructions, until crispy and golden. Serve immediately.

Fluffernutter Sandwich

This is a rich and sinful treat similar to the sweet, fluffy sandwich of the same name. I like to serve it with a side of Tempeh Bacon (page 38) and a tall glass of Orange Creamsicle Juice (page 46).

Tips

Be sure to use raw (not processed) agave nectar. It is a 100% natural (non-GMO) sweetener that contains naturally occurring fructose and is low on the glycemic scale, which means that it releases glucose slowly, providing sustained energy.

Organic vanilla powder can be found in most well-stocked supermarkets and natural food stores. It is made from dried and ground whole vanilla beans and will add a lot of flavor to your dishes. If you cannot find it, substitute ½ tsp (2 mL) alcohol-free organic vanilla extract.

Substitute 4 pieces of your favorite gluten-free toast for the English muffins.

½ cup	hazelnut butter	125 mL
¼ cup	raw cacao powder	60 mL
3 tbsp	raw agave nectar (see Tips, left)	45 mL
¼ tsp	organic vanilla powder (see Tips, left)	1 mL
½ cup	blueberries	125 mL
½ cup	hulled strawberries	125 mL
2	gluten-free English muffins, split and toasted (see Tips, left)	2

1. In a bowl, combine hazelnut butter, cacao powder, agave nectar and vanilla; stir until smooth. Gently fold in blueberries and strawberries, being careful not to break their skins.

2. Place 2 English muffin halves on a serving plate. Spread each with half of the hazelnut butter mixture. Place other halves of English muffins on top and spread tops with the remaining mixture, creating 2 layered open-face sandwiches. Serve immediately.

Breakfast Club Sandwich

Why relegate the club sandwich to lunch? Smoky tempeh bacon, creamy vegan mayonnaise and sliced avocado make this version a worthwhile start to your day.

MAKES 1 LARGE SERVING

Tips

Be sure to use raw (not processed) agave nectar. It is a 100% natural (non-GMO) sweetener that contains naturally occurring fructose and is low on the glycemic scale, which means that it releases glucose slowly, providing sustained energy.

Liquid smoke is a seasoning made from water vapor that has been exposed to wood smoke and then condensed. It adds a smoky flavor to foods without needing to use a smoker. You can find it in most well-stocked supermarkets and natural food stores.

To help hold the sandwich together, pierce each half with a wooden skewer.

Substitute an equal amount of Basic Chickpea Hummus (page 72) for the mayonnaise.

2 tbsp	wheat-free tamari	30 mL
1 tbsp	water	15 mL
4 tsp	grapeseed oil, divided	20 mL
2 tsp	raw agave nectar (see Tips, left)	10 mL
⅛ tsp	liquid smoke (see Tips, left)	0.5 mL
3	pieces thinly sliced (¼ inch/5 mm) firm tofu	3
3	pieces gluten-free bread, toasted	3
¼ cup	Vegan Mayonnaise (page 550), divided	60 mL
4	leaves romaine lettuce	4
¼	avocado, thinly sliced	¼
3	slices tomato	3
4	pieces Tempeh Bacon (page 38)	4

1. In a bowl, whisk together tamari, water, 1 tsp (5 mL) grapeseed oil, agave nectar and liquid smoke. Add tofu slices and toss to coat. Cover and set aside for 30 minutes or overnight (if overnight, refrigerate).

2. In a skillet over medium heat, heat remaining 3 tsp (15 mL) grapeseed oil. Remove tofu from marinade (discard marinade), shake off excess liquid and cook for 2 to 3 minutes per side, until lightly golden. Remove from heat and set aside.

3. Spread 2 tbsp (30 mL) mayonnaise on one piece of toast. Top with 2 lettuce leaves, avocado and tofu. Spread remaining 2 tbsp (30 mL) mayonnaise on second piece of toast and place, mayo side up, on top of tofu. Add remaining lettuce, tomato and bacon. Top with remaining piece of toast and cut in half. Serve immediately.

Breakfast Wrap

This wrap is perfect for those mornings when you are craving something hearty and filling.

Tip

To make a simple scrambled tofu that can be used for this recipe, crumble 1 package (16 oz/500 g) firm or extra-firm tofu. In a large skillet over medium heat, heat 3 tbsp (45 mL) grapeseed oil. Add crumbled tofu and cook, stirring frequently, until lightly browned. Add 1 tbsp (15 mL) chopped fresh thyme leaves, $\frac{1}{2}$ tsp (2 mL) ground cumin and $\frac{1}{4}$ tsp (1 mL) ground turmeric. Cook, stirring occasionally, for 2 to 3 minutes, until aromatic. Remove from heat and stir in $\frac{3}{4}$ to 1 cup (175 to 250 mL) nutritional yeast and $\frac{1}{4}$ cup (60 mL) wheat-free tamari. Store leftovers in the refrigerator in an airtight container for up to 5 days.

1½ cups	Scrambled Tofu with Caramelized Onions, Mushrooms and Peppers (page 30)	375 mL
8	pieces Tempeh Bacon (page 38)	8
½ cup	Vegan Shredded Mozzarella (page 537)	125 mL
2	Gluten-Free Pita Breads (page 474)	2
2 tbsp	grapeseed oil	30 mL

1. Lay pitas flat on a clean work surface. Spread $\frac{3}{4}$ cup (175 mL) scrambled tofu evenly across center of each pita, leaving a 1-inch (2.5 cm) border on each side. Top each with 4 pieces of bacon, followed by $\frac{1}{4}$ cup (60 mL) cheese.

2. Fold sides of one pita over filling; then, starting at the edge closest to you, roll up tightly to form a cylinder. Repeat with the remaining pita and filling.

3. In a large skillet over medium heat, heat oil. Place wraps in pan, seam side down, and cook for about 5 minutes, until bottoms are golden brown. Turn over and cook on other side until golden brown and pitas are heated through, about 5 minutes. Serve immediately.

The Elvis Wrap

Inspired by Elvis's favorite sandwich, this wrap combines creamy roasted bananas, chunky peanut butter and sweet maple syrup. It's a filling breakfast treat. You can also cut these wraps in half and serve them for dessert.

MAKES 2 WRAPS

Tips

If your bananas ripen too quickly, peel and transfer them to a resealable bag. Freeze for the next time you want a cold, creamy smoothie.

Use high-quality organic cinnamon. You'll get the freshest flavor by grinding whole cinnamon sticks in a clean spice grinder.

- **Preheat oven to 400°F (200°C)**
- **Baking sheet, lined with parchment paper**

2 to 3	bananas, cut into 1-inch (2.5 cm) chunks	2 to 3
2 to 3 tbsp	pure maple syrup	30 to 45 mL
1 cup	chunky peanut butter, divided	250 mL
1/4 tsp	ground cinnamon, divided (see Tips, left)	1 mL
2	Gluten-Free Pita Breads (page 474)	2

1. In a large bowl, toss bananas with maple syrup until well coated. Transfer to prepared baking sheet and bake in preheated oven until golden brown, 10 to 12 minutes. Remove from oven and set aside until cool enough to handle.

2. Lay 1 pita flat on a clean work surface. Spread 1/2 cup (125 mL) peanut butter across center of pita, leaving a 1/2-inch (1 cm) border on each side. Top with half of the roasted bananas and sprinkle with 1/8 tsp (0.5 mL) cinnamon.

3. Fold sides of pita over filling; then, starting at the edge closest to you, roll up tightly to form a cylinder. Repeat with the remaining pita and fillings. Serve immediately or transfer to an airtight container and refrigerate for 1 day.

Scrambled Tofu with Caramelized Onions, Mushrooms and Peppers

This cheesy-tasting (see Tips, page 31) breakfast dish is full of protein and healthy fats. Serve it with a side of Tempeh Bacon (page 38) and some crunchy toast.

MAKES 6 SERVINGS

Tips

To crumble tofu, break it into bite-size pieces. Then rub each piece between your fingers to break it into smaller bits.

To chop fresh thyme: Pinch the stem at the bottom with two fingers. Pulling upward with the finger and thumb of your other hand, strip the leaves. Reserve stems for soups or broths (discard after cooking). Use a sharp knife to chop the leaves, being careful not to chop too much or too hard, as this will bruise the leaves and cause the thyme to discolor.

Black salt (kala namak) comes from the Himalayas and northwest Pakistan. The salt contains sulfuric compounds that have an eggy flavor, which is why it is often used in vegan dishes that are similar to traditional egg dishes.

¼ cup	grapeseed oil	60 mL
4 cups	quartered button mushrooms	1 L
2 cups	chopped red bell pepper	500 mL
½ cup	chopped onion	125 mL
2 lbs	crumbled firm tofu (see Tips, left)	1 kg
2 tbsp	chopped fresh thyme leaves	30 mL
1½ tbsp	wheat-free tamari	22 mL
1 tsp	ground cumin	5 mL
⅛ tsp	ground turmeric	0.5 mL
⅓ cup	nutritional yeast	75 mL
⅛ tsp	black salt (optional; see Tips, left)	0.5 mL

1. In a large skillet over high heat, heat oil. Add mushrooms, red pepper and onion and cook, stirring occasionally, for 5 to 6 minutes or until vegetables are softened and light golden.

2. Stir in tofu and cook, stirring constantly, for 5 to 6 minutes, until heated through and lightly golden. Stir in thyme, tamari, cumin and turmeric and cook for 2 to 3 minutes, until spices are fragrant and most of the liquid has evaporated.

3. Remove from heat and stir in nutritional yeast and black salt (if using). Serve immediately or cover and refrigerate for up to 1 week.

Variations

Scrambled Curry Tofu: In Step 2, omit the thyme, increase the amount of cumin to 2 tsp (10 mL) and add 1 tbsp (15 mL) curry powder, 1 tsp (5 mL) ground coriander and 1 tsp (5 mL) minced gingerroot. At the end, stir in ¼ cup (60 mL) chopped tomato and cook until heated through.

Cheesy Broccoli Hemp Tofu Scramble: In Step 2, add 2 cups (500 mL) chopped broccoli (florets only). Increase the amount of nutritional yeast to 1 cup (250 mL) and stir in ½ cup (125 mL) raw shelled hemp seeds.

Cheesy Grits with Spinach

This version of a traditional Southern dish uses nutritious organic stone-ground grits to create a creamy, savory dish the whole family will love.

Tips

Naturally there is no cheese in this recipe, but the nutritional yeast adds an appealing cheese-like flavor. It also provides vitamin B_{12}, which is challenging to obtain if you are a vegan.

Substitute an equal amount of Cashew Milk (page 61) or Coconut Milk (page 62) for the almond milk.

1 cup	Almond Milk (page 61; see Tips, left)	250 mL
½ tsp	fine sea salt, divided	2 mL
¼ cup	organic stone-ground grits	60 mL
1 cup	nutritional yeast	250 mL
2 tbsp	Whipped Non-dairy Butter (page 554)	30 mL
2 tbsp	grapeseed oil, divided	30 mL
2 tbsp	finely chopped onion	30 mL
4 cups	packed baby spinach leaves	1 L
1	tomato, sliced 1 inch (2.5 cm) thick	1

1. In a small saucepan, bring almond milk and ¼ tsp (1 mL) salt to a boil. Add grits and whisk until thickened, 2 to 3 minutes. Reduce heat and simmer, stirring constantly with a wooden spoon, for 15 to 20 minutes or until mixture begins to thicken and pull away from sides of pan. Add nutritional yeast and butter and cook, stirring constantly, until well incorporated. Remove from heat and set aside.

2. In a skillet over medium heat, heat 1 tbsp (15 mL) grapeseed oil. Cook onion, stirring occasionally, until translucent, about 4 minutes. Add spinach and remaining salt and cook, stirring occasionally, until wilted, 1 to 2 minutes. Add spinach mixture to cooked grits and stir to combine. Transfer to a serving bowl and set aside.

3. In another skillet, over high heat, heat remaining 1 tbsp (15 mL) grapeseed oil. Add tomato slices and cook until bottoms are lightly blackened, about 5 minutes. Flip and cook on the other side for 2 to 3 minutes, until blackened and tomato is cooked through. Place on top of grits and serve.

Variation

Herbed Garlic Grits: Reduce the amount of nutritional yeast to 2 tbsp (30 mL). Add ¼ cup (60 mL) each chopped fresh flat-leaf (Italian) parsley and sliced fresh basil leaves, 1 tbsp (15 mL) chopped fresh thyme leaves and 2 tsp (10 mL) garlic powder.

Vegan Benedict

This is my take on classic eggs Benedict, complete with creamy hollandaise sauce and the addition of nutrient-rich spinach. It's one of my all-time favorite breakfast dishes.

MAKES 2 SERVINGS

Tips

Liquid smoke is a seasoning made from water vapor that has been exposed to wood smoke and then condensed. It provides a smoky flavor to foods without needing to use a smoker. You can find it in most well-stocked supermarkets and natural food stores.

Silken tofu is available in shelf-stable packages that do not require refrigeration. You can find it in most well-stocked supermarkets.

TOFU

2 tbsp	wheat-free tamari	30 mL
2 tbsp	water	30 mL
1 tbsp	raw agave nectar	15 mL
½ tsp	liquid smoke (see Tips, left)	2 mL
1½ tbsp	grapeseed oil	22 mL
½ lb	firm silken tofu, sliced lengthwise into 4 pieces (see Tips, left)	250 g

TOMATO

½ cup	coarse organic stone-ground cornmeal	125 mL
1 tbsp	garlic powder	15 mL
1½ tsp	fennel seeds	7 mL
¾ tsp	sweet paprika	3 mL
⅛ tsp	fine sea salt	0.5 mL
1	beefsteak tomato, cut into 4 thick slices	1
3 tbsp	grapeseed oil	45 mL

HOLLANDAISE SAUCE

¼ cup	melted coconut oil	60 mL
⅓ cup	brown rice flour	75 mL
⅛ tsp	ground turmeric	0.5 mL
3 tbsp	dry white wine (see Tips, page 33)	45 mL
2 tbsp	freshly squeezed lemon juice	30 mL
1½ cups	Almond Milk (page 61)	375 mL
1 tbsp	nutritional yeast	15 mL
1½ tsp	Dijon mustard	7 mL

SPINACH

2 tbsp	grapeseed oil	30 mL
1 tbsp	minced garlic	15 mL
8 cups	lightly packed baby spinach leaves	2 L
3 tbsp	dry white wine	45 mL
1 tsp	chopped fresh thyme leaves	5 mL
¼ tsp	fine sea salt	1 mL
2	gluten-free English muffins, split and toasted	2

Tips

I like to use a dry white wine such as a Chardonnay for this recipe.

Nutritional yeast is an inactive yeast that has been grown on beet molasses and then pasteurized. It provides a rich, cheesy flavor in sauces, stews, soups and dips. Look for it in well-stocked supermarkets and natural food stores.

1. *Tofu:* In a bowl, combine tamari, water, agave nectar, liquid smoke and grapeseed oil. Add tofu and turn to coat. Cover and set aside to marinate for 10 minutes or overnight (if overnight, refrigerate).

2. Remove tofu from marinade (discard marinade). In a nonstick skillet over medium-high heat, cook marinated tofu for about 2 minutes per side, until golden brown. Set aside.

3. *Tomato:* In a shallow bowl, whisk together cornmeal, garlic powder, fennel seeds, paprika and salt. Dredge each tomato slice in mixture until both sides are well coated.

4. In a skillet over medium-high heat, heat grapeseed oil. Cook coated tomatoes for 2 to 3 minutes per side, until golden brown and crisp. Remove from heat and transfer to a plate (tomatoes will become mushy if left in pan). Set aside.

5. *Hollandaise Sauce:* In a small saucepan over medium heat, combine coconut oil, flour and turmeric and cook, stirring constantly, for 3 to 4 minutes, until raw flavor of flour cooks out. Stir in wine and cook, stirring constantly, until mixture thickens and forms a paste, about 2 minutes. Stir in lemon juice and bring to a simmer. Cook for 1 minute, then stir in almond milk. Bring to a boil, reduce heat to a simmer and cook, uncovered and stirring occasionally, for 2 to 3 minutes, until mixture is thick enough to coat the back of a spoon. Turn off heat. Stir in nutritional yeast and mustard. Using a fine-mesh sieve, strain into a bowl (discard solids), cover surface with plastic wrap (to prevent a skin forming) and set aside.

6. *Spinach:* In a skillet over medium-high heat, heat grapeseed oil. Sauté garlic until golden but not brown, about 1 minute. Add spinach and wine, stirring occasionally, and cook until spinach is wilted and most of the liquid has evaporated, 2 to 3 minutes. Add thyme and salt and stir to combine. Remove from heat.

7. *Assembly:* Divide toasted English muffins between two serving plates. Place one-quarter of the spinach on each muffin half. Top each with a slice of crispy tomato and a piece of seared tofu. Ladle a generous portion of the hollandaise sauce over each half. Serve immediately.

Breakfast Frittata

Frittatas are traditionally made using eggs, flour, cheese and milk. This version reinvents the classic dish with tofu, a blend of gluten-free flours, nutritional yeast and almond milk for a delicious result.

MAKES 6 TO 8 SERVINGS

Tips

To crumble tofu, break it into bite-size pieces. Then rub each piece between your fingers to break it into smaller bits.

To strip the leaves from fresh thyme, hold sprig upside down by the stem and, using two fingers, firmly pull the leaves downward. Reserve stems for soups or broths (discard after cooking). Use a sharp knife to chop the leaves, being careful not to chop too much or too hard, as this will bruise the leaves and cause the thyme to discolor.

- **Preheat oven to 350°F (180°C)**
- **Blender**
- **10-inch (25 cm) deep-dish pie plate, greased**

2 tbsp	coconut oil	30 mL
3	cloves garlic, minced	3
½ cup	chopped onion	125 mL
1 lb	firm tofu, crumbled (see Tips, left)	500 g
1 tsp	ground turmeric, divided	5 mL
1 tsp	fine sea salt, divided	5 mL
1 tbsp	chopped fresh thyme leaves (see Tips, left)	15 mL
1 tbsp	wheat-free tamari	15 mL
¼ cup	nutritional yeast, divided	60 mL
1	package (12 oz/375 g) water-packed firm silken tofu	1
½ cup	Almond Milk (page 61)	125 mL
2 tbsp	brown rice flour	30 mL
2 tbsp	chickpea flour	30 mL
1 tbsp	ground raw flax seeds	15 mL
2 tsp	organic cornstarch	10 mL

1. In a skillet over medium heat, heat coconut oil. Sauté garlic until browned, about 2 minutes (be careful not to burn it). Add onion and cook, stirring often, until translucent, 4 to 5 minutes. Add firm tofu, ½ tsp (2 mL) turmeric, ½ tsp (2 mL) salt, and thyme. Cook, stirring occasionally, until tofu is slightly browned, 5 to 6 minutes. Remove pan from heat and stir in tamari and 2 tbsp (30 mL) nutritional yeast. Transfer to a mixing bowl.

2. In blender, combine silken tofu, almond milk, brown rice flour, chickpea flour, flax seeds, cornstarch, and remaining 2 tbsp (30 mL) nutritional yeast, ½ tsp (2 mL) turmeric and ½ tsp (2 mL) salt. Blend at high speed until smooth, stopping the motor to scrape down sides of blender jar as necessary. Pour over sautéed tofu and stir well.

Nutritional yeast is an inactive yeast that has been grown on beet molasses and then pasteurized. It provides a rich, cheesy flavor in sauces, stews, soups and dips. Look for it in well-stocked supermarkets and natural food stores.

3. Spread mixture evenly in prepared pie plate. Bake in preheated oven for 25 to 30 minutes or until a toothpick inserted in the center comes out clean. Remove from oven and let cool in pan for about 20 minutes. Slice into 6 to 8 equal pieces. Serve immediately or cool completely, cover and refrigerate for up to 1 week.

Variations

Spinach Mushroom Frittata: In a skillet over medium-high heat, heat 3 tbsp (45 mL) coconut oil. Sauté 2 cups (500 mL) sliced button mushrooms and 4 cups (1 L) lightly packed baby spinach leaves until mushrooms are soft and spinach is wilted. Add to sautéed tofu and seasonings in Step 1 and continue with recipe.

Black Olive and Sun-Dried Tomato Frittata: Omit the fresh thyme, and the salt, if you are concerned about sodium intake (the olives and sun-dried tomatoes are salty). Add 1 cup (250 mL) sliced kalamata olives, $\frac{1}{2}$ cup (125 mL) soaked sun-dried tomatoes and 1 tbsp (15 mL) dried oregano to sautéed tofu in Step 1. (To soak the sun-dried tomatoes, place in a bowl and cover with warm water. Set aside for 30 minutes, until softened.)

The Eggless Omelet

This dish is a great alternative for anyone who doesn't consume eggs. I like to stuff my omelet with caramelized onions and sautéed spinach, but you can use whatever you have on hand, such as your favorite store-bought pesto.

MAKES 3 INDIVIDUAL OMELETS

Tips

You can purchase flax seeds that are already ground (often described as "milled") in vacuum-sealed bags, or you can grind them yourself. To grind them, place 1 cup (250 mL) whole flax seeds in a blender and blend at high speed until finely ground. Cover and refrigerate any extra for up to 1 month.

Black salt (kala namak) is a salt that comes from the Himalayas and northwest Pakistan. It contains sulfuric compounds that lend dishes an eggy flavor, which is why it is used in vegan recipes that are similar to traditional egg recipes.

Be sure to use organic cornstarch, which contains no additives or preservatives and is GMO-free.

Food processor

4 oz	water-packed firm or medium silken tofu	125 g
¼ cup	Almond Milk (page 61)	60 mL
3 tbsp	medium organic stone-ground cornmeal	45 mL
1 tbsp	extra virgin olive oil	15 mL
1 tbsp	nutritional yeast	15 mL
1 tbsp	brown rice flour	15 mL
1 tbsp	ground raw flax seeds (see Tips, left)	15 mL
1½ tsp	organic cornstarch	7 mL
½ tsp	black salt (optional; see Tips, left)	2 mL
¼ tsp	ground turmeric	1 mL
1 to 3 tbsp	grapeseed oil	15 to 45 mL

1. In food processor fitted with the metal blade, combine tofu, almond milk, cornmeal, olive oil, nutritional yeast, flour, flax seeds, cornstarch, black salt (if using) and turmeric. Process until smooth, stopping the motor to scrape down sides of work bowl as necessary. Transfer to a bowl.

2. In a nonstick skillet over medium heat, heat 1 tbsp (15 mL) grapeseed oil. Drop about ½ cup (125 mL) of the mixture into pan, tilting it so mixture spreads evenly over bottom. Cook for 5 to 6 minutes, until bottom is firm and lightly golden. Flip and cook on the other side for 4 to 5 minutes or until lightly golden and omelet is cooked through — firm and pliable but not crisp. Repeat twice with the remaining mixture. Serve immediately.

Sweet Potato and Corn Hash

This decadent side dish is the perfect alternative to traditional roasted potatoes. I love to serve this with Scrambled Tofu with Caramelized Onions, Mushrooms and Peppers (page 30) or Eggless Omelet (page 36).

MAKES 6 SIDE SERVINGS

Tips

If using frozen corn, increase the cooking time to 10 to 12 minutes.

To strip the leaves from fresh thyme: Hold sprig upside down by the stem and, using two fingers, firmly pull the leaves downward. Using a sharp knife, chop gently. Do not use a dull knife or the thyme will oxidize and turn brown.

4 cups	chopped sweet potatoes (unpeeled)	1 L
3 tbsp	grapeseed oil	45 mL
6 to 8	cloves garlic, thinly sliced	6 to 8
½ cup	chopped onion	125 mL
½ tsp	fine sea salt	2 mL
1 cup	corn kernels (fresh or frozen; see Tips, left)	250 mL
2 tbsp	chopped fresh thyme leaves (see Tips, left)	30 mL

1. In a large saucepan filled with water, bring sweet potatoes to a boil. Reduce heat and simmer until potatoes are just tender, 6 to 8 minutes. Drain and set aside.

2. In a medium skillet over medium-high heat, heat oil. Sauté garlic until lightly browned, about 2 minutes (be careful not to burn it). Add onion and salt and cook, stirring occasionally, until slightly caramelized, 5 to 6 minutes. Add corn and cook, stirring occasionally, until corn is golden brown, 5 to 6 minutes. Stir in cooked sweet potatoes and cook for 2 to 3 minutes, until heated through. Stir in thyme and cook for 30 seconds or until thyme becomes fragrant. Serve immediately or transfer to an airtight container and refrigerate for up to 1 week.

Tempeh Bacon

Smoky, salty strips of crispy tempeh bacon are the perfect addition to most breakfast dishes. I like to serve this alongside Scrambled Tofu with Caramelized Onions, Mushrooms and Peppers (page 30) and some crusty toast.

Tips

You can find unpasteurized tempeh in the freezer section of well-stocked supermarkets and natural food stores.

It is important to use a blender for Step 2 to ensure that the ingredients are thoroughly emulsified.

Liquid smoke is a seasoning made from water vapor that has been exposed to wood smoke and then condensed. It provides a smoky flavor to foods without needing to use a smoker. You can find it in most well-stocked supermarkets and natural food stores.

To reheat refrigerated tempeh bacon: In a skillet over medium heat, heat 1 tbsp (15 mL) grapeseed oil. Cook tempeh until golden, about 2 minutes per side.

- **Blender**
- **Baking sheet, lined with parchment paper**

1	block (8.5 oz/240 g) frozen unpasteurized tempeh (see Tips, left)	1
8 cups	water	2 L
1 cup	wheat-free tamari, divided	250 mL
1/4 cup	water	60 mL
1/4 cup	raw agave nectar (see page 8)	60 mL
1/4 cup	grapeseed oil	60 mL
2 tsp	liquid smoke (see Tips, left)	10 mL

1. In a large saucepan, bring to a boil tempeh, 8 cups (2 L) water and 1/2 cup (125 mL) tamari. Reduce heat and simmer for 15 minutes. Using a slotted spoon, transfer tempeh to a bowl and set aside (discard cooking liquid).

2. In blender, combine 1/4 cup (60 mL) water, remaining 1/2 cup (125 mL) tamari, agave nectar, grapeseed oil and liquid smoke. Blend at high speed until smooth. Set aside.

3. Using a sharp knife, slice cooled tempeh into 26 to 28 equal pieces. Layer slices in a shallow dish and pour tamari mixture overtop. Cover and set aside for at least 30 minutes or refrigerate overnight.

4. Preheat oven to 400°F (200°C). Remove tempeh from marinade (discard marinade). Arrange in a single layer on prepared baking sheet. Bake in preheated oven for 15 to 20 minutes or until no liquid remains and tempeh is slightly crisp. Serve immediately or let cool, transfer to an airtight container and refrigerate for up to 1 week (see Tips, left).

Juices, Smoothies and Non-dairy Milks

Juices

Smoothies

Non-dairy Milks

Cucumber Aloe Watermelon Juice

Aloe vera isn't just for soothing burns — it's also a powerful digestive aid. Try it in this light and refreshing juice.

| | MAKES ABOUT 2 CUPS (500 ML) | |

Tips

Aloe vera plants are available at most nurseries.

To extract gel from an aloe vera leaf: Using a sharp knife, carefully peel the rind off the leaf and discard rind. Carefully peel away the yellow top layer (aloe latex) and discard. Using your fingers, squeeze the aloe gel into the blender.

● Electric juicer

½	English cucumber, halved crosswise	½
	Gel from 1 piece (6 inches/15 cm) fresh aloe vera (see Tips, left)	1
4 cups	chopped peeled watermelon	1 L

1. In juicer, process half each of the cucumber, aloe vera gel and watermelon. Repeat with the remaining cucumber, aloe vera and watermelon. Whisk well and serve immediately.

Variation

For an added burst of flavor, add ½ bunch fresh mint to the juicer.

Lemon-Lime Fusion Juice

This tropical drink pairs beautifully with creamy coconut dishes such as Tofu and Lemongrass Vegetable Coconut Curry (page 306).

| | MAKES 2 CUPS (500 ML) | |

Tips

A hand-held citrus reamer can be used to extract the juice from lemons and limes. Available in most kitchen supply stores, this tool would be ideal to use for the citrus in this recipe.

To purée the gingerroot, use a fine-toothed grater such as the kind made by Microplane.

1 cup	water	250 mL
¼ cup	freshly squeezed lemon juice	60 mL
¼ cup	freshly squeezed lime juice	60 mL
2 tbsp	pure maple syrup	30 mL
1 tbsp	wheat-free tamari	15 mL
1	½-inch (1 cm) piece peeled gingerroot, puréed (see Tips, left)	1
Pinch	cayenne pepper	Pinch

1. In a small bowl, combine water, lemon and lime juices, maple syrup, tamari, puréed ginger and cayenne pepper. Whisk well and serve immediately.

Matcha Me Green Juice

This juice is a refreshing aromatic blend of fresh green vegetables and cold Japanese green tea. Serve it alongside an Asian-inspired dishes such as Quick Sweet-and-Sour Tofu Stir-Fry (page 308).

(page 308)

MAKES ABOUT 2 CUPS (500 ML)

Tips

Matcha is available in most well-stocked supermarkets and natural food stores. It is known for its high antioxidant content and stimulating effects.

If you prefer a bigger kick of ginger, increase the quantity to 1 inch (2.5 cm).

● **Electric juicer**

1 tsp	matcha (green tea) powder (see Tips, left)	5 mL
½ cup	water	125 mL
2	kale leaves	2
1	stalk celery	1
¼	English cucumber	¼
1	½-inch (1 cm) piece gingerroot	1
¼	lemon, skin on	¼

1. In a small bowl, whisk together matcha powder and water until no lumps remain.
2. In juicer, process kale, celery, cucumber, ginger and lemon. Add to prepared green tea, whisk well and serve immediately.

Liquid Chlorophyll Juice

One of the best ways to start your day is with a fresh green juice. This one is packed with healthy greens. It's a perfect complement to almost any breakfast.

MAKES ABOUT 1¼ CUPS (300 ML)

Tip

Black kale, also called dinosaur or lacinato kale, is one of the most nutrient-dense green vegetables. I like to use it for this juice because it yields a deeper green color than other varieties of kale.

● **Electric juicer**

1	head black kale (see Tip, left)	1
¼	bunch fresh flat-leaf (Italian) parsley	¼
2	stalks celery	2
¼	lemon, skin on	¼
1	½-inch (1 cm) piece gingerroot	1

1. In juicer, process kale, parsley, celery, lemon and ginger. Whisk well and serve immediately.

Lawnmower Juice

This juice is a chlorophyll-rich blend that includes detoxifying wheatgrass. It's perfect with breakfast or as a midday pick-me-up.

MAKES ABOUT 2 CUPS (500 ML)

Tip

Wheatgrass is a living grass. You can buy wheatgrass juice either fresh or flash-frozen. Wheatgrass cannot be juiced in a standard electric juicer. You will need either a specialized wheatgrass juicer or a masticating juicer.

- **Electric juicer**

6 to 8	kale leaves (see Tips, page 43)	6 to 8
1	apple, sliced	1
2 to 3	stalks celery	2 to 3
2	romaine lettuce leaves	2
¼	lemon, skin on	¼
2 oz	wheatgrass juice (see Tip, left)	60 mL

1. In juicer, process ⅓ each of the kale, apple and celery, 1 lettuce leaf and lemon. Repeat until kale, apple, celery and lettuce have all been juiced. Whisk in wheatgrass juice. Serve immediately.

Detoxifier Juice

Start your day off right and boost your metabolism with this chlorophyll-rich juice that gets its kick of heat from cayenne pepper.

MAKES ABOUT 2 CUPS (500 ML)

Tips

When juicing vegetables that contain smaller amounts of water, such as kale, follow them through the juicer with vegetables or fruits that are higher in water, such as cucumber or celery. This helps to flush out the juicer.

For an even spicier kick, increase the quantity of cayenne to ⅛ tsp (0.5 mL).

- **Electric juicer**

6 to 8	kale leaves	6 to 8
4	stalks celery	4
1	English cucumber, quartered	1
4	large romaine lettuce leaves	4
1	1-inch (2.5 cm) piece gingerroot	1
½	lemon, skin on	½
½	bunch flat-leaf (Italian) parsley	½
Pinch	cayenne pepper (see Tips, left)	Pinch

1. In juicer, process 2 kale leaves, 1 celery stalk, ¼ of the cucumber, 1 lettuce leaf, ginger, lemon and ¼ of the parsley. Repeat until all of the vegetables are used up. Whisk in cayenne pepper and serve immediately.

Muddy Waters

Detoxifying kale, beta carotene–rich carrots, purifying beets, sweet apples and aromatic ginger combine to make this hearty and refreshing juice.

MAKES ABOUT 2 CUPS (500 ML)

Tips

Black (dinosaur or lacinato) kale has a strong flavor and tends to make juices taste bitter. For a milder flavor, use green curly kale.

I like to match the sweetness of carrot with firm, sweet apples such as Gala, Pink Lady or Macintosh.

● Electric juicer

4 to 6	kale leaves	4 to 6
2 to 3	carrots	2 to 3
1	red beet, quartered	1
1	apple, quartered	1
1	½-inch (1 cm) piece gingerroot	1

1. In juicer, process 1 kale leaf, 1 carrot, ¼ of the beet, ¼ of the apple and the ginger. Repeat until the remaining kale, carrots, beet and apple have been juiced. Whisk well and serve immediately.

Roots and Sticks Juice

This juice is a fresh blend of sweet carrots, creamy sweet potato, detoxifying burdock root and rich beets. It's a perfect midday pick-me-up.

MAKES ABOUT 2 CUPS (500 ML)

Tips

Depending on the juicer you are using, you may need to cut the vegetables into thin strips in order to process them. For juicers with large openings, the vegetables need only be washed, not cut.

Burdock root is known for its detoxifying effects. It looks like a long twig and is available in most well-stocked supermarkets and natural food stores.

● Electric juicer

3 to 4	medium carrots (see Tips, left)	3 to 4
½	sweet potato, cut into strips	½
1	12-inch (30 cm) piece burdock root (see Tips, left)	1
2 to 3	medium red beets	2 to 3

1. In juicer, process 1 carrot and ¼ each of the sweet potato, burdock root and beets. Repeat until all of the vegetables are used up. Whisk well and serve immediately.

The Gardener's Juice

This chlorophyll-rich juice is great for when you are craving something a little sweet but healthy. The juicy apples pair well with fresh sunflower sprouts and floral celery to make a satisfying drink.

Tips

Black kale, also called dinosaur or lacinato kale, has a strong flavor and tends to make juices taste slightly bitter. For a milder flavor, use green curly kale.

Substitute an equal amount of pea sprouts for the sunflower sprouts in this recipe.

- **Electric juicer**

2	apples, quartered	2
2 to 3	kale leaves (see Tips, left)	2 to 3
1 cup	sunflower sprouts	250 mL
1	½-inch (1 cm) piece gingerroot	1
2	stalks celery	2

1. In juicer, process 4 pieces of apple, 1 kale leaf, ½ cup (125 mL) sunflower sprouts, ginger and 1 stalk celery. Repeat until the remaining apple, kale, sprouts and celery have been juiced. Whisk well and serve immediately.

Pink Beet Delight

In this drink, fresh beet juice is blended with citrusy orange juice and sweet maple syrup to make a healthy pink-hued treat.

Tips

When the juice of golden beets is mixed with the orange juice, the result is a beautiful amber color.

Purchase beets with the leaves attached. The greens are delicious in salads, wraps or stir-fries. Cut them off, wash, wrap loosely in damp paper towels and refrigerate for up to 2 days.

- **Electric juicer**
- **Citrus reamer**

4 to 5	medium golden or red beets, quartered (see Tips, left)	4 to 5
2	medium oranges, halved (see Tips, page 45)	2
¼ cup	pure maple syrup	60 mL

1. In juicer, process enough beets to make 1¼ cups (300 mL) juice.
2. Using citrus reamer, juice oranges to make ½ cup (125 mL) juice.
3. In a glass, whisk together beet juice, orange juice and maple syrup. Serve immediately.

Piña Colada Juice

This tropical juice is a take on the classic island drink served with rum over crushed ice and coconut cream. It pairs well with a dish such as Jerk Tofu, Avocado and Plantain Wraps (page 360) or Eggplant and Tempeh Paella (page 244).

MAKES ABOUT 2 CUPS (500 ML)

Tip

There are many different brands of coconut water. I prefer cold-pressed unpasteurized organic coconut water for its superior flavor and nutritional value.

- Electric juicer

2 cups	chopped pineapple (about 1 medium; see Tips, page 46)	500 mL
½ cup	coconut water (see Tip, left)	125 mL
¼ cup	crushed ice	60 mL

1. In juicer, process pineapple.
2. In a pitcher, whisk together pineapple juice and coconut water.
3. Fill a glass with crushed ice. Pour pineapple mixture over ice and serve immediately.

Pink Sunset Juice

This juice is a perfect blend of tart grapefruit, rich and detoxifying beets and sweet, juicy apples. Enjoy it as a mid-afternoon snack when those three-o'clock cravings kick in.

MAKES ABOUT 2 CUPS (500 ML)

Tips

It is best to use apples that are firm and crisp. If an apple is mushy, it will not pass properly through the juicer.

A hand-held reamer can be used to extract the juice from citrus fruits. Available in most kitchen supply stores, this tool would be ideal to use for the grapefruit in this recipe and the oranges in Pink Beet Delight.

- Citrus reamer
- Electric juicer

1	pink grapefruit, halved	1
2 to 3	medium beets, quartered	2 to 3
1 to 2	apples, quartered (see Tips, left)	1 to 2

1. Using citrus reamer, juice grapefruit.
2. In juicer, process 3 to 4 beet quarters followed by 3 to 4 apple pieces. Repeat until the remaining apples and beets have been juiced.
3. In a glass, whisk together apple-beet juice and grapefruit juice. Serve immediately.

Island-Time Juice

In this juice, mango and pineapple are combined with celery, ginger and apple to give you a taste of the tropics any time of the year.

MAKES ABOUT 1½ CUPS (375 ML)

Tips

When juicing pineapple, it is acceptable to leave the skin on.

Juicing ripe mango can be tough — it can clog the gears and result in very little juice. For best results, use a firm under-ripe mango for this recipe.

- **Electric juicer**

½ cup	chopped pineapple (about ¼ medium; see Tips, left)	125 mL
2	stalks celery	2
1	apple, quartered	1
¼ cup	chopped mango (about ¼ medium; see Tips, left)	60 mL
1	½-inch (1 cm) piece gingerroot	1

1. In juicer, process ¼ cup (60 mL) pineapple, 1 stalk celery, 2 apple quarters, 2 tbsp (30 mL) mango and the ginger. Repeat with remaining pineapple, celery, apple and mango. Whisk and serve immediately.

Orange Creamsicle Juice

This blend of sweet orange juice and rich coconut oil will remind you of those creamy orange Popsicles from your childhood. Enjoy this as a mid-afternoon snack or dessert.

MAKES ABOUT 2 CUPS (500 ML)

Tips

Bring your ingredients to room temperature before making this juice. Cold juice will cause the melted coconut oil to solidify and it will not mix properly.

To melt the coconut oil, gently warm in a small skillet over low heat.

- **Citrus reamer**
- **Blender**

5	oranges (see Tips, page 47)	5
2 tbsp	freshly squeezed lime juice	30 mL
1 tbsp	freshly squeezed lemon juice	15 mL
2 tbsp	raw agave nectar (see page 8)	30 mL
2 tbsp	melted coconut oil (see Tips, left)	30 mL
½ tsp	alcohol-free organic vanilla extract	2 mL

1. Using citrus reamer, juice oranges to produce 1½ cups (375 mL) orange juice.
2. In blender, combine orange, lime and lemon juices with agave nectar, coconut oil and vanilla. Blend at high speed for 10 seconds, until well combined. Serve immediately.

Spicy Ginger Juice

This juice is perfect for when you feel a cold coming on. The ginger and cayenne will boost your metabolism.

MAKES ABOUT 1¼ CUPS (300 ML)

Tips

To get the maximum yield, let citrus fruit sit at room temperature for 30 minutes, then use the palm of your hand to roll it on the counter to release the juices before squeezing.

If you prefer a spicier drink, add as much as ¼ tsp (1 mL) cayenne pepper.

• Electric juicer

1	3-inch (7.5 cm) piece gingerroot	1
½	lemon, skin on	½
1 cup	hot water	250 mL
⅛ tsp	cayenne pepper	0.5 mL

1. In juicer, process ginger and lemon. Pour into a glass with hot water. Whisk in cayenne and serve immediately.

Variation

Spicy Ginger Green Juice: In juicer, process 1 head green kale and ½ English cucumber, sliced in half crosswise. Add ginger and lemon, omitting the water. Whisk in cayenne and serve.

Pop-Tart Juice

I love to serve this sweet juice alongside some fresh fruit such as mango, papaya or banana on a hot day.

MAKES ABOUT 2 CUPS (500 ML)

Tip

The strawberries for this recipe should be firm and not overly ripe. If they are too soft they will not juice properly. If your berries are very ripe, place them in the freezer for 3 hours and juice from frozen.

• Electric juicer

2 cups	hulled strawberries (see Tip, left)	500 mL
2 cups	red grapes	500 mL
1	apple, quartered	1
½ cup	chopped pineapple (about ¼ medium)	125 mL

1. In juicer, process strawberries, grapes, apple and pineapple. Whisk well and serve immediately.

Variation

Pop-Tart Smoothie: Transfer juice to a blender. Add 1 frozen banana and ¼ tsp (1 mL) organic vanilla powder or ½ tsp (2 mL) alcohol-free organic vanilla extract. Blend at high speed until smooth.

Kick-Me-Up Juice

In this juice, sweet fruits and floral celery get a cooling kick from fresh mint. Try this at lunch with a big bowl of crisp salad greens.

MAKES ABOUT 2 CUPS (500 ML)		

Tips

For a slightly tarter juice, use green apples.

The stalks of fresh mint are acceptable to use when juicing. Do not discard them.

● **Electric juicer**

3	apples, quartered (see Tips, left and page 49)	3
½ cup	grapes	125 mL
3 to 4	stalks celery	3 to 4
½	bunch fresh mint (see Tips, left)	½

1. In juicer, process 6 apple quarters, ¼ cup (60 mL) grapes, 2 stalks celery and half of the mint. Repeat with the remaining apple, grapes, celery and mint. Whisk well and serve immediately.

Spiced Apple Juice

The addition of cloves and nutmeg makes this juice a natural choice during the holiday season. Try adding a little rum or whiskey.

MAKES ABOUT 2 CUPS (500 ML)		

Tips

I like to use a sweeter variety of apple, such as Gala, Pink Lady or McIntosh.

The maple syrup adds sweetness; it is optional.

I like to use an electric juicer to make my cold-pressed juices. Since no blades are used, the enzymes in the fruits and vegetables are not damaged and the juice will not oxidize as quickly.

● **Electric juicer**

4	apples, quartered (see Tips, left)	4
1 tbsp	pure maple syrup (optional)	15 mL
⅛ tsp	ground cloves	0.5 mL
⅛ tsp	ground nutmeg	0.5 mL

1. In juicer, process apples.
2. Pour apple juice into a glass and add maple syrup (if using), cloves and nutmeg. Whisk well and serve immediately.

Variations

Spiced Apple Juice Smoothie: Transfer apple juice to a blender. Add ¼ cup (60 mL) raw shelled hemp seeds and 1 tsp (5 mL) chia seeds; blend at high speed until smooth.

Spiced Apple Chia Pudding: In a bowl, whisk together apple juice and 3 tbsp (45 mL) chia seeds. Cover and set aside for 10 minutes so chia seeds can absorb the liquid and swell.

Warming Apple Juice

This juice is perfect for those cold nights when you are craving something warming yet light. It's also great at breakfast.

Tip

Use apples that are firm and crisp. If an apple is mushy, it will not pass properly through the juicer, and the juice will be cloudy and have a poor texture.

● **Electric juicer**

4 to 5	apples, quartered (see Tip, left)	4 to 5
1 to 2	medium carrots, sliced	1 to 2
1	1-inch (2.5 cm) piece gingerroot	1
½	lemon, skin on	½

1. In juicer, process apples, carrots, ginger and lemon. Whisk well and serve immediately.

Spiced Holiday Juice

This is a delightful blend of fresh orange and apple juices and aromatic spices. Serve it with a spritz of soda water or your favorite spirit.

Tips

A hand-held citrus reamer is used to extract the juice from citrus fruits. Available in most kitchen supply stores, this tool would be ideal to use for the oranges in this recipe.

To grate the nutmeg, use a fine-toothed grater such as the kind made by Microplane.

● **Electric juicer**
● **Citrus reamer**

3	apples, quartered	3
2	medium oranges, halved (see Tips, left)	2
¼ tsp	ground allspice	1 mL
⅛ tsp	ground cloves	0.5 mL
Pinch	freshly grated nutmeg (see Tips, left)	Pinch
1 tbsp	pure maple syrup (optional)	30 mL

1. In electric juicer, process apples.
2. Using citrus reamer, juice oranges.
3. In a large glass, whisk together apple and orange juices, allspice, cloves, nutmeg and maple syrup (if using). Serve immediately.

Variation

Spiced Holiday Smoothie: Transfer mixture to a blender. Add 1 frozen banana and ⅛ tsp (0.5 mL) organic vanilla powder or ¼ tsp (1 mL) alcohol-free organic vanilla extract. Blend until smooth.

Chia-Spiked Berry Smoothie

If you keep berries in the freezer, this smoothie is quick and easy to make.

MAKES
2 CUPS (500 ML)

Tip

Buy organic frozen berries in bulk and keep them in your freezer to use as needed. Adding frozen berries to your smoothie will have the same chilling effect as using ice. They can be stored for up to 6 months in an airtight container.

• Blender

1 cup	freshly squeezed orange juice	250 mL
6	strawberries	6
10	blueberries	10
4	each blackberries and raspberries	4
1	Medjool date, pitted and chopped	1
1 tsp	chia seeds	5 mL

1. In blender, combine orange juice, berries, date and chia seeds. Blend at high speed until smooth. Serve immediately.

Variations

Substitute gooseberries, brambleberries or cranberries for one of the berries. If using a less sweet fruit, add 1 to 2 tbsp (15 to 30 mL) raw agave nectar.

Strawberry Kiwi Smoothie

Serve this luscious smoothie when these fruits are in season.

MAKES
2 CUPS (500 ML)

Tips

To extract the flesh from kiwifruit, use a paring knife to remove a small amount of skin from the bottom. Carefully insert a small spoon between the flesh and the skin and rotate it until the skin becomes loose. Scoop out the flesh.

For a creamy smoothie, substitute an equal amount of almond milk for the orange juice and add 3 tbsp (45 mL) melted coconut oil.

• Blender

1 cup	freshly squeezed orange juice	250 mL
2	kiwifruit, peel removed	2
1	banana	1
8 to 10	strawberries	8 to 10
1 tsp	raw agave nectar	5 mL
1 tsp	alcohol-free organic vanilla extract	5 mL

1. In blender, combine orange juice, kiwis, banana, strawberries, agave nectar and vanilla. Blend at high speed until smooth. Serve immediately.

Variations

Strawberry Grape Smoothie: Substitute 1 cup (250 mL) grapes for the kiwi fruit.

Strawberry Fig Smoothie: Substitute 1/2 cup (125 mL) chopped fresh figs for the kiwi fruit.

Classic Green Smoothie

This smoothie makes an easy breakfast, simple lunch or quick snack. I like to serve it with Quinoa Tabbouleh (page 219).

MAKES ABOUT 2 CUPS (500 ML)

Tips

To remove the stem from a kale leaf: Hold the leaf upside down by its stem. Using your fingers, gently pull down and strip away the leaf; discard stem.

I like to use raw vegan protein powders. You can find them in most well-stocked supermarkets and natural food stores. Use your favorite flavor in this recipe.

• Blender

1¼ cups	Almond Milk (page 61)	300 mL
1	frozen banana (see Tips, page 52)	1
3 to 4	kale leaves, stems removed (see Tips, left)	3 to 4
1	scoop protein powder (optional; see Tips, left)	1
½ cup	lightly packed baby spinach leaves	125 mL
¼ cup	chopped pineapple or mango	60 mL
½ tsp	alcohol-free organic vanilla extract	2 mL

1. In blender, combine almond milk, banana, kale, protein powder (if using), spinach, pineapple and vanilla. Blend at high speed until smooth. Serve immediately.

Avocado Spinach Smoothie

This creamy but light smoothie is a great way to start your day. It contains protein, healthy fat and greens that will leave you feeling full and satisfied.

MAKES ABOUT 2 CUPS (500 ML)

Tips

Substitute an equal amount of Almond Milk (page 61), Oat Milk (page 63), Cashew Milk (page 61) or Green Milk (page 64) for the hemp milk.

If your avocado is large or extra-large, use ½ cup (125 mL) chopped avocado (about ¼ to ⅙ of the whole).

• Blender

1¼ cups	Hemp and Chia Milk (page 64; see Tips, left)	300 mL
½	small to medium avocado, chopped (see Tips, left)	½
½ cup	lightly packed baby spinach leaves	125 mL
¼ cup	crushed ice	60 mL
1 tsp	pure maple syrup	5 mL
¼ tsp	alcohol-free organic vanilla extract	1 mL

1. In blender, combine hemp milk, avocado, spinach, ice, maple syrup and vanilla. Blend at high speed until smooth and creamy. Serve immediately.

Hibiscus Melon Smoothie

This refreshing floral-scented smoothie is bursting with flavor.

Tips

To brew the tea for this recipe: In a cup, pour ½ cup (125 mL) boiling water over a hibiscus teabag. Cover and set aside for 10 minutes. Remove and discard teabag. Refrigerate for 30 minutes.

Look for rose water in East Indian grocery stores. Choose an organic brand to ensure that it is food-grade.

Blender

¾ cup	Quinoa Milk (page 62)	175 mL
½ cup	steeped hibiscus tea, cooled (see Tips, left)	125 mL
2 tbsp	raw shelled hemp seeds	30 mL
¼ cup	chopped watermelon (rind removed)	60 mL
½ tsp	organic rose water (see Tips, left)	2 mL
⅛ tsp	ground cardamom	0.5 mL

1. In blender, combine quinoa milk, hibiscus tea, hemp seeds, watermelon, rose water and cardamom. Blend at high speed until smooth. Serve immediately.

Springtime Smoothie

This refreshing green smoothie is a wonderful way to drink your greens.

Tips

To freeze a banana: Peel banana, then transfer to a resealable bag, pushing as much air out of the bag as you can before sealing it. Freeze for up to 4 months.

Substitute 2 tbsp (30 mL) raw cashews and 1 tsp (5 mL) freshly squeezed lemon juice for the yogurt.

Blender

1¼ cups	Hemp and Chia Milk (page 64)	300 mL
1	frozen banana (see Tips, left)	1
½ cup	lightly packed baby spinach leaves	125 mL
½ cup	Lemon Vanilla Cashew Yogurt (page 18; see Tips, left)	125 mL
¼ tsp	organic peppermint extract	1 mL
½ tsp	alcohol-free organic vanilla extract	2 mL

1. In blender, combine hemp milk, banana, spinach, yogurt, peppermint extract and vanilla. Blend at high speed until smooth. Serve immediately.

Variation

Minty Green Smoothie: Increase the amount of baby spinach to 1 cup (250 mL). Add 2 to 3 kale leaves, stems removed, and ¼ tsp (1 mL) spirulina powder.

Lemonade Smoothie

This tart and refreshing drink will quench your thirst on a hot summer's day.

Tips

Substitute an equal amount of Cashew Milk (page 61) for the almond milk.

Coconut sugar is a low-glycemic sweetener that is available in most well-stocked supermarkets and natural food stores. It has a sweet taste, similar to brown sugar.

• Blender

1 cup	Almond Milk (page 61; see Tips, left)	250 mL
1	frozen banana (see Tip, below)	1
3 tbsp	freshly squeezed lemon juice	45 mL
2 tbsp	organic coconut sugar or pure maple syrup (see Tips, left)	30 mL
½ tsp	alcohol-free organic vanilla extract	2 mL

1. In blender, combine almond milk, banana, lemon juice, coconut sugar and vanilla. Blend at high speed until smooth. Serve immediately.

Kitchen Sink Smoothie

This nutrient-dense smoothie is the perfect quick breakfast for a busy day.

Tip

To freeze a banana: Peel banana, then transfer to a resealable bag, pushing as much air out of the bag as you can before sealing it. Freeze for up to 4 months.

• Blender

1 cup	Almond Milk (page 61)	250 mL
1	frozen banana (see Tip, left)	1
2	kale leaves, stems removed (see Tips, page 51)	2
¼	apple, peeled and cored	¼
¼ cup	frozen mango	60 mL
3 tbsp	frozen blueberries	45 mL
2 tbsp	frozen strawberries	30 mL
½ tsp	alcohol-free organic vanilla extract	2 mL

1. In blender, combine almond milk, banana, kale, apple, mango, blueberries, strawberries and vanilla. Blend at high speed until smooth. Serve immediately.

Double Detox Smoothie

The tart green apple in this smoothie provides sweetness to balance the bitterness of the dandelion and kale leaves. However, it is worth acquiring a taste for these leafy greens, as they are wonderful detoxifiers.

MAKES ABOUT 2 CUPS (500 ML)

Tips

Substitute an equal amount of Almond Milk (page 61), Oat Milk (page 63) or Cashew Milk (page 61) for the green milk.

Spirulina is a protein- and mineral-rich blue-green freshwater alga that is believed to help boost the immune system. Look for it in natural food stores.

• Blender

1¼ cups	Green Milk (page 64; see Tips, left)	300 mL
1	frozen banana (see Tip, page 53)	1
3 to 4	kale leaves, stems removed	3 to 4
1 to 2	dandelion leaves, tough stems removed	1 to 2
¼ cup	peeled, cored and chopped green apple	60 mL
½ tsp	alcohol-free organic vanilla extract	2 mL
⅛ tsp	spirulina or chlorella powder (see Tips, left)	0.5 mL

1. In blender, combine green milk, banana, kale and dandelion leaves, apple, vanilla and spirulina. Blend at high speed until smooth. Serve immediately.

Earl Grey Smoothie

This refreshing smoothie is one of my favorite pick-me-ups on a warm, sunny afternoon. I like to enjoy it with Simple Summery Sandwiches (page 96).

MAKES ABOUT 2 CUPS (500 ML)

Tip

To make the tea for this recipe: Bring some water to a boil. Place 2 Earl Grey teabags in a mug and pour ½ cup (125 mL) boiling water overtop. Cover and set aside for 10 minutes to steep. Remove and discard teabags. Refrigerate tea for 30 minutes or until cold.

• Blender

1 cup	Almond Milk (page 61)	250 mL
½ cup	steeped Earl Grey tea, cooled (see Tip, left)	125 mL
1	frozen banana (see Tip, page 53)	1
1 tbsp	organic coconut sugar, raw agave nectar or pure maple syrup	15 mL
1 tbsp	raw shelled hemp seeds	15 mL
½ tsp	alcohol-free organic vanilla extract	2 mL

1. In blender, combine almond milk, tea, banana, coconut sugar, hemp seeds and vanilla. Blend at high speed until smooth and creamy. Serve immediately.

Teatime Smoothie

If you like green tea lattes, you'll enjoy this refreshing smoothie.

**MAKES ABOUT
2 CUPS (500 ML)**

Tips

Substitute an equal amount of Hemp and Chia Milk (page 64) or Oat Milk (page 63) for the green milk.

To brew the green tea for this recipe: Just before water reaches the boiling point, remove from heat. Place green tea bag in a mug and pour ½ cup (125 mL) hot water overtop. Cover and set aside for 15 minutes to steep. Remove and discard teabag. Refrigerate tea for 30 minutes or until cold.

Blender

1 cup	Green Milk (page 64; see Tips, left)	250 mL
1	frozen banana (see Tip, page 53)	1
½ cup	steeped green tea, cooled (see Tips, left)	125 mL
3 tbsp	freshly squeezed lemon juice	45 mL
1 tbsp	raw agave nectar	15 mL
½ tsp	alcohol-free organic vanilla extract	2 mL

1. In blender, combine green milk, banana, green tea, lemon juice, agave nectar and vanilla. Blend at high speed until smooth. Serve immediately.

Variation

Chai Me Smoothie: Substitute an equal amount of cold chai tea for the green tea. Add ¼ tsp (1 mL) ground cinnamon.

Easy Apple Pie Smoothie

This recipe is a delicious and healthy alternative to dessert.

**MAKES ABOUT
2 CUPS (500 ML)**

Tips

Substitute an equal amount of Cashew Milk (page 61) for the almond milk.

To melt the coconut oil, gently warm it in a small skillet over low heat.

Blender

1 cup	Almond Milk (page 61; see Tips, left)	250 mL
1	frozen banana (see Tip, page 53)	1
¾ cup	peeled, cored and chopped apple	175 mL
2 tbsp	melted coconut oil (see Tips, left)	30 mL
2 tbsp	pure maple syrup	30 mL
1 tsp	ground cinnamon	5 mL
¼ tsp	organic vanilla powder (see page 7)	1 mL

1. In blender, combine almond milk, banana, apple, coconut oil, maple syrup, cinnamon and vanilla. Blend at high speed until smooth. Serve immediately.

Sweet Potato Pie Smoothie

Sweet potato, maple syrup, rich coconut oil, aromatic cinnamon and creamy banana make this a thick, filling drink that will remind you of fall.

MAKES ABOUT 2 CUPS (500 ML)

Tip

To cook the sweet potato: In a saucepan filled with water, bring peeled and cubed sweet potato to a boil. Reduce heat and simmer for 10 to 12 minutes or until tender. Drain and set aside to cool.

Blender

1¼ cups	Fall Harvest Squash Milk (page 69)	300 mL
1	frozen banana (see Tips, page 60)	1
⅓ cup	cooked cubed sweet potato (see Tip, left)	75 mL
2 tbsp	melted coconut oil (see Tips, page 57)	30 mL
1 tbsp	pure maple syrup	15 mL
¼ tsp	ground cinnamon	1 mL

1. In blender, combine squash milk, banana, sweet potato, coconut oil, maple syrup and cinnamon. Blend at high speed until smooth. Serve immediately.

Whoopie Pie Smoothie

This sinful smoothie is inspired by a childhood favorite of mine. I love to top it with a spoonful of Pure Chocolate Ice Cream (page 522).

MAKES ABOUT 2 CUPS (500 ML)

Tips

Substitute an equal amount of Almond Milk (page 61) for the cashew milk.

Be sure to use raw (not processed) agave nectar. It is a 100% natural (non-GMO) sweetener that contains naturally occurring fructose and is low on the glycemic scale, which means that it releases glucose slowly, providing sustained energy.

Blender

1 cup	Cashew Milk (page 61; see Tips, left)	250 mL
1	frozen banana (see Tips, page 60)	1
¼ cup	raw cacao powder (see Tips, page 57)	60 mL
3 tbsp	melted coconut oil	45 mL
3 tbsp	raw agave nectar (see Tips, left)	45 mL
2 tbsp	raw almonds	30 mL
1 tbsp	raw cacao nibs (see Tips, page 57)	15 mL
½ tsp	alcohol-free organic vanilla extract	2 mL

1. In blender, combine cashew milk, banana, cacao powder, coconut oil, agave nectar, almonds, cacao nibs and vanilla. Blend at high speed for 10 seconds (you want to retain some of the texture from the almonds and cacao nibs). Serve immediately.

Marshmallow Smoothie

Bananas blended with creamy coconut oil and cashews will remind you of soft, fluffy marshmallows.

MAKES ABOUT 2 CUPS (500 ML)

Tips

To melt the coconut oil, gently warm it in a small skillet over low heat.

Substitute 2 tbsp (30 mL) raw agave nectar for the coconut sugar.

● **Blender**

1 cup	White Chocolate Milk (page 68)	250 mL
2	frozen bananas (see Tips, page 60)	2
¼ cup	melted coconut oil (see Tips, left)	60 mL
3 tbsp	organic coconut sugar	45 mL
6 to 8	raw cashews	6 to 8
½ tsp	alcohol-free organic vanilla extract	2 mL

1. In blender, combine white chocolate milk, bananas, coconut oil, coconut sugar, cashews and vanilla. Blend at high speed until smooth. Serve immediately.

Cookie Dough Smoothie

Crunchy cacao nibs give this creamy smoothie the texture and flavor of cookie dough. For a sinful treat, add a scoop of Salted Caramel Ice Cream (page 520).

MAKES ABOUT 2 CUPS (500 ML)

Tips

Raw cacao powder, with its rich dark chocolate flavor and superior nutritional content, is best for this smoothie, but if you don't have any on hand, you can substitute 2 tsp (10 mL) good-quality cocoa powder.

Cacao nibs — broken pieces of hulled cacao beans — are similar to chocolate chips but contain no sugar. They are available in natural food stores and well-stocked supermarkets.

● **Blender**

1¼ cups	Almond Milk (page 61)	300 mL
1	frozen banana (see Tips, page 60)	1
3 tbsp	raw cacao nibs (see Tips, left)	45 mL
1 tbsp	melted coconut oil (see Tips, above left)	15 mL
1 tsp	raw cacao powder (see Tips, left)	5 mL
1 tbsp	raw agave nectar	15 mL
½ tsp	alcohol-free organic vanilla extract	2 mL

1. In blender, combine almond milk, banana, cacao nibs, coconut oil, cacao powder, agave nectar and vanilla. Blend at high speed until smooth. Serve immediately.

Puckery Peanut Butter Smoothie

Lime zest gives this smoothie a bit of pucker power, while the banana makes it creamy.

MAKES ABOUT 2 CUPS (500 ML)

Tips

Substitute an equal amount of Hemp and Chia Milk (page 64), Cashew Milk (page 61) or Coconut Milk (page 62) for the almond milk.

Substitute an equal amount of almond butter for the peanut butter.

● **Blender**

1¼ cups	Almond Milk (page 61; see Tips, left)	300 mL
1	frozen banana (see Tips, page 60)	1
¼ cup	smooth peanut butter (see Tips, left)	60 mL
¼ tsp	freshly grated lime zest	1 mL
3 tbsp	freshly squeezed lime juice	45 mL

1. In blender, combine almond milk, banana, peanut butter, lime zest and lime juice. Blend at high speed until smooth. Serve immediately.

Peanut Butter Parfait Smoothie

This smoothie is nutty and decadent. Enjoy it as a snack or for dessert after dinner.

MAKES 2 CUPS (500 ML)

Tips

Substitute an equal amount of Almond Milk or Cashew Milk (page 61) for the oat milk.

Substitute an equal amount of almond or cashew butter for the peanut butter.

To melt the coconut oil, gently warm it in a small skillet over low heat.

● **Blender**

1 cup	Oat Milk (page 63; see Tips, left)	250 mL
1	frozen banana (see Tips, page 60)	1
2 tbsp	crunchy peanut butter (see Tips, left)	30 mL
1 tbsp	melted coconut oil (see Tips, left)	15 mL
1 tbsp	raw cacao powder	15 mL
2 tsp	raw agave nectar	10 mL
½ tsp	alcohol-free organic vanilla extract	2 mL
1 tbsp	crushed peanuts (optional)	15 mL

1. In blender, combine oat milk, banana, peanut butter, coconut oil, cacao powder, agave nectar and vanilla. Blend at high speed until smooth.
2. Pour into glass and top with crushed peanuts (if using). Serve immediately.

Peachy Butterscotch Smoothie

In this smoothie, the combined flavors of fresh peaches, sweet dates and aromatic vanilla and cinnamon are reminiscent of butterscotch ripple ice cream.

**MAKES
2 CUPS (500 ML)**

Tip

To soak dates: Place in a small bowl with 1 cup (250 mL) warm water. Cover and set aside for 30 minutes or until soft. Drain. Using your fingers, remove pit from each date.

● **Blender**

1 cup	Coconut Milk (page 62)	250 mL
1/2 cup	chopped peach (about 1/2 medium; see Tips, page 22)	125 mL
4 to 5	Medjool dates, soaked and pitted (see Tip, left)	4 to 5
1 tbsp	melted coconut oil	15 mL
1/2 tsp	ground cinnamon	2 mL
1/2 tsp	alcohol-free organic vanilla extract	2 mL

1. In blender, combine coconut milk, peach, dates, coconut oil, cinnamon and vanilla. Blend at high speed until smooth. Serve immediately.

Thanksgiving Smoothie

This smoothie has all the warming flavors of fall. The cooked pumpkin makes it extra creamy.

**MAKES ABOUT
2 CUPS (500 ML)**

Tip

To cook the pumpkin: In a saucepan filled with water, bring peeled and cubed pumpkin to a boil. Reduce heat and simmer for 10 to 12 minutes or until tender. Drain and set aside to cool.

● **Blender**

1 cup	Almond Milk (page 61)	250 mL
1	frozen banana (see Tips, page 60)	1
1/3 cup	cooked pumpkin or canned organic pumpkin purée (see Tip, left)	75 mL
2 tbsp	pure maple syrup	30 mL
1 tbsp	melted coconut oil	15 mL
1/2 tsp	ground cinnamon	2 mL
1/4 tsp	freshly grated nutmeg	1 mL
1/2 tsp	alcohol-free organic vanilla extract	2 mL
1/8 tsp	ground allspice	0.5 mL

1. In blender, combine almond milk, banana, pumpkin, maple syrup, coconut oil, cinnamon, nutmeg, vanilla and allspice. Blend at high speed until smooth and creamy. Serve immediately.

Eggnog Smoothie

This festive smoothie is a delectable alternative to traditional eggnog-based drinks at holiday gatherings.

MAKES ABOUT 2 CUPS (500 ML)

Tips

Substitute an equal amount of cashew milk for the Holiday Milk.

To freeze a banana: Peel banana, then transfer to a resealable bag, pushing as much air out of the bag as you can before sealing it. Freeze for up to 4 months.

● Blender

1 cup	Holiday Milk (page 70; see Tips, left)	250 mL
1	frozen banana (see Tips, left)	1
2 tbsp	pure maple syrup	30 mL
1 tbsp	raw cashews	15 mL
½ tsp	freshly grated nutmeg	2 mL
½ tsp	alcohol-free organic vanilla extract	2 mL
¼ tsp	ground cinnamon	1 mL

1. In blender, combine Holiday Milk, banana, maple syrup, cashews, nutmeg, vanilla and cinnamon. Blend at high speed until smooth. Serve immediately.

Candy Cane Smoothie

The addition of peppermint makes this pink-hued smoothie the perfect festive treat. I like to serve it for breakfast or brunch during the holiday season.

MAKES ABOUT 2 CUPS (500 ML)

Tips

For the best flavor, use alcohol-free organic peppermint extract.

For a sinful treat, substitute ¼ cup (60 mL) crushed gluten-free candy canes for the beet juice.

● Blender

1¼ cups	Almond Milk (page 61)	300 mL
1	frozen banana (see Tips, above left)	1
¼ cup	fresh beet juice	60 mL
2 tbsp	pure maple syrup	30 mL
½ tsp	organic peppermint extract (see Tips, left)	2 mL
½ tsp	alcohol-free organic vanilla extract	2 mL

1. In blender, combine almond milk, banana, beet juice, maple syrup, peppermint extract and vanilla. Blend at high speed until smooth. Serve immediately.

Almond Milk

This non-dairy milk is very versatile. Use it to replace cow's milk in most recipes.

Tips

To soak the almonds: Place in a bowl and add 4 cups (1 L) water. Cover and set aside for 3 hours or refrigerate overnight. Drain, discarding water.

You can dry out the almond pulp in the oven and grind it in a food processor or blender to use as almond flour in many recipes.

- **Blender**
- **Fine-mesh sieve**

1 cup	raw whole almonds, soaked	250 mL
4 cups	water	1 L
Pinch	fine sea salt	Pinch

1. In blender, combine almonds, water and salt. Blend at high speed until smooth.
2. Place sieve over a pitcher and strain mixture. Discard pulp or save for another use (see Tips, left). Serve immediately or cover and refrigerate for up to 5 days.

Variation

Sweet Vanilla Almond Milk: Complete Step 1. Add 3 pitted Medjool dates or 2 tbsp (30 mL) raw agave nectar or pure maple syrup, and $\frac{1}{2}$ tsp (2 mL) alcohol-free organic vanilla extract. Blend until smooth, then complete Step 2.

Cashew Milk

Cashew milk is higher in fat than other non-dairy milks. It is best for most dessert recipes because it produces a creamier texture.

Tips

To soak the cashews: Place in a bowl and cover with 4 cups (1 L) water. Cover and set aside for 3 hours or overnight (if overnight, refrigerate). Drain, discarding water.

You can also strain this and other non-dairy milks through cheesecloth or use a nut-milk bag.

- **Blender**
- **Fine-mesh sieve**

1 cup	raw cashews, soaked	250 mL
4 cups	water	1 L
Pinch	fine sea salt	Pinch

1. In blender, combine cashews, water and salt. Blend at high speed until smooth.
2. Place sieve over a pitcher and strain mixture. Discard pulp. Serve immediately or cover and refrigerate for up to 5 days.

Variation

Sweet Vanilla Cashew Milk: Follow the instructions for Sweet Vanilla Almond Milk, above.

Coconut Milk

This luscious milk is a great alternative to dairy milk.

MAKES 4 CUPS (1 L)

- **Blender**
- **Fine-mesh sieve**

1 cup	unsweetened dried shredded coconut, soaked (see Tips, left)	250 mL
4 cups	water	1 L
Pinch	fine sea salt	Pinch

Tips

To soak the coconut: Place in a bowl and cover with 4 cups (1 L) water. Cover and set aside for 30 minutes. Drain, discarding water.

This milk cannot be substituted for canned coconut milk, which is much thicker. Enjoy this version in smoothies, tea or coffee, or with cereal, among other uses.

1. In blender, combine coconut, water and salt. Blend at high speed until smooth.
2. Place sieve over a pitcher and strain. Discard pulp. Serve immediately or cover and refrigerate for up to 5 days.

Variation

Sweet Vanilla Coconut Milk: Complete Step 1. Add 3 pitted Medjool dates or 2 tbsp (30 mL) raw agave nectar or pure maple syrup, and $\frac{1}{2}$ tsp (2 mL) alcohol-free organic vanilla extract. Blend until smooth, then complete Step 2.

Quinoa Milk

This nutrient-rich milk is perfect for oatmeal and porridge, or on its own, served chilled. It's a great alternative for people with nut allergies.

MAKES 4 CUPS (1 L)

- **Blender**
- **Fine-mesh sieve**

2 cups	cooked quinoa	500 mL
4 cups	water	1 L
Pinch	fine sea salt	Pinch

Tip

To cook quinoa: In a saucepan, bring to a boil 1 cup (250 mL) quinoa and 2 cups (500 mL) water. Reduce heat and simmer, uncovered, until no water remains, about 15 minutes. Cover and set aside so quinoa can absorb any remaining liquid, about 5 minutes. Set aside to cool.

1. In blender, combine quinoa, water and salt. Blend at high speed until smooth.
2. Place sieve over a pitcher and strain. Discard pulp. Serve immediately or cover and refrigerate for up to 5 days.

Variation

Sweet Vanilla Quinoa Milk: Follow the instructions for Sweet Vanilla Coconut Milk, above.

Oat Milk

This creamy milk is a great nut-free alternative.

MAKES 4 CUPS (1 L)

Tip

To soak the oats: Place in a bowl with 4 cups (1 L) water. Cover and set aside for 3 hours or overnight (if overnight, refrigerate). Drain through a fine-mesh sieve, then rinse under cool water until the water runs clear.

- **Blender**
- **Fine-mesh sieve**

1 cup	gluten-free steel-cut oats, soaked	250 mL
4 cups	water	1 L
Pinch	fine sea salt	Pinch

1. In blender, combine oats, water and salt. Blend at high speed until smooth.
2. Place sieve over a pitcher and strain. Serve immediately or cover and refrigerate for up to 5 days.

Variation

Maple Cinnamon Oat Milk: In Step 1, add 3 tbsp (45 mL) pure maple syrup, $\frac{1}{2}$ tsp (2 mL) ground cinnamon and $\frac{1}{2}$ tsp (2 mL) alcohol-free organic vanilla extract.

Flaxseed Milk

This nut-free milk is rich in healthy omega-3 fats.

MAKES 4 CUPS (1 L)

Tips

To soak the flax seeds: Place in a bowl with 4 cups (1 L) water. Cover and set aside for 30 minutes. Drain, discarding water.

Golden flax seeds will make lighter-colored milk; brown flax seeds will result in a darker color.

You can also strain this and other non-dairy milks through cheesecloth or use a nut-milk bag.

- **Blender**
- **Fine-mesh sieve**

1 cup	raw flax seeds, soaked	250 mL
4 cups	water	1 L
Pinch	fine sea salt	Pinch

1. In blender, combine flax seeds, water and salt. Blend at high speed until smooth.
2. Place sieve over a pitcher and strain. Discard pulp. Serve immediately or cover and refrigerate for up to 5 days.

Variation

Vanilla Cinnamon Flax Milk: In Step 1, add 1 tsp (5 mL) alcohol-free organic vanilla extract and $\frac{1}{4}$ tsp (1 mL) ground cinnamon.

Hemp and Chia Milk

Hemp and chia seeds are rich in brain-boosting omega-3 fats. To help maintain a healthy body, add this milk to tea or coffee, smoothies and cereal.

MAKES 4 CUPS (1 L)

Tips

Store hemp and chia seeds in the refrigerator to prevent the fats from going rancid.

Substitute 3 pitted Medjool dates for the maple syrup.

You can also strain this and other non-dairy milks through cheesecloth or use a nut-milk bag.

- Blender
- Fine-mesh sieve

¼ cup	raw shelled hemp seeds	60 mL
3 tbsp	chia seeds	45 mL
4 cups	water	1 L
2 tbsp	pure maple syrup	30 mL
½ tsp	alcohol-free organic vanilla extract	2 mL
Pinch	fine sea salt	Pinch

1. In blender, combine hemp and chia seeds, water, maple syrup, vanilla and salt. Blend at high speed until smooth.
2. Place sieve over a pitcher and strain mixture through it (see Tips, left). Discard pulp. Serve immediately or cover and refrigerate for up to 5 days.

Green Milk

This milk is packed full of nutrition, so drink it when you feel like you need a nutritional boost. It's a great addition to smoothies or cereal.

MAKES ABOUT 4 CUPS (1 L)

Tips

Substitute an equal amount of chlorella powder for the spirulina. Chlorella is a nutrient-rich freshwater alga that is believed to have detoxifying effects. You can find it in well-stocked supermarkets.

Substitute an equal amount of Cashew Milk (page 61) or Coconut Milk (page 62) for the almond milk.

- Blender
- Fine-mesh sieve

3½ cups	Almond Milk (page 61)	875 mL
1 cup	chopped kale leaves, stems removed	250 mL
1 tbsp	pure maple syrup	15 mL
½ tsp	spirulina powder (see Tips, left)	2 mL
½ tsp	alcohol-free organic vanilla extract	2 mL

1. In blender, combine almond milk, kale, maple syrup, spirulina and vanilla. Blend at high speed until smooth.
2. Place sieve over a pitcher and strain mixture through it (see Tips, left). Discard pulp. Serve immediately or cover and refrigerate for up to 5 days.

Carrot Cashew Ginger Milk

I like to serve this milk alongside Indian-inspired dishes. It also works well as a base for smoothies and other drinks, where it adds flavor as well as nutrients.

MAKES 4 CUPS (1 L)

Tips

To soak the cashews: Place in a bowl and cover with 4 cups (1 L) water. Cover and set aside for 30 minutes or overnight (if overnight, refrigerate). Drain, discarding water.

To peel fresh gingerroot with the least amount of waste, use the edge of a teaspoon. Scrape off the skin with a brushing motion to reveal the yellow root.

- Blender
- Fine-mesh sieve

1 cup	raw cashews, soaked (see Tips, left)	250 mL
3½ cups	water	875 mL
2 cups	chopped carrots	500 mL
2 tbsp	chopped peeled gingerroot (see Tips, left)	30 mL

1. In blender, combine cashews, water, carrots and ginger. Blend at high speed until smooth.
2. Place sieve over a pitcher and strain mixture through it (see Tips, page 64). Discard pulp. Serve immediately or cover and refrigerate for up to 5 days.

Strawberry Hazelnut Milk

This milk is perfect for satisfying that mid-afternoon craving for something sweet. It's also great on cereal and porridge or blended into your favorite smoothie.

MAKES 4 CUPS (1 L)

Tips

To soak the hazelnuts: Place in a bowl and cover with 4 cups (1 L) water. Cover and set aside for 30 minutes or overnight (if overnight, refrigerate). Drain, discarding water.

Substitute ½ cup (125 mL) hazelnut butter for the hazelnuts.

- Blender
- Fine-mesh sieve

1 cup	raw hazelnuts, soaked	250 mL
1 cup	hulled strawberries	250 mL
3 tbsp	raw agave nectar (see page 8)	45 mL
½ tsp	alcohol-free organic vanilla extract	2 mL
4 cups	water or almond milk	1 L
Pinch	fine sea salt	Pinch

1. In blender, combine hazelnuts, strawberries, agave nectar, vanilla, water and salt. Blend at high speed until smooth.
2. Place sieve over a pitcher and strain mixture through it (see Tips, page 64). Discard pulp. Serve immediately or cover and refrigerate for up to 5 days.

Cardamom Brazil Nut Milk

This spiced nut milk is a delicious treat.

Tips

To soak the Brazil nuts: Place in a bowl and cover with 4 cups (1 L) water. Cover and set aside for 30 minutes or overnight (if overnight, refrigerate). Drain, discarding water.

Store Brazil nuts in the fridge or freezer. Because they are high in fat, they can spoil easily.

You can also strain this and other non-dairy milks through cheesecloth or use a nut-milk bag.

- **Blender**
- **Fine-mesh sieve**

1 cup	raw Brazil nuts, soaked	250 mL
4 cups	water	1 L
1 tbsp	raw agave nectar	15 mL
½ tsp	ground cardamom	2 mL
¼ tsp	alcohol-free organic vanilla extract	1 mL
Pinch	fine sea salt	Pinch

1. In blender, combine nuts, water, agave, cardamom, vanilla and salt. Blend at high speed until smooth.
2. Place sieve over a pitcher and strain mixture. Discard pulp. Serve immediately or cover and refrigerate for up to 5 days.

Variation

Cardamom Brazil Nut Hot Chocolate: Using a blender, combine ½ cup (125 mL) Cardamom Brazil Nut Milk, ½ cup (125 mL) boiling water, 2 tbsp (30 mL) raw cacao powder, 2 tbsp (30 mL) raw agave nectar, 1 tbsp (15 mL) melted coconut oil and ½ tsp (2 mL) alcohol-free organic vanilla extract.

Chai Almond Milk

When gently heated, this milk makes a perfect alternative to afternoon tea.

Tip

To steep the tea: Bring water to a boil. Add teabag to a mug and pour ½ cup (125 mL) boiling water overtop. Set aside for 15 minutes to steep. Remove and discard teabag. Refrigerate until cold.

- **Blender**

3½ cups	Almond Milk (page 61)	875 mL
½ cup	steeped chai tea (see Tips, left)	125 mL

1. In blender, combine almond milk and tea. Blend at high speed until smooth. Serve immediately or cover and refrigerate for up to 5 days.

Salted Caramel Pistachio Milk

Enjoy this non-dairy dessert milk as a sweet treat. It's particularly good served with a slice of Pecan Pie (page 456) or Blueberry Cheesecake (page 458).

(page 456) ... (page 458)

MAKES 4 CUPS (1 L)

Tips

To soak the pistachios: Place in a bowl and cover with 4 cups (1 L) water. Cover and set aside for 30 minutes or overnight (if overnight, refrigerate). Drain, discarding water.

Coconut sugar is made from dried sap of the coconut palm. It is a low-glycemic sweetener that contains trace minerals and is similar in taste and texture to brown sugar.

- Blender
- Fine-mesh sieve

1 cup	raw pistachios, soaked (see Tips, left)	250 mL
4 cups	water	1 L
3 tbsp	organic coconut sugar (see Tips, left)	45 mL
2 tbsp	melted coconut oil	30 mL
2 tbsp	raw agave nectar (see page 8)	30 mL
1 tbsp	pure maple syrup	15 mL
1/2 tsp	fine sea salt	2 mL
1/2 tsp	alcohol-free organic vanilla extract	2 mL

1. In blender, combine pistachios, water, coconut sugar, coconut oil, agave nectar, maple syrup, salt and vanilla. Blend at high speed until smooth.
2. Place sieve over a pitcher and strain mixture through it (see Tips, page 66). Discard pulp. Serve immediately or cover and refrigerate for up to 5 days.

Hot Chocolate

Warm up after a cold day with a cup of this creamy hot chocolate. For a special treat, serve with Churros with Cinnamon Sugar (page 490).

MAKES ABOUT 1 1/2 CUPS (375 ML)

Tips

If you do not have coconut butter, substitute 1/3 cup (75 mL) soaked raw cashews and blend until smooth.

Cooling the water ensures that the heat won't pop the lid off the blender.

- Blender

1/3 cup	coconut butter (see Tips, left)	75 mL
1/4 cup	raw cacao powder (see page 15)	60 mL
1 tbsp	melted coconut oil	15 mL
2 tbsp	organic coconut sugar	30 mL
1/2 tsp	alcohol-free organic vanilla extract	2 mL
1 1/4 cups	boiled water, cooled slightly	300 mL

1. In blender, combine coconut butter, cacao powder, coconut oil, coconut sugar and vanilla. Add hot water and blend at high speed until smooth and creamy. Serve immediately.

White Chocolate Milk

Try this spin on chocolate milk with Lemon Vanilla Biscotti (page 437).

MAKES 4 CUPS (1 L)

Tips

To soak the cashews: Place in a bowl and cover with 6 cups (1.5 L) water. Cover and set aside for 30 minutes or refrigerate overnight. Drain, discarding water.

Cacao butter is the fat from pure cacao, and it's what helps give chocolate its flavor. To melt, heat gently in a small saucepan over low heat.

You can also strain any milk through cheesecloth or use a nut-milk bag.

- Blender
- Fine-mesh sieve

2 cups	raw cashews, soaked (see Tips, left)	500 mL
3 cups	water	750 mL
½ cup	melted cacao butter (see Tips, left)	125 mL
¼ cup	raw agave nectar (see page 8)	60 mL
1 tbsp	pure maple syrup	15 mL
½ tsp	alcohol-free organic vanilla extract	2 mL

1. In blender, combine cashews, water, cacao butter, agave nectar, maple syrup and vanilla. Blend at high speed until smooth.
2. Place sieve over a pitcher and strain mixture through it (see Tips, left). Discard pulp or save for another use. Serve immediately or cover and refrigerate for up to 5 days.

Pure Chocolate Hazelnut Milk

This smooth, rich, sweet chocolate milk is full of flavor and nutrients.

MAKES 4 CUPS (1 L)

Tips

To soak the hazelnuts: Place in a bowl and cover with 4 cups (1 L) water. Cover and set aside for 30 minutes or refrigerate overnight. Drain, discarding water.

Substitute ½ cup (125 mL) hazelnut butter for the hazelnuts.

- Blender
- Fine-mesh sieve

1 cup	raw hazelnuts, soaked (see Tips, left)	250 mL
¼ cup	raw agave nectar (see page 8)	60 mL
3 tbsp	raw cacao powder	45 mL
½ tsp	alcohol-free organic vanilla extract	2 mL
4 cups	water or Almond Milk (page 61)	1 L
Pinch	fine sea salt	Pinch

1. In blender, at high speed, blend nuts, agave, cacao powder, vanilla, water and salt until smooth.
2. Strain mixture. Discard pulp. Serve immediately or cover and refrigerate for up to 5 days.

Fall Harvest Squash Milk

This milk is a tasty — and healthy — alternative to a pumpkin spice latte, and it's easy to make at home. Naturally sweet squash and sweet potatoes are blended with allspice, nutmeg and vanilla to make a unique fall treat. Try it on its own or enjoy it over cereal or added to your favorite smoothie.

MAKES 4 CUPS (1 L)

Tips

To soak the almonds: Place in a bowl and cover with 4 cups (1 L) water. Cover and set aside for 30 minutes or overnight (if overnight, refrigerate). Drain, discarding water.

To grate the nutmeg, use a fine-toothed grater such as the kind made by Microplane.

You can also strain this and other non-dairy milks through cheesecloth or use a nut-milk bag.

- **Blender**
- **Fine-mesh sieve**

1 cup	raw almonds, soaked (see Tips, left)	250 mL
3 cups	water	750 mL
½ cup	finely chopped peeled raw sweet potato	125 mL
½ cup	finely chopped peeled raw squash	125 mL
3 tbsp	pure maple syrup	45 mL
½ tsp	ground allspice	2 mL
½ tsp	alcohol-free organic vanilla extract	2 mL
⅛ tsp	freshly grated nutmeg (see Tips, left)	0.5 mL

1. In blender, combine almonds, water, sweet potato, squash, maple syrup, allspice, vanilla and nutmeg. Blend at high speed until smooth.

2. Place sieve over a pitcher and strain mixture through it (see Tips, left). Discard pulp. Serve immediately or cover and refrigerate for up to 5 days.

Holiday Milk

This non-dairy milk captures all the flavors of the holidays. Serve it as a special treat at family gatherings. I like to heat it gently and serve it warm alongside a slice of Pecan Pie (page 456) or Triple Ginger Cookies (page 428).

MAKES 4 CUPS (1 L)

Tips

To soak the almonds: Place in a bowl and cover with 4 cups (1 L) water. Cover and set aside for 30 minutes or overnight (if overnight, refrigerate). Drain, discarding water.

To grate the nutmeg, use a fine-toothed grater such as the kind made by Microplane.

You can also strain this and other non-dairy milks through cheesecloth or use a nut-milk bag.

- **Blender**
- **Fine-mesh sieve**

1 cup	raw almonds, soaked (see Tips, left)	250 mL
4 cups	water	1 L
3 tbsp	pure maple syrup	45 mL
1 tsp	ground allspice	5 mL
1 tsp	ground cinnamon	5 mL
½ tsp	ground ginger	2 mL
¼ tsp	freshly grated nutmeg (see Tips, left)	1 mL
½ tsp	alcohol-free organic vanilla extract	2 mL
Pinch	fine sea salt	Pinch

1. In blender, combine almonds, water, maple syrup, allspice, cinnamon, ginger, nutmeg, vanilla and salt. Blend at high speed until smooth.
2. Place sieve over a pitcher and strain mixture through it (see Tips, left). Discard pulp. Serve immediately or cover and refrigerate for up to 5 days.

Appetizers

Basic Chickpea Hummus

Keep a batch of this creamy chickpea purée on hand in the refrigerator. It's so versatile! You can enjoy it as a snack, slathered over a piece of gluten-free bread or pita, as a healthy accompaniment to your favorite wrap, or as a dip for crunchy carrot and celery sticks.

MAKES ABOUT 2 CUPS (500 ML)

Tips

A hand-held citrus reamer can be used to extract the juice from citrus fruits. Available in most kitchen supply stores, this tool would be ideal to use for the lemon juice in this recipe.

I like to use dried chickpeas and cook them myself, but you can use canned chickpeas, drained and rinsed, for convenience.

To cook dried chickpeas: Place in a bowl with 3 cups (750 mL) water, cover and set aside to soak for 3 hours or overnight (if overnight, refrigerate). Drain, discarding water. In a saucepan of boiling water, cook soaked chickpeas for about 30 minutes or until tender. Drain.

● **Food processor**

¼ cup	freshly squeezed lemon juice (see Tips, left)	60 mL
1 tsp	ground cumin	5 mL
½ tsp	fine sea salt	2 mL
4 to 6	cloves garlic	4 to 6
2 tbsp	tahini	30 mL
1 cup	cooked chickpeas (see Tips, left)	250 mL
½ cup	extra virgin olive oil	125 mL

1. In food processor fitted with the metal blade, process lemon juice, cumin, salt and garlic until no large pieces of garlic remain. Add tahini and process until smooth, about 30 seconds. Add chickpeas and process until smooth, about 30 seconds.

2. With the motor running, add oil through the feed tube in a slow, steady stream. Process until mixture is creamy and smooth, stopping the motor to scrape down sides of work bowl as necessary. Serve immediately or transfer to an airtight container and refrigerate for up to 2 weeks.

Variation

Herbed Chickpea Hummus: Substitute ½ cup (125 mL) fresh basil leaves and ¼ cup (60 mL) fresh flat-leaf (Italian) parsley leaves for the cumin.

Edamame Hummus

Tender young soybeans provide creamy body for this protein-rich dip, and fresh citrus gives it a taste of summer. I like to serve this with crunchy carrot and celery sticks or crisp organic corn chips.

Tips

Look for precooked organic edamame in the freezer section of your supermarket. You can purchase the beans either whole (in the pods) or shelled. I like to buy them shelled and store them in my freezer.

To cook shelled edamame: Lightly steam or boil from frozen for about 5 minutes or until tender and bright green.

A hand-held citrus reamer can be used to extract the juice from lemons and limes. Available in most kitchen supply stores, this tool would be ideal to use for the citrus in this recipe.

- **Food processor**

2 cups	frozen edamame beans, lightly steamed (see Tips, left)	500 mL
¼ cup	freshly squeezed lime juice (see Tips, left)	60 mL
3 tbsp	freshly squeezed lemon juice	45 mL
1 tbsp	toasted sesame oil	15 mL
1 tsp	fine sea salt	5 mL
6	cloves garlic	6
¼ cup	tahini	60 mL
½ cup	extra virgin olive oil	125 mL

1. In food processor fitted with the metal blade, process edamame, lime and lemon juices, sesame oil, salt and garlic until smooth, stopping the motor to scrape down sides of work bowl as necessary. Add tahini and pulse to combine.

2. With the motor running, add olive oil through the feed tube in a slow, steady stream and process until mixture is smooth and creamy. Serve immediately or transfer to an airtight container and refrigerate for up to 1 week.

Variation

Spicy Wasabi Hummus: Add 1 tbsp (15 mL) wasabi powder and ⅛ tsp (0.5 mL) cayenne pepper. Increase the amount of sesame oil to ¼ cup (60 mL) and reduce the amount of olive oil to ⅓ cup + 1 tsp (80 mL).

Herbed Cashew and Kale Hummus

I love to serve this tasty dip with spears of cucumber and romaine lettuce leaves. To make a simple meal, you can toss it with some hot cooked pasta.

MAKES ABOUT 2 CUPS (500 ML)

Tips

To remove the stem from kale leaves: Hold the kale leaf upside down by the end of the stem. Using your fingers, gently pull down and strip away the leaf. Discard stem.

For a nut-free version, substitute 1¼ cups (300 mL) raw sunflower seeds for the cashews.

To strip the leaves from fresh thyme: Hold sprig upside down by the stem and, using two fingers, firmly pull the leaves downward. Reserve the stems for soups or broths (discard after cooking). Use a sharp knife to chop the leaves, being careful not to chop too much or too hard, as this will bruise the leaves and cause the thyme to discolor.

Food processor

3 cups	chopped kale leaves (center rib removed; see Tips, left)	750 mL
1 cup	raw cashews (see Tips, left)	250 mL
¼ cup	freshly squeezed lemon juice	60 mL
1 tbsp	chopped fresh thyme leaves (see Tips, left)	15 mL
¼ tsp	fine sea salt	1 mL
3	cloves garlic	3
2 tbsp	tahini	30 mL
½ cup	extra virgin olive oil	125 mL

1. In food processor fitted with the metal blade, process kale, cashews, lemon juice, thyme, salt and garlic until smooth, stopping the motor to scrape down sides of work bowl as necessary. Add tahini and pulse to combine.
2. With the motor running, add oil through the feed tube in a slow, steady stream and process until mixture is smooth and creamy. Serve immediately or transfer to an airtight container and refrigerate for up to 1 week.

Variation

Spicy Curried Cashew and Kale Hummus: Omit the thyme. Add 1 tbsp (15 mL) curry powder, ¼ tsp (1 mL) ground cumin, ⅛ tsp (0.5 mL) ground coriander and a pinch of cayenne pepper.

Curried Zucchini Hummus

This recipe is a legume-free version of classic hummus, which is traditionally made with chickpeas. It is best in the summer, when zucchini is at the height of its growing season.

Tips

You do not have to peel the zucchini for this recipe, but keep in mind that the color of the skin will affect the final color of the dip.

A hand-held citrus reamer can be used to extract the juice from citrus fruit. Available in most kitchen supply stores, this tool would be ideal to use for the lemon juice in this recipe.

Substitute an equal amount of hempseed, flaxseed or pumpkinseed oil for the olive oil.

Food processor

3	medium zucchini, peeled and chopped (about 4 cups/1 L; see Tips, left)	3
½ cup	freshly squeezed lemon juice (see Tips, left)	125 mL
2 tbsp	water	30 mL
1 tsp	curry powder	5 mL
½ tsp	ground cumin	2 mL
¼ tsp	organic coconut sugar	1 mL
4	cloves garlic	4
½ cup	tahini	125 mL
6 tbsp	extra virgin olive oil (see Tips, left)	90 mL

1. In food processor fitted with the metal blade, process zucchini, lemon juice, water, curry powder, cumin, coconut sugar and garlic until smooth, stopping the motor to scrape down sides of work bowl as necessary. Add tahini and pulse to combine.

2. With the motor running, add oil through the feed tube in a slow, steady stream and process until mixture is smooth and creamy. Serve immediately or transfer to an airtight container and refrigerate for up to 1 week.

White Bean and Roasted Garlic Purée

White kidney beans provide the perfect creamy consistency for this simple and tasty spread. Enjoy it as a snack, or serve at dinner parties with grilled gluten-free flatbreads or as a dip for crunchy vegetables such as carrots and celery sticks.

MAKES ABOUT 2½ CUPS (625 ML)

Tips

To soak the beans: Place in a bowl and cover with 8 cups (2 L) water. Cover and set aside for 1 hour or overnight (if overnight, refrigerate). Drain, discarding water.

When roasting whole garlic, use a serrated knife to remove the top ¼ inch (0.5 cm) of the bulb, exposing the flesh of the individual cloves.

You can substitute 1 tbsp (15 mL) garlic powder for the roasted garlic.

- Preheat oven to 325°F (160°C)
- Baking sheet, lined with parchment paper
- Food processor

2 cups	dried white kidney beans, soaked (see Tips, left)	500 mL
4	heads garlic, tops removed (see Tips, left)	4
¾ cup	olive oil, divided	175 mL
1 tsp	fine sea salt, divided	5 mL
¼ cup	freshly squeezed lemon juice	60 mL
¼ cup	chopped fresh flat-leaf (Italian) parsley	60 mL
1 tbsp	chopped fresh thyme leaves	15 mL

1. On prepared baking sheet, toss garlic bulbs with ¼ cup (60 mL) oil. Bake in preheated oven for 45 minutes or until garlic is lightly golden and soft. Remove from oven and set aside to cool. Once cool, squeeze softened garlic cloves out of their skins.

2. In a saucepan filled with water, bring beans and ¼ tsp (1 mL) salt to a boil. Reduce heat and simmer until beans are tender, about 30 minutes. Drain and set aside to cool.

3. In food processor fitted with the metal blade, combine cooked beans, roasted garlic, remaining ½ cup (125 mL) oil, lemon juice, parsley, and thyme, remaining ¾ tsp (3 mL) salt. Process until smooth, stopping the motor to scrape down sides of work bowl as necessary. Serve immediately or transfer to an airtight container and refrigerate for up to 10 days.

Mushroom and Spinach Duxelles

Duxelles is a classic French mixture made of finely chopped mushrooms sautéed with fresh herbs. It is usually used to stuff puff pastry, but I like to serve it with Glazed Lentil Loaf (page 210) or Cauliflower Gratin (page 169), or simply with some gluten-free whole-grain crackers.

MAKES 3 CUPS (750 ML)

Tips

An easy way to mince garlic is to use a food processor fitted with the metal blade. Process it twice, stopping the motor to scrape down sides of work bowl as necessary. You can also use a fine-toothed grater such as the kind made by Microplane.

Substitute 8 cups (2 L) lightly packed baby spinach leaves for the spinach bunches.

Substitute an equal quantity of cremini mushrooms for the button mushrooms.

● **Food processor**

3 tbsp	grapeseed oil	45 mL
½ cup	finely chopped onion	125 mL
2 tbsp	minced garlic (see Tips, left)	30 mL
2	bunches spinach, leaves only, tough stems trimmed off, chopped (see Tips, left)	2
4 cups	sliced button mushrooms (see Tips, left)	1 L
2 tbsp	chopped fresh thyme leaves	30 mL

1. In a large skillet over medium-high heat, heat oil. Sauté onion until tender, about 3 minutes. Add garlic and cook, stirring constantly, for 2 minutes, until fragrant (be careful not to burn the garlic).

2. Add spinach and mushrooms and cook, stirring occasionally, until most of the liquid has evaporated, about 15 minutes. Remove from heat and set aside to cool.

3. In food processor fitted with the metal blade, process spinach mixture and thyme until smooth, stopping the motor to scrape down sides of work bowl as necessary. Serve immediately or transfer to an airtight container and refrigerate for up to 1 week.

Roasted Garlic and Black Olive Tapenade

Salty olives complement sweet, rich roasted garlic in this classic Mediterranean tapenade. This makes a relatively large quantity, perfect to serve as an appetizer when you are entertaining. (If you prefer a smaller yield, feel free to halve the recipe.) Spread on your favorite crusty bread, it's a perfect accompaniment to a light lunch.

MAKES ABOUT 2 CUPS (500 ML)

Tips

When roasting whole garlic, use a serrated knife to cut off the top ¼ inch (0.5 cm) of the bulb, exposing the flesh of the individual cloves.

I like to use kalamata olives for this recipe, but you can use any kind you like.

Substitute an equal amount of chopped fresh cilantro or basil leaves for the parsley.

- Baking sheet, lined with parchment paper
- Preheat oven to 325°F (160°C)
- Food processor

12	heads garlic, tops removed (see Tips, left)	12
1 cup	extra virgin olive oil, divided	250 mL
½ tsp	fine sea salt	2 mL
3 cups	pitted kalamata olives	750 mL
½ cup	chopped flat-leaf (Italian) parsley	125 mL
1 tbsp	freshly squeezed lemon juice	15 mL

1. Toss garlic bulbs with ¼ cup (60 mL) oil. Arrange in a single layer on prepared baking sheet. Bake in preheated oven for 45 minutes or until light golden and softened. Remove from oven and set aside to cool. Once cool, squeeze softened cloves from their skins (discard the skins) and set aside.

2. In food processor fitted with the metal blade, process roasted garlic, salt, olives, parsley and lemon juice until smooth, stopping the motor to scrape down sides of work bowl as necessary.

3. With the motor running, add remaining ¾ cup (175 mL) oil through the feed tube in a slow, steady stream; process until well combined. Serve immediately or transfer to an airtight container and refrigerate for up to 1 week.

Creamy Cashew Tzatziki

Serve this creamy, garlicky dip with fresh vegetables as part of a crudités platter or use it as a tasty spread in your favorite sandwich or wrap.

MAKES ABOUT 3½ CUPS (825 ML)

Tip

To soak the cashews: Place in a bowl and cover with 3 cups (750 mL) water. Cover and set aside for 30 minutes or overnight (if overnight, refrigerate). Drain, discarding water.

● **Food processor**

2 cups	raw cashews, soaked (see Tip, left)	500 mL
¾ cup	water	175 mL
¼ cup	freshly squeezed lemon juice	60 mL
½ tsp	fine sea salt	2 mL
½ cup	shredded cucumber	125 mL
6 to 8	cloves garlic, minced	6 to 8
1 tbsp	dried dill or ¼ cup (60 mL) chopped fresh dill fronds	15 mL

1. In food processor fitted with the metal blade, combine cashews, water, lemon juice and salt. Process until smooth. Transfer to a bowl.

2. Add cucumber, garlic and dill and stir well. Serve immediately or transfer to an airtight container and refrigerate for up to 5 days.

Ranch Dip

Enjoy this creamy dip as part of a crudités platter with crunchy broccoli and cauliflower florets. It also makes a great spread for your favorite sandwich or wrap.

Tips

To make this dip even creamier, add ½ cup (125 mL) extra virgin olive oil to the blender in Step 2 after blending the other ingredients. With the motor running, add oil through the lid in a slow, steady stream and process until smooth.

Substitute 1 tbsp (15 mL) dried dill for the fresh dill.

● **Blender**

1 cup	raw cashews	250 mL
	Water	
3 tbsp	freshly squeezed lemon juice	45 mL
1 tbsp	red wine vinegar	15 mL
½ cup	finely sliced green onions (white and green parts)	125 mL
¼ cup	chopped flat-leaf (Italian) parsley	60 mL
3 tbsp	chopped fresh dill (about ¼ bunch; see Tips, left)	45 mL
2 tsp	garlic powder	10 mL
½ tsp	fine sea salt	2 mL
¼ tsp	freshly ground black pepper	1 mL

1. In a saucepan, cover cashews with water. Bring to a boil, remove from heat and drain. Set cashews aside to cool.

2. In blender, combine boiled cashews, ½ cup (125 mL) water, lemon juice, vinegar, green onions, parsley, dill, garlic powder, salt and pepper. Blend at high speed until smooth and creamy. Serve immediately or transfer to an airtight container and refrigerate for up to 1 week.

Pico de Gallo

Serve this fresh tomato salsa as a dip for chips, tossed with your favorite salad, to dress up your favorite wrap or as a side to any Mexican-themed meal.

Tip

Unlike fresh flat-leaf (Italian) parsley stems, which are tough and hard to break down, the top two-thirds of cilantro stems are soft and full of flavor — do not discard them.

2 cups	chopped tomatoes	500 mL
½ cup	finely chopped white onion	125 mL
½ cup	roughly chopped fresh cilantro, leaves and stems (see Tip, left)	125 mL
¼ cup	finely chopped jalapeño pepper	60 mL
3 tbsp	freshly squeezed lime juice	45 mL
2 tbsp	extra virgin olive oil	30 mL
½ tsp	fine sea salt	2 mL

1. In a bowl, toss together tomatoes, onion, cilantro, jalapeño, lime juice, olive oil and salt. Serve immediately or transfer to an airtight container and refrigerate for up to 2 days.

Perfect Guacamole

This simple, classic dip is one of the best flavor combinations possible, as well as being very nutritious. It is fabulous with Sunflower Beet Crackers (page 151), Baked Loaded Nachos (page 172) or Baked Sweet Potato Chips (page 148).

Tips

Don't over-mash the avocado. You want it to be a bit chunky.

To remove the pit from an avocado: Remove the nib at the top. Insert the blade of the knife where the nib was and rotate the avocado from top to bottom to cut it in half lengthwise. Twist the two halves apart. With one motion, stick the knife into the pit and turn it 90 degrees, pulling out the pit as you twist the knife.

3	ripe medium avocados	3
¼ cup	freshly squeezed lemon juice	60 mL
2 tbsp	finely diced red onion	30 mL
3	cloves garlic, minced	3
1 tsp	fine sea salt	5 mL
Pinch	freshly ground black pepper	Pinch

1. In a bowl, combine avocados, lemon juice, onion, garlic, salt and pepper. Using a wire whisk, fork or potato masher, mix until the avocado is crushed and the ingredients are evenly distributed. Serve immediately or cover and refrigerate for up to 2 days.

Variations

There are many variations of guacamole. Play around with the recipe to see what suits your taste buds best. I sometimes add ¼ cup (60 mL) chopped cilantro leaves, 2 tbsp (30 mL) chopped tomato and a pinch of cayenne pepper or some minced fresh chile pepper for a little heat.

Queso Dip

This spicy, cheesy sauce is perfect for dipping, spreading or layering in your favorite recipes. I like to serve it with crispy or organic corn chips.

Tips

Medium-starch (all-purpose) potatoes such as Yukon Gold or Yellow Finn are best in this recipe.

For a nut-free version, substitute an equal amount of Quinoa Milk (page 62) or Oat Milk (page 63) for the almond milk.

You can substitute an equal amount of your favorite store-bought salsa for the chopped tomato.

Food processor

2 cups	chopped peeled potatoes	500 mL
4 cups	water	1 L
1 tsp	fine sea salt, divided	5 mL
½ cup	Almond Milk (page 61)	125 mL
¼ cup	nutritional yeast	60 mL
1 tsp	chili powder	5 mL
1 tsp	ground cumin	5 mL
½ tsp	sweet smoked paprika	2 mL
¼ tsp	hot sauce	1 mL
2	cloves garlic, minced	2
¼ cup	extra virgin olive oil	60 mL
¼ cup	chopped tomato (see Tips, left)	60 mL
1	small red or green chile, finely minced (optional)	1

1. In a large saucepan, combine potatoes, water and ½ tsp (2 mL) salt and bring to a boil. Reduce heat and simmer until potatoes are tender, about 12 minutes. Using a colander, drain potatoes.

2. In food processor fitted with the metal blade, combine cooked potatoes, almond milk, nutritional yeast, chili powder, cumin, paprika, hot sauce, garlic and remaining ½ tsp (2 mL) salt. Process until smooth, stopping the motor to scrape down sides of work bowl as necessary.

3. With the motor running, slowly add oil and process until well combined (if you prefer a creamier sauce, add up to ½ cup/125 mL oil). Transfer to a bowl and stir in tomato and chile (if using). Serve immediately or transfer to an airtight container and refrigerate for up to 1 week.

Variation

Cashew Queso Sauce: Omit potatoes. Add 2 cups (500 mL) cashews, soaked, to the food processor in Step 2. To soak cashews, place in a bowl and cover with 4 cups (1 L) water. Cover and set aside for 30 minutes or overnight (if overnight, refrigerate). Drain, discarding water.

Spicy, Cheesy Nacho Dip

This dip is perfect to serve with organic corn chips while enjoying the big game, or spread it on some crusty bread with your favorite sandwich. You can also use it as a dip for crunchy carrot and celery sticks.

Tip

Nutritional yeast is an inactive yeast that has been grown on beet molasses and then pasteurized. It provides a rich, cheesy flavor in sauces, stews, soups and dips. Look for it in well-stocked supermarkets and natural food stores.

● **Food processor**

2 cups	raw cashews	500 mL
	Water	
1 cup	nutritional yeast (see Tip, left)	250 mL
½ cup	extra virgin olive oil	125 mL
3 tbsp	freshly squeezed lemon juice	45 mL
2 tsp	chili powder	10 mL
1 tsp	fine sea salt	5 mL
⅛ tsp	ground turmeric	0.5 mL
1 to 2	cloves garlic	1 to 2
Pinch	cayenne pepper	Pinch

1. In a saucepan filled with water, bring cashews to a boil. Remove from heat and drain. Set cashews aside to cool.

2. In food processor fitter with the metal blade, combine boiled cashews, 1 cup (250 mL) water, nutritional yeast, olive oil, lemon juice, chili powder, salt, turmeric, garlic and cayenne. Process until smooth and creamy, stopping the motor to scrape down sides of work bowl as necessary. Serve immediately or transfer to an airtight container and refrigerate for up to 1 week.

Variation

Spicy Curried Nacho Dip: In Step 2, increase the amount of cayenne pepper to ½ tsp (2 mL). Add 2 tsp (10 mL) curry powder, 1 tsp (5 mL) ground cumin and ¼ tsp (1 mL) ground coriander.

Cheesy Fondue

Serve this creamy dish with chunks of toasted gluten-free bread for dipping.

**MAKES ABOUT
3 CUPS (750 ML)**

Tips

I recommend using an organic Chardonnay for this recipe.

Nutritional yeast is an inactive yeast that has been grown on beet molasses and then pasteurized. It provides a rich, cheesy flavor in sauces, stews, soups and dips. Look for it in well-stocked supermarkets and natural food stores.

You can substitute an equal quantity of your favorite store-bought vegan mozzarella for the mozzarella called for.

½ cup	coconut oil	125 mL
½ cup	brown rice flour	125 mL
¼ cup	dry white wine (see Tips, left)	60 mL
¼ cup	freshly squeezed lemon juice	60 mL
3 cups	Almond Milk (page 61)	750 mL
1 cup	nutritional yeast (see Tips, left)	250 mL
1 cup	Vegan Shredded Mozzarella (page 537; see Tips, left)	250 mL
1 tbsp	Dijon mustard	15 mL
1 tsp	fine sea salt	5 mL

1. In a small saucepan over medium heat, melt coconut oil. Add brown rice flour and cook, stirring frequently, for 3 to 4 minutes, until raw taste of flour is cooked out. Remove from heat and whisk in almond milk, ½ cup (125 mL) at a time, until no lumps remain. Return to medium heat and simmer, stirring frequently, for 5 to 6 minutes.

2. Remove from heat and stir in nutritional yeast, vegan mozzarella, mustard and salt. Serve immediately or let cool, transfer to an airtight container and refrigerate for up to 1 week. Reheat in a saucepan over medium heat, stirring constantly, until just bubbling.

Chia Whiz

Serve this rich, cheesy red pepper dip with crispy gluten-free crackers or fresh vegetables.

Tips

Nutritional yeast is an inactive yeast that has been grown on beet molasses and then pasteurized. It provides a rich, cheesy flavor in sauces, stews, soups and dips. Look for it in well-stocked supermarkets and natural food stores.

I prefer to use white chia seeds for a lighter-colored dip. You may use dark chia seeds, but keep in mind that they will result in dark specks throughout the dip.

● **Food processor**

¾ cup	raw cashews	175 mL
1 cup	chopped red bell pepper	250 mL
	Water	
¼ cup	nutritional yeast (see Tips, left)	60 mL
2½ tbsp	freshly squeezed lemon juice	37 mL
2 tbsp	chia seeds (see Tips, left)	30 mL
¾ tsp	fine sea salt	3 mL
¼ tsp	ground turmeric	1 mL

1. In a saucepan filled with water, bring cashews to a boil. Remove from heat and drain. Set aside to cool.

2. In food processor fitted with the metal blade, combine boiled cashews, red pepper, 6 tbsp (90 mL) water, nutritional yeast, lemon juice, chia seeds, salt and turmeric. Process until smooth and creamy, stopping the motor to scrape down sides of work bowl as necessary. Serve immediately or transfer to an airtight container and refrigerate for up to 1 week.

Baked Polenta Fries

Here is the perfect alternative to french fries. They are easy to make and delicious, especially when served with a side of Maple Chipotle Barbecue Sauce (page 111) or Roasted Red Pepper Mole Sauce (page 108).

MAKES ABOUT 20 PIECES

Tip

Cornmeal is made from dried ground pieces of corn. Since most of the corn grown in North America in genetically modified, it is particularly important to purchase organically produced corn products to avoid GMOs.

- **13- by 9-inch (33 by 23 cm) jelly-roll pan, lined with parchment paper**
- **Baking sheet, lined with parchment paper**

4 cups	water	1 L
1 tsp	fine sea salt	5 mL
1 cup	fine organic stone-ground cornmeal (see Tips, left)	250 mL
3 tbsp	grapeseed oil	45 mL

1. In a medium skillet, bring water to a boil. Whisking constantly, add cornmeal in a slow, steady stream. Bring to a boil, still whisking constantly. Reduce heat and simmer for 12 to 15 minutes, until thickened, stirring constantly to ensure that cornmeal cooks evenly and does not stick to the pan.

2. Using a spatula, spread cooked cornmeal evenly in prepared pan. Cover with plastic wrap and refrigerate for at least 3 hours or until cool and firm.

3. Preheat oven to 400°F (200°C). Cut polenta into 18 to 20 pieces. Brush with oil and arrange in a single layer on prepared baking sheet.

4. Bake in preheated oven for 18 to 20 minutes, turning and brushing fries with oil halfway through the cooking time, until crisp and heated through. Serve immediately or let cool, transfer to an airtight container and refrigerate for up to 5 days.

Variations

Cheesy Polenta: After the cornmeal has finished cooking in Step 1, stir in 1/2 cup (125 mL) nutritional yeast and 1 tsp (5 mL) freshly grated lemon zest. Serve warm. I particularly enjoy this with Slow-Cooked Barbecued Jackfruit (page 369).

Spicy Chipotle Polenta: In a blender, process 1/2 cup (125 mL) chopped chipotle peppers with 2 tbsp (30 mL) wheat-free tamari and 1 tbsp (15 mL) olive oil, until smooth. Stir into cooked cornmeal at the end of Step 1. Serve warm with Ratatouille (page 333).

Baked Onion Rings

These crispy, guilt-free (baked, not fried) onion rings are perfect for serving at summer barbecues or get-togethers. The cornmeal gives the coating its crisp texture. Try these with Maple Chipotle Barbecue Sauce (page 111) for dipping.

MAKES 4 SERVINGS

Tips

I like to use Vidalia onions for this recipe, as their higher sugar content yields a sweeter onion ring.

Marinating the onions in the almond milk mixture before baking helps to soften them and reduce the raw onion flavor.

● **2 baking sheets, lined with parchment paper**

2	large onions (see Tips, left)	2
3 cups	Almond Milk, divided (page 61)	750 mL
2 tbsp	freshly squeezed lemon juice	30 mL
1 tbsp	raw (unpasteurized) apple cider vinegar	15 mL
1 cup	medium organic stone-ground cornmeal (see Tips, page 86)	250 mL
½ cup	brown rice flour	125 mL
1 tbsp	garlic powder	15 mL
1 tsp	sweet paprika	5 mL
½ tsp	fine sea salt	2 mL
¼ cup	Dijon mustard	60 mL

1. Using a sharp knife, slice onions into rounds 1 inch (2.5 cm) thick (discard root ends) and separate into rings.

2. In a bowl, whisk together 2 cups (500 mL) almond milk, lemon juice and vinegar. Add sliced onions and toss to coat well. Cover and set aside for 30 minutes or refrigerate overnight (see Tips, left).

3. In a bowl, whisk together cornmeal, brown rice flour, garlic powder, paprika and salt.

4. In another bowl, whisk together remaining 1 cup (250 mL) almond milk and mustard.

5. Preheat oven to 400°F (200°C). Remove onions from marinade (discard liquid). Using your fingers, dip each onion ring first in mustard mixture, then in cornmeal mixture. Arrange coated onions in a single layer on prepared baking sheets.

6. Bake in preheated oven for 20 minutes or until crisp on the outside and tender in the middle. Serve immediately.

Variation

Curried Onion Rings: In Step 3, add 2 tbsp (30 mL) curry powder, 1 tsp (5 mL) ground cumin, ½ tsp (2 mL) ground coriander and ¼ tsp (1 mL) ground turmeric.

Baked Jalapeño Poppers

These spicy little treats make a great appetizer, but to tone down the heat it might be best to serve them with some cooling snacks. They also work as a side dish with Chipotle Walnut Mushroom and Rice Burgers (page 228) or Cheesy Quesadillas (page 166) served with a side of Queso Dip (page 82).

MAKES 4 POPPERS

Tips

I use particularly large peppers when making this recipe. If yours are smaller, adjust the amount of filling accordingly.

If you don't have any Creamy Vegan Pepper Jack on hand, substitute the following mixture. Place 1 cup (250 mL) raw cashews in a food processor fitted with the metal blade. Add 2 tbsp (30 mL) freshly squeezed lemon juice, 2 tbsp (30 mL) nutritional yeast, 2 tbsp (30 mL) melted coconut oil, ¼ tsp (1 mL) fine sea salt and ⅛ tsp (0.5 mL) sweet paprika. Process until smooth.

Finely ground cornmeal will yield the crispest results, but any size of grind will work.

• **Preheat oven to 400°F (200°C)**
• **Baking sheet, lined with parchment paper**

4	jalapeño peppers	4
½ cup	Creamy Vegan Pepper Jack (page 534; see Tips, left)	125 mL
½ cup	non-dairy milk, such as Almond Milk (page 61)	125 mL
¼ cup	Dijon mustard	60 mL
¼ tsp	fine sea salt, divided	1 mL
¼ cup	brown rice flour	60 mL
¼ cup	fine organic stone-ground cornmeal (see Tips, left)	60 mL
2 tbsp	chopped fresh flat-leaf (Italian) parsley leaves	30 mL
1 tbsp	finely grated lemon zest	15 mL

1. Lay jalapeños on a cutting board. Using a small knife, cut the top (stem end) off each pepper and discard. Insert a small spoon and gently scrape out the seeds and ribs.

2. Carefully spoon 2 tbsp (30 mL) Pepper Jack into each pepper, filling to the top. Set aside.

3. In a small bowl, whisk together non-dairy milk, mustard and ⅛ tsp (0.5 mL) salt. Set aside.

4. In another small bowl, whisk together brown rice flour, cornmeal, parsley, lemon zest and remaining ⅛ tsp (0.5 mL) salt.

5. Dip each stuffed pepper in milk mixture, shake off excess liquid, and then roll in flour mixture until completely coated. Place on prepared baking sheet.

6. Bake in preheated oven for 15 to 18 minutes or until peppers are golden brown.

Sweet Potato Quinoa Fritters

These crispy little fritters are the perfect finger food or side dish. I like to serve them with African-style dishes such as Simple Simmered Moroccan Chickpeas (page 201) or Spicy African Millet Salad (page 217), or with Middle Eastern Platter (page 426).

(page 201) ... (page 217) ... (page 426).

MAKES 8 FRITTERS

Tips

You want the oil to be deep enough in the pan to cover the fritters.

To cook just enough quinoa for this recipe: In a small saucepan, bring 1½ cups (375 mL) water and ¾ cup (175 mL) quinoa to a boil. Reduce heat and simmer, uncovered, until almost all the liquid has been absorbed, 12 to 13 minutes. Cover and set aside for 5 minutes so quinoa can absorb any remaining liquid and swell. Fluff with a fork before using.

Golden flax seeds will produce lighter-colored fritters, while brown flax seeds will produce darker-colored ones.

- Candy/deep-fry thermometer
- Bowl, lined with paper towels

4 cups	cubed peeled sweet potatoes	1 L
1½ cups	cooked quinoa (see Tips, left)	375 mL
2 tbsp	brown rice flour	30 mL
2 tbsp	melted coconut oil	30 mL
2 tbsp	ground flax seeds (see Tips, left)	30 mL
2 tsp	ground cinnamon	10 mL
½ tsp	fine sea salt	2 mL
2 cups	(approx.) grapeseed oil	500 mL

1. In a large saucepan filled with water, bring sweet potatoes to a boil. Reduce heat and simmer until potatoes are tender, about 15 minutes. Drain and transfer to a large bowl.

2. Using a wire whisk or potato masher, mash cooked sweet potatoes until no large pieces remain (a few small lumps are okay). Add cooked quinoa, brown rice flour, coconut oil, flax seeds, cinnamon and salt and whisk until combined. Cover and set aside for 10 to 15 minutes so the flax seeds can absorb some of the liquid and swell.

3. In a skillet over medium-high heat, heat oil until it reaches 400°F (200°C).

4. Using a ¼ cup (60 mL) measure, divide sweet potato mixture into 8 equal portions. Using your hands, shape each portion into an oblong (don't worry if they aren't perfect).

5. Working in batches, carefully drop 4 portions into hot oil and fry for 3 to 4 minutes per side or until golden brown and crispy. Using a slotted spoon, transfer to prepared bowl to drain excess oil. Repeat with remaining portions. Serve immediately.

Mac and Cheese Bites

Crispy on the outside and with a soft, gooey center, these tasty little bites are sure to make your next party a hit! I love to serve them with Maple Chipotle Barbecue Sauce (page 111) for dipping.

(page 111)

MAKES ABOUT 22 BITES

Tips

Gluten-free pasta requires a lot of cooking water to ensure that it does not stick together. Be sure to cook it in a large pot with at least 4 to 5 times more water than pasta.

Nutritional yeast is an inactive yeast that has been grown on beet molasses and then pasteurized. It provides a rich, cheesy flavor in sauces, stews, soups and dips. Look for it in well-stocked supermarkets and natural food stores.

To melt the coconut oil for this recipe, gently warm it in a skillet over low heat.

- Blender
- Baking sheet, lined with parchment paper

½ lb	gluten-free dried elbow macaroni	250 g
	Water	
1	small to medium butternut squash, peeled, seeded and chopped (about 5 cups/1.25 L)	1
½ cup	chopped onion	125 mL
1 to 2	cloves garlic, chopped	1 to 2
1 tbsp	fine sea salt, divided	15 mL
¼ cup	extra virgin olive oil, divided	60 mL
1½ cups	nutritional yeast (see Tips, left), divided	375 mL
⅔ cup	melted coconut oil (see Tips, left), divided	150 mL
¼ cup	Almond Milk (page 61)	60 mL
3 tbsp	Dijon mustard	45 mL
½ cup	brown rice flour	125 mL
½ cup	medium organic stone-ground cornmeal	125 mL

1. In a large saucepan of boiling salted water (see Tips, left), cook macaroni according to package directions. Using a colander, drain and rinse under cold running water to stop the cooking. Transfer cooked pasta to a large bowl.

2. Meanwhile, in a medium saucepan, combine squash, onion, garlic and 1 tsp (5 mL) salt with water to cover. Bring to a boil, then reduce heat and simmer for 12 to 15 minutes or until squash is very tender. Remove from heat, drain and set aside.

3. Fill blender jar halfway with cooked squash. Add 1 tsp (5 mL) salt, 2 tbsp (30 mL) olive oil, ¾ cup (75 mL) nutritional yeast and ⅓ cup (75 mL) coconut oil. Blend at high speed until smooth.

4. Pour squash mixture over cooked pasta and toss to combine. Repeat with remaining squash, salt, olive oil, nutritional yeast and coconut oil. Cover and refrigerate for 15 to 20 minutes to cool.

5. Preheat oven to 400°F (200°C). In a shallow bowl, whisk together almond milk and mustard. Set aside.

6. In another shallow bowl, whisk together brown rice flour and cornmeal.

7. Using a 1/4-cup (60 mL) measuring cup, divide macaroni mixture into equal portions. Using your hands, form portions into balls. Dip each portion in almond milk mixture, then roll in cornmeal mixture until evenly coated. Place on prepared baking sheet.

8. Bake in preheated oven for 20 to 25 minutes or until crispy and slightly browned. Serve immediately.

Crisp Tomato Wafers

I like to make these thin, crisp tomato wafers in the summer, when heirloom tomatoes are at the height of their growing season and have the best flavor. Serve them with your favorite dip or spread as an appetizer with almost any meal (see Tip, below).

MAKES 10 TO 12 WAFERS

Tip

Try serving these with Cashew Cheddar Cheese (pages 535) or Creamy Cashew Ricotta (page 532).

- Preheat oven to 400°F (200°C)
- Baking sheet, lined with parchment paper

1	large hothouse or heirloom tomato	1
1/4 cup	extra virgin olive oil	60 mL
1 tsp	dried basil	5 mL
1 tsp	dried oregano	5 mL
1/2 tsp	fine sea salt	2 mL

1. Using a sharp knife, slice tomato into 10 to 12 equal rounds, each about 1/8 inch (3 mm) thick.

2. Arrange tomato slices in a single layer on prepared baking sheet. Sprinkle evenly with oil, basil, oregano and salt. Bake in preheated oven for 35 minutes or until crisp (keep an eye on them, as they can easily burn).

3. Remove from oven and let cool completely on baking sheet. Serve immediately or transfer to an airtight container and store at room temperature for up to 2 weeks.

Mini Soft Tacos

These delectable mini tacos are the perfect way to start a Mexican-themed dinner or party. I like to serve them as an appetizer with Fajitas with Spice-Rubbed Portobellos (page 368).

MAKES 8 TACOS

Tips

I like to use frozen corn kernels for this recipe. To defrost, place in a colander and rinse under hot running water. You can also use fresh corn kernels cut off the cob.

You can purchase flax seeds that are already ground (often described as "milled") in vacuum-sealed bags, or you can grind them yourself. To grind the flax seeds for this recipe, place 1 cup (250 mL) whole seeds in a blender and blend at high speed until finely ground.

To keep the tortillas a lighter color, use golden flax; for darker tortillas, use brown flax.

- Preheat oven to 350°F (180°C)
- Food processor
- Tortilla press (optional)
- 2 baking sheets, lined with parchment paper

4 cups	corn kernels (see Tips, left)	1 L
1¼ cups	ground flax seeds (see Tips, left)	300 mL
½ cup	chopped carrot	125 mL
¼ cup	extra virgin olive oil, divided	60 mL
2 tsp	chili powder	10 mL
1 tsp	ground cumin	5 mL
1	ripe medium avocado	1
¼ cup	freshly squeezed lemon juice, divided	60 mL
½ tsp	fine sea salt, divided	2 mL
1	clove garlic, minced	1
½ cup	chopped tomato	125 mL
¼ cup	chopped fresh flat-leaf (Italian) parsley leaves	60 mL
2 cups	finely sliced romaine lettuce	500 mL
½ cup	Vegan Sour Cream (page 555)	125 mL
1 cup	raw shelled hemp seeds (see Tip, page 93)	250 mL

1. In food processor fitted with the metal blade, combine corn, ground flax seeds, carrot, 3 tbsp (45 mL) oil, chili powder and cumin. Process until smooth, stopping the motor to scrape down sides of work bowl as necessary. Transfer to a bowl.

2. If using tortilla press, drop ¼ cup (60 mL) batter onto lightly floured press, close and gently press down on handle to shape tortilla. Transfer to prepared baking sheet. Repeat with remaining batter. If not using tortilla press, divide dough into 8 equal portions and place on prepared baking sheet, spaced about 2 inches (5 cm) apart. Using the palm of your hand, flatten each portion to about ¼ inch (0.5 cm) thick.

Hemp seeds offer a simple protein alternative. Just 1 tbsp (15 mL) hemp seeds contains up to 5 grams complete protein.

3. Bake in preheated oven for 20 minutes. Remove from oven and carefully turn over. Bake for 5 to 7 minutes more, or until slightly browned and firm but still pliable enough to fold. Remove from oven and set aside.

4. In a bowl, using a fork, mash avocado with 3 tbsp (45 mL) lemon juice, ¼ tsp (1 mL) salt and garlic.

5. In another bowl, toss together chopped tomato, remaining 1 tbsp (15 mL) lemon juice, ¼ tsp (1 mL) salt, 1 tbsp (15 mL) oil and parsley.

6. To serve, top each tortilla with ¼ cup (60 mL) lettuce, 2 tbsp (30 mL) mashed avocado, 1 tbsp (15 mL) sour cream, 1 tbsp (15 mL) tomato mixture and 2 tbsp (30 mL) hemp seeds. Serve immediately.

Singapore Summer Rolls

These simple fresh rolls are perfect for summertime entertaining. Serve them as an appetizer with Lemon Tamari Ginger Dip (page 113) or Yellow Coconut Curry Sauce (page 118) for dipping. They also make a nice side dish with Thai-Style Coconut Eggplant and Rice Noodles (page 278).

MAKES 8 ROLLS

Tips

Rice-paper wrappers are available in most well-stocked supermarkets and natural food stores.

Substitute an equal amount of finely sliced mango for the cucumbers, and fresh basil leaves for the mint.

4 cups	hot water	1 L
8	10-inch (25 cm) rice-paper wrappers (see Tips, left)	8
4 cups	shredded carrots	1 L
2 cups	finely sliced red bell peppers	500 mL
2 cups	finely sliced cucumbers (see Tips, left)	500 mL
1	bunch fresh mint leaves	1

1. Place hot water in a heatproof bowl. Working with one wrapper at a time, submerge wrapper in hot water until pliable, about 30 seconds. Remove and pat dry. Lay wrapper flat on a clean work surface.

2. In the middle of wrapper, place ½ cup (125 mL) carrot, ¼ cup (60 mL) red pepper, ¼ cup (60 mL) cucumber and 5 or 6 mint leaves.

3. Carefully fold bottom edge of wrapper over filling. Fold in sides and continue rolling up from the bottom, gently packing roll as you go. Press down firmly to ensure that roll holds together. Repeat with remaining wrappers and fillings. Serve immediately or cover with a damp paper towel, transfer to an airtight container and refrigerate for up to 3 days.

Nori Bites

These tasty bites make a great snack or finger food for parties.

| MAKES 8 BITES | | |

1 cup	Basic Rice (page 212)	250 mL
3 tbsp	rice wine vinegar (see Tips, left)	45 mL
2 tbsp	raw agave nectar	30 mL
1 tsp	raw white sesame seeds	5 mL
1	sheet nori	1
½ cup	shredded carrot	125 mL

Tips

You can substitute an equal amount of raw (unpasteurized) apple cider vinegar for the rice wine vinegar.

If you have a sushi mat, feel free to use it for this recipe.

1. In a bowl, combine cooked rice, vinegar, agave nectar and sesame seeds. Stir well.
2. On a clean work surface, lay nori shiny side down. Spread evenly with rice mixture to the edges. Top with carrot.
3. Starting at end of sheet, using your fingers to hold the filling in place, gently roll to form a cylinder. Using a sharp knife, cut crosswise into 8 equal pieces. Serve immediately.

Sushi Wraps

In this recipe, nori sheets take the place of traditional sandwich wraps. I like to serve these wraps with Lemon Tamari Ginger Dip (page 113) for dipping.

| MAKES 2 WRAPS | | |

2	sheets nori (see Tip, left)	2
2 cups	Brown Sushi Rice (page 213)	500 mL
2 tsp	raw white sesame seeds, divided	10 mL
1	medium avocado, cut into thin strips	1
½	English cucumber, cut into thin strips	½
½ cup	thinly sliced red bell pepper	125 mL

Tip

To avoid nori that has been roasted using genetically modified oils, be sure the nori you purchase is labeled "raw." You can find it in well-stocked supermarkets and health food stores.

1. Place 1 sheet nori, shiny side down, on a clean work surface. Spread 1 cup (250 mL) rice evenly on top, leaving a ½-inch (1 cm) border around edges. Sprinkle with 1 tsp (5 mL) sesame seeds. Arrange half of the cucumber and red pepper down the middle.
2. Starting at the edge closest to you, carefully fold nori in half so top and bottom edges meet; press down gently. Fold in half again crosswise and press down edges. Transfer to a serving plate. Repeat. Serve immediately.

Collard-Wrapped Sushi Rolls

Collard leaves are a fresh alternative to nori in this recipe. These rolls make perfect snacks and can also be served as an accompaniment to Creamy Coconut Thai Quinoa Salad (page 220) or Asian-Style Adzuki Bean Salad (page 185). They make a great appetizer for a dinner party.

MAKES 8 PIECES

Tips

To remove the stem from a collard leaf: Lay leaf on a flat work surface. Using a sharp knife and working from top to bottom, cut along each side of the center rib and pull away from leaf. Remove only enough stem to make the leaf pliable and able to be rolled without cracking.

To cook the rice for this recipe: In a saucepan, combine 1/2 cup (125 mL) short-grain brown rice and 1 cup (250 mL) water; bring to a boil. Cover, reduce heat and simmer for 40 minutes, until tender. Remove from heat and set aside, covered, for 10 minutes so rice can absorb any remaining liquid. If you prefer, use 1 cup (250 mL) Basic Rice (page 212).

Substitute an equal amount of raw (unpasteurized) apple cider vinegar for the rice wine vinegar.

1	large collard leaf, stem removed (see Tips, left)	1
1 cup	cooked rice (see Tips, left)	250 mL
3 tbsp	rice wine vinegar (see Tips, left)	45 mL
2 tbsp	raw agave nectar	30 mL
1 tsp	raw white sesame seeds	5 mL
1/2 cup	finely sliced red bell pepper	125 mL
1/4 cup	finely sliced cucumber	60 mL

1. In a large bowl, toss together cooked rice, vinegar, agave nectar and sesame seeds.

2. Lay collard leaf, upper side down and widthwise, on a clean work surface. Spread rice mixture evenly over leaf, right to the edges. Top with even layers of red pepper and cucumber.

3. Starting at the bottom (stem) end, roll up leaf to form a cylinder. Using a sharp knife, cut roll into 8 equal pieces. Serve immediately or transfer to an airtight container and refrigerate for up to 2 days.

Simple Summery Sandwiches

Serve these light and refreshing sandwiches, in which lettuce replaces the usual bread, with a side of Ranch Dip (page 80) or Miso Tahini Sauce (page 121) for dipping.

MAKES 4 SANDWICHES		

Tips

Carrots are extremely high in beta-carotene, a carotenoid, which your body converts to vitamin A. Because smoking and drinking alcohol reduce levels of beta-carotene in the blood, consuming adequate amounts of this nutrient is recommended if you drink alcohol on a regular basis and/or smoke tobacco.

Stock up on raw shelled hemp seeds. These little seeds are nutritional powerhouses, providing up to 5 grams complete protein per tablespoon (15 mL), as well as other nutritional benefits.

2 cups	shredded carrots (see Tips, left)	500 mL
2 cups	shredded beets	500 mL
1 cup	thinly sliced red bell pepper	250 mL
½ cup	chopped flat-leaf (Italian) parsley leaves	125 mL
¼ cup	extra virgin olive oil	60 mL
3 tbsp	raw (unpasteurized) apple cider vinegar	45 mL
2 tbsp	raw agave nectar	30 mL
2 tsp	dried oregano leaves	10 mL
1 tsp	dried basil leaves	5 mL
1 tsp	fine sea salt	5 mL
¼ cup	raw shelled hemp seeds, divided (see Tips, left)	60 mL
8	large romaine lettuce leaves	8

1. In a large bowl, combine carrots, beets, red pepper, parsley, oil, vinegar, agave nectar, oregano, basil and salt. Toss until well coated.

2. Lay 1 lettuce leaf flat on a clean work surface. Spread ¼ of the carrot mixture evenly overtop and sprinkle with 1 tbsp (15 mL) hemp seeds. Cover with a second lettuce leaf. Repeat with remaining lettuce and fillings. Serve immediately.

Variation

Make 8 smaller wraps by substituting 16 Boston lettuce leaves for the romaine.

Avocado Tempura

These tasty little treats are crispy on the outside and creamy on the inside. They make a great appetizer for special occasions.

Tips

Stir the batter before using to ensure that it remains emulsified.

You can also use a deep-fryer; follow the manufacturer's instructions.

Be sure to transfer cooked tempura to paper towels to drain excess oil.

Sprinkle with salt (if using) while tempura is still very hot, so that it adheres to the coating.

I like to serve these in shot glasses with a bit of drizzle in the bottom of the glass.

If you prefer, substitute 1 medium zucchini cut into 1/2-inch (1 cm) strips for the avocado.

- Blender
- Large bowl, lined with paper towels
- Candy/deep-fry thermometer

BATTER

1 cup	brown rice flour	250 mL
2 tbsp	nutritional yeast	30 mL
1 tbsp	sweet smoked paprika	15 mL
1/2 tsp	chili powder	2 mL
1/4 tsp	fine sea salt	1 mL
3/4 cup	cold water	175 mL
2 to 3	ice cubes	2 to 3
	Grapeseed oil	
2	medium avocados, quartered lengthwise	2
	Sea salt (optional)	

CHINESE FIVE-SPICE DATE DRIZZLE

1/4 cup	extra virgin olive oil	60 mL
1 tbsp	Chinese five-spice powder	15 mL
1 tbsp	wheat-free tamari	15 mL
1 tbsp	finely sliced green onion (green part only)	15 mL
1 tsp	finely chopped peeled gingerroot	5 mL
5	chopped pitted Medjool dates	5

1. *Batter:* In a bowl, whisk together brown rice flour, nutritional yeast, paprika, chili powder and salt. Add cold water and ice cubes and stir well. Set aside.

2. *Drizzle:* In blender, combine oil, five-spice powder, tamari, green onion, ginger and dates. Blend at high speed until smooth. Transfer to a bowl and set aside.

3. In a Dutch oven, add oil to a depth of about 2 inches (5 cm). Heat over medium-high heat until temperature reaches 375°F (190°C).

4. Working in batches, dip avocado pieces in batter (be sure to coat completely) and carefully lower into hot oil. Cook until crispy, 5 to 6 minutes.

5. Using a slotted spoon, transfer avocado to prepared bowl. Sprinkle with sea salt (if using). Repeat with remaining avocado and batter. Serve immediately, with drizzle.

Greek-Style Vegetable Skewers

These fire-roasted vegetables, seasoned with lemon, olive oil and oregano, make a perfect side dish to any meal. Serve with Ranch Dip (page 80).

Tips

To soak the skewers: Place in a bowl with 4 cups (1 L) water. Cover and set aside for at least 3 hours or overnight.

To ensure that the vegetables cook at an even rate, cut them into similar-sized pieces.

- Preheat barbecue to High
- Twelve 3-inch (7.5 cm) wooden skewers, soaked (see Tips, left)

½ cup	extra virgin olive oil	125 mL
¼ cup	freshly squeezed lemon juice	60 mL
2 tbsp	dried oregano	30 mL
6	cloves garlic, thinly sliced	6
2	medium red bell peppers, cut into 1-inch (2.5 cm) pieces	2
1	medium red onion, cut into 1-inch (2.5 cm) pieces	1
2	medium zucchini, cut into 1-inch (2.5 cm) pieces	2
12	medium white button mushrooms	12

1. In a small bowl, whisk together oil, lemon juice, oregano and garlic.

2. In a large bowl, combine red peppers, onion, zucchini and mushrooms. Add oil mixture and toss to coat well. Cover and set aside for 1 hour. If it is more convenient, marinate the vegetables for as long as overnight.

3. Transfer vegetables to a plate, reserving marinade. To assemble, slide 1 piece red pepper onto a skewer, followed by a piece of onion, a piece of zucchini and a mushroom. Repeat with remaining skewers.

4. Place skewers on preheated grill, directly over heat. Reduce heat to Medium and cook for 4 to 5 minutes. Brush lightly with reserved marinade and turn. Cook for 4 to 5 minutes. Brush with additional marinade, turning and cooking to ensure that vegetables are tender and caramelized on all sides.

5. Transfer skewers to a plate and brush with a little marinade. Serve immediately or transfer to an airtight container and refrigerate for up to 5 days.

Variation

Moroccan-Spiced Grilled Vegetables: Omit oregano in Step 1. Replace with 1 tbsp (15 mL) ground cumin, 1 tsp (5 mL) ground cinnamon, 1 tsp (5 mL) chili powder and ¼ tsp (1 mL) ground turmeric.

Grilled Tofu with Peanut Sauce

These delicious skewers are packed with protein.

MAKES 8 SKEWERS

Tips

To soak the skewers: Place in a bowl with 4 cups (1 L) water. Cover and set aside for at least 3 hours or overnight.

To cut tofu for this recipe: Using a sharp knife, cut tofu block in half lengthwise. Cut each half in half again and then repeat, ending up with 8 equal pieces.

You can also broil the tofu in the oven. Preheat broiler to High. Arrange marinated tofu in a single layer on a baking sheet lined with aluminum foil. Broil for 3 to 4 minutes per side, until lightly blackened.

- Blender
- 8 wooden skewers, soaked (see Tips, left)
- Preheat grill to Medium-High (see Tips, left)

TOFU

1 lb	firm tofu, cut into pieces (see Tips, left)	500 g
6 tbsp	wheat-free tamari, divided	90 mL

PEANUT SAUCE

½ cup	smooth peanut butter	125 mL
¼ cup	water	60 mL
3 tbsp	freshly squeezed lime juice	45 mL
2 tbsp	wheat-free tamari	30 mL
1 tbsp	raw agave nectar	15 mL
1 tsp	minced peeled gingerroot	5 mL
¼ tsp	fine sea salt	1 mL
⅛ tsp	cayenne pepper	0.5 mL

1. *Tofu:* In a saucepan, combine 8 cups (2 L) water, tofu and tamari. Bring to a boil. Reduce heat and simmer for 8 to 10 minutes. Set aside.

2. *Sauce:* In blender, combine peanut butter, water, lime juice, tamari, agave nectar, ginger, salt and cayenne. Blend at high speed until creamy. Transfer to a bowl.

3. Using a slotted spoon, transfer tofu to peanut sauce (discard cooking liquid). Cover and set aside for 30 minutes to marinate, or refrigerate overnight.

4. Using your fingers, thread one piece of tofu on each skewer, reserving marinade. Grill for 4 to 5 minutes per side, until lightly blackened. Serve immediately with reserved peanut sauce. Satay will keep for up to 5 days in an airtight container in the refrigerator.

Variation

Grilled Tofu with Coconut Curry Sauce: Complete Step 1. Bring to a boil 1 can (14 oz/400 mL) full-fat coconut milk, 3 tbsp (45 mL) lime juice, 2 tbsp (30 mL) curry powder, 1 tbsp (15 mL) each coconut sugar and tamari, ½ tsp (2 mL) ground cumin, ¼ tsp (1 mL) ground tumeric and a pinch of cayenne. Simmer until slightly thickened. Complete Steps 3 and 4, substituting curry for the peanut sauce.

Soba Chopsticks

This simple but flavorful Asian-influenced appetizer, served on chopsticks, is sure to wow your guests and be the talk of the party.

Tips

Most soba noodles sold in supermarkets contain some gluten. Check the label and choose a brand that is made from 100% buckwheat and is gluten-free.

Unlike fresh flat-leaf (Italian) parsley stems, which are tough and hard to break down, the top two-thirds of cilantro stems are soft and full of flavor — do not discard them.

Skip the chopsticks and serve this as a delicious cold salad.

- **7 to 8 pairs single-use chopsticks**

1	package (8 oz/250 g) gluten-free soba noodles (see Tips, left)	1
2 tbsp	wheat-free tamari	30 mL
1½ tbsp	toasted sesame oil	22 mL
½ cup	roughly chopped fresh cilantro leaves (see Tips, left)	125 mL
¼ cup	shredded carrot	60 mL
2 tbsp	finely sliced green onion (green part only)	30 mL
2 tsp	raw white sesame seeds	10 mL

1. In a medium saucepan of boiling salted water, cook soba noodles according to package directions. Using a colander, drain noodles and rinse under cold running water to remove excess starch. Transfer to a large bowl.

2. Add tamari and sesame oil to noodles and toss until well coated. Add cilantro, carrot, green onion and sesame seeds and toss to combine.

3. Keep chopsticks attached at the top (do not snap apart). Working with one set of chopsticks at a time, gently separate free ends with your fingers and insert into noodles, then let go so they grip some noodles. Twirl chopsticks three or four times to twist noodles around the ends.

4. Transfer to a serving plate. Repeat with remaining chopsticks and noodles. Serve immediately.

Crisp Soba Noodle Cakes

I love to serve these crispy noodle cakes as an appetizer at cocktail parties, or as part of a multicourse Asian-themed meal with Teriyaki Tofu (page 298), Pineapple and Coconut Fried Rice (page 309) and Ginger Lime Edamame Stir-Fry (page 300).

MAKES ABOUT 8 CAKES

Tips

Wheat-free tamari is similar to soy sauce except that it is brewed without using wheat or grain alcohol. Because it has a stronger flavor than soy sauce, you don't need to add as much to your dishes.

I like to use black sesame seeds for visual appeal, but white sesame seeds will work as well.

To bake the cakes instead of frying them, preheat oven to 400°F (200°C). Transfer noodle cakes to a baking sheet lined with parchment paper. Bake for 12 to 15 minutes or until golden brown and crisp on top.

• **Two 12-inch (30 cm) pizza pans, one lined with parchment paper**

1	package (½ lb/250 g) gluten-free soba noodles	1
2 tbsp	wheat-free tamari (see Tips, left)	30 mL
2 tbsp	toasted sesame oil	30 mL
2 tbsp	raw black sesame seeds	30 mL
1 cup	roughly chopped fresh cilantro leaves	250 mL
3 tbsp	(approx.) grapeseed oil	45 mL
	Sea salt, optional	

1. In a saucepan of boiling salted water, cook soba noodles according to package directions. Using a colander, drain but do not rinse.

2. Transfer noodles to a large bowl. Add tamari, sesame oil and sesame seeds and toss to coat well. Add cilantro and toss to combine.

3. Spread dressed noodles evenly on parchment-lined baking sheet to about ½ inch (1 cm) thick. Place second baking sheet on top of noodles and press down firmly with your hands (this will help form the cakes). Remove top sheet, cover noodles with plastic wrap and refrigerate for 1 hour or preferably overnight, until noodles are set.

4. Using a sharp knife, cut noodle cake into 8 equal portions.

5. In a skillet over medium-high heat, heat grapeseed oil. Working in batches and adding more oil if necessary, cook noodle cakes for about 3 minutes per side, until golden brown. Sprinkle with sea salt, if using. Serve immediately.

Mushroom Risotto Cakes

Wow your guests with these easy-to-make and tasty little tidbits.

Tips

I like to use wild and slightly exotic mushrooms such as chanterelle, hedgehog, oyster or blue-foot for this recipe, but you can also use more common varieties such as button or cremini mushrooms.

Arborio rice is most commonly used to make risotto, but you can substitute an equal amount of baldo, Calriso, carnaroli or Vialone Nano rice in this recipe (you want a starchy rice that will hold together and form a cake). Be aware that these types of polished white rice are not a whole food.

Instead of vegetable stock, you can substitute ½ cup (125 mL) wheat-free tamari whisked into 15½ cups (3.7 L) water.

If you prefer, cut the cakes into smaller "bites" as desired.

● **8-inch (20 cm) square baking pan**

6 tbsp	grapeseed oil, divided	90 mL
4 cups	sliced mushrooms (see Tips, left)	1 L
3 tbsp	wheat-free tamari, divided	45 mL
16 cups	Vegetable Stock (page 559; see Tips, left)	4 L
½ cup	finely diced onion	125 mL
2 cups	Arborio rice (see Tips, left)	500 mL
½ cup	dry white wine, such as Chardonnay (optional)	125 mL
¼ cup	chopped fresh thyme leaves	60 mL
2 tbsp	tahini	30 mL
1 tbsp	nutritional yeast	15 mL

1. In a medium saucepan over high heat, heat 2 tbsp (30 mL) oil. Add mushrooms and cook until brown, 5 minutes. Stir in 1 tbsp (15 mL) tamari and remove from heat. Transfer to a bowl and set aside. Reserve saucepan.

2. In a large saucepan over medium heat, bring stock to a simmer. Reduce heat to very low and cover.

3. In reserved saucepan over medium heat, heat 2 tbsp (30 mL) oil. Add onion and rice. Cook, stirring, until onion is golden, 5 minutes. Add wine (if using) and cook until completely absorbed.

4. Using a ladle, add one or two spoonfuls of warm stock to rice mixture, stirring constantly until liquid is absorbed. Repeat until all the stock has been used and rice is creamy and tender, about 20 minutes. Remove from heat.

5. Stir in remaining tamari, thyme, tahini and nutritional yeast. Using a spatula, spread evenly into baking pan to 1½ to 2 inches (4 to 5 cm) thick. Cover and refrigerate for 2 hours or until firm.

6. Invert baking pan onto a cutting board (mixture will hold together). Cut into 16 squares.

7. In a skillet over medium heat, heat remaining 2 tbsp (30 mL) oil. Working in batches, cook squares until golden brown, 4 to 5 minutes per side.

Seared King Oyster Mushroom Scallops

King oyster mushroom stems make a wonderful substitute for scallops. When marinated and pan-seared, they take on a lovely texture. Serve with Peppercorn Sauce (page 120) or Roasted Garlic Chimichurri (page 109).

Tips

King oyster mushrooms are available in most well-stocked supermarkets and Asian specialty stores. For this recipe, use the largest size available.

When searing food to create a golden-brown crust, make sure the food is dry before putting it in the pan. If not, the heat will release the water on the food and it will steam in the pan, not sear.

4	large king oyster mushrooms (see Tips, left)	4
3 tbsp	wheat-free tamari	45 mL
2 tbsp	olive oil	30 mL
1 tbsp	raw agave nectar	15 mL
5 to 6	sprigs fresh thyme	5 to 6
6 tbsp	grapeseed oil	90 mL
Pinch	fine sea salt	Pinch

1. Remove mushroom caps and reserve for another use. Using a sharp knife, remove and discard bottom inch (2.5 cm) from each mushroom stem. Cut trimmed stems into 1-inch (2.5 cm) thick rounds.

2. Transfer mushrooms to a bowl. Add tamari, olive oil, agave nectar and thyme and toss to coat well. Cover and set aside for 1 hour to marinate, or refrigerate overnight.

3. In a skillet over medium heat, heat grapeseed oil.

4. Remove mushroom rounds from marinade and pat dry with paper towels (discard marinade). Using a small, sharp knife, gently cut a shallow cross in the top of each round.

5. Carefully add mushroom rounds cut side down, to hot oil in pan and cook, without disturbing, until golden brown, 6 to 7 minutes. Turn over and cook until golden, 5 to 6 minutes. Using a slotted spoon, transfer to a plate lined with paper towels. Season both sides with salt to taste. Serve immediately.

Mini Quinoa Croquettes

These tasty little cakes are crispy on the outside and soft in the middle. You can make them up to 3 days in advance and then simply reheat them in the oven when guests arrive. I also like to pan-sear them in a little grapeseed oil and drizzle them with Miso Tahini Sauce (page 121).

MAKES ABOUT 10 CROQUETTES

Tips

In this recipe, the quinoa is cooked in more water than usual. This helps to hold the croquettes together.

Typically quinoa is cooked in a covered pot. For normal use, I bring 2 parts water and 1 part quinoa to a rapid boil, uncovered, reduce the heat and simmer until almost all the liquid has evaporated. Then I remove the pot from the heat, cover and set aside for 10 to 15 minutes. This technique consistently produces beautiful results.

You can purchase flax seeds that are already ground (often described as "milled"), or you can grind them yourself. To grind the flax seeds for this recipe, place ½ cup (125 mL) whole seeds in a blender. Blend at high speed until finely ground. Refrigerate extra for another use.

To reheat refrigerated croquettes, place on a baking sheet lined with parchment paper and bake in a preheated 350°F (180°C) oven for 8 to 10 minutes.

- Preheat oven to 350°F (180°C)
- Baking sheet, lined with parchment paper

1 cup	quinoa, rinsed and drained	250 mL
	Water	
1 tsp	fine sea salt, divided	5 mL
1 cup	chopped peeled sweet potato	250 mL
6 tbsp	ground flax seeds (see Tips, left)	90 mL
1 tbsp	tahini	15 mL
2 tsp	chopped fresh thyme leaves	10 mL
1 tsp	freshly grated lemon zest	5 mL
1 tbsp	freshly squeezed lemon juice	15 mL

1. In a large saucepan, combine quinoa, 2½ cups (625 mL) water and ¼ tsp (1 mL) salt; bring to a boil. Reduce heat and simmer for 12 to 15 minutes or until quinoa is tender and almost all the liquid has been absorbed. Cover and set aside for 10 minutes so quinoa can absorb any remaining liquid and swell.

2. In a small saucepan, combine 2 cups (500 mL) water, sweet potato and ¼ tsp (1 mL) salt; bring to a boil. Reduce heat and simmer for 8 to 10 minutes or until sweet potato is tender. Drain and transfer potato to a bowl.

3. In a large bowl, toss together cooked quinoa and sweet potato, ground flax seeds, tahini, thyme, lemon zest, lemon juice and remaining ½ tsp (2 mL) salt, until well combined. Set aside for 5 to 6 minutes so flax seeds can absorb some of the liquid and swell.

4. Using a ¼-cup (60 mL) measuring cup, drop about 10 portions of mixture onto prepared baking sheet. Using the palm of your hand, press down firmly on each cake until it holds together. Use your hands to shape, if desired.

5. Bake in preheated oven for 8 to 10 minutes, until lightly browned and crisp. Serve immediately or transfer to an airtight container and refrigerate for up to 5 days (see Tips, left).

Green Tomato Carpaccio with Balsamic Arugula

In colder climates, green tomatoes are in abundance at both the beginning and end of tomato season. Usually we wind up pickling or preserving them in some other fashion. As an alternative, I like to marinate them and serve as an appetizer alongside braised lentils or Spicy Angel-Hair Toss (page 255).

MAKES 3 TO 4 SERVINGS

Tips

If you do not have green tomatoes, you can substitute an equal amount of carrots or parsnips.

I like to use extra virgin cold-pressed olive oil in my recipes, as I find the flavor to be superior.

Substitute an equal amount of raw agave nectar or coconut nectar for the maple syrup.

● **Mandoline**

2	medium green tomatoes (see Tips, left)	2
½ cup	extra virgin olive oil, divided (see Tips, left)	125 mL
¼ cup	balsamic vinegar, divided	60 mL
1 tbsp	freshly squeezed lemon juice	15 mL
½ tsp	fine sea salt, divided	2 mL
2 tsp	pure maple syrup (see Tips, left)	10 mL
1 tsp	Dijon mustard	5 mL
¼ tsp	dried oregano	1 mL
2 cups	lightly packed fresh arugula leaves	500 mL

1. Using mandoline, slice tomatoes into paper-thin rounds about $\frac{1}{16}$ inch (2 mm) thick (discard end pieces).

2. In a bowl, gently toss tomato slices with ¼ cup (60 mL) oil, 2 tbsp (30 mL) vinegar, lemon juice and ¼ tsp (1 mL) salt. Cover and set aside for 15 minutes to marinate and soften tomato.

3. In another bowl, whisk together remaining ¼ cup (60 mL) oil, 2 tbsp (30 mL) vinegar and ¼ tsp (1 mL) salt, maple syrup, mustard and oregano. Add arugula and toss to coat evenly. Set aside.

4. Remove tomato slices from marinade and divide evenly among serving plates (discard marinade). Top tomatoes with dressed arugula. Serve immediately.

Mushroom Ceviche

Ceviche is a traditional Mexican dish made with fish. My version uses thinly sliced mushrooms, fresh limes and spicy chiles. For best results, make it when fresh corn is in season. The sweet raw kernels really pop on your palate. Serve with crispy crackers and some Vegan Sour Cream (page 555). To really wow your guests, serve in a martini glass, garnished with Roasted Garlic Chimichurri (page 109).

Tips

I like to use a mixture of button, oyster and shiitake mushrooms for this dish, but just button mushrooms will work as well.

If necessary, use frozen corn kernels, lightly steamed. However, fresh will produce the best results.

In this recipe I like to use an olive oil that is fruitier in flavor and lower in acidity. Look for a high-quality Spanish olive oil at your supermarket.

To remove the seeds and ribs from a jalapeño: Slice pepper in half lengthwise through the middle. Using a small spoon, gently scrape out the inside until only the flesh remains.

1 lb	assorted mushrooms, thinly sliced (see Tips, left)	500 g
¼ cup	fresh corn kernels (see Tips, left)	60 mL
3 tbsp	extra virgin olive oil (see Tips, left)	45 mL
2 tbsp	freshly squeezed lime juice	30 mL
2 tbsp	chopped fresh flat-leaf (Italian) parsley leaves	30 mL
1 tbsp	chopped fresh cilantro leaves	15 mL
1 tbsp	wheat-free tamari	15 mL
1 tsp	minced jalapeño pepper, ribs and seeds removed (see Tips, left)	5 mL
½ tsp	organic coconut sugar	2 mL
¼ tsp	fine sea salt	1 mL

1. In a large bowl, toss together mushrooms, corn, oil, lime juice, parsley, cilantro, tamari, jalapeño, coconut sugar and salt until well combined. Cover and set aside for 30 minutes to marinate. Serve immediately or transfer to an airtight container and refrigerate for up to 3 days.

Sauces, Butters and Spreads

Sauces

Butters and Spreads

Roasted Red Pepper Mole Sauce

Serve this authentic spicy Mexican sauce overtop rice dishes such as Dirty Brown Rice with Black Beans (page 222), or alongside an Easy Burrito (page 189).

MAKES		
2 CUPS (500 ML)		

Tips

Covering the bowl tightly with plastic wrap after roasting the peppers creates steam, which helps to separate the skin from the flesh, making the peppers easier to peel.

To reheat refrigerated mole sauce, place in a saucepan over medium heat and cook for 2 to 3 minutes, stirring often, until heated through.

Bruising cinnamon sticks helps to bring out the natural oils, increasing the flavor. To bruise a cinnamon stick, place it on a cutting board and tap it with the butt end of a chef's knife.

Chipotle peppers are smoked dried jalapeños. You can purchase them dried or canned with adobo sauce. If you prefer, use the canned version in this recipe, making sure to include 1 tbsp (15 mL) of the adobo.

To soak dried chipotle peppers: Place in a bowl and cover with 2 cups (500 mL) warm water. Cover and set aside for 30 minutes or overnight (if overnight, refrigerate). Drain.

- **Preheat oven to 400°F (200°C)**
- **Baking sheet, lined with parchment paper**
- **Blender**

2	red bell peppers	2
3 tbsp	grapeseed oil, divided	45 mL
½ cup	chopped onion	125 mL
½ tsp	ground cumin	2 mL
½ tsp	ground coriander	2 mL
1	3-inch (7.5 cm) cinnamon stick, bruised (see Tips, left)	1
2	cloves garlic, minced	2
2	dried chipotle peppers, soaked and chopped (see Tips, left)	2
¼ cup	dry white wine	60 mL
1 tsp	fine sea salt	5 mL
¼ cup	raw cacao powder	60 mL
3 tbsp	melted coconut oil	45 mL

1. In a bowl, toss red peppers with 2 tbsp (30 mL) grapeseed oil. Arrange on prepared baking sheet and bake in preheated oven until slightly shriveled and browned, about 15 minutes. Remove from oven and transfer to a bowl. Cover tightly with plastic wrap and set aside for 10 minutes (see Tips, left).

2. Carefully remove peppers from bowl (they may be hot) and, using your fingers, gently rub skins off flesh. Cut peppers in half and discard seeds and ribs.

3. In a skillet over medium heat, heat remaining 1 tbsp (15 mL) grapeseed oil. Add onion and cook, stirring frequently, until translucent, about 6 minutes. Stir in cumin, coriander and cinnamon and cook for 3 to 4 minutes, until aromatic. Stir in garlic and cook for 2 to 3 minutes, until softened. Add chipotles and wine and cook, stirring occasionally, until most of the liquid has evaporated, about 2 minutes. Remove from heat and discard cinnamon.

4. In blender, combine roasted peppers, onion mixture, salt, cacao powder and coconut oil. Blend at high speed until smooth. Serve immediately or transfer to an airtight container and refrigerate for up to 1 week.

Roasted Garlic Chimichurri

This fresh-tasting sauce pairs perfectly with grilled or roasted dishes such as Grilled King Oyster Mushrooms with Green Curried Sticky Rice Parcels (page 424) or Herbed Rösti Bake (page 168).

MAKES ABOUT 1½ CUPS (375 ML)

Tips

Before roasting whole garlic, use a serrated knife to cut off the top ¼ inch (0.5 cm) of the bulb, exposing the flesh of the individual cloves.

The quantity of raw garlic depends on the size of the cloves. If large, use 2. If small, 3 may be required.

Unlike flat-leaf (Italian) parsley stems, which are tough and hard to break down, the top two-thirds of cilantro stems are soft and full of flavor — do not discard them.

- Preheat oven to 325°F (160°C)
- Baking sheet, lined with parchment paper
- Food processor

6	bulbs garlic, tops removed (see Tips, left)	6
½ cup	extra virgin olive oil, divided	125 mL
1½ tbsp	freshly squeezed lemon juice	22 mL
1 tbsp	wheat-free tamari	15 mL
2 to 3	cloves garlic (see Tips, left)	2 to 3
2 cups	fresh cilantro, leaves and stems (see Tips, left)	500 mL
2 cups	flat-leaf (Italian) parsley leaves	500 mL
1½ tsp	chili powder	7 mL
½ tsp	ground cumin	2 mL
	Salt	

1. In a small bowl, toss garlic bulbs with 2 tbsp (30 mL) oil. Arrange in a single layer on prepared baking sheet and bake in preheated oven for 45 minutes or until lightly golden and soft. Set aside to cool. Once cool enough to handle, squeeze cloves from their skins and set aside.

2. In food processor fitted with the metal blade, process roasted garlic, lemon juice, tamari and garlic cloves until no large pieces of garlic remain. Add cilantro, parsley, chili powder, cumin and salt, to taste, and pulse to combine.

3. With the motor running, add remaining oil through the feed tube in a slow, steady stream. Process until smooth, stopping the motor to scrape down sides of work bowl as necessary.

4. Serve immediately or transfer to an airtight container and refrigerate for up to 1 week.

Classic Garlicky Tomato Sauce

Toss this fragrant tomato sauce with your favorite pasta, or use it as a simple but delicious dipping sauce.

MAKES ABOUT 6 CUPS (1.5 L)

Tips

The quantity of garlic depends on the size of the cloves. If large, use the smaller number. If small, more may be required.

Substitute 16 cups (4 L) chopped fresh tomatoes for the canned tomatoes.

2 tbsp	grapeseed oil	30 mL
½ cup	chopped onion	125 mL
½ tsp	fine sea salt	2 mL
6 to 8	cloves garlic, minced	6 to 8
2	cans (each 28 oz/796 mL) diced tomatoes, with juice	2

1. In a saucepan over medium heat, heat oil. Add onion and salt and cook, stirring frequently, until onion is softened and translucent, 5 to 6 minutes. Stir in garlic and cook until garlic is fragrant, 2 to 3 minutes.

2. Stir in tomatoes, with juice, and bring to a boil. Reduce heat and simmer for 15 minutes or until sauce has thickened. Serve immediately or transfer to an airtight container and refrigerate for up to 2 weeks.

Variation

Creamy Sweet Potato Tomato Sauce: Add 1 cup (250 mL) chopped peeled sweet potato to pan along with tomatoes. Cook until sweet potato is tender, about 20 minutes. Transfer half of the sauce to a blender and add 2 tbsp (30 mL) extra virgin olive oil. Blend until smooth. Repeat with remaining sauce and an additional 2 tbsp (30 mL) olive oil.

Maple Chipotle Barbecue Sauce

This is a great all-purpose smoky barbecue sauce. Brush it on foods before grilling, spread it in your favorite sandwich or use it as a dipping sauce.

MAKES ABOUT 6 CUPS (1.5 L)

Tips

Chipotle peppers are smoked dried jalapeños. You can purchase them dried or canned with adobo sauce. If you prefer, use the canned version in this recipe, making sure to include 1 tbsp (15 mL) of the adobo.

To soak dried chipotle peppers: Place in a bowl and cover with 2 cups (500 mL) warm water. Cover and set aside for 30 minutes or overnight (if overnight, refrigerate). Drain.

Blackstrap molasses is available in most well-stocked supermarkets and natural food stores. If you cannot find it, substitute an equal amount of regular molasses.

You can replace the ketchup in this recipe with 3 cans (28 oz/796 mL) diced tomatoes. Increase the cooking time to 45 minutes or until sauce has thickened. Use an immersion blender to purée the sauce.

1 tbsp	grapeseed oil	15 mL
½ cup	chopped onion	125 mL
1 tsp	fine sea salt	5 mL
1 tsp	chili powder	5 mL
10 to 12	cloves garlic, minced	10 to 12
2 tbsp	Dijon mustard	30 mL
4	dried chipotle peppers, soaked and chopped (see Tips, left)	4
¼ cup	raw agave nectar	60 mL
¼ cup	pure maple syrup	60 mL
¼ cup	blackstrap molasses (see Tips, left)	60 mL
¼ cup	wheat-free tamari	60 mL
2	bottles (24 oz/750 g) ketchup (see Tips, left)	2

1. In a saucepan over medium heat, heat oil. Add onion, salt and chili powder and cook, stirring frequently, until onion is softened and translucent, about 6 minutes.

2. Stir in garlic, mustard and chipotles and cook until garlic is fragrant, about 2 minutes. Stir in agave nectar, maple syrup, molasses and tamari; bring to a boil.

3. Reduce heat and simmer for 5 minutes, until mixture has thickened slightly. Add ketchup and simmer for 30 minutes, stirring occasionally, until sauce has thickened.

4. Serve immediately or transfer to an airtight container and refrigerate for up to 2 months.

Red Wine Tamari Jus

This is my take on a traditional French demi-glace, a sauce typically made with red wine and beef, veal or vegetable stock. I like to drizzle it over Herbed Roasted Potatoes (page 179) and my protein of choice. It is very rich and flavorful, so a little goes a long way.

MAKES ABOUT 1 CUP (250 ML)

Tips

If you prefer a thicker sauce, whisk together 1 tbsp (15 mL) organic cornstarch and 3 tbsp (45 mL) cold water; set aside. Bring strained sauce to a boil and whisk in cornstarch mixture. Cook for 2 to 3 minutes, until thickened.

This recipe can easily be doubled or tripled for dinner parties.

To reheat refrigerated jus, place in a saucepan over medium heat and cook for 2 to 3 minutes, stirring often, until heated through.

1 tbsp	grapeseed oil	15 mL
¼ cup	finely chopped onion	60 mL
¼ cup	finely chopped celery	60 mL
¼ cup	finely chopped carrot	60 mL
1 tbsp	tomato paste	15 mL
1 to 2	cloves garlic, minced	1 to 2
1 tbsp	chopped fresh thyme leaves	15 mL
½ cup	dry red wine	125 mL
1 cup	wheat-free tamari	250 mL
1 cup	water	250 mL

1. In a saucepan over medium heat, heat oil. Add onion, celery and carrot and cook, stirring frequently, until vegetables are tender, about 6 minutes.

2. Stir in tomato paste, garlic and thyme and cook for 3 to 4 minutes, until garlic is softened and fragrant. Add wine and cook, stirring often, until almost all the liquid has evaporated and mixture resembles a thick paste.

3. Stir in tamari and water and bring to a boil. Reduce heat and simmer for 20 minutes, until sauce has reduced and thickened.

4. Using a fine-mesh sieve, strain sauce (discard solids). Serve immediately or transfer to an airtight container and refrigerate for up to 2 weeks.

Lemon Tamari Ginger Dip

This recipe makes a great dipping sauce for Asian dishes such as sushi or fried rice. Serve it alongside Crispy Asian Noodle Wraps (page 283) or Pineapple and Coconut Fried Rice (page 309).

**MAKES ABOUT
¾ CUP (175 ML)**

Tips

Wheat-free tamari is a gluten-free seasoning made from fermented soybeans. It can be found in most well-stocked supermarkets and natural food stores.

Be sure to use raw (not processed) agave nectar. It is a 100% natural (non-GMO) sweetener that contains naturally occurring fructose and is low on the glycemic scale, which means that it releases glucose slowly, providing sustained energy.

2 tbsp	freshly squeezed lemon juice	30 mL
¼ cup	water	60 mL
½ cup	wheat-free tamari (see Tips, left)	125 mL
1 cup	raw agave nectar (see Tips, left)	250 mL
2 tsp	minced peeled gingerroot	10 mL

1. In a small saucepan over high heat, combine lemon juice, water, tamari, agave nectar and ginger; bring to a boil. Reduce heat and simmer for 25 to 30 minutes or until mixture thickens enough to coat the back of a spoon.

2. Remove from heat and set aside to cool completely. Serve immediately or transfer to an airtight container and refrigerate for up to 1 month.

Orange Ginger Sauce

Serve this citrusy sauce drizzled over crispy tofu, fried rice or Asian-style noodle dishes such as Thai-Style Coconut Eggplant and Rice Noodles (page 278). It also makes a great marinade for grilled tofu or sautéed eggplant.

**MAKES ABOUT
1 CUP (250 ML)**

Tips

A hand-held citrus reamer can be used to extract the juice from citrus fruits. Available in most kitchen supply stores, this tool would be ideal to use for the orange juice in this recipe.

Whenever using cornstarch to thicken a sauce, to avoid lumps, be sure to whisk it thoroughly into a liquid before adding it to your dish. Cornstarch reaches its maximum thickening power once the sauce has reached the boiling point.

Be sure to purchase organic cornstarch to avoid GMOs.

¾ cup	freshly squeezed orange juice (see Tips, left)	175 mL
3 tbsp	water	45 mL
3 tbsp	raw agave nectar	45 mL
2 tbsp	raw (unpasteurized) apple cider vinegar	30 mL
2 tbsp	minced peeled gingerroot	30 mL
2 tbsp	organic cornstarch (see Tips, left)	30 mL
½ tsp	fine sea salt	2 mL

1. In a small saucepan, whisk together orange juice, water, agave nectar, vinegar, ginger, cornstarch and salt, until no lumps of cornstarch remain.
2. Bring to a boil, reduce heat and simmer, stirring frequently, until thickened, 8 to 10 minutes. Serve immediately or transfer to an airtight container and refrigerate for up to 2 weeks.

Ginger Teriyaki Sauce

This sauce is extremely versatile. Use it as a stir-fry sauce for vegetables or tofu, drizzle it on steamed quinoa or brown rice, or toss it with crisp salad greens.

**MAKES
2½ CUPS (625 ML)**

Tips

Wheat-free tamari is a gluten-free seasoning made from fermented soybeans. It can be found in most well-stocked supermarkets and natural food stores.

Be sure to use raw (not processed) agave nectar. It is a 100% natural (non-GMO) sweetener that contains naturally occurring fructose and is low on the glycemic scale, which means that it releases glucose slowly, providing sustained energy.

To purée gingerroot, use a fine-toothed grater such as the kind made by Microplane.

Whisk or shake the sauce before using, to remix the oil, which may separate.

● **Blender**

1 cup	wheat-free tamari	250 mL
¾ cup	raw agave nectar	175 mL
¾ cup	toasted sesame oil	175 mL
¼ cup	puréed peeled gingerroot (see Tips, left)	60 mL
2 tsp	freshly squeezed lemon juice	10 mL
2	cloves garlic	2

1. In blender jar, combine tamari, agave nectar, sesame oil, ginger, lemon juice and garlic. Blend at high speed until smooth.
2. Serve immediately or transfer to an airtight container and refrigerate for up to 2 weeks.

Sweet-and-Sour Sauce

Serve this classic sauce as a dip for Avocado Tempura (page 97) instead of the drizzle, as a stir-fry sauce for dishes such as Classic Pad Thai (page 310) and Pineapple and Coconut Fried Rice (page 309), or simply drizzled over steamed rice.

MAKES ABOUT 1½ CUPS (375 ML)

Tips

Coconut sugar is a low-glycemic sweetener that is available in most well-stocked supermarkets and natural food stores. It has a sweet taste similar to brown sugar.

Substitute an equal amount of raw (unpasteurized) apple cider vinegar for the rice wine vinegar.

Wheat-free tamari is a gluten-free seasoning made from fermented soybeans. It can be found in most well-stocked supermarkets and natural food stores.

1½ cups	organic coconut sugar (see Tips, left)	375 mL
⅔ cup	rice wine vinegar (see Tips, left)	150 mL
¼ cup	wheat-free tamari (see Tips, left)	60 mL
2 tbsp	ketchup	30 mL
2 tbsp	organic cornstarch	30 mL

1. In a small saucepan, whisk together coconut sugar, vinegar, tamari, ketchup and cornstarch. Bring to a boil, reduce heat and simmer, stirring constantly, for 2 minutes, until thickened.

2. Serve immediately or transfer to an airtight container and refrigerate for up to 2 weeks.

Festive Cranberry Sauce

Cranberries are native to North America. Sour in flavor but rich in nutrients, they have long been associated with holiday festivities, particularly Thanksgiving, when early settlers celebrated the harvest. Serve this sauce at any holiday gathering to capture the festive spirit. I enjoy it with Glazed Lentil Loaf (page 210) or Holiday Lentil Loaf with Quinoa (page 382).

**MAKES ABOUT
2 CUPS (500 ML)**

Tips

A hand-held citrus reamer can be used to extract the juice from citrus fruits. Available in most kitchen supply stores, this tool would be ideal to use for the orange juice in this recipe.

Substitute an equal amount of pure maple syrup or ¾ cup (175 mL) coconut sugar for the agave nectar.

Use high-quality organic cinnamon. You will get the freshest flavor by grinding whole cinnamon sticks in a clean spice grinder.

To grate the nutmeg, use a fine-toothed grater such as the kind made by Microplane.

Feel free to double this recipe if desired.

3 cups	fresh cranberries	750 mL
¼ cup	freshly squeezed orange juice (see Tips, left)	60 mL
¼ cup	raw agave nectar (see Tips, page 115)	60 mL
2 tbsp	water	30 mL
¼ tsp	ground cinnamon (see Tips, left)	1 mL
Pinch	fine sea salt	Pinch
Pinch	freshly grated nutmeg (see Tips, left)	Pinch

1. In a saucepan, combine cranberries, orange juice, agave nectar, water, cinnamon, salt and nutmeg. Bring to a boil, reduce heat and simmer for 10 minutes, until thickened.

2. Serve immediately or transfer to an airtight container and refrigerate for up to 2 weeks.

Yellow Coconut Curry Sauce

For a match made in heaven, serve this fragrant Indian sauce with some crispy tofu and Basic Quinoa (page 235), Basic Rice (page 212) or Roasted Vegetables (page 177).

**MAKES
2 CUPS (500 ML)**

Tips

The quantity of garlic depends on the size of the cloves. If large, use the smaller number. If small, more may be required.

You will get the freshest flavor by buying fresh whole spices such as cumin and coriander seed and grinding them yourself in a clean spice grinder.

Substitute an equal amount of dry white wine for the water.

To reheat refrigerated curry sauce (or White Wine Spinach Cream Sauce, page 119), place in a saucepan over medium heat and cook for 2 to 3 minutes, stirring often, until heated through.

1 tbsp	grapeseed oil	15 mL
1/4 cup	chopped onion	60 mL
1/4 tsp	fine sea salt	1 mL
1/2 tsp	minced peeled gingerroot	2 mL
1 to 2	cloves garlic, minced	1 to 2
1 tbsp	curry powder	15 mL
1/4 tsp	ground cumin	2 mL
Pinch	ground coriander	Pinch
1/4 cup	water (see Tips, left)	60 mL
1	can (14 oz/400 mL) coconut milk	1
2 tsp	freshly squeezed lemon or lime juice	10 mL

1. In a saucepan over medium heat, heat oil. Add onion and salt and cook, stirring frequently, until onion is translucent, about 6 minutes. Stir in ginger and garlic and cook for 2 minutes, until fragrant. Add curry powder, cumin and coriander and cook, stirring constantly, for about 5 minutes, until fragrant. Add water and bring to a simmer. Cook for 2 to 3 minutes, until slightly thickened. Add coconut milk and bring to a boil.

2. Reduce heat and simmer until thickened, about 10 minutes. Stir in lemon juice and remove from heat. Serve immediately or transfer to an airtight container and refrigerate for up to 1 week.

Variation

Green Coconut Curry Sauce: Omit curry powder. After cooking ginger and garlic, stir in 1/2 cup (125 mL) chopped fresh cilantro; 1/2 small green chile, chopped; 1 lime leaf and 2 tsp (10 mL) chopped lemongrass. Continue with the recipe. Using a fine-mesh sieve, strain sauce (discard solids) before serving.

White Wine Spinach Cream Sauce

This creamy sauce is perfect to serve over Creamy Mashed Potatoes (page 178) or with Spanakopita Pie with Red Pepper Slaw and Lemon Dijon Arugula (page 422).

(page 178)... (page 422).

MAKES ABOUT 3 CUPS (750 ML)

Tips

The quantity of garlic depends on the size of the cloves. If large, use the smaller number. If small, more may be required.

Choose bunched (field) spinach for this recipe, as it stands up well to high heat and does not wilt as much as baby spinach. You can use baby spinach if desired, but you will need to increase the amount to 12 cups (3 L).

Replace the wine with ½ cup (125 mL) water and 1 tsp (5 mL) white wine vinegar.

● Blender

2 cups	raw cashews	500 mL
	Water	
3 tbsp	freshly squeezed lemon juice	45 mL
½ tsp	fine sea salt	2 mL
1 tbsp	grapeseed oil	15 mL
¼ cup	finely chopped onion	60 mL
4 to 5	garlic cloves, minced	4 to 5
8 cups	packed chopped spinach leaves (see Tips, left)	2 L
½ cup	dry white wine (see Tips, left)	125 mL
2 tbsp	nutritional yeast	30 mL

1. In a saucepan filled with water, bring cashews to a boil. Remove from heat and drain.

2. In blender, combine boiled cashews, lemon juice, salt and 1 cup (250 mL) water. Blend at high speed until smooth. Set blender aside.

3. In a skillet over medium heat, heat oil. Cook onion, stirring frequently, until translucent, about 6 minutes. Stir in garlic and cook until fragrant, about 2 minutes. Stir in spinach and cook just until wilted, 2 to 3 minutes. Add wine and cook, stirring constantly, until all of the liquid has evaporated. Stir in nutritional yeast and remove from heat.

4. Add half of the spinach mixture to blender with puréed cashews, reserving remaining spinach mixture in pan. Blend until smooth.

5. Pour puréed spinach into pan with reserved spinach mixture and stir to combine. Cook over medium heat just until heated through, 1 to 2 minutes. Serve immediately or transfer to an airtight container and refrigerate for up to 5 days (see reheating Tip, page 118).

Peppercorn Sauce

Serve this creamy sauce with grilled tofu or Roasted Vegetables (page 177).

Tips

Nutritional yeast is an inactive yeast that has been grown on beet molasses and then pasteurized. It provides a rich, cheesy flavor in sauces, stews, soups and dips. Look for it in well-stocked supermarkets and natural food stores.

To mince garlic: Place a whole clove on a cutting board. Using the butt end of a chef's knife, press firmly but gently on the clove to loosen the skin. Using your index finger and thumb, gently squeeze clove out of skin. Chop coarsely, then sprinkle with a bit of sea salt. Using the butt end of the knife, rub garlic into board (the salt will act as an abrasive and help to mince the garlic). Chop until fine.

To prevent the sauce from splitting, make sure the Whipped Non-dairy Butter is cold before swirling it in.

Blender

1 cup	raw cashews	250 mL
	Water	
2 tsp	nutritional yeast (see Tips, left)	10 mL
¼ tsp	fine sea salt	1 mL
2 tsp	grapeseed oil	10 mL
2 tbsp	finely chopped onion	30 mL
2 tbsp	black peppercorns	30 mL
1	clove garlic, minced (see Tips, left)	1
2 tbsp	dry white wine	30 mL
½ cup	Red Wine Tamari Jus (page 112)	125 mL
1 tbsp	Whipped Non-dairy Butter (page 554)	15 mL

1. In a saucepan filled with water, bring cashews to a boil. Remove from heat and drain. Set cashews aside to cool.

2. In blender, combine boiled cashews, 2 cups (500 mL) water, nutritional yeast and salt. Blend at high speed until smooth and creamy. Set aside.

3. In a small saucepan over medium heat, heat oil. Add onion and peppercorns and cook, stirring frequently, until onion is translucent, about 3 minutes. Stir in garlic and cook until fragrant, about 2 minutes. Add wine and cook until liquid has evaporated, about 2 minutes. Stir in Red Wine Tamari Jus and puréed cashews and simmer gently for 4 to 5 minutes or until mixture has thickened slightly.

4. Remove from heat and stir in butter (you want the butter to melt into the sauce without it splitting; see Tips, left). Serve immediately or transfer to an airtight container and refrigerate for up to 1 week. To reheat, place in a saucepan over medium heat for 2 to 3 minutes, stirring often, until heated through.

Miso Tahini Sauce

Serve this sauce over freshly cooked pasta, as a salad dressing or as a dip for fresh vegetables.

Tips

To use this as a dressing for salads, make the sauce thinner by increasing the amount of water to 2/3 cup (150 mL).

To make the sauce creamier, add 1/4 cup (60 mL) extra virgin olive oil.

Blender

1/2 cup	tahini	125 mL
1/2 cup	water (see Tips, left)	125 mL
3 tbsp	brown rice miso	45 mL
1 tbsp	freshly squeezed lemon juice	15 mL
1	clove garlic	1

1. In blender, combine tahini, water, miso, lemon juice and garlic. Blend at high speed until smooth and creamy. Serve immediately or transfer to an airtight container and refrigerate for up to 5 days.

Variation

Southwest Tahini Dressing: Omit miso. Increase lemon juice to 3 tbsp (45 mL). Add 1 bunch fresh cilantro, 1 tsp (5 mL) chili powder, 1/2 tsp (2 mL) ground cumin and a pinch of cayenne pepper.

Hollandaise Sauce

This is my vegan take on the classic sauce made with egg yolks and butter. The luscious combination is often served over steamed fresh asparagus. You can also drizzle it on breakfast potatoes, Basic Rice (page 212) or Basic Quinoa (page 235). If desired, use about 1½ cups (375 mL) to replace the recipe-specific hollandaise in Vegan Benedict (page 32).

**MAKES
3 CUPS (750 ML)**

Tips

I prefer to use Chardonnay in this recipe, but any dry white wine will do.

Substitute an equal amount of Hemp and Chia Milk (page 64), Cashew Milk (page 61) or Coconut Milk (page 62) for the almond milk.

Store-bought non-dairy milks will also work well in the recipe.

½ cup	coconut oil	125 mL
½ cup	brown rice flour	125 mL
¼ tsp	ground turmeric	1 mL
¼ cup	dry white wine (see Tips, left)	60 mL
¼ cup	freshly squeezed lemon juice	60 mL
3 cups	Almond Milk (page 61)	750 mL
2 tbsp	nutritional yeast	30 mL
1 tbsp	Dijon mustard	15 mL
1 tsp	fine sea salt	5 mL

1. In a small saucepan over medium heat, whisk together coconut oil, brown rice flour and turmeric. Cook, whisking constantly, for 5 to 6 minutes, until raw flavor of flour has been cooked out. Add wine and cook, stirring constantly, until liquid has evaporated, about 2 minutes. Add lemon juice and cook, stirring constantly, for 3 to 4 minutes.

2. Add almond milk, 1 cup (250 mL) at a time, stirring constantly after each addition until well combined. Bring to a boil, reduce heat and simmer for 10 minutes, until thickened. Remove from heat and stir in nutritional yeast, mustard and salt.

3. Using a fine-mesh sieve, strain sauce (discard solids). Serve immediately or transfer to an airtight container and refrigerate for up to 1 week. To reheat refrigerated sauce, place in a saucepan over medium heat for 2 to 3 minutes, stirring often, until heated through.

Easy Creamy Alfredo Sauce

Alfredo sauce is traditionally made with heavy cream, butter and cheese. In my quick and simple take on this classic, I use cashews to create the creamy texture and nutritional yeast to provide a cheesy flavor. Use this in any recipe that calls for Alfredo sauce.

**MAKES
1½ CUPS (375 ML)**

Tips

Nutritional yeast is an inactive yeast that has been grown on beet molasses and then pasteurized. It provides a rich, cheesy flavor in sauces, stews, soups and dips. Look for it in well-stocked supermarkets and natural food stores.

You may substitute 2 tsp (10 mL) unpasteurized brown rice miso for the nutritional yeast. Reduce the amount of salt to ½ tsp (2 mL).

To chop fresh thyme: Pinch the stem at the bottom with two fingers. Pulling upward with the finger and thumb of your other hand, strip the leaves. Reserve stems for soups or broths (discard after cooking). Use a sharp knife to chop the leaves, being careful not to chop too much or too hard, as this will bruise the leaves and cause the thyme to discolor.

● Blender

1 cup	raw cashews	250 mL
	Water	
¼ cup	nutritional yeast (see Tips, left)	60 mL
2 tbsp	freshly squeezed lemon juice	30 mL
1 tsp	chopped fresh thyme leaves (see Tips, left)	5 mL
1 tsp	fine sea salt	5 mL
½	clove garlic	½

1. In a saucepan filled with water, bring cashews to a boil. Remove from heat and drain.
2. In blender, combine cooked cashews, 1 cup (250 mL) water, nutritional yeast, lemon juice, thyme, salt and garlic. Blend at high speed until smooth.
3. Serve immediately or transfer to an airtight container and refrigerate for up to 5 days. To reheat refrigerated sauce, place in a saucepan over medium heat for 2 to 3 minutes, stirring often, until heated through.

Hemp, Garlic and Chia Butter

This creamy butter can be spread on toast, used as a dip for crunchy carrot and celery sticks or dolloped onto a baked potato.

MAKES ABOUT 1 CUP (250 ML)

Tips

If you use black chia seeds, the butter will contain black specks. If you use white chia, it will not. Choose according to your preference.

The quantity of garlic depends on the size of the cloves. If large, use the smaller number. If small, more may be required.

Substitute an equal amount of chia seed oil, pumpkinseed oil or flaxseed oil for the olive oil.

Food processor

¾ cup	raw shelled hemp seeds	175 mL
¼ cup	chia seeds (see Tips, left)	60 mL
6 to 8	cloves garlic	6 to 8
3 tbsp	freshly squeezed lemon juice	45 mL
1 tbsp	water	15 mL
½ tsp	fine sea salt	2 mL
¼ cup	extra virgin olive oil (see Tips, left)	60 mL

1. In food processor fitted with the metal blade, combine hemp seeds, chia seeds, garlic, lemon juice, water and salt. Process until smooth, about 10 minutes, stopping the motor to scrape down sides of work bowl as necessary.

2. With the motor running, add oil through the feed tube in a slow, steady stream. Process until mixture is thick and creamy, 5 to 6 minutes.

3. Transfer mixture to an airtight container and refrigerate for at least 3 hours to solidify. Store in the refrigerator for up to 2 weeks.

Roasted Garlic and Parsley Sunflower Seed Butter

This flavorful butter pairs floral parsley and rich, aromatic roasted garlic. I like to spread it on crusty bread or swirl it into some freshly cooked pasta for a simple meal.

MAKES ABOUT 1¼ CUPS (300 ML)

Tips

When roasting whole garlic, use a serrated knife to cut off the top ¼ inch (0.5 cm) of the bulb, exposing the flesh of the individual cloves.

To remove grit from your parsley: Before chopping, place it in a bowl, cover with cool water and set aside for 2 minutes. The dirt will sink to the bottom of the bowl. Lift out the parsley, rinse under cold running water, and pat dry or dry in a salad spinner to remove all excess moisture.

- Preheat oven to 325°F (160°C)
- 2 baking sheets, lined with parchment paper
- Food processor

12	bulbs garlic, tops removed (see Tip, left)	12
¼ cup	extra virgin olive oil, divided	60 mL
2 cups	raw sunflower seeds	500 mL
1 tsp	garlic powder	5 mL
½ tsp	fine sea salt	2 mL
1 cup	chopped flat-leaf (Italian) parsley leaves	250 mL
1 tbsp	freshly squeezed lemon juice	15 mL

1. In a bowl, toss garlic bulbs with 2 tbsp (30 mL) oil. Transfer to one prepared baking sheet and bake in preheated oven for 45 minutes or until lightly golden and softened. Set aside to cool. Once cool, squeeze softened cloves from their skins and set aside.

2. Spread sunflower seeds on second prepared baking sheet and bake in preheated oven for 12 to 15 minutes or until fragrant and lightly toasted. Immediately transfer to a bowl. Set aside for 10 to 15 minutes or until completely cooled.

3. In food processor fitted with the metal blade, process toasted sunflower seeds until flour-like in consistency, 2 to 3 minutes. With the motor running, add remaining 2 tbsp (30 mL) oil through the feed tube in a slow, steady stream. Process for 12 to 15 minutes, until smooth, stopping the motor to scrape down sides of work bowl as necessary.

4. Add roasted garlic, garlic powder, salt, parsley and lemon juice and process for about 5 minutes, until well combined.

5. Transfer mixture to an airtight container and refrigerate for at least 3 hours to solidify. Store in the refrigerator for up to 2 weeks.

Cinnamon Raisin Sunflower Seed Butter

This butter is the perfect companion for crunchy toast. I also like to serve it alongside Buckwheat Coconut Pancakes (page 23) or Quinoa Maple Berry Porridge (page 21).

MAKES ABOUT 2 CUPS (500 ML)

Tips

To melt the coconut oil, gently warm it in a small skillet over low heat.

For a savory butter, omit the coconut sugar.

Use high-quality organic cinnamon. You will get the freshest flavor by grinding whole cinnamon sticks in a clean spice grinder.

Organic vanilla powder can be found in most well-stocked supermarkets and natural food stores. It is made from dried and ground whole vanilla beans. If you cannot find it, substitute ¼ tsp (1 mL) alcohol-free organic vanilla extract.

- Preheat oven to 400°F (200°C)
- Baking sheet, lined with parchment paper
- Food processor

3 cups	raw sunflower seeds	750 mL
3 tbsp	melted coconut oil (see Tips, left)	45 mL
2 tbsp	organic coconut sugar (optional; see Tips, left)	30 mL
1 tsp	ground cinnamon (see Tips, left)	5 mL
⅛ tsp	organic vanilla powder (see Tips, left)	0.5 mL
⅛ tsp	fine sea salt	0.5 mL
½ cup	Thompson or sultana raisins	125 mL

1. Spread sunflower seeds on prepared baking sheet and bake in preheated oven for 12 to 15 minutes, or until fragrant and lightly toasted. Immediately transfer to a bowl. Set aside for 10 to 15 minutes or until completely cooled.

2. In food processor fitted with the metal blade, process sunflower seeds until flour-like in consistency, 2 to 3 minutes. With the motor running, add coconut oil through the feed tube in a slow, steady stream. Process for 12 to 15 minutes or until smooth, stopping the motor to scrape down sides of work bowl as necessary.

3. Add coconut sugar (if using), cinnamon, vanilla and salt; process for 3 to 4 minutes, until well combined.

4. Transfer mixture to a bowl and stir in raisins. The butter will keep for up to 2 weeks in an airtight container in the refrigerator.

Almond Beurre Blanc

This sauce is incredibly versatile. Use it as a salad dressing, as a dipping sauce or even as a spread for sandwiches.

MAKES ABOUT 2 CUPS (500 ML)

Tips

Apple cider vinegar has long been used in folk medicine. It is a great digestive aid, among its other benefits. When purchasing apple cider vinegar, make sure it is raw and unpasteurized.

Be sure to use raw (not processed) agave nectar. It is a 100% natural (non-GMO) sweetener that contains naturally occurring fructose and is low on the glycemic scale, which means that it releases glucose slowly, providing sustained energy.

Blender

1 cup	almond butter	250 mL
½ cup	water	125 mL
½ cup	raw (unpasteurized) apple cider vinegar (see Tips, left)	125 mL
¼ cup	raw agave nectar (see Tips, left)	60 mL
½ tsp	fine sea salt	2 mL
2	cloves garlic	2

1. In blender, combine almond butter, water, vinegar, agave nectar, salt and garlic. Blend at high speed until smooth and creamy.
2. Serve immediately or transfer to an airtight container and refrigerate for up to 2 weeks.

Variation

Thai Almond Beurre Blanc: Substitute 2 tbsp (30 mL) freshly squeezed lime juice for 2 tbsp (30 mL) of the apple cider vinegar. Add 1 tbsp (15 mL) wheat-free tamari, 1 tbsp (15 mL) melted coconut oil and a pinch of cayenne pepper.

Vanilla Almond Butter

Enjoy this creamy butter spread over Buckwheat Coconut Pancakes (page 23) or crisp apple slices.

(page 23)

MAKES ABOUT 1¼ CUPS (300 ML)

- **Preheat oven to 350°F (180°C)**
- **Baking sheet, lined with parchment paper**
- **Food processor**

2 cups	raw almonds (see Tips, left)	500 mL
2 tbsp	grapeseed oil (see Tips, left)	30 mL
2 tbsp	coconut sugar	30 mL
½ tsp	organic vanilla powder (see Tips, left)	2 mL
Pinch	fine sea salt	Pinch

Tips

To save time, you can use roasted almonds. Omit Step 1.

Grapeseed oil has a neutral flavor. If you don't mind the taste of coconut, substitute an equal amount of melted coconut oil.

Coconut sugar is a low-glycemic sweetener that is available in most well-stocked supermarkets and natural food stores. It has a taste similar to brown sugar.

Organic vanilla powder can be found in most well-stocked supermarkets and natural food stores. It is made from dried and ground whole vanilla beans and will add a lot of flavor to your dishes. If you cannot find it, substitute 1 tsp (5 mL) alcohol-free organic vanilla extract.

1. Spread almonds on prepared baking sheet and bake in preheated oven for 10 to 12 minutes, until fragrant and lightly toasted. Immediately transfer to a bowl. Set aside for 10 to 15 minutes or until completely cooled.

2. In food processor fitted with the metal blade, process roasted almonds until flour-like in consistency, about 3 minutes. With the motor running, add oil through the feed tube in a slow, steady stream. Process for about 15 minutes, until smooth, stopping the motor to scrape down sides of work bowl as necessary.

3. Add coconut sugar, vanilla and salt; process for 5 minutes or until smooth and creamy.

4. Serve immediately or transfer to an airtight container and store at room temperature for up to 1 month.

Variation

For a savory butter, omit the coconut sugar and increase the amount of salt to ⅛ tsp (0.5 mL).

Superfood Green Pistachio Butter

Spread this uber-healthy butter on crunchy carrot and celery sticks for a snack, or toss with some freshly cooked pasta for a quick and easy meal.

**MAKES ABOUT
1 CUP (250 ML)**

Tips

Chlorella is a nutrient-rich freshwater alga that is believed to have detoxifying effects. You can find it in well-stocked supermarkets and natural food stores.

Spirulina is a blue-green freshwater alga that is rich in protein and minerals and is believed to help boost the immune system. You can find the powder in well-stocked supermarkets and natural food stores.

- **Preheat oven to 400°F (200°C)**
- **Baking sheet, lined with parchment paper**
- **Food processor**

2 cups	raw pistachios	500 mL
1/4 tsp	fine sea salt	1 mL
2 tbsp	grapeseed oil	30 mL
1/2 tsp	freshly grated lemon zest	2 mL
1 tbsp	freshly squeezed lemon juice	15 mL
1 tsp	chlorella powder (see Tips, left)	5 mL
1/4 tsp	spirulina powder (see Tips, left)	1 mL

1. Spread pistachios on prepared baking sheet and bake in preheated oven for 8 to 10 minutes, or until fragrant and lightly toasted. Immediately transfer to a bowl. Set aside for 10 to 15 minutes or until completely cooled.

2. In food processor fitted with the metal blade, process toasted pistachios and salt until flour-like in consistency, 2 to 3 minutes. With the motor running, add oil through the feed tube in a slow, steady stream. Process for 12 to 15 minutes or until smooth, stopping the motor to scrape down sides of work bowl as necessary.

3. Add lemon zest, lemon juice, chlorella and spirulina; process until well incorporated, about 3 minutes.

4. Serve immediately or transfer to an airtight container and store at room temperature for up to 2 weeks.

Thai-Style Macadamia Butter

This butter combines creamy macadamia nuts and freshly squeezed lime juice for an exotic flavor. I love to serve it with salted crackers and a glass of Lemon-Lime Fusion Juice (page 40).

MAKES ABOUT 1¼ CUPS (300 ML)

Tips

If not consumed within a couple of weeks, raw macadamia nuts should be stored in the fridge or freezer. Because of their high fat content, they can become rancid very quickly if not refrigerated.

To melt the coconut oil, gently warm it in a small skillet over low heat.

Coconut sugar is a low-glycemic sweetener that is available in most well-stocked supermarkets and natural food stores. It has a taste similar to brown sugar.

- Preheat oven to 400°F (200°C)
- Baking sheet, lined with parchment paper
- Food processor

2 cups	raw macadamia nuts (see Tips, left)	500 mL
¼ cup	melted coconut oil (see Tips, left)	60 mL
3 tbsp	freshly squeezed lime juice	45 mL
2 tbsp	wheat-free tamari	30 mL
2 tbsp	organic coconut sugar (see Tips, left)	30 mL
⅛ tsp	fine sea salt	0.5 mL
⅛ tsp	cayenne pepper	0.5 mL

1. Spread macadamia nuts in a single layer on prepared baking sheet and bake in preheated oven for 8 to 10 minutes, or until fragrant and lightly toasted. Immediately transfer to a bowl. Set aside for 10 to 15 minutes or until completely cooled.

2. In food processor fitted with the metal blade, process roasted macadamia nuts until flour-like in consistency, about 3 minutes. With the motor running, add coconut oil through the feed tube in a slow, steady stream. Process for about 15 minutes, until smooth, stopping the motor to scrape down sides of work bowl as necessary.

3. Add lime juice, tamari, coconut sugar, salt and cayenne; process for 5 minutes, until well combined. Serve immediately or transfer to an airtight container and refrigerate for up to 1 month.

Roasted Red Pepper and Thyme Cashew Butter

This creamy, savory cashew butter is incredibly versatile. Slather it on crusty gluten-free bread, use it as a dressing for crisp salad greens and fresh veggies, or toss it with your favorite pasta.

MAKES ABOUT 2 CUPS (500 ML)

Tips

Covering the bowl tightly with plastic wrap after roasting the peppers captures the steam, which helps to separate the skin from the flesh, making the peppers easier to peel.

To roast cashews: Spread on a baking sheet and toast in preheated 400°F (200°C) oven for 8 to 10 minutes, or until golden brown and fragrant. Remove from oven and immediately transfer to a bowl. Set aside for 10 to 15 minutes or until completely cooled.

To chop fresh thyme: Pinch the stem at the bottom with two fingers. Pulling upward with the finger and thumb of your other hand, strip the leaves. Reserve stems for soups or broths (discard after cooking). Use a sharp knife to chop the leaves, being careful not to chop too hard, as this will bruise the leaves and cause them to discolor.

Substitute 3 to 4 garlic cloves, minced, for the garlic powder.

- Preheat oven to 400°F (200°C)
- Baking sheet, lined with parchment paper
- Food processor

2	red bell peppers	2
3 tbsp	grapeseed oil	45 mL
3 cups	roasted cashews (see Tips, left)	750 mL
1 tbsp	extra virgin olive oil	15 mL
2 tbsp	chopped fresh thyme leaves (see Tips, left)	30 mL
1 tbsp	wheat-free tamari	15 mL
1 tbsp	freshly squeezed lemon juice	15 mL
½ tsp	garlic powder (see Tips, left)	2 mL
½ tsp	fine sea salt	2 mL

1. In a bowl, toss peppers with grapeseed oil. Arrange on prepared baking sheet. Bake in preheated oven until skin is lightly blackened, 18 to 20 minutes. Remove from oven and transfer to a bowl. Cover tightly with plastic wrap and set aside for 10 minutes.

2. Carefully remove peppers from bowl (they may be hot) and, using your fingers, gently rub skins off flesh. Cut peppers in half and discard seeds and ribs.

3. In food processor fitted with the metal blade, process roasted cashews until flour-like in consistency, about 3 minutes. With the motor running, add olive oil through the feed tube in a slow, steady stream. Process until smooth, about 15 minutes, stopping the motor often to scrape down sides of work bowl.

4. Add thyme, tamari, lemon juice, garlic powder and salt; process until well combined, about 5 minutes. Add prepared peppers and process until combined, about 1 minute. Transfer to an airtight container and refrigerate for 1 hour to solidify. Serve immediately or transfer to an airtight container and refrigerate for up to 1 week.

Spiced Pumpkin Cashew Butter

I love to make this butter during the harvest months, when the air becomes a little crisper and the leaves are starting to change color. The creamy pumpkin and fragrant allspice bring out the natural sweetness of the cashews. Enjoy this for breakfast, spread on some crusty bread, or use it as a dip with fresh Gluten-Free Pita Bread (page 474) for a quick afternoon snack.

MAKES ABOUT 2 CUPS (500 ML)

Tips

Be sure to use a pie or sugar pumpkin. The large pumpkins used at Halloween are very watery and won't produce the desired results. If pumpkin is not available, substitute an equal quantity of butternut squash.

To melt the coconut oil for this recipe, gently warm it in a small skillet over low heat.

For the best flavor, use freshly grated nutmeg. I like to use a fine-toothed grater such as the type made by Microplane.

- **Preheat oven to 400°F (200°C)**
- **Baking sheet, lined with parchment paper**
- **Food processor**

2 cups	chopped peeled pumpkin (see Tips, left)	500 mL
2 cups	raw cashews	500 mL
3 tbsp	melted coconut oil (see Tips, left)	45 mL
½ tsp	fine sea salt	2 mL
½ tsp	ground allspice	2 mL
¼ tsp	freshly grated nutmeg (see Tips, left)	1 mL
⅛ tsp	ground cloves	0.5 mL

1. In a saucepan of boiling water, cook pumpkin until tender, about 15 minutes. Drain in a colander, then set aside to cool.

2. Spread cashews on prepared baking sheet and bake in preheated oven for 8 to 10 minutes, or until fragrant and lightly toasted. Immediately transfer to a bowl. Set aside for 10 to 15 minutes or until completely cooled.

3. In food processor fitted with the metal blade, process cashews until flour-like in consistency, 2 to 3 minutes. With the motor running, add coconut oil through the feed tube in a slow, steady stream. Process for 12 to 15 minutes or until smooth, stopping the motor to scrape down sides of work bowl as necessary.

4. Add cooked pumpkin, salt, allspice, nutmeg and cloves; process for about 5 minutes, until well combined. Serve immediately or transfer to an airtight container and refrigerate for up to 2 weeks.

Mixed Berry Cashew Butter

This sweet, creamy berry-filled butter is a versatile treat. Use it as a spread on gluten-free toast, as a dip for fresh fruit, or as a topping for Salted Caramel Ice Cream (page 520) or Vegan Vanilla Ice Cream (page 513).

MAKES ABOUT 2 CUPS (500 ML)

Tips

To melt the coconut oil, gently warm it in a small skillet over low heat.

Organic vanilla powder can be found in most well-stocked supermarkets and natural food stores. It is made from dried and ground whole vanilla beans and will add a lot of flavor to your dishes. If you cannot find it, substitute ½ tsp (2 mL) alcohol-free organic vanilla extract.

- Preheat oven to 400°F (200°C)
- Baking sheet, lined with parchment paper
- Food processor

2 cups	raw cashews	500 mL
⅛ tsp	fine sea salt	0.5 mL
¼ cup	melted coconut oil (see Tips, left)	60 mL
2 tbsp	pure maple syrup	30 mL
¼ tsp	organic vanilla powder (see Tips, left)	1 mL
½ cup	chopped hulled strawberries	125 mL
½ cup	blueberries	125 mL
½ cup	raspberries	125 mL
½ cup	blackberries	125 mL

1. Spread cashews on prepared baking sheet and bake in preheated oven for 8 to 10 minutes, or until fragrant and lightly toasted. Immediately transfer to a bowl. Set aside for 10 to 15 minutes or until completely cooled.

2. In food processor fitted with the metal blade, process toasted cashews and salt until flour-like in consistency, 2 to 3 minutes.

3. With the motor running, add coconut oil through the feed tube in a slow, steady stream. Process for 12 to 15 minutes or until smooth, stopping the motor to scrape down sides of work bowl as necessary.

4. Add maple syrup, vanilla, strawberries, blueberries, raspberries and blackberries. Process until well combined, about 5 minutes. Serve immediately or transfer to an airtight container and refrigerate for up to 1 week.

Black Olive and Walnut Butter

Serve this creamy, salty butter with crusty bread as an accompaniment to Mediterranean-inspired meals, as a garnish for grilled vegetables, or as a delicious salad dressing.

MAKES ABOUT 2 CUPS (500 ML)

Tip

I prefer to use kalamata olives in this recipe, but any type of pitted black olive will work.

- **Preheat oven to 400°F (200°C)**
- **Baking sheet, lined with parchment paper**
- **Food processor**

2 cups	raw walnut halves	500 mL
2 tbsp	extra virgin olive oil	30 mL
1 tsp	dried oregano	5 mL
2 cups	pitted kalamata olives (see Tip, left)	500 mL

1. Spread walnuts in a single layer on prepared baking sheet and bake in preheated oven for 6 to 8 minutes, or until fragrant and lightly toasted. Immediately transfer to a bowl. Set aside for 10 to 15 minutes or until completely cooled.

2. In food processor fitted with the metal blade, process walnuts until flour-like in consistency, about 2 minutes. With the motor running, add oil through the feed tube in a slow, steady stream. Process for 12 to 15 minutes or until smooth, stopping the motor to scrape down sides of work bowl as necessary.

3. Add oregano and olives and process for 5 minutes, until well combined. Serve immediately or transfer to an airtight container and refrigerate for up to 2 weeks.

Pecan Pie Butter

Enjoy this butter slathered over your favorite gluten-free toast. For a decadent treat during the holidays, spread it over Oatmeal Raisin Cookies (page 431) or Banana Goji Cookies (page 430).

MAKES ABOUT 2 CUPS (500 ML)

Tips

Substitute 1 tbsp (15 mL) agave nectar or 3 tbsp (45 mL) coconut sugar for the maple syrup.

Organic vanilla powder can be found in most well-stocked supermarkets and natural food stores. It is made from dried and ground whole vanilla beans and will add a lot of flavor to your dishes. If you cannot find it, substitute ½ tsp (2 mL) alcohol-free organic vanilla extract.

There are numerous varieties of dates, but Medjools are my favorite. Although they are generally more expensive, they are larger, softer and, in my opinion, more flavorful.

- **Preheat oven to 400°F (200°C)**
- **Baking sheet, lined with parchment paper**
- **Food processor**

2 cups	raw pecan halves	500 mL
3 tbsp	melted coconut oil	45 mL
2 tbsp	pure maple syrup (see Tips, left)	30 mL
½ tsp	ground cinnamon	2 mL
¼ tsp	fine sea salt	1 mL
¼ tsp	organic vanilla powder (see Tips, left)	1 mL
½ cup	chopped pitted Medjool dates (see Tips, left)	125 mL

1. Spread pecans on prepared baking sheet and bake in preheated oven for 8 to 10 minutes, or until fragrant and lightly toasted. Immediately transfer to a bowl. Set aside for 10 to 15 minutes or until completely cooled.

2. In food processor fitted with the metal blade, process pecans until flour-like in consistency, 2 to 3 minutes. With the motor running, add coconut oil through the feed tube in a slow, steady stream. Process for 12 to 15 minutes or until smooth, stopping the motor to scrape down sides of work bowl as necessary.

3. Add maple syrup, cinnamon, salt and vanilla; process until well incorporated, about 3 minutes. Add dates and process until smooth and creamy, about 5 minutes. Serve immediately or transfer to an airtight container and store at room temperature for up to 2 weeks.

Peanut Butter and Jelly Nut Butter

A classic combination, this butter can be spread on your favorite gluten-free bread or used as a dip for fresh fruit to satisfy a midday snack craving. I love to serve it alongside a glass of Pink Beet Delight (page 44).

MAKES ABOUT 2 CUPS (500 ML)

Tips

To melt the coconut oil, gently warm it in a small skillet over medium heat.

Substitute 2 tsp (10 mL) raw agave nectar for the maple syrup.

Organic vanilla powder can be found in most well-stocked supermarkets and natural food stores. It is made from dried and ground whole vanilla beans and will add a lot of flavor to your dishes. If you cannot find it, substitute ½ tsp (2 mL) alcohol-free organic vanilla extract.

- **Preheat oven to 400°F (200°C)**
- **Baking sheet, lined with parchment paper**
- **Food processor**

2 cups	raw peanuts	500 mL
3 tbsp	melted coconut oil	45 mL
2 tbsp	organic coconut sugar	30 mL
1 tbsp	pure maple syrup (see Tips, left)	15 mL
¼ tsp	organic vanilla powder (see Tips, left)	1 mL
¼ cup	raspberries	60 mL
¼ cup	chopped hulled strawberries	60 mL
¼ cup	blueberries	60 mL
¼ cup	chopped pitted Medjool dates	60 mL

1. Spread peanuts on prepared baking sheet and bake in preheated oven for 8 to 10 minutes, or until fragrant and lightly toasted. Immediately transfer to a bowl. Set aside for 10 to 15 minutes or until completely cooled.

2. In food processor fitted with the metal blade, process peanuts until flour-like in consistency, 2 to 3 minutes. With the motor running, add coconut oil through the feed tube in a slow, steady stream. Process for 12 to 15 minutes or until smooth, stopping the motor to scrape down sides of work bowl as necessary.

3. Add coconut sugar, maple syrup and vanilla; process until well combined, about 3 minutes. Add raspberries, strawberries, blueberries and dates. Process for 5 minutes, until smooth and creamy. Serve immediately or transfer to an airtight container and refrigerate for up to 1 week.

Variation

Peanut Butter and Peach Jelly Nut Butter: Substitute 1 cup (250 mL) thinly sliced peaches for the berries. Add ¼ tsp (1 mL) ground cinnamon.

Chocolate Hazelnut Butter

This heavenly spread can be slathered on your favorite crusty gluten-free bread and served as a sandwich — or eaten straight out of the jar with a spoon! It is perfect served with apple slices or grilled peaches for a nutritious snack or light dessert.

MAKES ABOUT 2 CUPS (500 ML)

Tips

To melt the coconut oil, gently warm it in a small skillet over medium heat.

Substitute an equal amount of Almond Milk (page 61) for the coconut milk.

Substitute 1/4 cup (60 mL) raw agave nectar or 1/3 cup (75 mL) pure maple syrup for the coconut sugar.

Organic vanilla powder can be found in most well-stocked supermarkets and natural food stores. It is made from dried and ground whole vanilla beans and will add a lot of flavor to your dishes. If you cannot find it, substitute 1/2 tsp (2 mL) alcohol-free organic vanilla extract.

- **Preheat oven to 350°F (180°C)**
- **Baking sheet, lined with parchment paper**
- **Food processor**

2 cups	raw hazelnuts	500 mL
1/2 cup	raw cacao powder	125 mL
3 tbsp	melted coconut oil	45 mL
1/2 cup	Coconut Milk (page 62; see Tips, left)	125 mL
1/2 cup	organic coconut sugar (see Tips, left)	125 mL
1/4 tsp	organic vanilla powder (see Tips, left)	1 mL
Pinch	fine sea salt	Pinch

1. Spread hazelnuts on prepared baking sheet and bake in preheated oven for 10 to 12 minutes, or until fragrant and lightly toasted. Transfer nuts to the middle of a clean, damp kitchen towel. Roll up towel, fold in both ends and, using your hands, gently roll on work surface to remove as much of the nut skins as possible (it's okay to leave some remaining). Unwrap and set aside for 10 to 15 minutes or until completely cooled.

2. In food processor fitted with the metal blade, process toasted hazelnuts and cacao powder until flour-like in consistency, 3 to 5 minutes.

3. With the motor running, add coconut oil through the feed tube in a slow, steady stream. Process until smooth and somewhat creamy, stopping the motor every few minutes to scrape down sides of work bowl as necessary (this step can take as long as 20 minutes).

4. Add coconut milk, coconut sugar, vanilla and salt; process for another 5 minutes, until well combined. Serve immediately or transfer to an airtight container and store at room temperature for up to 2 weeks.

Caramelized Onion and Cherry Tomato Relish

Top your favorite veggie burger, sandwich or freshly cooked pasta with this savory relish.

MAKES ABOUT 2 CUPS (500 ML)

Tips

Substitute an equal amount of chopped fresh regular tomatoes for the cherry tomatoes.

Be sure to use raw (not processed) agave nectar. It is a 100% natural (non-GMO) sweetener that contains naturally occurring fructose and is low on the glycemic scale, which means that it releases glucose slowly, providing sustained energy.

1 tbsp	grapeseed oil	15 mL
2	onions, thinly sliced	2
½ tsp	fine sea salt	2 mL
1½ cups	chopped cherry tomatoes (see Tips, left)	375 mL
½ cup	balsamic vinegar	125 mL
¼ cup	raw agave nectar (see Tips, left)	60 mL
2 tbsp	water	30 mL

1. In a large skillet over high heat, heat oil. Add onions and salt and cook, stirring frequently, until onions begin to brown, about 5 minutes. Reduce heat to low and cook for 25 to 30 minutes, until onions are golden.

2. Stir in cherry tomatoes, vinegar, agave nectar and water. Increase heat to high and simmer until mixture has thickened, about 15 minutes. Serve immediately or transfer to an airtight container and refrigerate for up to 2 weeks.

Pear, Date and Fig Jam

Spread this delicious jam on toast, dollop it over pancakes or serve it as an accompaniment to French toast.

**MAKES ABOUT
4 CUPS (1 L)**

Tips

Substitute an equal quantity of peeled chopped apples for the pears.

Coconut sugar is a low-glycemic sweetener that is available in most well-stocked supermarkets and natural food stores. It has a taste similar to brown sugar.

There are numerous varieties of dates, but Medjools are my favorite. Although they are generally more expensive, they are larger, softer and, in my opinion, more flavorful.

Do not lift the lid of your slow cooker while it is cooking. Each time you do, heat escapes, and you will need to add 20 to 30 minutes to the cooking time.

- **Medium (approximately 4 quart) slow cooker**

8 cups	peeled chopped pears (see Tips, left)	2 L
2 cups	chopped fresh figs	500 mL
2 cups	organic coconut sugar (see Tips, left)	500 mL
1 cup	chopped pitted Medjool dates (see Tips, left)	250 mL
½ cup	water	125 mL
1	3-inch (7.5 cm) cinnamon stick	1
¼ tsp	fine sea salt	1 mL

1. In slow cooker stoneware, combine pears, figs, coconut sugar, dates, water, cinnamon stick and salt. Cover and cook on Low for 6 hours or High for 3 hours. Discard cinnamon stick.

2. Transfer to an airtight container and refrigerate until cool. Serve immediately or refrigerate for up to 1 month.

Sicilian Eggplant Caponata

Caponata is a traditional Sicilian dish. It is usually served warm as a spread on crusty bread or crostini, but it is really multipurpose, making a wonderful dip for fresh vegetables or even a rich side dish.

**MAKES
3 CUPS (750 ML)**

Tips

To remove grit from your parsley: Before chopping, place it in a bowl, cover with cool water and set aside for 2 minutes. The dirt will sink to the bottom of the bowl. Lift out the parsley, rinse under cold running water, and pat dry or dry in a salad spinner to remove all excess moisture.

Do not lift the lid of your slow cooker while it is cooking. Each time you do, heat escapes, and you will need to add 20 to 30 minutes to the cooking time.

To reheat refrigerated caponata, place in a skillet over medium heat and cook for 2 to 3 minutes, until heated through.

● **Medium (about 4 quart) slow cooker**

6 tbsp	grapeseed oil, divided	90 mL
8 cups	chopped peeled eggplant (about 1 large)	2 L
1 cup	chopped onion	250 mL
1 tbsp	dried oregano	15 mL
1 tsp	fine sea salt	5 mL
8 to 10	cloves garlic, minced	8 to 10
12 cups	chopped tomatoes	3 L
1/3 cup	red wine vinegar	75 mL
1 tbsp	organic coconut sugar	15 mL
1/2 cup	chopped green olives	125 mL
1/2 cup	capers (drained)	125 mL
1/2 cup	chopped flat-leaf (Italian) parsley leaves	125 mL

1. In a large pot over high heat, heat 1/4 cup (60 mL) oil. Cook eggplant, stirring frequently, until soft and lightly browned, 8 to 10 minutes. Using a slotted spoon, transfer to a plate and set aside.

2. In same pot over medium heat, heat remaining 2 tbsp (30 mL) oil. Add onion, oregano and salt; cook, stirring constantly, until onion is translucent, about 6 minutes. Stir in garlic and cook for 2 to 3 minutes, until fragrant. Stir in tomatoes, vinegar and coconut sugar and bring to a simmer. Transfer to slow cooker stoneware.

3. Cover and cook on Low for 6 hours or High for 3 hours. Stir in olives and capers; cook, covered, for 20 minutes more. Stir in parsley. Serve immediately or transfer to an airtight container and refrigerate for up to 2 weeks.

Snacks and Sides

Snacks

Sides

Fresh Fruit Ice Pops

These frozen treats are a great way to cool off and enjoy a healthy serving of fruit during the heat of summer.

MAKES ABOUT 12 ICE POPS

Tips

Substitute an equal amount of pineapple juice, apple juice, cooled steeped tea, or water for the orange juice.

For added nutrition, add 2 tsp (10 mL) chia seeds or raw shelled hemp seeds to the fruit mixture in Step 1.

- Ice pop mold with 12 compartments
- Ice pop sticks

3 cups	freshly squeezed orange juice (see Tips, left)	750 mL
½ cup	chopped peeled kiwifruit	125 mL
½ cup	chopped pineapple	125 mL
½ cup	chopped hulled strawberries	125 mL
½ cup	roughly chopped blueberries	125 mL

1. In a bowl, combine orange juice, kiwi, pineapple, strawberries and blueberries. Stir gently.
2. Spoon fruit mixture into ice pop compartments until each is three-quarters full. Top up with any remaining fruit or juice. Cover and place in freezer until partially frozen and slushy, about 30 minutes.
3. Insert a stick in center of each compartment. Cover and freeze until solid, about 8 hours. Ice pops will keep for up to 2 months in the freezer.

Variation

Fresh Vegetable Ice Pops: Make ice pops with fresh vegetables instead of fruit. In a bowl, combine 3 cups (750 mL) fresh tomato juice, 2 tsp (10 mL) chopped fresh flat-leaf (Italian) parsley, 2 tsp (10 mL) chopped celery, 2 tsp (10 mL) finely chopped carrot and 2 tsp (10 mL) finely chopped red bell pepper. Continue recipe from Step 2. These ice pops may be slightly smaller than the fruit version because of the volume of the vegetables.

Cucumber Protein Cups

These cucumber cups are quick, healthy and delicious. The hemp seeds provide a boost of protein, which means that these are also a good post-workout recovery snack.

MAKES 14 TO 16 CUPS (ABOUT 4 SERVINGS)

Tips

A hand-held citrus reamer can be used to extract the juice from lemons and limes. Available in most kitchen supply stores, this tool would be ideal to use for the lemon juice in this recipe.

The cucumber pieces should be about 1¾ inches (4.5 cm) thick to allow room for the filling once the flesh is scooped out.

Flat-leaf (Italian) parsley has much more flavor and is easier to chew than curly parsley.

Save any extra cashew mixture to use as a dip with your favorite crunchy vegetables, such as carrots and celery.

- **Food processor**

2 cups	raw cashews	500 mL
½ cup	raw shelled hemp seeds	125 mL
1 cup	chopped red bell pepper	250 mL
½ cup	chopped celery	125 mL
¼ cup	freshly squeezed lemon juice (see Tips, left)	60 mL
1 tbsp	nutritional yeast	15 mL
1 tsp	fine sea salt	5 mL
2	cloves garlic	2
1	English cucumber, cut crosswise into 14 to 16 pieces (see Tips, left)	1
	Chopped fresh flat-leaf (Italian) parsley (see Tips, left)	

1. In food processor fitted with the metal blade, combine cashews, hemp seeds, red pepper, celery, lemon juice, nutritional yeast, salt and garlic. Process until smooth, stopping the motor to scrape down sides of work bowl as necessary. Set aside.

2. Place cucumber pieces flat on a clean work surface. Using a small spoon or melon baller, carefully scoop out some of the flesh, being careful not to go all the way through (discard scooped-out part).

3. Fill each cucumber cup with about 1 tbsp (15 mL) cashew mixture. Sprinkle with chopped parsley. Serve immediately or transfer to an airtight container and refrigerate for up to 2 days.

Hemp Apple Rings

Enjoy these protein-dense snacks as part of a complete breakfast along with your favorite bowl of cereal. They're also a healthy snack any time of day.

Tips

Choose crisp, firm apples for this recipe, such as McIntosh or Honeycrisp.

Using a mandoline ensures thin, even slices, but a knife works well too. The slices should be about ¼ inch (0.5 cm) thick.

Organic vanilla powder can be found in most well-stocked supermarkets and natural food stores. It is made from dried and ground whole vanilla beans and will add a lot of flavor to your dishes. If you cannot find it, substitute a dash of alcohol-free organic vanilla extract.

Do not slice the apples too early or they will turn brown. If you want to cut them ahead of time, place the slices in a bowl containing 1 cup (250 mL) water and 3 to 4 tbsp (45 to 60 mL) freshly squeezed lemon juice until ready to use. Pat dry with paper towels before dipping into maple syrup mixture.

- Mandoline (see Tips, left)

3 tbsp	pure maple syrup	45 mL
1 tsp	freshly squeezed lemon juice	5 mL
Pinch	organic vanilla powder (see Tips, left)	Pinch
½ cup	raw shelled hemp seeds	125 mL
2	apples, cored and thinly sliced (see Tips, left)	2

1. In a shallow bowl, whisk together maple syrup, lemon juice and vanilla.
2. Place hemp seeds in another shallow bowl.
3. Dip each apple slice in maple syrup mixture, ensuring that both sides are well coated, and then in hemp seeds, turning to coat well. Serve immediately.

Almond Oat Apple Wedges

Enjoy these apple treats as a midday snack or healthy dessert. They're also a great addition to children's lunchboxes — kids love them!

MAKES 4 SERVINGS

Tips

Almonds are very nutritious. They contain phytochemicals, protein, fiber and healthy fats, as well as vitamin E, magnesium, phosphorus, potassium, manganese and small amounts of B vitamins.

For sweeter wedges, use Gala, McIntosh, Ambrosia or Braeburn apples. If you prefer them less sweet, use Red Delicious or Granny Smith apples. Do not cut the wedges too early or they will turn brown (see Tips, page 144).

• Food processor

½ cup	raw almonds	125 mL
¼ cup	quick-cooking rolled oats	60 mL
½ cup	almond butter	125 mL
1 tbsp	pure maple syrup	15 mL
⅛ tsp	organic vanilla powder (see Tips, page 144)	0.5 mL
3	apples, cored and cut into 6 wedges (see Tips, left)	3

1. In food processor fitted with the metal blade, process almonds and oats until nuts are finely chopped (be careful not to overprocess, as you want to retain some texture). Transfer to a shallow bowl.

2. In a small bowl, combine almond butter, maple syrup and vanilla.

3. Dip each apple wedge in almond butter mixture, ensuring that all sides are well coated, and then in almond-oat mixture, turning to coat well. Transfer to a tray. Cover and refrigerate for 1 hour to set. Serve immediately.

Stuffed Medjool Dates

Cure your dessert cravings with these sweet, soft dates stuffed with a mixture of warm chocolate and almond butter.

**MAKES
15 STUFFED DATES
(5 TO 6 SERVINGS)**

Tip

If you don't have any non-dairy chocolate chips on hand, in a blender, combine ½ cup (125 mL) melted coconut oil, 3 tbsp (45 mL) raw agave nectar, ¼ cup (60 mL) raw cacao powder, 1 tbsp (15 mL) cool water and ⅛ tsp (0.5 mL) organic vanilla powder or ¼ tsp (1 mL) alcohol-free organic vanilla extract. Blend until smooth. If substituting for chocolate chips, skip Step 1 and add to almond butter in Step 2.

● **Baking sheet, lined with parchment paper**

½ cup	non-dairy chocolate chips (see Tip, left)	125 mL
¼ cup	almond butter	60 mL
15	Medjool dates, pitted	15

1. In a small saucepan over low heat, gently heat chocolate chips, stirring constantly, until completely melted and smooth (be careful not to burn the chocolate).
2. Add almond butter and stir until combined. Remove from heat and set aside.
3. Using your fingers, gently pull apart a date to expose the space left by the pit. Using a small spoon, drizzle chocolate mixture inside. Transfer to prepared baking sheet.
4. Repeat with remaining dates and chocolate mixture. Refrigerate until filling is slightly firm, about 30 minutes. Serve immediately or transfer to an airtight container and refrigerate for up to 2 weeks.

Easy Cheesy Kale Chips

Keep a stash of these crispy kale chips in the cupboard at home, in a desk drawer at the office, or in your bag for a quick and tasty on-the-go snack.

Tips

Heads of kale vary in size. If they are on the larger size, use only one. If smaller, use two.

Nutritional yeast is an inactive yeast that has been grown on beet molasses and then pasteurized. It provides a rich, cheesy flavor in sauces, stews, soups and dips. Look for it in well-stocked supermarkets and natural food stores.

To soak the cashews: Place in a bowl and cover with 2 cups (500 mL) water. Cover and set aside for 30 minutes or overnight (if overnight, refrigerate). Drain.

- **Preheat oven to 275°F (140°C)**
- **Food processor**
- **2 baking sheets, lined with parchment paper**

1 to 2	bunches green curly kale (see Tips, left)	1 to 2
1½ cups	chopped red bell peppers	375 mL
1 cup	nutritional yeast (see Tips, left)	250 mL
1 cup	water	250 mL
¾ cup	raw cashews, soaked (see Tips, left)	175 mL
¼ cup	extra virgin olive oil	60 mL
¼ cup	freshly squeezed lemon juice	60 mL
1½ tsp	fine sea salt	7 mL

1. Strip leaves from kale stems (discard stems and ribs). Tear or cut into large bite-size pieces about 1½ inches (4 cm) square. Transfer to a large bowl and set aside.

2. In food processor fitted with the metal blade, process red peppers, nutritional yeast, water, soaked cashews, oil, lemon juice and sea salt until smooth and creamy. Add to kale and toss to combine, ensuring that the pieces are completely coated with sauce.

3. Arrange kale in a single layer on prepared baking sheets and bake in preheated oven for 20 to 25 minutes, turning over halfway through, until thoroughly dried, with no wet spots. (If the chips are still wet, continue baking and check for doneness every 5 to 10 minutes.)

4. Remove from oven and set aside to cool completely. Serve immediately or transfer to an airtight container and refrigerate for up to 2 weeks.

Baked Sweet Potato Chips

Wafer-thin crispy sweet potato chips are one of my favorite snacks. This recipe makes perfect chips with only three ingredients, so you can indulge without feeling guilty.

MAKES 4 SERVINGS

Tips

If you like your chips a little spicier, add ¼ tsp (1 mL) cayenne pepper in Step 1.

There are lots of nutrients in the skin of sweet potatoes, so leave the skin on whenever possible. Just make sure you purchase organically grown sweet potatoes, to avoid pesticide residue.

- **Preheat oven to 275°F (140°C)**
- **Mandoline**
- **2 baking sheets, lined with parchment paper**

2	large sweet potatoes, skin on	2
2 tbsp	grapeseed oil	30 mL
¼ tsp	fine sea salt	1 mL

1. Using mandoline, cut sweet potatoes into slices about ⅛ inch (3 mm) thick. Transfer to a large bowl. Toss with oil and salt until evenly coated.

2. Arrange seasoned sweet potato slices in a single layer on prepared baking sheets. Bake in preheated oven until dry and crisp, about 1½ to 1¾ hours, turning halfway through the cooking time (slices will shrivel and brown lightly around the edges).

3. Remove from oven and set aside for 10 to 15 minutes to cool completely and crisp up. Serve immediately or transfer to an airtight container and refrigerate for up to 2 weeks.

Variation

Spicy, Smoky Baked Sweet Potato Chips: Toss sliced sweet potatoes with 1 tsp (5 mL) chili powder, ½ tsp (2 mL) smoked paprika, ¼ tsp (1 mL) chipotle powder and a pinch of cayenne pepper before baking.

Best Stovetop Protein Popcorn

One of my favorite snacks is a big bowl of crunchy popcorn coated with protein-dense hemp seeds, creamy coconut oil and cheesy nutritional yeast.

MAKES 3 SERVINGS

Tips

For added flavor, sprinkle a little garlic powder on the hot popcorn.

If the popcorn is chewy rather than crisp after being popped, this means that the kernels are old and should be discarded.

¼ cup	melted coconut oil, divided	60 mL
¼ cup	raw shelled hemp seeds, divided	60 mL
¼ cup	nutritional yeast, divided	60 mL
1 tsp	fine sea salt, divided	5 mL
3 tbsp	grapeseed oil	45 mL
⅓ cup	organic popcorn kernels	75 mL

1. In a large bowl, combine 2 tbsp (30 mL) coconut oil, 2 tbsp (30 mL) hemp seeds, 2 tbsp (30 mL) nutritional yeast and ½ tsp (2 mL) salt. Set aside.

2. In a large pot with a tight-fitting lid, heat grapeseed oil over high heat. Add corn kernels and cover. Cook, shaking pot constantly, until the popping reduces to once every 3 to 5 seconds. Remove from heat.

3. Pour popcorn into bowl with coconut oil mixture. Top with remaining coconut oil, hemp seeds, yeast and salt; toss to combine. Serve immediately or let cool, transfer to an airtight container and store at room temperature for up to 2 days.

Variation

Sweet and Spicy Stovetop Popcorn: Omit the nutritional yeast. Add 2 tbsp (30 mL) coconut sugar and 1 tsp (5 mL) chili powder to the mixture.

Chickpea Popcorn Mix

Enjoy this easy-to-make treat as a healthy snack or dessert.

MAKES 4 SERVINGS

Tip

Substitute an equal amount of peanut butter for the almond butter.

3 cups	Best Stovetop Protein Popcorn (above)	750 mL
1 cup	drained cooked chickpeas	250 mL
½ cup	almond butter (see Tip, left)	125 mL
3 tbsp	raw agave nectar or 2 tbsp (30 mL) pure maple syrup or organic coconut sugar	45 mL

1. In a large bowl, combine popcorn, chickpeas, almond butter and agave nectar. Toss to coat well. Serve immediately.

Teriyaki Almonds

I love the sweet-and-salty punch you get from these crunchy almonds. Make them to eat on the go or use them for a boost of protein, chopped and sprinkled over salads or side dishes.

	MAKES 2 CUPS (500 ML)		
¼ cup	wheat-free tamari (see Tips, left)	60 mL
3 tbsp	raw agave nectar	45 mL
3 tbsp	sesame oil (untoasted)	45 mL
1 tbsp	chopped peeled gingerroot	15 mL
2 cups	whole raw almonds (see Tips, left)	500 mL

Tips

Wheat-free tamari is similar to soy sauce except that it is brewed without using wheat or grain alcohol. Because it has a stronger flavor than soy sauce, you don't need to add as much to your dishes.

When purchasing nuts, be sure to look for products labeled "raw." Most nuts on the market have been roasted and do not qualify as raw food. If you have concerns, ask your purveyor.

If you are lucky enough to own an electric dehydrator, toss the almonds in the sauce and then place them in the dehydrator at 105°F (40°C) for 8 to 10 hours, or until all of the liquid has evaporated and the almonds are dry and slightly sticky. Cool completely. Store in an airtight container at room temperature for up to 14 days.

1. In a blender, combine tamari, agave nectar, sesame oil and ginger. Blend at high speed until smooth. Transfer to a large bowl.

2. Add almonds and toss to combine. Serve immediately or cover and refrigerate for up to 7 days.

Variation

Teriyaki Cashews: Substitute an equal amount of cashews for the almonds.

Sunflower Beet Crackers

Serve these flavorful crackers with your favorite dip or spread. They also make a great portable snack for when you are on the go. Pack them in your bag, keep them in a jar on the counter, or tuck them into an office drawer.

Tips

To soak the sunflower seeds: Place in a bowl and cover with 6 cups (1.5 L) water. Cover and set aside to soak for 30 minutes. Drain, discarding soaking water.

You can purchase flax seeds that are already ground (often called "milled") or you can grind them yourself. To grind the flax seeds for this recipe, place 2 cups (500 mL) whole seeds in a blender (or clean spice grinder in batches) and blend at high speed until finely ground. Cover and refrigerate any extra for up to a month.

Add a small silica gel pack to storage containers to help prevent dry baked goods from absorbing moisture. Silica gel packets are available in most restaurant supply stores.

Try seasoning these crackers with various fresh herbs or spices. I use 2 tbsp (30 mL) dried rosemary for a Mediterranean cracker or 1 tbsp (15 mL) ground cumin and 1 tsp (5 mL) chili powder for a Southwest flavor.

- **Preheat oven to 350°F (180°C)**
- **Food processor**
- **Baking sheet, lined with parchment paper**

4 cups	raw sunflower seeds, soaked (see Tips, left)	1 L
2 cups	shredded peeled beets	500 mL
½ cup	water	125 mL
¼ cup	wheat-free tamari	60 mL
1 tbsp	chopped fresh thyme leaves	15 mL
1 tsp	fine sea salt	5 mL
3 to 4	cloves garlic	3 to 4
¼ cup	extra virgin olive oil	60 mL
2 cups	ground raw flax seeds (see Tips, left)	500 mL

1. In food processor fitted with the metal blade, combine soaked sunflower seeds, beets, water and tamari. Process until smooth, stopping the motor to scrape down sides of work bowl as necessary. Add thyme, salt and garlic; process until no large pieces of garlic remain. With the motor running, add oil through the feed tube in a slow, steady stream. Transfer mixture to a large bowl.

2. Stir in ground flax seeds until well combined. Cover and set aside for about 10 minutes so the flax seeds can absorb the liquid and swell.

3. Spread dough evenly, about ¼ inch (0.5 cm) thick, on prepared baking sheet. Using a small knife, score dough into about 16 crackers.

4. Bake in preheated oven for 20 minutes. Remove from oven, break apart crackers at scored lines, and turn them over. Bake on other side for 10 minutes or until dry throughout.

5. Remove from oven and set aside to cool on baking sheet until crisp, 15 to 20 minutes. Serve immediately or let cool completely, transfer to an airtight container and store at room temperature for up to 2 weeks (see Tips, left).

Spiced Superfood Trail Mix

Keep this nutrient-dense superfood mix in the cupboard for a healthy treat anytime. It also makes a great high-protein post-workout snack.

Tips

You can substitute any of your favorites for the nuts and seeds in this recipe. Try pistachios, hazelnuts, pine nuts, peanuts and sesame seeds.

Always check the label to ensure that the dried fruits you are buying do not contain any preservatives, such as the sulfur compounds commonly used on apricots, sun-dried tomatoes and other dried ingredients.

1 cup	raw walnuts (see Tips, left)	250 mL
1 cup	raw cashews	250 mL
1 cup	raw Brazil nuts	250 mL
1 cup	raw shelled hemp seeds	250 mL
½ cup	raw sunflower seeds	125 mL
½ cup	raw pumpkin seeds	125 mL
½ cup	dried goji berries	125 mL
½ cup	chia seeds	125 mL
½ cup	roughly chopped dried apricots (see Tips, left)	125 mL
½ cup	Thompson or sultana raisins	125 mL
1 tbsp	extra virgin olive oil	15 mL
1 tsp	organic coconut sugar	5 mL
½ tsp	chili powder	2 mL
¼ tsp	fine sea salt	1 mL
⅛ tsp	organic vanilla powder (see Tips, page 153)	0.5 mL

1. In a large bowl, combine walnuts, cashews, Brazil nuts, hemp seeds, sunflower seeds, pumpkin seeds, goji berries, chia seeds, apricots, raisins, oil, coconut sugar, chili powder, salt and vanilla. Stir well.

2. Serve immediately or transfer to an airtight container and refrigerate for up to 1 month.

Spiced Apple Buckwheat Granola

Not just for breakfast, granola is rich in protein and fiber and makes a healthy snack any time of day. Keep a batch of this on hand and enjoy a handful as an easy snack on the go or a guilt-free treat. It's especially good after workouts.

MAKES ABOUT 8 CUPS (2 L) OR 12 TO 15 SERVINGS

Tips

To soak the dates: Place in a bowl and cover with 2 cups (500 mL) warm water. Cover and set aside for 1 hour. Drain, reserving ½ cup (125 mL) soaking water.

To soak the buckwheat: Place in a large bowl and cover with 12 cups (3 L) water. Cover and set aside for 1 hour or overnight (if overnight, refrigerate). Transfer to a fine-mesh sieve and drain. Rinse under cold running water for 2 minutes or until water runs clear.

Organic vanilla powder can be found in most well-stocked supermarkets and natural food stores. It is made from dried and ground whole vanilla beans and will add a lot of flavor to your dishes. If you cannot find it, substitute ½ tsp (2 mL) alcohol-free organic vanilla extract.

- Blender
- Baking sheet, lined with parchment paper

1 cup	pitted Medjool dates, soaked (see Tips, left)	250 mL
½ cup	date-soaking water	125 mL
4 cups	raw buckwheat groats, soaked (see Tips, left)	1 L
¼ cup	raw agave nectar	60 mL
2 tsp	ground cinnamon	10 mL
¼ tsp	freshly grated nutmeg	1 mL
¼ tsp	organic vanilla powder (see Tips, left)	1 mL
2 cups	finely chopped apples	500 mL
½ cup	raw pumpkin seeds	125 mL
¼ cup	raw shelled hemp seeds	60 mL

1. In blender, combine dates and reserved soaking liquid, agave nectar, cinnamon, nutmeg and vanilla. Blend at high speed until smooth.
2. Preheat oven to 275°F (140°C). In a large bowl, combine soaked buckwheat, date mixture, apples, pumpkin seeds and hemp seeds. Toss together until well mixed.
3. Spread evenly on prepared baking sheet and bake in preheated oven for 30 to 35 minutes, or until mixture is completely dry, stirring halfway through the cooking time.
4. Remove from oven and set aside to cool completely. Granola will keep in an airtight container at room temperature for up to 1 month.

Puffed Quinoa Peanut Butter Bites

Creamy peanut butter and air-puffed quinoa make these delectable bites a guilt-free treat you can reach for any time of the day.

MAKES 12 TO 15 BITES

Tips

Substitute an equal amount of almond, cashew or hazelnut butter for the peanut butter.

To melt the coconut oil, gently warm it in a small skillet over low heat.

For a nice crunch, add 3 tbsp (45 mL) raw buckwheat groats along with the quinoa.

- Blender
- Baking sheet, lined with parchment paper

1 cup	smooth peanut butter (see Tips, left)	250 mL
¼ cup	melted coconut oil (see Tips, left)	60 mL
3 tbsp	raw agave nectar	45 mL
¼ tsp	organic vanilla powder (see Tips, page 155)	1 mL
3 cups	puffed quinoa cereal	750 mL

1. In blender, combine peanut butter, coconut oil, agave nectar and vanilla. Blend at high speed until smooth and creamy.
2. In a large bowl, combine puffed quinoa and peanut butter mixture and stir well. Using your hands, divide mixture into 12 to 15 equal portions and shape into rough balls.
3. Transfer to prepared baking sheet. Refrigerate until firm, about 3 hours. Serve immediately or transfer to an airtight container and refrigerate for up to 1 month.

Power Balls

These protein-dense treats are a guilt-free way to satisfy your cravings for something sweet.

MAKES 12 TO 15 BALLS

Tips

The dates for this recipe should be soft and moist. If they are not, soak them in 1 cup (250 mL) warm water for 15 minutes before using.

Organic vanilla powder can be found in most well-stocked supermarkets and natural food stores. It is made from dried and ground whole vanilla beans and will add a lot of flavor to your dishes. If you cannot find it, substitute ½ tsp (2 mL) alcohol-free organic vanilla extract.

Food processor

1 cup	chopped pitted Medjool dates (see Tips, left)	250 mL
½ cup	raw almonds	125 mL
½ cup	raw cashews	125 mL
¼ cup	raw shelled hemp seeds	60 mL
2 tbsp	chia seeds	30 mL
¼ tsp	organic vanilla powder (see Tips, left)	1 mL
Pinch	fine sea salt	Pinch

1. In food processor fitted with the metal blade, process dates until smooth, stopping the motor to scrape down sides of work bowl as necessary. Add almonds, cashews, hemp seeds, chia seeds, vanilla and salt; process until well combined.

2. Transfer mixture to a bowl. Using your hands, divide into 12 to 15 equal portions and roll into balls. Serve immediately or transfer to an airtight container and refrigerate for up to 1 month.

Oat Clusters

These treats make a delicious afternoon snack together with a cup of tea and some fresh fruit.

Tips

Substitute an equal amount of peanut butter or cashew butter for the almond butter.

If you don't have a small ice-cream scoop, use 2 serving spoons.

- Small (2 ounces/60 mL) ice-cream scoop
- Baking sheet, lined with parchment paper

½ cup	almond butter (see Tips, left)	125 mL
½ cup	Almond Milk (page 61)	125 mL
¼ cup	organic coconut sugar	60 mL
2 cups	quick-cooking rolled oats	500 mL
1 tsp	alcohol-free organic vanilla extract	5 mL
½ tsp	ground cinnamon	2 mL
Pinch	fine sea salt	Pinch

1. In a small saucepan over medium heat, combine almond butter, almond milk and coconut sugar. Bring to a boil, then remove from heat and stir in oats, vanilla, cinnamon and salt, until well combined. Cover and set aside for about 10 minutes so the oats can absorb remaining liquid and swell.

2. Using ice-cream scoop or two spoons, drop 12 to 15 equal portions onto prepared baking sheet. Refrigerate until set, about 2 hours. Serve immediately or transfer to an airtight container and refrigerate for up to 1 month.

Variation

Chocolate Oat Clusters: In Step 1, add ½ cup (125 mL) non-dairy chocolate chips to the saucepan and reduce the amount of coconut sugar to 1 tbsp (15 mL).

Berry Oat Bars

Serve these moist, tasty bars in the morning with coffee or tea, as a midday snack or as a healthy dessert.

Tips

Steel-cut oats can stick to the bottom of the pot. Use a wooden spoon to stir frequently when cooking.

Organic vanilla powder can be found in most well-stocked supermarkets and natural food stores. It is made from dried and ground whole vanilla beans and will add a lot of flavor to your dishes. If you cannot find it, substitute 1 tsp (5 mL) alcohol-free organic vanilla extract.

Use high-quality organic cinnamon. You will get the freshest flavor by grinding whole cinnamon sticks in a spice grinder.

• **8-inch (20 cm) square glass baking dish, lined with parchment paper**

1 cup	steel-cut oats (see Tips, left)	250 mL
3 cups	Almond Milk (page 61)	750 mL
1 cup	blueberries	250 mL
½ cup	chopped hulled strawberries	125 mL
¼ cup	organic coconut sugar	60 mL
½ tsp	organic vanilla powder (see Tips, left)	2 mL
½ tsp	ground cinnamon (see Tips, left)	2 mL
Pinch	fine sea salt	Pinch
¼ cup	quick-cooking rolled oats	60 mL

1. In a small saucepan, combine steel-cut oats, almond milk, blueberries, strawberries, coconut sugar, vanilla, cinnamon and salt; bring to a boil. Reduce heat and simmer, stirring frequently, until oats are tender and mixture is creamy, about 40 minutes.

2. Remove from heat and stir in quick-cooking oats. Spread mixture evenly in baking dish. Refrigerate until firm, about 3 hours.

3. Preheat oven to 400° (200°C). Using a sharp knife, cut oat mixture into 8 equal bars. Transfer to prepared baking sheet and bake in preheated oven for 20 to 25 minutes or until golden brown.

4. Remove from oven and set aside to cool. Using parchment liner, lift from pan. With a sharp knife, cut into bars. Serve immediately or transfer to an airtight container and refrigerate for up to 2 weeks.

Date-Me Bars

These bars are fiber-rich and full of healthy fats. Keep them on hand for when that mid-afternoon crash threatens.

MAKES ABOUT 8 LARGE BARS

Tips

There are numerous varieties of dates, but Medjools are my favorite. Although they are generally more expensive, they are larger, softer and, in my opinion, more flavorful.

Organic vanilla powder can be found in most well-stocked supermarkets and natural food stores. It is made from dried and ground whole vanilla beans and will add a lot of flavor to your dishes. If you cannot find it, substitute 1 tsp (5 mL) alcohol-free organic vanilla extract.

- **Food processor**
- **8-inch (20 cm) square glass baking dish, lined with parchment**

2 cups	raw almonds	500 mL
½ cup	raw shelled hemp seeds	125 mL
¼ cup	raw walnuts	60 mL
Pinch	fine sea salt	Pinch
8 cups	chopped pitted Medjool dates (about 3 lbs/750 g) (see Tips, left)	2 L
½ tsp	organic vanilla powder (see Tips, left)	2 mL

1. In food processor fitted with the metal blade, combine almonds, hemp seeds, walnuts and salt; process until no large pieces of nuts remain. Add dates and vanilla; process until dates are smooth, stopping the motor to scrape down sides of work bowl as necessary.

2. Spread mixture evenly in prepared baking dish. Refrigerate until set, about 3 hours.

3. Using parchment liner, lift from pan. With a sharp knife, cut into 8 equal portions. Serve immediately or transfer to an airtight container and refrigerate for up to 1 month.

Vanilla Chai Power Bars

Energy bars are a great item to keep on hand for snacking on the go, or enjoy them as a quick breakfast with a cold glass of Almond Milk (page 61).

MAKES ABOUT 8 LARGE BARS

Tips

Puffed quinoa and millet are available in most well-stocked supermarkets and natural food stores.

This recipe can easily be doubled, tripled or quadrupled. Just adjust the size of the baking dish or use multiple dishes. You can freeze extra bars for up to 2 months.

> **8-inch (20 cm) square glass baking dish, lined with parchment**

3 cups	puffed quinoa cereal (see Tips, left)	750 mL
1 cup	puffed millet	250 mL
2 tbsp	chia seeds	30 mL
1 tbsp	raw shelled hemp seeds	15 mL
1 cup	brown rice syrup	250 mL
1/4 cup	raw agave nectar	60 mL
1/2 tsp	ground cinnamon	2 mL
1/4 tsp	ground cardamom	1 mL
1/4 tsp	ground ginger	1 mL
1/4 tsp	ground allspice	1 mL
1/4 tsp	organic vanilla powder (see Tips, page 158)	1 mL
1/8 tsp	ground cloves	0.5 mL

1. In a large bowl, toss together quinoa, millet, chia seeds and hemp seeds. Add brown rice syrup and agave nectar and stir well. Stir in cinnamon, cardamom, ginger, allspice, vanilla and cloves.

2. Spread mixture evenly in prepared baking dish. Cover and refrigerate until set, about 3 hours.

3. Using parchment liner, lift from pan. With a sharp knife, cut into 8 equal bars. Serve immediately or transfer to an airtight container and refrigerate for up to 1 month.

Variations

Chocolate Mint Power Bars: Omit the cinnamon, cardamom, ginger, allspice and cloves. Add 1/2 cup (125 mL) non-dairy chocolate chips and 1 tsp (5 mL) organic peppermint extract.

Lemon Blueberry Power Bars: Omit the cinnamon, cardamom, ginger, allspice and cloves. Add 2 tsp (10 mL) freshly grated lemon zest, 1 tbsp (15 mL) freshly squeezed lemon juice and 3 tbsp (45 mL) unsweetened dried blueberries.

Chewy Tropical Coconut Bars

Fresh, juicy mango and tropical coconut are a match made in heaven in these sweet snack bars. You can also enjoy them as a quick dessert. I like to eat them with a tall glass of White Chocolate Milk (page 68).

(page 68)

MAKES ABOUT 8 LARGE BARS

Tips

Coconut butter is a blend of coconut oil and coconut meat. Look for it in natural food stores, next to the coconut oil.

Use unsulfured, unsweetened medium shredded coconut. Not only is this type of coconut nutritionally beneficial, the medium shred size will help hold the bars together.

- Food processor
- Baking sheet, lined with parchment paper

½ cup	raw agave nectar	125 mL
½ cup	ground raw flax seeds	125 mL
1 cup	coconut butter (see Tips, left)	250 mL
2 cups	chopped mango	500 mL
2 cups	unsweetened dried shredded coconut (see Tips, left)	500 mL

1. In food processor fitted with the metal blade, process agave nectar, ground flax seeds and coconut butter until smooth, stopping the motor to scrape down sides of work bowl as necessary.

2. Add mango and coconut and process just until mixture comes together.

3. Spread mixture evenly, about 2 inches (5 cm) thick, on prepared baking sheet. Cover and freeze until set in the middle, about 10 minutes.

4. Using a sharp knife, cut into 8 equal bars. Serve immediately or transfer to an airtight container and refrigerate for up to 1 month.

Key Lime Pie Bars

If you like Key lime pie, you'll love these chewy bars. They're a delicious blend of tropical lime and coconut that you can enjoy as a quick snack or treat any time of the day.

MAKES ABOUT 8 LARGE BARS

Tips

Coconut butter is a blend of coconut oil and coconut meat. You can usually find it in natural food stores, next to the coconut oil.

Organic vanilla powder can be found in most well-stocked supermarkets and natural food stores. It is made from dried and ground whole vanilla beans and will add a lot of flavor to your dishes. If you cannot find it, substitute ½ tsp (2 mL) alcohol-free organic vanilla extract.

Use unsulfured, unsweetened medium shredded coconut. Not only is this type of coconut nutritionally beneficial, the medium shred size will help hold the bars together.

- Food processor
- 8-inch (20 cm) square glass baking dish, lined with parchment paper

½ cup	coconut butter (see Tips, left)	125 mL
½ cup	freshly squeezed Key lime juice	125 mL
¼ cup	raw agave nectar	60 mL
3 tbsp	melted coconut oil	45 mL
¼ tsp	organic vanilla powder (see Tips, left)	1 mL
4 cups	unsweetened dried shredded coconut (see Tips, left)	1 L

1. In food processor fitted with the metal blade, combine coconut butter, lime juice, agave nectar, coconut oil and vanilla; process until smooth. Add shredded coconut and pulse to combine.

2. Spread mixture evenly in prepared baking dish. Cover and refrigerate until firm, about 3 hours.

3. Using parchment liner, lift from pan. With a sharp knife, cut into 8 equal bars. Serve immediately or transfer to an airtight container and refrigerate for up to 2 weeks.

Chocolate Chip Treat Bars

These bars are packed full of goodness and studded with non-dairy chocolate chips.

MAKES ABOUT 8 LARGE BARS

Tips

Puffed quinoa is available in most well-stocked supermarkets and natural food stores.

This recipe can easily be doubled, tripled or quadrupled. Just adjust the size of the baking dish accordingly. You can freeze extra bars for up to 2 months.

8-inch (20 cm) square glass baking dish, lined with parchment paper

8 cups	puffed quinoa cereal (see Tips, left)	2 L
1 cup	brown rice syrup	250 mL
1 cup	non-dairy chocolate chips	250 mL
6 tbsp	raw shelled hemp seeds	90 mL
2 tbsp	chia seeds	30 mL
¼ tsp	organic vanilla powder or ½ tsp (2 mL) alcohol-free organic vanilla extract	1 mL

1. In a large bowl, combine puffed quinoa, brown rice syrup, chocolate chips, hemp seeds, chia seeds and vanilla; stir well.

2. Spread mixture evenly in prepared baking dish. Cover and refrigerate until set, about 3 hours.

3. Using parchment liner, lift from pan. With a sharp knife, cut into 8 equal bars. Serve immediately or transfer to an airtight container and refrigerate for up to 1 month.

Peanut Butter Hemp Power Bars

These protein-rich bars are a great post-workout snack. When served with a nice cold smoothie such as Avocado Spinach Smoothie (page 51), they can make a complete meal.

MAKES ABOUT 8 LARGE BARS

Tips

This may seem like a large amount of water for cooking the whole grains, but the added liquid facilitates binding.

Not all oats are gluten-free: some brands are processed in facilities where gluten is present. Be sure to check the label if you are following a completely gluten-free diet. Ask your purveyor if you have concerns.

Organic vanilla powder can be found in most well-stocked supermarkets and natural food stores. It is made from dried and ground whole vanilla beans and will add a lot of flavor to your dishes. If you cannot find it, substitute ½ tsp (2 mL) alcohol-free organic vanilla extract.

To melt the coconut oil for this recipe, warm it gently in a skillet over low heat.

- Food processor
- 8-inch (20 cm) square glass baking dish, lined with parchment paper

8 cups	water	2 L
½ cup	millet, rinsed and drained	125 mL
½ cup	steel-cut oats (see Tips, left)	125 mL
½ tsp	fine sea salt, divided	2 mL
2 cups	smooth peanut butter	500 mL
½ cup	raw agave nectar	125 mL
½ cup	raw shelled hemp seeds	125 mL
3 tbsp	raw sunflower seeds	45 mL
¼ tsp	organic vanilla powder (see Tips, left)	1 mL
½ cup	melted coconut oil (see Tips, left)	125 mL

1. In a saucepan, combine water, millet, oats and ¼ tsp (1 mL) salt; bring to a boil. Reduce heat and simmer until oats and millet are very tender and most of the liquid has been absorbed, about 25 minutes. Cover and set aside for about 10 minutes so grains can absorb any remaining liquid and swell.

2. In a large bowl, combine peanut butter, agave nectar, hemp seeds, sunflower seeds, remaining ¼ tsp (1 mL) salt and vanilla. Add coconut oil and stir well. Set aside.

3. In food processor fitted with the metal blade, combine cooked grains mixture and 1 cup (250 mL) of the peanut butter mixture. Process until smooth, stopping the motor to scrape down sides of work bowl as necessary. Add remaining peanut butter mixture and pulse to combine.

4. Spread mixture evenly in prepared baking dish. Cover and refrigerate until set, about 3 hours.

5. Using parchment paper, lift from pan. With a sharp knife, cut into 8 equal bars. Serve immediately or transfer to an airtight container and refrigerate for up to 1 month.

Fluffernutter Bars

These delectable bars are inspired by the famous sandwich made with peanut butter and marshmallow creme. Take these over the top by serving with a big dollop of Whipped Coconut Cream (page 565) on the side for dipping.

MAKES ABOUT 8 LARGE BARS

Tips

To melt the cacao butter for this recipe, warm it gently in a skillet over low heat.

Organic vanilla powder can be found in most well-stocked supermarkets and natural food stores. It is made from dried and ground whole vanilla beans and will add a lot of flavor to your dishes. If you cannot find it, substitute ½ tsp (2 mL) alcohol-free organic vanilla extract.

I use both a blender and a food processor when making this recipe, as the cashews need to be finely ground in Step 1.

Substitute an equal amount of almond, peanut, walnut or macadamia butter for the cashew butter.

- **Blender**
- **Food processor**
- **8-inch (20 cm) square glass baking dish, lined with parchment paper**

½ cup	melted cacao butter (see Tips, left)	125 mL
½ cup	raw cashews	125 mL
¼ cup	raw agave nectar	60 mL
¼ tsp	organic vanilla powder (see Tips, left)	1 mL
2 cups	whole raw almonds	500 mL
1 cup	cashew butter (see Tips, left)	250 mL
½ cup	brown rice syrup	125 mL
½ cup	non-dairy chocolate chips	125 mL

1. In blender, combine cacao butter, cashews, agave nectar and vanilla. Blend at high speed until smooth, stopping the motor to scrape down sides of blender jar as necessary.

2. In food processor fitted with the metal blade, process almonds until flour-like in consistency (be careful not to overprocess or they will turn into a paste). Add cashew butter and brown rice syrup and pulse 8 to 10 times, just until mixture comes together. Add cacao butter mixture and process just until combined. Transfer to a large bowl. Fold in chocolate chips.

3. Spread mixture evenly in prepared baking dish. Cover and refrigerate until set, about 3 hours.

4. Using parchment paper, lift from pan. With a sharp knife, cut mixture into 8 equal bars. Serve immediately or transfer to an airtight container and refrigerate for up to 1 month.

Crispy Rice Squares

A more wholesome version of classic Rice Krispie squares, these treats are sure to be devoured quickly. Make them ahead of time and freeze them for special occasions and family gatherings.

MAKES ABOUT 8 LARGE SQUARES

Tips

To melt the coconut oil, warm it gently in a small skillet over low heat.

You can substitute ¾ cup (175 mL) pure maple syrup for the agave nectar and increase the amount of coconut butter to ¼ cup (60 mL).

- Blender
- 9-inch (23 cm) square glass baking dish, lined with parchment paper

1 cup	melted coconut oil (see Tips, left)	250 mL
¾ cup	raw agave nectar	175 mL
3 tbsp	coconut butter	45 mL
½ tsp	organic vanilla powder or 1 tsp (5 mL) alcohol-free organic vanilla extract	2 mL
8 cups	puffed brown rice	2 L

1. In blender, combine coconut oil, agave nectar, coconut butter and vanilla. Blend at high speed until smooth and creamy.
2. In a large bowl, combine puffed rice and coconut mixture and stir well.
3. Spread evenly in prepared baking dish. Cover and refrigerate until set, about 3 hours.
4. Using parchment paper, lift from pan. With a sharp knife, cut into 8 equal squares. Serve immediately or transfer to an airtight container and refrigerate for up to 1 month (freeze for up to 2 months).

Variation

Chocolate Crispy Rice Squares: Add ¼ cup (60 mL) raw cacao powder to the blender in Step 1. Add ½ cup (125 mL) non-dairy chocolate chips in Step 2.

Cheesy Quesadillas

Crisp, warm and gooey, these quesadillas are perfect served with some fresh salsa, guacamole, Vegan Sour Cream (page 555) and thinly sliced green onions.

**MAKES
2 QUESADILLAS
(4 SERVINGS)**

Tips

If you prefer, use smaller (6 inches/15 cm) corn tortillas, which are more readily available. Adjust the quantity of filling accordingly.

Most commercially made tortillas dry out very quickly. They need to be kept in an airtight container until ready to use.

If you prefer, substitute your favorite store-bought vegan mozzarella for the homemade version.

You can also bake this wrap. Preheat oven to 400°F (200°C) and cook on a parchment-lined baking sheet for 8 to 10 minutes or until golden brown and crisp.

● **Blender**

1 cup	water	250 mL
1 cup	nutritional yeast	250 mL
½ cup	raw cashews	125 mL
¼ cup	tahini	60 mL
3 tbsp	freshly squeezed lemon juice	45 mL
1 tbsp	Dijon mustard	15 mL
1 tsp	fine sea salt	5 mL
2	large (10 inches/25 cm) gluten-free organic corn tortillas (see Tips, left)	2
1 cup	Vegan Shredded Mozzarella (page 537; see Tips, left)	250 mL
3 tbsp	grapeseed oil	45 mL

1. In blender, combine water, nutritional yeast, cashews, tahini, lemon juice, mustard and salt. Blend at high speed until smooth and creamy, stopping the motor to scrape down sides of blender jar as necessary.

2. Lay 1 tortilla flat on a clean work surface. Spread half of the mixture over one half of the tortilla, leaving a ½-inch (1 cm) border around the edge. Top with ½ cup (125 mL) vegan mozzarella. Fold over tortilla, matching edges. Repeat with remaining tortilla.

3. In a large skillet over medium heat, heat oil. Cook each quesadilla for 3 to 4 minutes on each side, until golden brown (see Tips, left). Cut each quesadilla in half. Serve immediately.

Thai Tofu Lettuce Snacks

In this recipe, romaine lettuce leaves are used instead of bread to make a sandwich of perfectly seasoned tofu. It's a quick and healthy lunch or snack for those days when you want something fresh and tasty but have limited time.

MAKES 4

Tips

The stems on the leaves closest to the bottom of a sprig of fresh cilantro are generally tough and need to be removed. The stems on leaves closer to the top are softer.

For shredding small amounts of vegetables, use the large holes of a box grater. For larger amounts, the shredding attachment on your food processor is probably more efficient.

1 cup	shredded firm tofu	250 mL
½ cup	shredded carrot	125 mL
½ cup	chopped fresh cilantro, leaves and stems (see Tips, left)	125 mL
3 tbsp	wheat-free tamari	45 mL
2 tbsp	freshly squeezed lime juice	30 mL
1 tbsp	melted coconut oil	15 mL
1 tsp	toasted sesame oil	5 mL
1 tsp	organic coconut sugar	5 mL
Pinch	cayenne pepper	Pinch
8	large romaine lettuce leaves	8
¼ cup	chopped raw almonds	60 mL

1. In a bowl, combine tofu, carrot, cilantro, tamari, lime juice, coconut oil, sesame oil, coconut sugar and cayenne. Stir well.

2. Lay 4 lettuce leaves flat on a clean work surface. Top each leaf with tofu mixture, dividing equally. Sprinkle each with 1 tbsp (15 mL) chopped almonds. Cover with remaining lettuce leaves and serve immediately.

Variation

Substitute cabbage leaves for the romaine lettuce and roll into tight cylinders.

Herbed Rösti Bake

Enjoy this crispy potato dish as a side with dishes such as Ratatouille (page 333), Black Bean and Sweet Potato Chili (page 346) or Tempeh and Roasted Pepper Sloppy Joes (page 350).

MAKES ABOUT 4 SERVINGS

Tips

Floury potatoes such as russets are best for making rösti.

To prevent fresh herbs from turning brown after chopping, use a sharp knife to prevent bruising.

- Preheat oven to 400°F (200°C)
- 8-inch (20 cm) square glass baking dish, greased

2 tbsp	grapeseed oil	30 mL
½ cup	chopped onion	125 mL
1 tsp	fine sea salt	5 mL
3 to 4	cloves garlic, minced	3 to 4
8 cups	shredded potatoes (see Tips, left)	2 L
¼ cup	chopped fresh chives	60 mL
¼ cup	nutritional yeast	60 mL
2 tbsp	chopped fresh thyme leaves	30 mL
1 tsp	chopped fresh rosemary	5 mL

1. In a large skillet over medium heat, heat oil. Add onion and salt and cook, stirring frequently, until onions are translucent, about 6 minutes. Add garlic and cook until fragrant, about 2 minutes.

2. Add potatoes and cook, stirring constantly, until tender but not mushy, 6 to 8 minutes. Stir in chives, nutritional yeast, thyme and rosemary. Spread evenly in prepared baking dish.

3. Bake in preheated oven for 45 minutes or until crisp around the edges and potatoes are cooked through. Serve immediately or transfer to an airtight container and refrigerate for up to 1 week. To reheat: Place leftovers on a parchment-lined baking sheet. Bake in a preheated oven (350°F/180°C) for about 12 minutes, until heated through.

Cauliflower Gratin

Serve this creamy dish at your next potluck or to dinner guests as part of a larger meal. It is particularly good as an accompaniment to Poached Tofu with Vegetables in Cheesy Hemp Sauce (page 402), Mushroom and Spinach Lasagna (page 274) or Simple Simmered Moroccan Chickpeas (page 201).

MAKES 4 TO 6 SERVINGS

Tip

For extra crunch, toss the final 2 tbsp (30 mL) nutritional yeast with ½ cup (125 mL) of your favorite breadcrumb mixture. Sprinkle on just before baking.

- **Preheat oven to 400°F (200°C)**
- **Food processor**
- **8-inch (20 cm) square glass baking dish, greased**

8 cups	finely chopped cauliflower (stems removed)	2 L
½ cup	nutritional yeast, divided	125 mL
¼ cup	raw cashews	60 mL
1 tbsp	grapeseed oil	15 mL
½ cup	chopped onion	125 mL
½ tsp	fine sea salt	2 mL
3 to 4	cloves garlic, minced	3 to 4
2 tsp	chopped fresh thyme leaves	10 mL

1. Place cauliflower in a large pot of water and bring to a boil. Reduce heat and simmer until tender, about 5 minutes. Drain. Transfer half to food processor fitted with the metal blade; reserve remainder.

2. Add 6 tbsp (90 mL) nutritional yeast and cashews to food processor. Process until mixture is broken down into fine pieces but not smooth. Set aside.

3. In a large skillet over medium heat, heat oil. Add onion, reserved cooked cauliflower and salt and cook, stirring frequently, until onion is translucent and cauliflower is lightly golden, 12 to 15 minutes. Stir in garlic and cook until fragrant, about 2 minutes. Stir in thyme and remove from heat.

4. Transfer to a large bowl and add reserved processed cauliflower; stir to combine. Spread evenly in prepared baking dish and sprinkle with remaining 2 tbsp (30 mL) nutritional yeast (see Tips, left).

5. Bake in preheated oven for 40 minutes or until golden brown and heated through. Serve immediately or let cool, transfer to an airtight container and refrigerate for up to 1 week. To reheat: Place leftovers on a parchment-lined baking sheet. Bake in a preheated oven (350°F/180°C) for about 12 minutes until heated through.

Exotic Spiced Layered Sweet Potatoes

These baked sweet potatoes work wonderfully as an accompaniment to a spicy dish such as African-Spiced Tempeh Chili (page 348), Simple Simmered Moroccan Chickpeas (page 201) or Spicy Southern-Style Slow-Cooked Collard Greens (page 173).

MAKES 4 TO 6 SERVINGS

Tips

Cutting the sweet potatoes into uniform slices will help this dish cook more evenly. Using a mandoline will make the task easier.

Use high-quality organic spices. You will get the freshest flavor by grinding whole cinnamon sticks and coriander seeds in a clean spice grinder.

- **Preheat oven to 400°F (200°C)**
- **11- by 7-inch (28 by 18 cm) glass baking dish, greased**

2 tbsp	grapeseed oil	30 mL
1/2 tsp	fine sea salt	2 mL
1/2 tsp	ground cumin	2 mL
1/2 tsp	fennel seeds	2 mL
1/4 tsp	chili powder	1 mL
1/4 tsp	ground cinnamon	1 mL
Pinch	ground coriander	Pinch
8 cups	thinly sliced sweet potatoes (about 4; see Tips, left)	2 L
1/2 cup	thinly sliced onion	125 mL

1. In a large bowl, whisk together oil, salt, cumin, fennel seeds, chili powder, cinnamon and coriander. Add sweet potatoes and onion and toss until well coated.

2. Spread evenly in baking dish and cover tightly with aluminum foil.

3. Bake in preheated oven for 45 minutes, until potatoes are lightly golden on top and soft in the middle. Uncover and bake for 10 minutes more, or until lightly browned on top. Serve immediately or transfer to an airtight container and refrigerate for up to 10 days.

Easy Baked Ratatouille

Serve this Italian-inspired dish with Pasta Aglio e Olio (page 249) for an easy meal. It's also a good dish to make ahead and have on hand for those busy days when you are short on time, or for when guests drop by and you want to put together a quick meal.

MAKES 4 TO 6 SERVINGS

Tips

The quantity of garlic depends on the size of the cloves. If large, use the smaller number. If small, more may be required.

Substitute 4 cups (1 L) chopped fresh tomatoes for the canned tomatoes and increase the cooking time to 1 hour.

• Preheat oven to 400°F (200°C)

3 tbsp	grapeseed oil	45 mL
1 cup	chopped red onions (1 inch/2.5 cm pieces)	250 mL
1 tsp	fine sea salt	5 mL
2 cups	chopped red pepper (1 inch/2.5 cm pieces)	500 mL
2 cups	chopped zucchini (1 inch/2.5 cm pieces)	500 mL
2 cups	chopped eggplant (1 inch/2.5 cm pieces)	500 mL
10 to 12	cloves garlic, minced	10 to 12
1	can (5½ oz/156 mL) tomato paste	1
1	can (28 oz/796 mL) diced tomatoes, with juice (see Tip, left)	1
2 tbsp	chopped fresh thyme leaves	30 mL
Pinch	cayenne pepper	Pinch

1. In a large ovenproof pot over medium heat, heat oil. Add onions and salt and cook, stirring frequently, until onions are lightly golden, 10 to 12 minutes. Add red pepper, zucchini and eggplant and cook just until vegetables begin to soften, 8 to 10 minutes.

2. Add garlic and tomato paste. Cook, stirring constantly, until garlic is fragrant, 3 to 4 minutes. Add tomatoes, thyme and cayenne and stir well.

3. Cover and bake in preheated oven for 45 minutes. Serve immediately or transfer to an airtight container and refrigerate for up to 1 week. To reheat, bring to a simmer over medium heat.

Variation

Easy Baked Lentil Ratatouille: Add 2 cups (500 mL) split red lentils and 4 cups (1 L) water along with the vegetables.

Baked Loaded Nachos

Who can resist loaded nachos? Serve these for the big game, at your next casual dinner party or as an appetizer with a Mexican-themed meal.

MAKES 4 SERVINGS

Tips

I always use organic products, but buying organic is particularly important with products made from corn (such as tortillas) in order to avoid GMOs.

If you do not have Vegan Shredded Mozzarella on hand, substitute an equal amount of your favorite vegan cheese, or simply omit.

I like to use kalamata olives for this recipe, but feel free to substitute an equal amount of your favorite olives.

- Preheat oven to 400°F (200°C)
- 2 baking sheets, lined with parchment paper
- Ovenproof serving platter

10 to 12	corn tortillas (6 inches/15 cm), cut into triangles	10 to 12
3 tbsp	grapeseed oil	45 mL
½ tsp	fine sea salt	2 mL
1 cup	Vegan Shredded Mozzarella (page 537; see Tips, left)	250 mL
1 cup	thinly sliced romaine lettuce leaves	250 mL
1 cup	chopped tomato	250 mL
¼ cup	chopped green onion (green part only)	60 mL
¼ cup	thinly sliced olives (see Tips, left)	60 mL
¼ cup	Vegan Sour Cream (page 555)	60 mL
¼ cup	Classic Garlicky Tomato Sauce (page 110)	60 mL

1. In a large bowl, toss tortilla pieces with oil and salt. Spread in a single layer on prepared baking sheets. Bake in preheated oven on upper and lower racks, switching halfway through baking, until crisp, about 15 minutes. Remove from oven and set aside to cool (do not turn off oven).

2. Spread one-quarter of the baked tortillas on serving platter. Top with ¼ cup (60 mL) vegan mozzarella, ¼ cup (60 mL) lettuce and ¼ cup (60 mL) tomato. Repeat layers until no ingredients remain.

3. Sprinkle with green onion and olives and dollop with sour cream and tomato sauce. Bake in preheated oven for 10 minutes, until mozzarella is soft and gooey. Serve immediately.

Spicy Southern-Style Slow-Cooked Collard Greens

For an easy meal, serve this spicy side dish with Basic Rice (page 212) and grilled tofu or tempeh.

(page 212)

MAKES 4 SIDE SERVINGS

Tips

Take care that you don't burn the garlic in Step 1. You want the slices to become lightly golden to provide good depth of flavor. Keep an eye out and, as soon as they reach that stage, add the onion.

Collard leaves have a long, thick vein that runs through the center. When working with them, keep the soft vein at the top of the leaf intact. However, as you move toward the bottom (stem) end of the leaf, the vein becomes larger and tougher and needs to be removed. Lay the leaf flat on a cutting board, use a paring knife to remove the thick part of the vein, and discard.

Apple cider vinegar has long been used in folk medicine. It is a great digestive aid, among its other benefits. When purchasing apple cider vinegar, make sure it is raw and unpasteurized.

- Medium (about 4 quart) slow cooker

¼ cup	grapeseed oil	60 mL
½ cup	sliced jalapeño peppers (½ inch/1 cm)	125 mL
½ cup	sliced garlic (½ inch/1 cm)	125 mL
1 cup	finely chopped onions	250 mL
2 tbsp	fennel seeds	30 mL
½ tsp	fine sea salt	2 mL
16 cups	collard greens, stems removed, cut into 1-inch (2.5 cm) pieces (see Tips, left)	4 L
½ cup	water	125 mL
¼ cup	raw (unpasteurized) apple cider vinegar (see Tips, left)	60 mL

1. In a large skillet over medium-high heat, heat oil. Add jalapeños and garlic and cook, stirring frequently, until peppers are light golden brown and softened, 6 to 8 minutes. Add onions, fennel seeds and salt and cook, stirring occasionally, until onions are light golden brown, 4 to 6 minutes. Transfer to slow cooker stoneware.

2. Add collard greens, water and vinegar. Cover and cook on Low for 6 hours or High for 3 hours. Serve immediately or let cool, transfer to an airtight container and refrigerate for up to 5 days. To reheat, combine cooked greens and ¼ cup (60 mL) of water in a saucepan. Bring to a simmer and stir until greens are heated through, about 5 minutes.

Spiced Whole Beets

Tender whole beets, slow-cooked in aromatic spices, make a perfect accompaniment to any meal.

MAKES 4 BEETS

Tips

Using a small paring knife, trim off the top ¼ inch (5 mm) and the bottom ⅛ inch (3 mm) of the beets so they will lie flat in the stoneware.

Raw (unpasteurized) apple cider vinegar is said to aid in detoxification.

Do not lift the lid of your slow cooker while it is cooking. Each time you do, heat will escape and you will need to add 20 to 30 minutes of cooking time to your recipe.

● **Medium (about 4 quart) slow cooker**

4	medium beets, trimmed (see Tips, left)	4
¼ cup	water	60 mL
2 tbsp	freshly squeezed lemon juice	30 mL
1 tbsp	raw (unpasteurized) apple cider vinegar	15 mL
½ tsp	fine sea salt	2 mL
1 tsp	fennel seeds	5 mL
1	3-inch (7.5 cm) cinnamon stick	1
2	whole star anise	2
1	clove garlic	1

1. In slow cooker stoneware, combine beets, water, lemon juice, vinegar, salt, fennel seeds, cinnamon, star anise and garlic. Cover and cook on Low for 8 hours.

2. Using a slotted spoon, transfer beets to a bowl (discard cooking liquid, cinnamon stick, star anise and garlic). Using a sharp paring knife, peel skins. Serve immediately or transfer to an airtight container and refrigerate for up to 1 week.

Braised Fennel and Onions with Lentils

In this recipe, anise-flavored fennel is first caramelized and then slowly simmered with whole onions and protein-dense lentils. It's a wonderful side dish or, served with a fresh green salad, a satisfying main dish.

MAKES 4 SERVINGS

Tips

Cut the fennel in half from top to bottom so you have two pieces with large, flat surfaces.

The onions are cooked whole so they remain soft and juicy throughout the process.

The quantity of garlic depends on the size of the cloves. If large, use the smaller number. If small, more may be required.

Substitute for the vegetable stock in this recipe with an equal amount of water and add 1 tbsp (15 mL) wheat-free tamari.

● Medium (about 4 quart) slow cooker

¼ cup	grapeseed oil, divided	60 mL
1	medium bulb fennel, halved (see Tips, left)	1
2	medium onions	2
1 tsp	fine sea salt	5 mL
1 cup	dried red lentils, rinsed and drained	250 mL
3 to 4	cloves garlic	3 to 4
1 cup	Vegetable Stock (page 559; see Tips, left)	250 mL
1 tbsp	organic coconut sugar	15 mL
1 tsp	chopped fresh thyme leaves	5 mL

1. In a large skillet over medium-high heat, heat 2 tbsp (30 mL) oil. Add fennel and cook until golden brown on one side, 5 to 6 minutes. Turn over and cook until other side is golden brown, 3 to 4 minutes. Transfer to slow cooker stoneware.

2. In same skillet, heat remaining 2 tbsp (30 mL) oil . Add onions and cook, stirring, until golden brown, 4 to 5 minutes. Transfer to slow cooker stoneware.

3. Add salt, lentils, garlic, vegetable stock and coconut sugar to stoneware. Cover and cook on Low for 8 hours or High for 4 hours. Stir in thyme and cook, covered, for 20 minutes more.

4. To serve, cut onions into quarters and fennel into halves and divide evenly among 4 serving plates. Spoon lentils overtop. If not serving immediately, let cool and then transfer to an airtight container and refrigerate for up to 1 week.

Beer-Braised Cabbage

Serve this aromatic cabbage dish as a side with Cheesy Broccoli, Red Pepper, Mushroom and Spinach Quiche (page 388), Poached Tofu with Vegetables in Cheesy Hemp Sauce (page 402) or Mushroom Colcannon (page 364).

MAKES 6 TO 8 SIDE SERVINGS

Tips

Either red or green cabbage works well in this recipe.

You can find gluten-free beers in most well-stocked liquor stores.

The quantity of garlic depends on the size of the cloves. If large, use the smaller number. If small, more may be required.

Do not lift the lid of your slow cooker while it is cooking. Each time you do, heat will escape and you will need to add 20 to 30 minutes of cooking time to your recipe.

● **Medium (about 4 quart) slow cooker**

16 cups	thinly sliced cabbage (see Tips, left)	4 L
1 cup	thinly sliced onions	250 mL
½ cup	water	125 mL
¼ cup	organic coconut sugar	60 mL
3 tbsp	raw (unpasteurized) apple cider vinegar	45 mL
2 tsp	fine sea salt	10 mL
1	bottle (330 mL/11 oz) gluten-free beer (see Tips, left)	1
3 to 4	cloves garlic	3 to 4
½ cup	chopped flat-leaf (Italian) parsley leaves	125 mL

1. In slow cooker stoneware, combine cabbage, onions, water, coconut sugar, vinegar, salt, beer and garlic. Cover and cook on High for 8 hours.

2. Stir in parsley. Serve immediately or transfer to an airtight container and refrigerate for up to 10 days.

Roasted Vegetables

To me there is nothing more comforting than simple roasted vegetables. You can enjoy them as an accompaniment to almost any meal. I like to serve these with Basic Rice (page 212) drizzled with a little extra virgin olive oil and sprinkled with some raw shelled hemp seeds, nutritional yeast and a pinch of fine sea salt.

MAKES ABOUT 4 SIDE SERVINGS

Tips

Substitute an equal amount of shiitake, cremini or oyster mushrooms for the button mushrooms.

I like to roast vegetables at a higher temperature for a shorter length of time, so they will develop color. However, if you prefer, you can cook them at 350°F (180°C) for 35 to 40 minutes or until tender.

- **Preheat oven to 425°F (220°C)**
- **Baking sheet, lined with parchment paper**

1 cup	button mushrooms (see Tips, left)	250 mL
1	red bell pepper, cut into 2-inch (5 cm) pieces	1
1	sweet potato, unpeeled, cut into ½-inch (1 cm) wedges	1
1	zucchini, cut into 2-inch (5 cm) pieces	1
¼ cup	grapeseed oil	60 mL
1 tbsp	chopped fresh thyme leaves	15 mL
½ tsp	fine sea salt	2 mL
¼ tsp	freshly ground black pepper	1 mL

1. In a large bowl, toss together mushrooms, red pepper, sweet potato, zucchini, oil, thyme, salt and pepper.

2. Spread evenly on prepared baking sheet. Bake in preheated oven for 20 to 25 minutes or until vegetables have softened and are lightly browned (see Tips, left).

3. Serve immediately or let cool, transfer to an airtight container and refrigerate for up to 1 week. To reheat, place in oven preheated to 350°F (180°C) for about 10 minutes, until heated through.

Variation

Curried Roasted Vegetables: In Step 1, omit thyme. Add 2 tsp (10 mL) curry powder, ½ tsp (2 mL) ground cumin and ¼ tsp (1 mL) ground coriander to the vegetables. This is a great side dish to serve with Coconut Green Curry Angel Hair (page 282) or Curried Soba Noodles (page 281).

Creamy Mashed Potatoes

Nothing says comfort food more than a big bowl of luscious mashed potatoes. This recipe is perfect for family gatherings or holiday meals. Serve with some piping-hot Holiday Gravy (page 558) alongside.

(page 558)

MAKES 4 SIDE SERVINGS

Tips

You will need about 3 lbs/1.5 kg of potatoes.

Generally, there are two different types of potatoes: waxy and starchy. Starchy potatoes are better for mashing — I prefer russets or Yukon Golds.

Before adding the coconut milk to the potatoes, I often flavor it with a little onion and garlic. In a skillet over medium heat, heat 1 tbsp (15 mL) grapeseed oil. Sauté ½ cup (125 mL) finely chopped onion and 6 minced garlic cloves until softened and lightly browned. Stir in coconut milk and bring to a boil. Reduce heat and simmer for about 10 minutes, until thickened.

8 cups	quartered unpeeled potatoes (see Tips left)	2 L
1	can (14 oz/400 mL) full-fat coconut milk (see Tips, left)	1
	Non-dairy milk, optional	
2 tsp	fine sea salt	10 mL

1. In a large pot filled with water, bring potatoes to a boil. Reduce heat and simmer until tender, about 25 minutes. Drain. Transfer to a large bowl.

2. Add coconut milk and salt. Using a potato masher, mash potatoes until no lumps remain. If desired, add non-dairy milk ¼ cup (60 mL) at a time, until desired consistency is reached. Serve immediately or let cool, cover and refrigerate for up to 5 days.

Variations

Herbed Creamy Mashed Potatoes: After adding the coconut milk in Step 2, add 1 cup (250 mL) chopped flat-leaf (Italian) parsley, 2 tbsp (30 mL) chopped fresh thyme leaves and 1 tbsp (15 mL) chopped fresh rosemary.

Roasted Garlic and Chipotle Mash: Before mashing the potatoes, add 2 bulbs roasted garlic and 2 tsp (10 mL) dried chipotle powder.

Herbed Roasted Potatoes

My memories of gathering around a dinner table for the holidays always feature roast potatoes. This basic recipe provides a foolproof method for producing the most delectable results — crispy on the outside and soft in the middle.

Tips

Medium-starch potatoes are best for roasting. I prefer Yukon Gold or white potatoes for this recipe.

Substitute an equal amount of melted coconut oil for the grapeseed oil.

- **Preheat oven to 400°F (200°C)**
- **Baking sheet, lined with parchment paper**

4	medium to large potatoes, cut into ½-inch (1 cm) wedges (see Tips, left)	4
¼ cup	grapeseed oil (see Tips left)	60 mL
2 tbsp	chopped fresh thyme leaves	30 mL
1 tbsp	chopped fresh rosemary	15 mL
1 tsp	fine sea salt	5 mL

1. In a bowl, toss potatoes with oil, thyme, rosemary and salt until evenly coated. Arrange in a single layer on prepared baking sheet.

2. Bake in preheated oven for about 45 minutes or until potatoes are golden brown, turning once to ensure even cooking. Serve immediately or let cool, transfer to an airtight container and refrigerate for up to 1 week.

Variations

Garlic Paprika Roasted Potatoes: Omit the thyme and rosemary. In a bowl, whisk grapeseed oil with 1 tbsp (15 mL) garlic powder, 1 tsp (5 mL) sweet paprika and the salt. Add potatoes and toss to combine. Roast as directed.

Indian-Spiced Potatoes: Omit the thyme and rosemary. In a bowl, whisk grapeseed oil with 1 tbsp (15 mL) curry powder, 1 tsp (5 mL) ground cumin, ½ tsp (2 mL) garlic powder, ¼ tsp (1 mL) turmeric and the salt. Add potatoes and toss to combine. Roast as directed.

Wild Rice Stuffing

This stuffing is a great gluten-free alternative to traditional holiday stuffings. The combination of herbs, apples and nutty wild rice is delicious.

MAKES ABOUT 6 CUPS (1.5 L)

Tips

To help bring out the flavor of the fresh herbs, use a sweeter apple for this recipe, such as Gala, Pink Lady or McIntosh.

The soaked flaxseed mixture in this recipe functions much as an egg would, to help bind the stuffing.

You'll need about 10 sage leaves for this recipe.

Serve this with Holiday Gravy (page 558) for a special treat.

To reheat chilled stuffing, place in oven preheated to 350°F (180°C) for about 10 minutes.

8-inch (20 cm) square glass baking dish, lined with aluminum foil

1½ cups	wild rice, rinsed and drained	375 mL
1 tsp	fine sea salt, divided	5 mL
2 tbsp	grapeseed oil	30 mL
½ cup	chopped onion	125 mL
½ cup	chopped carrot	125 mL
½ cup	chopped celery	125 mL
½ cup	chopped apple (see Tips, left)	125 mL
4 to 5	slices gluten-free bread, cut into 1-inch (2.5 cm) cubes (2 cups/500 mL)	4 to 5
2 tbsp	thinly sliced fresh sage leaves	30 mL
1 tbsp	chopped fresh thyme leaves	15 mL
⅔ cup	hot water	150 mL
3 tbsp	ground raw flax seeds	45 mL

1. In a large saucepan filled with water, combine wild rice and ½ tsp (2 mL) salt; bring to a boil. Reduce heat and simmer until rice is tender, about 45 minutes. Drain and set aside.

2. In a skillet over medium heat, heat oil. Add onion, carrot and celery and cook, stirring occasionally, for 4 to 5 minutes, until vegetables are softened. Add apple and bread and cook, stirring occasionally, until softened, 8 to 10 minutes. Remove from heat and stir in sage and thyme. Set aside.

3. Preheat oven to 350°F (180°C). In a small bowl, whisk together hot water and flax seeds. Set aside for about 5 minutes so flax can absorb liquid and swell.

4. In a large bowl, toss together cooked rice and vegetable-bread mixture. Add flaxseed mixture and remaining salt and toss well.

5. Spread evenly in prepared baking dish. Cover with aluminum foil and bake in preheated oven for 30 minutes. Remove foil and bake for about 8 minutes more, until slightly browned and crisp on top. Serve immediately or transfer to an airtight container and refrigerate for up to 1 week.

Beans and Grains

Beans

Grains

Basic Slow-Cooked Legumes

Beans can be a wonderful addition to any meal. They are easy to prepare, packed with protein and fiber, and leave you feeling fully satisfied. Cooking beans in a slow cooker requires very little effort. Put presoaked beans in the slow cooker before you go to bed; when you wake up, they'll be ready for use.

**MAKES ABOUT
2 CUPS (500 ML)
(SEE TIPS, BELOW)**

Tips

This recipe may be doubled or tripled. Remember to use the appropriate size of slow cooker.

If you prefer, cook legumes on your stovetop. Follow these soaking instructions, if required: Cover with about 4 cups (1 L) fresh water per 1 cup (250 mL) legumes. Bring to a boil, reduce heat and simmer until tender (about 30 minutes for lentils; up to 1½ hours for chickpeas).

Store legumes in an airtight container at room temperature. They lose their moisture over time and are best used within a year (beans are stale if their skins shrivel up when soaked). If your beans are still tough after a long cooking, they are probably old and should be discarded.

Canned beans are a good substitute for cooked dried beans. For 2 cups (500 mL) cooked beans, use a standard can, ranging from 14 oz (398 mL) to 19 oz (540 mL). Rinse well before use.

- **Small to medium (approx. 2 quart) slow cooker**

1 cup	dried beans or chickpeas, soaked (see box, below)	250 mL
3 cups	water	750 mL
	Herbs (optional)	
	Fine sea salt	

1. In slow cooker stoneware, combine soaked beans and water. Season with garlic, bay leaf or a bouquet garni of your favorite herbs tied together in a piece of cheesecloth, if desired. Add salt to taste.
2. Cover and cook on Low for 8 to 10 hours (or overnight) or on High for 4 to 5 hours, until beans are tender. Drain and rinse. If not using immediately, cover and refrigerate for up to 5 days or freeze for up to 6 months.

Variation

Basic Lentils: Do not presoak dried lentils, but rinse and drain. Reduce the cooking time to about 6 hours on Low or 3 hours on High.

How to Soak Dried Beans

Long Soak: Place rinsed, drained beans in a bowl with water. Cover and set aside for at least 6 hours or overnight (if overnight, refrigerate). Drain and rinse thoroughly under cold running water.

Quick Soak: In a pot, combine rinsed, drained beans and water. Cover and bring to a boil for 3 minutes. Remove from heat and let soak for 1 hour. Drain and rinse thoroughly under cold running water.

Chickpea "Tuna" Salad

This chickpea salad resembles tuna salad in flavor and texture. It's a perfect sandwich filling paired with your favorite gluten-free bread or crunchy toast, Dijon mustard, tomato slices, pickles and lettuce. I also like to use it as a dip for crunchy carrot and celery sticks.

**MAKES
3 CUPS (750 ML)**

Tips

To soak the chickpeas: Place in a bowl and cover with 8 cups (2 L) water. Cover and set aside for at least 6 hours or overnight (if overnight, refrigerate). Drain, discarding water.

If you prefer, cook the chickpeas in your slow cooker (see page 182).

The outer layer of raw celery is very fibrous and can be difficult to chew. Use a vegetable peeler to remove the outside strands. This will make the texture more pleasing and bring out the flavor.

For a lighter version of this recipe, omit the mayonnaise. You can either add ½ cup (125 mL) Basic Chickpea Hummus (page 72) or increase the amount of Dijon mustard to 3 tbsp (45 mL) and add ⅓ cup (75 mL) extra virgin olive oil.

● **Food processor**

2 cups	soaked chickpeas (see Tips, left)	500 mL
8 cups	water	2 L
1 tsp	fine sea salt, divided	5 mL
3 tbsp	freshly squeezed lemon juice	45 mL
½ cup	finely chopped celery (see Tips, left)	125 mL
¼ cup	finely chopped red onion	60 mL
¼ cup	chopped fresh dill	60 mL
1 tbsp	Dijon mustard	15 mL
¾ cup	Vegan Mayonnaise (page 550)	175 mL

1. In a large saucepan, combine soaked chickpeas, water and ¼ tsp (1 mL) salt. Bring to a boil, reduce heat and simmer until tender, about 1 hour. Drain, discarding water.

2. In food processor fitted with the metal blade, combine cooked chickpeas, lemon juice and remaining ¾ tsp (3 mL) salt. Process until chickpeas are broken down into small pieces (be careful not to overprocess — you want some texture). Transfer to a large bowl.

3. Add celery, red onion, dill, mustard and mayonnaise and stir until well combined. Serve immediately or transfer to an airtight container and refrigerate for up to 5 days.

Creamy Pinto Bean Salad

Nothing says summer like this creamy salad. I like to serve it with some crunchy greens and a tall glass of Matcha Me Green Juice (page 41).

MAKES 4 SERVINGS

Tips

To soak the beans: Place in a bowl and cover with 8 cups (2 L) water. Cover and set aside for at least 6 hours or overnight (if overnight, refrigerate). Drain, discarding water.

If you prefer, cook the beans in your slow cooker (see page 182).

Substitute an equal amount of canary beans for the pinto beans.

A citrus reamer is a hand-held tool used to extract the juice from lemons and limes. It is available in most kitchen supply stores and would be ideal to use for the lemon juice in this recipe.

Wheat-free tamari is a gluten-free seasoning made from fermented soybeans. It can be found in most well-stocked supermarkets and natural food stores.

• Blender

2 cups	pinto beans, soaked (see Tips, left)	500 mL
8 cups	water	2 L
½ tsp	fine sea salt, divided	2 mL
¾ cup	freshly squeezed lemon juice (see Tips, left)	175 mL
½ cup	tahini	125 mL
¼ cup	water	60 mL
¼ cup	extra virgin olive oil	60 mL
3 tbsp	wheat-free tamari (see Tips, left)	45 mL
2 tbsp	raw (unpasteurized) apple cider vinegar	30 mL
1 tbsp	chopped fresh thyme leaves	15 mL
½ cup	finely sliced green onion (green part only)	125 mL
½ cup	finely chopped red bell pepper	125 mL
¼ cup	chopped fresh flat-leaf (Italian) parsley	60 mL
3 tbsp	raw unshelled hemp seeds	45 mL

1. In a large saucepan, combine soaked beans, 8 cups (2 L) water and ¼ tsp (1 mL) salt. Bring to a boil, reduce heat and simmer until beans are tender, about 1 hour. Drain, discarding water. Set aside.

2. In blender, combine lemon juice, tahini, ¼ cup (60 mL) water, oil, tamari, vinegar, thyme and remaining salt. Blend at high speed until smooth. Set aside.

3. In a large bowl, toss together cooked beans, green onion, red pepper, parsley and hemp seeds. Add reserved dressing and toss to combine. Serve immediately or transfer to an airtight container and refrigerate for up to 5 days.

Asian-Style Adzuki Bean Salad

In this salad, protein-rich legumes are paired with crisp bok choy and crunchy sesame seeds for a perfectly satisfying dish.

MAKES 4 SERVINGS

Tips

To soak the adzuki beans, place in a bowl with 8 cups (2 L) water. Cover and set aside for at least 3 hours or overnight (if overnight, refrigerate). Drain, discarding water.

If you prefer, cook the beans in your slow cooker (see page 182).

Either black or white sesame seeds will work in this recipe. You can also use a mixture of both for visual appeal.

To toast the sesame seeds: Heat a dry skillet over medium heat. Add sesame seeds and cook, stirring constantly, until fragrant and just starting to turn brown, about 3 minutes. Remove from heat and immediately transfer to a plate to cool.

Mirin is a sweet Japanese cooking wine that can be found in most well-stocked supermarkets. It has a low alcohol content that is further reduced by cooking.

Blender

1 cup	adzuki beans, soaked (see Tips, left)	250 mL
8 cups	water	2 L
2 cups	thinly sliced baby bok choy	500 mL
½ cup	chopped fresh cilantro, leaves and stems	125 mL
2 tbsp	toasted sesame seeds (see Tips, left)	30 mL
2 tbsp	freshly squeezed lemon juice	30 mL
1 tbsp	mirin (see Tips, left)	15 mL
¼ cup	toasted sesame oil, divided	60 mL
¼ cup	wheat-free tamari	60 mL
2 tbsp	water	30 mL
1 tbsp	raw agave nectar	15 mL
2 tsp	minced peeled gingerroot	10 mL

1. In a large saucepan, combine soaked adzuki beans and water and bring to a boil. Reduce heat and simmer until beans are tender, 45 minutes to 1 hour. Drain, discarding water. Set aside.

2. In a large bowl, toss together cooked beans, bok choy, cilantro, sesame seeds, lemon juice, mirin and 1 tbsp (15 mL) sesame oil, until well combined. Set aside.

3. In blender, combine remaining 3 tbsp (45 mL) sesame oil, tamari, water, agave nectar and ginger. Blend at high speed until smooth. Add to bean mixture and toss well. Serve immediately or transfer to an airtight container and refrigerate for up to 3 days.

Grilled Pepper and Navy Bean Salad

Sweet peppers, rich, fragrant beans, bitter arugula and tangy balsamic vinegar combine to make this hearty and flavorful salad.

MAKES 4 SERVINGS

Tips

To soak the beans: Place in a bowl and cover with 8 cups (2 L) water. Cover and set aside for at least 6 hours or overnight (if overnight, refrigerate). Drain, discarding water.

If you prefer, cook the beans in your slow cooker (page 182).

If the peppers you are using are on the small side, use 3; if large, use 2.

Covering the bowl with plastic captures steam from the peppers. It will help to separate the skin from the flesh, making the peppers easier to peel.

You can make this salad ahead and refrigerate for up to 5 days — just hold off adding the arugula until right before serving, or it will get mushy.

Substitute 3 tbsp (45 mL) red wine vinegar for the balsamic vinegar.

Substitute 4 cups (1 L) baby spinach leaves for the arugula.

● Preheat grill or broiler to High

2 cups	navy beans, soaked (see Tips, left)	500 mL
8 cups	water	2 L
½ tsp	fine sea salt, divided	2 mL
2 to 3	red bell peppers (see Tips, left)	2 to 3
2 to 3 tbsp	grapeseed oil	30 to 45 mL
2 cups	packed baby arugula	500 mL
¼ cup	balsamic vinegar	60 mL
¼ cup	extra virgin olive oil	60 mL
3 tbsp	Dijon mustard	45 mL
1 tbsp	dried oregano	15 mL
2 tsp	pure maple syrup	10 mL

1. In a large saucepan, combine soaked beans, water and ¼ tsp (mL) salt. Bring to a boil, reduce heat and simmer until beans are tender, about 1 hour. Drain, discarding water. Let cool.

2. Meanwhile, in a bowl, toss peppers with grapeseed oil. Place on preheated grill and cook, turning frequently, until all sides are blistered and lightly blackened, about 8 minutes. (You can also broil the peppers on a baking sheet, turning often.) Transfer to a bowl and cover tightly with plastic wrap. Set aside for 10 minutes.

3. Carefully remove peppers from bowl (they may be hot) and, using your fingers, gently rub skins off flesh. Using a sharp knife, cut peppers in half and discard seeds and white pith. Cut the roasted pepper flesh into strips about ½ inch (1 cm) wide.

4. In a bowl, toss together cooled cooked beans, grilled peppers, remaining ¼ tsp (1 mL) salt, arugula, vinegar, olive oil, mustard, oregano and maple syrup. Serve immediately.

Mediterranean Bean Salad

This tricolor dish is the perfect marriage of protein-dense beans, fresh vegetables and aromatic herbs and spices. I love to serve it alongside Herbed Roasted Potatoes (page 179) or Stewed Onions and Mushrooms with Millet (page 336). Combined, these pairs make a perfect meal.

MAKES 4 SERVINGS

Tips

To soak the beans and chickpeas: Place in a bowl and cover with 8 cups (2 L) water. Cover and set aside for at least 6 hours or overnight (if overnight, refrigerate). Drain, discarding water.

If you prefer, cook the beans in your slow cooker (page 182).

To prepare the cucumber: Remove skin with a vegetable peeler, then cut in half lengthwise. Using a small spoon, carefully scoop out the seeds and discard.

Substitute an equal amount of maple syrup for the agave nectar.

8 cups	water	2 L
1 cup	kidney beans, soaked (see Tips, left)	250 mL
½ cup	chickpeas, soaked	125 mL
½ cup	cannellini beans, soaked	125 mL
1 tsp	fine sea salt, divided	5 mL
½ cup	chopped red bell pepper	125 mL
½ cup	chopped peeled and seeded cucumber (see Tips, left)	125 mL
¼ cup	extra virgin olive oil	60 mL
3 tbsp	red wine vinegar	45 mL
2 tsp	dried oregano	10 mL
1 tsp	raw agave nectar	5 mL

1. In a large saucepan, combine water, soaked kidney beans, chickpeas and cannellini beans and ½ tsp (2 mL) salt. Bring to a boil, reduce heat and simmer until tender, about 1 hour. Drain, discarding water. Let cool.

2. In a large bowl, combine cooked beans, remaining ½ tsp (2 mL) salt, red pepper, cucumber, oil, vinegar, oregano and agave nectar; toss until well combined. Serve immediately or transfer to an airtight container and refrigerate for up to 5 days.

Black Bean Santa Fe Wraps

This wrap is stuffed with creamy black bean purée and fresh tomatoes, avocado and red pepper. Serve with a side of Vegan Sour Cream (page 555), Queso Dip (page 82) or Roasted Red Pepper Mole Sauce (page 108).

MAKES 6 WRAPS

Tips

Use either black beans you have cooked yourself or canned cooked beans, preferably with no salt added. If using canned beans that contain salt, be sure to rinse and drain them thoroughly before using.

A hand-held citrus reamer can be used to extract the juice from lemons and limes. Available in most kitchen supply stores, this tool would be ideal to use for the lemon juice in this recipe.

I use gluten-free brown rice wraps for this recipe. You can also use corn tortillas, which may be only 6 inches (15 cm) in diameter, in which case increase the number and adjust the distribution of the filling accordingly.

Choose organic tortillas to avoid GMOs, and check the label to make sure they are gluten-free and do not contain any added wheat.

● **Food processor**

3 cups	drained cooked black beans, divided (see Tips, left)	750 mL
3 tbsp	freshly squeezed lemon juice (see Tips, left)	45 mL
1 tbsp	chili powder	15 mL
2 tsp	ground cumin	10 mL
1 tsp	fine sea salt	5 mL
2 to 3	cloves garlic	2 to 3
¼ cup	extra virgin olive oil	60 mL
6	large (10 inches/25 cm) gluten-free wraps (see Tips, left)	6
1	avocado, cut into 6 wedges	1
1	tomato, cut into 6 wedges	1
¾ cup	finely chopped red bell pepper	175 mL

1. In food processor fitted with the metal blade, combine 2 cups (500 mL) cooked black beans, lemon juice, chili powder, cumin, salt and garlic. Process until smooth, stopping the motor to scrape down sides of work bowl as necessary.

2. With the motor running, add oil through the feed tube in a slow, steady stream; process until smooth. Transfer to a large bowl. Add remaining 1 cup (250 mL) beans and stir well.

3. Divide bean mixture into 6 equal portions. Lay 1 wrap flat on a clean work surface. Spread 1 portion of the bean mixture along the bottom third of the wrap; top with a wedge of avocado, a wedge of tomato and 2 tbsp (30 mL) of the red pepper.

4. Fold about 1 inch (2.5 cm) of the sides of the wrap over the filling and, starting from the bottom, roll up wrap around the filling. Repeat with remaining wraps and filling. Serve immediately or wrap tightly in plastic and refrigerate for up to 1 day.

Easy Burritos

These burritos are simple to prepare yet delicious. Fresh tortillas are rolled around creamy hummus, chunky avocado, fresh tomatoes, crisp lettuce, soft rice and creamy Vegan Sour Cream.

Tips

The quantity of garlic depends on the size of the cloves. If large, use the smaller number. If small, more may be required.

Substitute an equal amount of cooked quinoa for the rice.

I use gluten-free brown rice wraps for this recipe. You can also use corn tortillas, which may be only 6 inches (15 cm) in diameter, in which case increase the number and adjust the distribution of the filling accordingly.

Choose organic tortillas to avoid GMOs, and check the label to make sure they are gluten-free and do not contain any added wheat.

Most commercially made gluten-free breads dry out very quickly, so keep them in an airtight container until ready to use.

1	ripe medium avocado	1
3 tbsp	freshly squeezed lemon juice	45 mL
½ tsp	fine sea salt	2 mL
1 to 2	cloves garlic, minced	1 to 2
2	large (10 inches/25 cm) gluten-free wraps (see Tips, left)	2
1 cup	Basic Chickpea Hummus (page 72)	250 mL
1 cup	Basic Rice (page 212; see Tips, left)	250 mL
½ cup	chopped tomato	125 mL
½ cup	thinly sliced romaine lettuce leaves	125 mL
½ cup	Vegan Sour Cream (page 555)	125 mL

1. In a large bowl and using a fork, mash together avocado, lemon juice, salt and garlic (you want the mixture to be somewhat chunky). Set aside.

2. Lay 1 wrap flat on a clean work surface. Spoon half of the hummus along the bottom third of the wrap. Top with half of the avocado mixture, ½ cup (125 mL) rice, ¼ cup (60 mL) tomato, ¼ cup (60 mL) lettuce and ¼ cup (60 mL) sour cream.

3. Fold about 1 inch (2.5 cm) of the sides of the wrap over the filling and, starting from the bottom, roll the wrap around the filling. Repeat.

4. Heat a large, dry skillet over medium heat. Add burritos, seam side down, and cook until bottom of each is golden brown, about 5 minutes. Turn over and cook until other side is golden brown and burrito is heated through. Serve immediately.

Variation

Cheesy Burritos: Add ½ cup (125 mL) Chia Whiz (page 85) to each burrito and serve with a side of Easy Cheesy Pasta Sauce (page 540).

Mediterranean Wraps

These wraps are full of fresh vegetables tossed with creamy olive oil, tangy lemon juice and fresh herbs.

Tips

For convenience, use premade pita breads or tortillas or other gluten-free wraps about 8 inches (20 cm) in diameter.

I like to use kalamata olives for this recipe, but feel free to substitute any type of olive you like.

To store raw hemp seeds: Place them in an airtight container and refrigerate. This will prevent the fats from turning rancid. Hemp seeds can also be frozen for up to 6 months. They are extremely high in protein, containing up to 5 grams per tablespoon (15 mL).

2	Gluten-Free Pita Breads (page 474; see Tips, page 191)	2
1 cup	Basic Chickpea Hummus (page 72)	250 mL
1 cups	Quinoa Tabbouleh (page 219),	250 mL
1 cup	thinly sliced romaine lettuce leaves	250 mL
½ cup	thinly sliced kalamata olives (see Tips, left)	125 mL
2 tbsp	raw shelled hemp seeds (see Tips, left)	30 mL

1. Lay 1 pita flat on a clean work surface. Place ½ cup (125 mL) hummus in center. Using the back of a spoon or spatula, spread evenly over the wrap, leaving a ½-inch (1 cm) border around the edge.

2. Spread ½ cup (125 mL) tabbouleh evenly over hummus. Lay half of the lettuce in a horizontal strip across the center. Sprinkle with half of the olives and hemp seeds.

3. Fold about 1 inch (2.5 cm) of the sides of the wrap over the filling and, starting from the bottom, roll up wrap around the filling. Repeat with remaining wrap and filling. Cut each wrap in half. Serve immediately or wrap tightly in plastic and refrigerate for up to 1 day.

Hummus Wraps

Simple yet delicious, these hummus-laden wraps can be enjoyed for lunch or dinner. You can also slice them into smaller pieces to serve as an appetizer at your next dinner party.

MAKES 4 WRAPS

Tips

Always use a very sharp knife when cutting tomatoes, and remove the core before chopping — insert the tip of a paring knife into the stem end and turn the tomato while holding the knife steady. Remove and discard the core.

If you prefer, use gluten-free brown rice wraps for this recipe. You can also use corn tortillas, which may be only 6 inches (15 cm) in diameter, in which case increase the number and adjust the distribution of the filling accordingly.

Most gluten-free breads dry out very quickly, so keep them in an airtight container until ready to use.

4	Gluten-Free Pita Breads (page 474; see Tips, left)	4
2 cups	Basic Chickpea Hummus (page 72)	500 mL
2 cups	thinly sliced romaine lettuce	500 mL
2 cups	chopped tomatoes, divided	500 mL
2 cups	thinly sliced English cucumber,	500 mL
¼ cup	raw shelled hemp seeds	60 mL

1. Lay 1 wrap flat on a clean work surface. Spread ½ cup (125 mL) hummus along the bottom third of the wrap; top with ½ cup (125 mL) each lettuce, tomato and cucumber and 1 tbsp (15 mL) hemp seeds.

2. Fold about 1 inch (2.5 cm) of the sides of the wrap over the filling and, starting from the bottom, roll up wrap around the filling. Repeat with remaining filling and wraps. Serve immediately or wrap tightly in plastic and refrigerate for up to 1 day.

Green Goddess Wraps

Serve this phytonutrient-dense wrap with a side of Ranch Dip (page 80) for an easy lunch any day of the week.

**MAKES 2 WRAPS
(4 SERVINGS)**

Tips

Kale and collard leaves have a long, thick rib that runs through the center. When working with these vegetables, try to keep the soft vein at the top of the leaf intact. However, toward the bottom (stem) end of the leaf, the vein becomes larger and tougher and needs to be removed. Lay the leaf flat on a cutting board and use a paring knife to remove the thick part of the rib and discard. For this recipe, slice the leafy green part of the kale into thin strips.

Kale comes in many different varieties. The most common, green kale, is widely available. Black kale, which is also called dinosaur or lacinato kale, is reputed to be the most nutrient-dense.

Substitute an equal amount of chard or mustard greens for the kale.

- Slotted spoon or spider
- Large bowl, half-filled with ice water

8 cups	water	2 L
1 tsp	fine sea salt	5 mL
4 cups	loosely packed thinly sliced kale leaves, stems and ribs removed (see Tips, left)	1 L
4 cups	loosely packed chopped spinach leaves	1 L
2	large collard leaves, stems removed (see Tips, left)	2
1 cup	Basic Chickpea Hummus (page 72)	250 mL
2 tbsp	raw shelled hemp seeds	30 mL

1. In a large covered saucepan, bring water and salt to a boil. Add kale and spinach and cook, uncovered, until just wilted, about 30 seconds. Using slotted spoon, transfer greens to ice bath to stop the cooking. Once they have cooled, drain, discarding water. Using your hands, squeeze as much water as you can from the greens. Set aside.

2. Lay 1 collard leaf flat on a clean work surface. Spoon $\frac{1}{2}$ cup (250 mL) hummus over the leaf, leaving a 1-inch (2.5 cm) border on each side. Top with half of the cooked greens and 1 tbsp (15 mL) hemp seeds.

3. Fold in sides of leaf over filling; then, starting at the edge closest to you, roll up tightly to form a cylinder. Repeat with remaining collard leaf and filling. Cut each wrap in half. Serve immediately or wrap tightly in plastic and refrigerate for up to 1 day.

Grilled Veggie Wraps

Freshly grilled marinated vegetables are a natural for entertaining friends in the summertime. Serve with your favorite cold beverage.

Tips

I use gluten-free brown rice wraps for this recipe. You can also use corn tortillas, which may be only 6 inches (15 cm) in diameter, in which case increase the number and adjust the distribution of the filling accordingly.

If using tortillas, choose organic to avoid GMOs, and check the label to make sure they do not contain any added wheat.

Preheat grill to High

1/4 cup	grapeseed oil	60 mL
1	red bell pepper	1
1	zucchini, cut crosswise into 1/2-inch (1 cm) pieces	1
1	portobello mushroom cap	1
3 to 4	1/4-inch (0.5 cm) slices eggplant (unpeeled)	3 to 4
2 tbsp	balsamic vinegar	30 mL
1 tbsp	chopped fresh thyme leaves	15 mL
1 tbsp	chopped fresh rosemary	15 mL
1 tsp	fine sea salt	5 mL
2 tbsp	Dijon mustard	30 mL
2	large (10 inches/25 cm) gluten-free wraps (see Tips, left)	2
1 cup	Basic Chickpea Hummus (page 72)	250 mL

1. In a large bowl, combine oil, red pepper, zucchini, mushroom, eggplant, vinegar, thyme, rosemary and salt; toss to coat well. Grill over high heat for 3 to 4 minutes per side, until vegetables are tender and have grill marks. Remove from heat and set aside to cool completely.

2. Using a sharp knife, cut vegetables into 1/4-inch (0.5 cm) strips. Transfer to a bowl and toss with mustard.

3. Lay 1 wrap flat on a clean work surface. Spread 1/2 cup (250 mL) hummus along the bottom of the wrap. Top with half of the grilled vegetables.

4. Fold about 1 inch (2.5 cm) of the sides of the wrap over the filling and, starting from the bottom, roll up wrap around the filling. Repeat with remaining wrap and filling. If desired, cut each wrap in half. Serve immediately or wrap tightly in plastic and refrigerate for up to 1 day.

Sweet Potato Burritos

In these hearty wraps, creamy sweet potato is paired with rich, cheesy Chia Whiz and crispy lettuce.

MAKES 2 LARGE BURRITOS (4 SERVINGS)

Tips

The sweet potato in this recipe is served intact, cut in half, with the skin on, so be sure to scrub it well before baking.

Substitute an equal amount of cooked quinoa for the rice.

I use gluten-free brown rice wraps for this recipe. You can also use corn tortillas, which may be only 6 inches (15 cm) in diameter, in which case increase the number and adjust the distribution of the filling accordingly.

Choose organic tortillas to avoid GMOs, and check the label to make sure they are gluten-free and do not contain any added wheat.

- **Preheat oven to 400°F (200°C)**
- **Baking sheet, lined with parchment paper**

1	large sweet potato, well scrubbed (see Tips, left)	1
2	large (10 inches/25 cm) gluten-free wraps (see Tips, left)	2
1 cup	Chia Whiz (page 85)	250 mL
½ cup	Basic Rice (page 212) (see Tips, left)	125 mL
1 cup	thinly sliced romaine lettuce leaves	250 mL
2 tbsp	raw shelled hemp seeds	30 mL
2 tbsp	grapeseed oil	30 mL

1. Using a fork, poke several holes in sweet potato. Wrap tightly in aluminum foil. Place on prepared baking sheet and bake in preheated oven until tender, 45 to 75 minutes, depending on the size of the sweet potato. Remove from oven and unwrap (discard foil). Set aside until cool enough to handle, about 10 minutes. Cut sweet potato in half lengthwise. Set aside.

2. Lay 1 wrap flat on a clean work surface. Spread ½ cup (125 mL) Chia Whiz evenly along the bottom third of the wrap; top with ¼ cup (60 mL) rice, one sweet potato half, ½ cup (125 mL) lettuce and 1 tbsp (15 mL) hemp seeds.

3. Fold about 1 inch (2.5 cm) of the sides of the wrap over the filling and, starting from the bottom, roll up wrap around the filling. Repeat with remaining wrap and filling.

4. Heat a large, dry skillet over medium heat. Add each burrito, seam side down, and cook for about 5 minutes, until bottom is golden brown. Turn over and cook until other side is golden brown and burrito is heated through. Cut each burrito in half. Serve immediately.

Chana Masala Wraps

Serve these Indian-inspired wraps as a simple dinner, with some fresh lime wedges on the side and a crisp green salad.

Tips

If you prefer, substitute prepared gluten-free wraps for the chapatis.

Substitute an equal amount of cooked quinoa for the rice.

Always use a very sharp knife when cutting tomatoes, and remove the core before chopping — insert the tip of a paring knife into the stem end and turn the tomato while holding the knife steady. Remove and discard the core.

Most gluten-free breads dry out very quickly, so keep them in an airtight container until ready to use.

2	Gluten-Free Chapatis (page 476)	2
1 cup	Baked Chana Masala (page 349)	250 mL
1/2 cup	Basic Rice (page 212), divided (see Tips, left)	125 mL
1/2 cup	Creamy Cashew Tzatziki (page 79)	125 mL
1/4 cup	chopped tomato (see Tips, left)	60 mL
1/4 cup	chopped fresh cilantro, leaves and stems	60 mL
	Lime wedges	
	Hot sauce (optional)	

1. Lay 1 chapati on a clean work surface. Spread 1/2 cup (125 mL) chana masala evenly along the bottom third of the wrap; top with 1/4 cup (60 mL) each rice and tzatziki and 2 tbsp (30 mL) each tomato and cilantro.

2. Fold about 1 inch (2.5 cm) of the sides of the wrap over the filling and, starting from the bottom, roll up wrap around the filling. Repeat with remaining wrap and filling.

Roasted Cauliflower and Chickpea Tacos

This new twist on traditional Mexican fare will add spice to your diet — along with a wide range of nutrients. I like to serve these with Queso Dip.

MAKES 8 TO 10 TACOS

Tips

Use either chickpeas you have cooked yourself or canned, preferably with no salt added. When using canned legumes that contain salt, be sure to rinse and drain them thoroughly before using.

If cooking dried chickpeas, you can use your slow cooker or cook them on the stovetop (see page 182).

A hand-held citrus reamer can be used to extract the juice from lemons and limes. Available in most kitchen supply stores, this tool would be ideal to use for the citrus in this recipe.

- **Preheat oven to 400°F (200°C)**
- **Baking sheet, lined with parchment paper**
- **Blender**

FILLING

¼ cup	grapeseed oil	60 mL
3 tbsp	freshly squeezed lime juice (see Tips, left)	45 mL
2 tsp	chili powder	10 mL
1 tsp	ground cumin	5 mL
½ tsp	fine sea salt	2 mL
Pinch	cayenne pepper	Pinch
2 cups	drained cooked chickpeas (see Tips, left)	500 mL
1	head cauliflower, cut into bite-size florets (about 4 cups/1 L)	1

SLAW

2 cups	thinly sliced red cabbage	500 mL
½ cup	roughly chopped fresh cilantro leaves	125 mL
½ cup	thinly sliced red bell pepper	125 mL
2 tbsp	extra virgin olive oil	30 mL
2 tbsp	freshly squeezed lemon juice	30 mL
¼ tsp	fine sea salt	1 mL

AVOCADO DRIZZLE

½	ripe medium avocado	½
½ cup	water	125 mL
½ cup	extra virgin olive oil	125 mL
3 tbsp	freshly squeezed lime juice	45 mL
1 tbsp	freshly squeezed lemon juice	15 mL
⅛ tsp	fine sea salt	0.5 mL
8 to 10	small gluten-free organic corn taco shells (see Tips, page 197)	8 to 10
	Lime wedges	
	Hot sauce	
	Queso Dip (page 82; optional)	

Choose organic taco shells to avoid GMOs, and check the label to make sure they are gluten-free and do not contain any added wheat.

If you prefer, serve the Avocado Drizzle alongside.

1. *Filling:* In a large bowl, whisk together grapeseed oil, lime juice, chili powder, cumin, salt and cayenne. Add chickpeas and cauliflower and toss well. Spread evenly over prepared baking sheet. Bake in preheated oven for 18 to 20 minutes or until golden brown.

2. *Slaw:* In a large bowl, toss together cabbage, cilantro, red pepper, olive oil, lemon juice and salt. Set aside.

3. *Avocado Drizzle:* In blender, combine avocado, water, olive oil, lime juice, lemon juice and salt. Process until smooth and creamy. (Store leftover drizzle in an airtight container in the refrigerator for up to 3 days.)

4. *Assembly:* Spoon chickpea-cauliflower filling into taco shells. Top with slaw and a liberal amount of avocado drizzle. Serve with lime wedges and hot sauce on the side, along with Queso Dip (if using).

Variation

Substitute an equal amount of Vegan Sour Cream (page 555) for the avocado drizzle.

Un-Tuna Wraps

The combination of chopped chickpeas and creamy mayonnaise in these protein-dense wraps is reminiscent of tuna salad. They are perfect for a summertime lunch or a light dinner.

MAKES 4 WRAPS

Tips

Use either chickpeas you have cooked yourself or canned chickpeas, preferably with no salt added. When using canned legumes that contain salt, be sure to rinse and drain them thoroughly before using.

If you prefer, use your slow cooker to cook the chickpeas for this recipe (see page 182).

A citrus reamer is a hand-held tool used to extract the juice from lemons and limes. It is available in most kitchen supply stores and would be ideal to use for the lemon juice in this recipe.

Whenever you are measuring fresh herbs, pack them firmly into the measuring cup to ensure an accurate amount.

● **Food processor**

2 cups	drained cooked chickpeas (see Tips, left)	500 mL
1 tsp	finely grated lemon zest	5 mL
¼ cup	freshly squeezed lemon juice (see Tips, left)	60 mL
1 tsp	fine sea salt	5 mL
1 cup	Vegan Mayonnaise (page 550)	250 mL
½ cup	chopped flat-leaf (Italian) parsley leaves	125 mL
½ cup	roughly chopped fresh dill	125 mL
½ cup	finely chopped celery	125 mL
¼ cup	finely chopped red onion	60 mL
2 tbsp	Dijon mustard	30 mL
4	Gluten-Free Pita Breads (page 474)	4
1 cup	chopped tomatoes, divided	250 mL
4	romaine lettuce leaves	4

1. In food processor fitted with the metal blade, combine cooked chickpeas, lemon zest, lemon juice and salt. Process until almost smooth (a few large pieces of chickpea are okay).

2. Transfer to a large bowl. Add mayonnaise, parsley, dill, celery, onion and mustard. Stir to combine.

3. Lay 1 pita on a clean work surface. Spread one-quarter of the chickpea mixture evenly along the bottom third of the wrap; top with ¼ cup (60 mL) of tomato and 1 lettuce leaf.

4. Fold about 1 inch (2.5 cm) of the sides of the wrap over the filling and, starting from the bottom, roll up wrap around the filling. Repeat with remaining pitas and filling. Serve immediately or wrap tightly in plastic and refrigerate for up to 1 day.

Mung Bean Daal

Slow-cooked legumes make a perfect dinner on a cold winter's night. Drizzle with your favorite hot sauce and enjoy with a piece of crusty gluten-free bread.

MAKES 2 SERVINGS

Tips

Substitute an equal amount of grapeseed oil for the coconut oil.

Substitute 2½ cups (625 mL) split red lentils for the mung beans.

Wheat-free tamari is a gluten-free seasoning made from fermented soybeans. It can be found in most well-stocked supermarkets and natural food stores.

Nutritional yeast is an inactive yeast that has been grown on beet molasses and then pasteurized. It provides a rich, cheesy flavor in sauces, stews, soups and dips. Look for it in well-stocked supermarkets and natural food stores.

2 tbsp	coconut oil (see Tips, left)	30 mL
½ cup	finely chopped onion	125 mL
¼ cup	finely chopped celery	60 mL
¼ tsp	fine sea salt	1 mL
1 tsp	minced peeled gingerroot	5 mL
1 tsp	minced garlic	5 mL
2 cups	split mung beans (see Tips, left)	500 mL
6 cups	water	1.5 L
¼ cup	wheat-free tamari (see Tips, left)	60 mL
¼ cup	nutritional yeast (see Tips, left)	60 mL
⅛ tsp	cayenne pepper (optional)	0.5 mL

1. In a medium saucepan over medium heat, heat coconut oil. Add onion, celery and salt and cook, stirring constantly, for about 5 minutes, until vegetables become softened and translucent. Stir in ginger and garlic and cook for 2 to 3 minutes, until fragrant. Add mung beans and stir to combine.

2. Add water and bring to a boil, then reduce heat and simmer until most of the liquid has been absorbed, about 20 minutes.

3. Remove from heat and stir in tamari, nutritional yeast and cayenne (if using). Serve immediately or transfer to an airtight container and refrigerate for up to 1 week. To reheat, place in a large skillet over medium heat and stir until heated through, 4 to 5 minutes.

Variation

Curried Mung Bean Daal: In Step 1, increase the amount of coconut oil to ¼ cup (60 mL) and add 2 tbsp (30 mL) curry powder, 1 tsp (5 mL) ground cumin, ½ tsp (2 mL) ground coriander, ¼ tsp (1 mL) ground cardamom and ⅛ tsp (0.5 mL) ground turmeric along with the onions.

Lemon Parsley Lupini Beans

This dish is full of fresh, bold flavors. It works well as part of a salad table or platter, which makes it perfect for serving at barbecues, holiday gatherings or other family functions.

MAKES 4 SERVINGS

Tips

To soak the beans: Place in a bowl and cover with 8 cups (2 L) water. Cover and set aside for at least 6 hours or overnight (if overnight, refrigerate). Drain, discarding water.

Use lupini beans you have cooked yourself or, if you prefer, substitute 2 cups (500 mL) canned lupini beans, preferably with no salt added. When using canned beans that contain salt, be sure to rinse them thoroughly before using.

To ensure that any grit is removed from your parsley before chopping, place it in a bowl, cover with cool water and set aside for 2 minutes. The dirt will sink to the bottom of the bowl. Lift out parsley, rinse under cold running water and pat dry (or dry in a salad spinner) to remove excess moisture.

1 cup	soaked, drained lupini beans (see Tips, left)	250 mL
8 cups	water	2 L
¾ tsp	fine sea salt, divided	3 mL
4 cups	chopped fresh flat-leaf (Italian) parsley leaves (see Tips left)	1 L
½ cup	extra virgin olive oil	125 mL
1 tsp	freshly grated lemon zest	5 mL
¼ cup	freshly squeezed lemon juice	60 mL
3 tbsp	raw hulled hemp seeds	45 mL

1. In a large saucepan, combine soaked beans, water and ¼ tsp (1 mL) salt. Bring to a boil, then reduce heat and simmer until tender, about 45 minutes. Drain, reserving ½ cup (125 mL) cooking liquid.

2. In a large bowl, combine cooked beans, remaining ½ tsp (2 mL) salt, parsley, olive oil, lemon zest, lemon juice and hemp seeds; toss until well combined. Serve immediately or transfer to an airtight container and refrigerate for up to 5 days.

Simple Simmered Moroccan Chickpeas

This is a hearty, protein-dense dish. When you use your slow cooker to make it, it's ready and waiting for you when you arrive home after a long day of work.

MAKES 4 TO 6 SERVINGS

Tips

Buy whole organic spices when possible and grind your own as you need them. Fresh, flavorful spices are essential to creating great dishes. When you buy pre-ground spices, their essential oils dissipate over time and they lose their flavor.

Use either chickpeas you have cooked yourself (see page 182) or canned chickpeas, preferably with no salt added. When using canned legumes that contain salt, be sure to rinse and drain them thoroughly before using.

Do not lift the lid of your slow cooker while it is cooking. Each time you do, heat will escape and you'll need to add 20 to 30 minutes of cooking time to your recipe.

Medium (about 4 quart) slow cooker

2 tbsp	grapeseed oil	30 mL
½ cup	chopped onion	125 mL
½ cup	chopped celery	125 mL
½ cup	chopped carrot	125 mL
1 tsp	fine sea salt	5 mL
3 to 4	cloves garlic, minced	3 to 4
2 tsp	ground cumin	10 mL
1 tsp	chili powder	5 mL
¼ tsp	ground turmeric	1 mL
1	3-inch (7.5 cm) cinnamon stick	1
1	can (28 oz/796 mL) diced tomatoes, with juice	1
2 tbsp	wheat-free tamari	30 mL
1 tbsp	freshly squeezed lemon juice	15 mL
2 cups	drained cooked chickpeas (see Tips, left)	500 mL
½ cup	water	125 mL
1 cup	chopped red bell pepper	250 mL
	Chopped flat-leaf (Italian) parsley leaves	

1. In a large skillet over medium heat, heat oil. Add onion, celery, carrot and salt and cook, stirring frequently, until vegetables are tender, 5 to 6 minutes. Stir in garlic and cook for 2 minutes, until fragrant. Add cumin, chili powder, turmeric and cinnamon; cook, stirring frequently, for 2 to 3 minutes, until fragrant. Stir in tomatoes, tamari, lemon juice and cooked chickpeas and bring to a simmer. Transfer to slow cooker stoneware.

2. Add water, cover and cook on Low for 6 hours or High for 3 hours. Add red pepper and cook, covered, for 20 minutes more, until pepper is tender. Discard cinnamon stick. Garnish with parsley and serve immediately, or transfer to an airtight container and refrigerate for up to 1 week.

Thyme and Mushroom Navy Bean Ragoût

Serve this hearty ragoût over Creamy Mashed Potatoes (page 178), Basic Rice (page 212) or Polenta (page 230).

MAKES 4 SERVINGS

Tips

Substitute an equal amount of pinto beans for the navy beans.

To soak the beans: Place in a bowl and cover with 8 cups (2 L) water. Cover and set aside for at least 6 hours or overnight (if overnight, refrigerate). Drain, discarding water.

If you prefer, use your slow cooker to cook the beans for this recipe (Step 1; page 182).

If desired, substitute an equal amount of Vegetable Stock (page 559) for the wine.

Unsweetened store-bought almond milk will also work well in this recipe.

2 cups	navy beans, soaked (see Tips, left)	500 mL
½ tsp	fine sea salt, divided (see Tips, left)	2 mL
8 cups	water	2 L
¼ cup	melted coconut oil	60 mL
1 cup	finely chopped onion	250 mL
6 to 8	cloves garlic, minced	6 to 8
2 cups	quartered button mushrooms	500 mL
3 tbsp	brown rice flour	45 mL
¼ cup	chopped fresh thyme leaves	60 mL
¼ cup	dry white wine (see Tips, left)	60 mL
1 cup	Almond Milk (page 61; see Tips, left)	250 mL
½ cup	nutritional yeast, divided	125 mL
3 tbsp	wheat-free tamari	45 mL

1. In a large saucepan, combine soaked beans, ¼ tsp (1 mL) salt and water. Bring to a boil, then reduce heat and simmer until beans are tender, about 1 hour. Drain, discarding water. Set aside.

2. In a skillet over medium-high heat, heat coconut oil. Sauté onion until slightly golden, 7 to 8 minutes. Add garlic and cook, stirring, for 2 minutes, until fragrant. Add mushrooms and cook, stirring often, until soft and most of their liquid has evaporated.

3. Add rice flour and thyme and cook, stirring constantly, for about 4 minutes, until mixture is lightly golden. Stir in wine and cook until liquid has evaporated. Stir in almond milk and ¼ cup (60 mL) nutritional yeast and bring to a simmer. Cook, stirring, for 5 to 6 minutes or until mixture has thickened slightly. Add cooked beans and cook, stirring constantly, for about 2 minutes, until heated through.

4. Remove from heat and stir in remaining ¼ tsp (1 mL) salt, ¼ cup (60 mL) nutritional yeast and tamari. Serve immediately or let cool, transfer to an airtight container and refrigerate for up to 1 week. To reheat, place in a large skillet over medium heat and stir until heated through, about 5 minutes.

Navy Bean Ratatouille

This is my take on the traditional French stew of slow-cooked vegetables in a rich tomato broth. The addition of navy beans helps make this dish a complete meal, full of fiber and protein.

MAKES 4 SERVINGS

Tips

To soak the beans: Place in a bowl and cover with 8 cups (2 L) water. Cover and set aside for at least 6 hours or overnight (if overnight, refrigerate). Drain, discarding water.

If you prefer, use your slow cooker to cook the beans for this recipe (Step 1; page 182).

I like to add 4 cups (1 L) chopped peeled sweet potatoes along with the rest of the vegetables in Step 2. I find that the starch in the potatoes gives this dish a nice consistency, as well as a healthy carbohydrate component.

To chop fresh thyme: Pinch the stem at the bottom with two fingers. Pulling upward with the finger and thumb of your other hand, strip the leaves. Reserve stems for soups or broths (discard after cooking). Use a sharp knife to chop the leaves, being careful not to chop too much or too hard, as this will bruise the leaves and cause the thyme to discolor.

2 cups	navy beans, soaked (see Tips, left)	500 mL
8 cups	water	2 L
1 tsp	fine sea salt, divided	5 mL
3 tbsp	grapeseed oil	45 mL
6 to 8	cloves garlic	6 to 8
½ cup	chopped red onion	125 mL
½ cup	cut-up (1-inch/2.5 cm pieces) eggplant	125 mL
½ cup	quartered button mushrooms	125 mL
1	zucchini, cut into 1-inch (2.5 cm) pieces	1
1	tomato, cut into 1-inch (2.5 cm) pieces	1
1	can (14 to 19 oz/398 to 540 mL) tomato purée	1
3 tbsp	chopped fresh thyme leaves, divided (see Tips, left)	45 mL

1. In a large saucepan, combine soaked beans, water and ¼ tsp (1 mL) salt. Bring to a boil, then reduce heat and simmer until beans are tender, about 1 hour. Drain, discarding water.

2. In a skillet over medium-high heat, heat oil. Add garlic and cook, stirring constantly, until browned on all sides, about 4 minutes. Add onion, eggplant, mushrooms, zucchini and remaining salt. Increase heat to high and cook, stirring constantly, until vegetables are lightly caramelized, 8 to 10 minutes.

3. Add cooked beans, tomato, tomato purée and 1 tbsp (15 mL) thyme. Reduce heat and simmer for 30 minutes, stirring occasionally, until mixture has thickened slightly and is rich and fragrant. Stir in remaining 2 tbsp (30 mL) thyme.

4. Serve immediately or transfer to an airtight container and refrigerate for up to 1 week. To reheat, place in a saucepan over medium heat and stir until heated through, about 5 minutes.

Maple Baked Beans

For much of my childhood I enjoyed baked beans with a crunchy piece of toast. Now, as an adult making them for myself, I still enjoy them, but without any of the refined sugar or hidden ingredients.

MAKES 4 SERVINGS

Tips

To soak beans: Place in a bowl and cover with 4 cups (1 L) water. Cover and set aside for at least 3 hours or overnight (if overnight, refrigerate). Drain, discarding water.

Substitute an equal amount of kidney beans for the navy beans.

● **Large ovenproof pot with tight-fitting lid**

1 cup	navy beans, soaked (see Tips, left)	250 mL
4 cups	water	1 L
2 tbsp	grapeseed oil	30 mL
1 cup	finely chopped onion	250 mL
1 tsp	dry mustard	5 mL
2	cans (each 14 to 19 oz/398 to 540 mL) crushed tomatoes	2
½ cup	pure maple syrup	125 mL
¼ cup	light (fancy) molasses	60 mL
½ tsp	fine sea salt	2 mL

1. In a large saucepan, bring soaked beans and water to a boil. Reduce heat and simmer until beans are tender, about 45 minutes.
2. Preheat oven to 350°F (180°C).
3. Meanwhile, in ovenproof pot, heat oil over medium heat. Add onion and cook, stirring occasionally, until lightly golden, 5 to 6 minutes. Stir in mustard powder and cook for 1 to 2 minutes. Add tomatoes, maple syrup, molasses and salt, then bring to a boil.
4. Cover and cook on middle rack of preheated oven for 1 hour, until beans are thick and rich and most of the liquid has been absorbed. Serve immediately or transfer to an airtight container and refrigerate for up to 1 week. To reheat, place in a saucepan over medium heat and stir until heated through, about 5 minutes.

Black Bean Tortilla Bake

Serve this dish with a big dollop of Vegan Sour Cream (page 555), Roasted Red Pepper Mole Sauce (page 108) and a fresh green side salad.

MAKES ABOUT 6 SERVINGS

Tips

To soak the beans: Place in a bowl and cover with 12 cups (3 L) water. Cover and set aside for at least 6 hours or overnight (if overnight, refrigerate). Drain, discarding water.

If you prefer, use your slow cooker (page 182) to cook the beans for this recipe (Step 1).

The liquid that the beans are cooked in is sometimes referred to as the "liquor." Infused with starch from the breaking down of the beans during the cooking process, it can be used to help thicken sauces and give body to simmered dishes.

Choose organic tortillas to avoid GMOs, and check the label to make sure they are gluten-free and do not contain any added wheat.

• **Large ovenproof pot with tight-fitting lid**

3 cups	black beans, soaked (see Tips, left)	750 mL
12 cups	water	3 L
1 tsp	fine sea salt, divided	5 mL
2 tbsp	coconut oil	30 mL
1 cup	finely chopped onion	250 mL
½ cup	finely chopped sweet potato	125 mL
6 to 8	cloves garlic	6 to 8
2 tsp	chili powder	10 mL
1 tsp	ground cumin	5 mL
1	can (14 to 19 oz/398 to 540 mL) tomato purée	1
2 tbsp	freshly squeezed lemon juice	30 mL
12	6-inch (15 cm) gluten-free organic corn tortillas (see Tips, left)	12

1. In a large saucepan, combine soaked beans, water and ¼ tsp (1 mL) salt. Bring to a boil, then reduce heat and simmer until beans are tender, about 1 hour. Drain, reserving ½ cup (125 mL) cooking liquid (see Tips, left).

2. In ovenproof pot, melt coconut oil over medium-high heat. Add onion, sweet potato and garlic and cook, stirring occasionally, until onion is softened, 5 to 6 minutes. Add chili powder and cumin and cook for 2 to 3 minutes, stirring constantly.

3. Add cooked beans, tomato purée, lemon juice, remaining salt and reserved cooking liquid. Bring to a boil, reduce heat and simmer for 15 to 20 minutes or until mixture is reduced by half.

4. Preheat oven to 400°F (200°C).

5. Using your hands, tear tortillas into bite-size pieces. Stir into bean mixture. Cover and bake in preheated oven for 30 minutes. Serve immediately or let cool, transfer to an airtight container and refrigerate for up to 1 week. To reheat, place in a saucepan over medium heat and stir until heated through, about 5 minutes.

Italian-Style Red Bean Meatballs

Adding these tasty meatballs to a pasta dish will provide a protein kick that will leave you feeling full for hours.

MAKES 10 TO 12 MEATBALLS

Tips

To soak the beans: Place in a bowl and cover with 8 cups (2 L) water. Cover and set aside for at least 6 hours or overnight (if overnight, refrigerate). Drain, discarding water.

If you prefer, use your slow cooker to cook the beans for this recipe (Step 1).

I like to use kidney beans for this recipe, but an equal quantity of cranberry beans will also work well.

The quantity of garlic depends on the size of the cloves. If large, use the smaller number. If small, more may be required.

When roasting a whole head of garlic, use a serrated knife to cut off the top ¼ inch (0.5 cm) so the flesh of the cloves is exposed.

- Preheat oven to 325°F (160°C)
- 2 baking sheets, lined with parchment paper
- Food processor

4	heads garlic, tops removed (see Tips, left)	4
¼ cup	extra virgin olive oil	60 mL
8 cups	water (see Tips, page 207)	2 L
2 cups	red kidney beans, soaked (see Tips, left)	500 mL
1 tsp	fine sea salt, divided	5 mL
¼ cup	millet, rinsed and drained	60 mL
1½ cups	Vegetable Stock (page 559)	375 mL
1 tbsp	grapeseed oil	15 mL
1 cup	finely chopped onion	250 mL
6 to 8	cloves garlic, minced	6 to 8
½ cup	chopped fresh flat-leaf (Italian) parsley	125 mL
¼ cup	ground raw flax seeds	60 mL
2 tbsp	brown rice flour	30 mL

1. On a prepared baking sheet, toss garlic heads with olive oil. Bake in preheated oven for 45 minutes or until lightly golden and soft. Remove from oven and set aside to cool. Once cool, squeeze softened cloves from skins; set aside.

2. In a saucepan, combine water, beans and ¼ tsp (1 mL) salt. Bring to a boil, then reduce heat and simmer until beans are tender, about 1 hour. Drain, discarding water. Set aside to cool.

3. In another saucepan, combine millet and vegetable stock and bring to a boil. Reduce heat and simmer until millet is tender, about 20 minutes. Set aside to cool.

Substitute an equal amount of vegetable stock for the water.

Substitute an equal amount of white kidney beans for the red beans.

4. In a skillet over medium heat, heat grapeseed oil. Sauté onion until translucent, 5 to 6 minutes. Add garlic and cook, stirring occasionally, for 2 to 3 minutes, until fragrant. Remove from heat and set aside to cool.

5. Preheat oven to 400°F (200°C).

6. In food processor fitted with the metal blade, combine roasted garlic, cooked beans, cooked millet, onion mixture, remaining salt and parsley. Process until smooth, stopping the motor to scrape down sides of work bowl as necessary. Transfer to a large bowl. Add ground flax seeds and rice flour and mix well.

7. Using your hands and working with about $1/4$ cup (125 mL) of the mixture at a time, shape into balls; you should end up with 10 to 12 equal portions.

8. Place on prepared baking sheet and bake in preheated oven until "meatballs" are firm to the touch, lightly golden on the outside, and heated through, 12 to 15 minutes. Serve immediately or transfer to an airtight container and refrigerate for up to 1 week. To reheat, place on a rimmed baking sheet lined with parchment and warm in oven preheated to 350°F (180°C) until heated through, about 10 minutes.

Black Bean Burgers

These protein-dense burgers are a favorite for summertime grilling. Glaze them with Maple Chipotle Barbecue Sauce (page 111) and serve with a side of Quinoa Tabbouleh (page 219) or Maple Baked Beans (page 204).

MAKES ABOUT 8 BURGERS

Tips

To soak the beans: Place them in a bowl with 8 cups (2 L) water. Cover and set aside for at least 6 hours or overnight (if overnight, refrigerate). Drain, discarding water.

If you prefer, use your slow cooker to cook the beans for this recipe (Step 1; page 182).

If you don't have any ketchup on hand, you can substitute 1 cup (250 mL) tomato purée and 3 tbsp (45 mL) agave nectar. Add in Step 3 with tamari and cook until thickened.

Typically, millet is cooked in a covered pot. For normal use, I bring the water and rice to a rapid boil, reduce the heat and simmer until almost all the liquid has been absorbed. Then I remove the pot from the heat, cover and set aside for 10 to 15 minutes. This technique consistently produces beautiful results.

- **Food processor**
- **Baking sheet, lined with parchment paper**

9 cups	water, divided	2.25 L
2 cups	black beans, soaked (see Tips, left)	500 mL
½ cup	millet, rinsed and drained	125 mL
1 tbsp	grapeseed oil	15 mL
1	medium onion, thinly sliced	1
1 tsp	chili powder	5 mL
½ tsp	ground cumin	2 mL
¼ cup	ketchup (see Tips, left)	60 mL
3 tbsp	wheat-free tamari	45 mL
¼ cup	raw sunflower seeds	60 mL
½ cup	brown rice flour	125 mL
¼ cup	ground raw flax seeds (see Tips, page 209)	60 mL

1. In a large saucepan, combine 6 cups (1.5 L) water and beans and bring to a boil. Reduce heat and simmer until beans are tender, about 1 hour. Drain, discarding water. Transfer to a large bowl and set aside.

2. Meanwhile, in another saucepan, combine millet and 3 cups (750 mL) water and bring to a boil. Reduce heat and simmer, until millet is tender and almost all of the liquid has been absorbed about 15 minutes. Cover and set aside. Transfer to bowl with beans.

3. In a skillet over medium heat, heat oil. Sauté onion until lightly golden, 3 to 4 minutes. Stir in chili powder and cumin and cook for 1 to 2 minutes, until fragrant. Stir in ketchup and tamari and simmer for 2 to 3 minutes. Remove from heat and set aside to cool slightly. Add to reserved beans, along with millet and sunflower seeds. Toss to combine.

Tip

You can use either brown or golden flax seeds in this recipe. To grind the flax for this recipe, process 3 tbsp (45 mL) whole raw flax seeds to a powder in either a clean spice grinder or a blender.

4. Preheat oven to 400°F (200°C).

5. Transfer bean mixture to food processor fitted with the metal blade (reserve bowl) and process until smooth, stopping the motor to scrape down sides of work bowl as necessary. Return to bowl. Add rice flour and ground flax seeds and stir until well incorporated.

6. Dip a $\frac{1}{2}$-cup (125 mL) ladle or measuring cup in water, then scoop 8 equal portions of bean mixture onto prepared baking sheet, re-wetting ladle as necessary. Using your hands, form burgers to desired shape.

7. Bake in preheated oven for 15 to 20 minutes or until lightly golden on the bottom and firm in the middle. Serve immediately or transfer to an airtight container and refrigerate for up to 1 week. To reheat, place on a rimmed baking sheet lined with parchment, and warm in oven preheated to 350°F (180°C) until heated through, about 10 minutes.

Glazed Lentil Loaf

Serve this protein-dense dish with a big helping of Creamy Mashed Potatoes (page 178) and Holiday Gravy (page 558). Using a slow cooker to prepare this dish makes the loaf moist and tender.

MAKES 4 TO 6 SERVINGS

Tips

Substitute 4 cups (1 L) Basic Quinoa (page 235) for the cooked millet.

Substitute an equal amount of black lentils for the green lentils.

Wheat-free tamari is a gluten-free seasoning made from fermented soybeans. It can be found in most well-stocked supermarkets and natural food stores.

Typically millet is cooked in a covered pot. For normal use, I bring the water and millet to a rapid boil, uncovered, reduce the heat and simmer until almost all the liquid has been absorbed. Then I remove the pot from the heat, cover and set aside for 10 to 15 minutes. This technique consistently produces beautiful results.

To grind flax seeds: Place ¼ cup (60 mL) whole raw flax seeds in a blender or clean spice grinder and grind until flour-like in consistency. Transfer to an airtight container and refrigerate for up to 1 month.

- Food processor
- 8- by 4-inch (20 by 10 cm) loaf pan, greased
- Medium (about 4 quart) slow cooker

1 cup	millet, rinsed and drained (see Tips, left)	250 mL
	Water	
2 cups	dried green lentils, rinsed and drained (see Tips, left)	500 mL
2 tbsp	grapeseed oil	30 mL
½ cup	chopped carrot	125 mL
½ cup	chopped celery	125 mL
½ cup	chopped onion	125 mL
½ tsp	fine sea salt	2 mL
4 to 5	cloves garlic, minced	4 to 5
¼ cup	wheat-free tamari (see Tips, left)	60 mL
¼ cup	nutritional yeast	60 mL
2 tbsp	chopped fresh thyme leaves	30 mL
½ cup	brown rice flour	125 mL
¼ cup	ground raw golden flax seeds (see Tips, left)	60 mL
1 cup	Maple Chipotle Barbecue Sauce (page 111)	250 mL
2 cups	water	500 mL

1. In a large saucepan, combine millet and 3 cups (750 mL) water and bring to a boil. Reduce heat and simmer until millet is tender and almost all of the liquid has been absorbed, about 15 minutes. Remove from heat. Cover and set aside to cool.

2. Meanwhile, in another large saucepan, combine lentils and 4 cups (1 L) water and bring to a boil. Reduce heat and simmer until lentils are tender, about 20 minutes. Drain, discarding water. Set aside to cool.

Do not lift the lid of your
slow cooker while it is
cooking. Each time you
do, heat will escape and
you will need to add 20 to
30 minutes of cooking time
to your recipe.

Make ahead and store for
up to 1 week in an airtight
container in the refrigerator.

3. In a skillet over medium heat, heat oil. Add carrot, celery, onion and salt; cook, stirring frequently, until vegetables are tender, 5 to 6 minutes. Stir in garlic and cook until fragrant, 2 to 3 minutes. Remove from heat and stir in tamari, nutritional yeast and thyme.

4. In food processor fitted with the metal blade, combine half of the cooked millet, half of the cooked lentils and half of the vegetable mixture. Process until smooth, scraping down sides of work bowl as necessary. Transfer to a large bowl. Add remaining cooked millet, lentils and vegetables, along with rice flour and flax seeds; stir well.

5. Transfer mixture to prepared loaf pan. Spread barbecue sauce evenly overtop. Place pan in slow cooker stoneware. Pour water into slow cooker so that it surrounds the pan.

6. Cover and cook on Low for 6 hours or High for 3 hours. Remove pan from slow cooker and set aside to cool for 10 minutes. Turn out loaf, slice and serve.

Basic Rice

I have always found a big pot of warm rice very comforting on a cold night. You can use it to complement so many dishes: soups, stews, stir-fries or rice bowls. I love to serve it with Black Bean and Sweet Potato Chili (page 346), Stewed Lentils with Mushrooms and Sweet Potatoes (page 337) or Teriyaki Tofu (page 298).

MAKES 4 SERVINGS

Tips

Substitute an equal amount of short-grain white rice for the brown rice. Reduce the amount of water to 3½ cups (875 mL) and cook for 20 minutes, until tender.

For a more flavorful rice, substitute an equal amount of Vegetable Stock (page 559) for the water. I also like to add 1 to 2 tbsp (15 to 30 mL) nutritional yeast to the cooking liquid.

2 cups	short-grain brown rice, rinsed and drained (see Tips, below)	500 mL
4 cups	water	1 L
½ tsp	fine sea salt	2 mL

1. In a large saucepan, bring rice, water and salt to a boil. Reduce heat to low, cover and simmer for 45 minutes, until tender and almost all the liquid has been absorbed.

2. Remove from heat. Using a fork, gently fluff rice to separate the grains. Cover and set aside for 10 minutes so rice can absorb any remaining liquid. Serve immediately or let cool, transfer to an airtight container and refrigerate for up to 3 days.

Variation

Basic Herbed Rice: Add 1 tbsp (15 mL) chopped fresh thyme leaves and 1 bay leaf in Step 1. Once rice is cooked, fold in ½ cup (125 mL) chopped flat-leaf (Italian) parsley leaves.

Brown Sushi Rice

Traditionally sushi rice is made with refined white rice tossed with sweeteners, such as white sugar, and rice vinegar. To produce a more nutritious result, in this recipe I substitute short-grain brown rice for the white rice, agave nectar for the sugar, and apple cider vinegar for the rice vinegar. Use to make Sushi Wraps (page 94).

MAKES ENOUGH FOR ABOUT 4 SUSHI ROLLS

Tips

To soak the rice: Place in a bowl and cover with 4 cups (1 L) water. Cover and set aside for 1 hour. Drain, discarding water.

Typically, rice is cooked in a covered pot. For normal use, I bring the water and rice to a rapid boil, reduce the heat and simmer, until almost all the liquid has evaporated. Then I remove the pot from the heat, cover and set aside for 10 to 15 minutes. This technique consistently produces beautiful results.

Substitute an equal amount of brown rice vinegar for the apple cider vinegar.

For added texture and nutrition, add 1 tbsp (15 mL) each raw sesame seeds and raw shelled hemp seeds to cooked rice after it has cooled in Step 2. Stir to incorporate.

2½ cups	water	625 mL
1 cup	short-grain brown rice, rinsed and soaked (see Tips, left)	250 mL
½ tsp	fine sea salt	2 mL
¼ cup	raw (unpasteurized) apple cider vinegar (see Tips, left)	60 mL
3 tbsp	raw agave nectar	45 mL

1. In a saucepan over high heat, combine water, rice and salt; bring to a rapid boil. Reduce heat to low, stir once and cover with a tight-fitting lid. Cook for about 50 minutes or until rice is very tender and all the liquid has been absorbed.

2. Remove from heat. Set aside, covered, for 10 minutes so rice can absorb any remaining liquid. Transfer to a large bowl and set aside to cool slightly.

3. In a small bowl, whisk together vinegar and agave nectar. Pour over cooked rice. Using a spatula, stir until well incorporated. Set aside to cool completely. Use immediately or transfer to an airtight container and refrigerate for up to 3 days.

Jasmine Rice Salad

This salad is bursting with fresh, bold flavors. Enjoy with a glass of Matcha Me Green Juice (page 41) or Cucumber Aloe Watermelon Juice (page 40).

(page 41) ... (page 40)

MAKES 4 SERVINGS

Tips

Jasmine rice, also known as fragrant Thai rice, is a long-grain rice that originally came from Thailand. It is sweet and nutty in flavor and pairs well with Asian and Indian flavors.

Makrut (also known by the offensive term "kaffir") lime leaves are available in Indian, Chinese and Thai food stores, as well as some large supermarkets. They are pungent in flavor, so a little goes a long way — 1 or 2 leaves per dish is usually more than enough.

You do not need to cool the rice before adding the cilantro and remaining ingredients. The rice will absorb more flavor if they are added while it is still warm.

2 cups	water	500 mL
1 cup	brown jasmine rice	250 mL
½ tsp	fine sea salt, divided	2 mL
1	makrut lime leaf (see Tips, left)	1
½ cup	roughly chopped fresh cilantro leaves	125 mL
3 tbsp	toasted sesame oil	45 mL
1 tbsp	olive oil	15 mL
3 tbsp	freshly squeezed lime juice	45 mL
2 tbsp	rice wine vinegar	30 mL
1 tbsp	raw white sesame seeds	15 mL
1 tsp	puréed peeled gingerroot	5 mL

1. In a saucepan over high heat, combine water, rice, ¼ tsp (1 mL) salt and lime leaf; bring to a rapid boil. Reduce heat to low, stir once, cover with a tight-fitting lid and cook for 45 minutes, until tender.

2. Remove from heat. Using a fork, fluff rice, then cover and set aside for 10 minutes to absorb any remaining liquid.

3. In a large bowl, combine cooked rice, cilantro, sesame oil, olive oil, lime juice, vinegar, sesame seeds, ginger and remaining ¼ tsp (1 mL) salt; toss until well combined.

4. Cover and refrigerate for about 30 minutes. Serve immediately or transfer to an airtight container and refrigerate for up to 3 days.

Red Rice and Bean Salad

Red rice is similar to brown rice in flavor and nutritional value, and it's a delicious alternative. It adds color to this hearty rice and bean salad, which can be served warm or cold.

Tips

Substitute an equal amount of water for the vegetable stock.

Many varieties of red rice are available and all cook differently. This recipe was tested using Bhutanese red rice. If you use a different variety, the results will likely vary.

Use either black beans you have cooked yourself or well-rinsed canned beans, preferably with no salt added.

When purchasing canned foods, look for BPA-free products. BPA is often found in packaging materials and has been linked to various forms of hormone imbalance and cancer.

You do not need to cool the rice before adding the bean mixture. The grains will absorb more flavor if it is added while the rice is still warm.

2 cups	Vegetable Stock (page 559; see Tips, left)	500 mL
1 cup	Bhutanese red rice, rinsed and drained (see Tips, left)	250 mL
1 tsp	fine sea salt, divided	5 mL
2 cups	drained cooked black beans (see Tips, left)	500 mL
1 cup	chopped fresh flat-leaf (Italian) parsley	250 mL
½ cup	chopped tomato	125 mL
½ cup	finely chopped red bell pepper	125 mL
¼ cup	freshly squeezed lemon juice	60 mL
½ tsp	ground cumin	2 mL
½ tsp	chili powder	2 mL
Pinch	cayenne pepper	Pinch

1. In a saucepan over high heat, combine vegetable stock, rice and ½ tsp (2 mL) salt; bring to a boil. Reduce heat to low, stir once, cover with a tight-fitting lid and cook for about 45 minutes, until rice is tender and almost all the liquid has been absorbed.

2. Meanwhile, in a large bowl, toss together beans, parsley, tomato, red pepper, lemon juice, cumin, chili powder, cayenne and remaining ½ tsp (2 mL) salt.

3. Remove pan from heat. Using a fork, fluff rice, then cover and set aside for 10 minutes to absorb any remaining liquid.

4. Add cooked rice to bean mixture and toss to combine. Serve immediately or transfer to an airtight container and refrigerate for up to 3 days.

Indonesian Black Rice Salad

Black rice makes a great gluten-free substitute for many grains. It has a slightly chewy texture and a nutty flavor that pairs well with fresh herbs, vegetables and lemon juice.

MAKES 4 SERVINGS

Tips

Be sure to use Chinese black rice in this recipe. It is a medium-grain rice with a white kernel inside the black bran. When cooked, it is slightly chewy, has a nutty flavor and takes on a deep purplish color. Do not use Thai black sticky rice in this recipe. It is too glutinous.

Dried coconut can be purchased in fine, medium or large shreds. I like to use finely shredded coconut in most salads to keep the texture uniform.

A hand-held citrus reamer can be used to extract the juice from lemons and limes. Available in most kitchen supply stores, this tool would be ideal to use for the lime juice in this recipe.

To melt the coconut oil, gently warm it in a small skillet over low heat.

You do not need to cool the rice before adding the pineapple mixture. The grains will absorb more flavor if it is added while the rice is still warm.

4 cups	water	1 L
1 cup	Chinese black rice, rinsed and drained (see Tips, left)	250 mL
½ tsp	fine sea salt, divided	2 mL
½ cup	chopped red bell pepper	125 mL
½ cup	finely chopped pineapple	125 mL
½ cup	roughly chopped fresh cilantro leaves	125 mL
¼ cup	finely shredded unsweetened dried coconut (see Tips, left)	60 mL
3 tbsp	freshly squeezed lime juice (see Tips, left)	45 mL
3 tbsp	melted coconut oil (see Tips, left)	45 mL
½ tsp	chili powder	2 mL

1. In a large saucepan, combine water, rice and ¼ tsp (1 mL) salt; bring to a boil. Reduce heat and simmer for about 40 minutes until tender and almost all of the liquid has been absorbed.

2. Remove pan from heat. Using a fork, fluff rice, then cover and set aside for 10 minutes to absorb any remaining liquid. Transfer to a large bowl.

3. Add red pepper, pineapple, cilantro, coconut, lime juice, coconut oil, chili powder and remaining ¼ tsp (1 mL) salt; stir well. Serve immediately or transfer to an airtight container and refrigerate for up to 3 days.

Spicy African Millet Salad

High in vitamins and minerals, millet is a perfect grain to serve in place of rice or quinoa. In this salad it's tossed with fragrant spices for a simple but flavorful lunch or side dish.

MAKES 4 SERVINGS

Tips

When cooking the millet for this recipe, I like to cover the pan because it creates more of a "salad" texture.

A hand-held citrus reamer can be used to extract the juice from lemons and limes. Available in most kitchen supply stores, this tool would be ideal to use for the lemon juice in this recipe.

To toast whole spices: Heat a dry skillet over medium-high heat. Add spices and cook, rolling the pan to keep the spices moving, until they are fragrant and begin to smoke slightly. Transfer immediately to a heatproof bowl or container and let cool.

2 cups	water	500 mL
1 cup	millet, rinsed and drained	250 mL
1 tsp	fine sea salt	5 mL
¼ cup	extra virgin olive oil	60 mL
1 tsp	freshly grated lemon zest	5 mL
3 tbsp	freshly squeezed lemon juice (see Tips, left)	45 mL
1 tsp	ground cumin	5 mL
½ tsp	toasted caraway seeds (see Tips, left)	2 mL
½ tsp	toasted fenugreek seeds	2 mL
¼ tsp	ground coriander	1 mL
¼ tsp	smoked sweet paprika	1 mL
⅛ tsp	cayenne pepper	0.5 mL
Pinch	ground dried chile (optional)	Pinch

1. In a saucepan over medium heat, combine water, millet and salt and bring to a boil. Reduce heat to low, stir once and cover with a tight-fitting lid. Cook for about 20 minutes or until tender and almost all of the liquid has been absorbed (see Tips, left).

2. Remove from heat and stir once with a fork. Cover and set aside for 10 minutes so the millet can absorb any remaining liquid and swell.

3. In a large bowl, combine cooked millet, oil, lemon zest, lemon juice, cumin, caraway, fenugreek, coriander, paprika, cayenne and chile (if using); toss until well combined.

4. Serve immediately or transfer to an airtight container and refrigerate for up to 3 days.

Festive Millet Cranberry Salad

Tart and refreshing cranberries mixed with light, fluffy millet make this a perfect combination for any holiday dinner table.

Tips

To soak the cranberries, place in a bowl and cover with 3 cups (750 mL) water. Cover and set aside for 30 minutes. Drain, discarding water.

By choosing unsweetened organic cranberries, you can control the amount of sugar in your recipe and avoid the preservatives that are found in most dried fruit.

You do not need to cool the millet before adding the cranberry mixture. The grains will absorb more flavor if it is added while the millet is still warm.

2 cups	water	500 mL
1 cup	millet, rinsed and drained	250 mL
½ tsp	fine sea salt	2 mL
1 cup	unsweetened dried cranberries, soaked (see Tips, left)	250 mL
½ cup	chopped fresh flat-leaf (Italian) parsley	125 mL
2 tsp	freshly grated lemon zest	10 mL
3 tbsp	freshly squeezed lemon juice	45 mL
2 tbsp	extra virgin olive oil	30 mL

1. In a saucepan, combine water, millet and salt and bring to a boil. Reduce heat, cover with a tight-fitting lid and simmer for about 20 minutes, until millet is tender and almost all the liquid has been absorbed.

2. Remove from heat. Using a fork, fluff millet then cover, and set aside, for 10 minutes so millet can absorb any remaining liquid and swell.

3. Transfer millet to a large bowl. Add cranberries, parsley, lemon zest, lemon juice and oil; toss until well combined.

4. Serve immediately or transfer to an airtight container and refrigerate for up to 5 days.

Variation

Festive Orange Ginger Millet Salad: Omit the cranberries in Step 3. Substitute 2 cups (500 mL) chopped orange segments, 2 tbsp (30 mL) grated peeled gingerroot and ⅛ tsp (0.5 mL) ground allspice.

Quinoa Tabbouleh

Tabbouleh is a Middle Eastern classic traditionally made with bulgur. In this recipe the wheat is replaced by protein-rich quinoa and hemp seeds.

MAKES 5 TO 6 SERVINGS

Tips

To rinse quinoa: Place in a fine-mesh sieve under cool running water until the water runs clear.

The white part of green onions has a stronger flavor and is best reserved for cooking. The milder green part can be used either raw or in cooked dishes.

To remove the seeds from a tomato: Use a sharp knife to remove the core at the stem end. Slice the tomato into quarters from the top. Lay each quarter on its side and scrape lengthwise from top to bottom to remove the seeds.

Don't cool the quinoa before adding the parsley mixture. The grains will absorb more flavor if it is added while the quinoa is warm.

3 cups	water	750 mL
1½ cups	quinoa, rinsed and drained (see Tips, left)	375 mL
½ tsp	fine sea salt, divided	2 mL
1 cup	chopped fresh flat-leaf (Italian) parsley (about 1 bunch)	250 mL
½ cup	finely chopped red bell pepper	125 mL
½ cup	finely chopped green onions, green part only (see Tips, left)	125 mL
½ cup	finely chopped seeded tomato (see Tips, left)	125 mL
¼ cup	extra virgin olive oil	60 mL
3 tbsp	freshly squeezed lemon juice	45 mL

1. In a large saucepan, combine water, quinoa and ¼ tsp (1 mL) salt; bring to a boil. Reduce heat and simmer for about 15 minutes, until quinoa is tender and almost all the liquid has been absorbed. Cover and set aside for about 10 minutes so quinoa can absorb any remaining liquid and swell.

2. In a large bowl, combine cooked quinoa, parsley, red pepper, green onions, tomato, oil, lemon juice and remaining ¼ tsp (1 mL) salt; toss until well combined.

3. Serve immediately or transfer to an airtight container and refrigerate for up to 5 days.

Creamy Coconut Thai Quinoa Salad

The big, bold flavors of Thai cuisine pair well with soft quinoa, crisp shredded carrot and floral cilantro. This salad is perfect for a light snack or simple lunch or as part of a main course.

MAKES 4 SERVINGS

Tips

To rinse the quinoa: Place in a fine-mesh sieve under cold running water until the water runs clear.

Before measuring the coconut milk, stir it well to ensure that the cream and liquid are blended.

The stems on the leaves closest to the bottom of a sprig of fresh cilantro are generally tough and need to be removed. The stems on leaves closer to the top are softer.

For more protein, add 3 to 4 tbsp (45 to 60 mL) raw hulled hemp seeds in Step 2.

You do not need to cool the quinoa before adding the cilantro mixture. The grains will absorb more flavor if it is added while the quinoa is warm.

3½ cups	water	875 mL
2 cups	quinoa, rinsed and drained (see Tips, left)	500 mL
½ cup	canned full-fat coconut milk (see Tips, left)	125 mL
½ tsp	fine sea salt, divided	2 mL
1 cup	roughly chopped cilantro leaves (see Tips, left)	250 mL
½ cup	shredded carrot	125 mL
3 tbsp	freshly squeezed lime juice	45 mL
1 tsp	raw agave nectar	5 mL
Pinch	cayenne pepper	Pinch

1. In a saucepan, combine water, quinoa, coconut milk and ¼ tsp (1 mL) salt; bring to a boil. Reduce heat and simmer for about 15 minutes until quinoa is tender and almost all the liquid has been absorbed.

2. Remove from heat. Cover and set side for 10 minutes so the quinoa can absorb any remaining liquid and swell.

3. In a bowl, combine cooked quinoa, cilantro, carrot, lime juice, agave nectar and cayenne; toss until well combined. Serve immediately or transfer to an airtight container and refrigerate for up to 5 days.

Black-Eyed Peas and Rice

This Southern favorite is perfect for barbecues in the summer. It's great served with a side of Maple Baked Beans (page 204) and Roots and Sticks Juice (page 43).

MAKES 4 SERVINGS

Tips

Substitute an equal amount of Vegetable Stock (page 559) for the water.

Use either dried black-eyed peas you have soaked and cooked yourself or well-rinsed canned ones, preferably with no salt added.

I like to leave the onion in one piece during cooking. You can break it up when serving.

Nutritional yeast is an inactive yeast that has been grown on beet molasses and then pasteurized. It provides a rich, cheesy flavor in sauces, stews, soups and dips. Look for it in well-stocked supermarkets and natural food stores.

To make this dish a little spicier, add ¼ tsp (1 mL) cayenne pepper to the saucepan.

Substitute an equal amount of cooked kidney beans for the black-eyed peas.

2 cups	water (see Tips, left)	500 mL
1 cup	short-grain brown rice, rinsed and drained	250 mL
2 cups	cooked black-eyed peas (see Tips, left)	500 mL
½	onion	½
½ cup	nutritional yeast (see Tips, left)	125 mL
1 tsp	fine sea salt	5 mL
½ tsp	chili powder	2 mL
1	bay leaf	1

1. In a saucepan, combine water, rice, peas, onion, nutritional yeast, salt, chili powder and bay leaf. Bring to a rapid boil, stirring once to coat grains of rice with seasonings (stirring too much will cause starch to be released from the rice, making it sticky). Reduce heat to low and cover with a tight-fitting lid.

2. Cook for about 45 minutes or until rice is tender and most of the liquid has been absorbed. Remove from heat, stir once and set aside, uncovered, for 5 minutes.

3. Serve immediately or transfer to an airtight container and refrigerate for up to 3 days.

Dirty Brown Rice with Black Beans

Serve this dish with Southwest-inspired recipes such as burritos, tacos or enchiladas. For the best flavor, make sure the spices you use are as fresh as possible.

MAKES 4 SERVINGS

Tip

To cook the black beans: Place in a bowl and cover with 3 cups (750 mL) water. Cover and set aside for at least 6 hours or overnight (if overnight, refrigerate). Drain, discarding water. In a saucepan filled with water, bring soaked beans to a boil. Reduce heat and simmer until tender, about 1 hour. Or use your slow cooker (see page 182).

2 cups	diced tomatoes, with juice (about half a 28 oz/796 mL can)	500 mL
1½ cups	water	375 mL
1 cup	short-grain brown rice	250 mL
1 cup	cooked black beans (see Tip, left)	250 mL
½ cup	chopped onion	125 mL
1 tbsp	ground cumin	15 mL
2 tsp	chili powder	10 mL
2	cloves garlic, peeled	2
Pinch	cayenne pepper	Pinch

1. In a saucepan over high heat, combine tomatoes, water, rice, beans, onion, cumin, chili powder, garlic and cayenne; bring to a rapid boil. Reduce heat to low, stir once and cover with a tight-fitting lid. Cook for 45 minutes, until rice is tender.

2. Serve immediately or let cool, transfer to an airtight container and refrigerate for up to 3 days. To reheat, place in a saucepan with ¼ cup (60 mL) water. Bring to a simmer over medium heat and warm until heated through, about 5 minutes.

Sticky Brown Rice Balls

These delicious sticky rice balls are perfect served alongside Thai dishes or simply as a snack on their own. I love them with Coconut Curried Plantains and Okra (page 338) or Tom Yum Soup (page 324).

MAKES 8 SERVINGS

Tips

Soaking the rice helps the grains swell and makes the final product stickier and softer. To soak the rice, place in a bowl and cover with 4 cups (1 L) water. Cover and set aside for 45 minutes. Drain, discarding water.

I like to use brown rice vinegar in this dish to give it an Asian twist, but raw (unpasteurized) apple cider vinegar will work too.

5 cups	water	1.25 L
2 cups	short-grain brown rice, soaked (see Tips, left)	500 mL
1/2 tsp	fine sea salt, divided	2 mL
1/4 cup	raw agave nectar	60 mL
3 tbsp	brown rice vinegar (see Tips, left)	45 mL
1 tbsp	raw white sesame seeds	15 mL

1. In a saucepan, combine water, rice and 1/4 tsp (1 mL) salt; bring to a rapid boil. Cover with a tight-fitting lid, reduce heat to low and simmer for about 45 minutes, until rice is tender and most of the liquid has been absorbed. Transfer to a large bowl.

2. In a small bowl, whisk together agave nectar, vinegar, sesame seeds and remaining 1/4 tsp (1 L) salt. Pour mixture over rice and stir until well combined. Set aside for 30 minutes to cool.

3. Divide mixture into 8 equal portions. Using your hands, shape into balls. Serve immediately or transfer to an airtight container and refrigerate for up to 3 days.

Variation

Creamy Coconut Sticky Brown Rice Balls: Reduce the amount of water in Step 1 to 3 cups (750 mL) and add 2 cups (500 mL) full-fat coconut milk.

Creamy Coconut Brown Rice Cakes

Serve these rice cakes alongside spicy dishes — the coconut provides a cooling effect on the palate. I like to pair them with Spicy Tempeh and Squash (page 372) or Stuffed Zucchini Blossoms with Spicy Queso Dip (page 380).

MAKES 4 SERVINGS

Tips

Soaking the rice helps the grains swell and makes the final product stickier and softer. To soak the rice, place in a bowl and cover with 4 cups (1 L) water. Cover and set aside for 45 minutes. Drain, discarding water.

To serve hot, preheat oven to 400°F (200°C). Place rice cakes on a baking sheet lined with parchment paper and bake for 20 minutes or until crisp.

For extra flavor, I like to add about 1 tsp (5 mL) whole coriander seeds to the rice before cooking.

To make this recipe a bit lighter, reduce the amount of coconut milk to ½ cup (125 mL) and increase the amount of water to 3½ cups (875 mL).

- **Two 8-inch (20 cm) square metal baking pans, one lined with parchment paper**

2 cups	water	500 mL
2 cups	coconut milk (see Tips, left)	500 mL
2 cups	short-grain brown rice, soaked (see Tips, left)	500 mL
½ tsp	fine sea salt	2 mL
1	clove garlic	1

1. In a saucepan over high heat, combine water, coconut milk, rice, salt and garlic. Bring to a boil, reduce heat to low and stir once. Cover with a tight-fitting lid and cook for about 45 minutes, until rice is tender and almost all of the liquid has been absorbed. Discard garlic clove.

2. Spread cooked rice evenly over bottom of prepared baking pan. Place second pan on top of rice and press firmly to pack it down. Leave second pan in place and refrigerate until completely cool, about 2 hours.

3. Using parchment liner, lift mixture from pan. Cut rice into 4 equal squares. Serve cold or hot (see Tips, left). The rice cakes will keep for up to 3 days in an airtight container in the refrigerator.

Squash Stuffed with Brown Rice and Onions

I love the hearty texture of the cooked rice and slow-cooked squash in this dish. Serve it with some simple steamed greens such as kale or broccoli.

MAKES 2 SERVINGS

Tips

Nutritional yeast is an inactive yeast that has been grown on beet molasses and then pasteurized. It provides a rich, cheesy flavor in sauces, stews, soups and dips. Look for it in well-stocked supermarkets and natural food stores.

Acorn squash is mild-tasting and has a great texture. It is available year-round in most well-stocked supermarkets. Do not peel off the skin when using; it is edible and full of nutrients.

● **Baking sheet, lined with parchment paper**

2 cups	water	500 mL
1 cup	short-grain brown rice	250 mL
1 cup	chopped white onion	250 mL
1 cup	thinly sliced red onion	250 mL
½ cup	nutritional yeast (see Tips, left)	125 mL
½ tsp	fine sea salt	2 mL
1 tbsp	chopped fresh thyme leaves	15 mL
6 to 8	cloves garlic	6 to 8
1	acorn, buttercup or kabocha squash, halved and seeds removed (see Tips, left)	1

1. In a saucepan over high heat, combine water, rice, white onion, red onion, nutritional yeast, salt, thyme and garlic; bring to a boil. Reduce heat to low, stir once, cover with a tight-fitting lid and cook for 45 minutes, until rice is tender and almost all of the liquid has been absorbed.

2. Remove from heat, stir once or twice and set aside, covered, for 10 minutes to allow rice to absorb any remaining liquid.

3. Preheat oven to 400°F (200°C). Fill each squash half equally with the rice-and-onion mixture. Transfer stuffed squash to prepared baking sheet and bake until squash is tender, about 45 minutes.

4. Serve immediately or transfer to an airtight container and refrigerate for up to 3 days.

Simple Wild Rice Pilaf

This classic side dish is perfect for any holiday gathering. When chilled, it also makes a delicious salad for eating on the go.

Tip

Adding nutritional yeast to simmering water gives it a flavor similar to that of chicken stock. I like to add some to my soup broths and to cooking water for rice to give it more flavor.

4 cups	Vegetable Stock (page 559)	1 L
1 cup	wild rice, rinsed and drained	250 mL
½ cup	nutritional yeast (optional; see Tip, left)	125 mL
½ cup	finely chopped onion	125 mL
¼ cup	finely chopped celery	60 mL
1 tsp	fine sea salt	5 mL

1. In a large saucepan, combine vegetable stock, rice, nutritional yeast (if using), onion, celery and salt; bring to a boil. Reduce heat, cover with a tight-fitting lid, and simmer until rice is tender and most of the liquid has been absorbed, about 50 minutes. Drain and discard any excess water.
2. Serve immediately or transfer to an airtight container and refrigerate for up to 5 days.

Variation

Wild Rice Pilaf with Herbs: In a large saucepan, combine 2 cups (500 mL) wild rice, 4 cups (1 L) water and ½ tsp (2 mL) fine sea salt. Bring to a boil, reduce heat and simmer for about 50 minutes or until kernels begin to burst. Drain, discarding any excess water. Transfer to a bowl. Fold in ½ cup (125 mL) roughly chopped Italian parsley leaves, 1 tbsp (15 mL) chopped fresh thyme leaves and 1 tsp (5 mL) chopped rosemary leaves. Serve immediately or transfer to an airtight container and refrigerate for up to 5 days.

Mushroom Wild Rice Pilaf

This rich and warming dish is one of my favorite recipes to make during the fall and winter months. I love the crunch and slight nuttiness of wild rice paired with savory roasted mushrooms. The addition of nutritional yeast and tahini provides creaminess that is reminiscent of risotto.

MAKES 4 SERVINGS

Tips

If you do not have any vegetable stock, substitute an equal amount of water.

Button mushrooms work well for this recipe, but any variety of mushroom will do. I like to use a mixture of button, cremini, shiitake and chanterelle mushrooms.

Never clean mushrooms with water. Washing mushrooms can make them turn brown and soggy. Simply brush off any dirt with a clean, damp cloth.

I like to use Chardonnay for this recipe, but any dry white wine will work.

Wheat-free tamari is a gluten-free seasoning made from fermented soybeans. It can be found in most well-stocked supermarkets and natural food stores.

3 tbsp	coconut oil	45 mL
8 cups	sliced mushrooms (see Tips, left)	2 L
1 cup	finely chopped onion	250 mL
6 to 8	cloves garlic, minced	6 to 8
2 cups	wild rice, rinsed and drained	500 mL
½ cup	dry white wine (optional; see Tips, left)	125 mL
6 cups	Dark Vegetable Stock (page 559)	1.5 L
½ cup	nutritional yeast	125 mL
3 tbsp	tahini	45 mL
2 tbsp	wheat-free tamari (see Tips, left)	30 mL
2 tbsp	chopped fresh thyme leaves	30 mL

1. In a large saucepan over medium-high heat, melt coconut oil. Sauté mushrooms until browned and most of the liquid has evaporated, about 10 minutes. Using a slotted spoon, transfer mushrooms to a bowl. Add onion to pan and cook, stirring occasionally, until translucent, about 3 minutes. Stir in garlic and cook for 1 to 2 minutes, until fragrant.

2. Add wild rice and cook, stirring constantly, for 4 to 5 minutes, until rice is fragrant and toasted. Stir in white wine (if using) and cook until liquid has evaporated.

3. Add vegetable stock and bring to a rapid boil. Cover, reduce heat to low and simmer until stock has been absorbed and rice is tender, about 50 minutes.

4. Remove from heat and stir in nutritional yeast, tahini, tamari and thyme. Serve immediately or transfer to an airtight container and refrigerate for up to 5 days.

Chipotle Walnut Mushroom and Rice Burgers

These burgers are perfect for summer barbecues or get-togethers. I love serving them with Maple Chipotle Barbecue Sauce (page 111), on a crusty bun with lettuce, tomato and pickles.

MAKES 8 BURGERS

Tips

Nutritional yeast is an inactive yeast that has been grown on beet molasses and then pasteurized. It provides a rich, cheesy flavor in sauces, stews, soups and dips. Look for it in well-stocked supermarkets and natural food stores.

The quantity of garlic depends on the size of the cloves. If large, use the smaller number. If small, more may be required.

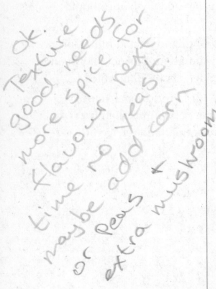

Food processor

5 cups	water	1.25 L
2 cups	short-grain brown rice, rinsed and drained	500 mL
¼ cup	nutritional yeast (see Tips, left)	60 mL
½ tsp	fine sea salt, divided	2 mL
6 tbsp	grapeseed oil, divided	90 mL
1 cup	finely chopped onion	250 mL
6 to 8	cloves garlic, minced	6 to 8
3 cups	thinly sliced mushrooms (see Tip, page 229)	750 mL
2 tsp	chipotle powder	10 mL
½ cup	tomato purée	125 mL
4 cups	raw walnuts	1 L
¼ cup	ground raw golden flax seeds	60 mL
	Burger trimmings, such as sliced tomato, onion, lettuce, optional	
	Gluten-free hamburger buns, optional	

1. In a saucepan over medium heat, combine water, rice, nutritional yeast and ¼ tsp (1 mL) salt. Cover with a tight-fitting lid and bring to a rapid boil. Reduce heat to low and cook for about 50 minutes, until rice is tender and almost all of the liquid has been absorbed. Using a fork, fluff rice, then cover and set aside for 10 minutes to absorb any remaining liquid.

2. In a skillet over medium heat, heat 3 tbsp (45 mL) oil. Add onion and remaining salt and sauté for about 5 minutes. Stir in garlic and cook for 2 minutes, until fragrant. Add mushrooms and chipotle powder and cook, stirring frequently, until most of the liquid has evaporated, about 10 minutes. Stir in tomato purée and simmer until mixture is slightly thickened, about 3 minutes.

Tip
──

Choose portobello,
cremini or white button
mushrooms for this recipe.
Their dense texture will
give the burgers body.

3. In food processor fitted with the metal blade, combine cooked rice, mushroom mixture and walnuts. Process until mostly smooth (small pieces of rice and walnut are fine).

4. Transfer to a large bowl. Stir in ground flax seeds until well incorporated. Using a $1/2$-cup (125 mL) measuring cup, divide mixture into 8 equal portions. With your hands, form into desired burger shape.

5. In a non-stick skillet over medium heat, heat 2 tbsp (30 mL) grapeseed oil. Cook burgers in batches, adding more oil as necessary, for about 3 minutes per side, until golden brown. Alternatively, cook on a baking sheet lined with parchment paper in a preheated 400°F (200°C) oven for 8 to 10 minutes, until golden brown, turning halfway through.

6. Serve immediately, on buns with trimmings if desired, or transfer to an airtight container and let cool. Refrigerate for up to 3 days or freeze for up to 2 months.

Polenta

Polenta is a classic and naturally gluten-free accompaniment to so many dishes. Try it with Coconut Curried Plantains and Okra (page 338), Eggplant, Lentil and Tomato Chili (page 345) or Sicilian Eggplant Caponata (page 140).

(page 338), (page 345), (page 140)

MAKES 6 SERVINGS

Tips

For a firmer polenta, decrease the amount of water to 4 cups (1 L).

Make sure to purchase organic cornmeal. Most corn is grown from genetically engineered seeds, so it is particularly important to buy organic.

5 cups	water (see Tips, left)	1.25 L
1 tsp	fine sea salt	5 ml
1 cup	medium or fine stone-ground organic yellow cornmeal (see Tips, left)	250 mL

1. In a large saucepan, bring water and salt to a rapid boil. In a slow, steady stream, pour cornmeal into water while whisking. Bring to a boil, whisking constantly. Reduce heat and simmer for 30 to 45 minutes, stirring often with a wooden spoon to ensure that cornmeal is not sticking to sides of pan or drying out. If necessary, add $1/2$ cup (125 mL) water to help loosen mixture. (Polenta should taste like corn and have a creamy, not gritty, consistency.)

2. Serve immediately or let cool and refrigerate in an airtight container for up to 1 week.

Variations

After the polenta is cooked, transfer it to molds or spread evenly in a baking dish and let cool. Cooled polenta can be cut into various shapes and roasted, pan-seared or even deep-fried. Use as a base for a canapés with toppings such as Vegan Sour Cream (page 555) and some thinly sliced green onion, or Herbed Tofu Ricotta (page 530) topped with Caramelized Onion and Cherry Tomato Relish (page 138).

Creamy Citrus Polenta

This recipe is a great addition to any summer meal and a lovely snack on its own. The bright citrus notes of lemon, lime and grapefruit add a nice flavor to the creamy polenta.

Tips

To make a smooth cornmeal and to reduce the cooking time slightly, use medium or finely ground cornmeal. Coarsely ground cornmeal will work, but it needs to be cooked for about 10 minutes longer, and the final product will not be as smooth.

A hand-held citrus reamer can be used to extract the juice from lemons and limes. Available in most kitchen supply stores, this tool would be ideal to use for the citrus in this recipe.

To melt the coconut oil, gently warm it in a small skillet over low heat.

3 cups	Almond Milk (page 61)	750 mL
¾ cup	medium stone-ground organic cornmeal (see Tips, left)	175 mL
1 tbsp	freshly grated lime zest	15 mL
2 tsp	freshly grated lemon zest	10 mL
1 tsp	freshly grated grapefruit zest	5 mL
2 tbsp	freshly squeezed lime juice (see Tips, left)	30 mL
1 tbsp	freshly squeezed lemon juice	15 mL
2 tbsp	melted coconut oil (see Tips, left)	30 mL
½ tsp	fine sea salt	2 mL

1. In a saucepan over medium heat, bring almond milk to a boil. Add cornmeal in a slow, steady stream and cook, stirring constantly, for about 5 minutes. Reduce heat to low and cook, stirring every few minutes, until polenta has thickened and begins to pull away from sides of pan, about 15 minutes.

2. Remove from heat and stir in lime zest, lemon zest, grapefruit zest, lime juice, lemon juice, coconut oil and salt. Serve immediately or let cool and refrigerate in an airtight container for up to 1 week.

Teff "Polenta" Cakes

Teff is an African grain that has a deep nutty flavor and is high in nutrients. I like to serve this recipe with Classic Garlicky Tomato Sauce (page 110) and some lightly sautéed greens such as kale or spinach.

MAKES 4 CAKES

Tips

Substitute an equal amount of water for the vegetable stock.

Nutritional yeast is an inactive yeast that has been grown on beet molasses and then pasteurized. It provides a rich, cheesy flavor in sauces, stews, soups and dips. Look for it in well-stocked supermarkets and natural food stores.

• **8-inch (20 cm) square glass baking dish, lined with parchment paper**

4 cups	Vegetable Stock (page 559; see Tips, left)	1 L
½ cup	nutritional yeast, divided (see Tips, left)	125 mL
1 tsp	garlic powder	5 mL
1 cup	teff	250 mL
2 tbsp	Whipped Non-dairy Butter (page 554)	30 mL
¼ tsp	fine sea salt	1 mL
2 tbsp	grapeseed oil	30 mL

1. In a large saucepan over high heat, combine vegetable stock, ¼ cup (60 mL) nutritional yeast and garlic powder. Bring to a boil.

2. In a slow, steady stream, whisk teff into boiling broth. Reduce heat to low and cook, stirring frequently, until teff is tender and there are no lumps, about 25 minutes. Remove from heat and stir in remaining ¼ cup (60 mL) nutritional yeast, butter and salt.

3. Spread mixture evenly in prepared baking dish and set aside until completely cool, then cover and refrigerate for 3 hours or overnight.

4. Using parchment liner, lift from pan. With a sharp knife, cut into 4 equal portions.

5. In a skillet over medium-high heat, heat oil. Cook teff cakes for 3 to 4 minutes per side, until golden brown. Serve immediately or transfer to an airtight container and refrigerate for up to 1 week. To reheat, place on a rimmed baking sheet lined with parchment paper in a 350°F (180°C) oven and heat until warmed through, about 12 minutes.

Millet Croquettes

I love millet for its versatility in the kitchen. This recipe is a perfect example of what can be done by slightly overcooking the grain and then forming it into cakes. I like to serve this with African-Spiced Tempeh Chili (page 348) or Ratatouille (page 333).

MAKES 6 SERVINGS

Tips

Millet tends to stick to the bottom of the pan when cooking. To help avoid this, reduce the heat to very low when simmering, and stir frequently with a wooden spoon.

I like to add chopped fresh herbs such as thyme, basil or rosemary to add flavor to cooked millet. You can also stir in chopped or shredded vegan cheese while the millet is still hot — try adding ½ cup (125 mL) Cashew Cheddar Cheese (page 535).

3 cups	water	750 mL
1 cup	millet, rinsed and drained	250 mL
½ tsp	fine sea salt, divided	2 mL
½ cup	nutritional yeast (see Tips, page 232)	125 mL
1 tbsp	chopped fresh thyme leaves	15 mL
2 to 3 tbsp	grapeseed oil	30 to 45 mL

1. In a saucepan, combine water, millet and ¼ tsp (1 mL) salt; bring to a boil. Reduce heat and simmer, stirring frequently, until porridge-like in consistency, about 15 minutes (see Tips, left).

2. Transfer to a bowl and stir in remaining ¼ tsp (1 mL) salt, nutritional yeast and thyme. Set aside until cool.

3. Using a ½-cup (125 mL) measure, divide mixture into 6 equal portions and, using your hands, form into patties.

4. In a skillet over medium heat, heat 2 tbsp (30 mL) of the oil. Add croquettes in batches and cook until golden brown on the bottom, 2 to 3 minutes, adding more oil as necessary. Flip and cook until other side is golden brown. Serve immediately or let cool, transfer to an airtight container and refrigerate for up to 1 week.

Amaranth and Millet Balls

This recipe is a great stand-in for the meatballs traditionally served with spaghetti. They are also good in baked pasta dishes with tomato sauce.

**MAKES ABOUT
20 BALLS**

Tips

Typically whole grains such as amaranth and millet are cooked in a covered pot. For normal use, I bring the water and grain(s) to a rapid boil, reduce the heat and simmer, uncovered, until almost all the liquid has evaporated. Then I remove the pot from the heat, cover and set aside for 10 to 15 minutes. This technique consistently produces beautiful results. In this recipe, to ensure that the grains hold together in the balls, I have increased both the quantity of liquid and the cooking time.

The quantity of garlic depends on the size of the cloves. If large, use the smaller number. If small, more may be required.

Use a sharp knife for chopping fresh herbs to help prevent them from bruising and turning brown.

Baking sheet, lined with parchment paper

1 cup	millet, rinsed and drained	250 mL
1 cup	amaranth, rinsed and drained	250 mL
8 cups	Vegetable Stock (page 559)	2 L
½ tsp	fine sea salt, divided	2 mL
2 tbsp	grapeseed oil	30 mL
1 cup	finely chopped onion	250 mL
6 to 8	cloves garlic, minced	6 to 8
1 tbsp	chopped fresh rosemary leaves (see Tips, left)	15 mL
1 tbsp	chopped fresh thyme leaves	15 mL
3 tbsp	ground raw flax seeds	45 mL
⅔ cup	hot water	150 mL
1 to 2 tbsp	brown rice flour	15 to 30 mL

1. In a saucepan, combine millet, amaranth, vegetable stock and ¼ tsp (1 mL) salt; bring to a boil. Reduce heat and simmer, stirring frequently, for about 30 minutes, until tender.

2. Using a fine-mesh sieve, drain millet and amaranth. Transfer to a large bowl and set aside.

3. Meanwhile, in a skillet over medium heat, heat oil. Add onion and remaining salt and cook, stirring frequently, until lightly golden, 8 to 10 minutes. Stir in garlic and cook until fragrant, 2 to 3 minutes. Remove from heat and set aside to cool.

4. Add onion mixture, rosemary and thyme to millet and amaranth and stir well. Set aside.

5. In a small bowl, whisk together ground flax seeds and hot water. Set aside for 10 minutes so the flax can absorb the liquid and swell (see Tip, page 235).

Flax seeds make a good substitute for egg when binding ingredients. For the equivalent of 1 egg, combine 1 tbsp (15 mL) ground flax seeds with 3 tbsp (45 mL) hot water. Set aside for 5 minutes so the flax can absorb the liquid and swell.

6. Preheat oven to 350°F (200°C). Add flaxseed mixture and 1 tbsp (15 mL) rice flour to amaranth and millet mixture. Stir until well combined. The mixture should not stick to your hands when rolling it into balls; if it is too sticky, stir in an additional 1 tbsp (15 mL) brown rice flour.

7. Working with about ¼ cup (60 mL) of the mixture at a time, roll into equal-sized balls and place on prepared baking sheet.

8. Bake in preheated oven for 18 to 20 minutes, or until lightly golden and hot in the center. Remove from oven and set aside to cool slightly to firm up. Serve immediately. These balls will keep for up to 5 days in an airtight container in the refrigerator.

Basic Quinoa

Soft, fluffy cooked quinoa can replace rice in nearly every application. Besides being a complete protein, quinoa is packed full of nutrition and can be enjoyed for breakfast, lunch or dinner.

**MAKES
2 CUPS (500 ML)**

Tip

There are several types of quinoa, but I prefer to use white or pearl quinoa because it cooks up light and fluffy. Both red and black quinoa are a little denser and more chewy, making them great for use in salads.

2 cups	water	500 mL
1 cup	quinoa, rinsed and drained (see Tip, left)	250 mL
½ tsp	fine sea salt	2 mL

1. In a saucepan, combine water, quinoa and salt and bring to a boil, uncovered. Reduce heat and simmer for 12 to 15 minutes, or until tender and almost all of the liquid has been absorbed. Remove from heat. Cover and set aside for 10 minutes so quinoa can absorb any remaining liquid and swell.

2. Serve immediately or let cool, transfer to an airtight container and refrigerate for up to 5 days.

Quinoa-Crusted Onion Rings

The quinoa in this recipe provides a crunchy coating for the soft, gooey thick-cut onions underneath.

Tips

Traditionally when making onion rings, the onions are marinated in buttermilk before being cooked. The acid in the buttermilk helps to break down the onions and soften them. The mixture of almond milk and lemon juice in this recipe does the same thing.

A hand-held citrus reamer can be used to extract the juice from lemons and limes. Available in most kitchen supply stores, this tool would be ideal to use for the lemon juice in this recipe.

• 2 baking sheets, lined with parchment paper

2	large Vidalia onions, peeled	2
3 cups	Almond Milk (page 61)	750 mL
¼ cup	freshly squeezed lemon juice (see Tips, left)	60 mL
1 tsp	fine sea salt, divided	5 mL
¾ cup	brown rice flour	175 mL
½ cup	quinoa (uncooked)	125 mL
½ cup	medium stone-ground organic cornmeal	125 mL
1 tbsp	garlic powder	15 mL
1 tsp	sweet paprika	5 mL
½ tsp	freshly ground black pepper	2 mL
3 tbsp	grapeseed oil	45 mL

1. Slice onions into 1-inch (2.5 cm) thick rounds. Using your fingers, separate the rounds into rings and transfer to a large bowl.

2. Pour almond milk and lemon juice over onion rings and sprinkle with ½ tsp (2 mL) salt. Toss to combine. Set aside for 1 hour to marinate, stirring 2 or 3 times to ensure equal marination.

3. Meanwhile, in another bowl, whisk together rice flour, quinoa, cornmeal, garlic powder, paprika, remaining ½ tsp (2 mL) salt and pepper. Set aside.

4. Preheat oven to 400°F (200°C). Using a fine-mesh sieve, drain onions, discarding liquid. Transfer to a large bowl. Drizzle with grapeseed oil and toss to coat. Add rice-flour mixture and toss until evenly coated.

5. Arrange in a single layer on prepared baking sheets. Bake in preheated oven on upper and lower racks, for 25 to 30 minutes or until golden brown, switching racks and turning onion rings halfway through to ensure even baking. Serve immediately.

Seared Quinoa Cakes

These crispy cakes make a perfect finger food for parties. Serve with Queso Dip (page 82), Roasted Red Pepper Mole Sauce (page 108) or Roasted Garlic Chimichurri (page 109).

Tips

Quinoa can be purchased in white, black or red varieties. White quinoa, also called "royal quinoa," is a little softer in texture and mellow in flavor when cooked. Both the red and black varieties are slightly denser and more chewy when cooked and have a nuttier flavor. I like to use red or black quinoa for salads and white quinoa as an all-purpose grain.

Overcooking the quinoa and using more water than usual helps the cakes hold together.

2 1/2 cups	water	625 mL
1 cup	quinoa, rinsed and drained (see Tips, left)	250 mL
1/2 tsp	fine sea salt, divided	2 mL
1/4 cup	ground raw flax seeds	60 mL
2 tbsp	tahini	30 mL
1 tsp	chopped fresh thyme leaves	5 mL
1/2 tsp	freshly grated lemon zest	2 mL
1/4 cup	grapeseed oil, divided	60 mL

1. In a saucepan, combine water, quinoa and 1/4 tsp (1 mL) salt; bring to a boil. Reduce heat and simmer until tender and almost all of the liquid has been absorbed, about 15 minutes. Cover and set aside so quinoa can absorb any remaining liquid and swell.

2. In a large bowl, toss together cooked quinoa, ground flax seeds, tahini, thyme and lemon zest. Using a 1/4-cup (60 mL) measuring cup, divide mixture into 8 equal portions. With your hands, form each portion into a firm cake.

3. In a skillet over medium heat, heat 2 tbsp (30 mL) oil. Working with 4 quinoa cakes at a time, cook for 6 to 8 minutes on each side, until golden brown. Transfer to a plate and cover to keep warm. Repeat with remaining cakes, adding more oil as necessary. Serve immediately.

Quinoa Sweet Potato Burgers

These delicious burgers can be enjoyed on their own or sandwiched in your favorite gluten-free bun with toppings of choice.

MAKES 8 BURGERS

Tips

Overcooking the quinoa and using more water than usual helps the burgers hold together.

Substitute an equal amount of squash for the sweet potato in this recipe.

To grind the flax for this recipe: Place ½ cup (125 mL) raw golden flax seeds in a high-powered blender or clean spice grinder; grind into a powder.

It's fine to use brown flax seeds for this recipe, but keep in mind that they will make the burgers darker than if using golden flax seeds.

● **Baking sheet, lined with parchment paper**

2 cups	quinoa, rinsed and drained	500 mL
	Water	
2 cups	cubed (1 inch/2.5 cm) peeled sweet potatoes (see Tips, left)	500 mL
1 tsp	fine sea salt, divided	5 mL
¾ cup	ground raw golden flax seeds (see Tips, left)	175 mL
2 tbsp	tahini	30 mL
1 tbsp	chopped fresh thyme leaves	15 mL
2 tsp	freshly grated lemon zest	10 mL

1. In a saucepan, combine quinoa, 4½ cups (1 L) water and a pinch of salt; bring to a boil. Reduce heat and simmer for 12 to 15 minutes, uncovered until quinoa is tender and almost all of the liquid has been absorbed. Remove from heat and cover with a tight-fitting lid. Set aside for 10 minutes so quinoa can absorb any remaining liquid and swell.

2. Meanwhile, in another saucepan, combine 4 cups (1 L) water, sweet potatoes and a pinch of salt; bring to a boil. Cook until potatoes are tender, about 15 minutes. Drain, discarding liquid. Transfer to a large bowl and set aside for 10 to 15 minutes or until cool enough to handle.

3. Preheat oven to 350°F (180°C).

4. To sweet potato, add cooked quinoa, ground flax seeds, tahini, thyme, lemon zest and remaining salt. Stir well (mixture should hold its shape when pressed together).

5. Using a ½-cup (125 mL) measuring cup, divide mixture into 8 equal portions. Using your hands, form each portion into a patty and transfer to prepared baking sheet. Bake in preheated oven for 10 to 12 minutes or until burgers are heated through. Serve immediately or transfer to an airtight container and refrigerate for up to 1 week.

Squash and Herb Baked Oats

This recipe is the perfect fall side dish with roasted root vegetables and fresh greens. I like to serve it with Simple Simmered Moroccan Chickpeas (page 201) or Slow-Cooked Barbecued Jackfruit (page 369).

MAKES 4 SERVINGS

Tips

For the butternut squash, substitute an equal amount of sweet potato, pumpkin or other varieties of squash such as kabocha or buttercup.

To chop fresh thyme: Pinch the stem at the bottom with two fingers. Pulling upward with the finger and thumb of your other hand, strip the leaves. Reserve stems for soups or broths (discard after cooking). Use a sharp knife to chop the leaves, being careful not to chop too much or too hard as this will bruise the leaves and cause the thyme to discolor.

- Preheat oven to 350°F (180°C)
- Ovenproof saucepan with tight-fitting lid

2 tbsp	grapeseed oil	30 mL
2 cups	chopped peeled butternut squash (see Tips, left)	500 mL
1 cup	chopped onion	250 mL
4 to 5	cloves garlic, minced	4 to 5
4 cups	water	1 L
2 cups	gluten-free steel-cut oats	500 mL
1 tsp	fine sea salt	5 mL
¼ cup	chopped fresh thyme leaves (about 1 bunch; see Tips, left)	60 mL
¼ cup	chopped fresh chives	60 mL

1. In a skillet over medium heat, heat oil. Add squash and onion and cook until onion is translucent, 3 to 4 minutes. Stir in garlic and cook for about 2 minutes, until fragrant.

2. Meanwhile, in saucepan, combine water, oats and salt and bring to a boil.

3. Add onion mixture to oats. Add thyme and chives and stir to combine.

4. Cover and bake in preheated oven for 45 minutes, until oats are soft and most of the liquid has been absorbed. Remove from oven and set aside for 15 minutes to cool. Serve immediately or let cool, transfer to an airtight container and refrigerate for up to 1 week.

Variation

Coconut and Cinnamon Squash Baked Oats: Omit garlic, onions, thyme and chives. When the oats have come to a boil (Step 2), stir in ½ cup (125 mL) coconut sugar, 1 tsp (5 mL) ground cinnamon and 2 tbsp (30 mL) melted coconut oil. Skip Step 1 and 3. Complete Step 4. This version is sweet, but delicious. I enjoy it for breakfast, but it is a real treat any time of the day.

Baked Chickpea Fritters

I love to serve these crispy little fritters with a side of Miso Tahini Sauce (page 121) or Roasted Garlic Chimichurri (page 109).

(page 121) or Roasted Garlic Chimichurri (page 109).

MAKES ABOUT 8 FRITTERS

Tips

To cook the chickpeas: Place in a bowl and cover with 4 cups (1 L) water. Cover and set aside for at least 6 hours or overnight (if overnight, refrigerate). Drain, discarding liquid. In a large pot of water, bring soaked chickpeas to a boil. Reduce heat and simmer until tender, about 1 hour. You can also cook the chickpeas in your slow cooker (see page 182).

You can substitute the chickpea flour in this recipe with a mixture of ½ cup (125 mL) coconut flour, ¼ cup (60 mL) tapioca starch and ¼ cup (60 mL) brown rice flour.

Nutritional yeast is inactive yeast that has been grown on beet molasses and then pasteurized. It provides a rich, cheesy flavor to sauces, stews, soups and dips. Look for it in well-stocked supermarkets and natural food stores.

- Preheat oven to 400°F (200°C)
- Food processor
- Baking sheet, lined with parchment paper

1 cup	drained cooked chickpeas, divided (see Tips, left)	250 mL
1 cup	chickpea flour (see Tips, left)	250 mL
⅓ cup	nutritional yeast (see Tips, left)	75 mL
1 tsp	fine sea salt	5 mL
1 cup	water	250 mL
2 tbsp	ground raw flax seeds	30 mL
½ cup	thinly sliced red bell pepper	125 mL
½ cup	thinly sliced zucchini	125 mL
¼ cup	thinly sliced red onion	60 mL

1. In food processor fitted with the metal blade, process ½ cup (125 mL) cooked chickpeas until roughly chopped. Add chickpea flour, nutritional yeast and salt; process until well incorporated. With the motor running, drizzle water through the feed tube and process until a smooth paste forms.

2. Transfer mixture to a large bowl. Add ground flax seeds and remaining ½ cup (125 mL) chickpeas; stir well. Cover and set aside for about 5 minutes so flax can absorb some of the liquid and swell.

3. Stir in red pepper, zucchini and red onion. Using a ¼-cup (60 mL) measuring cup, drop about 8 equal portions onto prepared baking sheet.

4. Bake in preheated oven until crisp and golden and hot in the center, about 20 minutes. Fritters will keep for up to 5 days in an airtight container in the refrigerator. To reheat, place on a baking sheet lined with parchment and bake in a 350°F (180°C) oven for about 12 minutes or until heated through.

Variation

Curried Baked Chickpea Fritters: In Step 1, add 1 tbsp (15 mL) chopped peeled gingerroot, 1 tbsp (15 mL) curry powder, 1 tsp (5 mL) ground cumin and ¼ tsp (1 mL) ground turmeric to the food processor.

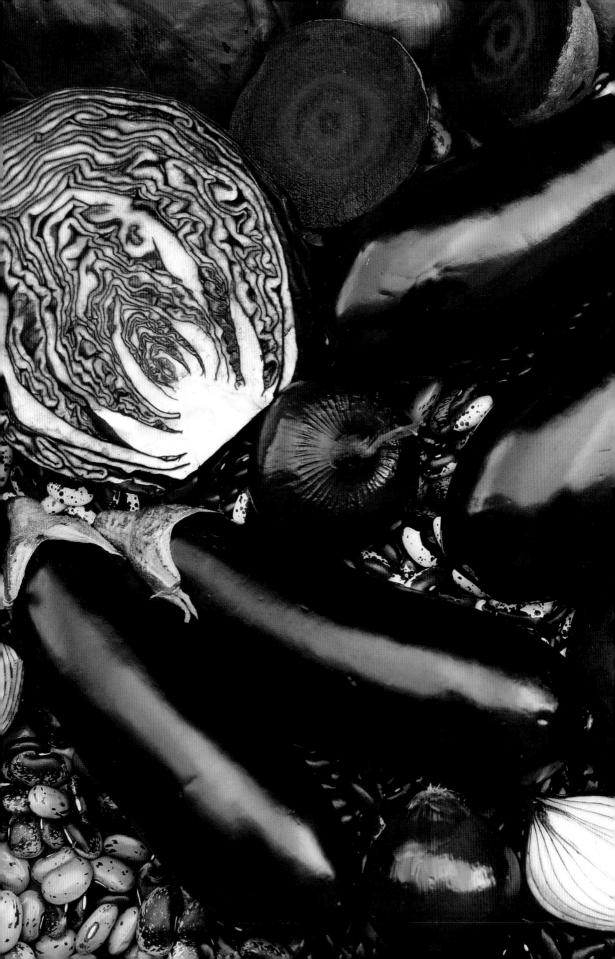

Açai Superfood Bowl (page 21)

Chocolate Hazelnut Waffles (page 25)
with Island-Time Juice (page 46)

Cucumber Aloe Watermelon Juice (page 40),
Classic Green Smoothie (page 51),
Sweet Potato Pie Smoothie (page 56)

Singapore Summer Rolls (page 93) with Yellow Coconut Curry Sauce (page 118)

Mini Quinoa Croquettes (page 104) with Miso Tahini Sauce (page 121)

Vanilla Chai Power Bars (page 159) with Almond Milk (page 61)

Braised Fennel and Onions with Lentils (page 175)

Roasted Cauliflower and Chickpea Tacos (page 196)

Chipotle Walnut Mushroom and Rice Burgers (page 228)
with Crunchy Cabbage and Carrot Slaw (page 545)

Tofu Squash Ravioli in Lemon Sage Cream Sauce (page 272)

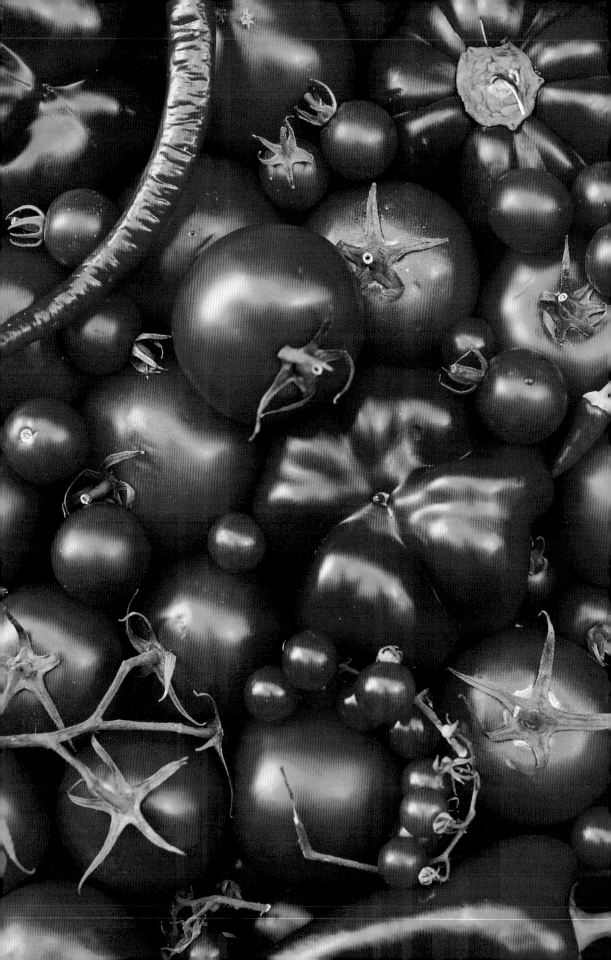

Buddhist Noodle Bowl (page 286)

Sautéed Ginger Miso Tempeh (page 297)
with Asian-Style Adzuki Bean Salad (page 185)

Crispy Curried Chickpeas

These crisp chickpeas are perfect scattered on top of salads, or on their own as a high-protein snack.

Tips

To soak the chickpeas: Place in a bowl and cover with 8 cups (2 L) water. Cover and set aside for at least 6 hours or overnight (if overnight, refrigerate). Drain, discarding water. If you prefer, use your slow cooker to cook the chickpeas (see page 182).

Substitute an equal amount of other Indian spices such as garam masala, chaat masala or goda masala for the curry powder.

Baking sheet, lined with paper towels

2 cups	dried chickpeas, soaked (see Tips, left)	500 mL
8 cups	water	2 L
¾ tsp	fine sea salt, divided	3 mL
½ cup	coconut oil	125 mL
1 tsp	curry powder	5 mL
¼ tsp	ground cumin	1 mL

1. In a large saucepan, combine chickpeas, water and ¼ tsp (1 mL) salt; bring to a boil. Reduce heat and simmer until tender, about 1 hour. Drain, discarding liquid.
2. In a small saucepan over medium heat, melt coconut oil. Add chickpeas and cook, stirring constantly, until golden brown, about 10 minutes.
3. Using a slotted spoon, transfer chickpeas to prepared baking sheet to absorb excess oil, then immediately transfer to a bowl. Toss with remaining ½ tsp (2 mL) salt, curry powder and cumin.
4. Serve immediately or transfer to an airtight container and refrigerate for up to 1 week.

Variation

Crispy Southwest Chickpeas: In Step 3, substitute an equal amount of chili powder for the curry powder. Increase the amount of ground cumin to ½ tsp (2 mL) and add a pinch of dried chipotle powder.

Traditional Mexican Pozole

This traditional Mexican dish makes a satisfying dinner any night of the week. I serve it with a crisp, refreshing slaw of cabbage and radishes with cilantro and lime juice.

MAKES 4 TO 6 SERVINGS

Tips

Hominy is dried corn that has been soaked in a solution of water and calcium oxide also known as quicklime. It is available in most supermarkets and in Mexican markets. Look for organic hominy to avoid genetically modified corn.

To soak the hominy: Place in a bowl and cover with 8 cups (2 L) water. Cover and refrigerate for 8 hours. Drain, discarding water.

For convenience, you can substitute about 2 cups (500 mL) drained canned hominy (do not soak, and skip Step 1).

For a more authentic taste, use Mexican oregano.

The quantity of garlic depends on the size of the cloves. If large, use the smaller number. If small, more may be required.

● **Medium (about 4 quart) slow cooker**

POZOLE

6 cups	water	1.5 L
1 cup	dried hominy, soaked (see Tips, left)	250 mL
2 tbsp	grapeseed oil	30 mL
1 cup	chopped onion	250 mL
1½ tsp	fine sea salt, divided	7 mL
2 tsp	dried oregano (see Tips, left)	10 mL
1 tsp	ground cumin	5 mL
1 tsp	organic coconut sugar	5 mL
1 tsp	chipotle powder	5 mL
3 to 4	cloves garlic	3 to 4
1	can (28 oz/796 mL) diced tomatoes, with juice	1
1 tsp	raw cacao powder (see Tips, page 243)	5 mL
4 cups	drained cooked kidney beans (see Tips, page 243)	1 L

SLAW

2 cups	thinly sliced cabbage	500 mL
½ cup	thinly sliced radishes	125 mL
½ cup	chopped fresh cilantro, leaves and stems	125 mL
¼ cup	freshly squeezed lime juice	60 mL
3 tbsp	extra virgin olive oil	45 mL
	Vegan Sour Cream (page 555; optional)	

1. *Pozole:* In a large saucepan, combine water and soaked, drained hominy; bring to a boil. Reduce heat and simmer until tender, about 40 minutes. Drain, discarding water, and set aside.

Tips

Cacao powder is powdered raw chocolate. It is similar to cocoa powder but tastes even better, with a deeper, richer flavor. Cacao powder is available in well-stocked supermarkets, natural food stores and online. If you can't find it, you may substitute an equal amount of good-quality cocoa powder.

Use either kidney beans you have cooked yourself or canned kidney beans, preferably with no salt added. When using canned beans that contain salt, be sure to rinse and drain them thoroughly before using.

Do not lift the lid of your slow cooker while it is cooking. Each time you do, heat will escape and you will need to add 20 to 30 minutes of cooking time to your recipe.

2. Meanwhile, in a large pot over medium heat, heat grapeseed oil. Add onion and 1 tsp (5 mL) salt; cook, stirring frequently, until onion is translucent, 5 to 6 minutes. Add oregano, cumin, coconut sugar, chipotle powder and garlic. Cook, stirring occasionally, for 4 to 5 minutes, until spices are fragrant.

3. Add tomatoes, with juice, and stir, using a wooden spoon to scrape up any brown bits on bottom of pan. Stir in cacao powder, cooked kidney beans and cooked hominy; bring to a boil. Remove from heat and transfer to slow cooker stoneware.

4. Cover and cook on High for 3 hours or Low for 6 hours.

5. *Slaw:* In a large bowl, toss together cabbage, radishes, cilantro, lime juice, olive oil and remaining ½ tsp (2 mL) salt.

6. *Assembly:* Ladle pozole into serving bowls and garnish with slaw and sour cream (if using).

Eggplant and Tempeh Paella

Serve this hearty dish with your favorite crusty gluten-free bread and a little Vegan Mayonnaise (page 550) for dipping.

MAKES 4 SERVINGS

Tips

Unpasteurized tempeh can be found in the freezer section of most well-stocked supermarkets and natural food stores. I prefer unpasteurized because I find it has a better texture. Pasteurized tempeh will work equally well.

Wheat-free tamari is a gluten-free seasoning made from fermented soybeans. It can be found in most well-stocked supermarkets and natural food stores.

The quantity of garlic depends on the size of the cloves. If large, use the smaller number. If small, more may be required.

Saffron is the world's most expensive spice. The tiny threads come from crocus flowers and are picked by hand. Because of saffron's strong but unique and enticing flavor, a little goes a long way in a recipe.

1	block (8.5 oz/240 g) frozen (unpasteurized) tempeh (see Tips, left)	1
4 cups	water	1 L
½ cup	wheat-free tamari, divided	125 mL
3 tbsp	grapeseed oil	45 mL
1 cup	chopped onion	250 mL
1 tsp	fine sea salt	5 mL
2 cups	cubed eggplant	500 mL
3 to 4	cloves garlic, minced	3 to 4
2 cups	short-grain brown rice	500 mL
4 cups	Vegetable Stock (page 559)	1 L
¼ tsp	saffron threads (see Tips, left)	1 mL
½ cup	frozen peas	125 mL
¼ cup	chopped flat-leaf (Italian) parsley leaves	60 mL

1. In a saucepan, combine tempeh, water and ¼ cup (60 mL) tamari. Cover and bring to a boil, then reduce heat and simmer for 15 minutes. Using a slotted spoon, transfer tempeh to a plate and set aside for 15 minutes to cool. Using a sharp knife, cut cooled tempeh into bite-size pieces.

2. In a large pot over medium heat, heat oil. Add onion, prepared tempeh and salt. Cook, stirring frequently, until onion is translucent, about 6 minutes. Add eggplant and cook for 2 to 3 minutes, stirring occasionally. Stir in garlic and cook until soft and fragrant, about 2 minutes. Stir in rice and cook for 1 to 2 minutes, until well coated. Stir in vegetable stock and saffron. Bring mixture to a boil, stirring once.

3. Cover, reduce heat and simmer for 45 minutes, until rice is tender. During the last 2 minutes, increase heat to high and cook until a crispy caramelized crust — the *socarrat* — forms on the bottom of the pot. Uncover and stir in peas.

4. Remove from heat and stir until peas are heated through, about 2 minutes. Sprinkle with parsley. Serve immediately or transfer to an airtight container and refrigerate for up to 1 week.

Pasta and Noodles

Three-Bean Pasta Salad

This hearty bean salad is full of fiber and protein. It makes a great quick but filling lunch — especially good after a long workout — and is a tasty addition to any buffet table.

Tips

Gluten-free pasta needs to be cooked in a lot of rapidly boiling water so it does not stick together. Make sure you use a large pot with at least 4 to 5 times more water than pasta.

Substitute an equal amount of your favorite legumes for any of the beans in this recipe (for example, use pinto, cannellini and kidney beans).

Use either beans you have cooked yourself or canned beans, preferably with no salt added. When using canned beans that contain salt, be sure to rinse and drain them thoroughly before using.

Make sure the red onion is finely chopped for this recipe. When using raw onion in salads, small pieces are best for providing a subtle flavor with just a little bite. If the pieces are too large, the flavor can overwhelm the dish.

1	package (16 oz/500 g) gluten-free penne or rigatoni	1
1 tsp	fine sea salt, divided	5 mL
½ cup	extra virgin olive oil	125 mL
¼ cup	freshly squeezed lemon juice	60 mL
½ cup	drained cooked black beans	125 mL
½ cup	drained cooked red kidney beans	125 mL
½ cup	drained cooked lupini beans	125 mL
½ cup	chopped red bell pepper	125 mL
½ cup	finely chopped red onion (see Tips, left)	125 mL
2 tbsp	raw agave nectar	30 mL
1 tsp	dried oregano	5 mL
1 tsp	dried basil	5 mL
¼ tsp	hot pepper flakes	1 mL

1. In a large covered pot, bring water to a rapid boil (see Tips, left). Add penne and ½ tsp (2 mL) salt and cook until pasta is al dente, as per package instructions. Drain, rinse well under cold running water and drain again. Transfer to a large bowl.

2. Add oil, lemon juice, black beans, kidney beans, lupini beans, red pepper, onion, agave nectar, oregano, basil, hot pepper flakes and remaining ½ tsp (2 mL) salt; toss to combine.

3. Serve immediately or transfer to an airtight container and refrigerate for up to 3 days.

Mediterranean Pasta Salad

With kalamata olives, cucumber and oregano, this salad is reminiscent of a classic Greek salad. Pasta makes it extremely portable — serve it as a light lunch or eat as a snack on the go.

MAKES 4 TO 6 SERVINGS

Tips

To remove the pit from an olive, use the butt end of your knife to gently press against the olive and pop the pit out of the middle.

A hand-held citrus reamer can be used to extract the juice from lemons and limes. Available in most kitchen supply stores, this tool would be ideal to use for the lemon juice in this recipe.

Gluten-free pasta needs to be cooked in a lot of rapidly boiling water so it does not stick together. Be sure to use a large pot with at least 4 to 5 times more water than pasta.

1	package (16 oz/500 g) gluten-free penne or rigatoni	1
¾ tsp	fine sea salt, divided	3 mL
½ cup	extra virgin olive oil	125 mL
¼ cup	freshly squeezed lemon juice (see Tips, left)	60 mL
1 cup	thinly sliced pitted kalamata olives (see Tips, left)	250 mL
1 cup	chopped red bell pepper	250 mL
½ cup	chopped English cucumber	125 mL
2 tbsp	raw shelled hemp seeds	30 mL
1 tbsp	dried oregano	15 mL

1. In a large covered pot, bring water to a rapid boil (see Tips, left). Add penne and ½ tsp (2 mL) salt and cook until pasta is al dente, as per package instructions. Drain, rinse well under cold running water and drain again. Transfer to a large bowl.

2. Add oil, lemon juice, olives, red pepper, cucumber, hemp seeds, oregano and remaining ¼ tsp (1 mL) salt; toss to combine.

3. Serve immediately or transfer to an airtight container and refrigerate for up to 3 days.

Santa Fe Macaroni Salad

This zesty macaroni salad is full of the flavors of the Southwest: chili powder, cumin, lime juice and fresh cilantro. Serve it for the big game or at family get-togethers and potlucks.

MAKES 4 TO 6 SERVINGS

Tips

Gluten-free pasta needs to be cooked in a lot of rapidly boiling water so it does not stick together. Make sure you use a large pot with at least 4 to 5 times more water than pasta.

For a lighter version of this recipe, replace the mayonnaise with 3 tbsp (45 mL) extra virgin olive oil and 2 tbsp (30 mL) Dijon mustard.

When using raw onion in salads, small pieces are best for providing a subtle flavor with just a little bite. If the pieces are too large, the flavor can overwhelm the dish.

1	package (16 oz/500 g) gluten-free macaroni	1
1¼ tsp	fine sea salt, divided	6 mL
1 cup	Vegan Mayonnaise (page 550; see Tips, left)	250 mL
1 cup	chopped red bell pepper	250 mL
1 cup	roughly chopped fresh cilantro, leaves and stems	250 mL
¼ cup	finely chopped red onion (see Tips, left)	60 mL
3 tbsp	raw shelled hemp seeds	45 mL
1 tbsp	freshly squeezed lime juice	15 mL
2 tsp	chili powder	10 mL
1 tsp	ground cumin	5 mL

1. In a large covered pot, bring water to a rapid boil (see Tips, left). Add macaroni and 1 tsp (5 mL) salt and cook, uncovered, until pasta is al dente, as per package instructions. Drain and rinse under cold running water until cool. Drain well.

2. Transfer cooled pasta to a large bowl. Add mayonnaise, red pepper, cilantro, onion, hemp seeds, lime juice, chili powder, cumin and remaining salt; stir well. Serve immediately or transfer to an airtight container and refrigerate for up to 3 days.

Pasta Aglio e Olio

Pasta tossed with olive oil and fresh herbs is an Italian classic. It has everything going for it: it's delicious, nutritious and economical, particularly if you grow the herbs in your garden. This makes a perfect summer lunch. Serve with Spinach Sautéed in White Wine and Garlic (page 292), Quick Garlic Cabbage Stir-Fry (page 303) or Leek, Potato and Lentil Soup (page 320).

MAKES 4 TO 6 SERVINGS

Tips

To ensure that any grit is removed from parsley before chopping, place it in a bowl, cover with cool water and set aside for about 2 minutes — the dirt will sink to the bottom of the bowl. Lift out parsley, rinse under cool running water and pat dry or dry in a salad spinner to remove excess moisture.

The residual starch in pasta cooking water helps to thicken and add body to sauces. Chefs usually scoop out a quantity before draining pasta. Then they add 1/4 to 1/2 cup (60 to 125 mL) to the sauce, depending on the desired result.

1/2 cup	extra virgin olive oil	125 mL
1 tbsp	grapeseed oil	15 mL
12 to 15	cloves garlic, thinly sliced	12 to 15
1 tbsp	fennel seeds	15 mL
1 tbsp	chopped fresh rosemary	15 mL
1/4 tsp	hot pepper flakes	1 mL
1 cup	chopped onion	250 mL
1 tsp	fine sea salt, divided	5 mL
1	package (16 oz/500 g) gluten-free spaghetti	1
1 cup	chopped flat-leaf (Italian) parsley leaves (see Tips, left)	250 mL

1. Place water for cooking pasta in a large covered pot and bring to a rapid boil (see Tips, page 248).

2. Meanwhile, in a skillet over medium heat, heat olive oil and grapeseed oil. Add garlic, fennel seeds, rosemary and hot pepper flakes. Cook, stirring constantly, until garlic is soft and light golden, 3 to 4 minutes. Add onion and 1/2 tsp (2 mL) salt. Cook, stirring, until onion is translucent, about 6 minutes. Remove from heat and set aside.

3. Add remaining 1/2 tsp (2 mL) salt to boiling water. Add spaghetti and cook until al dente, as per package instructions. Scoop out 1/2 cup (125 mL) pasta water and set aside (see Tips, left). Drain.

4. Return onion mixture to low heat. Add spaghetti and toss to combine. Add reserved pasta water and stir well. Serve immediately, garnished with chopped parsley.

Gluten-Free Pasta Dough

Making your own gluten-free pasta allows you to recreate your favorite fresh pasta recipes such as sauced cut pasta, cannelloni, ravioli and even lasagna.

MAKES ABOUT 1 LB (500 g) OR 6 SERVINGS

Tips

To grind flax seeds: Place ¼ cup (60 mL) whole flax seeds in a blender or spice grinder and blend until they become flour-like in consistency. Cover and refrigerate any extra for up to 1 month.

I prefer not to use already-ground (milled) flax seed in this recipe, because it is usually not fine enough. A larger grind will not bind well. If your milled flax seed is not powdery, place it in a blender or spice grinder and grind until the desired consistency is achieved.

When working with any flour, particularly those that are gluten-free, whisk before measuring. This aerates the flour and ensures more accurate measuring. Be sure to use a dry measure (not a glass measuring cup) and to level off with the side of a knife.

A wood pastry board is an excellent work surface for making pasta dough.

- Rolling pin
- Baking sheet, lined with parchment paper

3 tbsp	ground raw flax seeds (see Tip, left)	45 mL
½ cup + 6 tbsp	(approx.) hot water, divided	215 mL
1 cup	finely ground brown rice flour	250 mL
½ cup	tapioca starch	125 mL
½ cup	sorghum flour	125 mL
2 tbsp	extra virgin olive oil	30 mL
1 tsp	fine sea salt	5 mL
	Brown rice flour, for dusting	

1. In a small bowl, whisk together ground flax seeds and ½ cup (125 mL) hot water. Cover and set aside for 10 minutes so flax can absorb liquid and swell.

2. In another bowl, whisk together brown rice flour, tapioca starch and sorghum flour.

3. Place flour mixture on a clean work surface. Make a well in the center. Add flaxseed mixture, oil and salt. Using your hands, gradually work flour into flax mixture, adding 2 tbsp (30 mL) hot water at a time while kneading (up to about 6 tbsp/90 mL total), until a soft dough forms. Shape into a ball. Scrape up any bits of dough from work surface and discard.

4. Lightly dust work surface with brown rice flour. Knead dough for about 5 minutes, until smooth and homogeneous. Cover with plastic wrap and set aside for 30 minutes to rest.

5. After dough has finished resting, divide into 3 equal portions. If you have a pasta rolling machine, follow the manufacturer's instructions.

6. Dust work surface and rolling pin with brown rice flour. One portion at a time (keep remaining dough covered with plastic wrap so it doesn't dry out), dust lightly with flour and roll dough into a strip about 5 inches (12.5 cm) long. Turn 180 degrees so long side is facing you and roll into a rectangle. Turn dough again and continue to roll until it is about 1/16 inch (2 mm) thick. Repeat with remaining dough.

Tips

I like to use brown rice flour because it is a whole food, but sometimes the grind can be quite coarse, giving the final product a somewhat gritty texture. You can substitute an equal amount of white rice flour with good results, but keep in mind that white rice flour is a processed food.

Working with whole-food gluten-free flours can be tricky. Brands differ in how coarse or fine they grind their flours. That means you may need to add more water to a recipe (1 or 2 tbsp/ 15 to 30 mL at a time) to achieve the consistency of dough called for. Make adjustments as necessary.

Remember to dust the dough lightly with flour as you roll, to prevent sticking.

It is important to roll the dough as thinly as possible, because it will double in size when cooked. Also, if it is too thick you will not get the yield required for the recipes.

A bench scraper is very useful for releasing pasta that's become stuck to the board. One with a ruler marked on it is especially useful.

Keeping the dough from drying out is key to successful rolling. If necessary, roll dough out between sheets of plastic wrap to minimize the addition of flour.

7. *To make cut pasta:* Dust lightly with flour. Starting from the short edge, roll up pasta sheet like a jelly roll. Using a sharp knife, trim ends to make them even. Cut roll into strands or shapes as desired (see Variations, below) and transfer to prepared baking sheet. (To make pasta for ravioli, lasagna or cannelloni, see Variations, below.)

8. Dust fresh pasta with a little more brown rice flour. Set aside for 10 to 15 minutes to dry out before cooking. Use immediately or transfer to an airtight container and freeze for up to 1 month. Do not thaw before cooking.

Variations

Fettuccini: Cut rolled dough into thin ribbons about $\frac{1}{4}$ inch (5 mm) wide.

Linguine: Cut rolled dough into very thin ribbons about $\frac{1}{8}$ inch (3 mm) wide.

Pappardelle: Cut rolled dough into thick ribbons about $\frac{3}{4}$ inch (2 cm) wide.

Lasagna: Roll out dough and cut into 6- by 4-inch (15 by 10 cm) rectangles. Each batch of dough should produce 12 to 16 pieces, depending on how thinly you have rolled it out.

Ravioli: Roll out dough and cut into 8- by 5-inch (20 by 12.5 cm) sheets. Trim edges to straighten, then cut rectangles in half lengthwise, producing strips $2\frac{1}{2}$ inches (6 cm) wide and 8 inches (20 cm) long.

Cannelloni: Roll out dough and cut into sheets 8 inches (20 cm) square. Trim edges to straighten, then cut sheet in half. Cut each half in halves to produce four 4-inch (10 cm) squares.

Cooking Gluten-Free Pasta

Gluten-free pasta (fresh and dried) needs to be cooked in a lot of rapidly boiling water so it doesn't stick together. For every 1 lb (16 oz) pasta, place 32 cups (8 L) water and 1 tsp (5 mL) fine sea salt in a large pot and bring to a rapid boil. Add pasta and cook until al dente. (Note that fresh pasta cooks much more quickly than dried pasta: about 5 to 6 minutes, or 8 to 10 minutes from frozen.)

Sweet Potato Gnocchi

This recipe is a twist on traditional gnocchi made with white potatoes. Serve these light and airy morsels with your favorite sauce, such as Roasted Garlic Chimichurri (page 109), Classic Garlicky Tomato Sauce (page 110), Easy Creamy Alfredo Sauce (page 123) or White Wine Spinach Cream Sauce (page 119).

MAKES ABOUT 45 GNOCCHI

Tips

Using golden flax seeds will yield a lighter-colored dough, while dough made with brown flax will be darker. Choose according to your preference.

A spider is a type of strainer used for removing food from hot liquids or skimming foam. It has a wide, shallow wire-mesh basket at the end of a long handle and can be found in most kitchen supply stores. It is a useful tool for draining small pasta such as gnocchi that won't all be cooked at the same time. Use it to scoop out gnocchi as they are cooked.

If desired, you can freeze prepared gnocchi for later cooking. After rolling and cutting the gnocchi, arrange in a single layer on a baking sheet and freeze. To cook from frozen, increase the cooking time by 1 to 2 minutes.

- Preheat oven to 400°F (200°C)
- Potato ricer

3	large sweet potatoes	3
2 cups	brown rice flour, plus more for dusting	500 mL
1/3 cup	ground flax seeds (see Tips, left)	75 mL
1¾ tsp	fine sea salt, divided	8 mL

1. Wrap sweet potatoes in aluminum foil. Bake in preheated oven for 1 hour or until tender. Remove from oven and set aside for 10 minutes to cool.

2. Remove foil from sweet potatoes and peel away skin (keep potatoes as intact as possible). Pass potatoes through potato ricer into a large bowl.

3. Add rice flour, ground flax seeds and ¾ tsp (3 mL) salt. Stir until smooth and no traces of flour remain. Set aside until firm, about 10 minutes.

4. In a large covered pot, bring gnocchi cooking water to a rapid boil.

5. Divide dough into 4 equal pieces. Lightly dust a clean work surface with rice flour. With lightly floured hands and starting in the middle, gently roll each piece into a long cylinder about ½ inch (1 cm) in diameter. Using a sharp knife, cut each cylinder into 10 to 12 pieces, each about ½ inch (1 cm) long. Gently press the tines of a fork into each piece to make slight indentations (see Tips, page 253). Dust lightly with flour.

6. Add remaining 1 tsp (5 mL) salt to boiling water. Add gnocchi in batches to ensure that they don't stick together and cook just until they rise to the surface, 2 to 3 minutes. Using a spider (see Tips, left) scoop out gnocchi as they are cooked. Serve immediately with your favorite sauce.

Gnocchi in Tomato Sauce

Serve these soft, pillowy gnocchi (the ultimate comfort food) for dinner, sprinkled with nutritional yeast and a splash of your best extra virgin olive oil.

**MAKES ABOUT
80 GNOCCHI**

Tips

You will need two large potatoes weighing a total of about 2 lbs (1 kg). When peeling the skin after baking, keep the potatoes as intact as possible. Once they are riced, you should have about 4 cups (1 L) potato.

This recipe was tested using white rice flour, but I prefer to use brown rice flour because it is a whole food. You may need to adjust the quantity.

You need to give the flax time to absorb the liquid and swell.

Pressing the tines of a fork into the pieces of dough creates a bit of texture that helps sauce stick to the gnocchi.

These gnocchi are quite delicate. In my opinion, the best way to serve them is in individual bowls or plates, topped with tomato sauce. If placed in a serving bowl, they are likely to get crushed together and it may be difficult to get them out of the bowl intact.

- **Preheat oven to 400°F (200°C)**
- **Potato ricer**

2	baking (russet) potatoes	2
2 tbsp	ground raw flax seeds (see Tips, page 252)	30 mL
6 tbsp	hot water	90 mL
¾ cup	white rice flour, plus more for dusting	175 mL
2 tsp	fine sea salt, divided	10 mL
¼ tsp	xanthan gum	1 mL
3 cups	Classic Garlicky Tomato Sauce (page 110)	750 mL

1. Wrap potatoes in aluminum foil. Bake in preheated oven for 1 hour or until tender. Remove from oven and set aside for 10 minutes to cool.

2. Remove foil and peel away skin. Pass potatoes through ricer into a large bowl. Set aside.

3. In a small bowl, whisk together ground flax seeds and hot water until well combined. Cover and set aside for 10 minutes.

4. Add rice flour, 1 tsp (5 mL) salt, xanthan gum and soaked flax seeds to the potatoes. Stir until dough is smooth. Set aside for 10 minutes to absorb liquid and firm up.

5. Meanwhile, in a large covered pot, bring gnocchi cooking water to a rapid boil.

6. Divide dough into 4 equal pieces. Lightly dust a clean work surface with rice flour. With lightly floured hands, starting in the middle, gently roll each piece into a long cylinder about ¾ inch (2 cm) in diameter. Using a sharp knife, cut each cylinder into 18 to 20 pieces, each about ¾ inch (2 cm) long. Gently press the tines of a fork into each to make indentations. Dust lightly with flour and allow to rest 10 minutes.

7. Add remaining 1 tsp (5 mL) salt to boiling water. Add gnocchi, in batches, and cook just until they rise to the surface, 2 to 3 minutes. Using a slotted spoon or a spider, scoop out gnocchi as they are cooked. Serve immediately with hot tomato sauce.

Fettuccini with Lemon Parsley White Wine Sauce

This recipe is perfect for hot summer days when you are craving something lighter but still filling.

MAKES 4 SERVINGS

Tips

To make this dish a little richer, swirl 1/4 cup (60 mL) Whipped Non-dairy Butter (page 554) into the cooked pasta until melted.

To remove the skin from a clove of garlic, use the butt end of a chef's knife to press firmly but gently on the clove to loosen the skin. Using your index finger and thumb, gently squeeze off the skin.

The quantity of garlic depends on the size of the cloves. If large, use the smaller number. If small, more may be required.

To ensure that any grit is removed from parsley before chopping, place it in a bowl, cover with cool water and set aside for about 2 minutes — the dirt will sink to the bottom of the bowl. Lift out parsley, rinse under cool running water and pat dry or dry in a salad spinner to remove excess moisture.

2 tbsp	grapeseed oil	30 mL
1/2 cup	chopped onion	125 mL
1 tsp	fine sea salt, divided	5 mL
1/4 tsp	hot pepper flakes	1 mL
3 to 4	cloves garlic, minced (see Tips, left)	3 to 4
1 cup	chopped fresh flat-leaf (Italian) parsley leaves (see Tips, left)	250 mL
1/4 cup	capers (drained)	60 mL
1/2 cup	dry white wine	125 mL
1/4 cup	freshly squeezed lemon juice	60 mL
1	recipe Gluten-Free Pasta Dough (page 250), cut into fettuccini noodles	1

1. In a large covered pot, bring pasta cooking water to a rapid boil.
2. Meanwhile, in a large skillet over medium heat, heat oil. Add onion, 1/2 tsp (2 mL) salt and hot pepper flakes. Cook, stirring frequently, until onion is translucent, about 6 minutes. Stir in garlic and cook until fragrant, about 2 minutes.
3. Add parsley, capers, wine and lemon juice; stir to combine. Simmer until sauce has thickened slightly, 4 to 5 minutes. Remove from heat and set aside.
4. Add remaining 1/2 tsp (2 mL) salt to boiling water. Add fettuccini and cook until al dente, 5 to 6 minutes. Scoop out 1/2 cup (125 mL) cooking water and set aside (see Tips, page 255). Drain.
5. Return onion mixture to medium heat. Add cooked fettuccini and toss to combine. Add reserved pasta water and stir well. Serve immediately.

Spicy Angel-Hair Toss

Fans of spicy dishes will enjoy the fresh chiles and hot pepper flakes in this dish. It's a quick and simple dinner that's great for weeknights, when you may be short on time.

Tips

If you prefer a little less heat, remove the seeds and ribs from the chile.

Nutritional yeast is an inactive yeast that has been grown on beet molasses and then pasteurized. It provides a rich, cheesy flavor in sauces, stews, soups and dips. Look for it in well-stocked supermarkets and natural food stores.

Gluten-free pasta needs to be cooked in a lot of rapidly boiling water so it does not stick together. Make sure you use a large pot with at least 4 to 5 times more water than pasta.

The residual starch in pasta cooking water helps to thicken and add body to the sauce. Chefs usually scoop out a quantity before draining pasta. Then they add 1/4 to 1/2 cup (60 to 125 mL) to the sauce, depending on the desired result.

2 tbsp	grapeseed oil	30 mL
2 tbsp	extra virgin olive oil	30 mL
1 tbsp	chopped red chile (see Tips, left)	15 mL
1 tsp	hot pepper flakes	5 mL
1 tsp	fine sea salt, divided	5 mL
4 to 6	cloves garlic, minced	4 to 6
1	package (16 oz/500 g) gluten-free angel hair pasta	1
2 tbsp	nutritional yeast (see Tips, left)	30 mL

1. In a large covered pot, bring pasta cooking water to a rapid boil (see Tips, left).

2. Meanwhile, in a large skillet over medium heat, heat grapeseed oil and olive oil. Add chile, hot pepper flakes, 1/2 tsp (2 mL) salt and garlic. Cook, stirring constantly, until garlic is fragrant and lightly golden, 3 to 4 minutes. Remove from heat and set aside.

3. Add remaining 1/2 tsp (2 mL) salt to boiling water. Add pasta and cook until al dente, as per package instructions. Scoop out 1/2 cup (125 mL) cooking water and set aside (see Tips, left). Drain.

4. Return chile-garlic mixture to medium heat. Add pasta and toss to combine. Add reserved pasta water and stir well. Add nutritional yeast and toss to combine. Serve immediately.

Spaetzle in Lemon Garlic Sauce

Spaetzle is a kind of dumpling dish traditionally served in Germany, Austria and Switzerland. It is usually served as a side, but the dumplings make a nice lunch or light dinner with accompaniments. Here I've topped them with a slightly tart lemon, garlic and caper sauce. You can cook the dumplings ahead of time, then cool and refrigerate them for an easy meal any day of the week (see Tips, page 257).

<table>
<tr><td colspan="3">MAKES ABOUT
4 SERVINGS</td></tr>
</table>

Tips

Try to time preparation of the sauce so that it doesn't need to be reheated. Reheating after sitting might cause it to split. If you do need to reheat it, do so gently, over very low heat.

The quantity of garlic depends on the size of the cloves. If large, use the smaller number. If small, more may be required.

If your capers are packed in salt, rinse briefly under cold running water and drain well to remove excess salt before using.

To ensure that any grit is removed from parsley before chopping, place it in a bowl, cover with cool water and set aside for about 2 minutes — the dirt will sink to the bottom of the bowl. Lift out parsley, rinse under cool running water and pat dry or dry in a salad spinner to remove excess moisture.

- **Metal colander with small holes, or spaetzle maker**

LEMON GARLIC SAUCE

1 tbsp	grapeseed oil	15 mL
4 to 6	cloves garlic, minced	4 to 6
½ cup	capers (drained; see Tips, left)	125 mL
¼ cup	freshly squeezed lemon juice	60 mL
½ cup	roughly chopped flat-leaf (Italian) parsley leaves (see Tips, left)	125 mL
3 tbsp	Whipped Non-dairy Butter (page 554; see Tips, page 257)	45 mL
	Fine sea salt	

SPAETZLE

3 tbsp	ground raw flax seeds	45 mL
½ cup	hot water	125 mL
¼ cup	Almond Milk (page 61)	60 mL
½ cup	white rice flour	125 mL
½ cup	brown rice flour	125 mL
½ cup	arrowroot starch	125 mL
1 tbsp	extra virgin olive oil	15 mL
1 tsp	fine sea salt, divided	5 mL

1. *Lemon Garlic Sauce:* In a large skillet over medium heat, heat grapeseed oil. Add garlic and cook, stirring constantly, until fragrant and lightly golden brown, about 2 minutes. Add capers, lemon juice and parsley and cook for 1 to 2 minutes. Remove from heat and whisk in butter until melted. Season to taste with salt. Set aside (see Tips, left).

2. *Spaetzle:* In a small bowl, whisk together ground flax seeds and hot water until well combined. Cover and set aside for 10 minutes so flax can absorb the liquid and swell.

Tips

If your sauce tastes too strongly of capers to suit your palate, add an additional tablespoon (15 mL) of Whipped Non-dairy butter to improve the balance.

Spaetzle makers are available at most well-stocked restaurant supply stores. They are ideal to use for this recipe.

A spider is a type of strainer used for removing food from hot liquids or skimming foam. It has a wide, shallow wire-mesh basket at the end of a long handle and can be found in most kitchen supply stores.

You can make spaetzle ahead of time for most recipes. Once cooked, drain and transfer to a clean baking sheet to cool completely. Once cool, store refrigerated in an airtight container for up to 3 days. To reheat, toss with simmering sauce of your choice and cook until the spaetzle are heated through.

To reheat spaetzle for use with Lemon Garlic Sauce: In a small pan, bring water to a simmer, add spaetzle and cook for 2 to 3 minutes, until just heated through. Complete Step 6.

3. In a large bowl, combine almond milk, white rice flour, brown rice flour, arrowroot, olive oil, $\frac{1}{2}$ tsp (2 mL) salt and soaked flax seeds. Whisk until smooth (mixture should be thick but pourable; add almond milk 1 tbsp/15 mL at a time until desired consistency is achieved).

4. In a large covered pot, add remaining $\frac{1}{2}$ tsp (2 mL) salt to spaetzle cooking water and bring to a rapid boil.

5. Place colander (or spaetzle maker) over pot. Pour batter into colander and, using a rubber spatula, scrape batter through holes so it drips into boiling water. Once all the batter is pressed through, cook for 6 to 8 minutes, until dumplings float and texture is al dente. Using a slotted spoon or a spider (see Tips, left), scoop out spaetzle as they are cooked.

6. Add hot spaetzle to Lemon Garlic Sauce. Sprinkle with salt and toss to coat well. Serve immediately.

Squash Mac and Cheese

This is a creamy comfort food you can serve for lunch or dinner, at your next potluck or for a family gathering. Make it a complete meal by adding a side of Sautéed Vegetables with Three-Chile Blend (page 296) and Quick Garlic Cabbage Stir-Fry (page 303).

MAKES 4 TO 6 SERVINGS

Tips

Nutritional yeast is an inactive yeast that has been grown on beet molasses and then pasteurized. It provides a rich, cheesy flavor in sauces, stews, soups and dips. Look for it in well-stocked supermarkets and natural food stores.

The quantity of garlic depends on the size of the cloves. If large, use the smaller number. If small, more may be required.

Be cautious when adding the hot squash to the blender. Make sure it is no more than half full.

- Blender
- 13- by 9-inch (33 by 23 cm) glass baking dish

SAUCE

8 cups	chopped peeled butternut squash (1 to 2)	2 L
½ cup	chopped onion	125 mL
1 to 2	cloves garlic	1 to 2
2 tbsp	fine sea salt, divided	30 mL
	Water	
1½ cups	nutritional yeast (see Tips, left)	375 mL
½ cup	extra virgin olive oil	125 mL
¼ cup	melted coconut oil	60 mL

TOPPING

2	slices gluten-free bread, cut into 1-inch (2.5 cm) cubes	2
2 to 3 tbsp	grapeseed oil (see Tips, left)	30 to 45 mL
1 tbsp	nutritional yeast	15 mL
⅛ tsp	fine sea salt	0.5 mL
⅛ tsp	sweet paprika	0.5 mL

MACARONI

½ tsp	fine sea salt	2 mL
1	package (16 oz/500 g) gluten-free dried elbow macaroni, spirals or penne	1

1. *Sauce:* In a large saucepan, combine squash, onion, garlic and 1 tbsp (15 mL) salt. Cover liberally with water. Cover and bring to a boil. Uncover, reduce heat and simmer until squash is tender, about 15 minutes. Drain, discarding liquid.

2. Transfer squash mixture to blender in batches (see Tips, left). Add remaining 1 tbsp (15 mL) salt, nutritional yeast, olive oil and coconut oil. Blend at high speed until smooth and creamy. Transfer to a large bowl and set aside.

Tips

When cooking gluten-free pasta, remember that it needs to be cooked in copious amounts of rapidly boiling water. Otherwise, it will stick together. For every 1 lb (16 oz) pasta, bring about 8 quarts (8 L) water and 1 tsp (5 mL) fine sea salt to a rapid boil in a very large pot. Add pasta and cook until al dente.

If you prefer crisper breadcrumbs, use 3 tbsp (45 mL) grapeseed oil. If you are fine with softer breadcrumbs, use the smaller amount.

3. In a large covered pot, bring pasta cooking water to a rapid boil (see Tip, left).

4. *Topping:* Meanwhile, in a skillet over medium heat, heat grapeseed oil. Add bread cubes and cook until golden brown, 6 to 8 minutes. Remove from heat and stir in nutritional yeast, salt and paprika. Transfer to clean blender and process at medium speed until broken down into crumbs. Set aside.

5. Preheat oven to 400°F (200°C)

6. *Macaroni:* Add salt to boiling water. Add macaroni and cook until al dente, as per package instructions. Scoop out $1/2$ cup (125 mL) cooking water and set aside. Drain. Rinse under cold running water, stirring, until cold. Add cold macaroni to sauce and toss to coat well.

7. Spread sauced macaroni evenly in baking dish. Sprinkle breadcrumbs evenly overtop. Bake in preheated oven for 40 minutes or until top is golden brown and middle is bubbling hot. Serve immediately. This mac and cheese will keep for up to 5 days in an airtight container in the refrigerator.

Variation

Smoked Chipotle Tofu Mac and Cheese: In a skillet over medium heat, heat $1/4$ cup (60 mL) grapeseed oil. Add 1 cup (250 mL) cubed firm tofu and cook, stirring occasionally, until golden brown, 8 to 10 minutes. Remove from heat and stir in 3 tbsp (45 mL) nutritional yeast, 2 tbsp (30 mL) chopped chipotle peppers, 2 tbsp (30 mL) wheat-free tamari and 1 tsp (5 mL) chili powder. Stir mixture into squash sauce after blending.

Chile Garlic Spaghetti

This combination of pasta tossed with spicy chiles and fragrant garlic is sure to become a favorite. To transform it into a special-occasion dish, top it with Salt-and-Pepper Mushroom Sauté (page 293). The dish pairs well with a glass of dry red wine.

MAKES 4 TO 6 SERVINGS

Tips

To mince garlic: Place whole cloves on a cutting board. Using the butt end of a chef's knife, press firmly but gently on each clove to loosen the skin. Using your index finger and thumb, gently squeeze off the skins. Chop garlic coarsely, then sprinkle with a bit of sea salt. Using the butt end of the knife, rub the garlic into the cutting board. The salt will act as an abrasive and help to mince the garlic. Chop until fine.

The quantity of garlic depends on the size of the cloves. If large, use the smaller number. If small, more may be required.

Gluten-free pasta needs to be cooked in a lot of water so it does not stick together. Make sure you use a large pot with at least 4 to 5 times more water than pasta.

2 tbsp	grapeseed oil	30 mL
2 tbsp	extra virgin olive oil	30 mL
10 to 12	cloves garlic, minced (see Tips, left)	10 to 12
1 tbsp	hot pepper flakes	15 mL
½ cup	chopped onion	125 mL
1 tsp	fine sea salt, divided	5 mL
1	package (16 oz/500 g) gluten-free spaghetti	1

1. In a large covered pot, bring spaghetti cooking water to a rapid boil (see Tips, left).

2. Meanwhile, in a large skillet over medium heat, heat grapeseed oil and olive oil. Add garlic and hot pepper flakes. Cook, stirring constantly, until garlic is lightly browned and fragrant. Add onion and ½ tsp (2 mL) salt. Cook until onion is translucent, about 6 minutes. Remove from heat and set aside.

3. Add remaining ½ tsp (2 mL) salt to boiling water. Add spaghetti and cook until al dente, as per package instructions. Scoop out ½ cup (125 mL) cooking water and set aside (see Tips, page 261). Drain.

4. Return garlic mixture to medium heat. Add spaghetti and toss to combine. Add reserved pasta water and stir well. Serve immediately.

Spaghetti and Meatballs

This classic dish is best served hot, topped with nutritional yeast to add rich, cheesy flavor. Any vegan meatballs will do, but Italian-Style Red Bean Meatballs are particularly delicious.

MAKES 4 TO 6 SERVINGS

Tips

Gluten-free pasta needs to be cooked in a lot of water so it does not stick together. Make sure you use a large pot with at least 4 to 5 times more water than pasta.

The residual starch in pasta cooking water helps to thicken and add body to the sauce. Chefs usually scoop out a quantity before draining pasta. Then they add 1/4 to 1/2 cup (60 to 125 mL) to the sauce, depending upon the desired result.

To reheat the spaghetti and meatballs, bring about 1/2 cup (125 mL) water to a simmer in a large skillet. Add pasta and stir until heated through.

4 cups	Classic Garlicky Tomato Sauce (page 110)	1 L
12	Italian-Style Red Bean Meatballs (page 206) or prepared vegan meatballs	12
1/2 tsp	fine sea salt	2 mL
1	package (16 oz/500 g) gluten-free spaghetti	1
1/2 cup	nutritional yeast	125 mL

1. In a large covered pot, bring spaghetti cooking water to a rapid boil (see Tips, left).
2. Meanwhile, in a large saucepan over medium heat, combine tomato sauce and meatballs and cook, stirring frequently, until meatballs are heated through.
3. Add salt and spaghetti to boiling water and cook, uncovered, until pasta is al dente, as per package instructions. Scoop out 1/2 cup (125 mL) cooking water and set aside (see Tips, left). Drain.
4. Add spaghetti to sauce and meatballs and toss to combine. Add reserved pasta water and stir well. Serve immediately, sprinkled with nutritional yeast. The spaghetti and meatballs will keep for up to 5 days in an airtight container in the refrigerator.

Truffle-Flavored Fettuccini in Portobello Cream Sauce

Aromatic truffle oil pairs well with robust portobello mushrooms. Serve this with your favorite grilled bread on the side.

MAKES 4 TO 6 SERVINGS

Tips

If the mushrooms are large, use only 2; if they are small to medium, use 3.

If a portobello mushroom is large, trim off the bottom 1 inch (2.5 cm) of the stem — it's fibrous and tough.

Truffle oil is available in most well-stocked supermarkets. For the best flavor, look for an oil that has a small piece of either white or black truffle suspended in it.

If you do not have a barbecue, preheat the broiler in your oven. Cook the mushrooms on a baking sheet lined with aluminum foil, until lightly blackened and soft in the middle.

Whether cooking on the grill or under the broiler, the mushrooms will require 5 to 6 minutes per side.

You can also use fresh pasta dough to make this dish (see page 250).

- **Preheat grill to High (see Tips, left)**
- **Blender**

2 to 3	portobello mushrooms, stems trimmed (see Tips, left)	2 to 3
3 tbsp	extra virgin olive oil, divided	45 mL
1½ tsp	fine sea salt, divided	7 mL
¾ cup	water	175 mL
½ cup	tahini	125 mL
1 tsp	freshly grated lemon zest	5 mL
3 tbsp	freshly squeezed lemon juice	45 mL
2	cloves garlic	2
2 tbsp	truffle oil (see Tips, left)	30 mL
1	package (16 oz/500 g) gluten-free fettuccini (see Tips, left)	1
½ cup	nutritional yeast	125 mL
	Truffle oil for drizzling	

1. In a large covered pot, bring fettuccini cooking water to a rapid boil (see Tips, page 261).

2. Meanwhile, in a large bowl, toss mushrooms, 2 tbsp (30 mL) oil and ½ tsp (2 mL) salt. Place on preheated grill and cook until lightly blackened. Turn and cook until cooked throughout (see Tips, left). Remove from heat and set aside.

3. In blender, combine 1 grilled mushroom, water, tahini, lemon zest, lemon juice, garlic, truffle oil, ½ tsp (2 mL) salt and remaining 1 tbsp (15 mL) olive oil. Blend at high speed until smooth. Transfer to a large saucepan over low heat.

4. Add remaining ½ tsp (2 mL) salt to boiling water. Add fettuccini and cook until al dente. Scoop out ½ cup (125 mL) cooking water and set aside (see Tips, page 263). Drain.

5. Slice remaining mushroom(s) into thin strips.

6. Add cooked fettuccini and sliced mushroom(s) to mushroom sauce and toss to combine. Add reserved pasta water and nutritional yeast and stir well. Serve immediately, with a drizzle of truffle oil.

Fettuccini Carbonara

Tempeh bacon adds the perfect touch to this delicious plant-based version of a classic dish. The nutritional yeast and non-dairy butter create the great mouthfeel usually provided by cheese and eggs.

MAKES 4 TO 6 SERVINGS

Tips

Substitute an equal amount of your favorite store-bought non-dairy butter for the Whipped Non-dairy Butter.

The residual starch in pasta cooking water helps to thicken and add body to the sauce. Chefs usually scoop out a quantity before draining pasta. Then they add ¼ to ½ cup (60 to 125 mL) to the sauce, depending upon the desired result.

The fettuccine can easily be made ahead of time and refrigerated for later use. To reheat, bring about ½ cup (125 mL) water to a simmer in a large skillet. Add sauced pasta and stir until heated through.

2 tbsp	grapeseed oil	30 mL
1 cup	thinly sliced Tempeh Bacon (page 38)	250 mL
½ cup	chopped onion	125 mL
1 tsp	fine sea salt, divided	5 mL
2 to 3	cloves garlic, minced	2 to 3
1	package (16 oz/500 g) gluten-free fettuccini	1
½ cup	chopped flat-leaf (Italian) parsley leaves	125 mL
½ cup	nutritional yeast (see Tips, page 267)	125 mL
¼ cup	Whipped Non-dairy Butter (page 554; see Tips, left)	60 mL

1. In a large covered pot, bring fettuccini cooking water to a rapid boil (see Tips, page 264).
2. Meanwhile, in a large skillet over medium-low heat, heat oil. Add tempeh bacon and cook, stirring frequently, until bacon is crisp. Add onion and ½ tsp (2 mL) salt; cook until onion is translucent, about 6 minutes. Add garlic and cook until fragrant, about 2 minutes. Remove from heat and set aside.
3. Add remaining ½ tsp (2 mL) salt to boiling water. Add fettuccini and cook until al dente, as per package instructions. Scoop out ½ cup (125 mL) cooking water and set aside (see Tips, left). Drain.
4. Return bacon mixture to medium heat. Add cooked fettuccini and toss to combine. Add reserved pasta water and stir well. Add parsley, nutritional yeast and butter and toss until butter is melted completely. Serve immediately.

Creamy Sweet Potato Linguine

This hearty dish gets its creamy richness from heart-healthy sweet potatoes.

Tips

You will need 2 large or 3 medium sweet potatoes.

Replace the sweet potato with an equal amount of chopped peeled butternut squash.

You can also make this recipe using fresh pasta dough (see page 250).

Gluten-free pasta needs to be cooked in a lot of water so it does not stick together. Make sure you use a large pot with at least 4 to 5 times more water than pasta.

If the sauce becomes too thick while simmering, add a little more water, about ¼ cup (60 mL) at a time, until it reaches the right consistency.

Substitute an equal amount of fettuccini or spaghetti for the linguine.

- **Blender**

8 cups	chopped peeled sweet potatoes (see Tips, left)	2 L
1½ tsp	fine sea salt, divided	7 mL
3 tbsp	tahini	45 mL
1 tbsp	chopped fresh thyme leaves	15 mL
1 tsp	garlic powder	5 mL
1	package (16 oz/500 g) gluten-free linguine (see Tips, left)	1

1. In a large saucepan of water, combine sweet potatoes and ½ tsp (2 mL) salt. Bring to a boil, reduce heat and simmer until potatoes are tender, about 12 minutes. Drain, reserving 2 cups (500 mL) cooking liquid.

2. In a large covered pot, bring linguine cooking water to a rapid boil (see Tips, left).

3. Meanwhile, in blender, in batches, combine cooked sweet potatoes, reserved cooking liquid, tahini, thyme, garlic powder and ½ tsp (2 mL) salt. Blend at high speed until smooth and creamy. Transfer to a large skillet over low heat.

4. Add remaining ½ tsp (2 mL) salt to boiling water. Add linguine and cook until al dente, as per package instructions. Scoop out ½ cup (125 mL) cooking water and set aside (see Tips, page 263). Drain.

5. Add linguine and reserved pasta water to skillet. Toss to coat evenly and serve immediately.

Penne à la Vodka

This take on a classic dish is sure to impress your dinner guests. I like to use good-quality organic vodka and organic Italian plum tomatoes.

**MAKES 4 TO
6 SERVINGS**

Tips

You can replace the cashew purée in this recipe with 1 cup (250 mL) Almond Milk (page 61) and 3 to 4 tbsp (45 to 60 mL) Whipped Non-dairy Butter (page 554).

The quantity of garlic depends on the size of the cloves. If large, use the smaller number. If small, more may be required.

When cooking with alcohol over an open flame, always pull the pan off the stove and then add the spirit. This will help prevent unwanted flare-ups or fires.

Blender

1 cup	raw cashews (see Tips, left)	250 mL
2 tbsp	grapeseed oil	30 mL
3 to 4	cloves garlic, minced	3 to 4
1/4 tsp	hot pepper flakes	1 mL
1/2 cup	chopped onion	125 mL
1 tsp	fine sea salt, divided	5 mL
1 cup	organic vodka	250 mL
1	can (28 oz/796 mL) diced tomatoes, with juice	1
1	package (16 oz/500 g) gluten-free penne	1
1 cup	water	250 mL
1/2 cup	nutritional yeast	125 mL

1. In a saucepan filled with water, bring cashews to a boil. Remove from heat and drain, discarding liquid. Set cashews aside to cool.

2. In a large covered pot, bring pasta cooking water to a rapid boil (see Tips, page 264).

3. Meanwhile, in a large skillet over medium heat, heat oil. Add garlic and hot pepper flakes. Cook, stirring constantly, until garlic is golden brown, about 2 minutes. Stir in onion and 1/2 tsp (2 mL) salt. Cook until onion is translucent, about 3 minutes. Add vodka (see Tips, left) and cook until most of the liquid evaporates. Stir in tomatoes, with juice, and bring to a boil. Reduce heat and simmer for about 10 minutes, until sauce is thickened.

4. Add remaining 1/2 tsp (2 mL) salt to boiling water. Add penne and cook until al dente. Drain.

5. Meanwhile, in blender, combine cooked cashews and 1 cup (250 mL) water. Blend at high speed until smooth.

6. Add cashew purée to tomato mixture and stir well. Stir in nutritional yeast. Add cooked penne and toss to coat well. Serve immediately.

Roasted Mushroom Penne

The deep, rich flavors and meaty body of roasted mushrooms help to give this recipe not only great flavor but great texture as well.

MAKES 4 TO 6 SERVINGS

Tips

If the button mushrooms are large, cut them in half or even into quarters before roasting.

To trim the portobello mushrooms, cut off the bottom ½ inch (1 cm) of the stem.

The quantity of garlic depends on the size of the cloves. If large, use the smaller number. If small, more may be required.

Gluten-free pasta needs to be cooked in a lot of rapidly boiling water so it does not stick together. Make sure you use a large pot with at least 4 to 5 times more water than pasta.

The residual starch in pasta cooking water helps to thicken and add body to the sauce. Chefs usually scoop out a quantity before draining pasta. Then they add ¼ to ½ cup (60 to 125 mL) to the sauce, depending upon the desired result.

- Preheat oven to 450°F (230°C)
- Baking sheet, lined with parchment paper

4 cups	whole button mushrooms (see Tips, left)	1 L
4 cups	sliced portobello mushrooms (see Tips, left)	1 L
2 cups	thickly sliced shiitake mushroom caps	500 mL
2 cups	thickly sliced oyster mushrooms	500 mL
6 tbsp	grapeseed oil, divided	90 mL
3 tbsp	chopped fresh thyme leaves	45 mL
1½ tsp	fine sea salt, divided	7 mL
½ cup	chopped onion	125 mL
3 to 4	cloves garlic, minced	3 to 4
1	package (16 oz/500 g) gluten-free penne	1

1. In a large bowl, toss together button, portobello, shiitake and oyster mushrooms, 3 tbsp (45 mL) oil, thyme and 1 tsp (5 mL) salt. Transfer to prepared baking sheet. Bake in preheated oven until mushrooms are soft and lightly browned, about 30 minutes. Transfer mushrooms and their liquid to a large bowl. Set aside.

2. In a large covered pot, bring pasta cooking water to a rapid boil (see Tips, left). Add remaining ½ tsp (2 mL) salt and penne and cook, uncovered, until pasta is al dente. Scoop out ½ cup (125 mL) cooking water and set aside (see Tips, left). Drain.

3. Meanwhile, in a large skillet over medium heat, heat remaining 3 tbsp (45 mL) oil. Add onion and cook, stirring frequently, until translucent, about 6 minutes. Add garlic and cook until fragrant, about 2 minutes. Stir in roasted mushrooms.

4. Add reserved penne and pasta water to the skillet. Using a wooden spoon, stir to coat evenly. Serve immediately.

Baked Ziti

Prepare this dish ahead of time and refrigerate it so you can have a delicious meal on the table in the time it takes to cook it in the oven. With its combination of creamy cashew cheese and garlicky tomato sauce, this is a dish you will want to make time and again.

<table>
<tr><td>**MAKES 4 TO 6 SERVINGS**</td></tr>
</table>

Tips

Ziti is a medium-sized tubular pasta. If you cannot find gluten-free ziti, substitute an equal amount of penne.

Nutritional yeast is an inactive yeast that has been grown on beet molasses and then pasteurized. It provides a rich, cheesy flavor in sauces, stews, soups and dips. Look for it in well-stocked supermarkets and natural food stores.

For convenience use your favorite store-bought vegan mozzarella or ricotta.

Rinsing cooked pasta that will subsequently be baked stops the cooking process and helps to ensure over-cooking.

- Preheat oven to 400°F (200°C)
- 13- by 9-inch (33 by 23 cm) glass baking dish, greased

1	package (16 oz/500 g) gluten-free ziti (see Tips, left)	1
1 tsp	fine sea salt	5 mL
4 cups	Classic Garlicky Tomato Sauce (page 110), divided	1 L
2 cups	Creamy Cashew Ricotta (page 532)	500 mL
1 cup	Vegan Shredded Mozzarella (page 537)	250 mL
½ cup	nutritional yeast (see Tips, left)	125 mL

1. In a large covered pot, bring pasta cooking water to a rapid boil (see Tips, page 266). Add ziti and salt and cook until pasta is al dente. Drain. Rinse pasta under cold running water until water runs clear. Transfer to a large bowl.

2. Add 3 cups (750 mL) tomato sauce to ziti and toss well.

3. *Assembly:* Ladle one-third of the pasta mixture into prepared baking dish. Top with 1 cup (250 mL) cashew ricotta and ½ cup (125 mL) vegan mozzarella. Repeat. Top with remaining pasta, remaining 1 cup (250 mL) tomato sauce and nutritional yeast.

4. Bake in preheated oven for 45 minutes or until bubbling hot and golden brown on top. Serve immediately or transfer to an airtight container and refrigerate for up to 1 week.

Baked Penne Bolognese

Spiced ground tofu and rich, fragrant tomato sauce make this take on traditional pasta in a Bolognese sauce a surefire people-pleaser. You can prepare this ahead of time and bake it when you are ready to serve.

MAKES 4 TO 6 SERVINGS

Tips

To prepare the tofu for this recipe, cut it into 1-inch (2.5 cm) cubes. In a food processor fitted with the metal blade, process until broken down into small pieces.

The quantity of garlic depends on the size of the cloves. If large, use the smaller number. If small, more may be required.

To mince garlic: Place whole cloves on a cutting board. Using the butt end of a chef's knife, press firmly but gently on each clove to loosen the skin. Using your index finger and thumb, gently squeeze off the skins. Chop garlic coarsely, then sprinkle with a bit of sea salt. Using the butt end of the knife, rub the garlic into the cutting board. The salt will act as an abrasive and help to mince the garlic. Chop until fine.

- **Preheat oven to 350°F (180°C)**
- **Food processor**
- **13- by 9-inch (33 by 23 cm) square glass baking dish, greased**

¼ cup	grapeseed oil	60 mL
½ cup	chopped onion	125 mL
½ cup	chopped carrot	125 mL
½ cup	chopped celery	125 mL
1 tsp	fine sea salt, divided	5 mL
1	package (16 oz/450 g) firm tofu, crumbled until fine (see Tips, left)	1
8 to 10	cloves garlic, minced	8 to 10
3 tbsp	tomato paste	45 mL
2 cups	dry red wine	500 mL
1	can (28 oz/796 mL) tomato purée (see Tips, page 269)	1
1 tsp	dried oregano	5 mL
1 tsp	dried basil	5 mL
¼ tsp	dried thyme	1 mL
1	package (16 oz/500 g) gluten-free penne	1
½ cup	nutritional yeast	125 mL

1. In a large saucepan over medium heat, heat oil. Add onion, carrot, celery and ½ tsp (2 mL) salt. Cook, stirring frequently, until vegetables are soft and onion is translucent, about 6 minutes. Add crumbled tofu and cook until lightly browned, about 10 minutes. Add garlic and cook until fragrant, about 2 minutes.

2. Stir in tomato paste and cook for 2 to 3 minutes, until it is lightly browned. Add wine and cook for 6 to 7 minutes, until no liquid remains, using a wooden spoon to scrape up any brown bits from the bottom of the pan. Add tomato purée, oregano, basil and thyme. Bring to a boil, reduce heat and simmer for about 15 minutes, until sauce has thickened.

Tips

Tomato purée is often labeled "passata." It is different from tomato paste, which is also called for in this recipe. You may replace the canned tomato purée by placing 8 cups (2 L) chopped fresh tomatoes and $\frac{1}{4}$ cup (60 mL) water in a blender. Blend at high speed until smooth.

Rinsing cooked pasta that will subsequently be baked stops the cooking process and helps to ensure over-cooking.

3. Meanwhile, in a large covered pot, bring pasta cooking water and remaining $\frac{1}{2}$ tsp (2 mL) salt to a rapid boil. Add penne and cook until al dente, as per package instructions. Drain. Rinse under cold running water until pasta is cool. Transfer to a large bowl.

4. Add tomato sauce and toss to coat well. Spread evenly in prepared baking dish. Sprinkle with nutritional yeast. Bake in preheated oven for 40 to 45 minutes or until bubbling hot and top is golden brown. Serve immediately or transfer to an airtight container and refrigerate for up to 1 week.

Roasted Cauliflower Alfredo Bake

This creamy baked pasta dish is perfect to serve on a cold winter night. The velvety roasted cauliflower sauce coats the pasta to make it deliciously comforting.

MAKES 4 TO 6 SERVINGS

Tips

To ensure that the cauliflower cooks evenly, make sure the pieces are roughly the same size and shape.

Nutritional yeast is fortified with vitamin B$_{12}$ and helps to produce umami, a savory flavor sometimes lacking in vegetarian cuisine. Nutritional yeast flakes can be found in well-stocked supermarkets and natural food stores.

- Preheat oven to 400°F (200°C)
- Baking sheet, lined with parchment paper
- Blender
- 13- by 9-inch (33 by 23 cm) glass baking dish, greased

2	heads cauliflower, cut into 1-inch (2.5 cm) pieces (see Tips, left)	2
¼ cup	grapeseed oil	60 mL
½ cup	nutritional yeast, divided (see Tips, left)	125 mL
1½ tsp	fine sea salt, divided	7 mL
1 tsp	garlic powder	5 mL
1	package (16 oz/500 g) gluten-free penne	1
½ cup	water	125 mL
¼ cup	extra virgin olive oil	60 mL
1 tbsp	freshly squeezed lemon juice	15 mL
1 tsp	chopped fresh thyme leaves	5 mL

1. In a large bowl, toss together cauliflower, grapeseed oil, ¼ cup (60 mL) nutritional yeast, ½ tsp (2 mL) salt and garlic powder. Transfer to prepared baking sheet and bake in preheated oven until tender and golden brown, about 25 minutes. Remove from oven and set aside to cool.

2. In a large covered pot, bring pasta cooking water to a rapid boil (see Tip, page 271). Add ½ tsp (2 mL) salt to boiling water. Add penne and cook until al dente. Drain. Rinse pasta under cold running water until cool.

Tips

Gluten-free pasta needs to be cooked in a lot of rapidly boiling water so it does not stick together. Make sure you use a large pot with at least 4 to 5 times more water than pasta.

Rinsing cooked pasta that will subsequently be baked stops the cooking process and helps to ensure over-cooking.

3. Meanwhile, in blender, in batches if necessary, combine half of the cooked cauliflower, remaining ¼ cup (60 mL) nutritional yeast, reamining ½ tsp (2 mL) salt, water, olive oil, lemon juice and thyme. Blend at high speed until smooth. Set aside.

4. In a large bowl, toss together cooled penne, puréed cauliflower and remaining roasted cauliflower. Spread evenly in prepared baking dish.

5. Bake in preheated oven for 30 to 35 minutes, until lightly brown on top and bubbling hot in the middle. Serve immediately. The pasta will keep for up to 1 week in an airtight container in the refrigerator.

Tofu Squash Ravioli in Lemon Sage Cream Sauce

Few dishes are more impressive than ravioli created with your own homemade pasta dough! Serve it with White Wine Spinach Cream Sauce (page 119) or Easy Creamy Alfredo Sauce (page 123).

MAKES 24 RAVIOLI (4 SERVINGS)

Tips

A hand-held citrus reamer can be used to extract the juice from lemons and limes. Available in most kitchen supply stores, this tool would be ideal to use for the lemon juice in this recipe.

To mince garlic: Place whole cloves on a cutting board. Using the butt end of a chef's knife, press firmly but gently on each clove to loosen the skin. Using your index finger and thumb, gently squeeze off the skins. Chop garlic coarsely, then sprinkle with a bit of sea salt. Using the butt end of the knife, rub the garlic into the cutting board. The salt will act as an abrasive and help to mince the garlic. Chop until fine.

- **Food processor**
- **Blender**

TOFU SQUASH FILLING

2 cups	chopped peeled butternut squash	500 mL
1 tbsp	grapeseed oil	15 mL
¼ cup	chopped onion	60 mL
½ tsp	fine sea salt	2 mL
1	clove garlic, minced	1
¼ tsp	freshly grated nutmeg	mL
4 oz	firm tofu, chopped into small pieces (half 8 oz/250 g block)	125 g

LEMON SAGE CREAM SAUCE

1 cup	raw cashews	250 mL
4 cups	water, divided	1 L
¼ cup	freshly squeezed lemon juice (see Tips, left)	60 mL
2 tbsp	chopped fresh sage leaves	30 mL
½ tsp	fine sea salt	2 mL
2	cloves garlic	2

RAVIOLI

6	sheets Gluten-Free Pasta Dough (1 recipe), prepared for ravioli (see page 250)	6
½ tsp	fine sea salt	2 mL

1. *Tofu Squash Filling:* In a large saucepan of boiling salted water, cook squash until tender, about 20 minutes. Drain, discarding liquid. Set aside.

2. In a skillet over medium heat, heat oil. Add onion and salt; cook, stirring frequently, until onion is translucent, about 6 minutes. Add garlic and cook until fragrant, about 2 minutes. Add cooked squash and stir to combine. Stir in nutmeg and set aside to cool completely, about 15 minutes.

Tips

You will have some extra filling. Toss with your favorite salad, spread it into a sandwich or enjoy it as a dip with fresh vegetables such as carrot and celery sticks.

Make sure the ravioli are sealed well, so the filling does not come out during cooking.

To freeze ravioli for later use, once they are filled, arrange in a single layer on a baking sheet without letting them touch. Freeze for 8 hours or overnight. Transfer to an airtight container and store frozen for up to 2 months.

Gluten-free pasta needs to be cooked in a lot of rapidly boiling water so it does not stick together. Make sure you use a large pot with at least 4 to 5 times more water than pasta.

A spider is a type of strainer used for removing food from hot liquids or skimming foam. It has a wide, shallow wire-mesh basket at the end of a long handle and can be found in most kitchen supply stores.

3. Transfer squash mixture to food processor fitted with the metal blade. Process until smooth, stopping the motor to scrape down sides of work bowl as necessary. Add tofu and process until combined. Set aside.

4. *Lemon Sage Cream Sauce*: In a saucepan, combine cashews and 3 cups (750 mL) water and bring to a boil. Drain, discarding liquid, and transfer to blender. Add remaining 1 cup (250 mL) water, lemon juice, sage, salt and garlic. Blend at high speed until smooth and creamy. Transfer to a skillet and set aside.

5. In a large covered pot, bring pasta cooking water to a rapid boil (see Tips, left).

6. Place 1 ravioli sheet (8 by 2½ inches/20 by 6.25 cm) on a clean work surface, long side nearest you. Using a kitchen knife, lightly score the sheet to create 4 equal-sized rectangles. Brush sheet lightly with water. Place about ½ tbsp (7 mL) filling in the center of each division.

7. Place a second ravioli sheet on top. Wet your fingertips and gently press down between the dollops to stick the layers together. Using a knife or pasta cutter, cut straight lines between the dollops to make 4 ravioli. Press edges to seal well (see Tips, left). Repeat with remaining ravioli sheets and filling.

8. Add salt to boiling water. Drop in ravioli and cook just until they rise to the surface, 1 to 2 minutes. Using a slotted spoon or a spider (see Tips, left), remove ravioli as they are cooked, being careful not to break the shells. Scoop out ½ cup (125 mL) cooking water and set aside (see Tips, page 277).

9. In skillet over medium heat, heat sauce. Add reserved pasta water and ravioli and toss gently to coat well. Serve immediately or transfer to an airtight container and refrigerate for up to 1 week.

Mushroom and Spinach Lasagna

This hearty main course is perfect for large gatherings such as a birthday party, reunion or anniversary celebration. It works particularly well as part of a buffet — just cut smaller pieces.

MAKES 6 TO 8 SERVINGS

Tips

You can also make this lasagna using fresh pasta dough (see page 250).

The quantity of garlic depends on the size of the cloves. If large, use the smaller number. If small, more may be required.

To remove the skin from a clove of garlic, use the butt end of a chef's knife to press firmly but gently on the clove to loosen the skin. Using your index finger and thumb, gently squeeze off the skin.

Use button, cremini or portobello mushrooms for this dish. They are meaty and their texture holds up well when baked.

- **Preheat oven to 400°F (200°C)**
- **13- by 9-inch (33 by 23 cm) glass baking dish**

12	gluten-free lasagna noodles, divided (see Tips, left)	12
1 tbsp	fine sea salt, divided	15 mL
1/4 cup	coconut oil	60 mL
1/4 cup	brown rice flour	60 mL
2 cups	Almond Milk (page 61)	500 mL
1/2 cup	nutritional yeast, divided	125 mL
3 tbsp	grapeseed oil	45 mL
1/2 cup	chopped onion	125 mL
6 to 8	cloves garlic, minced	6 to 8
4 cups	thinly sliced mushrooms (see Tips, left)	1 L
8 cups	chopped spinach leaves	2 L
1 tbsp	chopped fresh thyme leaves	15 mL
3 1/4 cups	Classic Garlicky Tomato Sauce, divided (page 110)	800 mL
	Nutritional yeast for sprinkling	

1. In a large covered pot, bring pasta cooking water and 1 tsp (5 mL) salt to a rapid boil (see Tip, page 275). Add lasagna noodles and cook until al dente, as per package instructions. Drain. Rinse pasta under cold running water until cool (to stop the cooking). Spread out in a single layer on baking sheets lined with parchment paper and cover with damp kitchen towels (otherwise they will stick together). Set aside.

2. Meanwhile, in a saucepan over medium heat, melt coconut oil. Add rice flour and cook, stirring constantly, for about 5 minutes, until the raw taste of the flour has cooked out. Remove from heat and gradually whisk in almond milk, 1/4 cup (60 mL) at a time, until smooth. Bring mixture to a boil, reduce heat to low and simmer for 6 to 8 minutes, until thickened.

Gluten-free pasta needs to be cooked in a lot of rapidly boiling water so it does not stick together. Make sure you use a large pot with at least 4 to 5 times more water than pasta.

3. Remove from heat and stir in $\frac{1}{4}$ cup (60 mL) nutritional yeast and 1 tsp (5 mL) salt. Cover and set aside.

4. In a large skillet over medium heat, heat grapeseed oil. Add onion and remaining 1 tsp (5 mL) salt; cook, stirring constantly, until onion is translucent, about 5 minutes. Stir in garlic and cook until fragrant, about 2 minutes. Add mushrooms and toss to coat. Cook until they begin to soften (about 4 minutes), then add the spinach in batches. Cook until most of the liquid has evaporated, about 15 minutes.

5. Remove from heat and stir in remaining $\frac{1}{4}$ cup (60 mL) nutritional yeast and thyme. Transfer to a bowl and set aside.

6. *Assembly*: Pour just enough tomato sauce into baking dish to coat the bottom, about $\frac{1}{2}$ cup (125 mL). Lay 4 lasagna noodles lengthwise across bottom of dish, overlapping slightly. Spread half of the spinach-mushroom mixture evenly overtop. Cover with half of the almond milk sauce, followed by one-third of the remaining tomato sauce.

7. Repeat, following the same order. Finish with the remaining 4 noodles and top with remaining sauce. Sprinkle with additional nutritional yeast.

8. Bake in preheated oven for 45 minutes, until edges are golden brown and crisp and middle is bubbling hot. Serve immediately. The lasagna will keep for up to 1 week in an airtight container in the refrigerator.

Cannelloni

This is a great dish for entertaining. Creamy Cashew Ricotta is an excellent stand-in for the classic dairy cheese.

MAKES 4 TO 6 SERVINGS

Tips

Look for oven-ready gluten-free cannelloni shells in well-stocked supermarkets. If you can't find an oven-ready variety, cook regular gluten-free shells according to package instructions. Fill (Step 1), adjusting quantity of filling if necessary, when they are cool enough to handle.

You can replace the homemade vegan cheeses and tomato sauce with your favorite prepared vegan brands.

This dish can be prepared ahead of time and left in the fridge or freezer for an easy go-to meal any day of the week. To cook from frozen, preheat oven to 350°F (180°C) and bake for 45 to 60 minutes or until heated through.

If you are using fresh pasta (see Variation), use a small knife to pick up the bottom edge of the sheet to help you fold the pasta over the filling. Reduce the baking time by about 15 minutes.

- Preheat oven to 350°F (180°C)
- 13- by 9-inch (33 by 23 cm) glass baking dish, greased

16	ready-to-bake gluten-free cannelloni shells (see Tips, left)	16
2 cups	Creamy Cashew Ricotta (page 532; see Tips, left)	500 mL
4 cups	Classic Garlicky Tomato Sauce (page 110)	1 L
1 cup	Vegan Shredded Mozzarella (page 537)	250 mL
¼ cup	nutritional yeast	60 mL

1. Stuff each pasta shell with approximately 4 tbsp (60 mL) cashew ricotta. (When stuffed, the cannelloni shells should be full to both ends, leaving no extra room.)

2. Spread about 2 cups (500 mL) tomato sauce evenly over bottom of prepared baking dish. Lay filled cannelloni flat, shells touching. Top with remaining tomato sauce, mozzarella and nutritional yeast.

3. Bake in preheated oven for 1 hour or until pasta shells are soft and lightly browned and sauce is bubbling hot. Serve immediately or let cool, cover and refrigerate for up to 1 week.

Variation

Make the cannelloni with fresh Gluten-Free Pasta Dough (page 250). Cut the rolled dough into four 8-inch (20 cm) square sheets. Cut each of those sheets into quarters, making 16 pieces. Cook the pasta until it is almost al dente, 1 to 2 minutes. Drain and rinse under cold running water until cool. Spread out in a single layer on baking sheets. Cover with damp kitchen towels and set aside until cool enough to handle.

To fill, lay sheets one at a time on a clean work surface. Place about 4 tbsp (60 mL) Creamy Cashew Ricotta in the center of each sheet and spread into a thin strip. Roll up to form cannelloni. Continue with Step 2, placing seam side down in baking dish.

Mushroom Stroganoff with Noodles

Serve this rich, creamy pasta for a special lunch or dinner. The sour cream used is a vegan basic; it can be made anytime and stored in the fridge for a multitude of uses.

MAKES 4 TO 6 SERVINGS

Tips

The quantity of garlic depends on the size of the cloves. If large, use the smaller number. If small, more may be required.

Wheat-free tamari is a gluten-free seasoning made from fermented soybeans. It can be found in most well-stocked supermarkets and natural food stores.

You can also make this dish using fresh pasta dough (see page 250).

Gluten-free pasta needs to be cooked in a lot of rapidly boiling water so it does not stick together. Make sure you use a large pot with at least 4 to 5 times more water than pasta.

The residual starch in pasta cooking water helps to thicken and add body to the sauce. Chefs usually scoop out a quantity before draining pasta. Then they add $1/4$ to $1/2$ cup (60 to 125 mL) to the sauce, depending upon the desired result.

3 tbsp	grapeseed oil	45 mL
1 cup	chopped onion	250 mL
1 tsp	fine sea salt, divided	5 mL
4 to 6	cloves garlic, minced	4 to 6
4 cups	sliced cremini mushrooms	1 L
$1/4$ cup	wheat-free tamari (see Tips, left)	60 mL
1 cup	Vegan Sour Cream (page 555)	250 mL
1	package (16 oz/500 g) gluten-free fettuccini (see Tips, left)	1
	Chopped flat-leaf (Italian) parsley leaves	

1. In a large covered pot, bring pasta cooking water to a rapid boil (see Tips, left).
2. Meanwhile, in a skillet, heat oil over medium heat. Add onion and $1/2$ tsp (2 mL) salt. Cook, stirring frequently, until onion is translucent, about 6 minutes. Add garlic and cook until fragrant, about 2 minutes. Add mushrooms and cook until soft, retaining a bit of the liquid that comes from them. Remove from heat and stir in tamari and sour cream.
3. Add remaining $1/2$ tsp (2 mL) salt to boiling water. Add fettuccini and cook until al dente. Scoop out $1/2$ cup (125 mL) cooking water and set aside (see Tips, left). Drain.
4. Return mushroom mixture to low heat. Add noodles and toss to combine. Add reserved pasta water and stir well. Serve immediately, garnished with chopped parsley, or let cool, transfer to an airtight container and refrigerate for up to 5 days.

Thai-Style Coconut Eggplant and Rice Noodles

Fragrant coconut milk provides a perfect base to highlight the fresh, bold flavors of Thai cuisine. Spicy chiles, salty tamari, sweet coconut sugar, tart lime and aromatic garlic and ginger make this dish a real winner.

MAKES 3 TO 4 SERVINGS

Tips

To remove the skin from fresh gingerroot with the least amount of waste, use the edge of a teaspoon. With a brushing motion, scrape off the skin to reveal the yellow root.

The quantity of garlic depends on the size of the cloves. If large, use the smaller number. If small, more may be required.

To mince garlic: Place whole cloves on a cutting board. Using the butt end of a chef's knife, press firmly but gently on each clove to loosen the skin. Using your index finger and thumb, gently squeeze off the skins. Chop garlic coarsely, then sprinkle with a bit of sea salt. Using the butt end of the knife, rub the garlic into the cutting board. The salt will act as an abrasive and help to mince the garlic. Chop until fine.

¼ cup	grapeseed oil	60 mL
4 cups	chopped peeled eggplant	1 L
¼ cup	finely chopped onion	60 mL
½ tsp	fine sea salt	2 mL
2 tbsp	minced peeled gingerroot, divided (see Tips, left)	30 mL
6 to 8	cloves garlic, minced, divided (see Tips, left)	6 to 8
1	can (14 oz/400 mL) full-fat coconut milk	1
¼ cup	freshly squeezed lime juice, divided (see Tips, page 279)	60 mL
4 tsp	coconut sugar, divided	20 mL
2 tbsp	coconut oil	30 mL
1 tsp	minced fresh chile	5 mL
1	package (8 oz/250 g) medium rice noodles, soaked (see Tips, page 279)	1
3 tbsp	wheat-free tamari	45 mL
3 tbsp	water	45 mL

1. In a large saucepan over medium heat, heat grapeseed oil. Add eggplant and cook, stirring frequently, until golden brown and softened. Transfer to a plate lined with paper towels.

2. To the pan, add onion, salt, 1 tbsp (15 mL) ginger and half of the garlic. Cook, stirring occasionally, until onion is lightly golden and ginger and garlic are fragrant, about 5 minutes. Stir in coconut milk, 2 tbsp (30 mL) lime juice, 1 tsp (5 mL) coconut sugar and reserved eggplant. Bring to a boil, reduce heat and simmer until sauce has thickened, about 12 minutes.

Tips

A hand-held citrus reamer can be used to extract the juice from lemons and limes. Available in most kitchen supply stores, this tool would be ideal to use for the lime juice in this recipe.

To soak the rice noodles: Place in a bowl and cover with 8 cups (2 L) hot water. Cover and set aside for about 15 minutes, until softened. (You want them to remain firm.) Drain, discarding liquid.

3. In a large skillet over high heat, melt coconut oil. Add chile, remaining 1 tbsp (15 mL) ginger and remaining garlic. Cook, stirring constantly, until garlic is lightly golden, about 2 minutes (be careful not to burn it).

4. Add rice noodles and toss to coat. Stir in tamari, water, remaining 2 tbsp (30 mL) lime juice and remaining 1 tbsp (15 mL) coconut sugar. Reduce heat to medium and simmer for 2 to 3 minutes. Add eggplant mixture and toss to coat well. Serve immediately.

Peanut Sesame Soba Noodles

This recipe is Thai-inspired, with creamy peanut sauce enveloping healthy soba noodles. It is very versatile — serve warm or cold as an appetizer, a light lunch or part of a meal, accompanied by Ginger Lime Edamame Stir-Fry (page 300) and some Sautéed Vegetables with Three-Chile Blend (page 296).

MAKES 2 TO 3 SERVINGS

Tips

Most soba noodles contain added wheat, which means they are not gluten-free. Look for brands made from pure buckwheat flour. They are available in most well-stocked natural food stores and Japanese markets.

To remove the skin from fresh gingerroot with the least amount of waste, use the edge of a teaspoon. With a brushing motion, scrape off the skin to reveal the yellow root.

The stems on the leaves closest to the bottom of fresh cilantro are generally tough and need to be removed. The stems on leaves closer to the top of the herb are soft and full of flavor and can be left on.

Gluten-free noodles need to be cooked in a lot of rapidly boiling water so they do not stick together. Make sure you use a large pot with at least 4 to 5 times more water than noodles.

● **Blender**

1 tsp	fine sea salt, divided	5 mL
1	package (8 oz/250 g) gluten-free soba noodles (see Tips, left)	1
1 cup	smooth peanut butter	250 mL
½ cup	water	125 mL
3 tbsp	freshly squeezed lime juice (see Tips, page page 281)	45 mL
1 tbsp	raw (unpasteurized) apple cider vinegar	15 mL
1 tbsp	wheat-free tamari	15 mL
1 tbsp	toasted sesame oil	15 mL
½ tsp	minced peeled gingerroot (see Tips, left)	2 mL
2	cloves garlic	2
1 cup	chopped fresh cilantro, leaves and stems (see Tips, left)	250 mL
1 tbsp	raw white sesame seeds	15 mL

1. In a large covered pot, bring water for cooking noodles to a rapid boil (see Tips, left). Add ½ tsp (2 mL) salt and soba noodles and cook until noodles are al dente, as per package directions. Drain, rinse well under cold running water and drain again.

2. Meanwhile, in blender, combine peanut butter, water, lime juice, vinegar, tamari, sesame oil, ginger, garlic and remaining ½ tsp (2 mL) salt. Blend at high speed until smooth and creamy.

3. In a skillet over medium heat, combine drained soba noodles and peanut butter mixture. Using a wooden spoon, toss to combine. Garnish with cilantro and sesame seeds. Serve immediately or transfer to an airtight container and refrigerate for up to 2 days.

Curried Soba Noodles

In this recipe I've tossed soft and silky soba noodles with aromatic spices and fragrant garlic and ginger. It's a simple dish that I like to serve as a light lunch or as a main dish, accompanied by a salad and steamed or sautéed vegetables.

Tips

The quantity of garlic depends on the size of the cloves. If large, use the smaller number. If small, more may be required.

To mince garlic: Place whole cloves on a cutting board. Using the butt end of a chef's knife, press firmly but gently on each clove to loosen the skin. Using your index finger and thumb, gently squeeze off the skins. Chop garlic coarsely, then sprinkle with a bit of sea salt. Using the butt end of the knife, rub the garlic into the cutting board. The salt will act as an abrasive and help to mince the garlic. Chop until fine.

A hand-held citrus reamer can be used to extract the juice from lemons and limes. Available in most kitchen supply stores, this tool would be ideal to use for the citrus in this recipe.

1 tsp	fine sea salt, divided	5 mL
1	package (8 oz/250 g) gluten-free soba noodles (see Tips, page 280)	1
3 tbsp	grapeseed oil	45 mL
1/2 cup	chopped onion	125 mL
3 to 4	cloves garlic, minced (see Tips, left)	3 to 4
1 tsp	minced peeled gingerroot	5 mL
1 tbsp	curry powder	15 mL
1 tsp	ground cumin	5 mL
1/4 tsp	ground coriander	1 mL
1/2 cup	chopped tomatoes	125 mL
1/4 cup	water	60 mL
2 tbsp	freshly squeezed lime or lemon juice (see Tips, left)	30 mL
1 tbsp	raw agave nectar	15 mL

1. In a large covered pot, bring water for cooking noodles to a rapid boil. Add 1/2 tsp (2 mL) salt and soba noodles and cook until noodles are al dente, as per package directions. Drain, rinse well under cold running water and drain again.

2. Meanwhile, in a large skillet over medium heat, heat oil. Add onion and remaining 1/2 tsp (2 mL) salt; cook, stirring frequently, until onion is translucent, about 6 minutes. Add garlic, ginger, curry powder, cumin and coriander. Cook, stirring constantly, for 4 to 5 minutes.

3. Add tomatoes, water, lime juice and agave nectar. Simmer, stirring occasionally and using a wooden spoon to scrape up any brown bits from bottom of pan, until slightly thickened, about 5 minutes. Add drained soba noodles and stir to combine. Serve immediately or transfer to an airtight container and refrigerate for up to 2 days.

Coconut Green Curry Angel Hair

Fragrant green curry sauce tossed with silky smooth angel hair pasta will satisfy any craving for an authentic Indian dinner.

Tips

Use only the bottom 2 inches (5 cm) of the lemongrass stalk, as the rest is tough and fibrous. Save the remainder to use in other Thai-inspired recipes; for example, bruise with the butt of a knife and then add to a soup or stew (discard before serving).

The quantity of garlic depends on the size of the cloves. If large, use the smaller number. If small, more may be required.

Makrut (also known by the offensive term "kaffir") lime leaves are available in Indian, Chinese and Thai food stores, as well as some large supermarkets. They are pungent in flavor, so a little goes a long way — 1 or 2 leaves per dish is usually more than enough.

Gluten-free pasta needs to be cooked in a lot of rapidly boiling water so it does not stick together. Make sure you use a large pot with at least 4 to 5 times more water than pasta.

1 tsp	fine sea salt, divided	5 mL
1	package (16 oz/500 g) gluten-free angel hair pasta	1
3 tbsp	grapeseed oil	45 mL
½ cup	chopped onion	125 mL
1 tsp	minced peeled gingerroot	5 mL
3 to 4	cloves garlic, minced (see Tips, left)	3 to 4
1 cup	chopped fresh cilantro, leaves and stems (see Tips, page 283)	250 mL
1 tbsp	finely chopped lemongrass (see Tips, left)	15 mL
2 tbsp	wheat-free tamari	30 mL
1 tsp	raw agave nectar	5 mL
1	can (14 oz/400 mL) full-fat coconut milk	1
1	makrut lime leaf (see Tips, left)	1

1. In a large covered pot, bring pasta cooking water to a rapid boil (see Tips, left). Add ½ tsp (2 mL) salt and angel hair pasta and cook until pasta is al dente, as per package instructions. Drain, rinse well under cold running water and drain again.

2. Meanwhile, in a skillet, heat oil over medium heat. Add onion and remaining ½ tsp (2 mL) salt. Cook, stirring frequently, until onion is translucent, 4 to 5 minutes. Add ginger and garlic and cook until soft and fragrant, 2 to 3 minutes.

3. Add cilantro, lemongrass, tamari, agave nectar, coconut milk and lime leaf. Bring to a simmer and cook until thickened slightly, about 5 minutes. Add drained pasta and stir to combine. Serve immediately or transfer to an airtight container and refrigerate for up to 5 days.

Crispy Asian Noodle Wraps

These crisp cabbage wraps are the perfect lunch for when it is hot outside and you crave something light and refreshing.

Tips

The stems on the leaves closest to the bottom of a fresh cilantro sprig are generally tough and need to be removed.

To finely slice mint: Remove the leaves from the stems and stack them one on top of another. Roll the leaves into a cigar shape and, using a sharp chef's knife, slice into thin strips.

Mirin is a sweet Japanese cooking wine that can be found in most well-stocked supermarkets. It has a low alcohol content that is further reduced by cooking.

8 cups	hot water	2 L
8 oz	thin rice noodles	250 g
½ cup	roughly chopped fresh cilantro, leaves and stems (see Tips, left)	125 mL
½ cup	shredded carrot	125 mL
½ cup	thinly sliced red bell pepper	125 mL
½ cup	chopped raw cashews	125 mL
¼ cup	thinly sliced mint leaves (see Tips, left)	60 mL
3 tbsp	wheat-free tamari	45 mL
1 tbsp	freshly squeezed lime juice	15 mL
1 tbsp	mirin (see Tips, left)	15 mL
2 tsp	toasted sesame oil	10 mL
1 tsp	organic coconut sugar	5 mL
Pinch	red pepper flakes	Pinch
4 to 6	large napa cabbage leaves	4 to 6

1. In a large bowl, combine hot water and rice noodles. Cover and set aside for 15 to 20 minutes, until softened. Drain, using a colander. Rinse under cold running water until water runs clear.

2. Transfer noodles to a large bowl. Add cilantro, carrot, red pepper, cashews, mint, tamari, lime juice, mirin, sesame oil, coconut sugar and red pepper flakes. Toss to combine.

3. Lay a cabbage leaf on a clean work surface, rib side up. Top with seasoned noodle mixture, dividing equally and leaving a ¼-inch (0.5 cm) border around the edges.

4. Starting at the edge closest to you, roll up tightly to form a cylinder. Repeat with remaining cabbage leaves and filling. Serve immediately or wrap tightly in plastic wrap, transfer to an airtight container and refrigerate for up to 1 day.

Soba Noodles with Sesame Ginger Tempeh

One of my favorite meals is a simple bowl of fresh noodles and protein-rich tempeh with a delicious sauce. This makes an easy lunch or family dinner.

MAKES 4 SERVINGS

Tips

Unpasteurized tempeh can be found in the freezer section of most well-stocked supermarkets and natural food stores. I prefer unpasteurized, as I find it has a better texture. Pasteurized tempeh will work equally well for this recipe.

Wheat-free tamari is a gluten-free seasoning made from fermented soybeans. It can be found in most well-stocked supermarkets and natural food stores.

The quantity of garlic depends on the size of the cloves. If large, use the smaller number. If small, more may be required.

Be sure to use raw (not processed) agave nectar. It is a 100% natural (non-GMO) sweetener that contains naturally occurring fructose and is low on the glycemic scale, which means that it releases glucose slowly, providing sustained energy.

TEMPEH

4 cups	water	1 L
1	block (8½ oz/240 g) frozen (unpasteurized) tempeh (see Tips, left)	1
1 cup	wheat-free tamari, divided (see Tips, left)	250 mL
1 to 2	whole cloves garlic	1 to 2
1 tbsp	grapeseed oil	15 mL
¼ cup	finely chopped onion	60 mL
2 tbsp	minced peeled gingerroot	30 mL
2 to 3	cloves garlic, minced	2 to 3
½ cup	water	125 mL
¼ cup	raw agave nectar (see Tips, left)	60 mL
2 tbsp	brown rice vinegar (see Tips, page 285)	30 mL
2 tbsp	toasted sesame oil	30 mL
2 tbsp	organic cornstarch	30 mL
2 tbsp	cold water	30 mL

SOBA NOODLES

1	package (8 oz/250 g) gluten-free soba noodles	1
1 cup	roughly chopped fresh cilantro, leaves and stems	250 mL
¼ cup	finely sliced green onion (green parts only)	60 mL
3 tbsp	wheat-free tamari	45 mL
2 tbsp	toasted sesame oil	30 mL

1. *Tempeh*: In a saucepan, combine water, tempeh, ½ cup (125 mL) tamari and whole garlic. Bring to a boil, reduce heat and simmer for 15 minutes. Using a slotted spoon, transfer tempeh to a plate (discard cooking liquid and garlic) and set aside until cool enough to handle, about 10 minutes.

Substitute an equal amount of raw (unpasteurized) apple cider vinegar for the brown rice vinegar.

Gluten-free soba noodles need to be cooked in a lot of rapidly boiling water so they do not stick together. Make sure you use a large pot with at least 4 to 5 times more water than noodles.

2. Meanwhile, in a saucepan over medium heat, heat grapeseed oil. Add onion and ginger and cook, stirring frequently, until lightly browned, about 6 minutes. Stir in minced garlic and cook until fragrant, 2 to 3 minutes. Add water, agave nectar, vinegar and sesame oil; stir to combine. Bring to a boil, reduce heat and simmer for 2 to 3 minutes.

3. In a small a bowl, whisk together cornstarch and cold water until no lumps remain. Whisking constantly, pour into sesame-ginger mixture and bring to a boil. Reduce heat to low and simmer for 3 to 4 minutes, until thickened.

4. Using a sharp knife, cut poached tempeh in half widthwise across the middle. Cut each half into 2 triangles. Add to sauce and simmer for 3 to 4 minutes.

5. *Soba Noodles:* In a large pot, bring water for cooking noodles to a rapid boil (see Tips, left). Add soba noodles and cook until al dente, as per package instructions. Drain, but do not rinse. Transfer to a large bowl.

6. Add cilantro, green onion, tamari and sesame oil to noodles. Toss to combine.

7. Divide noodles among serving plates. Top with cooked tempeh and serve immediately.

Buddhist Noodle Bowl

Silky soba noodles combine perfectly with rich, salty broth, aromatic ginger and crunchy fresh vegetables in this very satisfying main-course dish.

MAKES 2 TO 3 SERVINGS

Tips

Wheat-free tamari is a gluten-free seasoning made from fermented soybeans. It can be found in most well-stocked supermarkets and natural food stores.

Dulse is a red seaweed. Look for it in well-stocked supermarkets, where it can be found in dried form in a shaker-type bottle. It has a salty flavor and makes a great substitute for salt in soups and sauces.

To remove the skin from fresh gingerroot with the least amount of waste, use the edge of a teaspoon. With a brushing motion, scrape off the skin to reveal the yellow root.

● **Blender**

BROTH

½ cup	wheat-free tamari (see Tips, left)	125 mL
½ cup	water	125 mL
2 tbsp	raw agave nectar	30 mL
1 tbsp	dulse flakes (see Tips, left)	15 mL
1 tbsp	brown rice vinegar	15 mL
1 tbsp	chopped peeled gingerroot (see Tips, left)	15 mL
1 tbsp	mirin	15 mL

NOODLES

1	package (8 oz/250 g) gluten-free soba noodles (see Tips, page 287)	1

VEGETABLES

2 tbsp	grapeseed oil	30 mL
1 tbsp	minced peeled gingerroot	15 mL
1 cup	thinly sliced baby bok choy	250 mL
½ cup	thinly sliced shiitake mushrooms	125 mL
½ cup	thinly sliced napa cabbage	125 mL
½ cup	thinly sliced red bell pepper	125 mL
½ cup	cooked adzuki beans (see Tips, page 287)	125 mL
2 tbsp	thinly sliced green onion	30 mL
2 tsp	raw white sesame seeds	10 mL
Dash	toasted sesame oil	Dash

1. *Broth:* In blender, combine tamari, water, agave nectar, dulse, vinegar, ginger and mirin. Blend at high speed until smooth. Transfer to a small saucepan and bring to a boil. Cover, reduce heat to low, and simmer until ready to use.

2. *Noodles:* In a large saucepan of boiling water, cook noodles according to package instructions. Using a colander, drain and immediately rinse under cold running water to remove excess starch. Set drained noodles aside.

Tips

Most soba noodles contain added wheat, which means they are not gluten-free. Look for brands made from pure buckwheat flour. They are available in most well-stocked natural food stores and Japanese markets.

Use either adzuki beans you have cooked yourself (see page 182) or canned beans, preferably with no salt added. When using canned beans that contain salt, be sure to rinse thoroughly under cold running water before adding.

3. *Vegetables:* In a large skillet over medium heat, heat grapeseed oil. Add ginger and cook until lightly golden, about 2 minutes. Add bok choy, mushrooms, cabbage and red pepper. Cook until soft, 2 to 3 minutes (be careful not to overcook, as you want the vegetables to retain their color).

4. Pour noodles and broth into individual serving bowls. Top with sautéed vegetables, beans, green onion, sesame seeds and a drizzle of sesame oil, divided equally. Serve immediately.

Classic Dashi Noodle Bowl

Silky smooth noodles and warm nutrient-dense greens highlight this classic Japanese broth.

Tips

Wheat-free tamari is a gluten-free seasoning made from fermented soybeans. It can be found in most well-stocked supermarkets and natural food stores.

Dulse is a red seaweed. Look for it in well-stocked supermarkets, where it can be found in dried form in a shaker-type bottle. It has a salty flavor and makes a great substitute for salt in soups and sauces.

This dish is best made with thin noodles such as soba noodles or spaghetti.

Gluten-free pasta needs to be cooked in a lot of rapidly boiling water so it does not stick together. Make sure you use a large pot with at least 4 to 5 times more water than pasta.

● **Blender**

DASHI

2 cups	water	500 mL
¼ cup	wheat-free tamari (see Tips, left)	60 mL
1 tbsp	raw agave nectar	15 mL
2 tsp	brown rice vinegar	10 mL
2 tsp	toasted sesame oil	10 mL
2 tsp	dulse flakes (see Tips, left)	10 mL
1 tsp	minced peeled gingerroot	5 mL

NOODLES AND GREENS

1	package (8 oz/250 g) gluten-free noodles (see Tips, left)	1
4 cups	thinly sliced baby bok choy	1 L
2 cups	cubed (½ inch/1 cm) firm tofu	500 mL
1 cup	broccoli florets	250 mL
¼ cup	thinly sliced green onion (green part only)	60 mL

1. *Dashi:* In blender, combine water, tamari, agave nectar, vinegar, sesame oil, dulse and ginger. Blend at high speed until smooth. Transfer to a small saucepan and bring to a boil. Cover and reduce heat to low to keep warm until ready to use.

2. *Noodles and Greens:* In a large covered pot, bring water for cooking noodles to a rapid boil (see Tips, left). Cook noodles until al dente, as per package instructions. Drain.

3. Return noodles to pot. Add bok choy, tofu, broccoli, green onion and prepared dashi. Bring to a simmer. Serve immediately or transfer to an airtight container and refrigerate for up to 5 days.

Sautés and Stir-Fries

Sautés

Stir-Fries

Sautéed Olives with Lemon, Garlic and Fresh Herbs

Rich garlic, aromatic herbs and tart lemon give these olives a boost of flavor. Serve as an easy appetizer or toss with hot pasta (see Gluten-Free Pasta Dough, page 250) for a quick and tasty dinner.

MAKES 4 SERVINGS

Tips

To chop fresh thyme: Pinch the stem at the bottom with two fingers. Pulling upward with the finger and thumb of your other hand, strip the leaves. Reserve stems for soups or broths (discard after cooking). Use a sharp knife to chop the leaves, being careful not to chop too much or too hard, as this will bruise the leaves and cause the thyme to discolor.

I prefer this combination of kalamata, green and niçoise olives, but you can substitute any type of olives you have on hand.

If you are storing this dish in the refrigerator, leave the lemon in until you are ready to serve.

¼ cup	extra virgin olive oil	60 mL
3 to 4	cloves garlic, thinly sliced	3 to 4
2 tbsp	roughly chopped fresh rosemary	30 mL
2 tbsp	roughly chopped fresh thyme leaves (see Tips, left)	30 mL
½ cup	kalamata olives	125 mL
½ cup	green olives	125 mL
½ cup	niçoise olives	125 mL
½ cup	thinly sliced lemon (unpeeled)	125 mL

1. In a large skillet over medium-low heat, heat oil. Add garlic and cook, stirring occasionally, until lightly golden. Stir in rosemary and thyme and cook for 1 to 2 minutes, until fragrant. Add kalamata, green and niçoise olives and cook, stirring occasionally, for 4 to 5 minutes, until well coated and heated through.

2. Stir in lemon and cook for 2 to 3 minutes, until lemon is heated through. Remove from heat and set aside to cool. Remove and discard lemon (see Tips, left). Serve immediately or transfer to an airtight container and refrigerate for up to 1 month.

Variation

Sautéed Olives with Orange, Chile and Fennel: Omit the garlic, rosemary, thyme and lemon. Add 1 tsp (5 mL) hot pepper flakes, ½ cup (125 mL) thinly sliced orange (unpeeled) and 1 tbsp (15 mL) fennel seeds.

Balsamic-Glazed Cherry Tomatoes in Red Wine Sauce

These sautéed balsamic tomatoes are delicious served over grilled or roasted dishes such as Cauliflower Gratin (page 169) or Grilled Tomato and Portobello Ragoût (page 340).

MAKES ABOUT 2 CUPS (500 ML)

Tips

Substitute an equal amount of chopped fresh tomatoes (with juice) for the cherry tomatoes.

Be sure to use raw (not processed) agave nectar. It is a 100% natural (non-GMO) sweetener that contains naturally occurring fructose and is low on the glycemic scale, which means that it releases glucose slowly, providing sustained energy.

Substitute 1½ tbsp (22 mL) raw almond butter for the non-dairy butter.

1 tbsp	grapeseed oil	15 mL
4 cups	cherry tomatoes, halved (see Tips, left)	1 L
½ cup	dry red wine	125 mL
¼ cup	balsamic vinegar	60 mL
¼ cup	water	60 mL
3 tbsp	raw agave nectar (see Tips, left)	45 mL
1 tsp	chopped fresh thyme leaves	5 mL
¼ tsp	fine sea salt	1 mL
3 tbsp	Whipped Non-dairy Butter (page 554; see Tips, left)	45 mL

1. In a large skillet over medium heat, heat oil. Add tomatoes and cook, stirring often, for 12 to 15 minutes or until most of the liquid has evaporated. Stir in wine, vinegar, water and agave nectar. Bring to a boil, then reduce heat and simmer for 20 minutes, stirring occasionally, until most of the liquid has evaporated.

2. Remove from heat and stir in thyme and salt. Whisk in butter, 1 to 2 tsp (5 to 10 mL) at a time, until well incorporated. Serve immediately.

Spinach Sautéed in White Wine and Garlic

Garlicky spinach makes a perfect accompaniment to your favorite roasted, braised or sautéed dishes. I like to serve it with Thyme and Mushroom Navy Bean Ragoût (page 202) or Mung Bean Daal (page 199).

MAKES 2 SERVINGS

Tips

Be careful not to burn the garlic. As soon as it begins to turn brown, add the spinach.

If using baby spinach for this recipe, increase the amount to 8 cups (2 L).

Substitute an equal amount of thinly sliced Swiss chard, beet greens or mustard greens for the spinach.

To chop fresh thyme: Pinch the stem at the bottom with two fingers. Pulling upward with the finger and thumb of your other hand, strip the leaves. Reserve stems for soups or broths (discard after cooking). Use a sharp knife to chop the leaves, being careful not to chop too much or too hard, as this will bruise the leaves and cause the thyme to discolor.

3 tbsp	grapeseed oil	45 mL
6 to 8	cloves garlic, minced	6 to 8
4 cups	packed chopped spinach leaves (see Tips, left)	1 L
¼ cup	dry white wine	60 mL
¼ tsp	fine sea salt	1 mL
2 tsp	chopped fresh thyme leaves (see Tips, left)	10 mL

1. In a large skillet over medium-high heat, heat oil. Add garlic and cook, stirring often, until fragrant and lightly golden, 2 to 3 minutes (see Tips, left).

2. Add spinach and cook just until wilted, 3 to 4 minutes. Add wine and cook until most of the liquid has evaporated, about 3 minutes. Add salt and thyme and toss to combine. Serve immediately.

Salt-and-Pepper Mushroom Sauté

Serve this simple yet satisfying sauté over some Chile Garlic Spaghetti (page 260) or alongside Teriyaki Tofu (page 298).

MAKES 2 SERVINGS

Tips

I like using a mixture of button, cremini, shiitake and chanterelle mushrooms for this recipe. You can also make it using only one type of mushroom, if that's all you have on hand.

To clean mushrooms, use a damp cloth to brush any dirt from the surface. Never clean mushrooms with water. Mushrooms are like sponges — they will absorb the water and turn gray.

3 tbsp	grapeseed oil	45 mL
¼ cup	finely chopped onion	60 mL
3 to 4	cloves garlic, minced	3 to 4
4 cups	thinly sliced assorted mushrooms (see Tips, left)	1 L
1 tsp	freshly ground black pepper	5 mL
½ tsp	fine sea salt	2 mL

1. In a large skillet over high heat, heat oil. Add onion and garlic and cook, stirring frequently, until onion is translucent, about 6 minutes.

2. Add mushrooms and cook, stirring frequently, until mushrooms are browned and all of the liquid has evaporated, 10 to 12 minutes. Remove from heat and season with pepper and salt. Serve immediately.

Ginger Cashew Carrot Sauté

For a simple and tasty meal, serve this sauté with Basic Quinoa (page 235) and a drizzle of wheat-free tamari.

Tips

To remove the skin from fresh gingerroot with the least amount of waste, use the edge of a teaspoon. With a brushing motion, scrape off the skin to reveal the yellow root.

Be sure to use raw (not processed) agave nectar. It is a 100% natural (non-GMO) sweetener that contains naturally occurring fructose and is low on the glycemic scale, which means that it releases glucose slowly, providing sustained energy.

3 tbsp	grapeseed oil	45 mL
2 tbsp	minced peeled gingerroot (see Tips, left)	30 mL
½ cup	raw cashews	125 mL
3 cups	thinly sliced carrots	750 mL
2 tbsp	raw agave nectar (see Tips, left)	30 mL
1 tbsp	water	15 mL
1 tbsp	wheat-free tamari	15 mL
1 tsp	toasted sesame oil	5 mL

1. In a large skillet over high heat, heat grapeseed oil. Add ginger and cashews and cook, stirring constantly, until nuts are lightly golden, 8 to 10 minutes. Add carrots and cook until just tender, 4 to 5 minutes.

2. Add agave nectar, water, tamari and sesame oil and cook for 2 minutes, until carrots are well coated. Serve immediately or let cool, transfer to an airtight container and refrigerate for up to 5 days.

Mushroom Fricassee

Try serving this classic dish over a large bowl of Polenta (page 230) with a sprinkling of Herb Salt (page 551) and some crusty bread for dipping.

MAKES 2 SERVINGS

Tips

The quantity of garlic depends on the size of the cloves. If large, use the smaller number. If small, more may be required.

Shiitake mushroom stems are fibrous and too tough to chew. However, they can be used to flavor soups or stocks. For this recipe, reserve the stems for another use or discard.

Any type of mushroom will work in this recipe. Try using chanterelle, hedgehog, portobello or maiitake mushrooms.

Wheat-free tamari is a gluten-free seasoning made from fermented soybeans. It can be found in most well-stocked supermarkets and natural food stores.

3 tbsp	grapeseed oil	45 mL
¼ cup	finely chopped onion	60 mL
¼ tsp	fine sea salt	1 mL
3 to 4	cloves garlic, minced	3 to 4
1 cup	sliced button mushrooms	250 mL
1 cup	sliced shiitake mushroom caps (see Tips, left)	250 mL
1 cup	sliced oyster mushrooms	250 mL
½ cup	dry red wine	125 mL
2 tbsp	wheat-free tamari (see Tips, left)	30 mL
1 tbsp	chopped fresh thyme leaves	15 mL
2 tbsp	Whipped Non-dairy Butter (page 554)	30 mL

1. In a large skillet over high heat, heat oil. Add onion, salt and garlic and cook, stirring frequently, until onion is translucent, about 6 minutes. Add button, shiitake and oyster mushrooms and cook, stirring frequently, until most of the liquid has evaporated, 8 to 10 minutes.

2. Stir in wine and cook until no liquid remains, 3 to 4 minutes. Remove from heat and add tamari, thyme and butter, stirring slowly so that the butter melts into the mushrooms. Serve immediately.

Sautéed Vegetables with Three-Chile Blend

These spicy vegetables are sure to bring any meal to life. Try serving them alongside Grilled King Oyster Mushrooms with Curried Sticky Rice Parcels (page 424).

Tips

Anaheim chiles are long, skinny red chiles that are available at most supermarkets. You can substitute an equal amount of fresh poblano chile, if desired.

Thinly sliced garlic can burn quickly when added to hot oil. To help prevent that from happening, slice the garlic about ⅛ inch (3 mm) thick.

3 tbsp	grapeseed oil	45 mL
1 tbsp	finely chopped jalapeño pepper	15 mL
1 tsp	finely chopped Anaheim chile (see Tips, left)	5 mL
½ tsp	hot pepper flakes	2 mL
2 to 3	cloves garlic, thinly sliced (see Tips, left)	2 to 3
½ cup	thinly sliced carrot	125 mL
½ cup	thinly sliced red bell pepper	125 mL
½ cup	thinly sliced zucchini	125 mL
½ cup	broccoli florets	125 mL
½ cup	thinly sliced kale leaves	125 mL
¼ tsp	fine sea salt	1 mL

1. In a large skillet over high heat, heat oil. Add jalapeño, Anaheim chile, hot pepper flakes and garlic. Cook, stirring constantly, until garlic is browned and chiles are fragrant, 2 to 3 minutes.

2. Add carrot, red pepper and zucchini and cook for 2 to 3 minutes, stirring occasionally, until carrot is tender. Add broccoli and kale and cook, stirring occasionally, for 2 to 3 minute, until vegetables are tender. Remove from heat and season with salt. Serve immediately or let cool, transfer to an airtight container and refrigerate for up to 5 days.

Sautéed Ginger Miso Tempeh

This protein-dense dish is ready in 20 minutes. Pair with another Asian-inspired dish such as Sweet-and-Sour Soup (page 325), Asian-Style Adzuki Bean Salad (page 185) or Soba Chopsticks (page 100).

MAKES 3 SERVINGS

Tips

Unpasteurized tempeh can be found in the freezer section of most well-stocked supermarkets and natural food stores. I prefer unpasteurized because I find it has a better texture. Pasteurized tempeh will work equally well in this recipe.

Wheat-free tamari is a gluten-free seasoning made from fermented soybeans. It can be found in most well-stocked supermarkets and natural food stores.

I like to use unpasteurized miso because it is living and contains healthy bacteria; do not boil it or you will kill the bacteria. Choose brown rice or chickpea miso for a gluten-free version (always check the labels, as some brands add barley).

1	block (8½ oz/240 g) frozen (unpasteurized) tempeh (see Tips, left)	1
4 cups	water	1 L
½ cup	wheat-free tamari, divided (see Tips, left)	125 mL
2	cloves garlic	2
3 tbsp	grapeseed oil	45 mL
¼ cup	unpasteurized brown rice miso or chickpea miso (see Tips, left)	60 mL
2 tbsp	pure maple syrup	30 mL
2 tbsp	minced peeled gingerroot	30 mL

1. In a small saucepan, combine tempeh, water, 6 tbsp (90 mL) wheat-free tamari and garlic. Bring to a boil, reduce heat and simmer for 15 minutes. Using a slotted spoon, transfer tempeh to a plate and set aside for 10 minutes to cool.

2. Using a sharp knife, cut tempeh into bite-size pieces.

3. In a large skillet over medium heat, heat oil. Add prepared tempeh and cook, stirring frequently, until golden brown on all sides, 8 to 10 minutes.

4. Meanwhile, in a small bowl, whisk together remaining tamari, miso, maple syrup and ginger. Add to browned tempeh in skillet and stir to combine. Serve immediately or let cool, transfer to an airtight container and refrigerate for up to 5 days.

Teriyaki Tofu

For a complete meal, serve this dish with Basic Rice (page 21) and some simple steamed greens such as broccoli or kale.

MAKES 4 SERVINGS

Tips

Freezing tofu: Although it is time-consuming, freezing, then thawing tofu creates a very appealing and unexpected texture. It is deliciously meaty and chewy. First, place tofu in the freezer overnight (or for at least 4 hours, until frozen through). When the tofu is frozen, place on a baking sheet and thaw at room temperature. Once thawed, cover with a clean kitchen towel and place another baking sheet (or a dinner plate) on top. Place a heavy weight (such as a large can of tomatoes or a brick) on top. Set weighted tofu aside in the refrigerator overnight (or for at least 6 hours).

Be sure to purchase organic cornstarch. Conventional cornstarch is likely made from genetically modified corn.

3 tbsp	grapeseed oil	45 mL
1 lb	firm tofu, preferably previously frozen, cut into 1-inch (2.5 cm) cubes (see Tips, left)	500 g
½ cup	Ginger Teriyaki Sauce (page 115)	125 mL
1 tbsp	chopped green onion (green part only)	15 mL
1 tsp	raw white sesame seeds	5 mL
3 tbsp	water	45 mL
1 tbsp	organic cornstarch (see Tips, left)	15 mL

1. In a large skillet over medium heat, heat oil. Add tofu and cook, stirring frequently, until golden brown on all sides, 10 to 12 minutes. Add teriyaki sauce, green onion and sesame seeds and cook for 2 to 3 minutes, until onion is softened.

2. In a small bowl, whisk together water and cornstarch until no lumps remain. Pour over tofu and simmer until thickened, 5 to 6 minutes. Serve immediately or let cool, transfer to an airtight container and refrigerate for up to 1 week.

Crispy Chickpea Stir-Fry

This protein-dense stir-fry pairs perfectly with a little Basic Rice (page 212) and some Stir-Fried Broccoli with Ginger and Hoisin (page 301).

MAKES 2 TO 3 SERVINGS

Tips

Use either chickpeas you have cooked yourself (see page 182) or canned chickpeas, preferably with no salt added. When using canned beans that contain salt, be sure to rinse and drain them thoroughly before using.

The outer layer of raw celery is very fibrous and can be difficult to chew. Use a vegetable peeler to remove the outside strands. This will make the texture more pleasing and bring out the flavor.

Wheat-free tamari is a gluten-free seasoning made from fermented soybeans. It can be found in most well-stocked supermarkets and natural food stores.

3 tbsp	grapeseed oil	45 mL
¼ tsp	hot pepper flakes	1 mL
2 to 3	cloves garlic, minced	2 to 3
2 cups	cooked chickpeas (see Tips, left)	500 mL
½ cup	thinly sliced celery (see Tips, left)	125 mL
1 tbsp	wheat-free tamari (see Tips, left)	15 mL

1. In a large skillet over high heat, heat oil. Add hot pepper flakes and garlic and cook, stirring constantly, until garlic is fragrant, about 30 seconds (be careful not to burn it). Add chickpeas and cook, stirring frequently, until crisp, 12 to 15 minutes.

2. Add celery and cook until tender, 2 to 3 minutes. Remove pan from heat and stir in tamari. Serve immediately or let cool, transfer to an airtight container and refrigerate for up to 1 week.

Ginger Lime Edamame Stir-Fry

Edamame are one of the most versatile foods in the vegan kitchen. Add them to soups, salads and stir-fries (such as this one) or blend them into dips and spreads. I like to serve this dish with Thai-Style Coconut Eggplant and Rice Noodles (page 278) or Thai Tofu Lettuce Snacks (page 167).

MAKES 2 SERVINGS

Tips

You can find precooked shelled organic edamame in the freezer section of your supermarket. Let thaw in the refrigerator overnight before cooking, or soak in 4 cups (1 L) warm water for 15 minutes, then drain well.

A citrus reamer is a hand-held tool used to extract the juice from lemons and limes. It is available in most kitchen supply stores and would be ideal to use for the lime juice in this recipe.

Once cooked, this dish can also be enjoyed cold as a protein-dense salad.

2 tbsp	grapeseed oil	30 mL
1 tbsp	minced peeled gingerroot	15 mL
¼ cup	chopped green onions (green part only)	60 mL
2 cups	shelled edamame beans (see Tips, left)	500 mL
1 tsp	freshly grated lime zest	5 mL
3 tbsp	freshly squeezed lime juice (see Tips, left)	45 mL
1 tbsp	water	15 mL
¼ tsp	fine sea salt	1 mL

1. In a large skillet over high heat, heat oil. Add ginger and cook, stirring frequently, for about 30 seconds or until fragrant. Add green onions and cook, stirring constantly, for about 2 minutes, until onions are lightly brown.

2. Stir in edamame and cook for 3 to 4 minutes, until bright green and tender. Stir in lime zest, lime juice, water and salt. Serve immediately or let cool, transfer to an airtight container and refrigerate for up to 5 days.

Variation

Chili Lime Black Beans: Substitute an equal amount of cooked black beans for the edamame and add 1 tsp (5 mL) chili powder.

Stir-Fried Broccoli with Ginger and Hoisin

Serve this Asian-inspired side with Teriyaki Tofu (page 298) and some Basic Rice (page 212).

Serve this Asian-inspired side with Teriyaki Tofu (page 298) and some Basic Rice (page 212).

MAKES 4 SERVINGS

Tips

To remove the skin from fresh gingerroot with the least amount of waste, use the edge of a teaspoon. With a brushing motion, scrape off the skin to reveal the yellow root.

Broccoli stems contain a lot of flavor and should not be thrown away. Use a vegetable peeler to remove the tough outer part and reveal the tender heart. Discard the bottom ½ inch (1 cm) of the stem, as it is fibrous and tough. After peeling, the tender stems can be substituted in virtually any recipe that calls for broccoli florets.

This recipe produces a real hit of hoisin flavor. If you prefer, reduce the quantity by up to half.

Look for gluten-free hoisin sauce that is free of preservatives and added sugars. Quality hoisin is made from soybeans and sweet potatoes, with the addition of molasses or other natural sugars.

3 tbsp	grapeseed oil	45 mL
3 tbsp	minced peeled gingerroot (see Tips, left)	45 mL
4 cups	broccoli florets (see Tips, left)	1 L
½ cup	hoisin sauce (see Tips, left)	125 mL
¼ cup	water	60 mL
1 tsp	rice wine vinegar	5 mL

1. In a large skillet over high heat, heat oil. Add ginger and cook, stirring frequently, until lightly browned, about 1 minute. Add broccoli and cook, stirring often, until it starts to turn bright green, 2 to 3 minutes.

2. Stir in hoisin sauce and water and cook for 2 to 3 minutes, until sauce has thickened slightly. Remove from heat and stir in vinegar. Serve immediately.

Light Summer Stir-Fry

This is a tasty light dish that can be made ahead of time and reheated just before serving your guests. The trick to keeping your vegetables crisp is to preheat the pan over high heat.

Tips

Thinly sliced garlic can burn quickly when added to hot oil. Slice the garlic about 1/8 inch (3 mm) thick.

The outer layer of raw celery is very fibrous and can be difficult to chew. Use a vegetable peeler to remove the outer strands. This will make the texture more pleasing and bring out the flavor.

Wheat-free tamari is a gluten-free seasoning made from fermented soybeans. It can be found in most well-stocked supermarkets and natural food stores.

To reheat leftovers: In a skillet, bring about 1/4 cup (60 mL) water to a simmer. Add leftovers and cook just until heated through, 3 to 4 minutes.

2 tbsp	grapeseed oil	30 mL
2 to 3	cloves garlic, thinly sliced (see Tips, left)	2 to 3
1 tbsp	minced peeled gingerroot	15 mL
1/2 cup	thinly sliced carrot	125 mL
1/2 cup	thinly sliced celery (see Tips, left)	125 mL
1/2 cup	thinly sliced red bell pepper	125 mL
1/2 cup	broccoli florets	125 mL
1/2 cup	thinly sliced baby bok choy	125 mL
3 tbsp	wheat-free tamari (see Tips, left)	45 mL
1 tbsp	raw agave nectar	15 mL
1 tbsp	rice wine vinegar	15 mL
2 tsp	toasted sesame oil	10 mL

1. In a large skillet over high heat, heat grapeseed oil. Add garlic and ginger; cook, stirring constantly, for about 1 minute or until garlic is fragrant. Add carrot, celery and red pepper; cook, stirring frequently, until carrot is tender, about 2 minutes.

2. Add broccoli and bok choy; cook, stirring frequently, until soft, about 2 minutes. Stir in tamari, agave nectar, vinegar and sesame oil. Remove from heat and serve immediately or let cool, transfer to an airtight container and refrigerate for up to 5 days.

Quick Garlic Cabbage Stir-Fry

Serve this simple dish for a light lunch or as a side with Braised Tofu in French Onions (page 344) or Simple Simmered Moroccan Chickpeas (page 201).

MAKES 2 TO 3 SERVINGS

Tips

I like to use a mandoline to cut the cabbage for this recipe.

To remove the skin from a clove of garlic: Use the butt end of a chef's knife to press firmly but gently on the clove to loosen the skin. Using your index finger and thumb, gently squeeze the clove out of its skin.

Wheat-free tamari is a gluten-free seasoning made from fermented soybeans. It can be found in most well-stocked supermarkets and natural food stores.

2 tbsp	grapeseed oil	30 mL
8 to 10	cloves garlic, minced (see Tips, left)	8 to 10
4 cups	thinly sliced cabbage (see Tips, left)	1 L
2 tbsp	wheat-free tamari (see Tips, left)	30 mL
1 tbsp	water	15 mL
2 tsp	toasted sesame oil	10 mL
1 tsp	raw white sesame seeds	5 mL

1. In a large skillet over high heat, heat grapeseed oil. Add garlic and cook just until golden, about 30 seconds (be careful not to burn it). Add cabbage and cook, stirring constantly, until it starts to wilt, 3 to 4 minutes.

2. Add tamari, water and sesame oil. Cook until all of the liquid has evaporated, about 5 minutes. Stir in sesame seeds. Serve immediately or let cool, transfer to an airtight container and refrigerate for up to 5 days.

Crispy Eggplant and Garlic Stir-Fry

Serve this with a bowl of steaming Basic Rice (page 212) and some Spinach Sautéed in White Wine and Garlic (page 292).

Tips

Japanese eggplant has a milder flavor than traditional Italian eggplant. Its skin is also softer, which helps it cook quickly when sautéed. Look for it in well-stocked supermarkets.

To thinly slice basil: Remove the leaves from the stems and stack them one on top of another. Roll the leaves into a cigar shape and, using a sharp chef's knife, slice into thin strips.

¼ cup	grapeseed oil	60 mL
8 to 10	cloves garlic, thinly sliced	8 to 10
3 cups	thinly sliced Japanese eggplant (see Tips, left)	750 mL
3 tbsp	wheat-free tamari (see Tips, page 305)	45 mL
2 tbsp	pure maple syrup	30 mL
1 tbsp	water	15 mL
1 tsp	toasted sesame oil	5 mL
1 tbsp	organic cornstarch	15 mL
¼ cup	thinly sliced fresh basil (see Tips, left)	60 mL

1. In a large skillet over high heat, heat grapeseed oil. Add garlic and cook, stirring constantly, until golden, about 30 seconds (be careful not to burn it). Add eggplant and cook, stirring frequently, until golden brown on all sides, 6 to 8 minutes.

2. In a small bowl, whisk together tamari, maple syrup, water and sesame oil. Add cornstarch and whisk until no lumps remain. Add to browned eggplant. Bring mixture to a simmer and cook for 2 to 3 minutes, until sauce has thickened. Stir in basil. Serve immediately.

Pan-Seared King Oyster Mushrooms with Tamari Glaze

In this recipe, pan-seared king oyster mushrooms bring to mind small scallops. With their meaty texture and ability to absorb flavors, they also have a similar ingredient profile. Serve this dish as an appetizer or as part of a multi-course meal with dishes such as Quick Sweet-and-Sour Tofu Stir-Fry (page 303) or Dashi Broth with Soba Noodles (page 322).

MAKES 2 SERVINGS

Tips

If the mushroom stems are very big, cut a cross into one side before cooking. This will allow them to cook more evenly.

Wheat-free tamari is a gluten-free seasoning made from fermented soybeans. It can be found in most well-stocked supermarkets and natural food stores.

Substitute an equal amount of pure maple syrup for the agave nectar.

1 to 2	king oyster mushrooms	1 to 2
3 tbsp	grapeseed oil, divided	45 mL
¼ tsp	fine sea salt	1 mL
3 tbsp	wheat-free tamari (see Tips, left)	45 mL
1 tbsp	raw agave nectar (see Tips, left)	15 mL
1 to 2 tbsp	water	15 to 30 mL
1 tsp	chopped fresh thyme leaves	5 mL

1. Using a sharp knife, remove cap from oyster mushroom and reserve for another use. Trim bottom ½ inch (1 cm) from stem and discard. Cut remaining stem into rounds 1 inch (2.5 cm) thick — you should end up with 4 to 6 pieces that resemble scallops (see Tips, left).

2. Drizzle 1 tbsp (15 mL) of the oil over both sides of the scallops and season with salt.

3. In a large skillet over medium-high heat, heat remaining 2 tbsp (30 mL) oil. Add mushroom slices and cook until golden brown on one side, 4 to 5 minutes. Turn over and cook on other side until golden brown, 3 to 4 minutes. Reduce heat to low and stir in tamari, agave nectar, water and thyme. Cook for 2 to 3 minutes or until no liquid remains. Serve immediately.

Tofu and Lemongrass Vegetable Coconut Curry

Creamy coconut milk and fragrant lemongrass make a perfect sauce for crispy tofu. This simple dish can be cooked in a flash and makes a lovely brunch or lunch.

MAKES 2 SERVINGS

Tips

Freezing tofu: Although it is time-consuming, freezing, then thawing tofu creates a very appealing and unexpected texture. It is deliciously meaty and chewy. First, place tofu in the freezer overnight (or for at least 4 hours, until frozen through). When the tofu is frozen, place on a baking sheet and thaw at room temperature. Once thawed, cover with a clean kitchen towel and place another baking sheet (or a dinner plate) on top. Place a heavy weight (such as a large can of tomatoes or a brick) on top. Set weighted tofu aside in the refrigerator overnight (or for at least 6 hours).

The combination and quantities of vegetables in this recipe are ideal, but for convenience feel free to use any combination of vegetables you have on hand. I like to feature the tofu in this recipe, but if you prefer, you can increase the quantity of mixed vegetables to as much as 2 cups (500 mL).

3 tbsp	grapeseed oil, divided	45 mL
8 oz	firm tofu, preferably previously frozen, cut into ½-inch (1 cm) cubes (see Tips, left)	250 g
½ cup	chopped onion	125 mL
1 tbsp	chopped lemongrass (see Tips, page 307)	15 mL
¼ tsp	fine sea salt	1 mL
2 to 3	cloves garlic, minced	2 to 3
1 tbsp	minced peeled gingerroot	15 mL
2 tsp	curry powder	10 mL
½ tsp	ground cumin	2 mL
¼ tsp	ground coriander	1 mL
¼ cup	small broccoli florets (see Tips, left)	60 mL
¼ cup	chopped carrot	60 mL
¼ cup	thinly sliced red bell pepper	60 mL
¼ cup	chopped zucchini	60 mL
¼ cup	water	60 mL
1	can (14 oz/400 mL) full-fat coconut milk	1
2 tbsp	wheat-free tamari	30 mL
1 tbsp	freshly squeezed lemon juice	15 mL

1. In a large skillet over medium-high heat, heat 2 tbsp (30 mL) oil. Add tofu and cook, stirring frequently, until golden brown, about 10 minutes. Transfer to a plate lined with paper towels and set aside.

2. In same pan, heat remaining 1 tbsp (15 mL) grapeseed oil. Add onion, lemongrass and salt; cook until onion is soft and translucent, about 5 minutes. Add garlic and ginger; cook for about 1 minute, until garlic is fragrant. Stir in curry powder, cumin and coriander. Cook, stirring constantly, for 1 minute, until spices are fragrant.

Tips

Not all parts of lemongrass are edible. Before use in recipes such as stir-fries, soups or curries, lemongrass needs to be trimmed. Discard the bottom inch (2.5 cm) of the stalk and remove the tough outside leaves. The top, fibrous part of the lemongrass stalk can be reserved for simmering in soups or sauces, but it must be discarded before serving. The middle 2 to 3 inches (5 to 7.5 cm) of the stalk are soft and can be chopped and consumed. Lemongrass must be cooked for at least 4 to 5 minutes before the stalk will be edible.

Replace the curry powder, cumin and coriander in this recipe with 1 tbsp (15 mL) of your favorite Indian spice blend, such as garam masala or chaat masala.

3. Add broccoli, carrot, red pepper and zucchini and cook, stirring for 1 minute. Stir in water and coconut milk and bring to a boil. Add reserved tofu and cook for 5 minutes, or until mixture has thickened slightly and vegetables are tender.

4. Remove from heat and stir in tamari and lemon juice. Serve immediately or let cool, transfer to an airtight container and refrigerate for up to 1 week.

Quick Sweet-and-Sour Tofu Stir-Fry

Enjoy this dish on its own as a quick lunch or as part of a larger meal, served with Peanut Sesame Soba Noodles (page 280) and Sautéed Vegetables with Three-Chile Blend (page 296).

MAKES 4 SERVINGS

Tip

If you do not have sweet-and-sour sauce on hand, make a substitute by whisking together 2 tbsp (30 mL) raw agave nectar, 1 tbsp (15 mL) rice wine vinegar or raw (unpasteurized) apple cider vinegar, 1 tbsp (15 mL) water, 1 tbsp (15 mL) cornstarch and a pinch of fine sea salt. Bring to a boil in a small saucepan over medium-high heat, stirring constantly until thickened.

3 tbsp	grapeseed oil	45 mL
1 lb	firm tofu, cut into ½-inch (1 cm) cubes (see Tips, page 306)	500 g
½ cup	thinly sliced red bell pepper	125 mL
½ cup	broccoli florets	125 mL
¼ cup	chopped pineapple	60 mL
½ cup	Sweet-and-Sour Sauce (page 116; see Tip, left)	125 mL

1. In a large skillet over high heat, heat oil. Add tofu and cook, stirring frequently, until golden brown on all sides, 8 to 10 minutes.

2. Add red pepper, broccoli and pineapple; cook, stirring frequently, for 3 to 4 minutes, until pepper and broccoli are tender. Add sweet-and-sour sauce and stir to combine. Serve immediately or let cool, transfer to an airtight container and refrigerate for up to 5 days.

Freezing Tofu

Although it is time-consuming, freezing, then thawing tofu creates a very appealing and unexpected texture. It is deliciously meaty and chewy. Use it anywhere a meaty texture is desired, in dishes such as stir-fries, soups, stews or salads. *To freeze tofu:* Place in the freezer overnight (or for at least 4 hours, until frozen through). When the tofu is frozen, place on a baking sheet and thaw at room temperature. Once thawed, cover with a clean kitchen towel and place another baking sheet (or a dinner plate) on top. Place a heavy weight (such as a large can of tomatoes or a brick) on top. Set weighted tofu aside in the refrigerator overnight (or for at least 6 hours).

Pineapple and Coconut Fried Rice

Serve this tropical dish as part of a main course or for lunch along with a tall glass of Spicy Ginger Juice (page 47).

**MAKES
2 MAIN-COURSE
SERVINGS OR
4 SIDE SERVINGS**

Tips

Replace Basic Rice with an equal amount of cooked brown jasmine rice.

For a nice color contrast, use equal parts white and black sesame seeds.

3 tbsp	grapeseed oil	45 mL
¼ cup	finely chopped onion	60 mL
2 to 3	cloves garlic, minced	2 to 3
1 tsp	minced peeled gingerroot	5 mL
2 cups	Basic Rice (page 212; see Tips, left)	500 mL
½ cup	drained chopped pineapple	125 mL
½ cup	unsweetened shredded coconut	125 mL
2 tbsp	wheat-free tamari	30 mL
2 tsp	toasted sesame oil	10 mL
1 tbsp	raw white sesame seeds (see Tips, left)	15 mL

1. In a large skillet over high heat, heat grapeseed oil. Add onion, garlic and ginger; cook, stirring constantly, for 2 to 3 minutes, until onion is translucent. Add rice and cook for 2 to 3 minutes, until heated through. Add pineapple and coconut; cook for 2 to 3 minutes, until pineapple is soft and fragrant.

2. Add tamari, sesame oil and sesame seeds and toss to coat well. Serve immediately.

Classic Pad Thai

This traditional Thai noodle dish comes together quickly and makes the perfect lunch or dinner.

Tips

To avoid additives and preservatives, purchase tamarind in blocks rather than jars of paste.

To soak the tamarind: Break off a 2-inch (5 cm) piece and place in a bowl with 1 cup (250 mL) hot water; set aside for 1 hour. Drain, discarding liquid. Transfer to a blender or food processor and add ½ cup (125 mL) warm water; process until smooth. Transfer to a fine-mesh sieve set over a bowl and, using the back of a spoon, press pulp through sieve (discard solids).

To soak the rice noodles: Place in a bowl with 8 cups (2 L) boiling water. Cover and set aside for 30 minutes. Drain.

If you prefer a little less heat, remove the seeds and ribs from the chile.

Be sure to use raw (not processed) agave nectar. It is a 100% natural (non-GMO) sweetener that contains naturally occurring fructose and is low on the glycemic scale, which means that it releases glucose slowly, providing sustained energy.

1	piece (2 inches/5 cm) block tamarind, soaked (see Tips, left)	1
8 oz	broad rice noodles, soaked (see Tips, left)	250 g
3 tbsp	grapeseed oil	45 mL
4	cloves garlic, minced	4
1 tsp	minced peeled gingerroot	5 mL
1	small Anaheim chile, finely chopped (see Tips, left)	1
½ cup	thinly sliced green onions, green part only	125 mL
¼ cup	thinly sliced green onion, white part only	60 mL
2 cups	bean sprouts	500 mL
½ cup	broccoli florets	125 mL
¼ cup	wheat-free tamari	60 mL
¼ cup	Vegetable Stock (page 559)	60 mL
3 tbsp	raw agave nectar (see Tips, left)	45 mL
¼ tsp	cayenne pepper	1 mL
8 oz	soft tofu, cut into ½-inch (1 cm) cubes	250 g
	Lime wedges	
	Crushed peanuts or almonds	

1. In a large skillet over medium-high heat, heat oil. Add garlic and ginger; cook, stirring constantly, until garlic is fragrant and golden, 2 to 3 minutes. Add chile, green onions, bean sprouts and broccoli. Cook, stirring frequently, for 2 to 3 minutes, until broccoli is slightly tender.

2. Add tamarind pulp, soaked noodles, tamari, vegetable stock, agave nectar and cayenne. Bring mixture to a simmer and cook for 2 to 3 minutes, stirring often, until noodles are well coated.

3. Stir in tofu and cook for 2 to 3 minutes, until tofu is heated through. Serve immediately, garnished with lime wedges and crushed peanuts.

Soups, Stews, Chilies and More

Soups

Stews

Chilies and More

Chilled Green Pea and Mint Soup

This cold soup is perfect for hot summer days or as part of a multiple-course meal.

**MAKES
6 CUPS (1.5 L)**

Tips

To thaw the frozen peas, place in a colander and rinse under cold running water.

If you prefer a thinner consistency, increase the amount of water to 6 cups (1.5 L).

● **Blender**

3 cups	frozen green peas, thawed, divided (see Tips, left)	750 mL
4 cups	water, divided (see Tips, left)	1 L
½ tsp	fine sea salt	2 mL
½ cup	fresh mint leaves	125 mL
1 tbsp	nutritional yeast	15 mL
	Vegan Sour Cream (page 555)	

1. In blender, combine half of the peas, half of the water and the salt. Blend at high speed until smooth. Transfer to an airtight container.

2. Add remaining peas and water to blender, along with mint and nutritional yeast. Blend at high speed until smooth. Add to container with first batch and stir well.

3. Cover and refrigerate until thoroughly chilled (about 30 minutes) or store refrigerated for up to 3 days. Serve garnished with sour cream.

Spicy Gazpacho

This refreshing summer soup is best served icy cold with some crusty bread.

Tips

Substitute 4 cups (1 L) chopped fresh tomatoes (field, hothouse or vine) for the canned tomatoes. Do not use Roma tomatoes, as their water content is too low for this recipe.

Substitute an equal amount of fresh cilantro, leaves and stems, for the parsley.

● Blender

1	can (28 oz/796 mL) diced tomatoes, with juice (see Tips, left)	1
¼ cup	water	60 mL
2 tbsp	freshly squeezed lime juice	30 mL
1 tbsp	extra virgin olive oil	15 mL
1 tbsp	wheat-free tamari	15 mL
1 tbsp	raw agave nectar	15 mL
½ tsp	fine sea salt	2 mL
¼ tsp	cayenne pepper	1 mL
1 cup	chopped red bell pepper	250 mL
½ cup	chopped flat-leaf (Italian) parsley leaves (see Tips, left)	125 mL
¼ cup	chopped red onion	60 mL
1 to 2	cloves garlic	1 to 2

1. In blender, combine tomatoes, water, lime juice, oil, tamari, agave nectar, salt and cayenne. Blend at high speed until smooth.

2. Add red pepper, parsley, onion and garlic. Blend until no large pieces remain (be careful not to overprocess — you want to retain some texture). Transfer to an airtight container and refrigerate until thoroughly chilled. Gazpacho can be stored in the refrigerator for up to 5 days.

Vegan Chicken Noodle Soup

This version of the classic soup delivers all the comfort you'd expect, thanks to its trio of traditional veggies (carrot, celery and onion), hearty noodles and a hit of nutritional yeast.

MAKES 4 SERVINGS

Tips

Nutritional yeast is an inactive yeast that has been grown on beet molasses and then pasteurized. It provides a rich, cheesy flavor in sauces, stews, soups and dips. Look for it in well-stocked supermarkets and natural food stores.

Gluten-free pasta needs to be cooked in a lot of rapidly boiling water to ensure that it does not stick together. Be sure to use a large pot with at least 4 to 5 times more water than pasta.

4 cups	water	1 L
1 cup	nutritional yeast (see Tips, left)	250 mL
½ cup	chopped carrot	125 mL
½ cup	chopped celery	125 mL
¼ cup	chopped onion	60 mL
1 tbsp	chopped fresh thyme leaves	15 mL
½ cup	gluten-free dried pasta such as penne or spirals	125 mL
½ tsp	fine sea salt	2 mL
½ cup	chopped fresh parsley leaves	125 mL

1. In a large pot, combine water, nutritional yeast, carrot, celery, onion and thyme. Bring to a boil, reduce heat and simmer until vegetables are tender, about 10 minutes.
2. In another large covered pot, bring pasta cooking water to a rapid boil (see Tips, left). Add pasta and salt and cook until pasta is al dente, as per package instructions. Drain.
3. Add cooked pasta to soup and stir to combine. Stir in parsley. Serve immediately or let cool, transfer to an airtight container and refrigerate for up to 5 days.

Avgolemono Soup

This take on a classic Greek egg-drop soup is made creamy with quinoa, tahini and vegetables. Serve with crusty bread.

MAKES 3 SERVINGS

Tips

I like to use unpasteurized miso because it is living and contains healthy bacteria; do not boil it or you will kill the bacteria. Choose brown rice or chickpea miso for a gluten-free version (always check the labels, as some brands add barley, which contains gluten).

Nutritional yeast is an inactive yeast that has been grown on beet molasses and then pasteurized. It provides a rich, cheesy flavor in sauces, stews, soups and dips. Look for it in well-stocked supermarkets and natural food stores.

2 tbsp	grapeseed oil	30 mL
½ cup	chopped onion	125 mL
½ cup	chopped carrot	125 mL
1 tsp	fine sea salt	5 mL
3 to 4	cloves garlic, minced	3 to 4
5 cups	Vegetable Stock (page 559)	1.25 L
½ cup	quinoa, rinsed and drained	125 mL
¼ cup	freshly squeezed lemon juice	60 mL
2 tbsp	tahini	30 mL
1 tbsp	unpasteurized miso (see Tips, left)	15 mL
¼ cup	roughly chopped fresh dill	60 mL
¼ cup	nutritional yeast (see Tips, left)	60 mL

1. In a large pot over medium heat, heat oil. Add onion, carrot and salt; cook, stirring frequently, until vegetables are softened, 6 to 8 minutes. Stir in garlic and cook for 2 to 3 minutes, until fragrant. Add vegetable stock and quinoa and stir to combine. Bring to a boil, reduce heat and simmer until quinoa is tender, about 20 minutes.

2. Meanwhile, in a small bowl, whisk together lemon juice, tahini and miso until no lumps remain.

3. Remove pot from heat and stir in lemon juice mixture, dill and nutritional yeast. Serve immediately or let cool, transfer to an airtight container and refrigerate for up to 5 days.

French Onion Soup

This twist on the classic soup is made rich with wheat-free tamari, fresh herbs and aromatic garlic. The croutons and vegan mozzarella make the perfect finish.

Tips

Wheat-free tamari is a gluten-free seasoning made from fermented soybeans. It can be found in most well-stocked supermarkets and natural food stores.

You can substitute a dash of white or red wine vinegar for the sherry.

1 tbsp	grapeseed oil	15 mL
4 cups	thinly sliced onions	1 L
¼ tsp	fine sea salt	1 mL
10 to 12	cloves garlic, minced	10 to 12
½ cup	dry white wine (optional)	125 mL
8 cups	water	2 L
½ cup	wheat-free tamari (see Tips, left)	125 mL
1 tbsp	chopped fresh thyme leaves	15 mL
Dash	dry sherry (optional)	Dash
	Gluten-Free Croutons (page 553)	
	Vegan Shredded Mozzarella (page 537)	

1. In a large pot over high heat, heat oil. Add onions and salt and cook, stirring often, until lightly brown, 10 to 12 minutes. Reduce heat to low and continue to cook, stirring occasionally, until onions are golden brown and softened, about 30 minutes.

2. Stir in garlic and cook for 2 to 3 minutes, until fragrant. Add wine (if using) and cook until liquid has evaporated. Add water, tamari and thyme and stir to combine. Bring to a boil, reduce heat and simmer for 12 to 15 minutes, until soup is dark brown and fragrant.

3. Remove from heat and stir in sherry (if using). Serve immediately, garnished with a few croutons and some shredded mozzarella. The ungarnished soup will keep in an airtight container in the refrigerator for up to 1 week.

Spring Minestrone

This hearty soup is perfect for a light lunch or even for dinner during the warm summer months. I like to serve it with my favorite crusty bread.

Tips

To mince garlic: Place a whole clove on a cutting board. Using the butt end of a chef's knife, press firmly but gently on the clove to loosen the skin. Using your index finger and thumb, gently squeeze clove out of skin. Chop coarsely, then sprinkle with a bit of sea salt. Using the butt end of the knife, rub garlic into board (the salt will act as an abrasive and help to mince the garlic). Chop until fine.

Substitute 4 cups (1 L) chopped fresh tomatoes for the canned tomatoes.

Gluten-free pasta needs to be cooked in a lot of rapidly boiling water to ensure that it does not stick together. Be sure to use a large pot with at least 4 to 5 times more water than pasta.

2 tbsp	grapeseed oil	30 mL
1/2 cup	finely chopped onion	125 mL
1/2 cup	finely chopped celery	125 mL
1/2 cup	finely chopped carrot	125 mL
1/2 cup	chopped peeled sweet potato	125 mL
1 tsp	fine sea salt, divided	5 mL
2 tsp	chopped fresh thyme leaves, divided	10 mL
1 tsp	dried oregano	5 mL
4 to 6	cloves garlic, minced (see Tips, left)	4 to 6
	Water	
1	can (28 oz/796 mL) diced tomatoes, with juice (see Tips, left)	1
1/2 cup	red lentils, rinsed and drained	125 mL
3 tbsp	wheat-free tamari	45 mL
1 tbsp	freshly squeezed lemon juice	15 mL
1 cup	gluten-free pasta such as penne or spirals	250 mL

1. In a large pot over medium heat, heat oil. Add onion, celery, carrot, sweet potato and 1/2 tsp (2 mL) salt. Cook, stirring frequently, until vegetables are softened, about 6 minutes. Stir in 1 tsp (5 mL) thyme, oregano and garlic; cook for 2 to 3 minutes, until fragrant.

2. Add 4 cups (1 L) water, tomatoes, lentils, tamari and lemon juice; stir to combine. Bring to a boil, reduce heat and simmer until lentils are tender, about 20 minutes.

3. Meanwhile, in a large covered pot, bring pasta cooking water and remaining 1/2 tsp (2 mL) salt to a rapid boil. Add pasta and cook until al dente. Drain.

4. Add cooked pasta and remaining 1 tsp (5 mL) thyme to lentil mixture and stir to combine. Serve immediately or let cool, transfer to an airtight container and refrigerate for up to 5 days.

Tomato and Sweet Potato Soup

Sweet potatoes boost the nutrition and provide the smooth, creamy texture in this take on a classic. Serve with gluten-free crackers.

Tips

The quantity of garlic depends on the size of the cloves. If large, use the smaller number. If small, more may be required.

To mince garlic: Place a whole clove on a cutting board. Using the butt end of a chef's knife, press firmly but gently on the clove to loosen the skin. Using your index finger and thumb, gently squeeze clove out of skin. Chop coarsely, then sprinkle with a bit of sea salt. Using the butt end of the knife, rub garlic into board (the salt will act as an abrasive and help to mince the garlic). Chop until fine.

To avoid having leftover tomatoes, use 1 large can (28 oz/796 mL) and 1 small (14 oz/398 mL).

Wheat-free tamari is a gluten-free seasoning made from fermented soybeans. It can be found in most well-stocked supermarkets and natural food stores.

Blending this soup twice ensures a smooth, velvety texture because the first blending emulsifies the oil.

- Immersion blender
- Blender

1 tbsp	grapeseed oil	15 mL
¼ cup	chopped carrot	60 mL
½ cup	thinly sliced onion	125 mL
¼ tsp	fine sea salt	1 mL
4 to 6	cloves garlic, minced (see Tips, left)	4 to 6
2 cups	chopped peeled sweet potatoes	500 mL
1½	cans (each 28 oz/796 mL) diced tomatoes, with juice (see Tips, left)	1½
1½ tbsp	wheat-free tamari (see Tips, left)	22 mL
¼ cup	balsamic vinegar	60 mL
6 tbsp	extra virgin olive oil	90 mL

1. In a large pot over medium heat, heat grapeseed oil. Add carrot, onion and salt; cook, stirring frequently, until vegetables are softened, 6 to 7 minutes. Stir in garlic and cook for 2 to 3 minutes, until fragrant.

2. Add sweet potatoes, tomatoes, tamari and vinegar; stir to combine. Bring to a boil, reduce heat and simmer, stirring frequently, until sweet potatoes are tender, about 25 minutes.

3. Using immersion blender, add olive oil in a slow, steady stream, blending soup until oil is emulsified (you shouldn't see any floating on top).

4. Fill blender halfway with soup. Blend at high speed until smooth and creamy (see Tips, left). Transfer puréed soup, in batches if necessary (see Tips, page 319) to a clean pot. Repeat with remaining soup. Place pot over medium heat and bring soup to a simmer. Serve immediately or let cool, transfer to an airtight container and refrigerate for up to 1 week.

Sweet Potato, Ginger and Coconut Soup

The fragrant flavor of ginger highlights the creamy sweet potatoes in this recipe. Serve with a nice cold Piña Colada Juice (page 45) to balance the spicy heat.

(page 45)

MAKES 6 SERVINGS

Tips

To remove the skin from fresh gingerroot with the least amount of waste, use the edge of a teaspoon. With a brushing motion, scrape off the skin to reveal the yellow root.

Substitute an equal amount of chopped peeled butternut squash for the sweet potatoes.

When blending hot liquids in a blender, make sure the blender jar is no more than half full. Also, place a folded towel over the lid and place your hand firmly on top. Otherwise, the pressure of the steam may cause the lid to blow off, spattering your soup all over the kitchen.

● Blender

1 tbsp	grapeseed oil	15 mL
½ cup	thinly sliced onion	125 mL
1 tbsp	minced peeled gingerroot (see Tips, left)	15 mL
½ tsp	fine sea salt	2 mL
6 cups	peeled chopped sweet potatoes (see Tips, left)	1.5 L
4 cups	water	500 mL
½ cup	full-fat coconut milk	125 mL

1. In a large pot over medium heat, heat oil. Add onion, ginger and salt. Cook, stirring frequently, until onion is translucent and ginger is fragrant, about 6 minutes.

2. Add sweet potatoes and water and bring to a boil. Reduce heat and simmer until sweet potatoes are tender, about 15 minutes. Remove from heat and stir in coconut milk.

3. Fill blender jar halfway with soup (see Tips, left). Blend at high speed until smooth and creamy. Transfer puréed soup to a clean pot. Repeat with remaining soup, in batches if necessary. Place pot over medium heat and bring soup to a simmer. Serve immediately or transfer to an airtight container and refrigerate for up to 5 days.

Leek, Potato and Lentil Soup

The creaminess of this classic soup will awaken childhood memories of cold nights and fuzzy blankets.

MAKES 8 SERVINGS

Tips

The green part of a leek is tough and fibrous and has little flavor. Typically it is discarded or saved for stock.

To chop fresh thyme: Pinch the stem at the bottom with two fingers. Pulling upward with the finger and thumb of your other hand, strip the leaves. Reserve stems for soups or broths (discard after cooking). Use a sharp knife to chop the leaves, being careful not to chop too much or too hard, as this will bruise the leaves and cause the thyme to discolor.

Nutritional yeast is an inactive yeast that has been grown on beet molasses and then pasteurized. It provides a rich, cheesy flavor in sauces, stews, soups and dips. Look for it in well-stocked supermarkets and natural food stores.

Blending this soup twice ensures a smooth, velvety texture.

- Immersion blender
- Blender

2 tbsp	grapeseed oil	30 mL
4 cups	coarsely chopped leeks (white part only; see Tips, left)	1 L
½ cup	chopped celery	125 mL
3 tbsp	chopped fresh thyme leaves (see Tips, left)	45 mL
1 tsp	fine sea salt	5 mL
10	cloves garlic, minced	10
8 cups	water	2 L
2 cups	chopped potatoes	500 mL
½ cup	red lentils, rinsed and drained	125 mL
¼ cup	nutritional yeast (see Tips, left)	60 mL
½ cup	extra virgin olive oil	125 mL

1. In a large pot over medium heat, heat oil. Add leeks, celery, thyme and salt; cook, stirring frequently, until softened, about 10 minutes. Stir in garlic and cook for 2 to 3 minutes, until fragrant.

2. Add water, potatoes, lentils and nutritional yeast; stir to combine. Bring to a boil, reduce heat and simmer until potatoes are tender, about 20 minutes.

3. Using immersion blender, add olive oil in a slow, steady stream, blending soup until oil is emulsified (you shouldn't see any floating on top).

4. Fill blender jar halfway with soup (see Tips, page 319). Blend at high speed until smooth and creamy. Transfer puréed soup to a clean pot. Repeat with remaining soup, in batches if necessary. Place pot over medium heat and bring soup to a simmer. Serve immediately or let cool, transfer to an airtight container and refrigerate for up to 5 days.

Quinoa and Lentil Borscht

This hearty and warming soup is a take on the Russian classic, which is often served cold. The addition of quinoa helps to thicken and add body to the soup, as well as protein and fiber.

MAKES 8 SERVINGS

Tips

When making soups, I like to add fresh herbs such as thyme at two different stages: at the beginning of the recipe, when cooking the aromatic vegetables, and at the end, after the pan is removed from the heat. I find that doing this helps the herbs impart a more sophisticated, layered flavor.

Any variety of quinoa will work in this recipe: white, black or red.

Wheat-free tamari is a gluten-free seasoning made from fermented soybeans. It can be found in most well-stocked supermarkets and natural food stores.

When adding the water (Step 2) use 8 cups (2 L) to start. After the borscht has cooked, add more water to thin, if necessary.

2 tbsp	grapeseed oil	30 mL
½ cup	finely chopped onion	125 mL
½ cup	finely chopped celery	125 mL
½ cup	finely chopped carrot	125 mL
½ tsp	fine sea salt	2 mL
4 to 5	cloves garlic, minced	4 to 5
2 tsp	chopped fresh thyme leaves, divided	10 mL
½ cup	chopped tomato	125 mL
1 cup	chopped peeled sweet potato	250 mL
2 cups	chopped peeled red beets	500 mL
½ cup	quinoa, rinsed and drained (see Tips, left)	125 mL
8 to 10 cups	water (see Tips, left)	2 to 2.5 L
¼ cup	wheat-free tamari (see Tips, left)	60 mL
2 tbsp	balsamic vinegar	30 mL
1 tbsp	freshly squeezed lemon juice	15 mL
	Vegan Sour Cream (page 555)	
	Fresh dill fronds	

1. In a large pot over medium heat, heat oil. Add onion, celery, carrot and salt; cook, stirring frequently, until vegetables are softened, about 6 minutes. Stir in garlic and 1 tsp (5 mL) thyme; cook for 2 to 3 minutes, until fragrant.

2. Add tomato, sweet potato, beets and quinoa. Cook, stirring frequently, for 2 to 3 minutes, until vegetables just begin to soften. Add water, tamari, vinegar and lemon juice; stir to combine. Bring to a boil, reduce heat and simmer until beets are soft, about 25 minutes.

3. Stir in remaining 1 tbsp (15 mL) thyme. Serve immediately, garnished with a dollop of sour cream and dill fronds. The borscht, without the added garnishes, will keep for up to 5 days in an airtight container in the refrigerator.

Dashi Broth with Soba Noodles

This simple soup is a warming blend of mineral-rich broth (from the dulse) and silky smooth soba noodles.

Tips

Wheat-free tamari is a gluten-free seasoning made from fermented soybeans. It can be found in most well-stocked supermarkets and natural food stores.

Most soba noodles contain added wheat, which means they are not gluten-free. Look for brands made from pure buckwheat flour. They are available in most well-stocked natural food stores and Japanese markets.

For added flavor, drizzle the soup with toasted sesame oil and garnish with some finely sliced green onions.

● **Blender**

2 cups	water	500 mL
¼ cup	wheat-free tamari (see Tips, left)	60 mL
1 tbsp	raw agave nectar	15 mL
2 tsp	brown rice vinegar	10 mL
2 tsp	toasted sesame oil	10 mL
2 tsp	dulse flakes	10 mL
1 tsp	minced peeled gingerroot	5 mL
1	package (8 oz/250 g) gluten-free soba noodles (see Tips, left)	1

1. In blender, combine water, tamari, agave nectar, vinegar, sesame oil, dulse and ginger. Blend until smooth. Transfer to a small saucepan and bring to a boil. Cover, reduce heat to low and simmer until flavors blend, about 3 minutes.

2. In a large covered pot, bring water for cooking noodles to a rapid boil. Add soba noodles and cook until al dente, as per package instructions. Drain, rinse well under cold running water, and drain again.

3. Transfer cooked noodles to serving bowls. Pour broth overtop and serve immediately.

Miso Soup with Shiitake Mushrooms

This classic soup makes a perfect light and nourishing meal. Serve it with Crisp Soba Noodle Cakes (page 101), Asian-Style Adzuki Bean Salad (page 185) or Thai-Style Coconut Eggplant and Rice Noodles (page 278).

MAKES 2 SERVINGS

Tips

I like to use unpasteurized miso because it is living and contains healthy bacteria. Do not boil it or you will kill the healthy bacteria.

Choose brown rice or chickpea miso, both of which are gluten-free.

¼ cup	unpasteurized miso (see Tips, left)	60 mL
3 cups	boiling water	750 mL
1 cup	thinly sliced shiitake mushroom caps	250 mL
½ cup	thinly sliced green onions (green part only)	125 mL
2 tsp	raw white sesame seeds	10 mL

1. In a large bowl, whisk together miso and boiling water until no lumps remain.
2. Divide mushrooms, green onions and sesame seeds between two serving bowls. Pour equal amounts of hot miso broth overtop. Serve immediately.

Tom Yum Soup

This creamy coconut-based soup is packed full of aromatic spices and fresh hot chiles. Serve it with Pineapple and Coconut Fried Rice (page 309).

(page 309)

MAKES 6 SERVINGS

Tips

Traditionally this soup is made with fresh galangal, but that can be difficult to find. If you wish, replace the ginger with an equal amount of fresh galangal; look for it in Southeast Asian supermarkets.

Typically bird's-eye chiles are used to make this soup, but any red chile peppers will do. If you like it spicier, add more chiles — up to 5 or 6, seeds and ribs included.

Not all parts of lemongrass are edible. Before use in recipes such as stir-fries, soups or curries, lemongrass needs to be trimmed. Discard the bottom inch (2.5 cm) of the stalk and remove the tough outside leaves. The top, fibrous part of the lemongrass stalk can be reserved for simmering in soups or sauces, but it must be discarded before serving. The middle 2 to 3 inches (5 to 7.5 cm) of the stalk are soft and can be chopped and consumed. Lemongrass must be cooked for at least 4 to 5 minutes before the stalk will be edible.

2 tbsp	grapeseed oil	30 mL
½ cup	finely chopped onion	125 mL
½ cup	chopped red bell pepper	125 mL
¼ cup	chopped celery	60 mL
3 tbsp	minced peeled gingerroot (see Tips, left)	45 mL
2	red chiles, chopped (see Tips, left)	2
2	cans (each 14 oz/400 mL) full-fat coconut milk	2
2 cups	water	500 mL
½ cup	chopped lemongrass (see Tips, left)	125 mL
3 tbsp	wheat-free tamari	45 mL
3 tbsp	freshly squeezed lime juice	45 mL
2 tbsp	raw agave nectar	30 mL
1 tsp	organic coconut sugar	5 mL
Pinch	cayenne pepper	Pinch
12 oz	firm tofu, cut into small cubes	375 g

1. In a large pot over medium heat, heat oil. Add onion, red pepper, celery, ginger and chiles. Cook, stirring frequently, until vegetables are softened, 6 to 8 minutes. Add coconut milk, water, lemongrass, tamari, lime juice, agave nectar, coconut sugar and cayenne; stir to combine. Bring to a boil, reduce heat and simmer for 20 minutes.

2. Add tofu and cook for 2 to 3 minutes, until heated through. Serve immediately or let cool, transfer to an airtight container and refrigerate for up to 5 days.

Sweet-and-Sour Soup

This traditional Asian soup is best served over freshly cooked noodles or rice. It's even better the next day, after the flavors have had a chance to meld.

MAKES 6 SERVINGS

Tips

Traditionally this soup is made using Chinese black vinegar, which is a bit sweeter and richer-tasting than rice vinegar. You can find it in Asian supermarkets. If desired, substitute an equal amount for the rice wine vinegar.

Use the quantity of hot pepper flakes that suits your taste.

Be sure to use raw (not processed) agave nectar. It is a 100% natural (non-GMO) sweetener that contains naturally occurring fructose and is low on the glycemic scale, which means that it releases glucose slowly, providing sustained energy.

6 cups	water	1.5 L
½ cup	rice wine vinegar (see Tips, left)	125 mL
¼ cup	raw agave nectar (see Tips, left)	60 mL
3 tbsp	wheat-free tamari	45 mL
2 tbsp	toasted sesame oil	30 mL
½ to 1 tsp	hot pepper flakes	2 to 5 mL
3 tbsp	organic cornstarch	45 mL
3 tbsp	cold water	45 mL
1 cup	thinly sliced shiitake mushrooms	250 mL
½ cup	thinly sliced green onions (green part only)	125 mL
12 oz	firm tofu, cut into small cubes	375 g
½ tsp	raw white sesame seeds	2 mL

1. In a large pot, combine water, vinegar, agave nectar, tamari, sesame oil and hot pepper flakes. Bring to a boil, reduce heat and simmer for 5 minutes.

2. In a small bowl, whisk together cornstarch and cold water until no lumps remain.

3. Bring soup back to a boil. Whisk in cornstarch mixture and cook for 2 minutes at a full boil. Remove from heat and stir in mushrooms, green onions, tofu and sesame seeds. Serve immediately or let cool, transfer to an airtight container and refrigerate for up to 5 days.

Variation

For a more authentic version of this recipe, add ½ cup (125 mL) each drained chopped and canned water chestnuts and drained and thinly sliced canned bamboo shoots.

Cream of Mushroom Soup

This soup gets its rich creaminess from blended red lentils, not added fat. Serve it to help uplift your soul on cold, dreary days.

MAKES 6 SERVINGS

Tips

If portobello mushrooms are quite large, the stems can be tough and fibrous. If this is the case, remove the bottom ½ inch (1 cm) with your knife. If the mushrooms are small there is no need to remove the stem ends.

To chop fresh thyme: Pinch the stem at the bottom with two fingers. Pulling upward with the finger and thumb of your other hand, strip the leaves. Reserve stems for soups or broths (discard after cooking). Use a sharp knife to chop the leaves, being careful not to chop too much or too hard, as this will bruise the leaves and cause the thyme to discolor.

Nutritional yeast is an inactive yeast that has been grown on beet molasses and then pasteurized. It provides a rich, cheesy flavor in sauces, stews, soups and dips. Look for it in well-stocked supermarkets and natural food stores.

• **Blender**

1 tbsp	grapeseed oil	15 mL
1 cup	thinly sliced onions	250 mL
¼ tsp	fine sea salt	1 mL
5	cloves garlic, minced	5
4 cups	thinly sliced button mushrooms	1 L
4 cups	thinly sliced cremini mushrooms	1 L
1	large portobello mushroom, chopped (see Tips, left)	1
¼ cup	red lentils	60 mL
1 tbsp	chopped fresh thyme leaves (see Tips, left)	15 mL
6 cups	water	1.5 L
¼ cup	nutritional yeast (see Tips, left)	60 mL
2 tbsp	wheat-free tamari	30 mL

1. In a large pot over medium-high heat, heat oil. Add onions and salt; cook, stirring frequently, until lightly golden, about 10 minutes. Stir in garlic and cook for 2 minutes, until fragrant.

2. Add button, cremini and portobello mushrooms. Cook, stirring frequently, until most of the liquid has evaporated and mushrooms are lightly golden, 10 to 12 minutes.

3. Add lentils, thyme, water, nutritional yeast and tamari, and stir well. Bring to a boil, reduce heat and simmer until lentils are tender, about 20 minutes.

4. Fill blender jar halfway with soup (see Tips, page 327). Blend at high speed until smooth and creamy. Transfer puréed soup to a clean pot. Repeat with remaining soup. Place pot over medium heat and bring soup to a simmer. Serve immediately or let cool, transfer to an airtight container and refrigerate for up to 5 days.

Cheesy Broccoli Quinoa Soup

I love the simplicity of this soup — fresh broccoli, light and tender quinoa, and rich, cheesy nutritional yeast make a perfect combination any time of year.

MAKES 6 SERVINGS

Tips

Broccoli stems have a lot of flavor, so don't throw them away. Trim and discard the bottom inch (2.5 cm), then peel the remaining stem to expose the tender flesh in the center. Chop and add to soups, stews or stir-fries.

When blending hot liquids in a blender, make sure the blender jar is no more than half full. Also, place a folded towel over the lid and place your hand firmly on top. Otherwise, the pressure of the steam may cause the lid to blow off, spattering your soup all over the kitchen.

● **Blender**

1 tbsp	grapeseed oil	15 mL
½ cup	thinly sliced onion	125 mL
¼ tsp	fine sea salt	1 mL
3 to 4	cloves garlic, minced	3 to 4
1 tbsp	chopped fresh thyme leaves	15 mL
6 cups	broccoli, cut into small pieces (see Tips, left)	1.5 L
6 cups	water	1.5 L
1½ cups	nutritional yeast (see Tips, page 326)	375 L
¼ cup	quinoa, rinsed and drained	60 mL
	Nutritional yeast for sprinkling	

1. In a large pot over medium heat, heat oil. Add onion and salt; cook, stirring frequently, until translucent, 5 to 6 minutes. Stir in garlic and thyme; cook for 2 to 3 minutes, until fragrant. Add broccoli, water and nutritional yeast and stir to combine. Bring to a boil, reduce heat and simmer until broccoli is tender, about 15 minutes.

2. Fill blender jar halfway with soup (see Tips, left). Blend at high speed until smooth and creamy. Transfer puréed soup to a clean pot. Repeat with remaining soup, in batches, if necessary.

3. Add quinoa and bring soup to a boil. Reduce heat and simmer until quinoa is tender, about 15 minutes. Serve immediately, sprinkled with nutritional yeast. Or, without adding the nutritional yeast, let cool, transfer to an airtight container and refrigerate for up to 5 days.

Roasted Cauliflower and Garlic Soup

Roasted cauliflower has a wonderful sweet, nutty flavor and meaty texture. Serve this hearty soup with a bowl of Basic Quinoa (page 235) or Basic Rice (page 212) drizzled with cold-pressed extra virgin olive oil and sprinkled with some high-quality sea salt.

MAKES 8 SERVINGS

Tips

I like to use a lot of roasted garlic in this recipe. If you prefer less garlic, reduce the quantity to as little as 2 heads.

When roasting whole heads of garlic, use a serrated knife to remove the top $\frac{1}{4}$ inch (0.5 cm) of the bulb to expose the flesh of the cloves. Cover with foil to make airtight.

- **Preheat oven to 425°F (220°C)**
- **2 baking sheets, lined with parchment paper**
- **Blender**

6	heads garlic, tops removed (see Tips, left)	6
$\frac{1}{4}$ cup	grapeseed oil, divided	60 mL
6 cups	chopped cauliflower florets	1.5 L
1 tsp	fine sea salt, divided	5 mL
$\frac{1}{2}$ cup	thinly sliced onion	125 mL
$\frac{1}{2}$ cup	chopped celery	125 mL
$\frac{1}{2}$ cup	chopped carrot	125 mL
$\frac{1}{2}$ cup	nutritional yeast (see Tips, page 329)	125 mL
2 tbsp	chopped fresh thyme leaves	30 mL
8 cups	water	2 L

1. In a small bowl, toss whole garlic heads with 1 tbsp (15 mL) oil until well coated. Transfer to a prepared baking sheet and bake in preheated oven for 30 minutes or until lightly golden and soft. Remove from oven and set aside to cool. Once cool, squeeze cloves from skins and set aside.

2. Meanwhile, in a large bowl, toss cauliflower with 2 tbsp (30 mL) oil and $\frac{1}{2}$ tsp (2 mL) salt. Arrange in a single layer on second prepared baking sheet and bake in preheated oven for about 20 minutes, until soft and lightly golden. Remove from oven and set aside.

3. In a large pot over medium heat, heat remaining 1 tbsp (15 mL) oil. Add onion, celery, carrot, nutritional yeast, thyme and remaining $\frac{1}{2}$ tsp (2 mL) salt. Cook, stirring frequently, until soft and translucent, about 6 minutes.

Tips

Nutritional yeast is an inactive yeast that has been grown on beet molasses and then pasteurized. It provides a rich, cheesy flavor in sauces, stews, soups and dips. Look for it in well-stocked supermarkets and natural food stores.

When blending hot liquids in a blender, make sure the blender jar is no more than half full. Also, place a folded towel over the lid and place your hand firmly on top. Otherwise, the pressure of the steam may cause the lid to blow off, spattering your soup all over the kitchen.

4. Add roasted cauliflower, roasted garlic and water; stir to combine. Bring to a boil, reduce heat and simmer for 20 minutes, until soup has thickened slightly.

5. Fill blender jar halfway with soup. (If you prefer, purée the soup in the saucepan, using an immersion blender.) Blend at high speed until smooth and creamy. Transfer puréed soup to a clean pot. Repeat with remaining soup in batches, if necessary (see Tips, left).

6. Place pot over medium heat and bring soup to a simmer. Serve immediately or let cool, transfer to an airtight container and refrigerate for up to 5 days.

Variation

Peppery Roasted Cauliflower and Garlic Soup: Add 1 tbsp (15 mL) chili powder and 1 tsp (5 mL) sweet paprika when sautéing the vegetables in Step 3. Use an immersion blender to purée soup slightly, keeping a chunky consistency. To do this, insert blender at one side of the pot and blend for 8 to 10 seconds. (If you do not have an immersion blender, transfer about half of the soup to a standard blender in batches, but be careful not to overprocess — you want to retain some texture. Return to saucepan.) Season soup with 1 tbsp (15 mL) freshly squeezed lemon juice and 1 tbsp (15 mL) wheat-free tamari.

Charred Cauliflower and White Bean Soup

Charred cauliflower adds a deep, smoky flavor to this fiber-rich and protein-dense soup. Serve it before the big game or as part of a family meal.

Tips

To soak the beans: Place in a bowl and cover with 4 cups (1 L) water. Cover and set aside for at least 6 hours or overnight (if overnight, refrigerate). Drain, discarding liquid.

To chop fresh thyme: Pinch the stem at the bottom with two fingers. Pulling upward with the finger and thumb of your other hand, strip the leaves. Reserve stems for soups or broths (discard after cooking). Use a sharp knife to chop the leaves, being careful not to chop too much or too hard, as this will bruise the leaves and cause the thyme to discolor.

Nutritional yeast is an inactive yeast that has been grown on beet molasses and then pasteurized. It provides a rich, cheesy flavor in sauces, stews, soups and dips. Look for it in well-stocked supermarkets and natural food stores.

- **Barbecue or grill pan, preheated to high**
- **Immersion blender**

1 cup	white beans, soaked (see Tips, left)	250 mL
	Water	
2	heads cauliflower, halved	2
1/4 cup	extra virgin olive oil	60 mL
2 tsp	fine sea salt, divided	10 mL
1 tbsp	grapeseed oil	15 mL
1 cup	chopped onion	250 mL
1/2 cup	chopped celery	125 mL
10 to 12	cloves garlic, minced	10 to 12
3 tbsp	chopped fresh thyme leaves (see Tips, left)	45 mL
1 cup	nutritional yeast (see Tips, left)	250 mL

1. In a large pot, combine 4 cups (1 L) water and soaked beans. Bring to a boil, reduce heat and simmer until beans are slightly tender, about 30 minutes. Drain, discarding liquid. Cover and set aside.

2. In a bowl, toss cauliflower with olive oil and 1 tsp (5 mL) salt. Cook on preheated grill for about 10 minutes per side, until grill marks appear and cauliflower becomes lightly blackened on all sides. Remove from heat and set aside.

3. In a large pot over medium heat, heat grapeseed oil. Add onion, celery and remaining salt; cook, stirring often, until softened, 4 to 5 minutes. Stir in garlic and cook for 2 to 3 minutes, until fragrant.

4. Add cooked beans, grilled cauliflower, 8 cups (2 L) water, thyme and nutritional yeast; stir. Bring to a boil, reduce heat and simmer for 30 minutes.

5. Using immersion blender, blend about one-third of the soup (don't purée it — it should be somewhat chunky; see Tips, page 331). Serve immediately or let cool, transfer to an airtight container and refrigerate for up to 5 days.

Smoky Corn Chowder

This rich and hearty soup will satisfy your craving for something warm and filling. Serve it with a drizzle of Vegan Sour Cream (page 555).

MAKES 8 SERVINGS

Tips

Substitute an equal amount of red or white potatoes for the sweet potatoes.

When using tahini in soups and sauces, heat it gently. If you boil it, it will split.

Blending about one-third of the soup breaks down some of the starch, while maintaining most of the texture. To do this, insert blender at one side of the pot and blend for about 10 seconds. If you do not have an immersion blender, transfer a portion of the soup to a standard blender.

Immersion blender

1 tbsp	grapeseed oil	15 mL
¼ cup	finely chopped onion	60 mL
¼ cup	finely chopped celery	60 mL
⅓ cup	finely chopped carrot	75 mL
½ cup	finely chopped red bell pepper	125 mL
1 tsp	fine sea salt	5 mL
2 to 3	cloves garlic, minced	2 to 3
5 cups	chopped peeled sweet potatoes (see Tips, left)	1.25 L
4 cups	Almond Milk (page 61)	1 L
1 cup	water	250 mL
2 cups	corn kernels (fresh or frozen)	500 mL
2 tbsp	chopped fresh dill	30 mL
¼ cup	tahini (see Tips, left)	60 mL
½ tsp	smoked sweet paprika	2 mL

1. In a large pot over medium heat, heat oil. Add onion, celery, carrot, red pepper and salt. Cook, stirring frequently, until vegetables are softened, 6 to 8 minutes.

2. Stir in garlic and cook for 2 to 3 minutes, until fragrant. Add sweet potatoes, almond milk, water and corn; stir to combine. Bring to a boil, reduce heat and simmer until sweet potatoes are tender, about 20 minutes.

3. Remove from heat. Stir in dill, tahini and paprika. Using immersion blender, blend about one-third of the soup (don't purée it — it should be somewhat chunky; see Tips, left). Serve immediately or let cool, transfer to an airtight container and refrigerate for up to 5 days.

Variation

Smoky Corn Chowder with Wild Rice: In a large pot of salted boiling water, cook ½ cup (125 mL) wild rice until tender, about 45 minutes. Drain, discarding liquid. Stir into soup in Step 3, then blend.

Black Bean and Sweet Potato Chowder

The spicy Mexican flavors of this soup are balanced by creamy, cooling sweet potato. Serve with a tall glass of Lemon-Lime Fusion Juice (page 40).

(page 40)

MAKES 6 SERVINGS

Tips

To soak the beans: Place in a bowl with 4 cups (1 L) water. Cover and set aside for at least 6 hours or overnight (if overnight, refrigerate). Drain, discarding liquid.

To mince garlic: Place a whole clove on a cutting board. Using the butt end of a chef's knife, press firmly but gently on the clove to loosen the skin. Using your index finger and thumb, gently squeeze clove out of skin. Chop coarsely, then sprinkle with a bit of sea salt. Using the butt end of the knife, rub garlic into board (the salt will act as an abrasive and help to mince the garlic). Chop until fine.

Substitute 4 cups (1 L) chopped fresh tomatoes for the canned tomatoes.

Some chipotle powders are spicier than others so be cautious when using this spice. Start by adding ½ tsp (2 mL) of chipotle powder. Taste and increase the amount if you prefer a zestier result.

5 cups	water, divided	1.25 L
1 cup	black beans, soaked (see Tips, left)	250 mL
3 tbsp	grapeseed oil	45 mL
1 cup	chopped onion	250 mL
½ cup	chopped celery	125 mL
1 tsp	fine sea salt	5 mL
8	cloves garlic, minced (see Tips, left)	8
1 tsp	ground cumin	5 mL
½ tsp	chipotle powder	2 mL
1	can (28 oz/796 mL) diced tomatoes, with juice (see Tips, left)	1
2 tbsp	freshly squeezed lemon juice	30 mL
1 tbsp	raw agave nectar	15 mL
4 cups	chopped peeled sweet potatoes	1 L

1. In a large saucepan, combine 4 cups (1 L) water and soaked beans. Bring to a boil, reduce heat and simmer until beans are tender, about 1 hour. Remove from heat and set aside.

2. In a large pot over medium heat, heat oil. Add onion, celery and salt; cook, stirring frequently, until softened, 6 to 8 minutes. Stir in garlic and cook for 2 to 3 minutes, until fragrant. Add cumin and chipotle powder; cook for 2 minutes, stirring constantly.

3. Add cooked beans and their cooking liquid, remaining 1 cup (250 mL) water, tomatoes, lemon juice, agave nectar and sweet potatoes; stir to combine. Bring to a boil, reduce heat and simmer for about 30 minutes, stirring every 5 minutes or so, until sweet potatoes are tender.

4. Using an immersion blender, purée about one-third of the soup to break down some of the starch in the sweet potatoes and beans (be careful not to blend too much — you want to retain some texture; see Tips, page 331). Serve immediately or let cool, transfer to an airtight container and refrigerate for up to 5 days.

Ratatouille

This traditional French vegetable stew is perfect over Basic Quinoa (page 235) with a drizzle of good-quality cold-pressed extra virgin olive oil.

MAKES ABOUT 4 SERVINGS

Tips

To chop fresh thyme: Pinch the stem at the bottom with two fingers. Pulling upward with the finger and thumb of your other hand, strip the leaves. Reserve stems for soups or broths (discard after cooking). Use a sharp knife to chop the leaves, being careful not to chop too much or too hard, as this will bruise the leaves and cause the thyme to discolor.

The quantity of garlic depends on the size of the cloves. If large, use the smaller number. If small, more may be required.

Substitute 4 cups (1 L) chopped fresh tomatoes for the canned tomatoes.

The vegetables in this recipe can also be grilled before being added to the tomato sauce. To do this, preheat grill to Medium-High. Toss vegetables with grapeseed oil and salt as in Step 1 and place in a large grilling basket, spreading them out in a single layer. Grill on all sides until soft and lightly brown, 7 to 8 minutes.

- Preheat oven to 450°F (230°C)
- Baking sheet, lined with parchment paper

3 tbsp	grapeseed oil, divided	45 mL
1 cup	chopped red bell pepper	250 mL
1 cup	chopped zucchini	250 mL
1 cup	chopped red onion	250 mL
1 cup	chopped eggplant	250 mL
1/4 cup	chopped fresh thyme leaves, divided (see Tips, left)	60 mL
1 tsp	fine sea salt, divided	5 mL
1/4 cup	chopped onion	60 mL
8 to 10	cloves garlic, minced	8 to 10
1	can (5 1/2 oz/156 mL) tomato paste	1
1	can (28 oz/796 mL) diced tomatoes, with juice (see Tips, left)	1
3 tbsp	wheat-free tamari	45 mL

1. In a bowl, combine 2 tbsp (30 mL) grapeseed oil, red pepper, zucchini, red onion, eggplant, 2 tbsp (30 mL) thyme and 1/2 tsp (2 mL) salt. Toss to coat well. Spread in a single layer on prepared baking sheet.

2. Bake in preheated oven until vegetables are tender and lightly browned, about 25 minutes. Remove from oven and set aside.

3. In a large pot over medium heat, heat remaining 1 tbsp (15 mL) oil. Add onion and remaining 1/2 tsp (2 mL) salt. Cook, stirring frequently, until onion is translucent, about 3 minutes. Stir in garlic and cook for 2 minutes, until fragrant. Stir in tomato paste, tomatoes and tamari.

4. Bring to a simmer and cook, stirring constantly, for about 5 minutes, until thickened. Add roasted vegetables and remaining 2 tbsp (30 mL) thyme. Stir until well coated with tomato sauce. Serve immediately or let cool, transfer to an airtight container and refrigerate for up to 1 week.

Berbere-Spiced Stewed Green Tomatoes

A fragrant berbere spice blend pairs perfectly with aromatic ginger and tender green tomatoes. I like to serve this with Spicy African Millet Salad (page 217).

page 217

MAKES 4 SIDE SERVINGS

Tips

To remove the skin from fresh gingerroot with the least amount of waste, use the edge of a teaspoon. With a brushing motion, scrape off the skin to reveal the yellow root.

Berbere is an Ethiopian spice blend available in specialty stores and well-stocked supermarkets.

Wheat-free tamari is a gluten-free seasoning made from fermented soybeans. It can be found in most well-stocked supermarkets and natural food stores.

Green tomatoes are available toward the end of the growing season, when the weather gets cooler. They are unripened tomatoes that stay green and firm.

3 tbsp	grapeseed oil	45 mL
½ cup	chopped onion	125 mL
¼ tsp	fine sea salt	1 mL
1 tbsp	minced peeled gingerroot (see Tips, left)	15 mL
2 tbsp	berbere (see Tips, left)	30 mL
¼ cup	water	60 mL
2 tbsp	wheat-free tamari (see Tips, left)	30 mL
1 tbsp	freshly squeezed lemon juice	15 mL
1 tbsp	raw agave nectar	15 mL
8 cups	chopped green tomatoes (see Tips, left)	2 L

1. In a large pot over medium-high heat, heat oil. Add onion and salt; cook, stirring frequently, until onion begins to brown, 8 to 10 minutes. Add ginger and berbere; cook for 3 to 4 minutes, until fragrant. Stir in water, tamari, lemon juice and agave nectar.

2. Bring mixture to a simmer and cook for 2 to 3 minutes, until slightly thickened. Stir in tomatoes.

3. Reduce heat to low and cover with a tight-fitting lid. Cook, stirring every 10 minutes, for 40 minutes or until tomatoes are soft. Serve immediately or let cool, transfer to an airtight container and refrigerate for up to 1 week.

Moroccan-Style Collard Greens

Fresh jalapeño peppers and aromatic fennel seeds and garlic add robust flavor to nutrient-dense collard greens. Serve this dish with Spicy African Millet Salad (page 217), African-Spiced Tempeh Chili (page 348) or Sweet Potato Quinoa Fritters (page 89).

(page 217), African-Spiced Tempeh Chili (page 348) or Sweet Potato Quinoa Fritters (page 89).

MAKES 4 SERVINGS

Tips

If you prefer less spice in your dish, remove the seeds and ribs from the jalapeños. To do this, slice each jalapeño through the middle and use a small spoon to scrape out the insides.

To reheat this dish, pour 1/2 cup (125 mL) water into a skillet and bring to a simmer. Add braised collards and cook, stirring occasionally, until heated through.

3 tbsp	grapeseed oil	45 mL
8 to 10	cloves garlic, thinly sliced	8 to 10
1/2 cup	chopped onion	125 mL
1/2 cup	thinly sliced jalapeño peppers (see Tips, left)	125 mL
3 tbsp	fennel seeds	45 mL
1/2 tsp	fine sea salt	2 mL
4 cups	trimmed collard greens, cut into strips (1 inch/2.5 cm)	1 L
1 cup	water	250 mL
1/2 cup	raw (unpasteurized) apple cider vinegar	125 mL

1. In a large pot over medium heat, heat oil. Add sliced garlic and cook, stirring constantly, until lightly browned and fragrant, about 5 minutes (be careful not to burn it). Add onion, jalapeños, fennel seeds and salt; cook, stirring frequently, until softened, about 5 minutes.

2. Stir in collard greens, water and vinegar; bring to a boil. Cover with a tight-fitting lid, reduce heat and simmer for 30 minutes, stirring every 5 or 6 minutes.

3. Uncover pot and cook for about 6 minutes, stirring frequently, until most of the liquid evaporates. Remove from heat and serve immediately or let cool, transfer to an airtight container and refrigerate for up to 1 week.

Stewed Onions and Mushrooms with Millet

Soft, sweet onions, tender mushrooms and nutritious millet combine to make a perfect addition to any meal.

Tips

If the mushrooms are small, you can leave them whole. If they are large, cut them into bite-size pieces.

To chop fresh thyme: Pinch the stem at the bottom with two fingers. Pulling upward with the finger and thumb of your other hand, strip the leaves. Reserve stems for soups or broths (discard after cooking). Use a sharp knife to chop the leaves, being careful not to chop too much or too hard, as this will bruise the leaves and cause the thyme to discolor.

2 tbsp	grapeseed oil	30 mL
4 cups	thinly sliced white onions	1 L
8 cups	quartered button mushrooms (see Tips, left)	2 L
3 to 4	cloves garlic, minced (see Tips, page 337)	3 to 4
½ tbsp	chopped fresh thyme leaves (see Tips, left)	7 mL
¼ cup	millet, rinsed and drained	60 mL
2 cups	Vegetable Stock (page 559)	500 mL

1. In a large pot over medium-high heat, heat oil. Add onions and mushrooms; cook, stirring frequently, until softened, about 10 minutes. Stir in garlic and thyme; cook for 2 minutes, until fragrant. Add millet and stir to combine.

2. Add vegetable stock and bring to a boil. Reduce heat and simmer, stirring occasionally, until millet is tender, about 15 minutes. Serve immediately or let cool, transfer to an airtight container and refrigerate for up to 1 week.

Quick Sweet-and-Sour Tofu Stir-Fry (page 308)

Spring Minestrone (page 317)

Jerk Tofu, Avocado and Plantain Wrap (page 360)

Loaded Baked Potatoes with Ginger Broccoli (page 370)

Okra and Squash Gumbo (page 342)

Polenta Cakes with Olive, Tomato and Spinach Ragoût (page 406)

Crispy Soba Cakes with Wakame Salad
and Umeboshi Dressing (page 420)

Pizza Rolls (page 468) with Vegan Shredded Mozzarella (page 537)

Triple Ginger Cookies (page 428)
and Lemon Vanilla Biscotti (page 437)

Chocolate Cherry Dream Bars (page 493)
with Whipped Coconut Cream (page 565)

Churros with Cinnamon Sugar (page 490)
with Easy Coconut Caramel Sauce (page 506)

Silky Chocolate Mousse (page 505)

Stewed Lentils with Mushrooms and Sweet Potatoes

This hearty dish is a perfect cold-weather dinner when served over Basic Rice (page 212) or with some Herbed Roasted Potatoes (page 179).

Tips

The quantity of garlic depends on the size of the cloves. If large, use the smaller number. If small, more may be required.

To mince garlic: Place a whole clove on a cutting board. Using the butt end of a chef's knife, press firmly but gently on the clove to loosen the skin. Using your index finger and thumb, gently squeeze clove out of skin. Chop coarsely, then sprinkle with a bit of sea salt. Using the butt end of the knife, rub garlic into board (the salt will act as an abrasive and help to mince the garlic). Chop until fine.

2 tbsp	grapeseed oil	30 mL
4 cups	sliced button mushrooms	1 L
1 cup	chopped onion	250 mL
½ cup	chopped celery	125 mL
½ cup	chopped carrot	125 mL
½ tsp	fine sea salt	2 mL
8 to 10	cloves garlic, minced (see Tips, left)	8 to 10
1	can (5½ oz/156 mL) tomato paste	1
1 cup	dry red wine	250 mL
3 cups	water	750 mL
½ cup	wheat-free tamari	125 mL
1 cup	chopped peeled sweet potatoes	250 mL
½ cup	red lentils, rinsed and drained	125 mL
3 tbsp	chopped fresh thyme leaves (see Tips, page 336)	45 mL

1. In a large pot over medium-high heat, heat oil. Add mushrooms, onion, celery, carrot and salt. Cook, stirring frequently, until vegetables are tender and most of the liquid has evaporated, about 10 minutes. Stir in garlic and cook for 2 to 3 minutes, until fragrant. Add tomato paste and cook, stirring constantly, for about 5 minutes, until tomato paste is lightly brown (be careful not to burn garlic).

2. Add wine and cook, stirring occasionally, until very little liquid remains, 4 to 5 minutes. Add water, tamari, sweet potatoes and lentils.

3. Bring to a boil, reduce heat and simmer until sweet potatoes and lentils are tender and mixture has thickened, about 25 minutes. Stir in thyme. Serve immediately or let cool, transfer to an airtight container and refrigerate for up to 1 week.

Coconut Curried Plantains and Okra

Sweet and creamy plantains help to make this dish a rich-tasting favorite. I like to serve it with steamed basmati rice and a crisp green salad.

Tips

Substitute 1½ cups (375 mL) chopped peeled sweet potato for the plantain.

Okra is a green vegetable common in Creole-style cooking. When slowly simmered, its starchy flesh helps to thicken and lend body to stews and casseroles.

A citrus reamer is a hand-held tool used to extract the juice from lemons and limes. It is available in most kitchen supply stores and would be ideal to use for the lime juice in this recipe.

2 tbsp	grapeseed oil	30 mL
1 cup	chopped onion	250 mL
½ cup	chopped celery	125 mL
½ tsp	fine sea salt	2 mL
1 tsp	minced peeled gingerroot	5 mL
6 to 8	cloves garlic, minced	6 to 8
2 tbsp	curry powder	30 mL
2 tsp	ground cumin	10 mL
½ tsp	ground coriander	2 mL
½ cup	dry white wine (optional)	125 mL
1 cup	sliced plantain (about 1 medium; see Tips, left)	250 mL
½ cup	thinly sliced okra (see Tips, left)	125 mL
½ cup	water	125 mL
3 tbsp	freshly squeezed lime juice (see Tips, left)	45 mL
1	can (14 oz/400 mL) full-fat coconut milk	1
	Lime wedges	
	Fine sea salt	

1. In a large saucepan over medium heat, heat oil. Add onion, celery and salt; cook, stirring frequently, until translucent, 7 to 8 minutes. Stir in ginger and garlic; cook for 2 to 3 more minutes, until fragrant. Add curry powder, cumin and coriander; cook, stirring constantly, for 5 to 6 minutes. Add wine (if using) and cook until liquid evaporates, 4 to 5 minutes.

2. Stir in plantain, okra, water, lime juice and coconut milk; bring mixture to a boil.

3. Reduce heat and simmer until plantain is soft and mixture has thickened slightly, about 15 minutes. Serve immediately with fresh lime wedges and a sprinkle of sea salt, or let cool, transfer to an airtight container and refrigerate for up to 5 days.

Mushroom, Black Bean and Sweet Potato Ragoût

This hearty stew makes a perfect dinner during the colder months, when you are craving comfort foods. I love to serve it ladled over Basic Quinoa (page 235).

MAKES 4 SERVINGS

Tips

To soak the black beans: Place in a bowl and cover with 4 cups (1 L) water. Cover and set aside for at least 6 hours or overnight (if overnight, refrigerate). Drain, discarding liquid.

Although it is an extra step, cooking the sweet potatoes before adding them to the ragoût ensures that they will break down in the second cooking, releasing starch to thicken the stew.

Wheat-free tamari is a gluten-free seasoning made from fermented soybeans. It can be found in most well-stocked supermarkets and natural food stores.

To prevent fresh herbs from turning brown after chopping, ensure that your knife is as sharp as possible, to prevent bruising.

1 cup	black beans, soaked (see Tips, left)	250 mL
2 cups	chopped peeled sweet potatoes	500 mL
3 tbsp	grapeseed oil	45 mL
1 cup	chopped onion	250 mL
1 cup	chopped carrot	250 mL
1 cup	chopped celery	250 mL
1/2 tsp	fine sea salt	2 mL
4 cups	quartered button mushrooms	1 L
6 to 8	cloves garlic, minced	6 to 8
1	can (5 1/2 oz/156 mL) tomato paste	1
1 cup	dry red wine	250 mL
1/4 cup	wheat-free tamari (see Tips, left)	60 mL
1 tbsp	chopped fresh thyme leaves	15 mL
2 cups	water	500 mL

1. In a large saucepan of water, bring soaked beans to a boil. Reduce heat and simmer until tender, about 1 hour. Drain, discarding liquid, and set aside.

2. Meanwhile, in another large saucepan of water, bring sweet potatoes to a boil. Reduce heat and simmer until tender, about 15 minutes. Drain, discarding liquid, and set aside.

3. In a large pot over medium heat, heat oil. Add onion, carrot, celery and salt. Cook, stirring frequently, until vegetables are softened, about 6 minutes. Stir in mushrooms and garlic; cook until liquid has evaporated, 5 to 6 minutes. Stir in tomato paste and cook for 2 to 3 minutes, until it is lightly brown and fragrant. Add wine and cook until sauce thickens.

4. Stir in cooked black beans, cooked sweet potatoes, tamari, thyme and water. Bring mixture to a boil, reduce heat and simmer for 15 to 20 minutes or until mixture has thickened slightly. Serve immediately or let cool, transfer to an airtight container and refrigerate for up to 5 days.

Grilled Tomato and Portobello Ragoût

Grilled tomatoes give this hearty dish a smoky flavor that pairs well with meaty portobello mushrooms.

MAKES 4 SERVINGS

Tips

Nutritional yeast is an inactive yeast that has been grown on beet molasses and then pasteurized. It provides a rich, cheesy flavor in sauces, stews, soups and dips. Look for it in well-stocked supermarkets and natural food stores.

To chop fresh thyme: Pinch the stem at the bottom with two fingers. Pulling upward with the finger and thumb of your other hand, strip the leaves. Reserve stems for soups or broths (discard after cooking). Use a sharp knife to chop the leaves, being careful not to chop too much or too hard, as this will bruise the leaves and cause the thyme to discolor.

- Preheat grill to High
- Medium (about 4 quart) slow cooker

10	tomatoes, halved lengthwise	10
6 tbsp	grapeseed oil, divided	90 mL
1½ tsp	fine sea salt, divided	7 mL
6	portobello mushroom caps	6
2 cups	chopped onions	500 mL
6 to 8	cloves garlic	6 to 8
½ cup	dried red lentils, rinsed and drained	125 mL
3 tbsp	tomato paste	45 mL
8 cups	Dark Vegetable Stock (page 559)	2 L
¼ cup	nutritional yeast (see Tips, left)	60 mL
3 tbsp	wheat-free tamari	45 mL
2 tbsp	chopped fresh thyme leaves (see Tips, left)	30 mL

1. In a large bowl, toss together tomatoes, 2 tbsp (30 mL) oil and ½ tsp (2 mL) salt. Set aside.

2. In another large bowl, toss together mushroom caps, 2 tbsp (30 mL) oil and ½ tsp (2 mL) salt. Set aside.

3. Grill tomato halves for 2 to 3 minutes per side, until blackened slightly. Transfer to a plate and set aside.

4. Grill mushrooms until tender and golden brown on one side, 4 to 5 minutes. Turn over and cook other side until golden, 3 to 4 minutes. Remove from heat and set aside until cool enough to handle, 8 to 10 minutes. Once cool, cut mushrooms into 2-inch (5 cm) strips.

Do not lift the lid of your slow cooker while it is cooking. Each time you do, heat will escape and you will need to add 20 to 30 minutes of cooking time to your recipe.

5. In a large skillet over medium heat, heat remaining 2 tbsp (30 mL) oil. Add onions and remaining $\frac{1}{2}$ tsp (2 mL) salt; cook, stirring frequently, until translucent, about 6 minutes. Add garlic, lentils and tomato paste; cook for 4 to 5 minutes, until tomato paste is lightly browned.

6. Stir in stock and bring to a simmer, using a wooden spoon to scrape up any brown bits from the bottom of the pan.

7. Transfer to slow cooker stoneware and add grilled tomatoes and mushrooms.

8. Cover and cook on Low for 6 hours or High for 3 hours. Stir in nutritional yeast, tamari and thyme; cook, covered, for 20 minutes. Serve immediately or let cool, transfer to an airtight container and refrigerate for up to 1 week.

Okra and Squash Gumbo

Serve this hearty dish on cold winter nights, with your favorite crusty bread for dipping.

Tips

Okra is a green vegetable common to Creole-style cooking. When slowly simmered, its starchy flesh helps to thicken and lend body to stews or casseroles.

Substitute an equal amount of chopped peeled sweet potatoes for the squash.

Wheat-free tamari is a gluten-free seasoning made from fermented soybeans. It can be found in most well-stocked supermarkets and natural food stores.

- Medium (about 4 quart) slow cooker

3 tbsp	grapeseed oil	45 mL
2 cups	sliced (½ inch/1 cm) okra (see Tips, left)	500 mL
1 cup	chopped onion	250 mL
1 cup	chopped celery	250 mL
1 cup	chopped green bell pepper	250 mL
1 tsp	fine sea salt	5 mL
2 tbsp	Cajun seasoning	30 mL
6 to 8	cloves garlic	6 to 8
¼ cup	tomato paste	60 mL
1	can (28 oz/796 mL) diced tomatoes, with juice	1
8 cups	chopped peeled butternut squash (see Tips, left)	2 L
2 tbsp	wheat-free tamari (see Tips, left)	30 mL
1 tsp	chopped fresh thyme leaves	5 mL
⅛ to ¼ tsp	cayenne pepper	0.5 to 1 mL

1. In a large skillet over medium-high heat, heat oil. Add okra, onion, celery, green pepper and salt. Cook, stirring frequently, until vegetables are softened, 5 to 6 minutes. Stir in Cajun seasoning, garlic and tomato paste. Cook for 5 to 6 minutes, until tomato paste is lightly browned.

2. Stir in tomatoes, with juice, and squash. Bring mixture to a simmer. Remove from heat and transfer to slow cooker stoneware.

3. Cover and cook for 8 hours on Low or 4 hours on High. Stir in tamari, thyme and cayenne. Serve immediately or let cool, transfer to an airtight container and refrigerate for up to 5 days.

Mushroom Sloppy Joes

Chewy mushrooms provide meaty texture for this dish. It's a perfect filling for sandwiches or as part of a main course, served on top of Creamy Mashed Potatoes (page 178), Polenta (page 230) or Squash and Herb Baked Oats (page 239).

(page 178), Polenta (page 230) or Squash and Herb Baked Oats (page 239).

MAKES 4 SERVINGS

Tips

To clean mushrooms: Use a damp cloth to brush any dirt from the surface. Never clean mushrooms with water. They are like sponges — they will absorb the water and turn gray.

Do not lift the lid of your slow cooker while it is cooking. Each time you do, heat will escape and you will need to add 20 to 30 minutes of cooking time to your recipe.

● **Medium (about 4 quart) slow cooker**

2 tbsp	grapeseed oil, divided	30 mL
8 cups	chopped button mushrooms (see Tips, left)	2 L
½ cup	finely chopped onion	125 mL
1½ cups	Classic Garlicky Tomato Sauce (page 110)	375 mL
¼ cup	Maple Chipotle Barbecue Sauce (page 111)	60 mL

1. In a large pot over high heat, heat 1 tbsp (15 mL) oil. Add half of the mushrooms and cook, stirring frequently, until lightly browned (there will be some liquid remaining).

2. Transfer mushrooms and liquid to slow cooker stoneware. Repeat with remaining oil and mushrooms. Add onion, tomato sauce and barbecue sauce to stoneware.

3. Cover and cook on Low for 6 hours or High for 3 hours. Serve immediately or let cool, transfer to an airtight container and refrigerate for up to 5 days.

Braised Tofu in French Onions

Dark, rich caramelized onions provide a flavorful base for protein-dense braised tofu. Serve with Basic Quinoa (page 235) and a crisp green salad for a complete meal.

MAKES 4 SERVINGS

Tips

Onions contain a considerable amount of natural sugar. Cooking them slowly for a long time results in a rich golden brown color and sweet flavor.

Use Vidalia or other sweet onions for this recipe. They have a higher sugar content than yellow onions, which is important for this dish.

Do not lift the lid of your slow cooker while it is cooking. Each time you do, heat will escape and you will need to add 20 to 30 minutes of cooking time to your recipe.

● **Medium (about 4 quart) slow cooker**

2 tbsp	grapeseed oil	30 mL
12 cups	thinly sliced sweet onions (see Tips, left)	3 L
1 tsp	fine sea salt	5 mL
12 to 15	cloves garlic, minced (see Tips, page 345)	12 to 15
½ cup	water	125 mL
2 tbsp	wheat-free tamari	30 mL
2 tbsp	nutritional yeast	30 mL
1 tbsp	raw (unpasteurized) apple cider vinegar	15 mL
1	block (16 oz/500 g) firm or extra-firm tofu, cut lengthwise into 4 strips	1
2 tbsp	chopped fresh thyme leaves	30 mL

1. In a large skillet over high heat, heat oil. Add onions and salt; cook, stirring frequently, until onions begin to brown, 5 to 6 minutes. Reduce heat to low and cook, stirring occasionally, until onions are soft and golden brown, about 45 minutes. Stir in garlic and cook for 2 to 3 minutes, until fragrant. Add water, tamari, nutritional yeast and vinegar; stir to combine.

2. Remove from heat and transfer to slow cooker stoneware. Lay slices of tofu on top of onion mixture.

3. Cover and cook on Low for 6 hours or High for 3 hours. Stir in thyme and cook, covered, for 30 minutes longer. Serve immediately or let cool, transfer to an airtight container and refrigerate for up to 5 days.

Eggplant, Lentil and Tomato Chili

Creamy, rich eggplant and protein-dense red lentils give this chili great body. I like to serve this over Roasted Vegetables (page 177) with a side of Creamy Mashed Potatoes (page 178).

MAKES 4 SERVINGS

Tips

Substitute an equal amount of coconut oil for the grapeseed oil in this recipe, but keep in mind that it will give the dish a slight coconut flavor.

To mince garlic: Place a whole clove on a cutting board. Using the butt end of a chef's knife, press firmly but gently on the clove to loosen the skin. Using your index finger and thumb, gently squeeze clove out of skin. Chop coarsely, then sprinkle with a bit of sea salt. Using the butt end of the knife, rub garlic into board (the salt will act as an abrasive and help to mince the garlic). Chop until fine.

The most common variety of eggplant is Italian eggplant, which has a black skin. You can also use Japanese eggplant, which has purple skin and is longer and thinner in shape.

¼ cup	grapeseed oil (see Tips, left)	60 mL
½ cup	chopped onion	125 mL
½ tsp	fine sea salt	2 mL
1 tbsp	chili powder	15 mL
1 tsp	ground cumin	5 mL
6 to 8	cloves garlic, minced (see Tips, left)	6 to 8
3 tbsp	wheat-free tamari	45 mL
2 cups	chopped peeled eggplant (see Tips, left)	500 mL
2 cups	chopped fresh tomatoes	500 mL
1 cup	red lentils, rinsed and drained	250 mL
3 cups	water	750 mL

1. In a skillet over medium-high heat, heat oil. Add onion and salt; cook, stirring frequently, until onion is translucent, about 3 minutes. Stir in chili powder and cumin; cook for 2 to 3 minutes, stirring constantly, until fragrant. Add garlic and cook, stirring constantly, for 1 to 2 minutes, until soft. Add tamari and stir, using a wooden spoon to scrape up any brown bits from bottom of pan.

2. Stir in eggplant, tomatoes and lentils; cook for 3 to 4 minutes. Add water and bring to a boil.

3. Reduce heat and simmer until eggplant is soft, lentils are tender and mixture has thickened, about 30 minutes. Serve immediately or let cool, transfer to an airtight container and refrigerate for up to 5 days.

Black Bean and Sweet Potato Chili

This hearty chili is great for cold winter nights over a bowl of Basic Rice (page 212) and topped with a dollop of Vegan Sour Cream (page 555).

MAKES 8 SERVINGS

Tips

This may seem like a massive amount of chili powder and cumin, but the quantity is nicely balanced by the citrus juices. This dish is very popular at my restaurant.

A hand-held citrus reamer can be used to extract the juice from citrus fruits. Available in most kitchen supply stores, this tool would be ideal to use for the citrus in this recipe.

Be sure to use raw (not processed) agave nectar. It is a 100% natural (non-GMO) sweetener that contains naturally occurring fructose and is low on the glycemic scale, which means that it releases glucose slowly, providing sustained energy.

• **Immersion or stand blender**

2 cups	cubed (1 inch/2.5 cm) peeled sweet potatoes	500 mL
3 tbsp	grapeseed oil	45 mL
1 cup	chopped onion	250 mL
½ cup	chopped celery	125 mL
½ cup	chopped red bell pepper	125 mL
½ tsp	fine sea salt	2 mL
2 tbsp	chopped garlic	30 mL
6 tbsp	chili powder	90 mL
3 tbsp	ground cumin	45 mL
½ cup	wheat-free tamari	125 mL
½ cup	freshly squeezed orange juice (see Tips, left)	125 mL
3 tbsp	raw agave nectar (see Tips, left)	45 mL
3 tbsp	freshly squeezed lemon juice	45 mL
1	can (28 oz/796 mL) diced tomatoes, with juice	1
2 cups	corn kernels	500 mL
4 cups	drained cooked black beans (see Tips, page 347)	1 L

1. In a large pot of boiling water, cook sweet potatoes until tender, about 12 minutes. Drain and set aside.

2. Meanwhile, in a large saucepan over medium-high heat, heat oil. Add onion, celery, red pepper and salt. Cook, stirring frequently, until onion is translucent and vegetables are tender, 5 to 6 minutes.

3. Stir in garlic and cook for 2 to 3 minutes, until fragrant. Stir in chili powder and cumin. Reduce heat to low and cook, stirring constantly, for 3 to 4 minutes, until spices are fragrant.

Tips

Replace the cooked black beans in this recipe with an equal amount of canned beans, preferably with no salt added. When using canned beans, be sure to rinse and drain them thoroughly before using.

Blending about one-third of the chili breaks down some of the starch, while maintaining most of the texture. To do this, insert blender at one side of the pot and blend for about 10 seconds. If you do not have an immersion blender, transfer a portion of the chili to a standard blender.

When blending hot liquids in a blender, make sure to your blender is no more than half full. Also, place a folded towel over the lid and place your hand firmly on top. Otherwise, the pressure of the steam may cause the lid to blow off, spattering your meal all over the kitchen.

4. Stir in tamari, orange juice, agave nectar, lemon juice and tomatoes. Increase heat to medium and bring mixture to a boil. Reduce heat and simmer for 10 to 12 minutes, until thickened slightly.
5. Add corn and beans. Stir well and simmer for 12 to 15 minutes or until chili is slightly thickened. Remove from heat.
6. Using an immersion blender, purée about one-third of the chili to break down some of the starch in the beans and corn while retaining most of the whole beans and vegetables for texture. If you do not have an immersion blender, transfer about half of the chili to a standard blender in batches (see Tips, left), but be careful not to overprocess — you want to retain some texture. Return to saucepan.)
7. Stir in cooked sweet potatoes and serve immediately.

African-Spiced Tempeh Chili

I like to serve this hearty dish simply, with steamed greens and drizzled with a little Roasted Garlic Chimichurri (page 109).

MAKES 4 TO 5 SERVINGS

Tips

Unpasteurized tempeh can be found in the freezer section of most well-stocked supermarkets and natural food stores. I prefer unpasteurized, as I find it has a better texture. Pasteurized tempeh will work equally well in this recipe.

Wheat-free tamari is a gluten-free seasoning made from fermented soybeans. It can be found in most well-stocked supermarkets and natural food stores.

Substitute 8 cups (2 L) chopped fresh tomatoes for the canned tomatoes.

1	block (8.5 oz/240 g) frozen (unpasteurized) tempeh (see Tips, left)	1
4 cups	water	1 L
½ cup	wheat-free tamari, divided	125 mL
2	whole cloves garlic, peeled	2
3 tbsp	grapeseed oil	45 mL
1 cup	chopped onion	250 mL
½ cup	chopped celery	125 mL
½ cup	chopped carrot	125 mL
6 to 8	cloves garlic, minced	6 to 8
1 tbsp	chili powder	15 mL
1 tsp	fenugreek seeds	5 mL
1 tsp	fennel seeds	5 mL
1 tsp	ground cumin	5 mL
½ tsp	caraway seeds	2 mL
½ tsp	ground coriander	2 mL
¼ tsp	sweet paprika	1 mL
1	can (28 oz/796 mL) diced tomatoes, with juice (see Tips, left)	1

1. In a saucepan, combine tempeh, water, ¼ cup (60 mL) tamari and garlic cloves. Cover and bring to a boil; reduce heat and simmer for 15 minutes. Using a slotted spoon, transfer tempeh to a plate (discard garlic and liquid). Set aside for 15 minutes. Chop finely.

2. In a skillet over medium-high heat, heat oil. Add prepared tempeh and cook, stirring frequently, until lightly golden, about 10 minutes. Add onion, celery and carrot. Cook, stirring occasionally, until vegetables are tender, 5 to 6 minutes. Stir in minced garlic and cook for 2 minutes, until fragrant.

3. Add chili powder, fenugreek, fennel seeds, cumin, caraway, coriander and paprika. Cook, stirring constantly, for about 5 minutes (be careful not to burn the garlic). Stir in tomatoes and remaining tamari. Bring to a boil, reduce heat and simmer until slightly thickened, about 15 minutes. Serve immediately or let cool, transfer to an airtight container and refrigerate for up to 5 days.

good

Baked Chana Masala

This fragrant dish is perfect with steamed basmati rice and Quick Garlic Cabbage Stir-Fry (page 303) topped with freshly chopped cilantro. Make it ahead and store in the fridge for an easy weekday dinner.

MAKES 4 TO 6 SERVINGS

Tips

Cilantro, like all herbs and spices, contains an abundance of phytonutrients that have antioxidant properties. Research suggests that it may help with digestion, ease bloating and relieve gas.

To remove the skin from fresh gingerroot with the least amount of waste, use the edge of a teaspoon. With a brushing motion, scrape off the skin to reveal the yellow root.

Replace the cooked chickpeas in this recipe with an equal amount of canned chickpeas, preferably with no salt added. When using canned legumes, be sure to rinse and drain them thoroughly before using.

Just OK very watery because of the fresh Tomatoes needs more salt & spice (handwritten note)

- **Large ovenproof pot with lid**
- **Preheat oven to 350°F (180°C)**

3 tbsp	coconut oil	45 mL
1 cup	chopped onion	250 mL
1 tsp	fine sea salt	5 mL
1 tbsp	ground cumin	15 mL
1 tsp	ground coriander	5 mL
½ tsp	ground cinnamon	2 mL
½ tsp	ground turmeric	2 mL
½ tsp	fennel seeds	2 mL
¼ tsp	ground cardamom	1 mL
⅛ tsp	ground cloves	0.5 mL
⅛ tsp	cayenne pepper	0.5 mL
½ cup	chopped fresh cilantro, leaves and stems	125 mL
1 tbsp	minced peeled gingerroot (see Tips, left)	15 mL
6 to 8	cloves garlic, minced	6 to 8
12 cups	chopped fresh tomatoes	3 L
½ cup	water	125 mL
2 tbsp	freshly squeezed lime juice	30 mL
1 tbsp	raw agave nectar	15 mL
4 cups	drained cooked chickpeas (see Tips, left)	1 L

1. In a pot over medium heat, melt coconut oil. Add onion and salt and cook until onion is lightly golden, 8 minutes. Add cumin, coriander, cinnamon, turmeric, fennel seeds, cardamom, cloves and cayenne. Cook, stirring constantly, for 3 minutes, until spices are fragrant. Stir in cilantro, ginger and garlic; cook for 2 minutes, until garlic is fragrant.

2. Add tomatoes, water, lime juice and agave nectar. Stir to combine, scraping up any brown bits from bottom of pan. Stir in chickpeas and bring to a boil.

3. Cover and bake in preheated oven for 45 minutes, until very fragrant. Serve immediately or let cool, transfer to an airtight container and refrigerate for up to 5 days.

Tempeh and Roasted Pepper Sloppy Joes

If you don't have gluten-free pita bread, this delicious combination of tempeh and roasted pepper is wonderful in a sandwich or served open-face on any favorite crusty bread. It is also great served over Basic Rice (page 212) with a dollop of Vegan Sour Cream (page 555).

MAKES 4 TO 6 SERVINGS

Tips

Unpasteurized tempeh can be found in the freezer section of most well-stocked supermarkets and natural food stores. I prefer unpasteurized, as I find it has a better texture. Pasteurized tempeh will work equally well for this recipe.

Wheat-free tamari is a gluten-free seasoning made from fermented soybeans. It can be found in most well-stocked supermarkets and natural food stores.

The quantity of garlic depends on the size of the cloves. If large, use the smaller number. If small, more may be required.

- Preheat oven to 400°F (200°C)
- Baking sheet lined with parchment paper
- Food processor

2	red peppers	2
1/4 cup	grapeseed oil, divided	60 mL
1 tsp	fine sea salt, divided	5 mL
1	block (8.5 oz/240 g) frozen (unpasteurized) tempeh (see Tips, left)	1
4 cups	water	1 L
1/2 cup	wheat-free tamari, divided (see Tips, left)	125 mL
2	whole cloves garlic, peeled	2
1 cup	chopped carrot	250 mL
1 cup	chopped onion	250 mL
1/2 cup	chopped celery	125 mL
10 to 12	cloves garlic, minced (see Tips, left)	10 to 12
1/2 cup	dry red wine (optional)	125 mL
1	can (28 oz/796 mL) diced tomatoes, with juice (see Tips, page 351)	1
1	can (5½ oz/156 mL) tomato paste	1
4 to 6	Gluten-Free Pita Breads (page 474)	4 to 6

1. In a bowl, toss together red peppers, 1 tbsp (15 mL) oil and ½ tsp (2 mL) salt. Place on prepared baking sheet and roast in preheated oven, turning several times, until skin is slightly blackened, about 25 minutes. Remove from oven. Transfer to a bowl and cover tightly with plastic wrap. Set aside for at least 10 minutes to sweat. Peel, discarding skins. Chop and set aside.

Tips

To mince garlic: Place a whole clove on a cutting board. Using the butt end of a chef's knife, press firmly but gently on the clove to loosen the skin. Using your index finger and thumb, gently squeeze clove out of skin. Chop coarsely, then sprinkle with a bit of sea salt. Using the butt end of the knife, rub garlic into board (the salt will act as an abrasive and help to mince the garlic). Chop until fine.

Substitute 4 cups (1 L) chopped fresh tomatoes for the canned tomatoes in this recipe.

This may seem like a lot of tomato paste, but it helps to flavor the tempeh while thickening the sauce.

If you are using flat pita breads, you can break them into large pieces and add to tempeh mixture or use them as a wrap, rolling around the tempeh. If using store-bought pita with a pocket, fill them with the tempeh.

2. Meanwhile, in a saucepan, combine tempeh, water, $\frac{1}{4}$ cup (60 mL) tamari and whole garlic cloves. Cover and bring to a boil; reduce heat and simmer for 15 minutes. Using a slotted spoon, transfer tempeh to a plate (discard garlic and liquid). Set aside for 10 to 15 minutes to cool.

3. Using a sharp knife, cut cooled tempeh into pieces. Transfer to food processor fitted with the metal blade, add carrot and process until roughly chopped. Set aside.

4. In a skillet over medium heat, heat remaining 3 tbsp (45 mL) oil. Add onion, celery and remaining $\frac{1}{2}$ tsp (2 mL) salt; cook, stirring frequently, until onion and celery are translucent, 7 to 8 minutes. Add minced garlic and cook for 2 to 3 minutes, until fragrant. Stir in wine (if using) and cook until liquid has evaporated.

5. Add tempeh and carrot mixture and stir to combine. Cook, stirring constantly, for 8 to 10 minutes, until tempeh is lightly browned and soft. Stir in remaining $\frac{1}{4}$ cup (60 mL) tamari, tomatoes and tomato paste. Reduce heat and simmer until thickened, about 10 minutes.

6. Serve tempeh mixture with pita. If not serving immediately, let mixture cool, transfer to an airtight container and refrigerate for up to 1 week.

Shepherd's Pie with Cauliflower Mash

Make this rich one-pot dish ahead of time and keep it in the fridge for an easy meal during the week. All it needs is a crisp green salad. If you want to gild the lily, add a drizzle of Holiday Gravy (page 558).

(page 558)

MAKES 4 SERVINGS

Tip

Unpasteurized tempeh can be found in the freezer section of most well-stocked supermarkets and natural food stores. I prefer unpasteurized, as I find it has a better texture. Pasteurized tempeh will work equally well for this recipe.

- **Food processor**
- **Blender**
- **13- by 9-inch (33 by 23 cm) glass baking pan**

TOPPING

6 cups	chopped cauliflower	1.5 L
1 tsp	fine sea salt, divided	5 mL
½ cup	nutritional yeast	125 mL

FILLING

2	blocks (each 8.5 oz/240 g) frozen (unpasteurized) tempeh (see Tip, left)	2
	Water	
½ cup	wheat-free tamari, divided	125 mL
2	whole cloves garlic, peeled	2
3 tbsp	grapeseed oil	45 mL
1 cup	chopped onion	250 mL
1 cup	chopped carrot	250 mL
1 cup	chopped celery	250 mL
½ tsp	fine sea salt	2 mL
3 to 4	cloves garlic, minced	3 to 4
3 tbsp	coconut oil	45 mL
¼ cup	brown rice flour	60 mL
½ cup	dry red wine	125 mL
1 tbsp	chopped fresh thyme leaves	15 mL
1 cup	corn kernels (fresh or frozen)	250 mL
	Sweet paprika	

1. *Topping:* Place cauliflower and ½ tsp (2 mL) salt in a large pot of water. Bring to a boil, reduce heat and simmer until tender, about 15 minutes. Drain, reserving 1 cup (250 mL) cooking liquid.

Carrot, celery and onion
are the three most common
ingredients you will find in
soups, stews and braises.
The classic term for this
combination is *mirepoix*.

2. In food processor fitted with the metal blade, combine cooked cauliflower, $\frac{1}{4}$ cup (60 mL) of the reserved cooking liquid, nutritional yeast and remaining $\frac{1}{2}$ tsp (2 mL) salt. Process until smooth, stopping the machine and adding additional cooking water 2 tbsp (30 mL) at a time, until creamy. (You likely won't need all of the cooking water.) Transfer to a bowl and set aside. Rinse out work bowl.

3. *Filling:* In a saucepan, combine tempeh, 4 cups (1 L) water, $\frac{1}{4}$ cup (60 mL) tamari and whole garlic cloves. Bring to a boil, reduce heat and simmer for 15 minutes. Using a slotted spoon, transfer tempeh to a plate (discard garlic and liquid). Set aside for 15 minutes to cool.

4. Using a sharp knife, cut cooled tempeh into pieces. Transfer to food processor fitted with the metal blade; process until broken down into small pieces.

5. In a large pot over medium heat, heat grapeseed oil. Add processed tempeh, onion, carrot, celery and salt. Cook, stirring frequently, until onion is translucent and tempeh is lightly browned, about 10 minutes. Stir in minced garlic and cook until fragrant, about 2 minutes.

6. Stir in coconut oil and rice flour; cook, stirring constantly, for 5 minutes, until the raw taste of the flour has been cooked out. Add wine and cook, stirring constantly, until no liquid remains. Add 2 cups (500 mL) water and remaining $\frac{1}{4}$ cup (60 mL) tamari. Bring mixture to a simmer and cook for 10 to 12 minutes. Remove from heat and stir in thyme and corn.

7. Preheat oven to 350°F (180°C).

8. Spread tempeh mixture evenly in prepared baking dish. Top with an even layer of cauliflower mixture. Sprinkle with paprika and bake in preheated oven for 25 to 30 minutes, until top is lightly golden brown and filling is bubbling. Serve immediately or let cool, cover and refrigerate for up to 1 week.

Baked Eggplant and Zucchini Napoleon

This dish delivers an authentic taste of Italy. It's also a perfect make-ahead dinner that can sit in your fridge for up to five days before being popped into the oven (see Tips, page 355).

(see Tips, page 355)

MAKES 4 TO 6 SERVINGS

Tips

Slicing the zucchini and eggplant to the same thickness ensures that they cook evenly. Using a mandoline will make this task easier.

Substitute an equal amount of your favorite store-bought tomato sauce for the Classic Garlicky Tomato Sauce.

- Preheat oven to 350°F (180°C)
- 13- by 9-inch (33 by 23 cm) glass baking dish, greased
- Baking sheet, lined with paper towels

1	medium Italian eggplant, cut lengthwise into ¼-inch (0.5 cm) slices	1
2	medium zucchini, cut lengthwise into ¼-inch (0.5 cm) slices (see Tips, left)	2
½ tsp	fine sea salt	2 mL
¼ cup	(approx.) grapeseed oil	60 mL
2 cups	Classic Garlicky Tomato Sauce (page 110; see Tips, left)	500 mL
1½ cups	nutritional yeast, divided (see Tips, page 355)	375 mL
½ cup	chopped flat-leaf (Italian) parsley leaves	125 mL
3 tbsp	extra virgin olive oil	45 mL
2 tbsp	freshly squeezed lemon juice	30 mL
1 tbsp	chopped fresh thyme leaves	15 mL
2 tsp	dried oregano leaves	10 mL

1. Lay eggplant and zucchini slices on a clean work surface. Sprinkle both sides with salt.

2. In a large skillet over medium-high heat, heat 2 tbsp (30 mL) grapeseed oil. Working in batches so as not to crowd the pan, cook zucchini slices for 1 to 2 minutes per side, until golden brown. Transfer to a plate lined with paper towels. Repeat with remaining zucchini and eggplant slices, adding more oil as necessary.

Tips

Nutritional yeast is an inactive yeast that has been grown on beet molasses and then pasteurized. It provides a rich, cheesy flavor in sauces, stews, soups and dips. Look for it in well-stocked supermarkets and natural food stores.

To assemble this dish ahead of time, complete the recipe to the end of Step 5. Cover and refrigerate for up to 2 days. Bake as instructed in Step 6.

3. In a small bowl, whisk together tomato sauce, 1 cup (250 mL) nutritional yeast and parsley.

4. In another small bowl, whisk together olive oil, lemon juice, thyme and oregano. Brush over cooked zucchini and eggplant slices, turning to coat as necessary.

5. Pour just enough seasoned tomato sauce into prepared baking dish to coat the bottom. Top with zucchini and eggplant slices, intermixing the two. Cover with another layer of tomato sauce. Repeat until no sauce and vegetables are left, finishing with a layer of tomato sauce. Sprinkle with remaining $\frac{1}{2}$ cup (125 mL) nutritional yeast.

6. Bake in preheated oven for 40 minutes or until bubbly and top is lightly golden. Serve immediately or let cool, transfer to an airtight container and refrigerate for up to 5 days.

Mushroom Pot Pie

This savory dish is perfect on cold winter nights when you are craving something hearty. The aromas of earthy mushrooms, red wine–infused gravy and the soft, flaky crust are sure to make your mouth water while it is baking.

MAKES 4 SERVINGS

Tips

To soak the dried mushrooms for this recipe: Place them in a bowl with 2 cups (500 mL) hot water. Cover and set aside to soak for 1 hour. Lift mushrooms out of the water carefully to ensure that any dirt or grit falls to the bottom of the bowl. Discard soaking water.

Dark Vegetable Stock will produce the richest flavor. If you do not have it, any vegetable stock, or even water, will do.

• 10-inch (25 cm) deep-dish pie plate, greased

½ cup	dried wild mushrooms, soaked (see Tips, left)	125 mL
¼ cup	coconut oil	60 mL
1 cup	chopped onion	250 mL
1 cup	chopped carrot	250 mL
½ cup	chopped celery	125 mL
½ tsp	fine sea salt	2 mL
6 to 8	cloves garlic, minced	6 to 8
4 cups	sliced button mushrooms	1 L
4 cups	sliced cremini mushrooms	1 L
⅓ cup	brown rice flour	75 mL
2 cups	Dark Vegetable Stock (page 559; see Tips, left)	500 mL
¼ cup	nutritional yeast (see Tips, page 357)	60 mL
2 tbsp	wheat-free tamari	30 mL
2 tbsp	chopped fresh thyme leaves	30 mL
½ cup	frozen green peas	125 mL
½	recipe Vegan Piecrust (page 562; see Tips, page 357)	½

1. In a large pot over medium heat, melt coconut oil. Add onion, carrot, celery and salt. Cook, stirring frequently, until vegetables become soft and translucent, about 6 minutes. Stir in garlic and cook until fragrant, about 2 minutes.

2. Add button, cremini and drained soaked mushrooms and cook until most of the liquid has evaporated, 12 to 15 minutes. Add rice flour and cook, stirring constantly, for 5 minutes, until the raw taste of the flour has cooked out. Remove from heat.

3. Add vegetable stock in a slow, steady stream, stirring constantly to prevent lumps. Return to medium heat and bring to a boil, then reduce heat and simmer for 4 to 5 minutes.

Tips

Nutritional yeast is an inactive yeast that has been grown on beet molasses and then pasteurized. It provides a rich, cheesy flavor in sauces, stews, soups and dips. Look for it in well-stocked supermarkets and natural food stores.

You can make your own piecrust from scratch or you can use a commercially prepared vegan pie crust, in which case follow the package instructions for rolling. You will need enough pastry for one top crust.

4. Remove from heat and stir in nutritional yeast, tamari and thyme until well combined. Stir in peas. Transfer to prepared pie plate and refrigerate until cold, about 1 hour.

5. Preheat oven to 350°F (180°C).

6. Roll out dough and cut into a 10-inch (25 cm) circle. Place crust over cooled filling. Pierce the top a few times to let steam escape.

7. Bake in preheated oven for 45 minutes or until crust is golden brown and filling is bubbling hot. Serve immediately.

Lentil Shepherd's Pie

This protein-rich baked meal is sure to become a favorite. Make it ahead and refrigerate for a comforting meal after a long day.

MAKES 4 TO 6 SERVINGS

Tips

To prevent fresh herbs from turning brown after chopping, ensure that your knife is as sharp as possible, to prevent bruising.

Substitute an equal amount of Dark Vegetable Stock (page 559) or water for the vegetable stock.

Replace the cooked lentils in this recipe with an equal amount of canned lentils, preferably with no salt added. When using canned legumes, be sure to rinse and drain them thoroughly before using.

You can make this recipe up to the end of Step 3, then cover and refrigerate for up to 2 days before baking as instructed.

- **Preheat oven to 400°F (200°C)**
- **13- by 9-inch (33 by 23 cm) glass baking dish, greased**

3 tbsp	grapeseed oil	45 mL
1 cup	chopped onion	250 mL
1/2 cup	chopped celery	125 mL
1/2 cup	chopped carrot	125 mL
1 tsp	fine sea salt	5 mL
6 to 8	cloves garlic, minced	6 to 8
2 tbsp	chopped fresh thyme leaves	30 mL
1	can (5 1/2 oz/156 mL) tomato paste	1
2 cups	Vegetable Stock (page 559; see Tips, left)	500 mL
4 cups	drained cooked green lentils (see Tips, left)	1 L
2 tbsp	wheat-free tamari	30 mL
1	recipe Creamy Mashed Potatoes (page 178)	1
1/4 tsp	sweet paprika	1 mL

1. In a large pot over medium heat, heat oil. Add onion, celery, carrot and salt. Cook, stirring frequently, until onion is translucent, about 6 minutes. Add garlic and thyme and cook until fragrant, about 2 minutes. Add tomato paste and cook, stirring constantly, for 2 to 3 minutes, until it is lightly brown.

2. Add vegetable stock, lentils and tamari. Bring to a boil, reduce heat and simmer for 3 to 5 minutes, until mixture has thickened.

3. Spread mixture evenly in prepared baking dish. Top with an even layer of mashed potatoes. Sprinkle with paprika.

4. Bake in preheated oven for 45 minutes, until bubbly and top is golden. Serve immediately or let cool, transfer to an airtight container and refrigerate for up to 5 days.

Potato Salad Wraps

Creamy potatoes and fresh herbs make up these delicious wraps filled with fiber and protein.

Tips

Always start with cold water when cooking potatoes. If you start with hot water, by the time the center of the potato is tender, the outside will be overcooked.

A hand-held citrus reamer can be used to extract the juice from lemons and limes. Available in most kitchen supply stores, this tool would be ideal to use for the lemon juice in this recipe.

To store fresh herbs, rinse well in cool water to remove any dirt. Dry in a salad spinner, wrap in slightly damp paper towels and refrigerate for up to 1 week.

● **Blender**

4 cups	cubed (1 inch/2.5 cm) red potatoes, skin on	1 L
½ cup	water	125 mL
½ tsp	fine sea salt	2 mL
½ cup	tahini	125 mL
¼ cup	freshly squeezed lemon juice (see Tips, left)	60 mL
2 tbsp	extra virgin olive oil	30 mL
1 tbsp	Dijon mustard	15 mL
1	clove garlic	1
½ cup	chopped fresh flat-leaf (Italian) parsley	125 mL
¼ cup	roughly chopped fresh dill	60 mL
¼ cup	raw shelled hemp seeds	60 mL
4	Gluten-Free Pita Breads (page 474)	4
	Hot sauce (optional)	

1. In a large saucepan of salted water, bring potatoes to a boil (see Tips, left). Reduce heat and simmer until tender, about 15 minutes. Drain, using a colander. Transfer to a large bowl and set aside to cool.

2. In blender, combine water, salt, tahini, lemon juice, oil, mustard and garlic. Blend at high speed until smooth and creamy. Pour over cooled potatoes. Add parsley, dill and hemp seeds and stir well. Set aside to allow potatoes to absorb the dressing.

3. Lay pitas flat on a clean work surface. Divide potato salad into 4 equal portions and spread across center of each pita, leaving a ¼-inch (0.5 cm) gap at each end. Fold in sides over filling. Serve immediately with hot sauce (if using).

Jerk Tofu, Avocado and Plantain Wraps

These wraps combine the delicious flavors and pleasing textures of creamy avocado, spiced tofu and sweet plantain. Enjoy them for either lunch or dinner.

MAKES 4 WRAPS

Tips

You want the plantains for this recipe to be black. They may look rotten to you, but they are perfectly ripe at this stage.

If you can't find Anaheim chiles, you can substitute 2 jalapeño peppers.

If you prefer your food spicier, leave the seeds in the chiles. If you want a little less heat, remove the seeds and ribs.

• Food processor

JERK TOFU

2 tbsp	extra virgin olive oil	30 mL
2 tbsp	grapeseed oil	30 mL
¼ cup	freshly squeezed lime juice	60 mL
½ cup	chopped red bell pepper	125 mL
2 tbsp	chopped fresh thyme leaves	30 mL
2 tbsp	wheat-free tamari	30 mL
1 tbsp	raw (unpasteurized) apple cider vinegar	15 mL
1 tbsp	chopped peeled gingerroot	15 mL
1 tbsp	organic coconut sugar	15 mL
2 tsp	ground allspice	10 mL
2	Anaheim chiles, chopped (see Tips, left)	2
3 to 4	cloves garlic	3 to 4
1	block (16 oz/500 g) firm or extra-firm tofu, cut in ¼-inch (0.5 cm) cubes	1

PLANTAINS

¼ cup	grapeseed oil	60 mL
2	ripe plantains, peeled and halved lengthwise (see Tips, left)	2
¼ tsp	fine sea salt	1 mL

ASSEMBLY

4	large (10 inches/25 cm) gluten-free wraps (see Tips, page 361)	4
2	medium ripe avocados, mashed	2
1 tbsp	grapeseed oil	15 mL

1. *Jerk Tofu:* In food processor fitted with the metal blade, combine olive oil, grapeseed oil, lime juice, red pepper, thyme, tamari, vinegar, ginger, coconut sugar, allspice, chiles and garlic. Process until smooth, stopping the motor to scrape down sides of work bowl as necessary.

Tips

If you prefer, substitute corn tortillas for the wraps. Tortillas are likely to be 6 inches (15 cm) in diameter, so adjust the filling amount accordingly.

Choose organic tortillas to avoid GMOs. Check the label to make sure they are gluten-free and do not contain any added wheat.

2. Transfer to a large bowl. Add tofu and toss to combine. Cover and set aside for 30 minutes to marinate or refrigerate overnight. Drain, discarding marinade, before adding to wraps.

3. *Plantains:* In a large skillet over medium heat, heat grapeseed oil. Add plantains and cook until golden brown on one side, 3 to 4 minutes. Turn over and cook until other side is golden brown, 2 to 3 minutes. Transfer to a plate, sprinkle with salt and set aside.

4. *Assembly:* Lay wraps flat on a clean work surface. Spoon an equal amount of avocado across the center of each wrap, leaving a 1-inch (2.5 cm) gap at each end. Top with equal amounts of jerk tofu and then cooked plantain. Fold in sides of wraps over filling, then, starting at the edge closest to you, roll up tightly to form cylinders.

5. In a large skillet over medium heat, heat grapeseed oil. Working in batches if necessary, add wraps, seam side down, and cook for 5 minutes per side, until golden brown and heated through. Serve immediately.

Greek-Style Gyro Wraps

Tart lemon and fragrant oregano paired with crisp lettuce, creamy tzatziki and fresh tomatoes make these wraps a perfect blend of delicious flavors and bold textures.

MAKES 4 WRAPS

Tips

Unpasteurized tempeh can be found in the freezer section of most well-stocked supermarkets and natural food stores. I prefer unpasteurized, as I find it has a better texture. Pasteurized tempeh will work equally well for this recipe.

Wheat-free tamari is a gluten-free seasoning made from fermented soybeans. It can be found in most well-stocked supermarkets and natural food stores.

Always use a very sharp knife when cutting tomatoes, and remove the core before chopping. Insert the tip of a paring knife into the stem end and turn the tomato while holding the knife steady. Remove and discard the core.

1	block (8.5 oz/240 g) frozen (unpasteurized) tempeh (see Tips, left)	1
4 cups	water	1 L
½ cup	wheat-free tamari (see Tips, left)	125 mL
2	whole cloves garlic, peeled	2
¼	lemon, sliced (unpeeled)	¼
¼ cup	extra virgin olive oil	60 mL
3 tbsp	freshly squeezed lemon juice	45 mL
1 tbsp	dried oregano	15 mL
½ tsp	fine sea salt	2 mL
4	Gluten-Free Pita Breads (page 474)	4
1 cup	Creamy Cashew Tzatziki (page 79)	250 mL
1 cup	chopped fresh tomato (see Tips, left)	250 mL
1 cup	thinly sliced romaine lettuce leaves	250 mL
½ cup	thinly sliced red onion	125 mL

1. In a small saucepan, combine tempeh, water, tamari, whole garlic cloves and lemon. Cover, bring to a boil, reduce heat and simmer for 15 minutes. Using a slotted spoon, transfer tempeh to a plate (discard garlic, lemon and liquid). Set aside for 15 minutes to cool.

2. Using a sharp knife, cut tempeh lengthwise into 8 equal strips. Transfer to a bowl. Add oil, lemon juice, oregano and salt; toss to combine. Cover and set aside for 30 minutes to marinate or refrigerate overnight.

3. Lay 1 pita flat on a clean work surface. Spread ¼ cup (60 mL) tzatziki across center, leaving a ½-inch (1 cm) gap at each end. Top with ¼ cup (60 mL) chopped tomato, ¼ cup (60 mL) lettuce, 2 tbsp (30 mL) onion and 2 strips marinated tempeh. Fold in sides of pita over filling, then, starting at the edge closest to you, roll up tightly to form a cylinder. Repeat with remaining pitas and fillings. Serve immediately.

Macrobiotic Platter

This recipe, based on traditional Japanese ingredients, is full of healing foods. Macrobiotic diets avoid refined flour and grains and instead focus on whole grains, legumes, greens and sea vegetables.

MAKES 4 SERVINGS

Tips

Wheat-free tamari is a gluten-free seasoning made from fermented soybeans. It can be found in most well-stocked supermarkets and natural food stores.

Arame is a nutritious sea vegetable. Most sea vegetables (also known as seaweed) are sold in a dry state. To rehydrate them, simply cover with twice their volume of warm water and set aside for 15 minutes or until softened.

Use either black beans you have cooked yourself or canned beans, preferably with no salt added. When using canned beans that contain salt, be sure to rinse and drain them thoroughly before using.

If your rice is freshly cooked, skip Step 3.

8 cups	water, divided	2 L
1	block (16 oz/500 g) firm tofu	1
½ cup	wheat-free tamari (see Tips, left)	125 mL
8 cups	cubed (1 inch/2.5 cm) peeled butternut squash	2 L
2 cups	Basic Rice (page 212)	500 mL
2 to 3 tbsp	water	30 to 45 mL
2 cups	arame, soaked (see Tips, left)	500 mL
2 cups	cooked black beans (see Tips, left)	500 mL
	Raw white sesame seeds	
	Wheat-free tamari	

1. In a large saucepan, combine 4 cups (1 L) water, tofu and tamari. Bring to a boil, reduce heat and simmer for 15 minutes. Drain and set aside.

2. In another large saucepan, bring to a boil remaining 4 cups (1 L) water and squash. Reduce heat and simmer until tender, about 15 minutes. Drain and set aside.

3. In a large skillet over medium heat, combine rice and 2 to 3 tbsp (30 to 45 mL) water. Simmer until rice is heated through (see Tips, left).

4. *Assembly:* On a large platter, arrange hot rice, cooked tofu, cooked squash, arame and beans. Garnish with sesame seeds and serve with a dish of wheat-free tamari.

Mushroom Colcannon

Colcannon is a traditional Irish dish of mashed potatoes and kale or cabbage. This version includes roasted mushrooms and crispy tempeh bacon — flavorful additions with a hit of protein.

MAKES 4 SERVINGS

Tip

Either Yukon Gold or russet potatoes work best in this dish. Keeping the skin on the potatoes helps retain nutrients during cooking.

- **Preheat oven to 400°F (200°C)**
- **Baking sheet, lined with parchment paper**
- **Food processor**

7 tbsp	grapeseed oil, divided	105 mL
4 cups	whole button mushrooms, trimmed	1 L
3 tbsp	wheat-free tamari	45 mL
1 tbsp	chopped fresh thyme leaves	15 mL
8 cups	chopped (1 inch/2.5 cm) unpeeled potatoes (see Tip, left)	2 L
1 tsp	fine sea salt, divided	5 mL
½ cup	chopped leeks (white part only; see Tip, page 365)	125 mL
½ cup	chopped onion	125 mL
1	bunch green curly kale, stems removed, chopped	1
3 to 4	cloves garlic, minced	3 to 4
½ cup	dry white wine (optional)	125 mL
1	can (14 oz/400 mL) full-fat coconut milk	1
2 cups	roughly chopped Tempeh Bacon (page 38)	500 mL
3 to 4 tbsp	Whipped Non-dairy Butter (page 554)	45 to 60 mL

1. In a large bowl, toss together ¼ cup (60 mL) oil, mushrooms, tamari and thyme. Spread evenly on prepared baking sheet and bake in preheated oven until mushrooms are soft and lightly golden brown, about 20 minutes. Set aside.

2. In a large pot of water, combine potatoes and ½ tsp (2 mL) salt. Bring to a boil, reduce heat and simmer until tender, about 20 minutes. Drain.

Tip

Place the sliced leeks in a bowl with 2 cups (500 mL) water and set aside for 5 minutes so any dirt can fall to the bottom of the bowl. Use a slotted spoon to remove from the water (discard water).

3. Meanwhile, in another large pot over medium heat, heat 2 tbsp (30 mL) oil. Add leeks, onion and remaining ½ tsp (2 mL) salt. Cook, stirring frequently, until onion is translucent, 5 to 6 minutes. Add kale and cook just until wilted, 2 to 3 minutes. Stir in garlic and cook until fragrant, about 2 minutes.

4. Add wine (if using) and cook until liquid has evaporated. Stir in coconut milk and bring to a boil. Reduce heat and simmer for 5 minutes, until mixture has thickened.

5. In food processor fitted with the metal blade, process tempeh bacon until broken into small pieces.

6. In a skillet over medium-high heat, heat remaining 1 tbsp (15 mL) oil. Add tempeh bacon and cook until golden brown, 5 to 6 minutes. Remove from heat and set aside.

7. In a large bowl, combine cooked potatoes, kale mixture and butter. Using a potato masher, mash together until no large pieces of potato remain. Gently stir in bacon and roasted mushrooms with their juices. Serve immediately or let cool, transfer to an airtight container and refrigerate for up to 5 days.

Stuffed Sweet Potatoes with Garlic-Braised Greens

A rich, hearty filling topped with crunchy tempeh bacon bits elevates this dish into something special.

Tips

Piercing the potatoes with a fork allows steam to escape, preventing them from exploding in the oven.

Kale and collard leaves have a long, thick vein that runs through the center. When working with these vegetables, keep the soft vein at the top of the leaf intact. However, as you move toward the bottom (stem) end of the leaf, the vein becomes larger and tougher and needs to be removed. Lay the leaf flat on a cutting board and use a paring knife to remove the thick part of the vein, discarding it. For this recipe, slice the remaining leaf into thin strips.

- Preheat oven to 400°F (200°C)
- 2 baking sheets, one lined with parchment paper
- Food processor

SWEET POTATOES

2	large sweet potatoes	2
1 cup	roughly chopped Tempeh Bacon (page 38)	250 mL
3 tbsp	grapeseed oil	45 mL
1/4 tsp	fine sea salt	1 mL
1/2 cup	Chia Whiz (page 85)	125 mL
1/2 cup	Vegan Sour Cream (page 555)	125 mL
1/4 cup	finely sliced green onions (green part only)	60 mL

BRAISED GREENS

2 tbsp	grapeseed oil	30 mL
6 to 8	cloves garlic, minced	6 to 8
4 cups	thinly sliced collard greens (see Tips, left)	1 L
4 cups	chopped spinach leaves	1 L
4 cups	thinly sliced kale leaves	1 L
1/2 cup	Vegetable Stock (page 559)	125 mL
1 tbsp	chopped fresh thyme leaves (see Tips, page 367)	15 mL
1/4 tsp	fine sea salt	1 mL

1. *Sweet Potatoes:* Using the tines of a fork, poke holes in potatoes. Wrap tightly in aluminum foil. Place on baking sheet and bake in preheated oven until tender, about 45 minutes. Remove from oven and set aside until cool enough to handle, 12 to 15 minutes.

2. Lower oven temperature to 350°F (180°C).

3. Meanwhile, in food processor fitted with the metal blade, process tempeh bacon until broken into small pieces.

To chop fresh thyme: Pinch the stem at the bottom with two fingers. Pulling upward with the finger and thumb of your other hand, strip the leaves. Reserve stems for soups or broths (discard after cooking). Use a sharp knife to chop the leaves, being careful not to chop too much or too hard, as this will bruise the leaves and cause the thyme to discolor.

4. In a large skillet over medium heat, heat oil. Add bacon and cook, stirring frequently, until golden brown and crispy, 5 to 6 minutes. Using a slotted spoon, transfer to a bowl. Toss with salt and set aside.

5. Cut sweet potatoes in half lengthwise and scoop out as much flesh as you can without damaging the skin. Reserve intact skins and transfer flesh to a large bowl. Add Chia Whiz. Using a potato masher, mash together until well combined.

6. Spoon an equal amount of filling into each reserved potato skin. Transfer filled skins to second (prepared) baking sheet and bake in preheated oven until golden brown on top and heated through, about 15 minutes.

7. *Braised Greens:* Meanwhile, in a large pot over medium heat, heat oil. Add garlic and cook, stirring constantly, until lightly golden, 2 to 3 minutes. Add collard greens, spinach and kale; cook just until wilted (be careful not to burn the garlic). Stir in vegetable stock, thyme and salt. Cover and cook for 10 to 15 minutes, until greens are soft and braising liquid has reduced slightly.

8. Garnish baked sweet potatoes with sour cream and sprinkle with green onion and bacon bits. Serve each person half a sweet potato with braised greens alongside.

Fajitas with Spice-Rubbed Portobellos

Serve these tasty wraps with a big dollop of Vegan Sour Cream and some Roasted Red Pepper Mole Sauce (page 108) for dipping. They are good to make for gatherings, where people can assemble their own fajitas.

MAKES 4 SERVINGS

Tips

Before slicing the mushrooms, discard the bottom ¼ to ½ inch (0.5 to 1 cm) of the stem.

If you prefer, substitute an equal quantity of your favorite store-bought vegan mozzarella or sour cream.

Look for gluten-free wraps or use organic corn tortillas that do not contain added wheat (check the label). Warm the wraps in a large covered dry skillet over low heat for 20 to 30 seconds per side, just before serving.

2	large portobello mushrooms, cut into thin strips (see Tips, left)	2
3 tbsp	wheat-free tamari	45 mL
¼ cup	extra virgin olive oil, divided	60 mL
2 tsp	chili powder	10 mL
1 tsp	ground cumin	5 mL
2 cups	chopped tomatoes	500 mL
½ cup	chopped flat-leaf (Italian) parsley leaves	125 mL
1 tsp	freshly squeezed lemon juice	5 mL
¼ tsp	fine sea salt	1 mL
2 tbsp	grapeseed oil	30 mL
1 cup	Vegan Shredded Mozzarella (page 537; see Tips, left)	250 mL
1 cup	thinly sliced romaine lettuce leaves	250 mL
½ cup	Vegan Sour Cream (page 555)	125 mL
¼ cup	finely sliced green onion (green and white parts)	60 mL
4	large (10 inches/25 cm) gluten-free wraps, warmed (see Tips, left)	4

1. In a bowl, toss together mushroom strips, tamari, 2 tbsp (30 mL) olive oil, chili powder and cumin. Cover and set aside for 30 minutes. Transfer mushrooms to a plate and set aside. Reserve marinade.

2. In a large bowl, toss together tomatoes, remaining 2 tbsp (30 mL) olive oil, parsley, lemon juice and salt.

3. In a large skillet over medium-high heat, heat grapeseed oil. Add marinated mushrooms and cook until soft, about 5 minutes. Add reserved marinade and bring to a simmer. Transfer to a plate.

4. Spread each warmed wrap with one-quarter of the sautéed mushrooms, ¼ cup (60 mL) mozzarella, ½ cup (125 mL) tomato mixture, ¼ cup (60 mL) lettuce, 2 tbsp (30 mL) sour cream and 1 tbsp (15 mL) green onion. Repeat with remaining wraps. Serve immediately.

Slow-Cooked Barbecued Jackfruit

Jackfruit is an Asian ingredient related to breadfruit. When rubbed together between your fingers, its flesh pulls apart just like slow-cooked meat. In this dish it is simmered all day in a sweet and smoky barbecue sauce. It can be served slathered inside a sandwich or served over a big bowl of Creamy Mashed Potatoes (page 178).

MAKES 4 TO 6 SERVINGS

Tips

Be sure to use raw (not processed) agave nectar. It is a 100% natural (non-GMO) sweetener that contains naturally occurring fructose and is low on the glycemic scale, which means that it releases glucose slowly, providing sustained energy.

When you remove the jackfruit pieces from the can, they will look like small pieces of pineapple. To give it the appearance of slow-cooked meat, simply rub the fruit between your fingers to break it into smaller pieces.

Do not lift the lid of your slow cooker while it is cooking. Each time you do, heat will escape and you will need to add 20 to 30 minutes of cooking time to your recipe.

• Medium (about 4 quart) slow cooker

1 tbsp	grapeseed oil	15 mL
1 cup	chopped onion	250 mL
1 tsp	fine sea salt	5 mL
6 to 8	cloves garlic, minced	6 to 8
1 tsp	chili powder	5 mL
1 tsp	chipotle powder	5 mL
1 tbsp	Dijon mustard	15 mL
¼ cup	raw (unpasteurized) apple cider vinegar	60 mL
¼ cup	pure maple syrup	60 mL
¼ cup	molasses	60 mL
2 tbsp	raw agave nectar (see Tips, left)	30 mL
2 cups	ketchup	500 mL
1	can (14 oz/398 mL) diced tomatoes, with juice	1
1	can (19 oz/540 mL) young green jackfruit (see Tips, left)	1

1. In a skillet over medium heat, heat oil. Add onion and salt; cook, stirring frequently, until onion is translucent, 5 to 6 minutes. Stir in garlic and cook until fragrant, about 2 minutes. Add chili powder and chipotle powder; cook, stirring constantly, for 2 to 3 minutes, until spices are fragrant.

2. Stir in mustard, vinegar, maple syrup, molasses, agave nectar and ketchup. Bring to a boil, reduce heat and simmer for 10 minutes. Stir in tomatoes and jackfruit. Transfer to slow cooker stoneware.

3. Cover and cook on Low for 8 hours or High for 4 hours. Serve immediately or transfer to an airtight container and refrigerate for up to 10 days.

Loaded Baked Potatoes with Ginger Broccoli

Serve these potatoes the next time you have friends over for a big game or get the family together for a picnic. A rich, hearty filling topped with crunchy tempeh bacon bits will make it a fan favorite.

MAKES 4 SERVINGS

Tips

Piercing the potatoes with a fork allows steam to escape, preventing them from exploding in the oven.

If you prefer, substitute an equal quantity of your favorite store-bought vegan mozzarella, cream cheese or non-dairy butter.

To remove the skin from fresh gingerroot with the least amount of waste, use the edge of a teaspoon. With a brushing motion, scrape off the skin to reveal the yellow flesh.

- **Preheat oven to 400°F (200°C)**
- **2 baking sheets, one lined with parchment paper**
- **Food processor**

POTATOES

2	large russet (baking) potatoes	2
1 cup	coarsely chopped Tempeh Bacon (see page 38)	250 mL
3 tbsp	grapeseed oil	45 mL
1/4 tsp	fine sea salt	1 mL
1 cup	Cashew Cream Cheese (page 535)	250 mL
1/2 cup	thinly sliced green onions (green part only)	125 mL
1/4 cup	Whipped Non-dairy Butter (page 554)	60 mL
1/2 cup	Vegan Shredded Mozzarella (page 537)	125 mL

BROCCOLI

2 tbsp	grapeseed oil	30 mL
1/4 cup	chopped peeled gingerroot (see Tips, left)	60 mL
4 cups	broccoli florets	1 L
1/4 cup	water	60 mL
1/4 cup	hoisin sauce (see Tips, page 371)	60 mL

1. *Potatoes:* Using the tines of a fork, poke holes in potatoes. Wrap tightly in aluminum foil. Place on baking sheet and bake in preheated oven until tender, about 60 minutes. Remove from oven and set aside until cool enough to handle, 20 to 25 minutes.

2. Lower oven temperature to 250°F (180°C).

3. In food processor fitted with the metal blade, process tempeh bacon until broken into small pieces.

Tip

Look for hoisin sauce that is free of preservatives, added sugar or gluten. Quality hoisin is made from soybeans and sweet potatoes with the addition of molasses or other natural sugars.

4. In a large skillet over medium heat, heat grapeseed oil. Add bacon and cook, stirring frequently, until golden brown and crispy, 5 to 6 minutes. Using a slotted spoon, transfer to a bowl. Add salt and toss to combine.

5. Cut baked potatoes in half lengthwise and scoop out as much flesh as you can without damaging the skin. Reserve skins intact and transfer flesh to a large bowl. Add cream cheese, green onions and butter. Using a potato masher, mash until well combined.

6. Spoon equal amounts of filling into reserved potato skins. Top with vegan mozzarella. Place on prepared baking sheet and bake in preheated oven until golden brown on top and heated through, about 15 minutes.

7. *Broccoli*: In a large skillet over medium heat, heat grapeseed oil. Add ginger and cook, stirring constantly, until golden brown, 5 to 6 minutes. Add broccoli and cook for 2 to 3 minutes, until just tender. Add water and hoisin sauce and cook, stirring constantly, until sauce has thickened, 2 to 3 minutes.

8. Top stuffed potatoes with crispy bacon. Serve each person half a potato with broccoli alongside.

Spicy Tempeh and Squash

There is something about adding squash to a slow-cooked dish that makes it hearty and comforting. In this dish the squash is paired with protein-dense tempeh to create a perfect weeknight meal to serve over Basic Rice (page 212).

(page 212)

MAKES 4 TO 6 SERVINGS

Tips

Unpasteurized tempeh can be found in the freezer section of most well-stocked supermarkets and natural food stores. I prefer unpasteurized, as I find it has a better texture. Pasteurized tempeh will work equally well for this recipe.

The skin on both delicata and acorn squash is edible. I serve roasted skin-on acorn squash as a vegetable at Christmas and my customers love it.

Nutritional yeast flakes can be found in well-stocked supermarkets and natural food stores. Nutritional yeast is fortified with vitamin B$_{12}$ and helps to produce umami, the savory flavor sometimes lacking in vegetarian cuisine.

• **Medium (about 4 quart) slow cooker**

1	block (8.5 oz/240 g) frozen (unpasteurized) tempeh (see Tips, left)	1
4 cups	water	1 L
½ cup	wheat-free tamari, divided	125 mL
2	whole cloves garlic, peeled	2
¼ cup	grapeseed oil, divided	60 mL
1 cup	chopped onion	250 mL
1 tsp	fine sea salt	5 mL
1 tsp	hot pepper flakes	5 mL
½ tsp	cayenne pepper	2 mL
4 to 6	cloves garlic, minced	4 to 6
½ cup	dried red lentils	125 mL
6 cups	Vegetable Stock (page 559)	1.5 L
4 cups	cubed (1 inch/2.5 cm) peeled butternut squash	1 L
2 cups	cubed (1 inch/2.5 cm) delicata or acorn squash, skin on	500 mL
¼ cup	nutritional yeast (see Tips, left)	60 mL
1 tbsp	chopped fresh thyme leaves	15 mL

1. In a saucepan, combine tempeh, water, ¼ cup (60 mL) tamari and whole garlic cloves. Cover and bring to a boil, reduce heat and simmer for 15 minutes. Using a slotted spoon, transfer tempeh to a plate (discard garlic and liquid). Set aside for 15 minutes to cool. Using a sharp knife, cut cooled tempeh into 1-inch (2.5 cm) cubes.

2. In a large skillet over high heat, heat 3 tbsp (45 mL) oil. Add prepared tempeh and cook, stirring frequently, until golden brown and crispy, 8 to 10 minutes. Using a slotted spoon, transfer to a plate lined with paper towels and set aside.

3. In same skillet, heat remaining 1 tbsp (15 mL) oil. Add onion, salt, hot pepper flakes, cayenne and minced garlic. Cook, stirring frequently, until onion is translucent, 5 to 6 minutes.

4. Stir in lentils and vegetable stock. Bring to a boil, then transfer to slow cooker stoneware. Add butternut and delicata squash.

5. Cover and cook on Low for 6 hours or High for 3 hours. Add remaining $\frac{1}{4}$ cup (60 mL) tamari, nutritional yeast and thyme; cook, covered, for 20 minutes longer. Serve immediately or let cool, transfer to an airtight container and refrigerate for up to 5 days.

Squash and Ginger Tofu

Serve this dish in the colder months when you are craving warm, hearty food. I like to pair it with Thai-Style Coconut Eggplant and Rice Noodles (page 278), Pineapple and Coconut Fried Rice (page 309) or Sautéed Vegetables with Three-Chile Blend (page 296).

MAKES 4 SERVINGS

Tips

To remove the skin from fresh gingerroot with the least amount of waste, use the edge of a teaspoon. With a brushing motion, scrape off the skin to reveal the yellow root.

Wheat-free tamari is a gluten-free seasoning made from fermented soybeans. It can be found in most well-stocked supermarkets and natural food stores.

Do not lift the lid of your slow cooker while it is cooking. Each time you do, heat will escape and you will need to add 20 to 30 minutes of cooking time to your recipe.

● **Medium (about 4 quart) slow cooker**

2 tbsp	grapeseed oil	30 mL
¼ cup	minced peeled gingerroot (see Tips, left)	60 mL
1 cup	thinly sliced onion	250 mL
1 tsp	fine sea salt	5 mL
8 cups	cubed (1 inch/2.5 cm) peeled butternut squash	2 L
1 cup	Vegetable Stock (page 559)	250 mL
2 tbsp	wheat-free tamari (see Tips, left)	30 mL
1 tbsp	organic coconut sugar	15 mL
1	block (16 oz/500 g) firm or extra-firm tofu, cut lengthwise into 4 pieces	1

1. In a large skillet over medium heat, heat oil. Add ginger and cook, stirring constantly, until golden brown, 3 to 4 minutes. Add onion and salt. Cook, stirring occasionally, until onion is translucent, about 6 minutes. Transfer to slow cooker stoneware.

2. Add squash, vegetable stock, tamari and coconut sugar; stir to combine. Place tofu on top of mixture.

3. Cover and cook on Low for 6 hours or High for 3 hours. Serve immediately or let cool, transfer to an airtight container and refrigerate for up to 1 week.

Entertaining

Beet Cakes with Braised Fennel and Creamed Swiss Chard

Serve this exotic dish as a main course or make the cakes smaller and serve as canapés or an appetizer at your next dinner party.

Tips

You can purchase raw flax seeds that are already ground (often described as "milled") in vacuum-sealed bags, or you can grind them yourself. To grind the flax for this recipe, place ¼ cup (60 mL) whole seeds in a blender or clean spice grinder. Blend at high speed until finely ground. Reserve any extra for other uses, such as adding to smoothies or sprinkling on cereal.

Using golden flax seeds will yield lighter-colored beet cakes, while brown flax will make them darker. Use whichever color you prefer.

- **Preheat oven to 400°F (200°C)**
- **Food processor**
- **Ovenproof saucepan with lid**
- **Blender**

BEET CAKES

2 tbsp	ground raw flax seeds (see Tips, left)	30 mL
6 tbsp	hot water	90 mL
½ cup	millet, rinsed and drained	125 mL
4 cups	water	1 L
½ tsp	fine sea salt	2 mL
4 cups	shredded beets, divided	1 L
½ tsp	ground coriander	2 mL
¼ tsp	fennel seeds	1 mL
1 to 2	cloves garlic, peeled	1 to 2
1 tbsp	brown rice flour	15 mL

BRAISED FENNEL

2 tbsp	grapeseed oil	30 mL
4 to 6	cloves garlic, minced	4 to 6
1	bulb fennel, halved crosswise	1
½ tsp	fine sea salt	2 mL
½ cup	water	125 mL
3 tbsp	red wine vinegar	45 mL
1 tbsp	wheat-free tamari	15 mL

CREAMED SWISS CHARD

1 cup	raw cashews	250 mL
4 cups	water, divided	1 L
½ tsp	fine sea salt	2 mL
2 tbsp	grapeseed oil	30 mL
½ cup	finely chopped onion	125 mL
1 to 2	cloves garlic, minced	1 to 2
8 cups	thinly sliced Swiss chard	2 L

ASSEMBLY

¼ cup	grapeseed oil	60 mL

Tips

The quantity of garlic depends on the size of the cloves. If large, use the smaller number. If small, more may be required.

The beet cakes may seem wet when mixed, but they hold together when cooked.

I like to braise fennel in larger pieces so it retains its texture. Cut each piece in half before serving.

1. *Beet Cakes:* In a bowl, whisk together ground flax seeds and hot water. Cover and set aside for about 10 minutes so flax can absorb the liquid and swell.

2. In a saucepan, combine millet, water and salt. Bring to a boil, reduce heat and simmer, stirring frequently, until tender, about 20 minutes. Cover and set aside for 10 minutes so millet can absorb any remaining liquid and swell.

3. In food processor fitted with the metal blade, combine cooked millet, 2 cups (500 mL) beets, coriander, fennel seeds and garlic. Process until smooth. Transfer to a bowl and stir in soaked flax, rice flour and remaining 2 cups (500 mL) beets. Set aside.

4. *Braised Fennel:* In ovenproof saucepan over medium heat, heat grapeseed oil. Add garlic and fennel and cook, stirring occasionally, until fennel is golden brown, 5 to 6 minutes. Stir in salt, water, vinegar and tamari. Cover and bake in preheated oven until fennel is soft, about 30 minutes. Remove from oven and set aside.

5. *Creamed Swiss Chard:* Meanwhile, in a saucepan, combine cashews and 3 cups (750 mL) water. Bring to a boil, then drain, discarding liquid. Transfer cashews to blender. Add remaining 1 cup (250 mL) water and salt. Blend at high speed until smooth. Set aside.

6. In a large skillet over medium heat, heat grapeseed oil. Add onion and garlic and cook until softened and fragrant, 5 to 6 minutes. Add chard and cook until tender, 3 to 4 minutes. Stir in puréed cashews; reduce heat to low and simmer for 3 to 4 minutes.

7. *Assembly:* Divide beet mixture into 4 equal portions. Using your hands, form them into puck shapes.

8. In a large skillet over medium-high heat, heat grapeseed oil. Cook beet cakes for 3 to 4 minutes per side, until golden brown. Transfer to a plate lined with paper towels and set aside.

9. Divide braised fennel among serving plates. Top each serving with equal portions Swiss chard and a beet cake. Serve immediately.

Crispy No-Crab Cakes with Creamy Coleslaw

These "let's pretend" crab cakes with all the trimmings make a terrific lunch or light Friday-night dinner with friends. The crisp cakes pair well with the creamy coleslaw and refreshing tartar sauce.

Tips

To save time, you can use your favorite store-bought vegan mayonnaise.

Finely chopping the red onion will soften the onion flavor in the no-crab cake. If you prefer a milder flavor, substitute ¼ cup (60 mL) finely sliced green onion (green parts only) for the red onion.

- Food processor
- Blender

NO-CRAB CAKES

1	block (16 oz/500 g) firm tofu	1
½ cup	Vegan Mayonnaise (page 550; see Tips, left)	125 mL
½ cup	chopped red bell pepper	125 mL
½ cup	chopped celery	125 mL
¼ cup	finely chopped red onion (see Tips, left)	60 mL
3 tbsp	Dijon mustard	45 mL
3 tbsp	freshly squeezed lemon juice (see Tip, page 379)	45 mL
1 tbsp	dried dill	15 mL
1 tsp	fine sea salt	5 mL
1 cup	coarse stone-ground organic cornmeal	250 mL

COLESLAW

4 cups	shredded cabbage	1 L
2 cups	shredded carrots	500 mL
½ cup	chopped flat-leaf (Italian) parsley	125 mL
2 tbsp	extra virgin olive oil	30 mL
2 tbsp	freshly squeezed lemon juice	30 mL
1 tsp	fine sea salt	5 mL
1 tsp	organic coconut sugar	5 mL
½ cup	Vegan Mayonnaise	125 mL

TARTAR SAUCE

1 cup	tahini	250 mL
¼ cup	freshly squeezed lemon juice	60 mL
¼ cup	water	60 mL
1 tbsp	white wine vinegar	15 mL
1 tbsp	raw agave nectar	15 mL
1 tbsp	prepared yellow ("ballpark") mustard	15 mL

A hand-held citrus reamer can be used to extract the juice from lemons and limes. Available in most kitchen supply stores, this tool would be ideal to use for the lemon juice in this recipe.

1 tsp	fine sea salt	5 mL
½ cup	finely chopped dill pickles	125 mL
½ cup	chopped fresh dill	125 mL

ASSEMBLY

| ¼ cup | grapeseed oil | 60 mL |
| | Lemon wedges | |

1. *No-Crab Cakes:* In food processor fitted with the metal blade, process tofu until roughly chopped. Transfer to a large bowl. Add mayonnaise, red pepper, celery, onion, Dijon mustard, lemon juice, dill and salt. Stir until well combined. Divide mixture into 6 equal portions. Using your hands, form them into puck shapes. Refrigerate for 30 minutes to firm up.

2. Place cornmeal in a shallow bowl. Roll each cake in cornmeal, coating evenly. Cover and refrigerate until ready to cook (this will also help firm up the cakes).

3. *Coleslaw:* In a large bowl, combine cabbage, carrots, parsley, olive oil, lemon juice, salt and coconut sugar. Toss together until well coated. Set aside for 5 to 10 minutes to marinate. Add mayonnaise and stir well. Set aside.

4. *Tartar Sauce:* In blender, combine tahini, lemon juice, water, vinegar, agave nectar, yellow mustard and salt. Blend at high speed until smooth. Transfer to a bowl. Add chopped pickles and dill; stir to combine.

5. *Assembly:* In a large skillet over medium-high heat, heat grapeseed oil. Cook cakes for 5 to 6 minutes per side, until golden brown and heated through.

6. Divide coleslaw among serving plates. Rest a crab cake on each serving and top with a dollop of tartar sauce. Serve with lemon wedges and additional tartar sauce alongside.

Stuffed Zucchini Blossoms with Spicy Queso Dip

Serve these yummy treats for a special lunch. They also make a great first course for four people when served as a prelude to dinner. The creamy cashew and quinoa filling is a cooling complement to the spicy queso sauce.

MAKES 4 SERVINGS

Tips

To soak the cashews: Place in a bowl and cover with 4 cups (1 L) water. Cover and set aside for 30 minutes or overnight (if overnight, refrigerate). Drain, discarding liquid.

The stems on the leaves closest to the bottom of fresh cilantro are generally tough and need to be removed. The stems on leaves closer to the top of the sprig are soft and full of flavor and can be left on.

Zucchini blossoms are available during late summer. Look for them in well-stocked supermarkets or your local farmers' market.

If you have leftover filling, use it as spread or as a high-protein dip with crisp vegetables. My favorites are cauliflower and broccoli florets and celery sticks.

- Preheat oven to 400°F (200°C)
- Food processor
- Baking sheet, lined with parchment paper

2 cups	raw cashews, soaked (see Tips, left)	500 mL
½ cup	chopped red bell pepper	125 mL
½ cup	chopped fresh cilantro, leaves and stems (see Tips, left)	125 mL
2 tbsp	freshly squeezed lemon juice	30 mL
2 tsp	chili powder	10 mL
1 tsp	fine sea salt	5 mL
1 tsp	ground cumin	5 mL
1 to 2	cloves garlic, peeled	1 to 2
Pinch	cayenne pepper	Pinch
⅓ cup	water	75 mL
1 cup	Basic Quinoa (page 235)	250 mL
8	zucchini blossoms (see Tips, left)	8
2 tbsp	extra virgin olive oil	30 mL
½ cup	Queso Dip (page 82)	125 mL

1. In food processor fitted with the metal blade, combine cashews, red pepper, cilantro, lemon juice, chili powder, salt, cumin, garlic and cayenne. Process until no large pieces of red pepper remain, stopping the motor to scrape down sides of work bowl as necessary. With the motor running, drizzle water through the feed tube and process until smooth and creamy. Transfer to a large bowl. Fold in cooked quinoa.

2. Using your fingers, gently open up each zucchini blossom and place in a large bowl. Drizzle with olive oil and toss gently to combine.

3. Using a small spoon, stuff each blossom with ¼ to ⅓ cup (60 to 75 mL) filling. Transfer to prepared baking sheet and bake in preheated oven for 25 to 30 minutes, or until slightly golden brown and heated through. Serve immediately with Queso Dip alongside.

Boxty

Boxty is a traditional potato pancake from Ireland. It makes a delicious special-occasion brunch or lunch, served with a big dollop of vegan sour cream, some finely sliced green onions and a little crispy tempeh bacon.

Tips

Substitute an equal amount of Cashew Milk (page 61), Oat Milk (page 63) or Coconut Milk (page 62) for the almond milk.

Grate the potatoes for this recipe using the side of a box grater or the shredding attachment of a food processor. Over a sink, use your hands to squeeze as much water out of the shredded potato as you can before adding to the rest of the ingredients.

After adding the rice flour (Step 3), the mixture should be thick and slightly dry. If it is still a little wet, add remaining rice flour and mix well.

- Preheat oven to 400°F (200°C)
- Baking sheet, lined with parchment paper

1 cup	Almond Milk (page 61; see Tips, left)	250 mL
1 tsp	raw (unpasteurized) apple cider vinegar	5 mL
1 tbsp	ground raw flax seeds	15 mL
3 tbsp	hot water	45 mL
4 cups	Creamy Mashed Potatoes (page 178), cooled	1 L
4 cups	shredded Yukon Gold potatoes (see Tips, left)	1 L
½ to ⅔ cup	brown rice flour (see Tips, left)	125 to 150 mL
2 tsp	gluten-free baking powder	10 mL
½ tsp	fine sea salt	2 mL
¼ cup	(approx.) grapeseed oil, divided	60 mL

1. In a small bowl, whisk together almond milk and vinegar until well combined. Cover and set aside for 10 minutes, until milk curdles slightly.

2. In another bowl, whisk together ground flax seeds and hot water. Cover and set aside for 8 to 10 minutes so flax can absorb the liquid and swell. Add to curdled almond milk and whisk well.

3. In a large bowl, combine mashed potatoes, shredded potatoes, ½ cup (125 mL) rice flour, baking powder, salt and almond milk mixture. Mix until well combined. Divide into 8 equal portions. Using your hands, shape each portion into a patty 4 to 5 inches (10 to 12.5 cm) in diameter and 2 inches (5 cm) thick.

4. In a large skillet over high heat, heat 2 tbsp (30 mL) oil. Working in batches, cook patties until golden brown on one side, about 4 minutes. Turn over and cook until golden brown on the other side. Repeat, adding more oil as necessary, until all patties are browned. Transfer to prepared baking sheet and bake in preheated oven for 12 to 15 minutes, or until cooked through and crisp on the outside. Serve immediately.

Holiday Lentil Loaf with Quinoa

This dish is perfect for holiday gatherings or family functions. I love to serve it with Creamy Mashed Potatoes (page 178) and Holiday Gravy (page 558).

(page 178) and Holiday Gravy (page 558)

MAKES 6 SERVINGS

Tips

Substitute an equal quantity of millet for the quinoa in this recipe.

Wheat-free tamari is a gluten-free seasoning made from fermented soybeans. It can be found in most well-stocked supermarkets and natural food stores.

To chop fresh thyme: Pinch the stem at the bottom with two fingers. Pulling upward with the finger and thumb of your other hand, strip the leaves. Reserve stems for soups or broths (discard after cooking). Use a sharp knife to chop the leaves, being careful not to chop too much or too hard, as this will bruise the leaves and cause the thyme to discolor.

- Preheat oven to 400°F (200°C)
- Food processor
- 9- by 5-inch (23 by 12.5 cm) loaf pan, greased

7 cups	water, divided	1.75 L
1 cup	quinoa, rinsed and drained (see Tips, left)	250 mL
½ tsp	fine sea salt, divided	2 mL
2 cups	dried green lentils, rinsed and drained	500 mL
3 tbsp	grapeseed oil	45 mL
1 cup	diced peeled apple	250 mL
½ cup	finely chopped onion	125 mL
½ cup	finely chopped carrot	125 mL
½ cup	finely chopped celery	125 mL
3 to 5	cloves garlic, minced	3 to 5
2 tbsp	chopped fresh thyme leaves (see Tips, left)	30 mL
¼ cup	wheat-free tamari (see Tips, left)	60 mL
¼ cup	nutritional yeast (see Tip, page 383)	60 mL
2 tbsp	chopped fresh sage	30 mL
1 tbsp	chopped fresh rosemary	15 mL
½ cup	brown rice flour	125 mL
⅓ cup	ground raw golden flax seeds	75 mL
½ cup	ketchup	125 mL

1. In a saucepan, combine 3 cups (750 mL) water, quinoa and ¼ tsp (1 mL) salt; bring to a boil. Reduce heat and simmer, stirring frequently, until quinoa is tender and almost all of the cooking liquid has been absorbed, about 15 minutes. Remove from heat and set side to cool.

2. Meanwhile, in another saucepan, combine remaining 4 cups (1 L) water and lentils. Bring to a boil, reduce heat and simmer until lentils are tender, about 20 minutes. Drain, discarding liquid. Set aside to cool.

Nutritional yeast is an inactive yeast that has been grown on beet molasses and then pasteurized. It provides a rich, cheesy flavor in sauces, stews, soups and dips. Look for it in well-stocked supermarkets and natural food stores.

3. In a skillet over medium heat, heat oil. Add apple, onion, carrot, celery and a pinch of salt; stir to combine. Cook, stirring, until onion and celery are translucent, 4 to 5 minutes. Stir in garlic and thyme and cook, stirring, for 2 minutes, until fragrant. Remove from heat, add tamari and nutritional yeast, and stir to combine.

4. In food processor fitted with the metal blade, combine cooked quinoa, half of the cooked lentils, half of the vegetable mixture and the sage and rosemary. Process until smooth, stopping the motor to scrape down sides of work bowl as necessary. Transfer to a bowl. Add remaining cooked lentils, remaining vegetable mixture, rice flour, ground flax seeds and remaining salt; stir well.

5. Spread mixture evenly in prepared loaf pan. Brush with ketchup. Bake in preheated oven for about 1 hour or until a light crust has formed on top and loaf is heated through. Remove from oven and serve immediately, or let cool, transfer to an airtight container and refrigerate for up to 1 week.

Spaghetti Squash Stuffed with Tofu and Spinach

Spaghetti squash serves as a delicious bake-and-eat bowl when filled with a creamy blend of tofu "ricotta" and spinach. You can make this ahead of time and refrigerate for a quick weeknight dinner.

MAKES 4 SERVINGS

Tips

Spaghetti squash is a great low-carbohydrate, gluten-free alternative to traditional pasta. When roasted, the flesh can be separated into spaghetti-like strands simply by using the tines of a fork.

For a soy-free version, substitute 4 cups (1 L) Creamy Cashew Ricotta (page 532) for the tofu in Step 3.

- Preheat oven to 350°F (180°C)
- Baking sheet, lined with parchment paper
- Food processor

1	medium to large spaghetti squash (see Tips, left)	1
2 tbsp	extra virgin olive oil	30 mL
1 tsp	fine sea salt, divided	5 mL
2 tbsp	grapeseed oil	30 mL
1 cup	chopped onion	250 mL
8 to 10	cloves garlic, minced	8 to 10
8 cups	chopped spinach leaves	2 L
1	block (10 oz/500 g) firm tofu, cut into ½-inch (1 cm) cubes (see Tips, left)	1
¼ cup	nutritional yeast	60 mL
1 tsp	dried oregano leaves	5 mL
½ tsp	dried basil leaves	2 mL

1. Using a sharp knife, cut spaghetti squash in half lengthwise. Scoop out seeds and discard. Rub with olive oil and season with ½ tsp (2 mL) salt. Wrap each squash half tightly in aluminum foil and place on prepared baking sheet, cut side up.

2. Bake in preheated oven for 35 to 40 minutes or until tender. Remove from oven and set aside, still wrapped in foil.

3. Meanwhile, in a large skillet over medium heat, heat grapeseed oil. Add onion and ¼ tsp (1 mL) salt and cook, stirring frequently, for 5 to 6 minutes, until onion is translucent. Stir in garlic and cook for 2 to 3 minutes, until fragrant. Add spinach and cook, stirring occasionally, until wilted, 5 to 6 minutes. Remove from heat and set aside.

4. In food processor fitted with the metal blade, process tofu until broken down into small pieces. Transfer to a large bowl. Stir in nutritional yeast, oregano, basil and remaining ¼ tsp (1 mL) salt. Add sautéed spinach and stir until well combined.

5. Remove squash from foil and return to baking sheet. Using a spoon, scoop out a bit of flesh from the center of each piece to make a bigger well.

6. Divide tofu mixture equally and spoon into squash halves. Bake in preheated oven for 30 minutes or until lightly golden brown on top and heated through.

7. Cut each squash piece in half. Serve immediately or transfer to an airtight container and refrigerate for up to 5 days. To reheat, place squash on a baking sheet and warm in a 350°F (180°C) oven for about 12 minutes, until heated through.

Cauliflower Steak with Celery Root Purée and Crispy Tofu

Make this vegan version of classic meat and potatoes. The celery root sauce brings out the natural flavors of the cauliflower.

MAKES 4 SERVINGS

Tips

You will need about 2½ lbs (1.25 kg) of celery root for this recipe. About a quarter of the weight of this vegetable is lost when it is trimmed and peeled.

The quantity of garlic depends on the size of the cloves. If large, use the smaller number. If small, more may be required.

Nutritional yeast is an inactive yeast that has been grown on beet molasses and then pasteurized. It provides a rich, cheesy flavor in sauces, stews, soups and dips. Look for it in well-stocked supermarkets and natural food stores.

- Preheat oven to 450°F (230°C)
- Baking sheet, lined with parchment paper
- Blender

CELERY ROOT PURÉE

12 cups	water	3 L
8 cups	cubed (1 inch/2.5 cm) peeled celery root (about 3; see Tips, left)	2 L
1 tbsp	caraway seeds	15 mL
½ tsp	fine sea salt	2 mL
2 to 3	cloves garlic, peeled	2 to 3

CAULIFLOWER STEAK

1	large head cauliflower	1
¼ cup	grapeseed oil, divided	60 mL
¼ cup	nutritional yeast (see Tips, left)	60 mL
1 tsp	chili powder	5 mL
1 tsp	fine sea salt	5 mL

TOFU

¼ cup	grapeseed oil	60 mL
1	block (1 lb/500 g) firm tofu, cut into ½-inch (1 cm) pieces	1
2 tbsp	nutritional yeast	30 mL
1 tsp	chopped fresh thyme leaves (see Tip, page 387)	5 mL
1½ tsp	fine sea salt	7 mL

ASSEMBLY

½ tsp	salt	2 mL
2 tbsp	nutritional yeast	30 mL
6 tbsp	extra virgin olive oil	90 mL

1. *Celery Root Purée:* In a large pot, combine water, celery root, caraway seeds, salt and garlic. Bring to a boil, reduce heat and simmer until celery root is tender, about 15 minutes.

2. Drain, reserving ½ cup (125 mL) of the cooking liquid. Return celery root, caraway seeds and garlic to warm pot. Cover and set aside.

Tips

To chop fresh thyme: Pinch the stem at the bottom with two fingers. Pulling upward with the finger and thumb of your other hand, strip the leaves. Reserve stems for soups or broths (discard after cooking). Use a sharp knife to chop the leaves, being careful not to chop too much or too hard, as this will bruise the leaves and cause the thyme to discolor.

When blending hot liquids in a blender, make sure the blender jar is no more than half full. Also, place a folded towel over the lid and place your hand firmly on top. Otherwise, the pressure of the steam may cause the lid to blow off, spattering your soup all over the kitchen.

3. *Cauliflower Steak:* Using a sharp knife, slice cauliflower in half lengthwise through the stem, then cut each half in half again so you end up with 4 large pieces. Place on prepared baking sheet.

4. Drizzle cauliflower with 2 tbsp (30 mL) grapeseed oil, then sprinkle with half each of the nutritional yeast, chili powder and salt. Flip cauliflower over and repeat with remaining ingredients. Bake in preheated oven until golden brown and tender, about 20 minutes.

5. *Tofu:* Meanwhile, in a large skillet over medium-high heat, heat grapeseed oil. Cook tofu, stirring frequently, until brown and crisp, about 10 minutes. Using a slotted spoon, transfer to a large bowl. Add nutritional yeast, thyme and salt; toss to coat well.

6. *Assembly:* Transfer cooked celery root to blender. Add $\frac{1}{4}$ cup (60 mL) of the reserved cooking water, including some caraway seeds and the garlic cloves. Add half of the salt, nutritional yeast and olive oil. Blend at high speed until smooth.

7. Transfer to a clean pot and repeat with remaining ingredients. Bring to a simmer over medium heat.

8. Divide celery root purée evenly among serving plates. Top with roasted cauliflower and crispy tofu. Serve immediately.

Cheesy Broccoli, Red Pepper, Mushroom and Spinach Quiche

Quiche is the perfect dish for a buffet or when you are entertaining guests for lunch or brunch. It is made complete with the simplest green salad. Leftovers can be refrigerated and make a great meal-on-the-go.

	MAKES 6 TO 8 SERVINGS

Tips

The rolled-out dough should be about 2 inches (5 cm) bigger in diameter than the pie plate you are using. Check by laying the prepared pie plate face down on top.

To save time, you can make this using your favorite store-bought gluten-free vegan piecrust or savory short crust.

Wheat-free tamari is a gluten-free seasoning made from fermented soybeans. It can be found in most well-stocked supermarkets and natural food stores.

For convenience, substitute an equal quantity of store-bought unsweetened almond milk for the homemade version called for.

- Preheat oven to 350°F (180°C)
- 9-inch (23 cm) pie plate, greased
- Food processor

CRUST

½	recipe Vegan Piecrust (page 562; see Tips, left)	½

FILLING

3 tbsp	grapeseed oil	45 mL
4 cups	sliced mushrooms	1 L
2 cups	chopped red bell peppers	500 mL
½ cup	chopped onion	125 mL
¼ tsp	fine sea salt	1 mL
2 cups	chopped spinach leaves	500 mL
2 cups	broccoli florets	500 mL
2 tbsp	wheat-free tamari (see Tips, left)	30 mL
1 tbsp	chopped fresh thyme leaves	15 mL
3 to 4	cloves garlic, minced (see Tips, page 389)	3 to 4
½ cup	Almond Milk (page 61), divided	125 mL
¼ cup	chickpea flour	60 mL
2	packages (each 12 oz/375 g) firm silken tofu	2
½ cup	nutritional yeast	125 mL
1 tbsp	freshly squeezed lemon juice	15 mL
1 tsp	black salt (kala namak; see Tips, page 389) or fine sea salt	5 mL
½ tsp	ground turmeric	2 mL

1. *Crust:* Dust a clean work surface lightly with rice flour and, using a rolling pin, roll out dough to about ¼ inch (0.5 cm) thick. Roll pastry loosely around rolling pin, then carefully unroll over prepared pie plate.

Tips

To mince garlic: Place a whole clove on a cutting board. Using the butt end of a chef's knife, press firmly but gently on the clove to loosen the skin. Using your index finger and thumb, gently squeeze clove out of skin. Chop coarsely, then sprinkle with a bit of sea salt. Using the butt end of the knife, rub garlic into board (the salt will act as an abrasive and help to mince the garlic). Chop until fine.

Black salt, or kala namak, comes from the Himalayas and northwest Pakistan. The salt contains sulfuric compounds that lend dishes an eggy flavor, which is why it is used in vegan dishes that are similar to traditional egg dishes.

2. Gently press piecrust into pie plate, evenly covering bottom and sides. Trim overhanging dough. Using the tines of a fork, poke several holes in dough to allow steam to escape when baking. Bake in preheated oven for about 6 minutes or until edges are dry and starting to turn golden. Remove from oven and set aside to cool.

3. *Filling:* In a large skillet over high heat, heat oil. Add mushrooms, red peppers, onion and salt. Cook, stirring frequently, until vegetables are lightly golden brown, 5 to 6 minutes. Add spinach and broccoli and cook, stirring occasionally, until most of the liquid has evaporated and spinach is wilted, 8 to 10 minutes.

4. Reduce heat to low and stir in tamari, thyme and garlic. Cook for 2 minutes, until garlic and thyme are fragrant. Remove from heat.

5. In a small bowl, whisk together $\frac{1}{4}$ cup (60 mL) almond milk and chickpea flour, until no lumps remain.

6. In food processor fitted with the metal blade, combine remaining $\frac{1}{4}$ cup (60 mL) almond milk, tofu, nutritional yeast, lemon juice, black salt and turmeric; process until smooth. Add $\frac{1}{4}$ cup (60 mL) of the vegetable mixture and process until smooth. Add chickpea flour mixture and pulse 8 to 10 times to combine.

7. Transfer to a large bowl and stir in remaining vegetable mixture. Spread evenly in prebaked piecrust.

8. Bake in preheated oven for 35 to 40 minutes, or until quiche is firmly set in the middle (it shouldn't jiggle too much when gently shaken). Remove from oven and set aside for 20 minutes to cool before serving. The quiche will keep for up to 2 days in an airtight container in the refrigerator.

Grilled Portobellos with Sweet Potato Gratin and Sautéed Green Beans

This multilayered dish is a crowd-pleaser. Smoky grilled portobellos, baked sweet potatoes and sautéed green beans, all topped with a creamy miso almond sauce, make a perfect combination to serve at any meal.

MAKES 6 SERVINGS

Tips

Nutritional yeast is an inactive yeast that has been grown on beet molasses and then pasteurized. It provides a rich, cheesy flavor in sauces, stews, soups and dips. Look for it in well-stocked supermarkets and natural food stores.

To remove the skin from a clove of garlic, use the butt end of a chef's knife to press firmly but gently on the clove to loosen the skin. Using your index finger and thumb, gently squeeze the clove out of its skin.

If portobello mushrooms are quite large, the stems can be tough and fibrous Remove the bottom ½ inch (1 cm) with a knife if this is the case. If the mushroom is small, there is no need to remove the stem.

- Preheat oven to 350°F (180°C)
- 8-inch (20 cm) square glass baking dish, lightly greased
- Blender

SWEET POTATO GRATIN

3 cups	Almond Milk (page 61)	750 mL
2 tbsp	nutritional yeast (see Tips, left)	30 mL
1 tbsp	chopped fresh thyme leaves	15 mL
1 tsp	fine sea salt	5 mL
8 cups	sliced (¼ inch/0.5 cm thick) sweet potatoes (about 3 large)	2 L

PORTOBELLOS

6	whole portobello mushrooms (see Tips, left)	6
3 tbsp	extra virgin olive oil	45 mL
1 tbsp	wheat-free tamari	15 mL
1 tbsp	chopped fresh thyme leaves	15 mL
¼ tsp	fine sea salt	1 mL

MISO ALMOND SAUCE

¾ cup	water	175 mL
½ cup	almond butter	125 mL
3 tbsp	raw (unpasteurized) apple cider vinegar	45 mL
3 tbsp	raw agave nectar	45 mL
2 tbsp	brown rice miso	30 mL
1 tbsp	wheat-free tamari	15 mL
1	clove garlic, peeled (see Tips, left)	1

GREEN BEANS

2 tbsp	grapeseed oil	30 mL
¼ cup	finely chopped onion	60 mL
2 to 3	cloves garlic, minced	2 to 3
4 cups	whole green beans	1 L

Tips

The quantity of garlic depends on the size of the cloves. If large, use the smaller number. If small, more may be required.

You can also broil the mushrooms in the oven. Preheat broiler to high. Arrange marinated mushrooms in a single layer on a baking sheet lined with aluminum foil. Broil for 3 to 4 minutes per side, until golden brown and tender.

1. *Sweet Potato Gratin:* In a large bowl, whisk together almond milk, nutritional yeast, thyme and salt. Add sweet potatoes and toss to coat well. Transfer to prepared baking dish and bake in preheated oven for 45 minutes, or until top is lightly golden brown and potatoes are tender. Remove from oven and set aside to firm up.

2. *Portobellos:* In a large bowl, toss mushrooms with olive oil, tamari, thyme and salt, until well combined. Cover and set aside for 10 minutes to marinate.

3. Preheat grill to High. Grill marinated mushrooms for 4 to 5 minutes per side, until golden brown and tender (see Tips, left). Remove from heat.

4. *Miso Almond Sauce:* Meanwhile, in blender, combine water, almond butter, vinegar, agave nectar, miso, tamari and garlic. Blend at high speed until smooth and creamy. Set aside.

5. *Green Beans:* In a large skillet over medium heat, heat grapeseed oil. Add onion and garlic and cook until translucent, about 3 minutes. Add beans and cook, stirring occasionally, until tender, about 5 minutes.

6. Divide sweet potato gratin among serving plates and top with cooked green beans. Arrange a grilled mushroom on top of each portion. Drizzle Miso Almond Sauce over everything and serve immediately.

Korean-Style Tofu Tacos

Tangy cabbage and cilantro slaw and quick-pickled cucumber enhance these delicious hand-held favorites. Serve them at your next picnic, potluck or family gathering. Everyone can have fun building their own tacos.

MAKES 8 TO 12 TACOS

Tips

The stems on the leaves closest to the bottom of fresh cilantro are generally tough and need to be removed. The stems on leaves closer to the top of the sprig are soft and full of flavor and can be left on.

Be sure to use raw (not processed) agave nectar. It is a 100% natural (non-GMO) sweetener that contains naturally occurring fructose and is low on the glycemic scale, which means that it releases glucose slowly, providing sustained energy.

- **Preheat oven to 400°F (200°C)**
- **Baking sheet, lined with parchment paper**

TOFU

3 tbsp	brown rice miso	45 mL
3 tbsp	pure maple syrup	45 mL
1 tbsp	wheat-free tamari	15 mL
1 tsp	toasted sesame oil	5 mL
1 lb	firm tofu, cut into thin strips	500 g

SLAW

4 cups	thinly sliced napa cabbage	1 L
1 cup	chopped fresh cilantro leaves (see Tips, left)	250 mL
¼ cup	thinly sliced green onions (green part only)	60 mL
3 tbsp	extra virgin olive oil	45 mL
2 tbsp	rice wine vinegar	30 mL
1 tbsp	freshly squeezed lime juice	15 mL
1 tsp	organic coconut sugar	5 mL
½ tsp	fine sea salt	2 mL

QUICK PICKLED CUCUMBER

4 cups	thinly sliced cucumber	1 L
3 tbsp	rice wine vinegar	45 mL
2 tbsp	raw agave nectar (see Tips, left)	30 mL
¼ tsp	fine sea salt	1 mL

ASSEMBLY

8 to 12	6-inch (15 cm) gluten-free organic corn tortillas (see Tip, page 393)	8 to 12
	Lime wedges	
	Hot sauce	

Make sure to purchase organic corn tortillas. Most corn is from genetically engineered crops, so it is particularly important to buy organic.

1. *Tofu:* In a bowl, whisk together miso, maple syrup, tamari and sesame oil. Add tofu strips and toss to coat evenly. Transfer to prepared baking sheet and bake in preheated oven for 12 to 15 minutes or until tofu is lightly browned.

2. *Slaw:* Meanwhile, in a large bowl, toss together cabbage, cilantro, green onion, olive oil, vinegar, lime juice, coconut sugar and salt. Set aside for 10 minutes to marinate.

3. *Quick Pickled Cucumber:* In another large bowl, toss together cucumber, vinegar, agave nectar and salt.

4. *Assembly:* Spoon cooked tofu onto tortillas and top with slaw and cucumber. Starting from the bottom edge, roll up to form a cylinder. Serve with lime wedges and hot sauce.

Tofu in Chilled Green Tea Broth with Crispy Bok Choy

This dish balances unique flavors and textures — silky, pudding-like tofu, aromatic broth and crisp greens. I enjoy this simple, light, refreshing meal with a Teatime Smoothie (page 55).

MAKES 4 SERVINGS

Tips

Mirin is a sweet Japanese cooking wine made from glutinous rice. Also known as rice wine, it has a low alcohol content that is further reduced by cooking. You can find it in most well-stocked supermarkets and Asian grocers.

Wheat-free tamari is a gluten-free seasoning made from fermented soybeans. It can be found in most well-stocked supermarkets and natural food stores.

- **Preheat oven to 425°F (220°C)**
- **Baking sheet, lined with parchment paper**

GREEN TEA BROTH

8 cups	water	2 L
¼ cup	green tea leaves	60 mL
2 tbsp	mirin (see Tips, left)	30 mL
2 tbsp	wheat-free tamari (see Tips, left)	30 mL
½ cup	thinly sliced green onions (green and white parts)	125 mL

BOK CHOY

2 tbsp	grapeseed oil	30 mL
2 tbsp	toasted sesame oil	30 mL
6	heads baby bok choy, leaves separated	6
1 tsp	hot pepper flakes	5 mL
Pinch	fine sea salt	Pinch

ASSEMBLY

1	package (12 oz/375 g) firm silken tofu, drained and cut into ½-inch (1 cm) cubes (see Tip, page 395)	1
	Toasted sesame oil, for drizzling	

1. *Green Tea Broth:* In a large pot, bring water to a boil. Remove from heat and stir in tea leaves, mirin and tamari. Cover and set aside for 12 to 15 minutes to allow tea to steep and release its flavor.

2. Using a fine-mesh strainer, strain tea into a clean pot. Stir in green onions. Refrigerate for 30 minutes or until cold.

3. *Bok Choy*: In a large bowl, combine grapeseed oil, sesame oil, bok choy leaves and hot pepper flakes; toss together until well coated. Spread in a single layer on prepared baking sheet (do not overlap the leaves, or they will steam instead of crisping up).

4. Bake in preheated oven for 6 to 8 minutes. Remove from oven and turn leaves over. Bake for 4 to 5 minutes more, or until dried and crisp. Remove from oven and set aside to cool completely, about 15 minutes.

5. *Assembly*: Divide tofu cubes among serving bowls. Ladle chilled broth overtop. Drizzle with toasted sesame oil and garnish with crispy bok choy. Serve immediately.

Tofu en Papillote

Your guests will be salivating when these steaming packets of heartwarming flavor arrive at the table. Serve with Basic Rice (page 212) or Basic Quinoa (page 235).

MAKES 6 SERVINGS

Tips

To clean sliced leeks, place in a bowl of water and soak for 5 minutes. The dirt will fall to the bottom of the bowl. Using a slotted spoon, remove leeks and discard water.

Wheat-free tamari is a gluten-free seasoning made from fermented soybeans. It can be found in most well-stocked supermarkets and natural food stores.

Nutritional yeast is an inactive yeast that has been grown on beet molasses and then pasteurized. It provides a rich, cheesy flavor in sauces, stews, soups and dips. Look for it in well-stocked supermarkets and natural food stores.

- Preheat oven to 400°F (200°C)
- Parchment paper
- Baking sheet, lined with parchment paper

1 cup	thinly sliced carrots	250 mL
1 cup	thinly sliced button mushrooms	250 mL
1 cup	thinly sliced leeks (white part only; see Tips, left)	250 mL
4 tsp	minced garlic	20 mL
2 lbs	medium-firm tofu, cut into 6 equal pieces	1 kg
4 tsp	nutritional yeast (see Tips, left)	20 mL
1 tsp	fine sea salt	5 mL
1 cup	Vegetable Stock (page 559)	250 mL
¼ cup	wheat-free tamari (see Tips, left)	60 mL

1. Fold a 15- by 24-inch (36 by 60 cm) piece of parchment paper in half to form a 15- by 12-inch (36 by 30 cm) rectangle. Using kitchen shears, cut out a half-heart the length and width of the paper (when you open it, it will form a whole heart). Discard trimmings. Repeat five more times.

2. Lay parchment hearts flat on a clean work surface. On one side of each, leaving a 1-inch (2.5 cm) border around the edges, mound one-sixth each of the carrots, mushrooms, leeks and garlic. Top with 1 piece of tofu and sprinkle with nutritional yeast and salt, dividing equally.

3. Working with one packet at a time, fold other half of parchment over filling and line up edges. Starting at the top of the heart and working your way around the edge, make overlapping folds about ½ inch (1 cm) deep, pressing firmly and creasing the edges so the folds hold. Before you seal it completely — when there is just one more fold to make — carefully lift the packet and pour in vegetable stock and tamari, dividing equally. Twist the end of the packet to seal completely. Repeat with remaining packets.

4. Transfer packets to prepared baking sheet and bake in preheated oven for 45 minutes. Serve immediately, letting your guests open their packet at the table.

Tofu Osso Buco with Braised Vegetables

Braised tofu replaces veal in this warm and comforting traditional Italian dish. Serve it with a side of Mushroom Wild Rice Pilaf (page 227).

MAKES 6 SERVINGS

Tips

Substitute an equal amount of water for the vegetable stock. Add 2 tbsp (30 mL) wheat-free tamari in Step 2.

Substitute 4 cups (1 L) chopped fresh tomatoes for the canned tomatoes.

The quantity of garlic depends on the size of the cloves. If large, use the smaller number. If small, more may be required.

- **Preheat oven to 350°F (180°C)**
- **4-quart Dutch oven with lid**

3 tbsp	grapeseed oil	45 mL
2 lbs	medium-firm tofu, cut into 6 equal pieces	1 kg
1 tsp	fine sea salt, divided	5 mL
1 cup	chopped onion	250 mL
1 cup	chopped celery	250 mL
1 cup	chopped carrot	250 mL
1	bay leaf	1
1 to 2	whole cloves garlic, peeled	1 to 2
1 cup	dry white wine	250 mL
2 cups	Vegetable Stock (see Tips, left)	500 mL
1	can (28 oz/796 mL) diced tomatoes, with juice (see Tips, left)	1
1 tbsp	finely grated lemon zest	15 mL
½ cup	chopped flat-leaf parsley leaves	125 mL
2 to 3	cloves garlic, minced	2 to 3

1. In Dutch oven over medium-high heat, heat oil. Season tofu with ½ tsp (2 mL) salt and cook in batches, about 2 minutes per side, until golden. Transfer to a plate lined with paper towels and set aside.

2. Add onion, celery, carrot, bay leaf, whole garlic and remaining salt to pot. Cook, stirring frequently, until vegetables are softened, 5 to 6 minutes. Add wine and simmer, stirring occasionally with a wooden spoon and scraping up brown bits on bottom of pan, until liquid has evaporated, 4 to 6 minutes. Add stock and tomatoes and stir well. Add reserved tofu and bring to a simmer.

3. Cover and bake in preheated oven for 45 minutes. Remove from oven, uncover and set aside for 10 minutes to cool slightly.

4. In a small bowl, whisk together lemon zest, parsley and minced garlic. Stir into tofu mixture. Serve immediately or transfer to an airtight container and refrigerate for up to 5 days.

Crispy Tofu and Zucchini Fritters with Corn and Red Pepper Relish

There is something festive and fun about fritters, which makes them the perfect thing to serve to guests. This sinfully delicious dish is easily completed by some simple steamed greens or a fresh, crunchy salad.

MAKES 6 SERVINGS

Tips

To remove the kernels from an ear of corn: Cut pieces from the top and bottom of the cob to create flat surfaces. Stand the cob up on end. Using a chef's knife, cut downward to gently strip away the kernels, making sure not to remove too much of the starchy white body of the cob. If fresh corn is not available, use frozen organic corn.

Be sure to use raw (not processed) agave nectar. It is a 100% natural (non-GMO) sweetener that contains naturally occurring fructose and is low on the glycemic scale, which means that it releases glucose slowly, providing sustained energy.

Use the side of a box grater or a food processor fitted with the metal shredding blade to shred the tofu and zucchini.

RELISH

2 cups	finely chopped red bell peppers	500 mL
2 cups	fresh organic corn kernels (see Tips, left)	500 mL
1 cup	finely chopped flat-leaf (Italian) parsley leaves	250 mL
¼ cup	finely chopped red onion	60 mL
¼ cup	red wine vinegar	60 mL
3 tbsp	raw agave nectar (see Tips, left)	45 mL
½ tsp	fine sea salt	2 mL

FRITTERS

3 tbsp	ground raw flax seeds	45 mL
½ cup + 2 tsp	hot water	135 mL
4 oz	firm tofu (half 8 oz/250 g block), shredded (see Tips, left)	125 g
2 cups	shredded zucchini	500 mL
1 tsp	fine sea salt	5 mL
1 tsp	garlic powder	5 mL
1 tsp	chili powder	5 mL
1 tsp	finely grated lemon zest	5 mL
1¼ cups	brown rice flour, divided (see Tip, page 399)	300 mL
1 cup	grapeseed oil	250 mL
¾ cup	cold water	175 mL

1. *Relish:* In a large bowl, toss together red peppers, corn, parsley, onion, vinegar, agave nectar and salt. Cover and set aside.
2. *Fritters:* In a small bowl, whisk together ground flax seeds and hot water. Cover and set aside for about 10 minutes so flax can absorb the liquid and swell.
3. In a large bowl, combine shredded tofu, zucchini, salt, garlic powder, chili powder, lemon zest, ¼ cup (60 mL) rice flour and soaked flax seeds. Stir to mix well.

I have used finely ground brown rice flour in these fritters because it is a whole food. The fritters may not be quite as crispy as they would be if an equal quantity of white rice flour were used. The decision is yours.

4. In a skillet over medium-high heat, heat oil.

5. Meanwhile, in a small bowl, whisk together remaining 1 cup (250 mL) rice flour and cold water.

6. Divide tofu and zucchini mixture into 6 equal portions. Using your hands, shape into patties.

7. Roll each portion in flour mixture, covering completely, and then carefully place in hot oil. Cook until golden brown and crisp, 5 to 6 minutes. Using a slotted spoon, transfer to a plate lined with paper towels. Sprinkle with sea salt.

8. Spoon relish onto serving plates, dividing equally. Top each serving with a fritter and serve immediately.

Variation

Tofu and Sweet Potato Fritters: Substitute an equal amount of shredded sweet potato for the zucchini.

Porcini-Crusted Tofu with Crispy Shallots and Red Wine Butter

Aromatic porcini mushrooms, ground to a powder, are used as a coating to give these tofu steaks their deep, rich flavor. Serve this substantial dish with a simple salad on the side. If you are so inclined, a glass of your favorite red wine will complement this luscious sauce, which is a vegan riff on the classic French *beurre rouge*, a reduction of red wine, vinegar and shallots, finished with butter.

MAKES 4 SERVINGS

Tips

The quantity of garlic depends on the size of the cloves. If large, use the smaller number. If small, more may be required.

To mince garlic: Place a whole clove on a cutting board. Using the butt end of a chef's knife, press firmly but gently on the clove to loosen the skin. Using your index finger and thumb, gently squeeze clove out of skin. Chop coarsely, then sprinkle with a bit of sea salt. Using the butt end of the knife, rub garlic into board (the salt will act as an abrasive and help to mince the garlic). Chop until fine.

Dried porcini mushrooms are a delicacy. They are available at finer retailers that sell imported products. They can be pricey, so you may want to save this dish for special occasions.

- Blender
- Baking sheet, lined with parchment paper
- Bowl, lined with paper towels

TOFU

1	block (16 oz/500 g) firm tofu	1
4¼ cups	water, divided	1.1 L
½ cup	wheat-free tamari	125 mL
1 to 2	cloves garlic, peeled	1 to 2
1 to 2	sprigs fresh thyme	1 to 2
¼ cup	grapeseed oil	60 mL
½ cup	Dijon mustard	125 mL
2 cups	dried porcini mushrooms	500 mL

CRISPY SHALLOTS

¼ cup	grapeseed oil	60 mL
2 cups	thinly sliced shallots	500 mL

RED WINE BUTTER

6 to 8	cloves garlic, minced	6 to 8
2 cups	dry red wine	500 mL
2 tbsp	red wine vinegar	30 mL
½ cup	cold Whipped Non-dairy Butter (page 554), cut into 4 pieces	125 mL
¼ tsp	fine sea salt	1 mL
2 tsp	chopped fresh thyme leaves (see Tip, page 401)	10 mL

1. *Tofu:* In a saucepan, combine tofu, 4 cups (1 L) water, tamari, garlic cloves and thyme. Bring to a boil, reduce heat and simmer for 15 minutes. Using a slotted spoon, transfer tofu to a plate (discard garlic, thyme and liquid). Set aside to cool completely, about 20 minutes.

2. Cut tofu in half crosswise. Then cut each piece in half lengthwise, so you are left with 4 equal pieces.

Tip

To chop fresh thyme: Pinch the stem at the bottom with two fingers. Pulling upward with the finger and thumb of your other hand, strip the leaves. Reserve stems for soups or broths (discard after cooking). Use a sharp knife to chop the leaves, being careful not to chop too much or too hard, as this will bruise the leaves and cause the thyme to discolor.

3. In a large skillet over high heat, heat oil. Add tofu pieces and cook for about 3 minutes per side, until golden. Transfer to a plate lined with paper towels. Set aside to cool completely.

4. In a shallow bowl, whisk together mustard and remaining 1/4 cup (60 mL) water. Set aside.

5. Preheat oven to 500°F (260°C).

6. In blender, process dried mushrooms at high speed until flour-like in consistency. Transfer to another shallow bowl.

7. Roll tofu in mustard mixture and then in ground mushrooms, until completely coated. Transfer to prepared baking sheet and bake in preheated oven for 20 minutes or until golden brown on top. Keep warm in oven.

8. *Crispy Shallots:* In a large skillet over high heat, heat oil. Add sliced shallots and cook, stirring frequently, until golden brown and crisp, 10 to 12 minutes. Using a slotted spoon, transfer to bowl lined with paper towels to absorb excess oil.

9. *Red Wine Butter:* Discard excess oil in skillet and return to high heat. Add minced garlic and cook, stirring constantly, for 1 to 2 minutes, until browned. Add wine and vinegar and cook, stirring frequently, until reduced to about 1/4 cup (60 mL), about 10 minutes. Remove from heat. Add butter and stir, slowly but constantly, until melted. Season with salt and stir in chopped thyme.

10. *Assembly:* Divide tofu among serving plates. Spoon wine butter evenly over tofu. Garnish with crispy shallots and serve immediately.

Poached Tofu with Vegetables in Cheesy Hemp Sauce

This is a perfect dish if you are entertaining people for lunch. As a nice light dessert afterward, serve Poached Pears Filled with Chocolate Ganache (page 484).

(page 484).

MAKES 4 SERVINGS

Tips

Wheat-free tamari is a gluten-free seasoning made from fermented soybeans. It can be found in most well-stocked supermarkets and natural food stores.

Hempseed oil is available in most well-stocked supermarkets and natural food stores. Once hemp oil has been opened, it must be refrigerated.

TOFU

8 cups	water	2 L
¾ cup	wheat-free tamari (see Tips, left)	175 mL
2 to 3	cloves garlic, peeled	2 to 3
2 to 3	sprigs fresh thyme	2 to 3
1	block (1 lb/500 g) firm tofu, cut into 1-inch (2.5 cm) cubes	1

VEGETABLES

8 cups	water	2 L
1 tsp	fine sea salt	5 mL
½ cup	chopped (1 inch/2.5 cm) peeled sweet potato	125 mL
½ cup	chopped (1 inch/2.5 cm) peeled carrot	125 mL
4 cups	thinly sliced kale, stems removed	1 L
2 cups	broccoli florets	500 mL
1 cup	chopped red bell pepper	250 mL

CHEESY HEMP SAUCE

¼ cup	cold-pressed hempseed oil (see Tips, left)	60 mL
½ cup	nutritional yeast (see Tip, page 403)	125 mL
3 tbsp	raw shelled hemp seeds	45 mL
½ tsp	fine sea salt	2 mL

ASSEMBLY

	Raw shelled hemp seeds, for garnish	
Pinch	cayenne pepper	Pinch

1. *Tofu:* In a large pot, combine water, tamari, garlic, thyme and tofu. Bring to a boil, reduce heat and simmer for 15 minutes. Remove from heat, cover and set aside.

Tip

Nutritional yeast is an inactive yeast that has been grown on beet molasses and then pasteurized. It provides a rich, cheesy flavor in sauces, stews, soups and dips. Look for it in well-stocked supermarkets and natural food stores.

2. *Vegetables:* In a large covered pot over high heat, combine water, salt, sweet potato and carrot. Bring to a boil, reduce heat to medium-low and cook until sweet potato is just tender, about 10 minutes. Add kale, broccoli and red pepper; stir to combine.

3. Cook, covered, for 3 to 4 minutes or until vegetables are tender. Drain, discarding liquid. Return vegetables to pot, cover and set aside (off heat) to keep warm.

4. *Cheesy Hemp Sauce:* In a large bowl, combine hemp oil, nutritional yeast, hemp seeds and salt. Add cooked vegetables and toss until well coated.

5. *Assembly:* Divide cooked tofu among warmed plates and top with vegetables. Serve immediately, garnished with additional hemp seeds and a light sprinkle of cayenne.

Miso-Glazed Tofu with Crispy Sushi Cakes and Braised Bok Choy

This Asian-inspired dish is a perfect balance of sweet, salty and rich flavors. Both the tofu and the rice cakes can be made ahead of time and reheated in the oven right before serving.

MAKES 4 SERVINGS

Tips

To soak the rice: Place in a bowl and cover with 4 cups (1 L) water. Cover and set aside for 1 hour. Drain, discarding liquid. Rinse rice under cold running water until water runs clear.

Be sure to use raw (not processed) agave nectar. It is a 100% natural (non-GMO) sweetener that contains naturally occurring fructose and is low on the glycemic scale, which means that it releases glucose slowly, providing sustained energy.

Substitute an equal amount of raw (unpasteurized) apple cider vinegar for the rice wine vinegar.

- Preheat oven to 450°F (200°C)
- 8-inch (20 cm) square glass baking dish, lined with parchment paper
- Baking sheet, lined with parchment paper
- Blender

SUSHI CAKES

1 cup	short-grain brown rice, soaked (see Tips, left)	250 mL
2½ cups	water	625 mL
1 tsp	fine sea salt	5 mL
¼ cup	raw agave nectar (see Tips, left)	60 mL
¼ cup	rice wine vinegar (see Tips, left)	60 mL
¼ cup	grapeseed oil, divided	60 mL

TOFU

¼ cup	grapeseed oil, divided	60 mL
1	block (1 lb/500 g) firm tofu, cut crosswise into 8 pieces	1
¼ cup	unpasteurized brown rice miso or chickpea miso	60 mL
3 tbsp	pure maple syrup	45 mL
2 tbsp	toasted sesame oil	30 mL
1 tbsp	wheat-free tamari	15 mL
1 tsp	rice wine vinegar	5 mL

BOK CHOY

2 tbsp	wheat-free tamari	30 mL
2 tbsp	water	30 mL
1 tbsp	raw agave nectar	15 mL
½ tsp	raw (unpasteurized) apple cider vinegar	2 mL
1 tbsp	grapeseed oil	15 mL
1 tbsp	minced peeled gingerroot	15 mL
2 to 3	cloves garlic, minced	2 to 3
4 cups	sliced baby bok choy (see Tips, page 405)	1 L

Tips

Replace the bok choy with an equal amount of broccoli florets or snow peas or 8 cups (2 L) chopped spinach leaves.

Use the bottom of a measuring cup to press the rice evenly into the baking dish.

This dish can be partially prepared ahead of time. Complete Steps 1 and 2 but do not cut sushi rice into squares. Complete Step 4. Cover and refrigerate sushi cakes and fried tofu until you are ready to cook, for as long as overnight. When you are ready to serve, cut the sushi rice into squares and complete Step 3. Brush tofu with miso mixture as in Step 5 and bake in preheated oven along with seared rice cakes (Step 6).

1. *Sushi Cakes:* In a saucepan, combine soaked rice, water and salt. Bring to a boil, stir once and reduce heat to low. Cover with a tight-fitting lid and cook for 45 to 50 minutes, until rice is tender. Remove from heat. Stir, cover and set aside for 5 to 10 minutes to allow rice to absorb any remaining liquid.

2. In a small bowl, whisk together agave nectar and vinegar until well combined. Transfer cooked rice to a large bowl and stir in agave-vinegar mixture. Using a silicone spatula, stir vigorously to slightly break down the grains. Press firmly into prepared baking dish (see Tips, left). Refrigerate for 2 hours or until cold. Lift mixture from pan using parchment paper. Cut into 4 square cakes.

3. In a large skillet over medium-high heat, heat 2 tbsp (30 mL) grapeseed oil. Add 2 rice cakes and cook for 5 to 6 minutes each side, until golden brown. Transfer to prepared baking sheet. Repeat with remaining oil and rice cakes. Set aside.

4. *Tofu:* In a large skillet over medium heat, heat 2 tbsp (30 mL) grapeseed oil. Working with 3 or 4 pieces at a time, cook tofu until golden brown on all sides, 2 to 3 minutes per side. Transfer to baking sheet with rice cakes. Repeat with remaining grapeseed oil and tofu.

5. In a small bowl, whisk together miso, maple syrup, sesame oil, tamari and vinegar, until no lumps of miso remain. Spread mixture evenly over tofu pieces.

6. Bake sushi cakes and tofu in preheated oven until miso glaze is bubbling hot and rice cakes are heated through and crisp, about 15 minutes.

7. *Bok Choy:* Meanwhile, in blender, combine tamari, water, agave nectar and vinegar. Blend until smooth. Set aside.

8. In a large skillet over medium heat, heat grapeseed oil. Add ginger and garlic and cook, stirring constantly, until garlic is lightly golden brown, about 3 minutes. Add sliced bok choy and toss to coat well. Stir in tamari mixture and cook for 1 to 2 minutes, until bok choy is heated through and tender. Remove from heat and set aside.

9. *Assembly:* Divide sushi cakes among serving plates. Pour braised bok choy and some of its cooking liquid over each. Top with glazed tofu. Serve immediately.

Polenta Cakes with Olive, Tomato and Spinach Ragoût

This Italian-inspired dish is perfect for a casual Friday-evening dinner with friends. All you need to add is a crisp green salad and, if you're feeling festive, a bottle of good wine. Classic polenta, nutritious on its own, gains a healthy dose of nutrients with the addition of protein-rich hemp seeds.

MAKES 6 SERVINGS

Tips

Wheat-free tamari is a gluten-free seasoning made from fermented soybeans. It can be found in most well-stocked supermarkets and natural food stores.

To chop fresh thyme: Pinch the stem at the bottom with two fingers. Pulling upward with the finger and thumb of your other hand, strip the leaves. Reserve stems for soups or broths (discard after cooking). Use a sharp knife to chop the leaves, being careful not to chop too much or too hard, as this will bruise the leaves and cause the thyme to discolor.

• **13- by 9-inch (33 cm by 23 cm) glass baking dish, lined with parchment**

POLENTA CAKES

4 cups	water	1 L
½ tsp	fine sea salt	2 mL
1½ cups	fine stone-ground organic cornmeal	375 mL
½ cup	raw shelled hemp seeds	125 mL
2 tbsp	nutritional yeast	30 mL
2 tbsp	Whipped Non-dairy Butter (page 554)	30 mL

RAGOÛT

2 tbsp	grapeseed oil	30 mL
3 to 4	cloves garlic, thinly sliced	3 to 4
½ cup	chopped onion	125 mL
¼ tsp	fine sea salt	1 mL
8 cups	packed chopped spinach leaves	2 L
1 cup	thinly sliced pitted black olives	250 mL
1	can (5½ oz/156 mL) tomato paste	1
1 cup	dry red wine	250 mL
3 tbsp	wheat-free tamari (see Tips, left)	45 mL
1 tbsp	nutritional yeast	15 mL
1 tsp	chopped fresh thyme leaves (see Tips, left)	5 mL
1	can (28 oz/796 mL) diced tomatoes, with juice (see Tip, page 407)	1

ASSEMBLY

¼ cup	(approx.) grapeseed oil	60 mL

Substitute 4 cups (1 L) chopped fresh tomatoes for the canned tomatoes.

1. *Polenta Cakes:* In a large saucepan, bring water and salt to a boil. In a slow, steady stream, pour cornmeal into boiling water. Cook, stirring constantly with a wooden spoon, for 12 to 15 minutes, or until polenta begins to pull away from sides of pan and mixture is thick.

2. Remove from heat and stir in hemp seeds, nutritional yeast and butter. Spread evenly in prepared baking dish. Cover and refrigerate until firm, about 1 hour.

3. *Ragoût:* In a large pot over medium heat, heat oil. Add garlic and cook, stirring constantly, until lightly golden brown, 2 to 3 minutes. Add onion and salt and cook, stirring occasionally, until onion is translucent. Add spinach and olives and cook, stirring occasionally, until spinach is wilted and most of the liquid has evaporated, about 10 minutes. Transfer mixture to a colander and drain off excess liquid. Set aside.

4. Return pan to element. Add drained spinach mixture. Stir in tomato paste and cook for 2 to 3 minutes. Add wine and tamari and cook, stirring occasionally with a wooden spoon to scrape up any brown bits on bottom of pan, until most of the liquid has evaporated, about 5 minutes. Add nutritional yeast, thyme and tomatoes and stir to combine. Bring mixture to a simmer and cook, stirring frequently, until thickened, about 15 minutes.

5. *Assembly:* Using parchment handles, lift polenta out of baking dish and cut into 6 equal portions.

6. In a large skillet over medium-high heat, heat 2 tbsp (30 mL) grapeseed oil. Working in batches, cook polenta cakes for 3 to 4 minutes each side, until golden brown. Repeat until all polenta cakes have been fried, adding more oil as necessary. Divide among serving plates and top each with a large ladleful of ragoût.

Coconut-Crusted Tempeh with Sweet Potato Mash

This dish makes a perfect dinner on a cold winter's night when you and your guests are craving something warm and hearty. The apple ginger relish pairs perfectly with the crisp coconut tempeh and rich sweet potato mash.

MAKES 4 SERVINGS

Tips

Unpasteurized tempeh can be found in the freezer section of most well-stocked supermarkets and natural food stores. I prefer unpasteurized, as I find it has a better texture. Pasteurized tempeh will work equally well for this recipe.

Since unpasteurized tempeh is a living food, it needs to be kept frozen until just before cooking. If you leave it in the refrigerator for more than 1 day, bacteria will grow; it will become hot and must be discarded.

The tempeh in this recipe can be coated ahead of time and refrigerated in an airtight container for up to 1 week. When ready to serve, pan-sear and bake as instructed.

● Baking sheet, lined with parchment paper

TEMPEH

1	block (8½ oz/240 g) frozen (unpasteurized) tempeh	1
4 cups	water	1 L
¼ cup	wheat-free tamari	60 mL
2	whole star anise	2
1	3-inch (7.5 cm) cinnamon stick	1
1	clove garlic, peeled	1
1 cup	unsweetened shredded coconut	250 mL
½ cup	brown rice flour	125 mL
1 tbsp	finely grated lemon zest	15 mL
¼ tsp	fine sea salt, divided	1 mL
1 cup	Almond Milk (page 61)	250 mL
¼ cup	Dijon mustard	60 mL

APPLE GINGER RELISH

2 tbsp	coconut oil	30 mL
½ cup	finely chopped onion	125 mL
¼ tsp	fine sea salt	1 mL
2 tbsp	chopped peeled gingerroot	30 mL
2 tbsp	dry white wine (optional)	30 mL
3 cups	chopped green apples	750 mL
¼ cup	raw agave nectar	60 mL
1½ tbsp	raw (unpasteurized) apple cider vinegar	22 mL
1 tbsp	chopped fresh thyme leaves	15 mL

SWEET POTATO MASH

6 cups	cubed (2 inches/5 cm) peeled sweet potatoes (see Tips, page 409)	1.5 L
8 cups	water	2 L
2 tsp	fine sea salt, divided	10 mL
½ cup	melted coconut oil	125 mL
2 tsp	ground cinnamon	10 mL

ASSEMBLY

¼ cup	grapeseed oil, divided	60 mL

Tips

Don't be tempted to cut the sweet potatoes into cubes smaller than 2 inches (5 cm). Small pieces will absorb more water and result in a soft, runny mash.

Be sure to use raw (not processed) agave nectar. It is a 100% natural (non-GMO) sweetener that contains naturally occurring fructose and is low on the glycemic scale, which means that it releases glucose slowly, providing sustained energy.

1. *Tempeh:* In a covered saucepan, combine tempeh, water, tamari, star anise, cinnamon stick and garlic. Bring to a boil, reduce heat and simmer for 15 minutes. Using a slotted spoon, transfer tempeh to a plate (discard garlic, spices and liquid). Set aside for 15 minutes to cool.

2. Meanwhile, in a small bowl, combine coconut, rice flour, lemon zest and 1/8 tsp (0.5 mL) salt.

3. In another bowl, whisk together almond milk, mustard and remaining 1/8 tsp (0.5 mL) salt.

4. Cut cooled tempeh in half. Cut each piece in half again so you end up with 4 equal rectangular pieces. Cut each piece on the diagonal to make 8 equal triangles.

5. Dip each piece of tempeh first in almond milk mixture and then in coconut and rice flour mixture, coating completely. Place on a large plate. Refrigerate for 10 to 15 minutes to firm up.

6. *Apple Ginger Relish:* In a large skillet over medium heat, melt coconut oil. Add onion and salt and cook, stirring frequently, until onion is translucent, 5 to 6 minutes. Add ginger and cook for 2 to 3 minutes. Add wine (if using) and cook until liquid has evaporated. Add apples, agave nectar and vinegar; stir to combine. Bring mixture to a simmer and cook until apples begin to break down and mixture thickens slightly, 5 to 6 minutes. Remove from heat and stir in thyme. Set aside.

7. *Sweet Potato Mash:* In a large pot, combine sweet potatoes, water and 1 tsp (5 mL) salt. Bring to a boil, reduce heat and simmer until potatoes are tender, about 15 minutes. Drain, discarding liquid. Return potatoes to pot. Stir in remaining 1 tsp (5 mL) salt, coconut oil and cinnamon. Using a potato masher, mash until no large pieces of sweet potato remain. Cover and set aside to keep warm.

8. *Assembly:* Preheat oven to 400°F (200°C).

9. In a large skillet over medium heat, heat 2 tbsp (30 mL) grapeseed oil. Working in batches of 4, cook tempeh for 4 to 5 minutes each side, until golden brown. Transfer to prepared baking sheet. Repeat with remaining oil and tempeh. Bake in preheated oven for 10 minutes, until heated through.

10. Divide sweet potato mash among 4 serving plates. Arrange 2 pieces of tempeh on each. Top with apple ginger relish and serve immediately.

Tempeh Croquettes with Vegetables and Rice

These protein-dense croquettes are similar in texture and taste to traditional crab cakes. Here they are served over seasoned rice and fresh vegetables.

Tips

To make the rice for this recipe: Before starting the croquettes, prepare half a recipe of Basic Rice (page 212), adding 3 tbsp (45 mL) nutritional yeast, 1 tbsp (15 mL) chopped fresh thyme leaves and 1 tsp (5 mL) fine sea salt to 2 cups (500 mL) water and 1 cup (250 mL) short-grain brown rice.

Unpasteurized tempeh can be found in the freezer section of most well-stocked supermarkets and natural food stores. I prefer unpasteurized, as I find it has a better texture. Pasteurized tempeh will work equally well.

Since unpasteurized tempeh is a living food, it needs to be kept frozen until just before cooking. If you leave it in the refrigerator for more than 1 day, bacteria will grow; it will become hot and must be discarded.

- Baking sheet

CROQUETTES

1	1 block (8½ oz/240 g) frozen (unpasteurized) tempeh	1
½ cup	wheat-free tamari (see Tips, page 411)	125 mL
1 to 2	cloves garlic, peeled	1 to 2
¼ cup	each finely chopped celery, red bell pepper and red onion	60 mL
2 tbsp	freshly squeezed lemon juice	30 mL
2 tbsp	Dijon mustard	30 mL
1 tbsp	dried dillweed (see Tips, page 411)	15 mL
1 tbsp	chili powder	15 mL
2 tsp	fine sea salt	10 mL
2 tsp	sweet paprika	10 mL

BREADING

½ cup	Almond Milk (page 61)	125 mL
¼ cup	Dijon mustard	60 mL
¾ tsp	fine sea salt, divided	3 mL
½ cup	brown rice flour	125 mL
½ cup	fine stone-ground organic cornmeal	125 mL
1 tbsp	finely grated lemon zest	15 mL
1 tsp	dried dillweed	5 mL
½ tsp	sweet paprika	2 mL

VEGETABLES

2 tbsp	grapeseed oil	30 mL
3 to 4	cloves garlic, minced	3 to 4
½ cup	thinly sliced red bell pepper	125 mL
½ cup	thinly sliced carrot	125 mL
½ cup	thinly sliced kale leaves	125 mL
½ cup	small broccoli florets	125 mL
1 tsp	chopped fresh thyme leaves	5 mL

ASSEMBLY

¼ cup	grapeseed oil	60 mL

Tips

The croquettes can be made ahead of time and stored, uncooked and prior to breading, for up to 3 days in an airtight container in the refrigerator. You can also cook them ahead of time; simply reheat in a preheated 400°F (200°C) oven for 12 minutes.

Wheat-free tamari is a gluten-free seasoning made from fermented soybeans. It can be found in most well-stocked supermarkets and natural food stores.

Substitute ½ cup (125 mL) roughly chopped fresh dill for the dried dill in the croquettes.

1. *Croquettes:* In a saucepan, combine tempeh, 4 cups (1 L) water, tamari and whole garlic; bring to a boil. Reduce heat and simmer for 15 minutes. Using a slotted spoon, transfer tempeh to a plate (discard garlic and liquid). Set aside until cool enough to handle, about 10 minutes. Chop into fine pieces.

2. In a bowl, combine cooked tempeh, celery, red pepper, onion, lemon juice, mustard, dill, chili powder, salt and paprika. Stir well. Divide mixture into 4 equal portions. Using your hands, form into puck shapes. Set aside.

3. *Breading:* In a small bowl, whisk together almond milk, mustard and ¼ tsp (1 mL) salt. In another small bowl, whisk together rice flour, cornmeal, lemon zest, dill, paprika and remaining ½ tsp (2 mL) salt.

4. Dip each tempeh cake in almond milk mixture and then in cornmeal mixture, coating completely. Place on baking sheet as completed. Refrigerate for about 15 minutes to firm up.

5. *Vegetables:* When croquettes are firm and rice is cooked, in a large skillet over medium heat, heat oil. Add minced garlic and cook, stirring constantly, until lightly golden brown, about 2 minutes. Stir in red pepper, carrot, kale and broccoli. Cook, stirring constantly, until vegetables are tender, 4 to 5 minutes.

6. Add 3 tbsp (45 mL) water and thyme and cook for 2 minutes, stirring, until thyme is fragrant and vegetables are evenly coated. Remove from heat, cover and keep warm.

7. *Assembly:* Meanwhile, in a second large skillet over medium heat, heat oil. Cook croquettes until golden brown on one side, 4 to 5 minutes. Turn over and cook for 3 to 4 minutes, until golden brown on other side.

8. To serve, divide hot rice among 4 plates. Spoon sautéed vegetables overtop and finish each serving with a croquette. Serve immediately.

Variation

To serve the croquette mixture as canapés, divide it into 1 tbsp (15 mL) portions and form into small cakes. Cook, in batches, reducing cooking time accordingly. Serve with a drizzle of Roasted Red Pepper Mole Sauce (page 108) overtop.

Jerk Tempeh with Plantains and Mango Salsa

Your guests will love the way the robust flavors of lime, chile and allspice are balanced by starchy plantain and sweet salsa in this Jamaican-inspired dish.

MAKES 4 SERVINGS

Tips

Unpasteurized tempeh can be found in the freezer section of most well-stocked supermarkets and natural food stores. I prefer unpasteurized, as I find it has a better texture. Pasteurized tempeh will work equally well for this recipe.

Since unpasteurized tempeh is a living food, it needs to be kept frozen until just before cooking. If you leave it in the refrigerator for more than 1 day, bacteria will grow; it will become hot and must be discarded.

If you prefer a little less heat, remove the seeds and ribs from the chiles before chopping.

The quantity of garlic depends on the size of the cloves. If large, use the smaller number. If small, more may be required.

- **Food processor**
- **Baking sheet, lined with parchment paper**

TEMPEH

1	1 block (8½ oz/240 g) frozen (unpasteurized) tempeh	1
4 cups	water	1 L
6 tbsp	wheat-free tamari, divided	90 mL
5 to 7	cloves garlic, peeled, divided	5 to 7
2 tbsp	extra virgin olive oil	30 mL
2 tbsp	grapeseed oil	30 mL
¼ cup	freshly squeezed lime juice	60 mL
½ cup	chopped red bell pepper	125 mL
2 tbsp	chopped fresh thyme leaves	30 mL
2 tbsp	wheat-free tamari	30 mL
1 tbsp	raw (unpasteurized) apple cider vinegar	15 mL
1 tbsp	chopped peeled gingerroot	15 mL
1 tbsp	organic coconut sugar	15 mL
2 tsp	ground allspice	10 mL
2	Anaheim chiles, chopped	2

PLANTAINS

¼ cup	grapeseed oil	60 mL
2	ripe plantains, peeled and sliced in half lengthwise (see Tips, page 413)	2
¼ tsp	fine sea salt	1 mL

SALSA

1 cup	chopped mango	250 mL
½ cup	finely chopped red bell pepper	125 mL
¼ cup	chopped fresh cilantro, leaves and stems (see Tips, page 413)	125 mL
2 tbsp	finely chopped red onion	30 mL
1 tbsp	extra virgin olive oil	15 mL
½ tsp	fine sea salt	2 mL

Tips

Plantains look like large bananas, but they should not be consumed raw. Use very ripe (black) plantains; they may look rotten but they are perfect for this dish.

The stems on the leaves closest to the bottom of fresh cilantro are generally tough and need to be removed. The stems on leaves closer to the top of the sprig are soft and full of flavor and can be left on.

1. *Tempeh:* In a covered saucepan, combine tempeh, water, 1/4 cup (60 mL) tamari and 2 to 3 cloves garlic. Bring to a boil, reduce heat and simmer for 15 minutes. Using a slotted spoon, transfer tempeh to a plate (discard garlic and liquid). Set aside for 15 minutes to cool.

2. In food processor fitted with the metal blade, combine olive oil, grapeseed oil, lime juice, red pepper, thyme, remaining 2 tbsp (30 mL) tamari, vinegar, ginger, coconut sugar, allspice, chiles and remaining 3 to 4 cloves garlic. Process until smooth, stopping the motor to scrape down sides of work bowl as necessary. Transfer to a bowl and set aside.

3. Cut cooled tempeh into 4 equal rectangular pieces. Cut each piece on the diagonal to make 8 equal triangles. Add to red pepper mixture and toss gently until well coated. Cover and set aside for 1 hour to marinate or refrigerate overnight.

4. *Plantains:* In a large skillet over medium heat, heat oil. Cook plantains until golden brown on one side, about 3 to 4 minutes. Turn over and cook until golden brown on other side, 2 to 3 minutes. Transfer to prepared baking sheet and sprinkle with salt.

5. *Salsa:* In a large bowl, toss together mango, red pepper, cilantro, onion, olive oil and salt. Set aside.

6. *Assembly:* Preheat oven to 350°F (180°C).

7. Remove tempeh from marinade (reserve marinade) and place in center of a large piece of aluminum foil. Gather corners of foil and pull up to make a pouch. Pour reserved marinade overtop and tightly seal pouch (you do not want any steam to escape).

8. Place tempeh pouch on prepared baking sheet alongside plantains. Bake in preheated oven for 20 minutes, until tempeh is bubbling hot. Remove from oven.

9. Divide plantains among serving plates and top with tempeh pieces. Spoon salsa overtop and serve immediately.

Not Your Grandmère's Tourtière

Tourtière is a traditional Quebec meat (and sometimes fish) pie usually served on Christmas Eve. This vegan version is a perfect substitute if you are looking for a festive dish to serve during the holiday season.

MAKES 6 TO 8 SERVINGS

Tips

If your dough is extremely cold, it may be too firm to roll properly. Allow it to rest at room temperature for a few minutes before rolling it out.

Unpasteurized tempeh can be found in the freezer section of most well-stocked supermarkets and natural food stores. I prefer unpasteurized, as I find it has a better texture. Pasteurized tempeh will work equally well for this recipe.

Since unpasteurized tempeh is a living food, it needs to be kept frozen until just before cooking. If you leave it in the refrigerator for more than 1 day, bacteria will grow; it will become hot and must be discarded.

The filling for this recipe can be made ahead of time and kept refrigerated for up to 5 days or frozen for up to 2 months.

- **9-inch (23 cm) pie plate, greased**
- **Preheat oven to 350°F (180°C)**
- **Food processor**

1	recipe Vegan Piecrust (page 562)	1
1	block (8½ oz/240 g) frozen (unpasteurized) tempeh (see Tips, left)	1
4 cups	water	1 L
½ cup	wheat-free tamari, divided (see Tips, page 415)	125 mL
2	whole cloves garlic, peeled	2
3 tbsp	grapeseed oil	45 mL
1 cup	finely chopped onion	250 mL
1 cup	finely chopped carrot	250 mL
1 cup	finely chopped celery	250 mL
2 cups	sliced button mushrooms	500 mL
½ tsp	fine sea salt	2 mL
3 to 4	cloves garlic, minced	3 to 4
3 tbsp	Dijon mustard	45 mL
1 tbsp	chopped fresh thyme leaves	15 mL
½ tsp	ground cinnamon	2 mL
¼ tsp	ground cloves	1 mL
¼ tsp	freshly grated nutmeg	1 mL
	Almond milk, for brushing	

1. Divide piecrust dough in half. (Cover remaining dough with plastic wrap to prevent it from drying out.) On a clean, floured work surface, roll out one portion into a circle 12 inches (30 cm) in diameter. Gently press into prepared pie plate, evenly covering bottom and sides. Trim overhanging dough. Using the tines of a fork, poke several holes in dough to allow steam to escape while baking.

2. Bake in preheated oven for 15 minutes or until crust is golden brown. Remove from oven and set aside to cool.

Wheat-free tamari is a gluten-free seasoning made from fermented soybeans. It can be found in most well-stocked supermarkets and natural food stores.

To prevent the edges of your crust from over-browning, place a foil ring (available in baking stores) over the crust. You can also make your own, using heavy-duty aluminum foil. It should be about 3 inches (7.5 cm) wide.

3. Meanwhile, in a covered saucepan, combine tempeh, water, $\frac{1}{4}$ cup (60 mL) tamari and whole garlic cloves. Bring to a boil, reduce heat and simmer for 15 minutes. Using a slotted spoon, transfer tempeh to a plate (discard garlic and liquid). Set aside for 15 minutes to cool.

4. Using a sharp knife, cut cooled tempeh into small pieces. In food processor fitted with the metal blade, process until finely chopped.

5. In a large skillet over medium heat, heat oil. Add chopped tempeh and cook, stirring constantly, until lightly browned, 10 to 12 minutes. Add onion, carrot, celery, mushrooms and salt. Cook, stirring frequently, until vegetables are tender, about 6 minutes. Stir in minced garlic and cook for 2 minutes, until fragrant. Remove from heat and stir in mustard, thyme, cinnamon, cloves, nutmeg and remaining $\frac{1}{4}$ cup (60 mL) tamari. Set aside to cool completely.

6. Spread mixture evenly in prepared pie shell, pressing down firmly with the back of a spoon. Set aside.

7. Preheat oven to 400°F (200°C).

8. On a clean, floured work surface, roll out remaining piecrust dough into a circle 12 inches (30 cm) in diameter. Top filled pie shell with second crust. Trim overhanging dough and pinch together edges to seal. Using a sharp knife, cut several slits in top to allow steam to escape. Brush with almond milk.

9. Place foil ring (see Tips, left) over top, if using. Bake in preheated oven for 10 minutes, then reduce to 350°F (180°C) and bake for 20 to 25 minutes, until top is golden brown and filling is bubbling hot. Remove from oven and set aside to cool for 10 minutes before serving.

Greek-Style Potatoes with Charred Eggplant

Rich, meaty eggplant stands in for the traditional lamb or chicken in this twist on Greek souvlaki, complete with a cashew-based tzatziki. The trick is to slice the eggplant thickly and to marinate it overnight so it can soak up the flavorings.

MAKES 4 SERVINGS

Tips

The quantity of garlic depends on the size of the cloves. If large, use the smaller number. If small, more may be required.

To mince garlic: Place a whole clove on a cutting board. Using the butt end of a chef's knife, press firmly but gently on the clove to loosen the skin. Using your index finger and thumb, gently squeeze clove out of skin. Chop coarsely, then sprinkle with a bit of sea salt. Using the butt end of the knife, rub garlic into board (the salt will act as an abrasive and help to mince the garlic). Chop until fine.

A citrus reamer is a hand-held tool used to extract the juice from lemons and limes. It is available in most kitchen supply stores and would be ideal to use for the lemon juice in this recipe.

- **13- by 9-inch (33 by 23 cm) glass baking dish**
- **Blender**

SOUVLAKI

1	large eggplant, peeled	1
½ cup	extra virgin olive oil	125 mL
3 tbsp	freshly squeezed lemon juice (see Tips, left)	45 mL
3 tbsp	red wine vinegar	45 mL
1 tbsp	dried oregano	15 mL
1 tsp	fine sea salt	5 mL
3 to 4	cloves garlic, minced (see Tips, left)	3 to 4

POTATOES

4 cups	water	1 L
1 tbsp	finely grated lemon zest	15 mL
½ cup	freshly squeezed lemon juice	125 mL
¼ cup	nutritional yeast	60 mL
2 tbsp	dried oregano	30 mL
1 tbsp	chopped fresh rosemary	15 mL
1 tsp	fine sea salt	5 mL
8 to 10	cloves garlic, minced	8 to 10
8 cups	sliced (½ inch/1 cm) potatoes	2 L

TZATZIKI

2 cups	raw cashews	500 mL
4 cups	water, divided	1 L
½ cup	freshly squeezed lemon juice	125 mL
½ tsp	fine sea salt	2 mL
½ cup	shredded cucumber (see Tips, left)	125 mL
8 to 10	cloves garlic, finely grated (see Tips, page 417)	8 to 10
½ cup	chopped fresh dill	125 mL

Tips

To shred the cucumber: Use the large holes on the side of a box grater or a food processor fitted with the metal shredding disk.

All-purpose or starchy potatoes such as Yukon Gold or russet work best for this recipe. Waxy potatoes will not produce a crisp exterior.

Use a fine-toothed grater, such as the type made by microplane, to grate the garlic for this recipe.

1. *Eggplant:* Using a sharp knife, cut eggplant lengthwise into slices 1½ inches (4 cm) thick (3 to 4 pieces in total). Place in an airtight container. In a small bowl, whisk together oil, lemon juice, vinegar, oregano, salt and garlic. Pour over eggplant. Cover and refrigerate for 8 hours or overnight.

2. *Potatoes:* Preheat oven to 375°F (190°C).

3. In a large bowl, whisk together water, lemon zest, lemon juice, nutritional yeast, oregano, rosemary, salt and garlic. Add potatoes and toss to coat well.

4. Transfer to baking dish and cover tightly with aluminum foil. Bake in preheated oven for 45 minutes. Remove foil and bake for 12 to 15 minutes longer, or until the top is golden brown. Set aside to cool slightly, about 15 minutes.

5. *Tzatziki:* In a saucepan, combine cashews and 3½ cups (875 mL) water; bring to a boil. Drain, discarding liquid.

6. In blender, combine boiled cashews, remaining ½ cup (125 mL) water, lemon juice and salt. Blend at high speed until smooth and creamy. Transfer to a large bowl. Add cucumber, grated garlic and dill; stir well.

7. *Assembly:* Preheat grill to High.

8. Remove eggplant from marinade (reserve marinade) and pat dry with paper towels. Grill, brushing with reserved marinade while cooking, for 5 to 6 minutes per side, until lightly charred on the outside and soft in the middle.

9. Divide cooked potatoes among serving plates. Arrange grilled eggplant slices on top. Garnish with tzatziki and serve immediately.

Layered Tortillas

Layers of beans, guacamole and salsa piled on tortillas made from corn kernels rather than flour are a sure crowd-pleaser. Serve these when having friends over for a big game or for a special Mexican treat.

Tips

To grind flax seeds for this recipe, place 1½ cups (375 mL) whole seeds in a blender and blend until they become flour-like in consistency, stopping the machine and scraping down the sides of the container as necessary. Cover and refrigerate any extra ground flax seeds for up to 1 month.

Use either black beans you have cooked yourself or canned beans, preferably with no salt added. When using canned beans, be sure to rinse and drain them thoroughly before using.

A citrus reamer is a hand-held tool used to extract the juice from lemons and limes. It is available in most kitchen supply stores and would be ideal to use for the lemon juice in this recipe.

- Preheat oven to 350°F (180°C)
- Food processor
- 2 baking sheets, lined with parchment paper

TORTILLAS

4 cups	corn kernels (fresh or frozen)	1 L
½ cup	chopped carrot	125 mL
2 tbsp	extra virgin olive oil	30 mL
2 tsp	chili powder	10 mL
1 tsp	ground cumin	5 mL
1	clove garlic, peeled	1
1¼ cups	ground raw flax seeds (see Tips, left)	300 mL

BEANS

2 cups	cooked black beans (see Tips, left)	500 mL
3 tbsp	freshly squeezed lemon juice (see Tips, left)	45 mL
2 tbsp	wheat-free tamari (see Tips, page 419)	30 mL
1 tbsp	chili powder	15 mL
2 tsp	ground cumin	10 mL
2 to 3	cloves garlic, minced	2 to 3
¼ cup	extra virgin olive oil	60 mL

GUACAMOLE

2	large avocados (see Tips, page 419)	2
⅓ cup	freshly squeezed lemon juice	75 mL
1 to 2	cloves garlic, minced	1 to 2
½ tsp	fine sea salt	2 mL

SALSA

2 cups	chopped tomatoes	500 mL
½ cup	chopped flat-leaf (Italian) parsley	125 mL
2 tbsp	extra virgin olive oil	30 mL
1 tbsp	freshly squeezed lemon juice	15 mL
¼ tsp	fine sea salt	1 mL

ASSEMBLY

2 cups	thinly sliced romaine lettuce	500 mL
½ cup	Vegan Sour Cream (page 555)	125 mL

Wheat-free tamari is a gluten-free seasoning made from fermented soybeans. It can be found in most well-stocked supermarkets and natural food stores.

To ripen avocados, place them in a brown paper bag with a tomato or an apple. If your avocado is ripe and won't be consumed within a day or two, place it in the coolest part of the refrigerator to lengthen its life by 3 to 4 days. Once you take an avocado out of the fridge, do not put it back in — it will turn black.

Use your judgment when dividing up the toppings and spreading them on the tortillas. Depending on the total yields, you will need from 3 tbsp (45 mL) to 1/4 cup (60 mL) of each topping.

The tortillas will take as long as 30 minutes to cook if you have used frozen corn.

1. *Tortillas:* In food processor fitted with the metal blade, combine corn, carrot, oil, chili powder, cumin and garlic. Process until well combined (about 3 minutes), stopping the motor to scrape down sides of work bowl as necessary. Transfer to a large bowl. Stir in ground flax seeds until well combined. Cover and set aside so flax can absorb the liquid and swell, 10 to 12 minutes. Rinse out work bowl.

2. Using a 1/4-cup (60 mL) measure, drop batter onto prepared baking sheets (you should end up with 12 portions). Using the palm of your hand, flatten each into a circle about 1/8 inch (3 mm) thick. Bake in preheated oven for 15 to 30 minutes (see Tips, left) or until dry all the way through. Remove from oven and set aside on baking sheets to cool.

3. *Beans:* In clean work bowl, combine beans, lemon juice, tamari, chili powder, cumin and garlic. Process for 2 to 3 minutes, until smooth. With the motor running, drizzle oil through feed tube in a slow, steady stream; process until smooth. Transfer mixture to a bowl and set aside.

4. *Guacamole:* In a large bowl, using a potato masher, roughly mash avocados. Add lemon juice, garlic and salt and mash until well combined. Cover and set aside.

5. *Salsa:* In a large bowl, toss together tomatoes, parsley, oil, lemon juice and salt.

6. *Assembly:* Place 1 tortilla on a serving plate. Spread with about 3 tbsp (45 mL) each of the bean mixture, guacamole, salsa and lettuce. Place a second tortilla on top and repeat. Finish with a dollop of sour cream. Repeat for additional servings. Serve immediately.

Crispy Soba Cakes with Wakame Salad and Umeboshi Dressing

The unique flavor of the umeboshi dressing makes this a standout dish to serve guests. The trick to making the cakes is not to rinse the cooked noodles — the natural starch from the buckwheat helps bind them together.

MAKES 4 SERVINGS

Tips

Wakame is a nutritious sea vegetable (seaweed) that needs to be soaked before using. To soak, place in a bowl and add 2 cups (500 mL) water. Cover and set aside for 30 minutes. Drain, discarding liquid. Rinse under cold running water until the water runs clear, to ensure that any particles of sand are removed.

The stems on the leaves closest to the bottom of fresh cilantro are generally tough and should be removed. The stems on leaves closer to the top of the plant are softer and do not need to be removed.

- **8-inch (20 cm) square glass baking dish, greased**
- **Blender**

SOBA CAKES

2	packages (each 8 oz/250 g) gluten-free soba noodles	2
2 tbsp	wheat-free tamari	30 mL
2 tbsp	toasted sesame oil	30 mL
1 tbsp	raw white sesame seeds	15 mL

WAKAME SALAD

1 cup	dried wakame, soaked (see Tips, left)	250 mL
1 cup	roughly chopped fresh cilantro, leaves and stems (see Tips, left)	250 mL
¼ cup	finely sliced green onion (green and white parts)	60 mL
1 tbsp	toasted sesame oil	15 mL
2 tsp	wheat-free tamari	10 mL

DRESSING

2 tbsp	water	30 mL
2 tbsp	toasted sesame oil	30 mL
2 tbsp	extra virgin olive oil	30 mL
2 tbsp	chopped umeboshi plums (see Tips, page 421)	30 mL
1½ tbsp	raw agave nectar (see Tips, page 421)	22 mL
1 tbsp	brown rice vinegar	15 mL
1½ tsp	wheat-free tamari	7 mL

ASSEMBLY

3 tbsp	grapeseed oil	45 mL

Tips

Umeboshi plums are available in most natural food stores and Japanese markets. If you cannot find the plums, substitute an equal amount of umeboshi vinegar for the brown rice vinegar and increase the amount of tamari to 2 tbsp (30 mL).

Be sure to use raw (not processed) agave nectar. It is a 100% natural (non-GMO) sweetener that contains naturally occurring fructose and is low on the glycemic scale, which means that it releases glucose slowly, providing sustained energy.

1. *Soba Cakes:* In a large covered pot, bring water for cooking noodles to a rapid boil. Add noodles and cook, uncovered, according to package directions, until al dente. Drain but do not rinse. Immediately transfer to a large bowl and stir in tamari, sesame oil and sesame seeds.

2. Spread noodle mixture evenly in prepared baking dish and, using a wooden spoon or measuring cup, press down. Refrigerate until noodles are firm and hold together, about 1 hour.

3. *Wakame Salad:* In a bowl, combine soaked wakame, cilantro, green onions, sesame oil and tamari. Toss together until well combined. Cover and set aside.

4. *Dressing:* In blender, combine water, sesame oil, olive oil, plums, agave nectar, vinegar and tamari. Blend at high speed until smooth and creamy. Set aside.

5. *Assembly:* Turn noodles out onto a cutting board and cut into 4 equal squares. In a large skillet over medium heat, heat grapeseed oil. Cook soba cakes for 3 to 4 minutes on each side, until golden brown and heated through, 3 to 4 minutes.

6. Drizzle each serving plate with dressing. Place a soba cake on top of dressing and top with equal portions of wakame salad. Serve immediately.

Spanakopita Pie with Red Pepper Slaw and Lemon Dijon Arugula

Spanakopita is a traditional Greek meze made with spinach, onions and feta cheese encased in phyllo pastry. Here the phyllo pastry is replaced by gluten-free vegan piecrust and tofu stands in for the feta. Served with arugula and a roasted pepper slaw, it makes an impressive entrée for a dinner party.

MAKES 6 TO 8 SERVINGS

Tips

To mince garlic: Place a whole clove on a cutting board. Using the butt end of a chef's knife, press firmly but gently on the clove to loosen the skin. Using your index finger and thumb, gently squeeze clove out of skin. Chop coarsely, then sprinkle with a bit of sea salt. Using the butt end of the knife, rub garlic into board (the salt will act as an abrasive and help to mince the garlic). Chop until fine.

Nutritional yeast is an inactive yeast that has been grown on beet molasses and then pasteurized. It provides a rich, cheesy flavor in sauces, stews, soups and dips. Look for it in well-stocked supermarkets and natural food stores.

If your dough is extremely cold, it may be too firm to roll properly. Allow it to rest at room temperature for a few minutes before rolling it out.

- **Preheat oven to 350°F (180°C)**
- **10-inch (25 cm) deep-dish pie plate, greased**
- **Food processor**
- **Blender**

SPANAKOPITA

1	recipe Vegan Piecrust (page 562)	1
2 tbsp	grapeseed oil	30 mL
1 cup	chopped onion	250 mL
1 tsp	fine sea salt, divided	5 mL
8	cloves garlic, minced (see Tips, left)	8
8 cups	packed chopped spinach leaves	2 L
1	block (1 lb/500 g) firm tofu, cut into ½-inch (1 cm) cubes	1
¼ cup	nutritional yeast (see Tips, left)	60 mL
1 tbsp	dried oregano leaves	15 mL
1 tsp	dried basil leaves	5 mL
¼ tsp	freshly grated nutmeg	1 mL

RED PEPPER SLAW

4	roasted red bell peppers (see Tips, page 423)	4
3 tbsp	grapeseed oil	45 mL
¼ cup	raw (unpasteurized) apple cider vinegar	60 mL
3 tbsp	raw agave nectar	45 mL
½ cup	chopped flat-leaf (Italian) parsley	125 mL
¼ tsp	fine sea salt, divided	1 mL

LEMON DIJON ARUGULA

½ cup	extra virgin olive oil	125 mL
¼ cup	freshly squeezed lemon juice (see Tips, page 423)	60 mL
3 tbsp	Dijon mustard	45 mL
¼ tsp	fine sea salt	1 mL
8 cups	lightly packed baby arugula	2 L

Tips

Pricking holes in the dough before baking the bottom crust allows steam to escape.

A citrus reamer is a hand-held tool used to extract the juice from lemons and limes. It is available in most kitchen supply stores and would be ideal to use for the lemon juice in this recipe.

To roast peppers: Preheat oven to 450°F (230°C). Brush peppers with oil and sprinkle with ¾ tsp (3 mL) salt. Place on a baking sheet and roast in preheated oven, turning several times, until skin is slightly blackened, about 25 minutes. Transfer to a bowl and cover tightly with plastic wrap. Set aside for 10 minutes. Peel.

Covering the bowl tightly with plastic wrap after roasting the peppers captures the steam, which helps to separate the skin from the flesh, making the peppers easier to peel.

To prevent the edges of your crust from over-browning, place a foil ring (available in baking stores) over the crust. You can also make your own, using heavy-duty aluminum foil. It should be about 3 inches (7.5 cm) wide.

1. *Spanakopita:* On a clean, floured work surface, roll out half the piecrust dough into a circle 14 inches (35 cm) in diameter. Gently press into prepared pie plate. Using the tines of a fork, poke holes in the dough. Bake in preheated oven for 15 minutes or until crust is golden brown. Remove from oven and set aside to cool.

2. In a large skillet over medium heat, heat oil. Add onion and ½ tsp (2 mL) salt; cook, stirring frequently, until onion is translucent, 3 minutes. Stir in garlic and cook until fragrant, 2 to 3 minutes. Add spinach and cook, stirring occasionally, until wilted, 4 to 5 minutes. Remove from heat and set aside.

3. In food processor fitted with the metal blade, process tofu until broken down into small pieces. Transfer to a large bowl. Stir in nutritional yeast, oregano, basil, nutmeg and remaining ½ tsp (1 mL) salt. Add sautéed spinach and stir to combine. Set aside.

4. Preheat oven to 400°F (200°C).

5. Spread tofu-spinach mixture evenly in baked pie shell. Set aside.

6. On a clean, floured work surface, roll out the remaining dough into a circle 14 inches (35 cm) in diameter. Top filled shell with crust. Trim overhanging dough and pinch together edges to seal. Using a sharp knife, cut several slits in the top to allow steam to escape. Place foil ring (see Tips, left) over top (if using). Bake in preheated oven for 10 minutes, then reduce heat to 350°F (180°C) and bake until golden brown and filling is bubbling hot, 15 to 20 minutes.

7. *Red Pepper Slaw:* Using a sharp knife, slice peeled roasted peppers into strips about ⅛ inch (3 mm) wide. Transfer to a bowl. Add vinegar, agave nectar, parsley and salt; toss gently to coat.

8. *Lemon Dijon Arugula:* In blender, combine olive oil, lemon juice, mustard and salt. Blend at high speed until smooth and creamy. Place arugula in a large bowl and toss with dressing.

9. Cut spinach pie into wedges and divide among serving plates. Serve with slaw and arugula alongside.

Grilled King Oyster Mushrooms with Curried Sticky Rice Parcels

Creamy coconut milk–infused rice paired with meaty grilled mushrooms makes a substantial and pleasing meal. Serve this with a side of Ginger Lime Edamame Stir-Fry (page 300).

MAKES 4 SERVINGS

Tips

To soak the rice: Place in a large saucepan with 3½ cups (875 mL) water. Cover and set aside for 1 hour. The rice is cooked in its soaking water (see Step 1).

To remove the skin from fresh gingerroot with the least amount of waste, use the edge of a teaspoon. With a brushing motion, scrape off the skin to reveal the yellow root.

A citrus reamer is a hand-held tool used to extract the juice from lemons and limes. It is available in most kitchen supply stores and would be ideal to use for the lime juice in this recipe.

• Baking sheet

STICKY RICE PARCELS

2 cups	sweet rice, soaked (see Tips, left)	500 mL
1 tsp	fine sea salt, divided	5 mL
2 tbsp	grapeseed oil	30 mL
½ cup	chopped onion	125 mL
2 to 3	cloves garlic, minced	2 to 3
1 tsp	minced peeled gingerroot (see Tips, left)	5 mL
1 cup	chopped fresh cilantro, leaves and stems	250 mL
¼ cup	chopped green onion (green and white parts)	60 mL
1 tsp	ground cumin	5 mL
½ tsp	ground coriander	2 mL
1	can (14 oz/400 mL) full-fat coconut milk	1
2 tbsp	freshly squeezed lime juice (see Tips, left)	30 mL
1 tbsp	wheat-free tamari	15 mL
1 tsp	organic coconut sugar	5 mL
⅛ tsp	cayenne pepper	0.5 mL
4	large banana leaves, cut into squares (see Tips, page 425)	4

MUSHROOMS

8	large king oyster mushrooms (see Tips, page 425)	8
¼ cup	extra virgin olive oil	60 mL
1 tsp	fine sea salt	5 mL

Tips

Banana leaves are sold in large sheets. Cut the leaves into 6-inch (15 cm) squares.

If you can't find banana leaves, use parchment paper. However, be aware that it will not impart any flavor to the dish.

Remove the bottom ½ to 1 inch (1 to 2.5 cm) from the stems of king oyster mushrooms — they are tough and inedible.

1. *Sticky Rice Parcels:* In a large covered saucepan, combine soaked rice, soaking water and ½ tsp (2 mL) salt. Bring to a boil, with lid slightly ajar so some steam can escape. Reduce heat and simmer until tender and almost all of the liquid has been absorbed, about 20 minutes. Remove from heat, cover and set aside for 10 minutes so rice can absorb any remaining liquid.

2. In a large pot over medium heat, heat grapeseed oil. Add onion and remaining ½ tsp (2 mL) salt; cook, stirring frequently, until onion is translucent, 5 to 6 minutes. Add garlic and ginger; cook until soft and fragrant, 2 to 3 minutes. Add cilantro, green onion, cumin and coriander. Cook, stirring frequently, for 3 to 4 minutes, until fragrant.

3. Stir in coconut milk, lime juice, tamari, coconut sugar and cayenne. Simmer, stirring occasionally with a wooden spoon to scrape up any brown bits from bottom of pan, until slightly thickened, 8 to 10 minutes. Remove from heat. Add cooked rice and stir until well combined. Set aside to cool completely, about 30 minutes.

4. Preheat oven to 400°F (200°C).

5. Lay banana leaves flat on a clean work surface. Divide rice mixture into 4 equal portions and place a portion in center of each leaf. Gently tuck corners of each leaf into center of rice. Wrap each parcel tightly in aluminum foil. Transfer to prepared baking sheet and bake in preheated oven for 25 minutes, until heated through. Remove from oven and set aside.

6. *Mushrooms:* Preheat grill to High.

7. In a bowl, toss together mushrooms, olive oil and salt. Grill mushrooms for 3 to 4 minutes per side, until tender and grill marks appear.

8. *Assembly:* Remove foil and place one banana leaf parcel on each serving plate. Top each parcel with 2 grilled mushrooms. Serve immediately.

Middle Eastern Platter

This special-occasion dish is the perfect platter for family gatherings or to serve at get-togethers during major sports events.

Tips

A citrus reamer is a hand-held tool used to extract the juice from lemons and limes. It is available in most kitchen supply stores and would be ideal to use for the lemon juice in this recipe.

To shred the cucumber, use the large holes on the side of a box grater or a food processor fitted with the metal shredding disk.

To mince garlic: Place a whole clove on a cutting board. Using the butt end of a chef's knife, press firmly but gently on the clove to loosen the skin. Using your index finger and thumb, gently squeeze clove out of skin. Chop coarsely, then sprinkle with a bit of sea salt. Using the butt end of the knife, rub garlic into board (the salt will act as an abrasive and help to mince the garlic). Chop until fine.

- **Food processor**
- **Large serving platter**

CASHEW DIP

2 cups	raw cashews	500 mL
4 cups	water, divided	1 L
½ cup	freshly squeezed lemon juice (see Tips, left)	125 mL
½ tsp	fine sea salt	2 mL
½ cup	shredded cucumber (see Tips, left)	125 mL
8 to 10	cloves garlic, minced (see Tips, left)	8 to 10
½ cup	chopped fresh dill	125 mL

ASSEMBLY

2 cups	Basic Chickpea Hummus (page 72)	500 mL
4 cups	Quinoa Tabbouleh (page 219)	1 L
1 cup	Sautéed Olives with Lemon, Garlic and Fresh Herbs (page 290)	250 mL
1	recipe Caramelized Onion and Olive Flatbread (page 470)	1
¼ cup	extra virgin olive oil	60 mL

1. *Cashew Dip:* In a saucepan, combine cashews and 3½ cups (875 mL) water; bring to a boil. Drain, discarding liquid. Transfer cashews to food processor fitted with the metal blade.

2. Add remaining ½ cup (125 mL) water, lemon juice and salt. Blend at high speed until smooth and creamy. Transfer to a large bowl. Add cucumber, garlic and dill; stir well.

3. *Assembly:* On a large serving platter, arrange cashew dip, hummus, tabbouleh, olives and flatbread. Drizzle everything with olive oil and serve immediately.

Baked Goods

Triple Ginger Cookies

Serve these fragrant cookies around the holidays or for family gatherings. They also make a delicious snack or on-the-run treat.

MAKES 24 COOKIES

- **2 baking sheets, lined with parchment paper**
- **Electric mixer**

Tips

When working with any flour, particularly those that are gluten-free, whisk before measuring. This aerates the flour and ensures more accurate measuring. Be sure to use a dry measure (not a glass measuring cup) and to level off with the side of a knife.

To melt the coconut oil, gently warm it in a small skillet over low heat.

Candied ginger can be found in most well-stocked supermarkets and natural food stores.

Research supports ginger's ability to reduce inflammation, much like low-dose analgesics such as ibuprofen. It is also a great digestive.

3 tbsp	warm water	45 mL
1 tbsp	ground raw flax seeds	15 mL
2 cups	All-Purpose Gluten-Free Flour Blend (page 561)	500 mL
2 tsp	ground ginger	10 mL
1½ tsp	ground cinnamon	7 mL
1 tsp	chopped peeled gingerroot	5 mL
1 tsp	baking soda	5 mL
½ tsp	ground allspice	2 mL
¼ tsp	xanthan gum	1 mL
¼ tsp	freshly ground black pepper	1 mL
¼ tsp	fine sea salt	1 mL
1 cup	organic coconut sugar, divided	250 mL
⅓ cup	blackstrap molasses	75 mL
¼ cup	melted coconut oil (see Tips, left)	60 mL
1 tsp	alcohol-free organic vanilla extract	5 mL
1 cup	candied organic ginger, chopped (see Tips, left)	250 mL

1. In a small bowl, whisk together warm water and ground flax seeds. Cover and set aside for about 10 minutes, so flax can absorb the liquid and swell.

2. In a large bowl, combine flour blend, ground ginger, cinnamon, chopped ginger, baking soda, allspice, xanthan gum, pepper and salt.

3. In mixer bowl, combine ⅔ cup (150 mL) coconut sugar, molasses, coconut oil, vanilla and soaked flax. Beat at medium speed until well combined. At low speed, gradually add flour mixture and candied ginger and mix until well combined.

4. Place dough on a large piece of plastic wrap and shape into a disk. Wrap tightly in plastic and refrigerate for 2 hours or until firm.

When baking more than
1 sheet of cookies, position
oven racks in upper and
lower thirds of oven and
switch sheets at half time,
rotating them front to back.

5. Preheat oven to 350°F (180°C).

6. Place remaining $\frac{1}{3}$ cup (75 mL) coconut sugar in
   a shallow bowl. Working with about 2 tbsp (30 mL)
   dough at a time, form it into balls. Roll balls in sugar
   to coat completely. Place on prepared baking sheets,
   spacing about 2 inches (5 cm) apart.

7. Bake in preheated oven for 10 minutes or until
   cookies appear dry and cracked.

8. Remove from oven and cool completely on baking
   sheets. Serve immediately or store for up to 3 days
   in an airtight container at room temperature.

Banana Goji Cookies

These soft cookies make the perfect breakfast treat when served with a tall glass of Almond Milk (page 61).

Tips

To warm the almond butter, gently heat it in a small skillet over low heat.

Goji berries are bright red berries native to Tibet and China. They are sold dried, not fresh, and are available in most well-stocked supermarkets and natural food stores. If you cannot find them, substitute an equal amount of dried blueberries or dried strawberries.

- **Preheat oven to 350°F (180°C)**
- **Baking sheet, lined with parchment paper**

½ cup	chopped banana	125 mL
½ cup	almond butter, warmed gently (see Tips, left)	125 mL
½ cup	Coconut Milk (page 62)	125 mL
¼ cup	raw agave nectar (see page 8)	60 mL
⅓ cup	unsweetened applesauce	75 mL
1 tsp	raw (unpasteurized) apple cider vinegar	5 mL
¼ tsp	alcohol-free organic vanilla extract	2 mL
¾ cup	All-Purpose Gluten-Free Flour Blend (page 561)	175 mL
1 tbsp	ground raw golden flax seeds	15 mL
½ tsp	gluten-free baking powder (see Tips, page 431)	2 mL
1 tsp	ground ginger	5 mL
1 tsp	ground cinnamon	5 mL
Pinch	fine sea salt	Pinch
2 tbsp	goji berries (see Tips, left)	30 mL

1. In a bowl, whisk together banana, almond butter, coconut milk, agave nectar, applesauce, vinegar and vanilla.

2. In a large bowl, whisk together flour blend, ground flax seeds, baking powder, ginger, cinnamon and salt. Make a well in the center and add almond butter mixture. Stir until combined. Fold in goji berries.

3. Working with about 2 tbsp (30 mL) dough at a time, form it into balls. Place on prepared baking sheet, spacing about 2 inches (5 cm) apart.

4. Bake in preheated oven for 10 minutes or until golden (cookies will be soft to the touch but will firm up once cool).

5. Remove from oven and let cool on baking sheet for 5 minutes or until firm enough to handle. Transfer to a wire rack to cool completely. Store for up to 3 days in an airtight container at room temperature.

Oatmeal Raisin Cookies

Serve these home-style cookies with a tall glass of cold Almond Milk (page 61).

MAKES ABOUT 36 COOKIES

Tips

Baking powder is a rising agent made from an alkali (bicarbonate of soda) and an acid (cream of tartar), plus a filler such as cornstarch or sometimes wheat starch to absorb moisture. Check the label to ensure that the brand you are buying is gluten-free.

Most oats are processed in a facility that contains gluten. Look for oats that are certified gluten-free.

When baking more than 1 sheet of cookies, position oven racks in upper and lower thirds of oven and switch sheets at half time, rotating them front to back.

- Preheat oven to 375°F (190°C)
- 2 large baking sheets, lined with parchment paper
- Electric mixer

2 tbsp	ground raw flax seeds	30 mL
6 tbsp	warm water	90 mL
1½ cups	organic coconut sugar	375 mL
¾ cup	unsalted non-dairy butter alternative, chilled	175 mL
1 tsp	alcohol-free organic vanilla extract	5 mL
1¾ cups	All-Purpose Gluten-Free Flour Blend (page 561)	425 mL
2 tsp	xanthan gum	10 mL
1 tsp	gluten-free baking powder (see Tips, left)	5 mL
1 tsp	ground cinnamon	5 mL
¼ tsp	baking soda	1 mL
¼ tsp	fine sea salt	1 mL
2 cups	quick-cooking gluten-free rolled oats (see Tips, left)	500 mL
1 cup	raisins	250 mL

1. In a small bowl, whisk flax seeds and warm water. Cover and set aside for 10 minutes.

2. In mixer bowl, combine coconut sugar, butter and vanilla. Beat at high speed until light and fluffy. Add soaked flax and mix until well combined.

3. In a bowl, whisk together flour blend, xanthan gum, baking powder, cinnamon, baking soda and salt. Gradually add dry ingredients to butter mixture, beating low speed until incorporated. Add oats and mix until combined. Fold in raisins.

4. Drop about 2 tbsp (30 mL) dough at a time onto prepared baking sheets, spacing about 2 inches (5 cm) apart.

5. Bake in preheated oven for 10 to 12 minutes, until edges are crisp. Remove from oven and let cool on sheets until firm enough to handle, 10 to 15 minutes. Transfer to wire racks to cool completely. Serve immediately or store for up to 7 days at room temperature in an airtight container.

Flourless Cashew Butter Cookies

For a delicious snack, serve these rich, delicious cookies with a tall glass of cold Cashew Milk (page 61) and some fresh fruit such as strawberries and peaches.

MAKES 12 COOKIES

Tips

You can easily purchase flax seeds already ground. They are often described as "milled." If you prefer to grind your own, place 1/4 cup (60 mL) whole flax seeds in a blender or spice grinder and process until flour-like in consistency. Cover and refrigerate any extra for up to 1 month.

Cashew butter is made from ground cashews. It is available in most well-stocked supermarkets and natural food stores.

- **Preheat oven to 325°F (160°C)**
- **Baking sheet, lined with parchment paper**

3 tbsp	warm water	45 mL
1 tbsp	ground raw flax seeds (see Tips, left)	15 mL
3/4 cup	organic coconut sugar	175 mL
1 cup	cashew butter (see Tips, left)	250 mL

1. In a bowl, whisk together water and ground flax seeds until well combined. Cover and set aside for about 10 minutes, so flax can absorb the liquid and swell.

2. Add coconut sugar and cashew butter to flaxseed mixture and, using a wooden spoon, mix well.

3. Drop about 2 tbsp (30 mL) dough at a time onto prepared baking sheet, spacing about 2 inches (5 cm) apart. Flatten with the tines of a fork.

4. Bake in preheated oven for 22 to 25 minutes, until edges are slightly golden.

5. Remove from oven and let cool on baking sheet for 10 to 15 minutes, then transfer to a wire rack to cool completely. Serve immediately or store for up to 5 days in an airtight container at room temperature.

White Chocolate Macadamia Cookies

Serve these soft, chewy cookies, which have a tantalizing white chocolate flavor, with a tall glass of cold Strawberry Hazelnut Milk (page 65).

MAKES ABOUT 24 COOKIES

Tips

To melt the coconut oil, gently warm it in a small skillet over low heat.

When baking more than 1 sheet of cookies, position oven racks in upper and lower thirds of oven and switch sheets at half time, rotating them front to back.

Non-dairy white chocolate chips can be found in most natural food stores. They are usually made with rice or soy milk and are formed like traditional chocolate chips.

Store macadamia nuts in the refrigerator. Otherwise, their sensitive fats may become rancid.

- **Preheat oven to 350°F (180°C)**
- **2 baking sheets, lined with parchment paper**

½ cup	melted coconut oil (see Tips, left)	125 mL
¼ cup	Almond Milk (page 61)	60 mL
1 tbsp	ground raw flax seeds	15 mL
1 tsp	alcohol-free organic vanilla extract	5 mL
1¼ cups	All-Purpose Gluten-Free Flour Blend (page 561)	300 mL
½ cup	organic coconut sugar	125 mL
1 tsp	gluten-free baking powder (see Tips, page 431)	5 mL
½ tsp	xanthan gum	2 mL
¼ tsp	fine sea salt	1 mL
½ cup	non-dairy white chocolate chips (see Tips, left)	125 mL
½ cup	chopped macadamia nuts (see Tips, left)	125 mL

1. In a large bowl, whisk together coconut oil, almond milk, flax seeds and vanilla. Cover and set aside for about 10 minutes.

2. Meanwhile, in another large bowl, whisk together flour blend, coconut sugar, baking powder, xanthan gum and salt. Add coconut oil mixture and stir until just combined. Fold in white chocolate chips and macadamia nuts.

3. Drop about 2 tbsp (30 mL) dough at a time onto prepared baking sheets, spacing about 2 inches (5 cm) apart.

4. Bake in preheated oven for 10 minutes, until golden brown around the edges (cookies will be soft to the touch but will firm up once cool).

5. Remove from oven and let cool on baking sheets for 5 minutes or until firm enough to handle, then transfer to a wire rack to cool completely. Store cookies for up to 3 days in an airtight container at room temperature.

Perfect Chocolate Chip Cookies

These soft, chewy cookies are simply perfect.

Tips

To melt the coconut oil, gently warm it in a small skillet over low heat.

Higher-fat non-dairy milks, such as Almond Milk (page 61), Cashew Milk (page 61) or Hemp and Chia Milk (page 64), work best in this recipe.

Bring both the maple syrup and the non-dairy milk to room temperature before using. If they are cold, they could seize the coconut oil, and the ingredients won't mix properly.

When baking more than 1 sheet of cookies, position oven racks in upper and lower thirds of oven and switch sheets at half time, rotating them front to back.

- Preheat oven to 375°F (190°C)
- Electric mixer
- Baking sheets, lined with parchment paper

2¾ cups	All-Purpose Gluten-Free Flour Blend (page 561)	675 mL
1 tsp	gluten-free baking powder	5 mL
½ tsp	baking soda	2 mL
½ tsp	fine sea salt	2 mL
½ cup	melted coconut oil (see Tips, left)	125 mL
1¼ cups	organic coconut sugar	300 mL
¼ cup	non-dairy milk (see Tips, left)	60 mL
2 tbsp	pure maple syrup (see Tips, left)	30 mL
2 tsp	alcohol-free organic vanilla extract	10 mL
1¼ cups	non-dairy semisweet chocolate chips	300 mL

1. In a mixing bowl, whisk together flour blend, baking powder, baking soda and salt.
2. In mixer bowl, combine coconut oil and sugar. Beat at high speed until creamy. Add milk, maple syrup and vanilla; mix at high speed until blended.
3. Gradually add dry ingredients, mixing at low speed until blended (you do not want to see any dry spots in the dough). Stir in chocolate chips until just combined.
4. Drop about 2 tbsp (30 mL) dough at a time onto prepared baking sheets, spacing about 2 inches (5 cm) apart.
5. Bake in preheated oven for 10 minutes or until golden (cookies will be soft to the touch but will firm up once cool).
6. Remove from oven and let cool on baking sheet for 5 minutes or until firm enough to handle, then transfer to a wire rack to cool completely. Store for up to 3 days in an airtight container at room temperature.

Variation

Peanut Butter Chocolate Chip Cookies: Add ½ cup (125 mL) smooth peanut butter along with the milk in Step 2.

Peanut Butter Cookies

These sweet, chewy cookies are a satisfying between-meal snack served with a cup of your favorite tea.

Tips

Substitute an equal amount of Coconut Milk (page 62) or Cashew Milk (page 61) for the almond milk.

When beating the dry ingredients (Step 3), the dough should hold together without being too crumbly — if it seems dry, add 1 to 2 tbsp (15 to 30 mL) almond milk and mix well.

- Preheat oven to 350°F (180°C)
- Electric mixer
- 2 baking sheets, lined with parchment paper

1½ cups	All-Purpose Gluten-Free Flour Blend (page 561)	375 mL
1 tsp	baking soda	5 mL
¼ tsp	fine sea salt	1 mL
¾ cup	organic coconut sugar	175 mL
½ cup	smooth natural peanut butter	125 mL
¼ cup	grapeseed oil	60 mL
2 to 4 tbsp	Almond Milk (page 61; see Tips, left)	30 to 60 mL

1. In a large bowl, whisk together flour blend, baking soda and salt. Set aside.

2. In mixer bowl, combine coconut sugar, peanut butter and oil. Beat at high speed until light and fluffy.

3. Gradually add dry ingredients to peanut butter mixture. Beat at low speed until well combined, 2 to 3 minutes. Add 2 tbsp (30 mL) almond milk and mix until well combined.

4. Drop about 3 tbsp (45 mL) dough at a time onto prepared baking sheets, spacing about 2 inches (5 cm) apart. Gently press the tines of a fork into each cookie to create a crisscross pattern.

5. Bake in preheated oven for 10 minutes, until golden brown.

6. Remove from oven and let cool completely on baking sheet. Serve immediately or transfer to an airtight container and store at room temperature for up to 1 week.

Variation

Double Chocolate Peanut Butter Cookies: Add 3 tbsp (45 mL) raw cacao powder to the dry ingredients in Step 1. Fold in ½ cup (125 mL) non-dairy chocolate chips to the mixing bowl after the dough has been mixed (Step 3).

Chocolate-Dipped Coconut Shortbreads

These sweet treats are sure to win fans.

MAKES ABOUT 24 COOKIES

Tips

The coconut oil should be firm but not cold for this recipe. Assuming that you live in a temperate climate, room temperature is fine. (In warmer climes, coconut oil is likely to be liquid at room temperature.)

Measure coconut oil when it has a soft and creamy consistency. If this is not possible, melt the oil before measuring, measure, then refrigerate until creamy.

To grind the coconut sugar, place in a clean coffee grinder, spice grinder or blender and process until flour-like in consistency.

To roll out dough: Lay a piece of parchment paper on a clean work surface. Place 1 portion of dough on top, flatten slightly, and cover with a second piece of parchment.

When baking more than 1 sheet of cookies, position oven racks in upper and lower thirds of oven and switch sheets at half time, rotating them front to back.

- Preheat oven to 350°F (180°C)
- 2-inch (5 cm) round cookie cutter
- 2 baking sheets, lined with parchment paper

1 cup + 2 tbsp	coconut oil, at room temperature (see Tips, left)	280 mL
1 tsp	alcohol-free organic vanilla extract	5 mL
3½ cups	All-Purpose Gluten-Free Flour Blend (page 561)	875 mL
¾ cup	organic coconut sugar, finely ground (see Tips, left)	175 mL
¾ tsp	fine sea salt	3 mL
8 oz	non-dairy semisweet chocolate chips	250 g

1. In a bowl, beat together coconut oil and vanilla.
2. In a large bowl, whisk together flour blend, coconut sugar and salt. Make a well in the center and add coconut oil mixture. Stir until a smooth, uniform dough forms. Divide dough into 4 equal portions.
3. Roll out dough to ¼ inch (0.5 cm) thickness. Cut out circles, using cookie cutter. Transfer to prepared baking sheets, spacing about 1 inch (2.5 cm) apart. Repeat with remaining dough, rerolling scraps.
4. Bake in preheated oven for 10 minutes or until firm to the touch, being careful not to let cookies brown.
5. Remove from oven and let cool for 5 minutes on baking sheets, then transfer to a wire rack to cool completely.
6. Set a small bowl over a pot of simmering water, making sure it doesn't touch the water. Add chocolate chips and stir until just melted.
7. Dip each cooled cookie in melted chocolate several times, until well coated. Place on a clean parchment-lined baking sheet and refrigerate until set. Serve immediately or store for up to 5 days in a cool place in an airtight container.

Lemon Vanilla Biscotti

Enjoy these crispy cookies with your morning coffee or as a treat any time of the day. These also make a great gift during the holiday season.

MAKES 14 COOKIES

Tips

Blanched almond flour is available in most well-stocked supermarkets and natural food stores.

Organic vanilla powder can be found in most well-stocked supermarkets and natural food stores. It is made from dried and ground whole vanilla beans and will add a lot of flavor to your dishes. If you cannot find it, add 2½ tsp (12 mL) alcohol-free organic vanilla extract along with the agave nectar.

To toast the almonds: Heat a dry skillet over medium heat. Add almonds and cook, stirring constantly, for 3 to 5 minutes or until fragrant and golden brown. Immediately transfer to a plate and let cool.

The biscotti may seem soft when removed from the oven, but they will firm up on cooling.

- Preheat oven to 350°F (180°C)
- Food processor
- Baking sheet, lined with parchment paper

1¼ cups	blanched almond flour (see Tips, left)	300 mL
1 tbsp	arrowroot starch	15 mL
1 tbsp	freshly grated lemon zest	15 mL
1⅛ tsp	organic vanilla powder (see Tips, left)	5.5 mL
¼ tsp	fine sea salt	1 mL
¼ tsp	baking soda	1 mL
¼ cup	raw agave nectar	60 mL
¼ cup	toasted almonds, roughly chopped (see Tips, left)	60 mL

1. In food processor fitted with the metal blade, combine almond flour, arrowroot, lemon zest, vanilla powder, salt and baking soda. Process until well combined.

2. With the motor running, pour agave nectar through the feed tube in a slow, steady stream. Process until dough comes together. Add toasted almonds and pulse 2 to 3 times to combine.

3. Divide dough into 2 equal portions. Form each into a log about 1 inch (2.5 cm) high, 1½ inches (4 cm) wide and 4 inches (10 cm) long. Place on prepared baking sheet, spacing 3 inches (7.5 cm) apart. Bake on middle rack of preheated oven for 20 minutes, until set but still soft. Remove from oven and let cool completely on baking sheet, about 1 hour.

4. Preheat oven to 300°F (150°C).

5. Using a serrated knife, slice each log crosswise into 7 equal pieces. Return slices to baking sheet and bake in preheated oven for 20 to 25 minutes, until dried and golden brown.

6. Remove from oven and let cool on baking sheet for 5 minutes. Transfer to a wire rack to cool completely. Serve immediately or store in an airtight container at room temperature for up to 5 days.

Chocolate Almond Biscotti

These crisp cookies are perfect for serving with Hot Chocolate (page 67).

MAKES 14 COOKIES

Tips

Blanched almond flour is available in most well-stocked grocery supermarkets and natural food stores. It is made from skinless almonds that have been ground finely.

Be sure to use raw (not processed) agave nectar. It is a 100% natural (non-GMO) sweetener that contains naturally occurring fructose and is low on the glycemic scale, which means that it releases glucose slowly, providing sustained energy.

Cacao powder is powdered raw chocolate. It is similar to cocoa powder but tastes even better, with a deeper, richer flavor. Cacao powder is available in well-stocked supermarkets, natural food stores and online. You may substitute an equal quantity of good-quality cocoa powder.

The biscotti may seem soft when removed from the oven, but they will firm up on cooling.

- **Preheat oven to 350°F (180°C)**
- **Food processor**
- **Baking sheet, lined with parchment paper**

1¼ cups	blanched almond flour (see Tips, left)	300 mL
1 tbsp	arrowroot starch	15 mL
3 tbsp	raw cacao powder (see Tips, left)	45 mL
1 tsp	alcohol-free organic vanilla extract	5 mL
¼ tsp	fine sea salt	1 mL
¼ tsp	baking soda	1 mL
⅓ cup	raw agave nectar (see Tips, left)	75 mL
2 tbsp	raw cacao nibs	30 mL

1. In food processor fitted with the metal blade, combine almond flour, arrowroot, cacao powder, vanilla, salt and baking soda. Process until well combined.

2. With the motor running, pour agave nectar through the feed tube in a slow, steady stream. Process just until dough comes together. Add cacao nibs and pulse 2 to 3 times to combine.

3. Divide dough into 2 equal portions. Form each into a log about 2 inches (5 cm) high, 1½ inches (4 cm) wide and 4 inches (10 cm) long.

4. Place on prepared baking sheet spacing 3 inches (7.5 cm) apart. Bake on middle rack of preheated oven for 20 minutes, until dried and golden brown. Remove from oven and let cool completely on baking sheet, about 1 hour.

5. Preheat oven to 300°F (150°C).

6. Using a serrated knife, slice each log diagonally into 7 equal pieces. Return slices to baking sheet and bake in preheated oven for 20 to 25 minutes, until dried and crisp.

7. Remove from oven and let cool on baking sheet for 5 minutes, then transfer to a wire rack to cool completely. Biscotti will keep in an airtight container at room temperature for up to 5 days.

Chai-Spiced Muffins

These heavenly spiced muffins are sure to become your favorite go-to snack. They are perfect in the afternoon with a nice cup of tea.

MAKES 8 MUFFINS

Tips

To grind flax seeds: Place ¼ cup (60 mL) whole raw flax seeds in a blender or clean spice grinder and process until flour-like in consistency. Transfer to an airtight container and refrigerate for up to 1 month.

Blanched almond flour is available in most well-stocked supermarkets and natural food stores. It is made from blanched almonds (skins removed) that have been finely ground.

- Preheat oven to 350°F (180°C)
- Food processor
- 12-cup standard muffin pan, 8 cups greased or lined with silicone or paper cups

6 tbsp	warm water	90 mL
2½ tbsp	ground raw flax seeds (see Tips, left)	37 mL
2	medium ripe bananas	2
3 tbsp	pure maple syrup	45 mL
¼ cup	Almond Milk (page 61)	60 mL
1 cup	blanched almond flour (see Tips, left)	250 mL
½ cup	All-Purpose Gluten-Free Flour Blend (page 561)	125 mL
1 tsp	gluten-free baking powder	5 mL
¾ tsp	ground cinnamon	3 mL
½ tsp	ground cardamom	2 mL
½ tsp	ground ginger	2 mL
½ tsp	ground cloves	2 mL

1. In a small bowl, whisk together warm water and ground flax seeds until well combined. Cover and set aside for 10 minutes, so flax can absorb the liquid and swell.

2. In food processor fitted with the metal blade, combine bananas, maple syrup and almond milk; process until smooth. Add flaxseed mixture and process until incorporated.

3. In another large bowl, whisk together almond flour, flour blend, baking powder, cinnamon, cardamom, ginger and cloves. Add to banana mixture and pulse just until combined (don't overprocess).

4. Divide batter equally among 8 prepared muffin cups. Bake in preheated oven for 30 to 35 minutes or until tops spring back when lightly touched.

5. Remove from oven and let cool in pan on a wire rack for 10 minutes. Serve immediately or let cool completely and store for up to 2 days in an airtight container at room temperature, or for up to 5 days in the refrigerator.

Lemon Poppyseed Muffins

These fragrant muffins make a perfect snack any time of the day.

Tips

Using golden flax seeds for this recipe will make the muffins lighter in color, while brown flax will make them darker. Either is acceptable.

A hand-held citrus reamer can be used to extract the juice from lemons and limes. Available in most kitchen supply stores, this tool would be ideal to use for the lemon juice in this recipe.

Higher-fat non-dairy milks, such as Almond Milk (page 61), Cashew Milk (page 61) or Hemp and Chia Milk (page 64), work best for this recipe.

Be sure to use raw (not processed) agave nectar. It is a 100% natural (non-GMO) sweetener that contains naturally occurring fructose and is low on the glycemic scale, which means that it releases glucose slowly, providing sustained energy.

- **Preheat oven to 375°F (190°C)**
- **12-cup standard muffin pan, greased or lined with silicone or paper cups**

2 tbsp	ground raw flax seeds (see Tips, left)	30 mL
6 tbsp	warm water	90 mL
¾ cup	unsweetened applesauce	175 mL
1 tbsp	freshly grated lemon zest	15 mL
⅓ cup	freshly squeezed lemon juice (see Tips, left)	75 mL
⅓ cup	organic coconut sugar	75 mL
¼ cup	non-dairy milk (see Tips, left)	60 mL
¼ cup	raw agave nectar (see Tips, left)	60 mL
¼ cup	melted coconut oil (see Tips, page 441)	60 mL
1½ tsp	baking soda	7 mL
¼ tsp	fine sea salt	1 mL
2⅓ cups	All-Purpose Gluten-Free Flour Blend (page 561)	575 mL
1 tbsp	gluten-free baking powder (see Tips, page 441)	15 mL
1 tsp	xanthan gum	5 mL
1 tbsp	poppy seeds	15 mL

1. In a small bowl, whisk together ground flax seeds and warm water. Cover and set aside for about 10 minutes, so flax can absorb the liquid and swell.

2. In another bowl, whisk together applesauce, lemon zest, lemon juice, coconut sugar, milk, agave nectar, coconut oil, baking soda and salt. Mix until well combined (mixture should be a little foamy from the baking soda).

3. In a large bowl, whisk together flour blend, baking powder and xanthan gum. Add applesauce mixture and stir until just combined, being careful not to overmix. The batter should be scoopable but not too thick — if it's too thick, add 1 to 2 tbsp (15 to 30 mL) milk to reach desired consistency. Stir in poppy seeds.

Tips

To melt the coconut oil, gently warm it in a small skillet over low heat.

Baking powder is a rising agent made from an alkali (bicarbonate of soda) and an acid (cream of tartar), plus a filler such as corn flour or rice flour to absorb moisture. The powder is activated when liquid is added, producing carbon dioxide, which forms bubbles that cause the mixture to expand. Check the label to ensure that the brand you are buying is gluten-free.

4. Spoon batter into prepared muffin cups, filling each about three-quarters full. Bake in preheated oven for 17 to 22 minutes or until tops spring back when lightly touched.

5. Remove from oven and let cool in pan for 10 minutes. Serve immediately or let cool completely and store for up to 5 days in an airtight container at room temperature.

Variation

Lemon Poppyseed Loaf: Transfer batter to a greased 9- by 5-inch (23 by 12.5 cm) loaf pan and bake in preheated oven until a toothpick inserted in the center comes out clean, about 50 minutes. Let cool in pan for 30 minutes. Serve immediately or store for up to 2 days in an airtight container at room temperature.

Morning Glory Muffins

Prepare these muffins ahead of time for a nutrient-dense breakfast on the go. The fresh carrots and apples make this a truly flavorful and particularly moist muffin.

MAKES 12 MUFFINS

Tips

To melt the coconut oil, gently warm it in a small skillet over low heat.

Baking powder is a rising agent made from an alkali (bicarbonate of soda) and an acid (cream of tartar), plus a filler such as cornstarch or sometimes wheat starch to absorb moisture. Check the label to ensure that the brand you are buying is gluten-free.

- **Preheat oven to 350°F (180°C)**
- **12-cup standard muffin pan, greased or lined with silicone or paper cups**

1 cup	melted coconut oil (see Tips, left)	250 mL
½ cup + 2 tsp	warm water	135 mL
3 tbsp	ground raw flax seeds	45 mL
1½ tsp	alcohol-free organic vanilla extract	7 mL
2¼ cups	All-Purpose Gluten-Free Flour Blend (page 561)	550 mL
½ cup	organic coconut sugar	125 mL
1 tbsp	ground cinnamon	15 mL
2 tsp	baking soda	10 mL
1 tsp	xanthan gum	5 mL
1 tsp	gluten-free baking powder (see Tips, left)	5 mL
½ tsp	fine sea salt	2 mL
2 cups	shredded carrots	500 mL
1 cup	shredded apple (see Tips, page 443)	250 mL
1 cup	chopped pineapple	250 mL
¾ cup	raisins	175 mL
½ cup	unsweetened shredded coconut	125 mL
½ cup	chopped raw walnuts	125 mL

1. In a bowl, whisk together coconut oil, warm water, ground flax seeds and vanilla. Cover and set aside for about 10 minutes, so flax can absorb the liquid and swell.

2. In a large bowl, whisk together flour blend, coconut sugar, cinnamon, baking soda, xanthan gum, baking powder and salt.

Tip

Use Fuji, Rome, Granny Smith or Golden Delicious apples for this recipe. Their firm texture and higher levels of pectin will help them stand up to the oven temperature when baked.

3. In another large bowl, combine carrots, apple, pineapple, raisins, coconut and walnuts. Stir until well combined. Add to dry ingredients. Add coconut oil mixture and stir until well combined.

4. Spoon batter into prepared muffin cups, dividing equally. Bake in preheated oven for 25 to 30 minutes, or until tops spring back when lightly touched.

5. Let cool in pan for 10 minutes. Serve immediately or let cool completely and store for up to 3 days in an airtight container at room temperature.

Variation

For an extra-special treat, fold in $\frac{1}{2}$ cup (125 mL) non-dairy semisweet chocolate chips at the end of Step 3.

Deep Chocolate Brownies

Serve these chewy, fudgy chocolate treats à la mode — with a big scoop of Vegan Vanilla Ice Cream (page 513) — for a truly decadent treat.

MAKES ABOUT 12 BROWNIES

Tips

Cacao powder is powdered raw chocolate. It is similar to cocoa powder but tastes even better because it has a deeper, richer flavor. Cacao powder is available in well-stocked supermarkets, natural food stores and online.

To grind the coconut sugar, place it in a clean coffee grinder, spice grinder or blender and process until flour-like in consistency.

To melt the coconut oil, gently warm it in a small skillet over low heat.

Baking powder is a rising agent made from an alkali (bicarbonate of soda) and an acid (cream of tartar), plus a filler such as corn flour or rice flour to absorb moisture. The powder is activated when liquid is added, producing carbon dioxide, which forms bubbles that cause the mixture to expand. Check the label to ensure that the brand you are buying is gluten-free.

- Preheat oven to 350°F (180°C)
- Food processor
- 8-inch (20 cm) square metal baking pan, greased

6 tbsp	warm water	90 mL
2½ tbsp	ground raw flax seeds	37 mL
1¾ cups	drained cooked black beans	425 mL
¾ cup	raw cacao powder (see Tips, left)	175 mL
½ cup	ground organic coconut sugar (see Tips, left)	125 mL
3 tbsp	melted coconut oil (see Tips, left)	45 mL
1½ tsp	gluten-free baking powder (see Tips, left)	7 mL
1 tsp	alcohol-free organic vanilla extract	5 mL
¼ tsp	fine sea salt	1 mL

1. In a small bowl, whisk together warm water and flax seeds. Cover and set aside for about 10 minutes, so flax can absorb the liquid and swell.

2. In food processor fitted with the metal blade, combine beans, cacao powder, coconut sugar, coconut oil, baking powder, vanilla, salt and flaxseed mixture. Process until smooth, stopping the motor to scrape down sides of work bowl as necessary.

3. Spread batter evenly in prepared baking pan. Bake in preheated oven for 20 to 25 minutes, until set and edges are pulling away from sides of pan.

4. Remove from oven and let cool in pan on a wire rack for 30 minutes. Serve immediately or store for up to 3 days in an airtight container at room temperature.

Variation

Walnut Brownies: Add 1 cup (250 mL) roughly chopped raw walnuts to the batter after processing in Step 2.

Banana Bread

This moist bread is simply delicious served warm, right out of the oven, with some vegan butter spread on top. It also works as part of a healthy breakfast — I particularly enjoy it with Açai Superfood Bowl (page 21).

**MAKES 1 LOAF
(12 TO 16 SLICES)**

Tips

Be sure to use raw (not processed) agave nectar. It is a 100% natural (non-GMO) sweetener that contains naturally occurring fructose and is low on the glycemic scale, which means that it releases glucose slowly, providing sustained energy.

Almond Milk (page 61), Coconut Milk (page 62), Hemp and Chia Milk (page 64) or Cashew Milk (page 61) will work well in this recipe.

To melt the coconut oil, gently warm in a small skillet over low heat.

- **Preheat oven to 350°F (180°C)**
- **9- by 5-inch (23 by 12.5 cm) loaf pan, greased**

2½ cups	All-Purpose Gluten-Free Flour Blend (page 561)	625 mL
1 tsp	xanthan gum	5 mL
1 tsp	ground cinnamon	5 mL
1 tsp	baking soda	5 mL
1½ tsp	gluten-free baking powder, divided	7 mL
½ tsp	fine sea salt	2 mL
½ cup	unsweetened applesauce	125 mL
½ cup	raw agave nectar (see Tips, left)	125 mL
½ cup	unsweetened non-dairy milk (see Tips, left)	125 mL
¼ cup	melted coconut oil (see Tips, left)	60 mL
1 tsp	alcohol-free organic vanilla extract	5 mL
4	ripe bananas, mashed	4

1. In a bowl, whisk together flour blend, xanthan gum, cinnamon, baking soda, 1 tsp (5 mL) baking powder and salt.

2. In another bowl, whisk together applesauce, remaining ½ tsp (2 mL) baking powder, agave nectar, milk, coconut oil, vanilla and mashed bananas. Add to dry ingredients and stir until just combined.

3. Pour batter into prepared pan and bake on middle rack of preheated oven for 55 to 60 minutes, or until a toothpick inserted in center of loaf comes out clean.

4. Remove from oven and let cool in pan for 30 minutes. Serve immediately or store for up to 2 days in an airtight container at room temperature.

Variation

Chocolate Walnut Banana Bread: After the applesauce mixture and dry ingredients have been incorporated in Step 2, fold in ½ cup (125 mL) non-dairy chocolate chips and ¼ cup (60 mL) chopped raw walnuts.

Zucchini Bread

The addition of shredded zucchini gives this sweet bread a healthy dose of vegetable and fiber, making it a particularly nutritious snack.

**MAKES 1 LOAF
(12 TO 16 SLICES)**

Tips

To melt the coconut oil, gently warm it in a small skillet over low heat.

Baking powder is a rising agent made from an alkali (bicarbonate of soda) and an acid (cream of tartar), plus a filler such as corn flour or rice flour to absorb moisture. The powder is activated when liquid is added, producing carbon dioxide, which forms bubbles that cause the mixture to expand. Check the label to ensure that the brand you are buying is gluten-free.

After shredding the zucchini, use your hands to squeeze as much water from it as you can. Place on paper towels to drain off any excess liquid before measuring and adding to the recipe.

To make zucchini muffins: Divide batter into a 12-cup muffin pan, greased or lined with silicone or paper cups. Bake at 375°F (190°C) for 25 minutes or until tops spring back when lightly touched.

- Preheat oven to 350°F (180°C)
- 9- by 5-inch (23 by 12.5 cm) loaf pan, greased

2 tbsp	ground raw flax seeds	30 mL
6 tbsp	warm water	90 mL
1½ cups	All-Purpose Gluten-Free Flour Blend (page 561)	375 mL
2 tsp	gluten-free baking powder (see Tips, left)	10 mL
2 tsp	ground cinnamon	10 mL
¾ tsp	xanthan gum	3 mL
½ tsp	baking soda	2 mL
½ tsp	fine sea salt	2 mL
1 cup	organic coconut sugar	250 mL
⅓ cup	melted coconut oil (see Tips, left)	75 mL
¼ cup	Coconut Milk (page 62)	60 mL
1 tbsp	alcohol-free organic vanilla extract	15 mL
1 tsp	freshly squeezed lemon juice	5 mL
1 cup	drained shredded zucchini (see Tips, left)	250 mL

1. In a small bowl, whisk together ground flax seeds and warm water. Cover and set aside for about 10 minutes, so flax can absorb the liquid and swell.

2. In a large bowl, whisk together flour blend, baking powder, cinnamon, xanthan gum, baking soda and salt.

3. In another large bowl, whisk together coconut sugar, coconut oil, coconut milk, vanilla and lemon juice. Add soaked flax and stir until well combined and no lumps remain. Add dry ingredients and stir until well combined. Fold in shredded zucchini.

4. Pour batter into prepared pan and bake on middle rack of preheated oven for 55 to 60 minutes, or until a toothpick inserted in center of loaf comes out clean.

5. Remove from oven and let cool in pan for 5 minutes, then transfer to a wire rack to cool completely. Serve immediately or store for up to 7 days in an airtight container at room temperature.

Blueberry Squares

This summery dessert is the perfect finish to any warm-weather meal. I particularly enjoy these squares with a nice glass of chilled white wine.

Tips

You can replace the fresh blueberries with an equal quantity of frozen. You will need to increase the baking time by 5 minutes.

To melt the coconut oil, gently warm it in a small skillet over low heat.

Baking powder is a rising agent made from an alkali (bicarbonate of soda) and an acid (cream of tartar), plus a filler such as corn flour or rice flour to absorb moisture. The powder is activated when liquid is added, producing carbon dioxide, which forms bubbles that cause the mixture to expand. Check the label to ensure that the brand you are buying is gluten-free.

- Preheat oven to 350°F (180°C)
- 13- by 9-inch (33 by 23 cm) baking pan, greased

1½ cups	fresh blueberries	375 mL
3½ cups	All-Purpose Gluten-Free Flour Blend, divided (page 561)	875 mL
1½ cups	Almond Milk (page 61)	375 mL
2 tsp	freshly grated lemon zest	10 mL
3 tbsp	freshly squeezed lemon juice	45 mL
1½ cups	organic coconut sugar	375 mL
½ cup	unsweetened applesauce	125 mL
⅓ cup	melted coconut oil (see Tips, left)	75 mL
1½ tsp	alcohol-free organic vanilla extract	7 mL
1½ tsp	alcohol-free organic lemon oil or extract	7 mL
2 tsp	gluten-free baking powder (see Tips, left)	10 mL
1 tsp	baking soda	5 mL
½ tsp	fine sea salt	2 mL

1. In a bowl, toss blueberries with 1 tbsp (15 mL) flour blend until evenly coated. Set aside.

2. In another bowl, whisk together almond milk and lemon juice. Set aside for 5 minutes so the milk can curdle. Add lemon zest, coconut sugar, applesauce, coconut oil, vanilla and lemon oil. Whisk until well combined.

3. In a large bowl, whisk together remaining flour blend, baking powder, baking soda and salt. Make a well in the center. Add curdled milk mixture and stir until well combined. Fold in floured blueberries.

4. Spread batter evenly in prepared pan. Bake on middle rack in preheated oven for 28 to 30 minutes, or until a toothpick inserted in the center comes out clean.

5. Remove from oven and let cool in pan on a wire rack for 10 minutes, then invert onto rack to cool completely. Cut into squares. Serve immediately or store for up to 2 days in an airtight container at room temperature.

Apple Strudel Loaf

This loaf makes a great dessert for a dinner party or simply a delicious sweet treat.

Tips

Baking powder is a rising agent made from an alkali (bicarbonate of soda) and an acid (cream of tartar), plus a filler such as corn flour or rice flour to absorb moisture. The powder is activated when liquid is added, producing carbon dioxide, which forms bubbles that cause the mixture to expand. Check the label to ensure that the brand you are buying is gluten-free.

Higher-fat non-dairy milks, such as Almond Milk (page 61), Cashew Milk (page 61) or Hemp and Chia Milk (page 64), work best in this recipe.

- **Preheat oven to 350°F (180°C)**
- **9- by 5-inch (23 by 12.5 cm) loaf pan, greased**

LOAF

2½ cups	All-Purpose Gluten-Free Flour Blend (page 561)	625 mL
1 tsp	gluten-free baking powder (see Tips, left)	5 mL
1 tsp	ground cinnamon	5 mL
½ tsp	xanthan gum	2 mL
½ tsp	baking soda	2 mL
½ tsp	fine sea salt	2 mL
¼ tsp	ground cardamom	1 mL
¼ tsp	ground ginger	1 mL
¼ tsp	ground cloves	1 mL
1 cup	non-dairy milk (see Tips, left)	250 mL
1 tbsp	freshly squeezed lemon juice	15 mL
2 tbsp	ground raw flax seeds	30 mL
6 tbsp	hot water	90 mL
1 cup	organic coconut sugar	250 mL
⅓ cup	melted coconut oil (see Tips, page 449)	75 mL
1½ tsp	alcohol-free organic vanilla extract	7 mL
1	apple, peeled, cored and shredded (see Tips, page 449)	1

TOPPING

¼ cup	brown rice flour	60 mL
¼ cup	organic coconut sugar	60 mL
3 tbsp	melted coconut oil	45 mL
2½ tbsp	tapioca flour	37 mL
1 tsp	ground cinnamon	5 mL
⅛ tsp	ground cardamom	0.5 mL
⅛ tsp	ground ginger	0.5 mL
⅛ tsp	ground cloves	0.5 mL
Pinch	fine sea salt	Pinch

Tips

To melt the coconut oil, gently warm it in a small skillet over low heat.

Use the large holes on a box grater to shred the apple. Use your hands to squeeze out excess moisture before adding to the recipe.

The topping on this loaf will adhere better if it is chilled before baking. If you have time, cover in plastic wrap and refrigerate for 3 hours or overnight. Scatter and bake as directed.

1. *Loaf:* In a large bowl, whisk together flour blend, baking powder, cinnamon, xanthan gum, baking soda, salt, cardamom, ginger and cloves. Set aside.

2. In a medium bowl, whisk together milk and lemon juice. Set aside for 5 minutes to curdle.

3. In a small bowl, whisk together ground flax seeds and hot water. Cover and set aside for about 10 minutes, so flax can absorb the liquid and swell.

4. Add soaked flax, coconut sugar, coconut oil and vanilla to the curdled milk and stir well. Add to dry ingredients and, using a spatula, fold until just combined. Fold in apple. Transfer mixture to prepared loaf pan.

5. *Topping:* In a clean bowl, whisk together rice flour, coconut sugar, coconut oil, tapioca flour, cinnamon, cardamom, ginger, cloves and salt, until well combined. Scatter topping mixture evenly over loaf batter.

6. Bake on middle rack of preheated oven for 65 minutes, or until a toothpick inserted into center of loaf comes out clean. Remove from oven and let cool in pan for 30 minutes, then turn out onto a wire rack and cool completely. Serve immediately or store for up to 2 days in an airtight container at room temperature.

Variation

Apple Strudel Muffins: Divide batter into a 12-cup muffin pan, greased or lined with silicone or paper cups, and sprinkle each portion with topping mixture. Bake in preheated oven for 25 to 30 minutes, or until tops are brown and spring back when lightly touched.

Peach Crumble

This summer-fresh dessert is perfect served with a big scoop of Salted Caramel Ice Cream (page 520).

MAKES 4 SERVINGS

Tips

To melt the coconut oil, gently warm it in a small skillet over low heat.

To peel peaches: Fill a bowl with ice water and set aside. In a small saucepan, bring to a boil 8 cups (2 L) water. Using a paring knife, score the bottom of each peach with a small X, just piercing the skin. Blanch peaches in boiling water for 30 seconds. Transfer immediately to ice water to stop cooking. When peaches are cool, use your fingers to peel off the skins.

To ripen peaches more quickly, leave them in a warm, sunny place in your kitchen. Once they ripen, refrigerate them to extend their shelf life.

This recipe also works well in four 3- to 4-inch (7.5 cm to 10 cm) ramekins, for individual servings, or an 8-inch (20 cm) soufflé dish. If using ramekins, reduce the cooking time to about 15 minutes.

- **Preheat oven to 350°F (180°C)**
- **6-cup (1.5 L) casserole dish, greased (see Tips, left)**

CRUMBLE

1½ cups	almond flour	375 mL
1 tbsp	melted coconut oil (see Tips, left)	15 mL
1 tsp	organic coconut sugar	5 mL
¼ tsp	fine sea salt	1 mL

FILLING

4	peaches, peeled (see Tips, left)	4
¼ cup	organic coconut sugar	60 mL
3 tbsp	melted coconut oil	45 mL
1 tsp	alcohol-free organic vanilla extract	5 mL
½ tsp	ground cinnamon	2 mL
¼ tsp	ground cardamom	1 mL
⅛ tsp	fine sea salt	0.5 mL

1. *Crumble:* In a mixing bowl, whisk together almond flour, coconut oil, coconut sugar and salt. Divide mixture in half.

2. Press half of the crumble mixture into bottom of prepared casserole dish. Bake in preheated oven for 7 minutes, until golden brown. Remove from oven and set aside to cool.

3. *Filling:* Cut each peeled peach in half lengthwise and remove the stone. Cut each half lengthwise into 4 or 5 slices. Lay peach slices evenly over cooled crust.

4. In a bowl, whisk together coconut sugar, coconut oil, vanilla, cinnamon, cardamom and salt. Spoon mixture over peaches. Spread reserved crumble mixture evenly overtop.

5. Bake in preheated oven for 25 minutes, until top is golden brown and filling is bubbling hot. Remove from oven and set aside for 10 minutes to cool. Serve immediately or let cool completely, then cover and refrigerate for up to 3 days.

Strawberry Rhubarb Crumble

Make this treat in summer, when local strawberries are in season.

MAKES 6 SERVINGS

Tips

The coconut oil in this recipe should be firm. Measure it at room temperature, when it has a soft and creamy consistency. Then place in the refrigerator for 1 hour prior to using.

Placing the ramekins on a parchment-lined baking sheet protects the oven (and the baking sheet) from any fruit juices that may leak out, making cleanup a cinch.

If you prefer your fruit soft and gooey, increase the baking time to 35 minutes.

- Preheat oven to 350°F (180°C)
- Six ¾-cup (175 mL) ramekins, greased
- Baking sheet, lined with parchment paper (see Tips, left)

2 cups	sliced hulled strawberries	500 mL
1 cup	chopped rhubarb	250 mL
1 tsp	organic coconut sugar	5 mL
½ cup	quinoa flakes	125 mL
½ cup	millet flour	125 mL
½ cup	chopped raw pecans	125 mL
½ cup	packed organic raw cane sugar, such as turbinado or muscovado	125 mL
½ tsp	ground cinnamon	2 mL
¼ tsp	fine sea salt	1 mL
¼ cup	coconut oil, refrigerated (see Tips, left)	60 mL
1 tbsp	coconut butter	15 mL

1. In a large bowl, toss together strawberries, rhubarb and coconut sugar. Divide mixture among prepared ramekins.

2. In another large bowl, whisk together quinoa flakes, millet flour, pecans, cane sugar, cinnamon and salt.

3. In a small bowl, combine coconut oil and coconut butter. Using your fingers, rub mixture into dry ingredients until a crumbly texture is achieved. Sprinkle evenly over fruit.

4. Place ramekins on prepared baking sheet and bake in preheated oven for 25 minutes, until tops are golden brown and filling is bubbling hot. Serve immediately or set aside to cool, then cover and refrigerate for up to 3 days.

Variations

Gingered Pear Rhubarb Crumble: Substitute 3 cups (750 mL) thinly sliced pears for the strawberries and add 1 tbsp (15 mL) minced gingerroot in Step 1.

Substitute an equal amount of blueberries, blackberries or raspberries for the strawberries.

Apple Crisp

This is a warm and comforting dessert the whole family will love. Oats spiced with cinnamon are baked to crispiness over sweet apples.

MAKES 6 TO 8 SERVINGS

Tips

I like to use Pink Lady, Mutsu or Granny Smith apples for this recipe, as they hold their shape when baked.

Be sure to purchase organic cornstarch in order to avoid GMOs.

Most oats are processed in facilities that contain gluten. Look for certified gluten-free oats.

To make the almond flour for this recipe: Place 5 tbsp (75 mL) raw almonds in a food processor fitted with the metal blade. Process until flour-like in consistency. (Be careful not to overprocess into a paste.) If you prefer, purchase prepared almond flour.

To melt the coconut oil, gently warm it in a small skillet over low heat.

- **Preheat oven to 350°F (180°C)**
- **11- by 7-inch (28 by 18 cm) glass baking dish, greased**

8 cups	thinly sliced peeled, cored apples (see Tips, left)	2 L
6 tbsp	organic coconut sugar	90 mL
1 tbsp	organic cornstarch	15 mL
1 tsp	ground cinnamon	5 mL
1 tsp	freshly squeezed lemon juice	5 mL
½ tsp	alcohol-free organic vanilla extract	2 mL
Pinch	fine sea salt	Pinch

TOPPING

⅔ cup	organic coconut sugar	150 mL
⅔ cup	quick-cooking gluten-free rolled oats (see Tips, left)	150 mL
⅓ cup	All-Purpose Gluten-Free Flour Blend (page 561)	75 mL
⅓ cup	almond flour (see Tips, left)	75 mL
½ tsp	ground cinnamon	2 mL
1 tbsp	ground raw flax seeds	15 mL
Pinch	fine sea salt	Pinch
6 tbsp	melted coconut oil (see Tips, left)	90 mL

1. In a bowl, combine apples, coconut sugar, cornstarch, cinnamon, lemon juice, vanilla and salt. Toss together until well combined. Transfer to prepared baking dish.

2. *Topping:* In a large bowl, whisk together coconut sugar, oats, flour blend, almond flour, cinnamon, ground flax seeds and salt. Add coconut oil and stir to combine. The mixture should hold together when pressed in your hand — if it is too dry, add 1 to 2 tbsp (15 to 30 mL) more coconut oil.

3. Sprinkle topping evenly over filling. Bake in preheated oven for 40 to 45 minutes or until apples are bubbling and top is golden brown. Serve immediately or set aside to cool, then cover and refrigerate for up to 3 days.

Pineapple Upside-Down Cake

This upside-down cake whips up in no time at all. Juicy pineapple is paired with flavorful vanilla and sweet coconut sugar for a delicious and satisfying treat. For a true guilty pleasure, serve it with a big scoop of Vegan Vanilla Ice Cream (page 513).

MAKES ONE 8-INCH (20 CM) CAKE

Tips

For an even sweeter treat, substitute an equal amount of freshly squeezed pineapple juice for the water.

You can use drained canned organic pineapple rings. Look for a brand with no sugar added (check the label).

- **Preheat oven to 350°F (180°C)**
- **8-inch (20 cm) springform pan, greased**

6	slices pineapple, each about ¼ inch (1 cm) thick	6
1¼ cups	organic coconut sugar, divided	300 mL
1½ cups	All-Purpose Gluten-Free Flour Blend (page 561)	375 mL
1 tsp	baking soda	5 mL
½ tsp	fine sea salt	2 mL
1 cup	water (see Tips, left)	250 mL
⅓ cup	grapeseed oil	75 mL
1 tbsp	raw (unpasteurized) apple cider vinegar	15 mL
1 tsp	alcohol-free organic vanilla extract	5 mL

1. Arrange pineapple slices side by side in a single layer in prepared pan, making sure to cover the bottom completely. Sprinkle with ¼ cup (60 mL) coconut sugar. Set aside.

2. In a large bowl, whisk together flour blend, remaining 1 cup (250 mL) coconut sugar, baking soda and salt.

3. In another bowl, whisk together water, oil, vinegar and vanilla. Add to dry ingredients and whisk until no lumps remain.

4. Pour evenly over pineapple slices. Bake in preheated oven for 30 to 35 minutes or until a toothpick inserted into the center comes out clean. Remove from oven and set aside to cool completely, about 1 hour.

5. To remove cake from pan, run a knife around the edges. Loosen hinges on pan and invert a serving platter overtop. Tightly holding plate and pan together, turn over to invert cake onto plate; carefully remove pan. Serve immediately or cover and refrigerate for up to 3 days.

Apple Pie

Apple pie is the ultimate classic dessert. It is best served à la mode, with some delicious Vegan Vanilla Ice Cream (page 513) and — to gild the lily — a drizzle of maple syrup.

MAKES 8 SERVINGS

Tips

Use Fuji, Rome, Granny Smith or Golden Delicious apples for this recipe. Their firm texture and higher level of pectin will help them stand up to the oven temperature and retain their shape.

You should have about 12 cups (3 L) sliced apples.

- 10-inch (25 cm) deep-dish pie plate, greased
- Mandoline
- Baking sheet, lined with parchment paper

CRUST

1½ cups	All-Purpose Gluten-Free Flour Blend (page 561)	375 mL
2 tbsp	organic coconut sugar	30 mL
½ tsp	xanthan gum	2 mL
½ tsp	fine sea salt	2 mL
¼ tsp	ground nutmeg	1 mL
½ cup	unsalted non-dairy butter or margarine, chilled and cut into ½-inch (1 cm) cubes	125 mL
2 tbsp	unsweetened applesauce	30 mL
½ tsp	alcohol-free organic vanilla extract	2 mL
¼ cup to 6 tbsp	ice water	60 to 90 mL

FILLING

8 to 9	baking apples (see Tips, left)	8 to 9
½ cup	organic coconut sugar	125 mL
1 tbsp	ground cinnamon	15 mL
2 tbsp	brown rice flour	30 mL
½ tsp	ground allspice	2 mL
¼ cup	unsalted non-dairy butter or margarine, chilled and cut into small pieces	60 mL
2 tbsp	freshly squeezed lemon juice	30 mL
½ tsp	alcohol-free organic vanilla extract	2 mL

TOPPING

¼ cup	organic coconut sugar	60 mL
1 tsp	ground cinnamon	5 mL
	Non-dairy milk, for brushing	

Tips

Use brown rice flour or sorghum flour for dusting the work surface when rolling out the dough.

If your dough is extremely cold, it may be too firm to roll properly. Allow it to rest at room temperature for a few minutes before rolling it out.

Baking the pie on a baking sheet lined with parchment makes cleanup easy, especially since this generously filled pie is likely to drip.

1. *Crust:* In a large bowl, whisk together flour blend, coconut sugar, xanthan gum, salt and nutmeg. Add butter, applesauce and vanilla. Using two knives, a pastry cutter or your fingers, work into dry ingredients until butter is the size of small peas. Add $\frac{1}{4}$ cup (60 mL) ice water and knead until a dough is formed, being careful not to overmix (if dough is still crumbly, add more ice water, up to 2 tbsp (30 mL), until it holds together).

2. Divide dough into 2 equal portions. Wrap each portion in plastic wrap and refrigerate for 1 hour or overnight.

3. *Filling:* Peel and core apples. Using mandoline, slice about $\frac{1}{8}$ inch (3 mm) thick. Place in a large bowl and add coconut sugar, cinnamon, rice flour and allspice. Toss until evenly coated. Add butter, lemon juice and vanilla and toss until evenly coated.

4. *Topping:* In a small bowl, whisk together coconut sugar and cinnamon. Set aside.

5. Preheat oven to 400°F (200°C).

6. Divide dough in half. On a lightly floured work surface (see Tips, left), roll out one portion into a circle about 12 inches (30 cm) in diameter and $\frac{1}{8}$ inch (3 mm) thick. Roll pastry loosely around rolling pin, then unroll over pie plate. Press into pie plate, bringing it up the sides of the pan and just over the edges. Trim edges as necessary.

7. Pour apple mixture, including accumulated liquid, into pastry-lined pie plate. (It will seem like a lot of apples, but don't worry — they will shrink when baked.)

8. Roll out remaining dough as in Step 6. Roll pastry loosely around rolling pin, then unroll over filling, covering apples completely. Using the tines of a fork, push down gently around edges to seal crust. Trim excess dough as necessary. Using a knife, cut a few slits in the top of the pie to allow steam to escape.

9. Brush top crust with a little non-dairy milk and sprinkle with topping mixture.

10. Place on prepared baking sheet (see Tips, left). Bake in preheated oven for 15 minutes, then reduce heat to 350°F (180°C) and bake for 40 to 50 minutes longer, until crust is golden brown and apples are bubbling hot. Remove from oven and set aside to cool. Serve immediately or store for up to 2 days in an airtight container at room temperature.

Pecan Pie

This sweet, rich treat is perfect for special occasions and holidays. Serve with a dollop of Whipped Coconut Cream (page 565).

(page 565)

MAKES 8 SERVINGS

Tips

You can substitute an equal amount of buckwheat, sorghum or oat flour for the brown rice flour.

Be sure to use raw (not processed) agave nectar. It is a 100% natural (non-GMO) sweetener that contains naturally occurring fructose and is low on the glycemic scale, which means that it releases glucose slowly, providing sustained energy.

To melt the coconut oil, gently warm it in a small skillet over low heat.

- **Preheat oven to 350°F (180°C)**
- **Food processor**
- **9-inch (23 cm) pie plate, greased**
- **Baking sheet, lined with parchment paper**

PRESS PASTRY

1 cup	raw almonds	250 mL
1 cup	brown rice flour	250 mL
¼ cup	raw agave nectar (see Tips, left)	60 mL
¼ cup	melted coconut oil (see Tips, left)	60 mL
2 tsp	ground cinnamon	10 mL
6	pitted Medjool dates	6

FILLING

1 cup	raw pecans	250 mL
⅔ cup	cashew butter (see Tips, 457)	150 mL
¼ cup	pure maple syrup	60 mL
12	pitted Medjool dates	12
¼ cup	water	60 mL

TOPPING

1 cup	raw pecans, chopped	250 mL
2 tbsp	pure maple syrup	30 mL
1 tsp	ground cinnamon	5 mL
¼ tsp	fine sea salt	1 mL

1. *Press Pastry:* In food processor fitted with the metal blade, process almonds until flour-like in consistency. Add rice flour, agave nectar, coconut oil, cinnamon and dates. Process until well combined and mixture holds together.

2. Using your hands or a spatula, press dough evenly into prepared pie plate. Bake in preheated oven for 15 minutes, until crust is browned and firm to the touch. Remove from oven and set aside to cool completely.

3. *Filling:* Meanwhile, in clean food processor work bowl, process pecans into a meal (the nuts should stick together, almost like pecan butter). Add cashew butter and process until well combined. Add maple syrup and dates and process until smooth.

4. With the motor running, pour water through the feed tube in a slow, steady stream and process until smooth. Spread filling evenly over cooled crust and set aside.

5. *Topping:* In a bowl, toss together chopped pecans, maple syrup, cinnamon and salt. Spread evenly over prepared baking sheet and bake in preheated oven for 5 minutes or until lightly browned.

6. Crumble evenly over filling. Refrigerate pie for at least 1 hour, to set. Serve immediately or refrigerate for up to 3 days in an airtight container.

Blueberry Cheesecake

Serve this light, creamy cheesecake at your next special occasion. It's sure to please even the most discerning palate.

Tips

To make the Triple Ginger Cookie crumbs, place 2 or 3 cookies in a food processor fitted with the metal blade and process until no large pieces remain (be careful not to overprocess — you want to retain some texture).

To melt the coconut oil, gently warm it in a small skillet over low heat.

To soak the cashews: Place them in a bowl and cover with 4 cups (1 L) water. Cover and set aside for 30 minutes or overnight (refrigerate if overnight). Drain, discarding liquid.

- **Preheat oven to 325°F (160°C)**
- **Food processor**
- **8-inch (20 cm) springform pan, greased and wrapped in aluminum foil (see Tips, page 459)**
- **13- by 9-inch (33 by 23 cm) metal baking pan**

CRUST

¾ cup	ground Triple Ginger Cookies (page 428; see Tips, left)	175 mL
¼ cup	melted coconut oil (see Tips, left)	60 mL
2 tbsp	organic coconut sugar	30 mL

FILLING

1¼ cups	Almond Milk (page 61), divided	300 mL
¾ cup	organic coconut sugar	175 mL
3 tbsp	arrowroot starch	45 mL
1 tsp	alcohol-free organic vanilla extract	5 mL
1 cup	raw cashews, soaked (see Tips, left)	250 mL
1 cup	drained cooked white beans (see Tips, page 459)	250 mL
½ cup	blueberries	125 mL
2 tbsp	melted coconut oil	30 mL
1 tbsp	raw (unpasteurized) apple cider vinegar	15 mL
1 tsp	agar powder (see Tips, page 459)	5 mL
¼ tsp	fine sea salt	1 mL

1. In food processor fitted with the metal blade, combine cookie crumbs, coconut oil and coconut sugar. Process until crumbly (you can also do this in a mixing bowl, using a wooden spoon). Press firmly over bottom and sides of prepared springform pan. Set aside.

2. *Filling:* In a bowl, whisk together ¼ cup (60 mL) almond milk, coconut sugar, arrowroot and vanilla. Set aside. Rinse out work bowl.

Tips

Navy or cannellini beans work best for this recipe. Make sure they have been cooked until soft, or you will get small pieces of bean in the cheesecake.

Agar powder is made from a seaweed and is sometimes referred to as "sea gelatin." It is available in most well-stocked supermarkets and natural food stores.

To ensure that water doesn't seep into the cake during cooking, place the springform pan on one large, seamless piece of foil, then wrap the foil up the sides and over the top edge.

3. In clean work bowl, combine remaining 1 cup (250 mL) almond milk, soaked cashews, beans, blueberries, coconut oil, vinegar, agar and salt. Process until smooth, stopping the motor to scrape down sides of work bowl as necessary. Add reserved almond milk mixture and process until well combined. Spread evenly over crust.

4. Place baking pan on middle rack of preheated oven. Place cheesecake in center of pan. Pour about 2 cups (500 mL) hot water into pan, ensuring that it does not overflow (it should reach halfway up the springform pan; add more water if necessary).

5. Bake in preheated oven for 55 to 60 minutes, until edges are set and center jiggles slightly.

6. Remove from oven and set springform pan on a wire rack to cool for at least 1 hour.

7. To remove cake from pan, run a knife around the edges and then loosen hinge and remove side piece. Refrigerate cake for 1 hour to set. Serve immediately or transfer to an airtight container and refrigerate for up to 4 days.

Carrot Cake

This is a classic carrot cake — lightly spiced, moist and flavorful, and topped with a rich caramel frosting.

MAKES 10 TO 12 SERVINGS

- **Preheat oven to 350°F (180°C)**
- **Food processor**
- **Two 9-inch (23 cm) round cake pans, greased**

Tips

Baking powder is a rising agent made from an alkali (bicarbonate of soda) and an acid (cream of tartar), plus a filler such as cornstarch or wheat starch to absorb moisture. The powder is activated when liquid is added, producing carbon dioxide, which forms bubbles that cause the mixture to expand. Check the label to ensure that the brand you are buying is gluten-free.

To shred the carrots, use the large holes on a box grater.

To melt the coconut oil, gently warm it in a small skillet over low heat.

CAKE

¾ cup	warm water	175 mL
¼ cup	ground raw flax seeds	60 mL
2¾ cups	All-Purpose Gluten-Free Flour Blend (page 561)	425 mL
1 tbsp	ground cinnamon	15 mL
1¼ tsp	gluten-free baking powder (see Tips, left)	6 mL
1¼ tsp	baking soda	6 mL
1 tsp	fine sea salt	5 mL
½ tsp	ground nutmeg	2 mL
Pinch	ground cloves	Pinch
Pinch	ground ginger	Pinch
4 cups	shredded carrots (see Tips, left)	1 L
1¼ cups	organic coconut sugar	300 mL
¾ cup	melted coconut oil (see Tips, left)	175 mL

FROSTING

4 cups	organic coconut sugar, finely ground (see Tips, page 461)	1 L
¼ cup	organic cornstarch	60 mL
¾ cup	unsalted non-dairy butter or margarine, chilled	175 mL
2 tbsp	Almond Milk (page 61)	30 mL
2 tsp	raw (unpasteurized) apple cider vinegar	10 mL
1 tsp	alcohol-free organic vanilla extract	5 mL
1 tsp	freshly squeezed lemon juice	5 mL
Pinch	fine sea salt	Pinch

1. *Cake:* In a small bowl, whisk together warm water and ground flax seeds. Cover and set aside for about 10 minutes, so flax can absorb the liquid and swell.

Tips

To grind the coconut sugar: In a blender, process 4 cups (1 L) coconut sugar at high speed until flour-like in consistency. Transfer to a bowl.

For a professional presentation, first apply a thin coating of icing on top and all around the layered cake, sealing in the crumbs — this is called a "crumb coat." Then add a thicker layer of icing overtop and smooth it out.

2. In a large bowl, whisk together flour blend, cinnamon, baking powder, baking soda, salt, nutmeg, cloves and ginger. Add carrots and stir until well combined.

3. In food processor fitted with the metal blade, combine flaxseed mixture and coconut sugar; process until well combined. With the motor running, pour coconut oil through the feed tube in a slow, steady stream; process until combined. Add to carrot mixture and, using a spatula, stir until well combined.

4. Spread batter evenly in prepared pans, dividing equally. Bake in preheated oven for 25 to 30 minutes, or until a toothpick inserted into center of cakes comes out clean. Remove pans from oven and place on wire racks to cool completely, about 1 hour. Run a knife around the inside edge of each cake pan to loosen. Turn out onto racks.

5. *Frosting:* In food processor fitted with the metal blade, pulse coconut sugar and cornstarch to combine. Add chilled butter, almond milk, vinegar, vanilla, lemon juice and salt. Process until smooth and creamy. Transfer to an airtight container and refrigerate until firm, about 30 minutes.

6. *Assembly:* Place one cake layer on a serving platter. Place one-third of the frosting on top. Using a small offset spatula or butter knife, spread it in an even layer over cake.

7. Place second cake layer on top (some frosting will squeeze out the sides). Cover top and sides of cake with remaining frosting, smoothing it out and aligning and balancing cake overall (see Tips, left).

8. Refrigerate frosted cake for 30 minutes to set. Serve immediately or cover and refrigerate for up to 3 days.

Variation

The coconut sugar frosting has a luscious caramel flavor that may not be what you are accustomed to in a carrot cake frosting. While I avoid the use of refined sugar, if you prefer, feel free to substitute an equal quantity of organic confectioner's (icing) sugar for both the coconut sugar and cornstarch in the frosting. Check the label to make sure it is suitable for vegans.

Basic Scones

These soft, flaky scones are perfect for a weekend brunch, smeared with peanut butter as a snack, or served as a dessert, accompanied by Whipped Coconut Cream (page 565) and fresh berries.

MAKES 16 SCONES

Tips

When working with any flour, particularly those that are gluten-free, whisk before measuring. This aerates the flour and ensures more accurate measuring. Be sure to use a dry measure (not a glass measuring cup) and to level off with the side of a knife.

Baking powder is a rising agent made from an alkali (bicarbonate of soda) and an acid (cream of tartar), plus a filler such as cornstarch or wheat starch to absorb moisture. The powder is activated when liquid is added, producing carbon dioxide, which forms bubbles that cause the mixture to expand. Check the label to ensure that the brand you are buying is gluten-free.

- Preheat oven to 400°F (200°C)
- Large baking sheet, lined with parchment paper

3 cups	All-Purpose Gluten-Free Flour Blend (page 561)	750 mL
¼ cup	organic coconut sugar, divided	60 mL
2 tsp	gluten-free baking powder (see Tips, left)	10 mL
½ tsp	fine sea salt	2 mL
1 cup	unsalted non-dairy butter or margarine, chilled	250 mL
1¼ cups	non-dairy milk (approx.; see Tips, page 463)	300 mL
	Brown rice flour, for dusting	
	Additional non-dairy milk, for brushing	

1. In a bowl, whisk together flour blend, 3 tbsp (45 mL) coconut sugar, baking powder and salt. Using two knives, a pastry cutter or your fingers, cut in cold butter until mixture resembles small peas.

2. Make a well in the center. Add milk and stir just until combined (dough should be sticky to the touch).

3. Lightly dust work surface with rice flour. Turn out dough and knead gently until it just begins to stick together, about 10 times. If dough is too sticky, add a bit more brown rice flour. Do not overmix — it is okay if a little flour is showing in the dough.

4. Divide dough into 2 equal portions. Using your hands, form each portion into a rectangle about 6 inches (15 cm) long and 2 inches (5 cm) wide. Cut each rectangle in half crosswise, then cut each half in half diagonally, to end up with 8 triangles.

Tips

Higher-fat non-dairy milks, such as Almond Milk (page 61), Cashew Milk (page 61) or Hemp and Chia Milk (page 64), work best in this recipe.

Because gluten-free flours vary so much among brands, it is hard to be precise about the quantity of liquid required in any recipe. If your dough is sticky, add brown rice flour as noted in Step 3.

5. Place scones on prepared baking sheet. Brush tops with a little milk and sprinkle lightly with remaining sugar.

6. Bake in preheated oven for about 25 minutes, until golden brown and tops are firm. Serve immediately or transfer to a wire rack to cool completely. The scones will keep for up to 3 days in an airtight container at room temperature.

Variations

Sun-Dried Tomato and Olive Scones: After adding the milk in step 2, mix in ⅓ cup (75 mL) chopped drained, reconstituted sun-dried tomatoes, ¼ cup (60 mL) chopped black olives, 1 tbsp (15 mL) finely chopped fresh rosemary and ½ tsp (2 mL) freshly ground black pepper. Reduce sugar to 2 tbsp (30 mL) and do not sprinkle any on top.

Dark Chocolate and Berry Scones: After adding the milk in Step 2, mix in 1 cup (250 mL) fresh raspberries, blueberries, strawberries or blackberries and ½ cup (125 mL) non-dairy chocolate chips.

Buttermilk Biscuits

These soft and fluffy biscuits are a perfect accompaniment to almost any meal. They are especially good served Southern style, with a large helping of Holiday Gravy (page 558).

MAKES 8 BISCUITS

Tips

When working with any flour, particularly those that are gluten-free, whisk before measuring. This aerates the flour and ensures more accurate measuring. Be sure to use a dry measure (not a glass measuring cup) and to level off with the side of a knife.

Baking powder is a rising agent made from an alkali (bicarbonate of soda) and an acid (cream of tartar), plus a filler such as cornstarch or sometimes wheat starch to absorb moisture. Check the label to ensure that the brand you are buying is gluten-free.

- Preheat oven to 450°F (230°C)
- 3- to 4-inch (7.5 to 10 cm) biscuit cutter (see Tips, page 465)
- Baking sheet, lined with parchment paper

1½ cups	Almond Milk (page 61)	375 mL
1 tbsp	freshly squeezed lemon juice	15 mL
2½ cups	All-Purpose Gluten-Free Flour Blend (page 561)	625 mL
1 tbsp	gluten-free baking powder (see Tips, left)	15 mL
1 tsp	xanthan gum	5 mL
¾ tsp	fine sea salt	3 mL
½ tsp	baking soda	2 mL
¼ cup	unsalted non-dairy butter or margarine, chilled	60 mL
	Brown rice flour, for dusting	
	Melted non-dairy butter or margarine, for brushing	

1. In a bowl, whisk together almond milk and lemon juice. Set aside for about 10 minutes, to let almond milk curdle.

2. In a separate large bowl, whisk together flour blend, baking powder, xanthan gum, salt and baking soda.

3. Using two knives, a pastry cutter or your fingers, cut in cold butter until mixture resembles small peas. Make a well in the center. Add milk mixture in a slow, steady stream, stirring constantly with a wooden spoon, and mix just until dough comes together and is slightly sticky.

4. Dust work surface generously with rice flour. Turn out dough onto floured surface and gently fold 5 or 6 times to form a disk 1 inch (2.5 cm) thick, handling the dough as little as possible. If dough seems too sticky, gently knead in a bit more flour, keeping in mind that the less you add, the fluffier and more tender the biscuits will be.

If you don't have a biscuit cutter, use an object of a similar shape and size that has sharp edges (such as a cocktail shaker lid or an empty can).

5. Using biscuit cutter, cut out biscuits by pushing straight down through dough. Repeat until all the dough is used up, reshaping and cutting leftover bits. Place biscuits on prepared baking sheet in two rows, making sure they just touch, so they will rise uniformly.

6. Brush tops of biscuits with melted butter. Using two fingers, gently press a small divot in the center of each (this helps them rise evenly and keeps the middle from puffing up).

7. Bake in preheated oven for about 15 minutes or until slightly golden brown. Serve immediately or let cool completely, then store for up to 3 days in an airtight container at room temperature.

Cheddar and Chive Biscuits

Serve these flaky biscuits slathered with a dollop of fresh non-dairy butter. For a real treat, dunk them in some Ranch Dip (page 80) as well.

MAKES 6 BISCUITS

Tips

When working with any flour, particularly those that are gluten-free, whisk before measuring. This aerates the flour and ensures more accurate measuring. Be sure to use a dry measure (not a glass measuring cup) and to level off with the side of a knife.

Baking powder is a rising agent made from an alkali (bicarbonate of soda) and an acid (cream of tartar), plus a filler such as cornstarch or sometimes wheat starch to absorb moisture. Check the label to ensure that the brand you are buying is gluten-free.

Place coconut oil in a small bowl and refrigerate until cold, about 15 minutes.

- **Preheat oven to 475°F (240°C)**
- **3- to 4-inch (7.5 to 10 cm) biscuit cutter**
- **Baking sheet, lined with parchment paper**

⅔ cup	Almond Milk (page 61)	150 mL
1 tsp	raw (unpasteurized) apple cider vinegar	5 mL
1 cup	All-Purpose Gluten-Free Flour Blend (page 561)	250 mL
1 tbsp	gluten-free baking powder (see Tips, left)	15 mL
1 tsp	fine sea salt	5 mL
½ tsp	xanthan gum	2 mL
2 tbsp	unsalted non-dairy butter or margarine, chilled	30 mL
2 tbsp	cool coconut oil (see Tips, left)	30 mL
1 cup	chopped Cashew Cheddar Cheese (page 535)	250 mL
½ cup	chopped fresh chives (see Tips, page 467)	125 mL
	Brown rice flour, for dusting	
	Melted non-dairy butter or margarine, for brushing	

1. In a small bowl, whisk together almond milk and vinegar. Set aside for about 10 minutes, to let almond milk curdle.

2. In a large bowl, whisk together flour blend, baking powder, salt and xanthan gum. Using two knives, a pastry cutter or your fingers, cut in cold butter and coconut oil until mixture resembles small peas. Make a well in the center. Add curdled milk in a slow, steady stream, stirring constantly with a wooden spoon, and mix just until dough comes together and is slightly sticky.

3. Transfer dough to a lightly floured surface. Knead in chives and cheese until well distributed. Return dough to bowl, cover with a damp cloth or plastic wrap, and refrigerate for 30 minutes.

Substitute ¼ cup (60 mL) dried chives for the fresh chives.

For convenience, substitute an equal quantity of your favorite store-bought vegan Cheddar.

When cutting out the biscuits, do not "twist" the cutter. Cut straight down through the dough.

4. Dust work surface lightly with rice flour. Turn out dough and gently fold 5 or 6 times to form a disk ½ inch (1 cm) thick, handling dough as little as possible. If dough seems too sticky, gently knead in a bit more flour, keeping in mind that the less you add, the fluffier and more tender the biscuits will be.

5. Once dough is uniformly flattened, using biscuit cutter, cut out biscuits (see Tips, left). Repeat until all the dough is used up, reshaping and cutting leftover bits. Place biscuits on prepared baking sheet in two rows, making sure they just touch, so they will rise uniformly.

6. Brush tops of biscuits with melted non-dairy butter. Using two fingers, gently press a small divot in the center of each (this helps the biscuits rise evenly and keeps the middle from puffing up).

7. Bake in preheated oven for about 15 minutes, until dark golden brown. Serve immediately or let cool completely, then store for up to 3 days in an airtight container at room temperature. To reheat, place on a baking sheet lined with parchment paper and warm in a preheated 350°F (180°C) oven for about 8 minutes.

Variation

Olive and Herb Biscuits: Substitute 2 tbsp (30 mL) chopped fresh rosemary and 1 tbsp (15 mL) chopped fresh thyme leaves for the chives. Replace the Cashew Cheddar with 1 cup (250 mL) chopped kalamata olives.

Pizza Rolls

Serve these delicious Italian-inspired treats to your guests at your next party or gathering. The addition of vegan mozzarella makes this a particularly enjoyable snack.

MAKES ABOUT 8 ROLLS

Tips

Substitute a blend of ½ tsp (2 mL) dried oregano, ¼ tsp (1 mL) dried basil and ¼ tsp (1 mL) dried parsley flakes for the Italian seasoning.

You can replace the Garlicky Tomato Sauce in this recipe with an equal amount of your favorite store-bought tomato or pizza sauce.

- Stand mixer, fitted with dough hook
- Baking sheet, lined with parchment paper

3¼ cups	All-Purpose Gluten-Free Flour Blend (page 561)	800 mL
1½ tbsp	cane sugar	22 mL
2½ tsp	xanthan gum	12 mL
2¼ tsp	instant (fast-acting) yeast	11 mL
1 tsp	fine sea salt	5 mL
1 tsp	Italian seasoning (see Tips, left)	5 mL
¼ tsp	garlic powder	1 mL
6 tbsp	warm water	90 mL
2 tbsp	ground raw flax seeds	30 mL
1 cup	water	250 mL
¼ cup	extra virgin olive oil	60 mL
1 tsp	raw (unpasteurized) apple cider vinegar	5 mL
	Brown rice flour, for dusting	
1½ cups	Classic Garlicky Tomato Sauce (page 110; see Tips, left)	375 mL
1½ cups	Vegan Shredded Mozzarella (page 537; see Tip, page 469)	375 mL

1. In mixer bowl, combine flour blend, sugar, xanthan gum, yeast, salt, Italian seasoning and garlic powder. Attach dough hook and mix at medium speed until well combined.

2. In a small bowl, whisk together warm water and ground flax seeds. Cover and set aside for 8 to 10 minutes, so flax can absorb the liquid and swell.

3. In a large bowl, whisk together 1 cup (250 mL) water, oil, vinegar and soaked flax.

4. With mixer running at medium speed, add flaxseed mixture to dry ingredients. Mix until dough starts to pull away from sides of bowl, about 5 minutes. Cover bowl with a damp cloth and set aside for 20 minutes.

5. Lay a piece of parchment paper on a clean work surface and dust with rice flour. Turn out rested dough onto parchment. Dust with flour and cover with another piece of parchment. Using a rolling pin, roll out into a rectangle about 12 inches (30 cm) long and 10 inches (25 cm) wide — the dough should be about $\frac{1}{4}$ inch (0.5 cm) thick. Remove top piece of parchment.

6. Spread tomato sauce evenly overtop dough, leaving a 1-inch (2.5 cm) border around the edges. Sprinkle evenly with cheese.

7. Starting at nearest long side of rectangle, using the parchment to lift and guide, roll up dough as tightly as possible into a long cylinder. Pinch ends to seal. Cut cylinder crosswise into 1-inch (2.5 cm) slices.

8. Lay rolls flat on prepared baking sheet, spacing about 1 inch (2.5 cm) apart. Cover with a clean kitchen towel and set aside in a warm place for 30 minutes to rise.

9. Preheat oven to 400°F (200°C).

10. Remove towel and bake in preheated oven for 15 to 20 minutes, or until golden brown on top and slightly firm to the touch. Serve immediately or cool completely and store for up to 3 days in an airtight container at room temperature.

Caramelized Onion and Olive Flatbread

Serve this crispy bread with your favorite dip or sauce. I like it with Chia Whiz (page 85), Ranch Dip (page 80) or Black Olive and Walnut Butter (page 134).

**MAKES ABOUT
16 PIECES**

Tips

When working with any flour, particularly those that are gluten-free, whisk before measuring. This aerates the flour and ensures more accurate measuring. Be sure to use a dry measure (not a glass measuring cup) and to level off with the side of a knife.

I like to use kalamata olives for this recipe, but feel free to substitute any type of olive in the same quantity.

• **Baking sheet, lined with parchment paper**

1½ cups	warm water, divided	375 mL
¼ cup	ground raw flax seeds, divided	60 mL
1 tbsp	active dry yeast	15 mL
1 tbsp	organic coconut sugar	15 mL
3 tbsp	extra virgin olive oil	45 mL
3¼ cups	All-Purpose Gluten-Free Flour Blend (page 561)	800 mL
2 tsp	chopped fresh rosemary	10 mL
1 tsp	fine sea salt	5 mL
	Brown rice flour, for dusting	
1 tbsp	grapeseed oil	15 mL
2 cups	thinly sliced onions	500 mL
Pinch	fine sea salt	Pinch
½ cup	thinly sliced pitted kalamata olives	125 mL

1. In a mixing bowl, whisk together ½ cup (125 mL) warm water and 2 tbsp (30 mL) ground flax seeds. Cover and set aside for about 10 minutes, so flax can absorb the liquid and swell.

2. In another bowl, whisk together remaining 1 cup (250 mL) warm water, yeast and coconut sugar. Let stand until yeast begins to foam, about 5 minutes.

3. When flax has swelled, add to bloomed yeast. Add olive oil and whisk until combined.

4. In a large bowl, whisk together flour blend, rosemary, 1 tsp (5 mL) salt and remaining (unsoaked) flax seeds. Make a well in the center, add yeast mixture and stir well.

5. Lightly dust work surface with rice flour. Turn out dough onto floured surface and, using your hands, knead well. Shape into a round. Place dough in a clean bowl and cover with a clean, damp kitchen towel. Set aside for 30 minutes to rest.

6. Meanwhile, in a skillet over high heat, heat grapeseed oil. Add onions and pinch of salt; cook, stirring constantly, until just beginning to turn golden brown, about 5 minutes. Reduce heat to low and cook, stirring occasionally, until soft and golden, about 25 minutes. Remove from heat and set aside to cool.

7. When you are ready to bake, preheat oven to 425°F (220°C).

8. Uncover dough and punch down several times to remove air bubbles. Transfer to prepared baking sheet.

9. Using your hands, carefully flatten out dough — it should be about 1/8 inch (3 mm) thick and cover entire surface of sheet. Using the tines of a fork, poke holes in surface of dough to allow steam to escape.

10. Bake in preheated oven for 25 minutes or until golden on the bottom (lift up a corner to check). Remove from oven and reduce temperature to 350°F (180°C).

11. Spread caramelized onions and olives evenly overtop, right to the edges. Return to oven and bake for 10 minutes, or until bottom is golden brown and crispy. Let cool for 3 to 4 minutes before serving. Leftover flatbread can be stored for up to 3 days in an airtight container in the refrigerator.

Irish Soda Bread

This is a wonderful bread to serve with stews and soups — perfect for sopping up the flavors in the bottom of your bowl.

MAKES 1 LOAF (ABOUT 10 TO 12 SLICES)

Tips

Substitute an equal amount of raisins for the currants.

When working with any flour, particularly those that are gluten-free, whisk before measuring. This aerates the flour and ensures more accurate measuring. Be sure to use a dry measure (not a glass measuring cup) and to level off with the side of a knife.

- **Preheat oven to 350°F (180°C)**
- **Baking sheet, lined with parchment paper**

2¼ cups	All-Purpose Gluten-Free Flour Blend (page 561)	550 mL
¼ cup	ground raw flax seeds	60 mL
2 tsp	baking soda	10 mL
½ tsp	fine sea salt	2 mL
½ cup	dried currants (see Tip, left)	125 mL
1 tbsp	caraway seeds	15 mL
1 cup	non-dairy milk	250 mL
2 tbsp	extra virgin olive oil	30 mL
2 tsp	pure maple syrup	10 mL
2 tsp	freshly squeezed lemon juice	10 mL
	Brown rice flour, for dusting	

1. In a mixing bowl, combine flour blend, ground flax seeds, baking soda, salt, currants and caraway seeds. Whisk well.

2. In a large measuring cup, whisk together non-dairy milk, olive oil, maple syrup and lemon juice. Make a well in the center of dry ingredients and add milk mixture; mix until a smooth, uniform dough forms. The dough should pull away from the sides of the bowl easily. Set dough aside for 5 minutes to rest.

3. Dust a clean work surface with rice flour. Turn out dough onto floured surface and gently knead it, with a few turns. Shape into a round loaf about 6 inches (15 cm) in diameter. Place on prepared baking sheet. Using a knife, make shallow X cuts along top of loaf.

4. Bake in preheated oven for about 35 minutes or until crust is brown and firm to the touch. Remove from oven and set aside to cool completely. Serve immediately or store for up to 3 days in an airtight container at room temperature.

Variation

Garlic and Chive Irish Soda Bread: Omit the currants and caraway seeds. Add ¼ cup (60 mL) dried chives and 1 tbsp (15 mL) minced garlic in Step 1.

Mushroom and Asparagus Bread Pudding

This savory bread pudding is a wonderful addition to any meal. I serve it with Holiday Gravy (page 558) and Creamy Mashed Potatoes (page 178).

Tips

To clean leeks: Place sliced leeks in a bowl with 4 cups (1 L) water. Allow dirt from leeks to fall to bottom of bowl. Use a strainer to remove leeks, leaving the dirt behind at bottom of bowl.

Substitute an equal quantity of portobello, shiitake, chanterelle or cremini mushrooms for the button mushrooms.

- **Preheat oven to 350°F (180°C)**
- **13- by 9-inch (33 by 23 cm) metal baking pan, greased**

¾ cup	warm water	175 mL
¼ cup	ground raw flax seeds	60 mL
2 tbsp	grapeseed oil	30 mL
1 cup	chopped leeks (white part only; see Tips, left)	250 mL
1 tsp	fine sea salt	5 mL
3 to 4	cloves garlic, minced	3 to 4
2 cups	sliced button mushrooms	500 mL
4 cups	chopped asparagus	1 L
1 tbsp	chopped fresh thyme leaves	15 mL
16 cups	Gluten-Free Croutons (page 553)	4 L
4 cups	Almond Milk (page 61)	1 L
2 tbsp	thinly sliced fresh basil leaves	30 mL
2 tsp	Dijon mustard	10 mL

1. In a small bowl, whisk together warm water and ground flax seeds. Cover and set aside for about 10 minutes, so flax can absorb the liquid and swell.

2. In a large skillet over medium heat, heat oil. Add leeks and salt. Cook, stirring frequently, until softened and translucent, about 8 minutes. Stir in garlic and cook until fragrant, about 2 minutes. Add mushrooms and asparagus and cook, stirring occasionally, until most of the liquid has evaporated, about 10 minutes.

3. Transfer cooked vegetables to a large bowl. Add thyme, croutons, almond milk, basil, mustard and soaked flax. Stir to combine.

4. Spread evenly in prepared pan and bake in preheated oven for 30 minutes, until edges are lightly golden. Serve immediately or let cool, transfer to an airtight container and refrigerate for up to 1 week.

Gluten-Free Pita Breads

Scoop up your favorite dip with chunks of these soft, fluffy breads — I particularly like Basic Chickpea Hummus (page 72) and Hemp, Garlic and Chia Butter (page 124). Or try a pita for breakfast alongside Cheesy Grits with Spinach (page 31).

MAKES 8 PITAS

Tips

To grind flax seeds: Place ¼ cup (60 mL) flax seeds in a blender or clean spice grinder and process until flour-like in consistency. Transfer to an airtight container and refrigerate for up to 1 month.

When working with any flour, particularly those that are gluten-free, whisk before measuring. This aerates the flour and ensures more accurate measuring. Be sure to use a dry measure (not a glass measuring cup) and to level off with the side of a knife.

- **Stand mixer**
- **Baking sheet, greased (or nonstick)**

1 tbsp	ground raw flax seeds (see Tips, left)	15 mL
3 tbsp	hot water	45 mL
1	package (¼ oz/7 g) quick-rising (instant) yeast	1
½ cup	warm water	125 mL
1 tsp	organic cane sugar	5 mL
1 cup	brown rice flour	250 mL
1 cup	sorghum flour	250 mL
½ cup	white rice flour	125 mL
½ cup	tapioca flour	125 mL
2 tsp	xanthan gum	10 mL
1 tsp	fine sea salt	5 mL
1 cup	water	250 mL
	Brown rice flour, for dusting	

1. In a small bowl, whisk together ground flax seeds and hot water. Cover and set aside for about 15 minutes, so flax can absorb the liquid and swell.

2. In another small bowl, stir together yeast, warm water and sugar until well combined. Set aside for 10 minutes, until yeast is activated and becomes frothy.

3. In stand mixer bowl, whisk brown rice flour, sorghum flour, white rice flour, tapioca flour, xanthan gum and salt.

4. Fit mixer with flat beater and attach mixer bowl to the mixer. Add soaked flax and activated yeast to mixer bowl. With mixer running at medium speed, add 1 cup (250 mL) water and mix for 2 to 3 minutes, until a sticky dough forms (it should just pull away from sides of bowl).

Because the baking sheet
is preheated in a hot
oven, when greasing it,
be sure to use an oil with
a high smoke point, such
as grapeseed oil.

5. Transfer dough to an oiled bowl and turn to coat with oil. Cover with a clean kitchen towel and set aside in a warm place for 2 hours to let dough proof.

6. Place prepared baking sheet on lowest rack in oven. Preheat oven to 500°F (260°C).

7. Lightly dust a clean work surface with brown rice flour. Divide proofed dough into 6 to 8 equal portions. Using your hands and adding more flour as needed, shape each portion into a circle 6 to 8 inches (15 to 20 cm) in diameter and 1/4 inch (0.5 cm) thick.

8. Carefully, remove hot baking sheet from oven. Transfer 4 pitas to baking sheet, spacing about 1 inch (2.5 cm) apart. Return sheet to bottom rack and bake for about 6 minutes, until light brown and crisp. Flip and cook for about 4 minutes more, until surface has bubbled slightly and is lightly browned and crisp at the edges.

9. Remove from oven and poke a hole in any large air bubbles so pita can lie flat. Transfer to a wire rack to cool. Repeat with remaining pitas. Serve immediately or transfer to an airtight container and store at room temperature for up to 5 days.

Variation

Cheesy Gluten-Free Pita Breads: In Step 3, after dough has been mixed and pulls away from sides of bowl, add 1/2 cup (125 mL) nutritional yeast and 1/4 cup (60 mL) Vegan Shredded Mozzarella (page 537) or store-bought alternative.

Gluten-Free Chapatis

These traditional Indian breads are perfect for dipping into soups or stews, slathering with your favorite spread or wrapping around sandwich fillings. I often have them with Tofu and Lemongrass Vegetable Coconut Curry (page 306), Okra and Squash Gumbo (page 342) or as an accompaniment to Tempeh and Roasted Pepper Sloppy Joes (page 350) instead of pita.

MAKES 6 CHAPATIS

Tip

If using chapatis as wraps, fold them while still warm. Because this recipe is gluten-free, the breads may crack and break if folded when cold.

* **Large nonstick skillet**

1½ cups	chickpea flour	375 mL
1 cup	water	250 mL
2 tbsp	extra virgin olive oil	30 mL
½ tsp	fine sea salt	2 mL

1. In a large bowl, combine chickpea flour, water, olive oil and salt, mixing until smooth.
2. Preheat skillet over high heat.
3. Using a ½-cup (125 mL) measure, tip batter into hot pan and spread around until even. Cook until bubbles start to form on top and bottom is browned, 2 to 3 minutes. Flip and cook until dough is brown on other side, 1 to 2 minutes.
4. Serve immediately or let cool and store for up to 3 days in an airtight container at room temperature.

Variation

Cumin-Spiced Chapatis: Add 1 tsp (5 mL) whole cumin seeds in Step 1.

Desserts

Ice Creams, Sorbets and Frozen Desserts

Watermelon "Cake"

Watermelon dressed up as cake is a crisp, refreshing summertime dessert.

	MAKES
	1 MEDIUM "CAKE"

Tips

You want the watermelon to resemble a rectangle more than a sphere. So slice off as much at the ends as necessary. Enjoy the leftover watermelon as a refreshing snack while you work, or cover and refrigerate.

If you can't find coconut cream, substitute 3 cans (each 14 oz/400 mL) full-fat coconut milk that has been frozen. To extract the cream, turn a frozen can of coconut milk upside down. Open bottom end and, using a spoon, gently scoop out cream that has separated out (save the liquid for another use). You should have about 1⅔ cups (400 mL) cream.

To toast almonds: Heat a dry skillet over medium heat. Add almonds and cook, stirring constantly, until fragrant and just starting to turn brown, about 3 minutes. Remove from heat and immediately transfer to a plate to cool.

Replace the sliced almonds in this recipe with an equal amount of toasted shredded coconut.

• **Stand mixer, with whisk attachment, bowl chilled in freezer**

WATERMELON

1	seedless watermelon	1

FROSTING

1	can (14 oz/400 mL) chilled coconut cream (see Tips, left)	1
3 tbsp	pure maple syrup	45 mL
½ tsp	alcohol-free organic vanilla extract	2 mL
1 cup	sliced blanched almonds, toasted (see Tips, left)	250 mL

TOPPING

½ cup	fresh raspberries	125 mL
½ cup	sliced hulled strawberries	125 mL

1. *Watermelon*: Using a sharp knife, cut substantial slices from the top and bottom of the fruit to create large flat ends. (You want it to be stable when served and to provide enough space to accommodate the topping.) Stand watermelon on a cutting board and, starting from the top, cut downward to remove the green skin and white rind (see Tips, left).

2. *Frosting*: In chilled mixer bowl, beat coconut cream at high speed for 4 to 5 minutes or until medium peaks form. Add maple syrup and vanilla and whip until stiff peaks form, 4 or 5 minutes longer.

3. Place watermelon a serving tray on one flat side. Pat melon dry. Using a spatula, spread whipped coconut cream over entire surface, just as you would ice a cake. Sprinkle sides with almonds. Distribute topping evenly over top. Serve immediately.

Variations

Cacao Crunch Cherry Watermelon Cake: In a small bowl, whisk together ¼ cup (60 mL) cold coconut cream and 2 tbsp (30 mL) raw cacao powder, until no lumps remain. Add to cold mixer bowl and complete Step 2. Substitute 1 cup (250 mL) raw cacao nibs for the almonds. Top with 1 cup (250 mL) roughly chopped pitted cherries.

Salted Superfood Cinnamon Watermelon Cake:
Add 1 tsp (5 mL) ground cinnamon and ¼ tsp (1 mL) fine sea salt to cold mixer bowl and complete Step 2. Substitute ¼ cup (60 mL) raw chia seeds and ¼ cup (60 mL) raw shelled hemp seeds for the almonds. Top cake with ½ cup (125 mL) goji berries and ½ cup (125 mL) dried mulberries.

Almond Banana Watermelon Cake: Add 1 tsp (5 mL) alcohol-free organic almond extract to cold mixer bowl and complete Step 2. Spread mixture over entire surface. Top cake with about 2 cups (500 mL) thinly sliced bananas and sprinkle with ½ cup (125 mL) sliced blanched almonds, toasted

Chocolate Mint Watermelon Cake: In a small bowl, whisk together ¼ cup (60 mL) cold coconut cream with 2 tbsp (30 mL) raw cacao powder, until no lumps remain. Add to cold mixer bowl along with ½ tsp (2 mL) pure mint extract. Complete Step 2. Spread mixture over entire surface. Top cake with 1 cup (250 mL) fresh raspberries and garnish with a few leaves of fresh mint.

Panna Cotta

This silky smooth and creamy dessert is perfect to serve with a drizzle of maple syrup and fresh berries.

MAKES 4 SERVINGS

Tips

Agar flakes are available in most well-stocked supermarkets and natural food stores. You can substitute 2 tsp (10 mL) agar powder for the flakes.

This recipe can easily be doubled, tripled or quadrupled. You can also make it in smaller molds to serve as mini desserts.

● **Four ½-cup (125 mL) ramekins or custard cups**

2 tbsp	agar flakes (see Tips, left)	30 mL
2 tbsp	hot water	30 mL
1	can (14 oz/400 mL) full-fat coconut milk	1
⅓ cup	pure maple syrup	75 mL
½ tsp	alcohol-free organic vanilla extract	2 mL

1. In a small bowl, whisk together agar flakes and hot water until combined.

2. In a small saucepan, combine coconut milk, maple syrup, vanilla and agar mixture. Bring to a simmer and cook, stirring occasionally, for 5 to 6 minutes or until agar is completely dissolved.

3. Transfer to ramekins and refrigerate until firm, about 3 hours. To unmold, place bottoms of ramekins in warm water for about 1 minute. Serve immediately or cover ramekins and refrigerate for up to 5 days.

Crème Caramel

This traditional French custard, made here with creamy coconut milk, fragrant vanilla and sweet coconut sugar, is sure to please.

MAKES 6 SERVINGS

Tips

Coconut sugar is a low-glycemic sweetener that is available in most well-stocked supermarkets and natural food stores. It has a sweet taste similar to brown sugar.

Agar flakes are available in most well-stocked supermarkets and natural food stores. You can substitute 2 tsp (10 mL) agar powder for the flakes.

This recipe can easily be double, tripled or quadrupled. You can also make it in smaller molds to serve as mini desserts.

- Blender
- Six ¾-cup (175 mL) ramekins or custard cups

½ cup	organic coconut sugar (see Tips, left)	125 mL
2 tbsp	agar flakes (see Tips, left)	30 mL
2 tbsp	hot water	30 mL
2 cups	Coconut Milk (page 62)	500 mL
2 tbsp	pure maple syrup	30 mL
1	block (12 oz/375 g) soft silken tofu	1
1 tsp	alcohol-free organic vanilla extract	5 mL
Pinch	fine sea salt	Pinch

1. In a skillet over medium heat, heat coconut sugar, stirring constantly, until melted and lightly golden brown, 6 to 8 minutes. Divide melted sugar evenly among ramekins. Set aside to cool completely, about 30 minutes.

2. Meanwhile, in a small bowl, whisk together agar flakes and hot water until combined.

3. In a saucepan, combine agar mixture, coconut milk and maple syrup. Bring to a simmer and cook, stirring occasionally, for 5 to 6 minutes or until agar is completely dissolved. Transfer to blender and add tofu, vanilla and salt. Blend until smooth and creamy.

4. Divide coconut milk mixture evenly among prepared ramekins. Refrigerate until firm, about 3 hours.

5. To unmold, place bottoms of ramekins in warm water for 1 minute. Serve immediately or cover ramekins and refrigerate for up to 5 days.

Fresh Berry Sabayon

This whipped dessert is a perfect airy summertime treat when berries are in season.

Tips

Silken tofu is available in most well-stocked supermarkets and natural food stores. It is stored in aseptic boxes, so look for it in the dry foods section of your store rather than the refrigerator.

A hand-held citrus reamer can be used to extract the juice from lemons and limes. Available in most kitchen supply stores, this tool would be ideal to use for the lemon juice in this recipe.

Be sure to use raw (not processed) agave nectar. It is a 100% natural (non-GMO) sweetener that contains naturally occurring fructose and is low on the glycemic scale, which means that it releases glucose slowly, providing sustained energy.

Substitute an equal amount of pure maple syrup for the agave nectar.

● Blender

1 cup	raspberries	250 mL
1 cup	chopped hulled strawberries	250 mL
½ cup	blueberries	125 mL
1	package (12 oz/375 g) firm silken tofu (see Tips, left)	1
1 tsp	finely grated lemon zest	5 mL
½ cup	freshly squeezed lemon juice (see Tips, left)	125 mL
6 tbsp	raw agave nectar (see Tips, left)	90 mL
1 tbsp	dry white wine	15 mL
Pinch	fine sea salt	Pinch
1 cup	grapeseed oil	250 mL

1. In a bowl, combine raspberries, strawberries and blueberries.
2. In blender, combine tofu, lemon zest, lemon juice, agave nectar, wine and salt. Blend at high speed until smooth.
3. With the motor running, slowly drizzle oil through the feed tube. Process until mixture is thick and creamy.
4. Divide berries evenly among serving bowls. Top with sabayon and serve immediately.

Variation

Chocolate Vanilla Sabayon: Omit the lemon zest and wine in Step 2. Instead add 3 tbsp (45 mL) raw cacao powder and 1 tsp (5 mL) alcohol-free organic vanilla extract.

Coconut Cream Pineapple

In this dish, pineapple is cooked slowly to bring out all of its natural sweetness. Paired with rich, creamy coconut milk, it's perfect to serve on its own as a snack, as part of a dessert course served with your favorite cookies, or as a spread or condiment on a buffet table.

MAKES 4 TO 6 SERVINGS

Tips

To peel and core a pineapple: Place pineapple on a cutting board and use a sharp knife to cut off top and bottom, removing leaves and stem and creating flat surfaces (this will also reveal the thickness of the skin). Rest pineapple on a flat end; slide knife under skin and, with a downward motion, cut away peel in strips. Using knife, shave off any remaining bits of peel. Cut pineapple in half, then in quarters. Lay quarters flat on cutting board and, with knife held sideways, cut the core from each piece.

Coconut cream is similar to coconut milk but contains less water and has a higher fat content. Look for it in well-stocked supermarkets and Indian grocery stores.

Do not lift the lid of your slow cooker while it is cooking. Each time you do, heat will escape and you will need to add 20 to 30 minutes of cooking time to your recipe.

• **Medium (about 4 quart) slow cooker**

2	pineapples, peeled, cored and cut into 1-inch (2.5 cm) cubes (see Tips, left)	2
2 cups	water	500 mL
½ cup	organic coconut sugar (see Tips, page 483)	125 mL
¼ tsp	fine sea salt	1 mL
1	3-inch (7.5 cm) cinnamon stick	1
1	can (14 oz/400 mL) coconut cream (see Tips, left)	1

1. In slow cooker stoneware, combine pineapple, water, coconut sugar, salt and cinnamon. Cover and cook on Low for 6 hours or High for 3 hours, until pineapple is very soft and falling apart.

2. Stir in coconut cream and cook, covered, for 30 minutes more, until rich and creamy. Discard cinnamon stick. Serve immediately.

Poached Peaches

Serve this luscious dessert when juicy peaches are in season. Fragrant orange-flavored syrup spiked with vanilla makes this a perfect combination.

MAKES 4 TO 6 SERVINGS

Tips

Coconut sugar is a low-glycemic sweetener that is available in most well-stocked supermarkets and natural food stores. It has a sweet taste similar to brown sugar.

If you prefer, substitute 1 tsp (5 mL) alcohol-free organic vanilla extract for the vanilla bean.

If the peaches are very ripe and soft, reduce the cooking time to 3 or 4 minutes. If they are very hard, increase the cooking time to 10 or 12 minutes.

For extra flavor, add ½ cup (125 mL) white wine, brandy or cognac to the poaching liquid in Step 1.

8-inch (20 cm) square glass baking dish

3 cups	water	750 mL
3	2-inch (5 cm) strips orange peel	3
1 cup	freshly squeezed orange juice	250 mL
1 cup	organic coconut sugar (see Tips, left)	250 mL
2 tbsp	freshly squeezed lemon juice	30 mL
1	vanilla bean (see Tips, left)	1
4 to 6	medium to large ripe peaches, unpeeled (see Tips, left)	4 to 6

1. In a large, wide pot, combine water, orange peel, orange juice, coconut sugar and lemon juice. Using a paring knife, cut vanilla bean in half lengthwise. Scrape seeds into juice mixture. Add pod and bring to a boil. Reduce heat and simmer for 6 to 8 minutes, until coconut sugar is completely dissolved.

2. Add peaches and cook for 8 to 10 minutes, until soft. Using a slotted spoon, transfer poached peaches to a serving dish. Remove vanilla pod and save for another use.

3. Return poaching liquid to a boil and cook until thickened, 10 to 12 minutes (liquid should coat and hold on to a spoon dipped into the pot).

4. Using a fine-mesh sieve, strain poaching liquid into a bowl (discard solids). Set aside to cool completely. Once cool, drizzle over peaches. Serve immediately or cover and refrigerate for up to 3 days.

Poached Pears Filled with Chocolate Ganache

Soft, fragrant poached pears filled with rich chocolate ganache are a perfect way to end a dinner party. Since this dessert is served chilled, you can make it ahead and have it ready to take out of the fridge at the end of dinner.

MAKES 4 SERVINGS

Tips

A grapefruit spoon or apple corer makes quick work of hollowing out the pears.

Substitute 1 tbsp (15 mL) white wine vinegar for the white wine.

To melt the coconut oil, gently warm it in a small skillet over low heat.

Be sure to use raw (not processed) agave nectar. It is a 100% natural (non-GMO) sweetener that contains naturally occurring fructose and is low on the glycemic scale, which means that it releases glucose slowly, providing sustained energy.

When poaching pears, make sure they are completely submerged in the liquid, or they will discolor.

To give the pears a beautiful pink hue, replace 4 cups of the water with fresh beet juice.

> **Blender**

4	Bosc pears	4
8 cups	water (see Tips, left)	2 L
1 cup	organic coconut sugar (see Tips, page 485)	250 mL
½ cup	white wine (see Tips, left)	125 mL
3 tbsp	freshly squeezed lemon juice	45 mL
1 tbsp	freshly grated orange zest	15 mL
1	vanilla bean, split down the middle	1
½ cup	melted coconut oil (see Tips, left)	125 mL
½ cup	raw cacao powder	125 mL
½ cup	raw agave nectar (see Tips, left)	125 mL
2 tbsp	cold water	30 mL
¼ tsp	alcohol-free organic vanilla extract	1 mL

1. Peel pears and cut a small slice from the bottom of each to make ends flat. Using a spoon, carefully hollow out the pears from the bottom, keeping them whole.

2. In a saucepan, combine water, coconut sugar, wine, lemon juice, orange zest and vanilla bean. Bring to a boil, reduce heat and simmer for 5 minutes, stirring occasionally, until sugar is completely dissolved. Add pears and cook until tender, 10 to 12 minutes (see Tips, left).

3. Using a slotted spoon, gently transfer pears to a plate to cool, standing them upright. Reserve cooking liquid in pan and set aside.

4. In blender, combine coconut oil, cacao powder, agave nectar, cold water and vanilla. Blend at high speed until smooth.

5. Using a tablespoon (15 mL), fill each pear with 2 to 3 tbsp (30 to 45 mL) ganache. Cover and refrigerate until filling is set, about 20 minutes.

6. Meanwhile, return pan with poaching liquid to medium-high heat. Bring to a boil, reduce heat and simmer until thickened, 5 to 6 minutes. Remove from heat and set aside.

7. To serve, divide pears among serving plates and drizzle with reserved syrup. Serve immediately or store for up to 3 days in an airtight container in the refrigerator.

Caramelized Papaya Boats

Serve these delicious treats with Vegan Vanilla Ice Cream (page 513) and a drizzle of Easy Coconut Caramel Sauce (page 506). I also like to stuff them with fresh fruit and top with a dollop of Whipped Coconut Cream (page 565).

MAKES 2 BOATS

Tips

Many papayas sold in supermarkets have been genetically modified. To avoid GMOs, be sure to purchase organic papayas.

Coconut sugar is a low-glycemic sweetener that is available in most well-stocked supermarkets and natural food stores. It has a sweet taste similar to brown sugar.

If the papaya is very ripe, do not cover the baking dish with foil. Reduce the cooking time to 20 to 25 minutes.

- Preheat oven to 400°F (200°C)
- 8-inch (20 cm) square glass baking dish
- Aluminum foil

1	underripe organic papaya, peeled (see Tips, left)	1
½ cup	organic coconut sugar (see Tips, left)	125 mL
¼ cup	Whipped Non-dairy Butter (page 554)	60 mL
1 cup	water	250 mL

1. Cut papaya in half lengthwise through the middle. Using a spoon, scoop out the seeds and discard. Place papaya in baking dish.

2. In a small bowl, whisk together coconut sugar and butter until well combined. Spread equal amounts over each papaya half.

3. Add water to bottom of baking dish and cover dish tightly with aluminum foil (see Tips, left). Bake in preheated oven for 25 to 30 minutes or until papaya is tender when pierced with a fork. Uncover and bake for 10 to 15 minutes more, or until papaya is golden brown and caramelized. Serve immediately or let cool, transfer to an airtight container and refrigerate for up 5 days. Bring to room temperature before serving.

Caramelized Balsamic Figs and Berries

Make these delicious treats in late summer and fall, when fresh figs are at the height of their season. Serve warm over a big bowl of Vegan Vanilla Ice Cream (page 513).

MAKES 4 SERVINGS

Tips

Fresh figs do not have a long shelf life, so be sure to use them within a week of purchasing. They can be found in most well-stocked supermarkets and Italian markets.

Be sure to use raw (not processed) agave nectar. It is a 100% natural (non-GMO) sweetener that contains naturally occurring fructose and is low on the glycemic scale, which means that it releases glucose slowly, providing sustained energy.

You can substitute 2 tbsp (30 mL) pure maple syrup for the agave nectar.

For a special treat, add about 1 cup (250 mL) sliced fresh peaches when they are in season.

- Preheat oven to 500°F (260°C)
- Baking sheet, lined with parchment paper

2 cups	fresh figs, quartered (about 15 small; see Tips, left)	500 mL
½ cup	quartered hulled strawberries	125 mL
½ cup	raspberries	125 mL
3 tbsp	raw agave nectar (see Tips, left)	45 mL
2 tbsp	balsamic vinegar	30 mL
1 tbsp	organic coconut sugar (see Tips, page 485)	15 mL
½ tsp	alcohol-free organic vanilla extract	2 mL
Pinch	fine sea salt	Pinch

1. In a large bowl, gently toss together figs, strawberries, raspberries, agave nectar, vinegar, coconut sugar, vanilla and salt, until fruit is well coated.

2. Transfer to prepared baking sheet and bake in preheated oven for 5 to 6 minutes, until figs just begin to brown and sugar starts to harden.

3. Remove from oven and set aside for 2 to 3 minutes to cool. Serve immediately or transfer to an airtight container and refrigerate for up to 3 days.

Raspberry and Chocolate Sauté

Warm raspberries combined with rich, dark chocolate are simply perfect, and extra-special topped with a large dollop of Whipped Coconut Cream (page 565).

MAKES 4 SERVINGS

Tips

Substitute an equal amount of blackberries for the raspberries.

Substitute an equal amount of Coconut Milk (page 62) or Cashew Milk (page 61) for the almond milk.

1 tbsp	grapeseed oil	15 mL
3 cups	raspberries (see Tips, left)	750 mL
½ cup	non-dairy chocolate chips	125 mL
3 to 4 tbsp	Almond Milk (page 61; see Tips, left)	45 to 60 mL
2 tbsp	Whipped Non-dairy Butter (page 554)	30 mL

1. In a large skillet over high heat, heat oil. Add raspberries and cook for 2 to 3 minutes, stirring frequently, until they just begin to break down and release their juice. Remove from heat and add chocolate chips and almond milk. Stir continuously until chocolate has melted. Add butter and stir until melted. Serve immediately.

Hot Fudge Sundae

Serve this creamy sundae with White Chocolate Macadamia Cookies (page 433) or Perfect Chocolate Chip Cookies (page 434) crumbled overtop.

MAKES 4 SERVINGS

Tip

This sauce is an emulsion: a smooth blend of two or more ingredients that would not normally mix well (in this case, coconut oil and cacao powder). If the emulsion splits, causing the oil to separate while in the pan, return mixture to blender and add 2 to 3 tbsp (30 to 45 mL) cold water. Blend until smooth, then reheat in pan.

- **Blender**
- **4 ice-cream sundae dishes**

HOT FUDGE SAUCE

½ cup	melted coconut oil (see Tips, page 488)	125 mL
½ cup	raw agave nectar (see Tips, page 486)	125 mL
½ cup	raw cacao powder	125 mL
¼ tsp	alcohol-free organic vanilla extract	1 mL
4 cups	Vegan Vanilla Ice Cream (page 513)	1 L

1. *Hot Fudge Sauce:* In blender, combine coconut oil, agave nectar, cacao powder and vanilla. Blend at high speed until smooth and creamy. Transfer to a small saucepan and warm over low heat (see Tip, left).

2. Divide ice cream among sundae dishes. Pour warm chocolate sauce overtop. Serve immediately.

Chocolate Banana Parfaits

This fun and yummy dessert will make you feel like a kid again. Creamy banana is blended with coconut and vanilla and layered with chocolate sauce and strawberries — what's not to love?

MAKES 2 PARFAITS

Tips

To melt the coconut oil, gently warm it in a small skillet over low heat.

Replace the Easy Chocolate Sauce with melted chocolate chips. In a medium skillet over low heat, melt 1 cup (250 mL) chocolate chips, stirring constantly and taking care not to burn the chocolate. Remove from heat when only a few chips still hold their shape; continue stirring until smooth.

- **Blender**
- **2 parfait glasses**

3 cups	chopped bananas, divided	750 mL
1/2 cup	melted coconut oil (see Tips, left)	125 mL
1 tsp	raw agave nectar	5 mL
1/2 tsp	alcohol-free organic vanilla extract	2 mL
1 cup	Easy Chocolate Sauce (below)	250 mL
1 cup	chopped hulled strawberries	250 mL

1. In blender, combine 2 cups (500 mL) banana, coconut oil, agave nectar and vanilla. Blend at high speed until smooth and creamy.
2. Place 1/4 cup (60 mL) banana mixture in bottom of each parfait glass. Top with 1/4 cup (60 mL) each chocolate sauce and strawberries. Repeat, ending with a layer of strawberries. Top each with 1/2 cup (125 mL) chopped banana. Serve immediately or cover and refrigerate for up to 4 hours.

Easy Chocolate Sauce

Use this simple sauce to drizzle over fresh fruit, desserts, snacks or your favorite baked goods.

MAKES ABOUT 1 1/2 CUPS (375 ML)

- **Blender**

1/2 cup	raw agave nectar	125 mL
1/2 cup	raw cacao powder	125 mL
1/2 cup	melted coconut oil	125 mL
3 tbsp	cold water	45 mL
1/2 tsp	alcohol-free organic vanilla extract	2 mL

1. In blender, combine agave nectar, cacao powder, coconut oil, water and vanilla. Blend at the highest speed until smooth and creamy. Serve immediately or cover and store at room temperature for up to 5 days.

Banana Tempura

The trick to these crispy, sinfully delicious treats is to make sure the batter is cold and the oil is hot before battering and frying the banana.

MAKES 4 TO 8 SERVINGS

Tips

A spider is a type of strainer used for removing food from hot liquids or skimming foam. It has a wide, shallow wire-mesh basket at the end of a long handle and can be found in most kitchen supply stores.

Oils that have a high smoke point, such as grapeseed oil, are best for high-heat cooking such as frying or searing. They can stand up to high temperatures without having their fat molecules break down.

Test the oil temperature by dropping in about 1 tsp (5 mL) cold batter. If the batter sizzles right away and floats to the top, the oil is ready.

- Candy/deep-fry thermometer
- Slotted spoon or spider (see Tips, left)

8 cups	grapeseed oil (see Tips, left)	2 L
1 cup	brown rice flour	250 mL
¼ tsp	ground cinnamon	1 mL
Pinch	fine sea salt	Pinch
¾ cup	cold water	175 mL
¼ cup	crushed ice cubes	60 mL
4	very ripe bananas	4
	Organic coconut sugar, for sprinkling	

1. In a heavy-bottomed pot over medium-high heat, heat grapeseed oil to 375°F (190°C) — it will take 12 to 15 minutes for oil to reach correct temperature (see Tips).

2. In a deep bowl, whisk together rice flour, cinnamon and salt. Stir in water and crushed ice until smooth.

3. Cut each banana in half lengthwise. Dip into batter to coat evenly. Shake off excess batter and gently lower into hot oil. Cook until golden brown on all sides. (It won't take much more than a minute.)

4. Using a slotted spoon, transfer to a plate lined with paper towels to drain excess oil. Sprinkle with coconut sugar. Repeat with remaining bananas, frying only 2 to 3 pieces at a time and ensuring that oil returns to the correct temperature after each batch. Serve immediately.

Churros with Cinnamon Sugar

Churros and hot chocolate make a fabulous combination. To gild the lily, serve these with Easy Coconut Caramel Sauce (page 506) for dipping.

Tips

Coconut sugar is a low-glycemic sweetener that is available in most well-stocked supermarkets and natural food stores. It has a sweet taste similar to brown sugar.

It will take about 15 minutes for oil to reach correct temperature. (Test by dropping in a small piece of dough; if it floats and bubbles right away, the oil is ready.

If you do not have a piping bag, you can use a zipper-top plastic bag with about $1/4$ inch (0.5 cm) of a bottom corner snipped off.

- Candy/deep-fry thermometer
- Piping bag fitted, with star tip

¾ cup + 2 tbsp	brown rice flour	200 mL
2 tbsp	tapioca starch	30 mL
1 cup	water	250 mL
3 tbsp	coconut oil	45 mL
Dash	alcohol-free organic vanilla extract	Dash
2 cups	grapeseed oil	500 mL
½ cup	organic coconut sugar (see Tips, left)	125 mL
2 tsp	ground cinnamon	10 mL
Pinch	fine sea salt	Pinch

1. In a bowl, whisk together rice flour and tapioca starch.
2. In a small saucepan, combine water and coconut oil. Bring to a boil, then reduce heat to a simmer. Stir in vanilla. Add flour mixture and stir until dough comes away from sides of pan, 1 to 2 minutes. Remove from heat and transfer to a large bowl. Set aside to cool completely.
3. In a large saucepan over medium heat, heat oil to 375°F (190°C).
4. Meanwhile, in a large bowl, whisk together coconut sugar, cinnamon and salt. Set aside.
5. Fill piping bag with dough (see Tips, left). Working in batches of 2 or 3, squeeze strips of dough 2 to 3 inches (5 to 7.5 cm) long and about ½ inch (1 cm) in diameter into hot oil. Cook for 6 to 7 minutes, or until churros are crisp and golden brown.
6. Using a slotted spoon, transfer to bowl with cinnamon sugar and toss to coat well. Transfer to a serving plate. Repeat with remaining batter. Serve immediately.

Variation

Chocolate Churros: Add 2 tbsp (30 mL) raw cacao powder to the flour mixture in Step 1.

Dessert Pancakes

Delectable and sinful, these pancakes are the perfect treat when you are craving something on the sweet side. Serve them with a big dollop of Whipped Coconut Cream (page 565) and some Easy Coconut Caramel Sauce (page 506).

MAKES 8 TO 10 PANCAKES

Tips

Cacao powder is powdered raw chocolate. It is similar to cocoa powder but tastes even better, with a deeper, richer flavor. Cacao powder is available in well-stocked supermarkets and natural food stores and online. If you can't find it, you may substitute an equal quantity of good-quality cocoa powder.

Replace the chocolate chips with other ingredients such as chopped walnuts or pecans, candied fruit, goji berries or fresh fruit such as blueberries or raspberries.

Blender

1 cup	buckwheat flour	250 mL
½ cup	white rice flour	125 mL
2 tbsp	arrowroot starch	30 mL
2 tbsp	coconut flour	30 mL
2 tbsp	raw cacao powder (see Tips, left)	30 mL
½ tsp	baking soda	2 mL
⅛ tsp	fine sea salt	0.5 mL
⅛ tsp	ground cinnamon	0.5 mL
1½ cups	water	375 mL
2 tbsp	raw agave nectar (see page 8)	30 mL
1	large ripe banana, chopped	1
½ tsp	alcohol-free organic vanilla extract	2 mL
¼ cup	non-dairy chocolate chips (see Tips, left)	60 mL
1 tbsp	grapeseed oil	15 mL

1. In a large bowl, whisk together buckwheat flour, rice flour, arrowroot, coconut flour, cacao powder, baking soda, salt and cinnamon.

2. In blender, combine water, agave nectar, banana and vanilla. Blend at high speed until smooth and creamy. Add to dry ingredients and stir until smooth (there should be no lumps). Stir in chocolate chips.

3. Lightly grease a skillet with grapeseed oil. Heat over medium heat until a drop of water bounces on the surface before evaporating. Working in batches, drop about ¼ cup (60 mL) batter into skillet and cook until bubbles appear all over the surface, 4 to 5 minutes. Turn over and cook other side until browned, about 1 minute. Transfer to a plate and keep warm. Repeat with remaining batter. Serve immediately.

Indian-Spiced Date Squares

Sweet Medjool dates combined with fragrant spices pair with crumbled walnuts and crisp oats to take this traditional favorite to a whole new level.

**MAKES
16 SQUARES**

Tips

There are numerous varieties of dates, but Medjools are my favorite. Although they are generally more expensive, they are larger and softer.

Buy whole organic spices when possible and grind them as you need them. Fresh, flavorful spices are essential to creating great recipes. The oils in pre-ground spices have already begun to dissipate, and over time they lose their flavor.

Be sure to use raw (not processed) agave nectar. It is a 100% natural (non-GMO) sweetener that contains naturally occurring fructose and is low on the glycemic scale, which means that it releases glucose slowly, providing sustained energy.

- Food processor
- 8-inch (20 cm) square glass baking dish, lined with parchment paper

4 cups	chopped pitted Medjool dates, divided (see Tips, left)	1 L
½ cup	freshly squeezed orange juice	125 mL
¼ cup	pure maple syrup	60 mL
¼ cup	melted coconut oil (see Tips, page 493)	60 mL
½ tsp	minced gingerroot	2 mL
¼ tsp	ground cardamom	1 mL
⅛ tsp	ground coriander	0.5 mL
2 cups	raw walnuts	500 mL
¼ tsp	ground cinnamon	1 mL
Pinch	fine sea salt	Pinch
2 tbsp	raw agave nectar (see Tips, left)	30 mL

1. In food processor fitted with the metal blade, combine 3¾ cups (925 mL) dates, orange juice, maple syrup, coconut oil, ginger, cardamom and coriander. Process until smooth, stopping the motor to scrape down sides of work bowl as necessary. Spread mixture evenly in baking dish. Set aside.

2. In clean food processor work bowl, combine walnuts, cinnamon and salt. Process until no large pieces remain (be careful not to overprocess, or you will end up with walnut butter). Add remaining ¼ cup (60 mL) dates and pulse 8 to 10 times, until no large pieces of date remain. With the motor running, drizzle agave nectar through the feed tube and process until ingredients hold together when pressed between two fingers.

3. Spread walnut mixture evenly over date mixture. Cover and refrigerate for about 3 hours, until firm.

4. Using parchment liner, lift mixture from dish. Cut into 16 squares. Serve immediately or transfer to an airtight container and refrigerate for up to 1 week.

Chocolate Cherry Dream Bars

Serve these creamy, rich treats with a big dollop of Whipped Coconut Cream (page 565).

(page 565).

MAKES 16 BARS

Tips

Puffed brown rice is available in most well-stocked supermarkets and natural food stores. If you cannot find it, you can substitute an equal amount of puffed millet or puffed quinoa.

To melt the coconut oil, gently warm it in a small skillet over low heat.

To soak the cashews: Place in a bowl and cover with 2 cups (500 mL) water. Cover and set aside for 1 hour or overnight (if overnight, refrigerate). Drain, discarding liquid.

To pit cherries, use the butt end of a chef's knife. Place fruit on a clean cutting board and gently tap end of handle on cherries to expose pits. Remove and discard pits.

- **8-inch (20 cm) square glass baking dish, lined with parchment paper**
- **Blender**

CRUST

2 cups	puffed brown rice (see Tips, left)	500 mL
¼ cup	raw cacao powder	60 mL
3 tbsp	raw agave nectar (see Tips, page 492)	45 mL
3 tbsp	melted coconut oil (see Tips, left)	45 mL
Dash	alcohol-free organic vanilla extract	Dash
Pinch	fine sea salt	Pinch

FILLING

1 cup	raw cashews, soaked (see Tips, left)	250 mL
1 cup	cashew butter	250 mL
¾ cup	raw agave nectar	175 mL
¼ cup	melted coconut oil	60 mL
½ tsp	alcohol-free organic vanilla extract	2 mL
1 cup	chopped pitted cherries, divided (see Tips, left)	250 mL

1. *Crust:* In a large bowl, combine puffed rice, cacao powder, agave nectar, coconut oil, vanilla and salt; stir well. Spread evenly in prepared dish, cover and freeze for about 1 hour, until firm.

2. *Filling:* In blender, combine cashews, cashew butter, agave nectar, coconut oil and vanilla. Blend at high speed until smooth and creamy. Add ½ cup (125 mL) cherries and blend until smooth. Transfer mixture to a bowl and stir in remaining ½ cup (125 mL) cherries.

3. Spread filling over chilled crust. Cover and return to freezer for 3 hours or overnight.

4. Using parchment liner, lift mixure from dish. Bring to room temperature, then cut into 16 squares. Serve immediately or transfer to an airtight container and refrigerate for up to 5 days.

Apricot Almond Squares

Serve these tasty treats for dessert or as a snack at any time of the day.

**MAKES
16 SQUARES**

Tips

When purchasing dried apricots, make sure to look for ones that are darker in color. This means that they have not been treated with sulfites to preserve color. Read the label to be sure they are sulfite-free, or ask your purveyor if you have concerns.

To soak the apricots: Place them in a bowl and cover with 4 cups (1 L) hot water. Cover and set aside for 30 minutes. Drain, discarding liquid.

Coconut butter is a blend of coconut oil and coconut meat. You can find it in natural food stores, next to the coconut oil.

Pure almond extract can be found in most well-stocked supermarkets and natural food stores. For the best flavor possible, choose one that is alcohol-free and contains no additives.

- **Food processor**
- **8-inch (20 cm) square glass baking dish, lined with parchment paper**

1 cup	dried apricots, soaked (see Tips, left)	250 mL
½ cup	raw agave nectar (see Tips, page 495)	125 mL
½ cup	melted coconut oil (see Tips, page 495)	125 mL
¼ cup	coconut butter (see Tips, left)	60 mL
¼ tsp	alcohol-free organic almond extract (see Tips, left)	1 mL
½ tsp	alcohol-free organic vanilla extract	2 mL
2 cups	raw almond butter, at room temperature	500 mL

1. In food processor fitted with the metal blade, combine apricots, agave nectar, coconut oil, coconut butter, almond extract and vanilla. Process until smooth, stopping to scrape down sides of work bowl as necessary.

2. In a large bowl, combine apricot mixture and almond butter and stir well. Spread evenly in prepared baking dish and freeze until firm, about 3 hours.

3. Let sit at room temperature for 45 minutes, then, using parchment liner, lift mixture from dish. Cut into 16 squares. Serve immediately or transfer to an airtight container and refrigerate for up to 5 days.

Peanut Butter Fudge Squares

Creamy peanut butter and rich chocolate fudge are a match made in heaven. These bars are hard to resist.

Tips

Be sure to use raw (not processed) agave nectar. It is a 100% natural (non-GMO) sweetener that contains naturally occurring fructose and is low on the glycemic scale, which means that it releases glucose slowly, providing sustained energy.

To melt the coconut oil, gently warm it in a small skillet over low heat.

Cacao powder is powdered raw chocolate. It is similar to cocoa powder but tastes even better, with a deeper, richer flavor. Cacao powder is available in well-stocked supermarkets and natural food stores and online. If you can't find it, substitute an equal quantity of good-quality cocoa powder.

- **8-inch (20 cm) square glass baking dish, lined with parchment paper**

1 cup	raw agave nectar, divided (see Tips, left)	250 mL
1 cup	melted coconut oil, divided (see Tips, left)	250 mL
½ cup	raw cacao powder (see Tips, left)	125 mL
1 tsp	alcohol-free organic vanilla extract	5 mL
4 cups	chunky peanut butter	1 L

1. In a small bowl, whisk together ¼ cup (60 mL) agave nectar, ¼ cup (60 mL) coconut oil, cacao powder and vanilla.

2. In a large bowl, combine peanut butter, remaining ¾ cup (175 mL) agave nectar and remaining ¾ cup (175 mL) coconut oil. Stir until well combined. Swirl in chocolate mixture.

3. Spread evenly in prepared baking dish and freeze until firm, about 3 hours or overnight.

4. Using parchment liner, lift mixture from dish. Bring to room temperature before cutting into 16 squares. Store in an airtight container in the refrigerator for up to 2 months.

Variation

For a crunchier texture, in Step 2 stir in 1 cup (250 mL) puffed brown rice or ½ cup (125 mL) raw buckwheat groats.

Fudge Bites

These delicious bites pack a punch of velvety smooth deep, dark chocolate with hints of coconut and cashew.

Tips

To melt the coconut oil, gently warm it in a small skillet over low heat.

Coconut butter is a blend of coconut oil and coconut meat. You can find it in natural food stores, next to the coconut oil.

Use unsweetened medium-shred unsulfured coconut. Not only is this type of coconut nutritionally beneficial, the medium shred size will help the bites hold together.

- Blender
- Food processor
- Baking sheet, lined with parchment paper

½ cup	melted coconut oil (see Tips, left)	125 mL
1 cup	raw cacao powder	250 mL
½ cup	raw agave nectar (see Tips, page 497)	125 mL
¼ cup	coconut butter (see Tips, left)	60 mL
½ tsp	alcohol-free organic vanilla extract	2 mL
2 cups	raw cashews	500 mL
1 cup	unsweetened shredded coconut (see Tips, left)	250 mL

1. In blender, combine coconut oil, cacao powder, agave nectar, coconut butter and vanilla. Blend at high speed until smooth and creamy. Set aside.

2. In food processor fitted with the metal blade, process cashews until flour-like in consistency. Add coconut and process until combined. Add chocolate mixture and process until well combined. Transfer to a bowl.

3. Using a tablespoon (15 mL), drop 18 to 20 equal portions onto prepared baking sheet. Freeze until firm, about 2 hours. Serve immediately or transfer to an airtight container and refrigerate for up to 1 week.

Millet and Sweet Potato No-Bake Brownies

These rich, delicious brownies are full of healthful ingredients. I like to serve them with a big bowl of fresh fruit and Whipped Coconut Cream (page 565) on the side.

MAKES
MAKES 16 BROWNIES

Tips

Substitute 1¼ cups (300 mL) cocoa powder for the raw cacao.

Be sure to use raw (not processed) agave nectar. It is a 100% natural (non-GMO) sweetener that contains naturally occurring fructose and is low on the glycemic scale, which means that it releases glucose slowly, providing sustained energy.

To melt the coconut oil, gently warm it in a small skillet over low heat.

For a classic twist, add 1 cup (250 mL) chopped walnuts at the end of Step 3, after the mixture has been puréed.

- Food processor
- 8-inch (20 cm) square glass baking dish, lined with parchment paper

	Water	
1 cup	millet, rinsed and drained	250 mL
2 cups	cubed peeled sweet potatoes	500 mL
1 cup	raw cacao powder (see Tips, left)	250 mL
¾ cup	raw agave nectar (see Tips, left)	175 mL
½ cup	melted coconut oil (see Tips, left)	125 mL
¼ cup	Almond Milk (page 61)	60 mL
¼ cup	pure maple syrup	60 mL
1 tsp	alcohol-free organic vanilla extract	5 mL
Pinch	fine sea salt	Pinch

1. In a large saucepan, combine 3 cups (750 L) water and millet. Bring to a boil, reduce heat and simmer, stirring frequently, until millet is tender and all of the liquid has been absorbed, about 25 minutes. Cover and set aside.

2. In another large saucepan, combine sweet potatoes and 4 cups (1 L) water. Bring to a boil, reduce heat and simmer until tender, about 15 minutes. Drain, using a colander.

3. In food processor fitted with the metal blade, combine cooked millet and sweet potatoes, cacao powder, agave nectar, coconut oil, almond milk, maple syrup, vanilla and salt. Process until smooth, stopping the motor to scrape down sides of work bowl as necessary.

4. Spread mixture evenly in prepared baking dish. Refrigerate for 3 hours, until firm.

5. Using parchment liner, lift mixture from dish. Cut into 16 equal portions. Serve immediately or cover and refrigerate for up to 3 days.

Raspberry Cream Cheese No-Bake Brownies

These delectable treats are perfect for enjoying with a cup of coffee or tea.

MAKES
16 BROWNIES

Tips

Substitute an equal amount of strawberries or blackberries for the raspberries.

Coconut sugar is a low-glycemic sweetener that is available in most well-stocked supermarkets and natural food stores. It has a sweet taste similar to brown sugar.

Cacao powder is powdered raw chocolate. It is similar to cocoa powder but tastes even better, with a deeper, richer flavor. Cacao powder is available in well-stocked supermarkets and natural food stores and online. If you can't find it, substitute an equal quantity of good-quality cocoa powder.

- Blender
- Food processor
- 8-inch (20 cm) square glass baking dish, lined with parchment paper

FROSTING

1 cup	fresh raspberries (see Tips, left)	250 mL
1/2 cup	organic coconut sugar (see Tips, left)	125 mL
2 cups	raw cashews	500 mL
3 tbsp	freshly squeezed lemon juice	45 mL
1/4 tsp	fine sea salt	1 mL
1/2 tsp	alcohol-free organic vanilla extract	2 mL
1/2 cup	water	125 mL

BROWNIES

2 cups	raw walnuts	500 mL
1/2 cup	raw cacao powder (see Tips, left)	125 mL
1 cup	chopped pitted Medjool dates	250 mL
1/2 tsp	alcohol-free organic vanilla extract	2 mL
1/4 cup	raw agave nectar (see Tip, page 499)	60 mL

1. *Frosting:* In a skillet over medium-high heat, combine raspberries and coconut sugar. Cook, stirring frequently, until berries break down and a thick sauce forms, about 10 minutes. Remove from heat and set aside to cool.

2. In a saucepan filled with water, bring cashews to a boil. Drain, discarding liquid.

3. In blender, combine boiled cashews, lemon juice, salt, vanilla and water. Blend at high speed until smooth, stopping the motor to scrape down sides of blender jar as necessary.

Tip

Be sure to use raw (not processed) agave nectar. It is a 100% natural (non-GMO) sweetener that contains naturally occurring fructose and is low on the glycemic scale, which means that it releases glucose slowly, providing sustained energy.

4. Transfer to a bowl. Add cooked raspberries and stir until just combined (you do not want the mixture to be completely smooth). Set aside.

5. *Brownies:* In food processor fitted with the metal blade, process walnuts and cacao powder until nuts are broken down into small pieces (be careful not to overprocess, or you will end up with walnut butter). Add dates and vanilla; process until mixture is smooth and holds together. With the motor running, drizzle agave nectar through the feed tube and process until incorporated.

6. Spread mixture evenly in prepared baking dish. Spread frosting overtop. Refrigerate for 3 hours or overnight.

7. Using parchment liner, lift mixture from dish. Cut into squares and serve immediately or refrigerate for up to 5 days in an airtight container.

Pumpkin Toffee Cheesecake

Serve this creamy dessert with freshly grated nutmeg and a big dollop of Whipped Coconut Cream (page 565).

MAKES 1 CAKE (ABOUT 16 SLICES)

Tips

Be sure to use raw (not processed) agave nectar. It is a 100% natural (non-GMO) sweetener that contains naturally occurring fructose and is low on the glycemic scale, which means that it releases glucose slowly, providing sustained energy.

To soak the cashews: Place in a bowl and cover with 8 cups (2 L) water. Cover and set aside for 1 hour or overnight (if overnight, refrigerate). Drain, discarding liquid.

Substitute 2 cups (500 mL) cooked peeled, cubed pumpkin for the canned pumpkin.

- Food processor
- 9-inch (23 cm) springform pan, greased

CRUST

2 cups	raw walnuts	500 mL
1 cup	raw almonds	250 mL
1 cup	chopped pitted Medjool dates	250 mL
½ tsp	alcohol-free organic vanilla extract	2 mL
¼ tsp	ground cinnamon	1 mL
⅛ tsp	freshly grated nutmeg	0.5 mL
Pinch	fine sea salt	Pinch
2 to 3 tbsp	raw agave nectar (see Tips, left)	30 to 45 mL

FILLING

4 cups	raw cashews, soaked (see Tips, left)	1 L
1 cup	water	250 mL
1 cup	raw agave nectar	250 mL
1	can (14 oz/398 mL) canned organic pumpkin purée (see Tips, left)	1
1 tsp	ground cinnamon	5 mL
2 tsp	alcohol-free organic vanilla extract	10 mL
¼ tsp	freshly grated nutmeg	1 mL
1 cup	melted coconut oil (see Tip, page 501)	250 mL

1. *Crust:* In food processor fitted with the metal blade, combine walnuts, almonds, dates, vanilla, cinnamon, nutmeg and salt. Process until no large pieces of nut remain and mixture holds together.

2. With the motor running, pour agave nectar through the feed tube and process until combined (the mixture should hold together when pressed between two fingers). Transfer to prepared pan and press firmly into bottom. Set aside. Rinse out work bowl.

Tip

To melt the coconut oil, gently warm it in a small skillet over low heat.

3. *Filling:* In clean work bowl, combine soaked cashews, water, agave nectar, pumpkin, cinnamon, vanilla and nutmeg. Process until smooth, stopping the motor to scrape down sides of work bowl as necessary. Add coconut oil and blend until smooth.

4. Spread filling evenly over crust in pan and smooth top with a spatula. Refrigerate for 8 hours or overnight.

5. To remove cake from pan, run a knife around the edges. Loosen hinges on pan and remove side piece. Serve immediately or cover and refrigerate for up to 5 days.

Berry Cheesecake

This cheesecake boasts a rich, crumbly nut-and-date crust topped with a creamy filling bursting with berries. Make it for a special treat.

MAKES 1 CAKE (ABOUT 16 SLICES)

Tips

When processing ingredients for the crust, make sure there are no large pieces remaining and that the mixture holds together when pressed between two fingers.

To soak the cashews: Place in a bowl and cover with 8 cups (2 L) water. Cover and set aside for 1 hour or overnight (if overnight, refrigerate). Drain, discarding liquid.

Use a total of 1 cup (250 mL) berries. My other favorite combinations include raspberries and strawberries, as well as blueberries and blackberries. This cheesecake is also lovely made with just one type of berry.

To melt the coconut oil, gently warm it in a small skillet over low heat.

- Food processor
- 10-inch (25 cm) springform pan, greased

CRUST

2 cups	raw walnuts	500 mL
1 cup	raw almonds	250 mL
1 cup	chopped pitted Medjool dates	250 mL
½ tsp	alcohol-free organic vanilla extract	2 mL
Pinch	fine sea salt	Pinch
3 tbsp	raw agave nectar (see Tips, page 500)	45 mL

FILLING

4 cups	raw cashews, soaked	1 L
1 cup	water	250 mL
1 cup	raw agave nectar	250 mL
½ cup	blueberries (see Tips, left)	125 mL
½ cup	chopped hulled strawberries	125 mL
3 tbsp	freshly squeezed lemon juice	45 mL
2 tsp	alcohol-free organic vanilla extract	10 mL
1 cup	melted coconut oil (see Tips, left)	250 mL

1. *Crust:* In food processor fitted with the metal blade, combine walnuts, almonds, dates, vanilla and salt. Process until well combined (see Tips, left). With the motor running, drizzle agave nectar through the feed tube; process until combined.

2. Transfer to prepared pan and press evenly into bottom. Set aside. Rinse out work bowl.

3. *Filling:* In clean work bowl, combine soaked cashews, water, agave nectar, berries, lemon juice and vanilla. Process until smooth, stopping the motor to scrape down sides of work bowl as necessary. Add coconut oil and process until smooth.

4. Spread filling evenly over crust, using a spatula to smooth out. Refrigerate for 8 hours or overnight.

5. Remove from pan (see Tips, page 503). Serve immediately or cover and refrigerate for up to 5 days.

Chocolate Banana Cake

Garnish this silky, rich cake with a dollop of Whipped Coconut Cream.

MAKES 1 CAKE (ABOUT 20 SLICES)

Tips

To remove cake from pan, run a knife around the edges. Loosen hinges on pan and remove side piece.

To soak the cashews: Place in a bowl and cover with 4 cups (1 L) water. Cover and set aside for 1 hour or overnight (if overnight, refrigerate). Drain, discarding liquid.

Cacao powder is powdered raw chocolate. It is similar to cocoa powder but tastes even better, with a deeper, richer flavor. Cacao powder is available in well-stocked supermarkets and natural food stores and online. If you can't find it, you may substitute an equal quantity of good-quality cocoa powder.

To melt the coconut oil, gently warm it in a small skillet over low heat.

10-inch (25 cm) springform pan, greased

CRUST

2 cups	raw walnuts	500 mL
1 cup	raw almonds	250 mL
1 cup	chopped pitted Medjool dates	250 mL
½ tsp	alcohol-free organic vanilla extract	2 mL
Pinch	fine sea salt	Pinch
3 tbsp	raw agave nectar (see Tips, page 500)	45 mL

FILLING

2 cups	raw cashews, soaked (see Tips, left)	500 mL
8 cups	chopped bananas	2 L
1 cup	raw cacao powder	250 mL
1 cup	raw agave nectar	250 mL
1 cup	melted coconut oil (see Tips, left)	250 mL
½ tsp	alcohol-free organic vanilla extract	2 mL

1. *Crust:* In food processor fitted with the metal blade, combine walnuts, almonds, dates, vanilla and salt. Process until well combined. With the motor running, drizzle agave nectar through the feed tube; process until combined.

2. Transfer to prepared pan and press evenly into bottom. Set aside. Rinse out work bowl.

3. *Filling:* In clean work bowl, combine 1 cup (250 mL) soaked cashews, 4 cups (1 L) bananas, ½ cup (125 mL) cacao powder, ½ cup (125 mL) agave nectar, ½ cup (125 mL) coconut oil and ¼ tsp (1 mL) vanilla. Process until smooth, stopping the motor to scrape down sides of work bowl as necessary. Spread evenly over crust in pan. Repeat with remaining ingredients.

4. Smooth top with spatula. Refrigerate for 8 hours or overnight.

5. Remove from pan (see Tips, left). Serve immediately or cover and refrigerate for up to 5 days.

Grasshopper Pie

Creamy avocados are blended with soft, sweet bananas to make this light and fluffy chocolate mint pie. Serve it at your next family gathering or potluck.

Tips

When processing ingredients for the crust, make sure there are no large pieces remaining and that the mixture holds together when pressed between two fingers.

If your bananas ripen before you can use them, peel and freeze them in a resealable bag for the next time you want a cold, creamy smoothie.

To melt the coconut oil, gently warm it in a small skillet over low heat.

To remove cake from pan, run a knife around the edges. Loosen hinges on pan and remove side piece.

- Food processor
- 10-inch (25 cm) springform pan, greased

CRUST

2 cups	raw walnuts	500 mL
1 cup	raw almonds	250 mL
2 tbsp	raw cacao powder (see Tips, page 505)	30 mL
½ tsp	alcohol-free organic vanilla extract	2 mL
Pinch	fine sea salt	Pinch
1 cup	chopped pitted Medjool dates	250 mL
3 tbsp	raw agave nectar (see Tips, page 505)	45 mL

FILLING

4 cups	chopped ripe bananas (about 3 large; see Tips, left)	1 L
2	ripe medium avocados, chopped	2
1 cup	raw agave nectar	250 mL
¾ cup	melted coconut oil (see Tips, left)	175 mL
2 tsp	alcohol-free organic peppermint extract	10 mL
1 tsp	spirulina powder	5 mL
½ tsp	alcohol-free organic vanilla extract	2 mL

1. *Crust:* In food processor fitted with the metal blade, combine walnuts, almonds, cacao powder, vanilla and salt. Process until flour-like. Add dates and process until combined. With the motor running, drizzle agave nectar through the feed tube and process until combined. Transfer to prepared pan and press firmly into bottom. Set aside. Rinse out work bowl.

2. *Filling:* In clean work bowl, combine bananas, avocados, agave nectar, coconut oil, peppermint extract, spirulina and vanilla. Process until smooth, stopping the motor to scrape down sides of work bowl as necessary.

3. Pour filling evenly over crust. Using a spatula, smooth top. Refrigerate for 8 hours or overnight. Remove from pan (see Tips, left). Serve immediately or cover and refrigerate for up to 5 days.

Silky Chocolate Mousse

This creamy and decadent dessert is made with only a few ingredients — it's both simple and delicious.

MAKES 4 SERVINGS

Tips

Cacao powder is powdered raw chocolate. It is similar to cocoa powder but tastes even better, with a deeper, richer flavor. Cacao powder is available in well-stocked supermarkets and natural food stores and online. You may substitute an equal quantity of good-quality cocoa powder, but note that the flavor may not be as rich.

Be sure to use raw (not processed) agave nectar. It is a 100% natural (non-GMO) sweetener that contains naturally occurring fructose and is low on the glycemic scale, which means that it releases glucose slowly, providing sustained energy.

Food processor

1	block (12 oz/375 g) medium-firm silken tofu	1
1 cup	raw cacao powder (see Tips, left)	250 mL
¾ cup	raw agave nectar (see Tips, left)	175 mL
½ tsp	alcohol-free organic vanilla extract	2 mL

1. In food processor fitted with the metal blade, combine tofu, cacao powder, agave nectar and vanilla. Process until smooth, stopping the motor to scrape down sides of work bowl as necessary.
2. Transfer to a serving bowl. Serve immediately or cover and refrigerate for up to 5 days.

Variation

Chocolate Avocado Mousse: Substitute 2 ripe avocados for the tofu.

Easy Coconut Caramel Sauce

Drizzle this creamy sauce over Vegan Vanilla Ice Cream (page 513), Maca Crunch Ice Cream (page 523) or Salted Caramel Ice Cream (page 520).

MAKES ABOUT 1¼ CUPS (300 ML)

Tip

Coconut sugar is a low-glycemic sweetener that is available in most well-stocked supermarkets and natural food stores. It has a sweet taste similar to brown sugar.

1	can (14 oz/400 mL) full-fat coconut milk	1
½ cup	organic coconut sugar (see Tip, left)	125 mL
1 tsp	alcohol-free organic vanilla extract	5 mL

1. In a saucepan over medium heat, combine coconut milk and coconut sugar. Bring to a simmer and cook until thickened slightly and golden brown, 8 to 10 minutes. Remove from heat and stir in vanilla.

2. Serve immediately or let cool, transfer to an airtight container and refrigerate for up to 1 week.

Variation

Salted Caramel Sauce: Add 1 tsp (5 mL) fine sea salt to the pan before cooking.

Cookie Dough Pudding

This delicious pudding is perfect to serve as a dessert on its own, or drizzle it with some Easy Chocolate Sauce (page 488) and serve it as a dip with slices of fresh fruit such as melon, apples or fresh cherries.

MAKES ABOUT 1½ CUPS (375 ML)

Tips

Coconut butter is a blend of coconut oil and coconut meat. You can usually find it in natural food stores, next to the coconut oil.

Cacao nibs are bits of roasted cacao beans that have been broken into pieces. They provide a great crunchy texture and dark chocolate flavor.

● **Food processor**

¼ cup	raw almonds	60 mL
1 cup	coconut butter (see Tips, left)	250 mL
1 cup	pure maple syrup	250 mL
¼ cup	raw cacao nibs (see Tips, left)	60 mL
1 tsp	alcohol-free organic vanilla extract	5 mL

1. In food processor fitted with the metal blade, process almonds until flour-like in consistency (be careful not to overprocess, or you will end up with almond butter).

2. Add coconut butter, maple syrup, cacao nibs and vanilla; process until smooth and creamy. Transfer to a serving bowl and serve immediately or cover and refrigerate for up to 1 week.

Traditional Bread Pudding

Filling your slow cooker with this sweet and aromatic mix of spices and gluten-free bread is an easy and stress-free way to make a favorite comfort food. Try it drizzled with Easy Coconut Caramel Sauce (page 506).

MAKES 6 SERVINGS

Tips

To melt the coconut oil, gently warm it in a small skillet over low heat.

Use high-quality organic cinnamon. You will get the freshest flavor by grinding whole cinnamon sticks in a clean spice grinder.

Any type of sliced gluten-free bread will work for this recipe. However, before using, take it out of the package and leave it on the counter for 1 hour to become a little stale. This will allow it to soak up more of the milk mixture.

Make this ahead and store for up to 5 days in an airtight container in the refrigerator. To reheat the pudding, place it on a baking sheet lined with parchment paper. Bake in a preheated oven at 300°F (150°C) until warm in the center, about 20 minutes.

● **Medium (about 4 quart) slow cooker, stoneware greased**

3 tbsp	ground flax seeds	45 mL
½ cup + 2 tsp	hot water	135 mL
1½ cups	Almond Milk (page 61)	375 mL
½ cup	melted coconut oil (see Tips, left)	125 mL
½ cup	organic coconut sugar (see Tips, page 509)	125 mL
1 tsp	ground cinnamon (see Tips, left)	5 mL
1 tsp	alcohol-free organic vanilla extract	5 mL
1	loaf (16 oz/500 g) brown rice bread, cut into 1-inch (2.5 cm) cubes (see Tips, left)	1

1. In a small bowl, whisk together ground flax seeds and hot water. Cover and set aside for about 10 minutes, so flax can absorb the liquid and swell.

2. In a large bowl, whisk together almond milk, coconut oil, coconut sugar, cinnamon, vanilla and flaxseed mixture. Add bread and stir gently until well coated. Transfer to prepared slow cooker stoneware.

3. Cover and cook on Low for 6 hours or High for 3 hours. Serve immediately (see Tips, left).

Minted Grapefruit Granita

Granita is an Italian ice. It is a light, refreshing dessert that can be enjoyed any day of the week. In this version the bright, tart flavor of fresh grapefruit juice is married with refreshing mint.

MAKES ABOUT 4 CUPS (1 L)

Tips

Coconut sugar is a low-glycemic sweetener that is available in most well-stocked supermarkets and natural food stores. It has a sweet taste similar to brown sugar.

A hand-held citrus reamer can be used to extract the juice from citrus fruit. Available in most kitchen supply stores, this tool would be ideal to use for the citrus juices in this recipe.

In Step 4, instead of using a food processor, you can use a fork to scrape the frozen mixture into fine granules.

- Blender
- 11- by 7-inch (28 by 18 cm) glass baking dish
- Food processor

1 cup	water	250 mL
1/2 cup	organic coconut sugar (see Tips, left)	125 mL
2 tbsp	freshly squeezed lemon juice (see Tips, left)	30 mL
1/2 cup	thinly sliced mint leaves, divided	125 mL
1 tsp	alcohol-free organic peppermint extract	5 mL
3 cups	freshly squeezed grapefruit juice (see Tips, left)	750 mL

1. In a small saucepan, combine water, coconut sugar and lemon juice; bring to a boil. Remove from heat and whisk until sugar is dissolved. Transfer to blender.

2. Add 1/4 cup (60 mL) mint and peppermint extract. Blend at high speed until smooth. Add grapefruit juice and blend to combine.

3. Transfer to baking dish. Stir in remaining 1/4 cup (60 mL) mint. Cover and freeze until firm, about 6 hours or overnight.

4. Using a sharp knife, cut frozen mixture into large pieces. Transfer to food processor fitted with the metal blade and process until snow-like in consistency (see Tips, left). Serve immediately or transfer to an airtight container and keep frozen for up to 2 weeks.

Watermelon Lime Granita

Granita is a refreshing semi-frozen dessert that can be served as a palate cleanser during a multi-course meal or as a simple dessert anytime. It makes a perfect cooling finish to peppery meals such as Spicy Tempeh and Squash (page 372) and Spicy Angel-Hair Toss (page 255).

MAKES ABOUT 4 CUPS (1 L)

Tips

Coconut sugar is a low-glycemic sweetener that is available in most well-stocked supermarkets and natural food stores. It has a sweet taste similar to brown sugar.

In Step 3, instead of a food processor, you can use a fork to scrape the frozen mixture into fine granules.

- **Food processor**
- **6-cup (1.5 L) casserole dish**

1 cup	water	250 mL
1 cup	organic coconut sugar (see Tips, left)	250 mL
4 cups	chopped watermelon	1 L
1 tbsp	freshly squeezed lime juice	15 mL

1. In a saucepan, combine water and coconut sugar. Bring to a simmer, stirring constantly, until sugar is completely dissolved, about 5 minutes. Transfer to a bowl, cover and refrigerate until cooled completely.

2. In food processor fitted with the metal blade, combine cooled sugar syrup, watermelon and lemon juice; process until smooth. Transfer to casserole dish, cover and freeze until firm, about 6 hours or overnight.

3. Using a sharp knife, cut frozen mixture into large pieces. Transfer to food processor fitted with the metal blade and process until snow-like in consistency (see Tips, left). Serve immediately or transfer to an airtight container and keep frozen for up to 2 weeks.

Variations

Replace the watermelon with an equal amount of chopped hulled strawberries, raspberries, mango, peaches or blueberries.

Citrus Sorbet

Enjoy this light, refreshing sorbet as a cool treat on a hot summer's day, as a simple, healthy dessert or as a palate-cleansing course during a large meal.

MAKES ABOUT 4 CUPS (1 L)

Tips

A citrus reamer is a hand-held tool used to extract the juice from lemons and limes. It is available in most kitchen supply stores and would be ideal to use for the citrus in this recipe.

If you do not have an ice-cream maker, pour the cooled mixture into a 6-cup (1.5 L) casserole dish and freeze until solid. Transfer to a food processor fitted with the metal blade and process until smooth. Serve immediately or transfer to an airtight container and store in the freezer for up to 2 weeks.

* **Ice-cream maker**

3 cups	water	750 mL
1 cup	organic coconut sugar (see Tips, page 510)	250 mL
1 tsp	finely grated lemon zest	5 mL
1 tsp	finely grated lime zest	5 mL
½ cup	freshly squeezed lemon juice (see Tips, left)	125 mL
½ cup	freshly squeezed lime juice	125 mL

1. In a saucepan, combine water, coconut sugar, lemon juice and lime juice. Bring to a simmer, stirring constantly until sugar is completely dissolved, about 5 minutes. Remove from heat and stir in lemon zest and lime zest.
2. Transfer to a bowl, cover and refrigerate until cooled completely, at least 4 hours or overnight.
3. Transfer to ice-cream maker and freeze according to manufacturer's instructions (see Tips, left). Transfer to an airtight container and store in the freezer for up to 2 weeks.

Variation

Ginger Citrus Sorbet: In Step 1, add 2 tbsp (30 mL) chopped peeled ginger to the saucepan before simmering. Using a slotted spoon, scoop out and discard before cooling mixture. Before transferring to ice-cream maker, add 1 tsp (5 mL) minced gingerroot.

Cashew Vanilla Ice Cream

This is a simple way to make raw ice cream, which is very delicious — as creamy and rich as its dairy counterpart. I love the strong vanilla flavor combined with the luscious cashews. I often serve this with Easy Coconut Caramel Sauce (page 506), Dessert Pancakes (page 491) or Banana Tempura (page 489). If you are lucky enough to own a high-powered blender, use it to make this recipe; it will produce the creamiest result.

MAKES 4 CUPS (1 L)

Tips

To soak the cashews: Place in a bowl and cover with 2 cups (500 mL) water. Cover and set aside for 1 hour or overnight (if overnight, refrigerate). Drain, discarding liquid.

To melt the coconut oil, gently warm it in a small skillet over low heat.

Be sure to use raw (not processed) agave nectar. It is a 100% natural (non-GMO) sweetener that contains naturally occurring fructose and is low on the glycemic scale, which means that it releases glucose slowly, providing sustained energy.

Substitute ½ tsp (2 mL) organic vanilla powder for the extract.

A hand-held citrus reamer can be used to extract the juice from lemons and limes. Available in most kitchen supply stores, this tool would be ideal to use for the lemon juice in this recipe.

- **Blender**
- **Ice-cream maker**

1 cup	raw cashews, soaked (see Tips, left)	250 mL
¾ cup	melted coconut oil (see Tips, left)	175 mL
½ cup	raw agave nectar (see Tips, left)	125 mL
¼ cup	Cashew Milk (page 61)	60 mL
1 tsp	alcohol-free organic vanilla extract (see Tips, left)	5 mL
1 tsp	freshly squeezed lemon juice (see Tips, left)	5 mL

1. In blender, combine soaked cashews, coconut oil, agave nectar, cashew milk, vanilla and lemon juice. Blend at high speed until smooth and creamy.
2. Transfer to ice-cream maker and freeze according to manufacturer's instructions. Transfer to an airtight container and store in the freezer for up to 2 weeks.

Vegan Vanilla Ice Cream

This ice cream is just as rich and luscious as the traditional version, but with none of the dairy or refined sugars. Try it with some fresh berries and a large spoonful of Whipped Coconut Cream (page 565).

MAKES 4 CUPS (1 L)

Tips

Coconut cream is similar to coconut milk but contains less water and has a higher fat content. Look for it in well-stocked supermarkets and Indian grocery stores.

Using organic vanilla powder rather than vanilla extract in this recipe will make a huge difference in the flavor and visual appeal — you will see specks of vanilla in the ice cream. If you don't have it, substitute about 2 tsp (10 mL) alcohol-free organic vanilla extract.

When blending hot liquids in a blender, make sure your blender is no more than half full. Also, place a folded towel over the lid and place your hand firmly on top. Otherwise, the pressure of the steam may cause the lid to blow off, spattering liquid all over the kitchen.

Although it is an extra step, blending the ice cream mixture before chilling it emulsifies the solution and helps to prevent ice crystals from forming.

- Blender
- Ice-cream maker

1	can (14 oz/400 mL) full-fat coconut milk	1
1	can (14 oz/400 mL) coconut cream (see Tips, left)	1
½ cup	organic coconut sugar (see Tips, page 515)	125 mL
¼ cup	raw agave nectar (see Tips, page 512)	60 mL
1 tsp	organic vanilla powder (see Tips, left)	5 mL
⅛ tsp	fine sea salt	0.5 mL

1. In a small saucepan over medium heat, combine coconut milk, coconut cream, coconut sugar, agave nectar, vanilla and salt. Bring to a simmer and cook for 2 to 3 minutes, stirring occasionally, until sugar is completely dissolved. Remove from heat.
2. Transfer mixture to blender in batches (see Tips, left). Blend at high speed for 30 seconds. Transfer to a bowl, cover and refrigerate for at least 4 hours or overnight.
3. Stir well. Transfer to ice-cream maker and freeze according to manufacturer's instructions. Transfer to an airtight container and store in the freezer for up to 2 weeks.

Basil Lemon Ice Cream

Both basil and lemon have very pungent flavors. Together, in combination with a sweet, creamy coconut base, they create an ice cream with mouthwatering oomph. This is one treat that can't be beat.

MAKES ABOUT 4 CUPS (1 L)

Tips

To finely slice the basil, remove the leaves from the stems and stack them one on top of another. Roll the leaves into a cigar shape and, using a sharp chef's knife, slice into thin strips.

Be sure to use raw (not processed) agave nectar. It is a 100% natural (non-GMO) sweetener that contains naturally occurring fructose and is low on the glycemic scale, which means that it releases glucose slowly, providing sustained energy.

Using organic vanilla powder rather than vanilla extract in this recipe will make a huge difference in the flavor and the visual appeal — you will see specks of vanilla in the ice cream. If you don't have it, substitute ½ tsp (2 mL) alcohol-free organic vanilla extract.

- Blender
- Ice-cream maker

1	can (14 oz/400 mL) full-fat coconut milk	1
1	can (14 oz/400 mL) coconut cream (see Tips, page 515)	1
½ cup	packed thinly sliced basil leaves, divided (see Tips, left)	125 mL
½ cup	organic coconut sugar (see Tips, page 515)	125 mL
¼ cup	raw agave nectar (see Tips, left)	60 mL
1 tsp	finely grated lemon zest	5 mL
¼ cup	freshly squeezed lemon juice	60 mL
¼ tsp	organic vanilla powder (see Tips, left)	1 mL
⅛ tsp	fine sea salt	0.5 mL

1. In a small saucepan over medium heat, combine coconut milk, coconut cream, ¼ cup (60 mL) basil, coconut sugar, agave nectar, lemon zest, lemon juice, vanilla and salt. Bring to a simmer and cook for 2 to 3 minutes, or until sugar is completely dissolved.

2. Transfer mixture to blender in batches (see Tips, page 517). Blend at high speed for 30 seconds. Transfer to a bowl, cover and refrigerate for at least 4 hours or overnight.

3. Stir well. Transfer to ice-cream maker and freeze according to manufacturer's instructions. Add remaining ¼ cup (60 mL) basil just before the last 5 minutes of freezing and let the machine stir it in. Transfer to an airtight container and store in the freezer for up to 2 weeks.

Lemongrass Ice Cream

Coconut and lemongrass are a traditional combination in Thai cuisine. Here these exotic flavors become comfort food when transformed into the familiar texture of ice cream.

MAKES ABOUT 4 CUPS (1 L)

Tips

Coconut cream is similar to coconut milk but contains less water and has a higher fat content. Look for it in well-stocked supermarkets and Indian grocery stores.

Coconut sugar is a low-glycemic sweetener that is available in most well-stocked supermarkets and natural food stores. It has a sweet taste similar to brown sugar.

Use only the bottom 2 inches (5 cm) of the lemongrass stalk, as the rest is tough and fibrous. Save the remainder to use in other Thai-inspired recipes; for example, bruise with the butt of a knife and then add to a soup or stew (discard before serving).

Although it is an extra step, blending the ice cream mixture before chilling it emulsifies the solution and helps to prevent ice crystals from forming.

- **Blender**
- **Ice-cream maker**

1	can (14 oz/400 mL) full-fat coconut milk	1
1	can (14 oz/400 mL) coconut cream (see Tips, left)	1
1/2 cup	organic coconut sugar (see Tips, left)	125 mL
1/4 cup	raw agave nectar (see Tips, page 514)	60 mL
1/4 tsp	organic vanilla powder (see Tips, page 514)	1 mL
1/8 tsp	fine sea salt	0.5 mL
3	stalks lemongrass, chopped (see Tips, left)	3

1. In a small saucepan over medium heat, combine coconut milk, coconut cream, coconut sugar, agave nectar, vanilla, salt and lemongrass. Bring to a simmer and cook, stirring occasionally, for 2 to 3 minutes, or until sugar is completely dissolved.

2. Remove from heat and set aside for 30 minutes so lemongrass can infuse liquid. Using a fine-mesh sieve, strain (discard lemongrass).

3. Transfer mixture to blender in batches (see Tips, page 517). Blend at high speed for 30 seconds. Transfer to a bowl, cover and refrigerate until well chilled, for at least 4 hours or overnight.

4. Stir well. Transfer to ice-cream maker and freeze according to manufacturer's instructions. Transfer to an airtight container and store in the freezer for up to 2 weeks.

Strawberry Goji Berry Ice Cream

This combination of strawberries and goji berries is an antioxidant powerhouse. Here's a creamy treat that's perfect to serve when sweet, juicy strawberries are at the height of their season. Nutrient-dense goji berries, which have acquired a reputation as a superfood, are the perfect addition.

MAKES ABOUT 4 CUPS (1 L)

Tips

Coconut cream is similar to coconut milk but contains less water and has a higher fat content. Look for it in well-stocked supermarkets and Indian grocery stores.

To soak the goji berries: Place in a bowl and cover with 2 cups (500 mL) hot water. Cover and set aside for 30 minutes. Drain, discarding liquid.

Be sure to use raw (not processed) agave nectar. It is a 100% natural (non-GMO) sweetener that contains naturally occurring fructose and is low on the glycemic scale, which means that it releases glucose slowly, providing sustained energy.

Organic vanilla powder can be found in most well-stocked supermarkets and natural food stores. It is made from dried and ground whole vanilla beans and will add a lot of flavor to your dishes. Alcohol-free organic vanilla extract may be substituted.

- Blender
- Ice-cream maker

1	can (14 oz/400 mL) full-fat coconut milk	1
1	can (14 oz/400 mL) coconut cream (see Tips, left)	1
1 cup	finely chopped hulled strawberries, divided	250 mL
1/2 cup	goji berries, soaked, divided (see Tips, left)	125 mL
1/2 cup	organic coconut sugar (see Tips, page 517)	125 mL
1/4 cup	raw agave nectar (see Tips, left)	60 mL
1/4 tsp	organic vanilla powder or 1/2 tsp (2 mL) alcohol-free organic vanilla extract (see Tips, left)	1 mL
1/8 tsp	fine sea salt	0.5 mL

1. In a small saucepan over medium heat, combine coconut milk, coconut cream, 1/2 cup (125 mL) strawberries, 1/4 cup (60 mL) soaked goji berries, coconut sugar, agave nectar, vanilla and salt. Bring to a simmer and cook, stirring occasionally, for 2 to 3 minutes or until sugar is completely dissolved. Remove from heat.

2. Transfer mixture to blender in batches (see Tips, page 517). Blend at high speed for 30 seconds. Transfer to a bowl, cover and refrigerate for at least 4 hours or overnight.

3. Stir well. Transfer to ice-cream maker and freeze according to manufacturer's instructions. Add remaining 1/2 cup (125 mL) strawberries and 1/4 cup (60 mL) goji berries just before the last 5 minutes of freezing and let the machine stir them in. Transfer to an airtight container and store in the freezer for up to 2 weeks.

Raspberry Beet Ice Cream

You may think raspberries and beets make an odd pair, but they complement each other's flavors very well and also give this ice cream a lovely pink hue. Sweet beet juice and slightly tart raspberries make a wonderful ice cream that will please any palate. I like to serve it garnished with a few fresh raspberries and a drizzle of Easy Coconut Caramel Sauce (page 506).

MAKES ABOUT 4 CUPS (1 L)

Tips

Coconut sugar is a low-glycemic sweetener that is available in most well-stocked supermarkets and natural food stores. It has a sweet taste similar to brown sugar.

To make the beet juice for this recipe: Cut 2 to 3 medium beets into quarters and process in an electric juicer. Or purchase fresh beet juice from a juice bar.

When blending hot liquids in a blender, make sure your blender is no more than half full. Also, place a folded towel over the lid and place your hand firmly on top. Otherwise, the pressure of the steam may cause the lid to blow off, spattering liquid all over the kitchen.

Although it is an extra step, blending the ice cream mixture before chilling it emulsifies the solution and helps to prevent ice crystals from forming.

- **Blender**
- **Ice-cream maker**

1	can (14 oz/400 mL) full-fat coconut milk	1
1	can (14 oz/400 mL) coconut cream (see Tips, page 516)	1
½ cup	organic coconut sugar (see Tips, left)	125 mL
1 cup	raspberries, divided	250 mL
¼ cup	raw agave nectar (see Tips, page 516)	60 mL
¼ tsp	organic vanilla powder (see Tips, page 516)	1 mL
⅛ tsp	fine sea salt	0.5 mL
¼ cup	fresh beet juice (see Tips, left)	60 mL

1. In a small saucepan over medium heat, combine coconut milk, coconut cream, coconut sugar, ½ cup (125 mL) raspberries, agave nectar, vanilla and salt. Bring to a simmer and cook, stirring occasionally, for 4 to 5 minutes or until sugar is completely dissolved and raspberries are broken down. Remove from heat.

2. Transfer mixture to blender, in batches (see Tips, left), and add beet juice. Blend at high speed for 30 seconds. Transfer to a bowl, cover and refrigerate until well chilled, for at least 4 hours or overnight.

3. Stir well. Transfer to ice-cream maker and freeze according to manufacturer's instructions. Add remaining ½ cup (125 mL) raspberries just before the last 5 minutes of freezing and let the machine stir them in. Transfer to an airtight container and store in the freezer for up to 2 weeks.

Variation

Strawberry Beet Ice Cream: Substitute an equal quantity of chopped hulled strawberries for the raspberries.

Wild Blueberry Ice Cream

Make this fresh, fruity ice cream during the height of summer, when wild blueberries are in season.

Tips

If you can't find wild blueberries, substitute an equal quantity of cultivated organic highbush blueberries.

Coconut sugar is a low-glycemic sweetener that is available in most well-stocked supermarkets and natural food stores. It has a sweet taste similar to brown sugar.

Be sure to use raw (not processed) agave nectar. It is a 100% natural (non-GMO) sweetener that contains naturally occurring fructose and is low on the glycemic scale, which means that it releases glucose slowly, providing sustained energy.

Organic vanilla powder can be found in most well-stocked supermarkets and natural food stores. It is made from dried and ground whole vanilla beans and will add a lot of flavor to your dishes. If you cannot find it, substitute 1/2 tsp (2 mL) alcohol-free organic vanilla extract.

- **Blender**
- **Ice-cream maker**

1	can (14 oz/400 mL) full-fat coconut milk	1
1	can (14 oz/400 mL) coconut cream (see Tips, page 520)	1
1 cup	wild blueberries, divided (see Tips, left)	250 mL
1/2 cup	organic coconut sugar (see Tips, left)	125 mL
1/4 cup	raw agave nectar (see Tips, left)	60 mL
1/4 tsp	organic vanilla powder (see Tips, left)	1 mL
1/8 tsp	fine sea salt	0.5 mL
1 tbsp	freshly squeezed lemon juice	15 mL

1. In a small saucepan over medium heat, combine coconut milk, coconut cream, 1/2 cup (125 mL) blueberries, coconut sugar, agave nectar, vanilla and salt. Bring to a simmer and cook, stirring occasionally, for 2 to 3 minutes or until coconut sugar is completely dissolved.

2. Transfer mixture to blender, in batches, and add lemon juice. Blend at high speed for 30 seconds (see Tips, page 519). Transfer to a bowl, cover and refrigerate until well chilled, for at least 4 hours or overnight.

3. Stir well. Transfer to ice-cream maker and freeze according to manufacturer's instructions. Add remaining 1/2 cup (125 mL) blueberries just before the last 5 minutes of freezing and let the machine stir them in. Transfer to an airtight container and store in the freezer for up to 2 weeks.

Cinnamon Peach Ice Cream

The peach season is short where I live, so when these luscious orbs are fresh and plentiful, I like to use them as often as I can. This cinnamon-spiked ice cream is the perfect treat — the aromatic spice is especially peach-friendly.

**MAKES ABOUT
4 CUPS (1 L)**

Tips

To slice a peach, run a paring knife around its middle, through to the stone. Use your hands to twist and divide into two halves. Slice the half without the stone into the desired number of pieces. For the half with the stone, use your knife to loosen and remove it before slicing.

Use high-quality organic cinnamon. You will get the freshest flavor by grinding whole cinnamon sticks in a spice grinder.

When blending hot liquids in a blender, make sure your blender is no more than half full. Also, place a folded towel over the lid and place your hand firmly on top. Otherwise, the pressure of the steam may cause the lid to blow off, spattering liquid all over the kitchen.

Although it is an extra step, blending the ice cream mixture before chilling it emulsifies the solution and helps to prevent ice crystals from forming.

- **Blender**
- **Ice-cream maker**

1	can (14 oz/400 mL) full-fat coconut milk	1
1	can (14 oz/400 mL) coconut cream (see Tips, page 520)	1
1 cup	sliced unpeeled peaches, divided (see Tips, left)	250 mL
½ cup	organic coconut sugar (see Tips, page 518)	125 mL
¼ cup	raw agave nectar (see Tips, page 518)	60 mL
1 tsp	ground cinnamon (see Tips, left)	5 mL
¼ tsp	organic vanilla powder (see Tips, page 518)	1 mL
⅛ tsp	fine sea salt	0.5 mL
1 tbsp	freshly squeezed lemon juice	15 mL

1. In a small saucepan over medium heat, combine coconut milk, coconut cream, peaches, coconut sugar, agave nectar, cinnamon, vanilla and salt. Bring to a simmer and cook, stirring occasionally, for 2 to 3 minutes, or until coconut sugar is completely dissolved and peaches are soft and slightly brown. Remove from heat. Using a slotted spoon, transfer ½ cup (125 mL) cooked peaches to a bowl and set aside.

2. Transfer coconut mixture to blender, in batches (see Tips, left), and add lemon juice. Blend at high speed for 30 seconds. Transfer to a bowl, cover and refrigerate until well chilled, for at least 4 hours or overnight.

3. Stir well. Transfer to ice-cream maker and freeze according to manufacturer's instructions. Add reserved peaches just before the last 5 minutes of freezing and let the machine stir them in. Transfer to an airtight container and store in the freezer for up to 2 weeks.

Salted Caramel Ice Cream

This creamy coconut milk ice cream has an added swirl of sweet and salty caramel sauce that is sure to bring you back for seconds. Coconut products work well for virtually any recipe where dairy is usually called for. In particular, coconut milk and coconut cream replicate the mouthfeel of traditional ice cream. Try this recipe for an irresistible flavor combination!

MAKES ABOUT 4 CUPS (1 L)

Tips

Coconut cream is similar to coconut milk but contains less water and has a higher fat content. Look for it in well-stocked supermarkets and Indian grocery stores.

Coconut sugar is a low-glycemic sweetener that is available in most well-stocked supermarkets and natural food stores. It has a sweet taste similar to brown sugar.

Be sure to use raw (not processed) agave nectar. It is a 100% natural (non-GMO) sweetener that contains naturally occurring fructose and is low on the glycemic scale, which means that it releases glucose slowly, providing sustained energy.

Organic vanilla powder can be found in most well-stocked supermarkets and natural food stores. It is made from dried and ground whole vanilla beans and will add a lot of flavor to your dishes. If you cannot find it, substitute 1 tsp (5 mL) alcohol-free organic vanilla extract.

- Blender
- Ice-cream maker

1	can (14 oz/400 mL) full-fat coconut milk	1
1	can (14 oz/400 mL) coconut cream (see Tips, left)	1
½ cup	organic coconut sugar (see Tips, left)	125 mL
¼ cup	raw agave nectar (see Tips, left)	60 mL
¾ tsp	fine sea salt	3 mL
½ tsp	organic vanilla powder or 1 tsp (5 mL) alcohol-free organic vanilla extract (see Tips, left)	2 mL
½ cup	Easy Coconut Caramel Sauce (page 506), cooled	125 mL

1. In a small saucepan over medium heat, combine coconut milk, coconut cream, coconut sugar, agave nectar, salt and vanilla. Bring to a simmer and cook, stirring occasionally, until sugar is completely dissolved, 2 to 3 minutes.

2. Transfer mixture to blender in batches (see Tips, page 521). Blend at high speed for 30 seconds. Transfer to a bowl, cover and refrigerate for at least 4 hours or overnight.

3. Stir well. Transfer to ice-cream maker and freeze according to manufacturer's instructions. Add the Coconut Caramel Sauce in a slow, steady stream just before the last 5 minutes of freezing and let the machine stir it in. Transfer to an airtight container and store in the freezer for up to 2 weeks.

Cookie Dough Ice Cream

Creamy, cold and studded with crunchy bits that remind me of chocolate chip cookies, this ice cream is the perfect treat.

MAKES ABOUT 4 CUPS (1 L)

Tips

Cacao nibs are bits of roasted cacao beans that have been broken into pieces. They provide a great crunchy texture and dark chocolate flavor.

Cacao powder is powdered raw chocolate. It is similar to cocoa powder but tastes even better, with a deeper, richer flavor. Cacao powder is available in well-stocked supermarkets and natural food stores and online. If you can't find it, substitute an equal quantity of good-quality cocoa powder.

When blending hot liquids in a blender, make sure your blender is no more than half full. Also, place a folded towel over the lid and place your hand firmly on top. Otherwise, the pressure of the steam may cause the lid to blow off, spattering liquid all over the kitchen.

Although it is an extra step, blending the ice cream mixture before chilling it emulsifies the solution and helps to prevent ice crystals from forming.

- Blender
- Ice-cream maker

1	can (14 oz/400 mL) full-fat coconut milk	1
1	can (14 oz/400 mL) coconut cream (see Tips, page 520)	1
½ cup	organic coconut sugar (see Tips, page 520)	125 mL
½ cup	raw cacao nibs, divided (see Tips, left)	125 mL
¼ cup	raw agave nectar (see Tips, page 520)	60 mL
½ tsp	organic vanilla powder (see Tips, page 520)	2 mL
¼ tsp	raw cacao powder (see Tips, left)	1 mL
⅛ tsp	fine sea salt	0.5 mL

1. In a small saucepan over medium heat, combine coconut milk, coconut cream, coconut sugar, ¼ cup (60 mL) cacao nibs, agave nectar, vanilla, cacao powder and salt. Bring to a simmer and cook, stirring occasionally, for 2 to 3 minutes or until sugar is completely dissolved.

2. Transfer mixture to blender in batches (see Tips, left). Blend at high speed for 30 seconds. Transfer to a bowl, cover and refrigerate for at least 4 hours or overnight.

3. Stir well. Transfer to ice-cream maker and freeze according to manufacturer's instructions. Add remaining ¼ cup (60 mL) cacao nibs before the last 5 minutes of freezing and let the machine stir them in. Transfer to an airtight container and store in the freezer for up to 2 weeks.

Pure Chocolate Ice Cream

Creamy dark chocolate ice cream is made even more decadent with pure raw cacao powder. Serve this in a bowl or a gluten-free cone for a sweet treat anytime. For a real indulgence, add a drizzle of chocolate sauce.

> **MAKES ABOUT 4 CUPS (1 L)**

Tips

Organic vanilla powder can be found in most well-stocked supermarkets and natural food stores. It is made from dried and ground whole vanilla beans and will add a lot of flavor to your dishes. If you cannot find it, substitute ½ tsp (2 mL) alcohol-free organic vanilla extract.

Cacao powder is powdered raw chocolate. It is similar to cocoa powder but tastes even better, with a deeper, richer flavor. Cacao powder is available in well-stocked supermarkets and natural food stores and online. If you can't find it, substitute an equal quantity of good-quality cocoa powder.

For a version with less added sugar, substitute 3 tbsp (45 mL) raw cacao nibs for the chocolate chips.

- Blender
- Ice-cream maker

1	can (14 oz/400 mL) full-fat coconut milk	1
1	can (14 oz/400 mL) coconut cream (see Tips, page 520)	1
½ cup	organic coconut sugar (see Tips, page 520)	125 mL
¼ cup	raw agave nectar (see Tips, page 520)	60 mL
¼ tsp	organic vanilla powder (see Tips, left)	1 mL
⅛ tsp	fine sea salt	0.5 mL
¼ cup	raw cacao powder (see Tips, left)	60 mL
½ cup	non-dairy chocolate chips	125 mL

1. In a small saucepan over medium heat, combine coconut milk, coconut cream, coconut sugar, agave nectar, vanilla and salt. Bring to a simmer, reduce heat and cook, stirring occasionally, for 2 to 3 minutes or until sugar is completely dissolved.

2. Transfer mixture to blender, in batches (see Tips, page 523), and add cacao powder. Blend at high speed for 30 seconds. Transfer to a bowl, cover and refrigerate until well chilled, for at least 4 hours or overnight.

3. Stir well. Transfer to ice-cream maker and freeze according to manufacturer's instructions. Add chocolate chips before the last 5 minutes of freezing and let the machine stir them in. Transfer to an airtight container and store in the freezer for up to 2 weeks.

Variation

Chocolate Mint Ice Cream: Add 1 tsp (5 mL) alcohol-free pure peppermint extract to the blender in Step 2.

Maca Crunch Ice Cream

Maca root is believed to help alleviate stress and fatigue and to balance hormone levels. Its slightly malty, burnt sugar flavor nicely complements cinnamon and vanilla. The buckwheat groats not only add pleasing texture but also provide a particularly delicious way to up your intake of wholesome whole grains!

**MAKES ABOUT
4 CUPS (1 L)**

Tips

Maca root comes from the Andes Mountains in Peru. It has long been used to increase fertility and as an adaptogen to treat stress. It has a flavor similar to butterscotch or burnt sugar and works well in sweets, sauces and smoothies.

When blending hot liquids in a blender, make sure your blender is no more than half full. Also, place a folded towel over the lid and place your hand firmly on top. Otherwise, the pressure of the steam may cause the lid to blow off, spattering liquid all over the kitchen.

Although it is an extra step, blending the ice cream mixture before chilling it emulsifies the solution and helps to prevent ice crystals from forming.

- **Blender**
- **Ice-cream maker**

1	can (14 oz/400 mL) full-fat coconut milk	1
1	can (14 oz/400 mL) coconut cream (see Tips, page 520)	1
½ cup	organic coconut sugar (see Tips, page 520)	125 mL
¼ cup	raw agave nectar (see Tips, page 520)	60 mL
1 tbsp	maca root powder (see Tips, left)	15 mL
1 tsp	ground cinnamon	5 mL
¼ tsp	organic vanilla powder (see Tips, page 522)	1 mL
⅛ tsp	fine sea salt	0.5 mL
¼ cup	raw buckwheat groats	60 mL

1. In a small saucepan over medium heat, combine coconut milk, coconut cream, coconut sugar, agave nectar, maca powder, cinnamon, vanilla and salt. Bring to a simmer and cook, stirring occasionally, for 2 to 3 minutes or until sugar is completely dissolved.

2. Transfer mixture to blender in batches (see Tips, left). Blend at high speed for 30 seconds. Transfer to a bowl, cover and refrigerate for at least 4 hours or overnight.

3. Stir well. Transfer to ice-cream maker and freeze according to manufacturer's instructions. Add buckwheat just before the last 5 minutes of freezing and let the machine stir it in. Transfer to an airtight container and store in the freezer for up to 2 weeks.

Peanut Butter Fudge Ice Cream

This creamy recipe is a decadent treat that any peanut-butter lover will enjoy. Serve it with a big dollop of Whipped Coconut Cream (page 565).

MAKES ABOUT 4 CUPS (1 L)

Tips

Be sure to use raw (not processed) agave nectar. It is a 100% natural (non-GMO) sweetener that contains naturally occurring fructose and is low on the glycemic scale, which means that it releases glucose slowly, providing sustained energy.

Organic vanilla powder can be found in most well-stocked supermarkets and natural food stores. It is made from dried and ground whole vanilla beans and will add a lot of flavor to your dishes. If you cannot find it, substitute ½ tsp (2 mL) alcohol-free organic vanilla extract.

For added crunch, use crunchy peanut butter.

For a nut-free version, substitute an equal amount of sunflower seed butter for the peanut butter.

To melt the coconut oil, gently warm it in a small skillet over low heat.

- **Blender**
- **Ice-cream maker**

1	can (14 oz/400 mL) full-fat coconut milk	1
1	can (14 oz/400 mL) coconut cream (see Tips, page 526)	1
½ cup	organic coconut sugar (see Tips, page 525)	125 mL
¼ cup	raw agave nectar (see Tips, left)	60 mL
¼ tsp	organic vanilla powder (see Tips, left)	1 mL
⅛ tsp	fine sea salt	0.5 mL
½ cup	smooth peanut butter (see Tips, left)	125 mL
¼ cup	melted coconut oil (see Tips, left)	60 mL
2 tbsp	pure maple syrup	30 mL

1. In a small saucepan over medium heat, combine coconut milk, coconut cream, coconut sugar, agave nectar, vanilla and salt. Bring to a simmer and cook, stirring occasionally, for 2 to 3 minutes or until sugar is completely dissolved.

2. Transfer mixture to blender in batches (see Tips, page 523). Blend at high speed for 30 seconds. Transfer to a bowl, cover and refrigerate for at least 4 hours or overnight.

3. Stir well. Transfer to ice-cream maker and freeze according to manufacturer's instructions.

4. Meanwhile, in a small bowl, whisk together peanut butter, coconut oil and maple syrup. Cover and freeze for 20 minutes, until firm. Using a knife, cut into ¼- to ½-inch (0.5 to 1 cm) pieces. Refrigerate until ready to use.

5. Add pieces of peanut butter mixture just before the last 5 minutes of freezing and let the machine stir them in. Transfer to an airtight container and store in the freezer for up to 2 weeks.

Pecan Pie Ice Cream

For many people, pecan pie topped with whipped cream is a holiday tradition. This creamy, rich, dairy- and gluten-free treat is sure to be equally satisfying. For real decadence, candy the pecans before adding them to the ice cream (see Tips, below).

MAKES ABOUT 4 CUPS (1 L)

Tips

There are numerous varieties of dates, but Medjools are my favorite. Although they are generally more expensive, they are larger, softer and, in my opinion, more flavorful.

Coconut sugar is a low-glycemic sweetener that is available in most well-stocked supermarkets and natural food stores. It has a sweet taste similar to brown sugar.

To toast the pecans: Heat a dry skillet over medium heat. Add pecans and cook, stirring frequently, until they just start to turn golden brown. Transfer to a plate and set aside to cool completely.

To candy the pecans: Toss with ½ cup (125 mL) pure maple syrup and a pinch of fine sea salt. Arrange in a single layer on a baking sheet lined with parchment paper. Bake in a preheated 400°F (200°C) oven for 6 to 8 minutes or until golden brown. Immediately transfer to a bowl and set aside to cool.

- Blender
- Ice-cream maker

1	can (14 oz/400 mL) full-fat coconut milk	1
1	can (14 oz/400 mL) coconut cream (see Tips, page 526)	1
½ cup	chopped pitted Medjool dates, divided (see Tips, left)	125 mL
½ cup	organic coconut sugar (see Tips, left)	125 mL
¼ cup	raw agave nectar (see Tips, page 524)	60 mL
½ tsp	ground cinnamon	2 mL
¼ tsp	organic vanilla powder (see Tips, page 524)	1 mL
⅛ tsp	fine sea salt	0.5 mL
¼ cup	raw buckwheat groats	60 mL
½ cup	chopped toasted pecans (see Tips, left)	125 mL

1. In a small saucepan over medium heat, combine coconut milk, coconut cream, ¼ cup (60 mL) dates, coconut sugar, agave nectar, cinnamon, vanilla and salt. Bring to a simmer and cook, stirring occasionally, for 2 to 3 minutes or until sugar is completely dissolved and dates are soft.

2. Transfer mixture to blender, in batches (see Tips, page 523). Blend at high speed for 30 seconds. Transfer to a bowl, cover and refrigerate for at least 4 hours or overnight.

3. Stir well. Transfer to ice-cream maker and freeze according to manufacturer's instructions. Add buckwheat and remaining ¼ cup (60 mL) dates and pecans just before the last 5 minutes of freezing and let the machine stir them in. Transfer to an airtight container and store in the freezer for up to 2 weeks.

Minty Hemp and Chia Ice Cream

Hemp and chia seeds are emerging as superfoods. Why not capture their nutritious qualities in a refreshing ice cream that is chock-full of healthy proteins and fats?

MAKES ABOUT 4 CUPS (1 L)

Tips

Coconut sugar is a low glycemic sweetener that is available in most well stocked supermarkets and natural food stores. It has a sweet taste similar to brown sugar.

Coconut cream is similar to coconut milk but contains less water and has a higher fat content. Look for it in well-stocked supermarkets and Indian grocery stores.

Organic vanilla powder can be found in most well-stocked supermarkets and natural food stores. It is made from dried and ground whole vanilla beans and will add a lot of flavor to your dishes. If you cannot find organic vanilla powder, substitute ½ tsp (2 mL) alcohol-free organic vanilla extract.

When purchasing pure extracts, look for alcohol-free brands, to avoid the taste of raw alcohol in your dish.

- **Blender**
- **Ice-cream maker**

1	can (14 oz/400 mL) full-fat coconut milk	1
1	can (14 oz/400 mL) coconut cream (see Tips, left)	1
½ cup	organic coconut sugar (see Tips, left)	125 mL
½ cup	packed thinly sliced mint leaves	125 mL
¼ cup	raw agave nectar (see Tips, page 527)	60 mL
¼ tsp	organic vanilla powder (see Tips, left)	1 mL
⅛ tsp	fine sea salt	0.5 mL
1 tsp	alcohol-free organic peppermint extract (see Tips, left)	5 mL
3 tbsp	raw shelled hemp seeds	45 mL
1 tbsp	chia seeds	15 mL

1. In a small saucepan over medium heat, combine coconut milk, coconut cream, coconut sugar, mint, agave nectar, vanilla and salt. Bring to a simmer and cook, stirring occasionally, for 2 to 3 minutes or until sugar is completely dissolved.

2. Transfer mixture to blender in batches (see Tips, page 523). Blend at high speed for 30 seconds. Transfer to a bowl, cover and refrigerate for at least 4 hours or overnight.

3. Stir well. Transfer to ice-cream maker and freeze according to manufacturer's instructions. Add hemp seeds and chia seeds just before the last 5 minutes of freezing and let the machine stir them in. Transfer to an airtight container and store in the freezer for up to 2 weeks.

Strawberry Sherbet

This dairy-free frozen dessert is bursting with fresh strawberries. Try it sprinkled with some hemp and chia seeds for a healthy treat.

MAKES ABOUT 4 CUPS (1 L)

Tips

Substitute an equal amount of fresh raspberries for the strawberries. For a smooth sherbet, after blending, strain the mixture through a fine-mesh sieve to remove the seeds.

Substitute an equal amount of Cashew Milk (page 61) or Strawberry Hazelnut Milk (page 65) for the almond milk.

Be sure to use raw (not processed) agave nectar. It is a 100% natural (non-GMO) sweetener that contains naturally occurring fructose and is low on the glycemic scale, which means that it releases glucose slowly, providing sustained energy.

Organic vanilla powder can be found in most well-stocked supermarkets and natural food stores. It is made from dried and ground whole vanilla beans, and they add a lot of natural flavor to ice creams. If you cannot find it, substitute ½ tsp (2 mL) alcohol-free organic vanilla extract.

- Blender
- Ice-cream maker

3 cups	chopped hulled strawberries (see Tips, left)	750 mL
2 cups	Almond Milk (page 61; see Tips, left)	500 mL
¼ cup	raw agave nectar (see Tips, left)	60 mL
1 tbsp	pure maple syrup	15 mL
½ tsp	freshly grated lemon zest	2 mL
1 tbsp	freshly squeezed lemon juice	15 mL
¼ tsp	organic vanilla powder (see Tips, left)	1 mL

1. In blender, combine strawberries, almond milk, agave nectar, maple syrup, lemon zest, lemon juice and vanilla. Blend at high speed until smooth. Transfer to a bowl, cover and refrigerate for at least 4 hours or overnight.

2. Transfer to ice-cream maker and freeze according to manufacturer's instructions. Transfer to an airtight container and store in the freezer for up to 2 weeks.

Variation

Strawberry Double Chocolate Sherbet: Add 3 tbsp (45 mL) raw cacao powder to the blender in Step 1. Add 1 tbsp (15 mL) raw cacao nibs or 2 tbsp (30 mL) non-dairy chocolate chips in Step 2, just before the last 5 minutes of freezing, and let the machine stir them in.

Peach Cinnamon Sherbet

The combination of fresh peaches, cinnamon and vanilla in this creamy frozen treat will remind you of peach pie. For the best flavor, make it when local peaches are in season. Try it drizzled with Easy Coconut Caramel Sauce (page 506).

MAKES 4 CUPS (1 L)

Tips

To slice a peach: Run a paring knife around its middle, through to the stone. Use your hands to twist and divide into two halves. Slice the half without the stone into the desired number of pieces. For the half with the stone, use your knife to loosen and remove it before slicing.

Use high-quality organic cinnamon. You will get the freshest flavor by grinding whole cinnamon sticks in a clean spice grinder.

Organic vanilla powder can be found in most well-stocked supermarkets and natural food stores. It is made from dried and ground whole vanilla beans and will add a lot of flavor to your dishes. If you cannot find it, substitute ¼ tsp (1 mL) alcohol-free organic vanilla extract.

- Blender
- Ice-cream maker

3 cups	sliced peaches, frozen (see Tips, left)	750 mL
2 cups	Almond Milk (page 61)	500 mL
¼ cup	raw agave nectar	60 mL
1 tbsp	pure maple syrup	15 mL
1 tsp	ground cinnamon (see Tips, left)	5 mL
½ tsp	freshly squeezed lemon juice	2 mL
⅛ tsp	organic vanilla powder (see Tips, left)	0.5 mL

1. In blender, combine peaches, almond milk, agave nectar, maple syrup, cinnamon, lemon juice and vanilla. Blend at high speed until smooth.
2. Transfer to ice-cream maker and freeze according to manufacturer's instructions. Transfer to an airtight container and store in the freezer for up to 2 weeks.

Vegan Basics

Cheeses

Salads and Dressings

Staples

Herbed Tofu Ricotta

Use this tofu ricotta in any dish that calls for traditional ricotta cheese. I like it in Mushroom and Spinach Lasagna (page 274) and cannelloni, or as a simple spread on crusty gluten-free baguette. For a great appetizer, use it as the centerpiece for an antipasto platter, surrounded with olives, roasted vegetables, artichokes . . . there are so many possibilities!

(page 274)

**MAKES ABOUT
4 CUPS (1 L)**

Tips

Nutritional yeast is an inactive yeast that is grown on beet molasses and then pasteurized. It helps to provide a cheesy, rich flavor in sauces, stews, soups and dips. Look for it in most well-stocked supermarkets and natural food stores.

You will need 1 package (11 oz/325 g) baby spinach to make the White Wine, Garlic and Spinach Tofu Ricotta.

● **Food processor**

1	block (16 oz/500 g) firm tofu, cut into 1-inch (2.5 cm) cubes	1
¼ cup	nutritional yeast (see Tips, left)	60 mL
1 tbsp	dried oregano leaves	15 mL
1½ tsp	fine sea salt	7 mL
1 tsp	dried basil leaves	5 mL

1. In food processor fitted with the metal blade, process tofu until broken down into small pieces. Transfer to a bowl.
2. Add nutritional yeast, oregano, salt and basil; stir until well combined. Serve immediately or transfer to an airtight container and refrigerate for up to 1 week.

Variation

White Wine, Garlic and Spinach Tofu Ricotta: In a large skillet over medium heat, heat 2 tbsp (30 mL) grapeseed oil. Add 3 to 4 minced garlic cloves and cook, stirring occasionally, until just brown. Add 8 cups (2 L) packed chopped baby spinach (see Tips, left) and cook, stirring occasionally, until soft, about 1 minute. Stir in ½ cup (125 mL) dry white wine and cook for 5 to 6 minutes, until alcohol is cooked off. Stir into prepared Herbed Tofu Ricotta. Serve immediately or transfer to an airtight container and refrigerate for up to 1 week. Use the same way that you would traditional ricotta.

Cashew Cream Cheese

Cashews stand in for dairy in this vegan version of a classic. Smear it on a gluten-free bagel, spread it in your favorite wrap or sandwich, or use it as a dip for fresh vegetables.

**MAKES
3 CUPS (750 ML)**

Tip

A citrus reamer is a hand-held tool used to extract the juice from lemons and limes. It is available in most kitchen supply stores and would be ideal to use for the lemon juice in this recipe.

Food processor

4½ cups	water, divided	1.1 L
4 cups	raw cashews	1 L
2 tbsp	freshly squeezed lemon juice (see Tip, left)	30 mL
2 tsp	fine sea salt	10 mL

1. In a saucepan, combine 4 cups (1 L) water and cashews and bring to a boil. Remove from heat. Drain, discarding liquid.

2. In food processor fitted with the metal blade, process boiled cashews, remaining ½ cup (125 mL) water, lemon juice and salt until smooth, stopping the motor to scrape down sides of work bowl as needed. Serve immediately or cover and refrigerate for up to 10 days.

Creamy Cashew Ricotta

This rich and creamy vegan cheese is a soy-free alternative to tofu ricotta. Use it as a topping for pizza, a filling for calzones, a dressing for pasta, a dip for fresh vegetables or a spread in your favorite sandwich.

**MAKES ABOUT
3 CUPS (750 ML)**

Tips

To soak the cashews: Place in a bowl and cover with 8 cups (2 L) water. Cover and set aside for 3 hours or overnight (if overnight, refrigerate). Drain, discarding liquid.

A hand-held citrus reamer can be used to extract the juice from lemons and limes. Available in most kitchen supply stores, this tool would be ideal to use for the lemon juice in this recipe.

Nutritional yeast is an inactive yeast that is grown on beet molasses and then pasteurized. It helps to provide a cheesy, rich flavor in sauces, stews, soups and dips. Look for it in most well-stocked supermarkets and natural food stores.

- **Food processor**
- **Blender**

3 cups	raw cashews, soaked, divided (see Tips, left)	750 mL
1 cup	water, divided	250 mL
1/4 cup	freshly squeezed lemon juice (see Tips, left)	60 mL
1/4 cup	nutritional yeast (see Tips, left)	60 mL
1 tsp	fine sea salt	5 mL
1 to 2	cloves garlic	1 to 2
1/4 cup	extra virgin olive oil	60 mL

1. In food processor fitted with the metal blade, process 2 cups (500 mL) soaked cashews, 1/4 cup (60 mL) water, lemon juice, nutritional yeast, salt and garlic until no large pieces of cashew remain. Transfer to a bowl.

2. In blender, combine remaining cashews, oil and remaining water. Blend at high speed until smooth and creamy, stopping to scrape down sides of blender jar as necessary.

3. Add to mixture with nutritional yeast and stir until well combined. Serve immediately or transfer to an airtight container and refrigerate for up to 10 days.

Variations

Herbed Cashew Ricotta: In Step 1, add 2 tbsp (30 mL) chopped fresh thyme leaves and 1 tsp (5 mL) chopped fresh rosemary to the food processor.

Spicy Roasted Red Pepper Cashew Ricotta: In Step 1, add 1/2 tsp (2 mL) cayenne pepper and 1/2 cup (125 mL) roasted red bell peppers to the food processor.

Sun-Dried Tomato and Olive Pesto Cashew Cheese

This is more like a cream cheese spread than a real cheese. It is great served on crackers, on your favorite bread as a sandwich spread, or tossed with hot fresh pasta.

MAKES ABOUT 2 CUPS (500 ML)

Tips

To soak the cashews: Place in a bowl and cover with 4 cups (1 L) water. Cover and set aside for 3 hours or overnight (if overnight, refrigerate). Drain, discarding liquid.

To soak the sun-dried tomatoes: Place in a bowl and cover with 4 cups (1 L) water. Cover and set aside for 3 hours or overnight (if overnight, refrigerate). Drain, discarding liquid.

● **Food processor**

2 cups	raw cashews, soaked (see Tips, left)	500 mL
½ cup	sun-dried tomatoes, soaked (see Tips, left)	125 mL
¼ cup	freshly squeezed lemon juice (see Tips, page 532)	60 mL
3 tbsp	nutritional yeast (see Tips, page 532)	45 mL
1 tsp	fine sea salt	5 mL
4 to 6	cloves garlic	4 to 6
2 cups	packed fresh basil leaves	500 mL
½ cup	thinly sliced pitted kalamata olives	125 mL
¼ cup	extra virgin olive oil	60 mL

1. In food processor fitted with the metal blade, combine soaked cashews, soaked sun-dried tomatoes, lemon juice, nutritional yeast, salt and garlic. Process until smooth, stopping the motor to scrape down sides of work bowl as necessary. Add basil and olives and pulse 8 to 10 times to combine.

2. With the motor running, drizzle oil through the feed tube and process until smooth and creamy. Serve immediately or transfer to an airtight container and refrigerate for up to 10 days.

Creamy Vegan Pepper Jack

Use this peppery cheese in any dish that calls for the traditional dairy version. It's also great cut into cubes and served with crisp toast points and fresh fruit, as a simple appetizer or healthy snack.

MAKES ABOUT 3 CUPS (750 ML)

Tips

To soak the cashews: Place in a bowl and cover with 4 cups (1 L) water. Cover and set aside for 8 hours or overnight (if overnight, refrigerate). Drain, discarding liquid.

To melt the coconut oil, gently warm it in a small skillet over low heat.

Either sunflower or soy lecithin will work well in this recipe. Just make sure it is organic, as most lecithins are extracted using chemical processes.

If you prefer your cheese not to have a subtle taste of coconut, use refined coconut oil.

Agar is made from a seaweed and is sometimes referred to as "sea gelatin." It is available in both powder and flake forms at most well-stocked supermarkets and natural food stores. Use agar flakes in this recipe.

- Blender
- 8-inch (20 cm) square glass baking dish

1 cup	raw cashews, soaked (see Tips, left)	250 mL
1 cup	Almond Milk (page 61)	250 mL
¼ cup	nutritional yeast (see Tips, page 535)	60 mL
3 tbsp	melted coconut oil (see Tips, left)	45 mL
1 tbsp	freshly squeezed lemon juice	15 mL
1 tsp	fine sea salt	5 mL
1 tsp	garlic powder	5 mL
½ tsp	onion powder	2 mL
½ tsp	sunflower lecithin granules (see Tips, left)	2 mL
½ cup	chopped red bell pepper	125 mL
½ cup	chopped seeded jalapeño peppers	125 mL
1 cup	water	250 mL
½ cup	agar flakes (see Tips, left)	125 mL

1. In blender, combine soaked cashews, almond milk, nutritional yeast, coconut oil, lemon juice, salt, garlic powder, onion powder and sunflower lecithin. Blend at high speed until smooth and creamy, stopping the motor to scrape down sides of blender jar as necessary. Add red pepper and jalapeño peppers; pulse to combine.

2. In a small saucepan, combine water and agar flakes. Bring to a boil, stirring constantly until agar is completely dissolved. Pour into blender and pulse 2 to 3 times to combine.

3. Transfer mixture to baking dish. Refrigerate until firm, about 8 hours or overnight. Serve immediately or transfer to an airtight container and refrigerate for up to 2 weeks.

Cashew Cheddar Cheese

This creamy version of Cheddar cheese can be used to replace milk-based cheese sauces in most recipes that call for melting or spreadable Cheddar. It is delicious drizzled over nachos, layered in baked dishes, or as a dip.

MAKES 4 CUPS (1 L)

Tips

Nutritional yeast is an inactive yeast that is grown on beet molasses and then pasteurized. It helps to provide a cheesy, rich flavor in sauces, stews, soups and dips. Look for it in most well-stocked supermarkets and natural food stores.

A hand-held citrus reamer can be used to extract the juice from lemons and limes. Available in most kitchen supply stores, this tool would be ideal to use for the lemon juice in this recipe.

- **Food processor**
- **8-inch (20 cm) square glass baking dish**

4 cups	water, divided	1 L
3 cups	raw cashews	750 mL
1 cup	nutritional yeast (see Tips, left)	250 mL
2 tbsp	freshly squeezed lemon juice (see Tips, left)	30 mL
1 tsp	ground turmeric	5 mL
1 tsp	fine sea salt	5 mL

1. In a large saucepan, combine 3 cups (750 mL) water and cashews. Bring to a boil, then drain, discarding liquid.

2. In food processor fitted with the metal blade, process boiled cashews, remaining 1 cup (250 mL) water, nutritional yeast, lemon juice, turmeric and salt until smooth and creamy. Serve immediately or refrigerate for up to 10 days in an airtight container.

Variations

Firm Cashew Cheddar Cheese: If you need a cheese that can be sliced or shredded, make this version. In a small bowl, whisk together $\frac{1}{2}$ cup (125 mL) agar flakes and $\frac{1}{2}$ cup (125 mL) hot water. Transfer to a small saucepan and add $\frac{1}{2}$ cup (125 mL) water. Simmer, stirring constantly, until agar dissolves completely, 2 to 3 minutes. Add to food processor with other ingredients in Step 2 and process until smooth. Transfer to baking dish. Cover and refrigerate until firm, about 8 hours, or overnight. Serve immediately or transfer to an airtight container and refrigerate for up to 10 days.

Chipotle Cheddar Dip: Increase the amount of lemon juice to $\frac{1}{4}$ cup (60 mL) and salt to 2 tsp (10 mL). Add $\frac{1}{2}$ cup (125 mL) chia seeds. Soak 2 dried chipotle peppers in 1 cup (250 mL) hot water until soft, about 30 minutes. Chop and add to food processor in Step 2.

Vegan White Cheddar

This is a soft, sharp Cheddar-type cheese that you can spread in your favorite sandwich, fold into a pasta dish or roll into balls and serve as part of your next cheese platter.

Tips

To soak the cashews: Place in a bowl and cover with 4 cups (1 L) water. Cover and set aside for 3 hours or overnight (if overnight, refrigerate). Drain, discarding liquid.

A hand-held citrus reamer can be used to extract the juice from lemons and limes. Available in most kitchen supply stores, this tool would be ideal to use for the lemon juice in this recipe.

Nutritional yeast is an inactive yeast that is grown on beet molasses and then pasteurized. It helps to provide a cheesy, rich flavor in sauces, stews, soups and dips. Look for it in most well-stocked supermarkets and natural food stores.

To melt the coconut oil, gently warm it in a small skillet over low heat.

● **Food processor**

2 cups	raw cashews, soaked (see Tips, left)	500 mL
¼ cup	water	60 mL
¼ cup	freshly squeezed lemon juice (see Tips, left)	60 mL
½ cup	nutritional yeast (see Tips, left)	125 mL
3 tbsp	white miso (see page 7)	45 mL
1 tbsp	tahini	15 mL
1 tbsp	raw (unpasteurized) apple cider vinegar	15 mL
1 tsp	fine sea salt	5 mL
1 tsp	dry mustard powder	5 mL
½ cup	melted coconut oil (see Tips, left)	125 mL

1. In food processor fitted with the metal blade, process soaked cashews, water, lemon juice, nutritional yeast, miso, tahini, vinegar, salt and mustard powder until smooth and creamy, stopping the motor to scrape down sides of work bowl as necessary. Add coconut oil and blend until smooth.

2. Transfer to a 2-cup (500 mL) airtight container. Cover and refrigerate until set, about 3 hours. Serve immediately or refrigerate for up to 10 days.

Vegan Shredded Mozzarella

This vegan mozzarella cheese can be used in the same ways you would use traditional mozzarella. Sprinkle it on top of nachos, pizza or pasta. I also like to toss it with a nice big crisp green salad.

Tips

Agar is available in both powder and flake forms at most well-stocked supermarkets and natural food stores. Use agar flakes in this recipe.

Either sunflower or soy lecithin will work for this recipe. Just make sure it is organic, as most lecithins are extracted using chemical processes.

If you prefer your cheese not to have a subtle taste of coconut, use refined coconut oil.

This recipe can easily be doubled, tripled or quadrupled according to your needs.

A 4½-inch (11 cm) square dish is the perfect size to create a nice firm block of cheese, but any similar-sized dish will work. Just make sure it's small enough to produce a block that will be easy to shred.

- Blender
- **4½-inch (11 cm) square dish (see Tips, left)**

1 cup	raw cashews, soaked (see Tips, page 536)	250 mL
1¼ cups	hot water, divided	300 mL
½ cup	agar flakes (see Tips, left)	125 mL
3 tbsp	melted coconut oil (see Tips, page 536)	45 mL
2 tbsp	nutritional yeast (see Tips, page 536)	30 mL
1 tbsp	freshly squeezed lemon juice	15 mL
1 tsp	fine sea salt	5 mL
½ tsp	sunflower lecithin granules (see Tips, left)	2 mL

1. In a small bowl, whisk together ¼ cup (60 mL) hot water and agar flakes.

2. In a small saucepan, combine remaining 1 cup (250 mL) water and agar mixture. Bring to a simmer and cook until agar is dissolved, 3 to 4 minutes.

3. In blender, combine agar mixture, soaked cashews, coconut oil, nutritional yeast, lemon juice, salt and lecithin. Blend at high speed until smooth and creamy, stopping the motor to scrape down sides of blender jar as necessary. Transfer to dish, cover and refrigerate until set, about 8 hours or overnight.

4. Shred the cheese right away or transfer to an airtight container and refrigerate for up to 2 weeks.

Variations

Roasted Garlic Vegan Mozzarella: In Step 3, add ½ cup (125 mL) roasted garlic and ¼ tsp (1 mL) freshly grated lemon zest to the blender.

Parsley and Olive Vegan Mozzarella: After the cheese has been blended in Step 3, stir in ½ cup (125 mL) roughly chopped flat-leaf (Italian) parsley and ¼ cup (60 mL) thinly sliced pitted black olives. After it has set, cut into cubes or slice.

Vegan Cheese Curds

This cheese is similar to fresh buffalo-milk mozzarella. It can be served cold or melted on pizza, bruschetta or open-face sandwiches.

Tips

To quickly dissolve salt in water: In a small bowl, combine salt and 1 cup (250 mL) boiling water. Stir until salt has completely dissolved. Add to 3 cups (750 mL) cold water and set aside to cool, or add a few ice cubes to speed cooling.

If you are using purchased almond milk, make sure it contains no emulsifiers or preservatives, as they will prevent this recipe from working. For best results, make your own almond milk (page 61).

Agar is made from a seaweed and is sometimes referred to as "sea gelatin." It is available in both powder and flake forms at most well-stocked supermarkets and natural food stores. Use agar powder in this recipe.

Citric acid is available from specialty food retailers and online. Make sure the type you purchase is organic, as most citric acid is made from genetically modified corn. Substitute 2 tbsp (30 mL) freshly squeezed lemon juice for the citric acid.

- **Blender**

BRINE

4 cups	cold water	1 L
1 tbsp	fine sea salt	15 mL

CURDS

2⅔ cups	Almond Milk (page 61; see Tips, left)	650 mL
⅔ cup	tapioca flour	150 mL
⅔ cup	melted coconut oil (see Tips, page 536)	150 mL
2 tbsp	agar powder (see Tips, left)	30 mL
2½ tsp	fine sea salt	12 mL
1¼ tsp	organic citric acid (see Tips, left)	6 mL

1. *Brine:* In a large bowl, whisk together water and salt until salt has completely dissolved (see Tips, left). Cover and refrigerate until ready to use.

2. *Curds:* In blender, combine almond milk, tapioca flour, coconut oil, agar powder and salt. Blend at high speed until smooth, stopping the motor to scrape down sides of blender jar as necessary. Transfer to a saucepan over medium heat and cook, stirring constantly, until thick and creamy, 5 to 6 minutes. Remove from heat and whisk in citric acid.

3. Drop 2 tbsp (30 mL) portions of mixture directly into cold brine, until all of the mixture has formed curds. Leave in brine and refrigerate until curds are cold, about 3 hours.

4. When ready to use, use a slotted spoon to remove desired quantity of curds from brine. Blot dry with paper towels. Leave unused curds in brine and store, refrigerated, for up to 1 week, changing the brine once or twice to ensure that it stays fresh.

Spicy Pumpkinseed Parmesan

Ground pumpkin seeds, nutritional yeast and spices are transformed into a soft, fluffy topping that's perfect for your favorite pasta or salad. Use this cheese wherever you would use traditional Parmesan. While it's not quite the same as shaved aged Parmesan, it is easy to make, stores well and is handy to use in a pinch.

Tips

Nutritional yeast is an inactive yeast that is grown on beet molasses and then pasteurized. It helps to provide a cheesy, rich flavor in sauces, stews, soups and dips. Look for it in most well-stocked supermarkets and natural food stores.

The cayenne pepper provides a subtle hint of spice. If you prefer, you can omit it.

Food processor

1½ cups	raw pumpkin seeds	375 mL
2 tbsp	nutritional yeast (see Tips, left)	30 mL
1 tsp	fine sea salt	5 mL
¼ tsp	cayenne pepper (see Tips, left)	1 mL
2 tbsp	extra virgin olive oil	30 mL

1. In food processor fitted with the metal blade, combine pumpkin seeds, nutritional yeast, salt and cayenne. Process until flour-like in consistency. With the motor running, drizzle oil through the feed tube and process until mixture resembles finely grated Parmesan cheese. Serve immediately or transfer to an airtight container and refrigerate for up to 1 month.

Variations

Herbed Pumpkinseed Parmesan: Omit the cayenne pepper. Add 2 tsp (10 mL) chopped fresh thyme leaves and 1 tsp (5 mL) chopped fresh rosemary. Reduce storage time to 2 weeks.

Almond Parmesan: Omit the cayenne pepper and oil. Substitute an equal quantity of almonds for the pumpkin seeds.

Easy Cheesy Pasta Sauce

Enjoy this cheesy sauce tossed with your favorite pasta, as a dip for fresh vegetables or as a spread on a sandwich or wrap.

MAKES ABOUT
3 CUPS (750 ML)

Tips

To soak the cashews: Place in a bowl and cover with 4 cups (1 L) water. Cover and set aside for 3 hours or overnight (if overnight, refrigerate). Drain, discarding liquid.

A hand-held citrus reamer can be used to extract the juice from lemons and limes. Available in most kitchen supply stores, this tool would be ideal to use for the lemon juice in this recipe.

This sauce will simmer well in a pan, but do not bring it to a full boil — it will split. If adding to a cooked dish, reduce the heat to low and stir it in toward the end of cooking.

• Blender

2 cups	water	500 mL
1 cup	raw cashews, soaked (see Tips, left)	250 mL
⅔ cup	freshly squeezed lemon juice (see Tips, left)	150 mL
1 cup	nutritional yeast (see Tips, page 539)	250 mL
½ cup	tahini	125 mL
½ cup	extra virgin olive oil	125 mL
1 tbsp	Dijon mustard	15 mL
2 tsp	fine sea salt	10 mL
1 to 2	cloves garlic	1 to 2

1. In blender, combine water, soaked cashews, lemon juice, nutritional yeast, tahini, oil, mustard, salt and garlic. Blend at high speed until smooth and creamy, stopping the motor to scrape down sides of blender jar as necessary. Serve immediately or transfer to an airtight container and refrigerate for up to 10 days.

The Big Salad

This salad is a beautiful combination of crisp romaine lettuce, healthy kale and colorful vegetables. The shredded carrot and beet, mixed with tomato wedges, cucumber and avocado, provide a perfect base for any fresh salad greens plus your favorite dressing. Consider this a blank canvas on which to create your masterpiece salads. For a pleasant crunch, add some Gluten-Free Croutons (page 553).

Tips

Virtually any dressing works well on this salad. My favorites are Lemon Dill Cucumber Dressing (page 547), Basic Vinaigrette (page 548) and Easy Italian Dressing (page 546).

When chopping lettuce for a salad, make sure to cut it into bite-sized pieces, about 1 inch (2.5 cm) square. Dressing spills are more likely to occur with larger pieces.

Before chopping the kale, use a sharp knife to remove the tough center rib. Use only the leafy green parts.

2 cups	chopped romaine lettuce (see Tips, left)	500 mL
1 cup	chopped trimmed kale (see Tips, left)	250 mL
1/4 cup	shredded carrot (about 1 small)	60 mL
1/4 cup	shredded beet (about 1/2 small)	60 mL
1/4 cup	salad dressing (see Tips, left)	60 mL
1/2 cup	tomato wedges (about 1 small)	125 mL
1/2 cup	sliced cucumber (about 1/2 small)	60 mL
1/2 cup	sliced avocado (about 1/2 small)	60 mL
1/4 cup	Basic Chickpea Hummus (page 72)	60 mL

1. In a large serving bowl, toss together lettuce, kale, carrot, beet and dressing. Arrange tomato wedges, cucumber slices, avocado slices and dollops of hummus on top. Serve immediately.

Variations

Substitute Black Olive and Walnut Butter (page 134) or Ranch Dip (page 80) for the hummus.

For an additional boost of protein, add 2 tbsp (30 mL) raw shelled hemp seeds.

Wilted Spinach Salad

This is a wonderful, simple salad. It can be served on its own or used as a base for nutritious toppings such as Creamy Cashew Tzatziki (page 79), Queso Dip (page 82) or Edamame Hummus (page 73).

**MAKES
2 MAIN-COURSE
OR 4 SIDE SALADS**

Tips

If you are using baby spinach, double the amount, because it is lighter and less dense.

You can replace the lemon juice with an equal amount of lime juice.

6 cups	tightly packed chopped spinach leaves (see Tips, left)	1.5 L
½ cup	extra virgin olive oil	125 mL
¼ cup	freshly squeezed lemon juice (see Tips, page 543)	60 mL
1 tsp	fine sea salt	5 mL

1. In a large serving bowl, toss together spinach, oil, lemon juice and salt. Set aside for 15 minutes, until spinach wilts. Serve immediately or transfer to an airtight container and refrigerate for up to 2 days.

Avocado and Cucumber Salad

This light, creamy salad will delight your taste buds. I like to serve it over crisp romaine lettuce or baby spinach leaves.

Tips

Do not chop the parsley too finely. You want it to be a main ingredient in this salad, as opposed to a side note. Similarly, keep the avocado and cucumber chunky to ensure a salad-like result. If the ingredients are diced, it turns out more like a salsa.

A citrus reamer is a hand-held tool used to extract the juice from lemons and limes. It is available in most kitchen supply stores and would be ideal to use for the citrus juice in this recipe.

2 cups	cubed (1 inch/2.5 cm) avocado (about 3 medium)	500 mL
1 cup	cubed (1 inch/2.5 cm) peeled, seeded cucumber (about ½ large)	250 mL
⅓ cup	coarsely chopped flat-leaf (Italian) parsley leaves (see Tips, left)	75 mL
3 tbsp	cold-pressed flaxseed oil	45 mL
2 tbsp	freshly squeezed lemon or lime juice (see Tips, left)	30 mL
1½ tsp	fine sea salt	7 mL
Pinch	freshly ground black pepper	Pinch

1. In a serving bowl, toss together avocado, cucumber, parsley, oil, lemon juice, salt and pepper. Serve immediately.

Variations

Add ½ cup (125 mL) chopped tomato.

To give this salad a Southwestern spin, replace the parsley with an equal amount of coarsely chopped fresh cilantro leaves. Add 1 tsp (5 mL) chili powder and ½ tsp (2 mL) ground cumin, stirring into the lemon juice before combining the ingredients.

You can replace the oil and lemon juice with Easy Italian Dressing (page 546) or Basic Vinaigrette (page 548).

Shred-Me-Up Slaw

I love the simplicity of combining common ingredients to create a hearty, healthy dish. This slaw can be enjoyed as a snack or a main course.

Tips

For shredding small amounts of vegetables, use the large holes on a box grater. For larger amounts you can use the shredding attachment of your food processor.

I like to use peeled butternut squash for this recipe.

I prefer to use organic sea salt, which is classified as a whole food and is said to contain many trace minerals. If salt intake is something you are concerned about, feel free to use less than called for, or omit it completely.

½ cup	shredded carrot (see Tips, left)	125 mL
½ cup	shredded beet	125 mL
½ cup	finely sliced kale	125 mL
¼ cup	shredded squash (see Tips, left)	60 mL
3 tbsp	freshly squeezed lemon juice (see Tips, page 545)	45 mL
½ tsp	fine sea salt (see Tips, left)	2 mL

1. In a serving bowl, toss together carrot, beet, kale and squash. Add lemon juice and salt and toss well. Set aside for 10 minutes, until softened. Serve immediately or transfer to an airtight container and refrigerate for up to 2 days.

Variations

Substitute an equal quantity of lime juice for the lemon juice.

Replace the kale with an equal quantity of finely sliced chard.

For a boost of protein, add 3 tbsp (45 mL) raw shelled hemp seeds.

Crunchy Cabbage and Carrot Slaw

This crunchy slaw will remind you of family picnics and summer barbecues. Enjoy it knowing that it contains none of the hidden ingredients present in most store-bought coleslaws.

**MAKES
1 MAIN-COURSE
OR 2 SIDE SALADS**

Tips

A citrus reamer is a hand-held tool used to extract the juice from lemons and limes. It is available in most kitchen supply stores and would be ideal to use for the lemon juice in this recipe.

For a boost of protein, add ¼ cup (60 mL) raw cashews.

Use either red or green cabbage in this recipe.

2 cups	shredded cabbage (see Tips, page 544)	500 mL
1 cup	shredded carrots	250 mL
¼ cup	freshly squeezed lemon juice (see Tips, left)	60 mL
3 tbsp	extra virgin olive oil	45 mL
2 tbsp	raw agave nectar (see page 8)	30 mL
¼ tsp	fine sea salt	1 mL

1. In a large serving bowl, combine cabbage, carrots, lemon juice, oil, agave nectar and salt. Toss until well combined. Cover and set aside for 10 minutes, until cabbage has softened slightly. Serve immediately or cover and refrigerate for up to 3 days.

Easy Italian Dressing

When I was a kid, I loved Italian salad dressing. I put it on everything from hot dogs and hamburgers to mac 'n' cheese. As an adult I have fallen in love with this healthier alternative made with unpasteurized apple cider vinegar, which may aid in digestion and provide healthy bacteria to improve the health status of your gut. Try this dressing over a big bowl of crisp romaine lettuce and juicy tomatoes.

MAKES ABOUT 1¼ CUPS (300 ML)

Tips

I like to use unpasteurized apple cider vinegar in this recipe for its superior flavor and nutritional benefits, but conventional apple cider vinegar will work as well.

Substitute ⅓ cup (75 mL) freshly squeezed lemon juice for the vinegar.

You can substitute 3 tbsp (45 mL) fresh oregano leaves for the dried.

I prefer to use organic sea salt, which is classified as a whole food and is said to contain many trace minerals. If salt intake is something you are concerned about, feel free to use less than called for, or omit it completely.

● Blender

¾ cup	extra virgin olive oil	175 mL
¼ cup	raw (unpasteurized) apple cider vinegar (see Tips, left)	60 mL
2 tbsp	water	30 mL
1 tbsp	raw agave nectar (see page 8)	15 mL
1 tbsp	dried oregano (see Tips, left)	15 mL
1 tsp	fine sea salt	5 mL
2	cloves garlic	2

1. In blender, combine oil, vinegar, water, agave nectar, oregano, salt and garlic. Blend at high speed until smooth. Serve immediately or cover and refrigerate for up to 7 days. Whisk before serving.

Lemon Dill Cucumber Dressing

This light and refreshing dressing is a mixture of cooling cucumber, fresh and flavorful dill and tangy lemon. When the temperature climbs, I like to serve this with a big bowl of fresh baby spinach, juicy cherry tomatoes and creamy avocado.

MAKES ABOUT 1¼ CUPS (300 ML)

Tips

A citrus reamer is a hand-held tool used to extract the juice from lemons and limes. It is available in most kitchen supply stores and would be ideal to use for the lemon juice in this recipe.

Using a food processor gives this dressing a bit of texture, which I prefer. If you like a smoother dressing, by all means use a blender.

Food processor (see Tips, left)

1 cup	chopped cucumber	250 mL
½ cup	extra virgin olive oil	125 mL
¼ cup	freshly squeezed lemon juice (see Tips, left)	60 mL
¼ cup	water	60 mL
1 tsp	fine sea salt	5 mL
1	bunch fresh dill, stems removed, roughly chopped	1
2	cloves garlic, peeled	2

1. In food processor fitted with the metal blade, process cucumber, oil, lemon juice, water, salt, dill and garlic until smooth, stopping the motor to scrape down sides of work bowl as necessary. Serve immediately or cover and refrigerate for up to 3 days. Whisk before serving.

Variation

Substitute 2 small bunches of fresh basil, stems removed, for the dill.

Basic Vinaigrette

This vinaigrette is perfect drizzled over crisp lettuce, as well as many other fresh vegetables such as carrots, beets, broccoli and dark green kale. I like to keep it on hand and stir in whatever fresh herbs are available, such as thyme, rosemary or basil, for a new variation every time I use it.

**MAKES ABOUT
1 CUP (250 ML)**

Tips

For a more robust dressing, substitute an equal amount of red wine vinegar for the white wine vinegar.

To vary the nutrients and flavor, substitute an equal amount of flaxseed, hemp or avocado oil for the olive oil.

You can substitute an equal amount of pure maple syrup or coconut nectar for the agave nectar.

Blender

¾ cup	extra virgin olive oil (see Tips, left)	175 mL
¼ cup	white wine vinegar (see Tips, left)	60 mL
1 tbsp	Dijon mustard	15 mL
1 tsp	raw agave nectar (see page 8)	5 mL
¼ tsp	fine sea salt	1 mL

1. In blender, combine oil, vinegar, mustard, agave nectar and salt. Blend at high speed until smooth. Use immediately or transfer to an airtight container and store at room temperature for up to 1 week or in the refrigerator for up to 1 month. Whisk before serving.

Variations

Balsamic Vinaigrette: For a very robust dressing that is particularly well suited to baby spinach or romaine, substitute an equal amount of vegan-friendly balsamic vinegar for the white wine vinegar. Increase the amount of mustard to 2 tbsp (30 mL) and the agave nectar to 1 tbsp (15 mL). Add 1 tsp (5 mL) dried oregano leaves.

Citrus Vinaigrette: For a dressing with a nice citrusy tang, substitute 2 tbsp (30 mL) each freshly squeezed lemon juice, orange juice and grapefruit juice for the white wine vinegar.

Creamy Oil-Free Salad Dressing

This creamy dressing is a nice oil-free alternative to vinaigrette. Serve it over crisp romaine lettuce garnished with Gluten-Free Croutons (page 553) and some hemp or chia seeds for protein. It also works well drizzled over Basic Quinoa (page 235) and greens.

MAKES ABOUT 3 CUPS (750 ML)

Tips

Use regular yellow or golden Dijon mustard for this recipe. If you use the grainy kind, it will not emulsify or be as creamy.

I like to use unpasteurized apple cider vinegar in this recipe for its superior flavor and nutritional benefits, but conventional apple cider vinegar will work as well.

Look for unpasteurized brown rice miso in the refrigerated section of your health food store or supermarket. It is gluten-free and, since it is not pasteurized, has more health benefits than shelf-stable varieties.

Blender

2 cups	water	500 mL
1 cup	Dijon mustard (see Tips, left)	250 mL
¼ cup	raw (unpasteurized) apple cider vinegar (see Tips, left)	60 mL
2 tbsp	brown rice miso (see Tips, left)	30 mL
2 tbsp	raw agave nectar (see page 8)	30 mL
2 tbsp	ground cumin	30 mL

1. In blender, combine water, mustard, vinegar, miso, agave nectar and cumin. Blend at high speed until smooth and creamy. Serve immediately or transfer to an airtight container and refrigerate for up to 2 weeks. Whisk before serving.

Variation

Herbed Red Wine Vinegar Oil-Free Dressing: Substitute an equal amount of red wine vinegar for the apple cider vinegar and add 1 tsp (5 mL) each chopped fresh thyme and rosemary.

Vegan Mayonnaise

A good mayonnaise is indispensable in the kitchen: it can be used as a spread and to make dressings, sauces and dips. Leaving out the eggs not only makes it vegan-friendly but also removes a common allergen.

**MAKES ABOUT
4 CUPS (1 L)**

Tips

This recipe can be halved. If you do so, be sure to scrape down the sides of the blender jar when puréeing the cashews (the smaller quantity may cause them to stick to the sides). Blend until the mixture is smooth and creamy.

I like to use unpasteurized apple cider vinegar in this recipe for its superior flavor and nutritional benefits, but conventional apple cider vinegar will work as well.

Use regular Dijon mustard for this recipe, not the grainy brown type, which will not emulsify well.

You can substitute an equal amount of grapeseed oil for the olive oil.

• Food processor

1½ cups	raw cashews	375 mL
¼ cup	water	60 mL
2 tbsp	freshly squeezed lemon juice	30 mL
1 tbsp	raw (unpasteurized) apple cider vinegar (see Tips, left)	15 mL
1 tbsp	Dijon mustard (see Tips, left)	15 mL
2 tsp	raw agave nectar (see Tips, page 549)	10 mL
1 tsp	fine sea salt	5 mL
2	cloves garlic	2
1½ cups	extra virgin olive oil (see Tips, left)	375 mL

1. In a saucepan filled with water, bring cashews to a boil. Remove from heat and drain, discarding liquid. Set cashews aside to cool.

2. In food processor fitted with the metal blade, process cooled cashews, ¼ cup (60 mL) water, lemon juice, vinegar, mustard, agave nectar, salt and garlic until smooth, scraping down sides of work bowl as necessary.

3. With the motor running, add oil through the feed tube in a slow, steady stream. Process until smooth and creamy. Transfer to an airtight container and refrigerate for 2 to 3 hours or until firm. Use immediately or keep refrigerated for up to 3 weeks.

Variation

Roasted Garlic Vegan Mayonnaise: In Step 2, omit the garlic. Add ¼ cup (60 mL) roasted garlic cloves and ¼ tsp (1 mL) garlic powder to the blender.

Herb Salt

Seasoned salts are a great way to add flavor — all you need to do is sprinkle some over the finished dish. I love to use this herb salt on a crisp green salad or lightly steamed vegetables with a drizzle of good-quality olive oil.

Tips

To remove the zest from a lemon, I use a fine-tooth grater like the kind made by Microplane. Be careful not to remove the white pith, as it is bitter.

You will need 1½ tsp (7 mL) fresh lemon zest to yield this quantity of dried.

To dry the lemon zest, preheat oven to 300°F (150°C). Place grated zest on a baking sheet lined with parchment paper and heat for 20 to 25 minutes or until completely dried out.

• Food processor

½ cup	fine sea salt	125 mL
1 tsp	dried finely grated lemon zest (see Tips, left)	5 mL
½ tsp	dried basil leaves	2 mL
½ tsp	dried oregano leaves	2 mL
¼ tsp	dried thyme leaves	1 mL
⅛ tsp	garlic powder	0.5 mL

1. In food processor fitted with the metal blade, combine salt, dried lemon zest, basil, oregano, thyme and garlic powder. Process until well incorporated, about 1 minute. Transfer to an airtight container and store at room temperature for up to 2 months.

Variation

Citrus Salt: Omit the basil, oregano, thyme and garlic powder. Increase the amount of dried lemon zest to 1 tbsp (15 mL) and add 1 tbsp (15 mL) dried lime zest, 1 tbsp (15 mL) dried orange zest and 1 tsp (5 mL) dried grapefruit zest. You will need 1 tbsp + 1 tsp (20 mL) each fresh lemon, lime and orange zest and 1½ tsp (7 mL) fresh grapefruit zest to yield these quantities. Use this salt with exotically spiced dishes such as Mediterranean Bean Salad (page 187), Ratatouille (page 333) and Berbere-Spiced Stewed Green Tomatoes (page 334).

Preserved Lemons

These soft citrusy preserves are the perfect topping for dishes such as Sicilian Eggplant Caponata (page 140) and Braised Fennel and Onions with Lentils (page 175). They also make a good addition to soups and stews with Middle Eastern flavors.

Tips

To sterilize the jar, wash it with hot, soapy water and rinse well. Place in a pot and cover with cold water. Bring to a rapid boil and boil for 10 minutes. Using tongs, transfer to a clean kitchen towel and place upside down to dry and cool completely.

For an exotic sweeter variation, use Meyer lemons.

Experiment with different flavorings. For example, add 2 cinnamon sticks or 3 to 4 whole star anise or 1 tsp (5 mL) hot pepper flakes.

One 32 oz (1 L) glass jar with tight-fitting lid, sterilized (see Tips, left)

5	organic lemons (see Tips, left)	5
½ cup	fine sea salt	125 mL
1 tbsp	organic coconut sugar	15 mL

1. Using a sharp knife, cut each lemon almost lengthwise almost into quarters, leaving ½ inch (1 cm) at the bottom intact so the lemon holds together. Gently open up.

2. In a bowl, whisk together salt and sugar. Using your hands, generously coat all surfaces of each lemon with the mixture until evenly covered. Pack lemons into jar. Fill jar with remaining salt and sugar mixture.

3. Gently press down on lemons so they are evenly packed (if necessary, add more salt to make sure they are well covered). Seal jar and set aside in a warm, dark place for 30 days.

4. Once cured, remove lemons from jar and rinse under cool running water to remove excess salt. Discard the pulp — only the rind of preserved lemons is used. Return to a clean, airtight container and refrigerate for up to 1 year.

Gluten-Free Croutons

Croutons give salads body and texture, and they are great scattered over soups, stews and chilis. For a crunchy addition to soups, use them to top French Onion Soup (page 316) or Spring Minestrone (page 317).

Tip

Substitute 1 tbsp (15 mL) chopped fresh thyme leaves for the dried thyme.

- Preheat oven to 425°F (220°C)
- Baking sheet, lined with parchment paper

5 cups	cubed (1 inch/2.5 cm) gluten-free bread	1.25 L
¼ cup	extra virgin olive oil	60 mL
½ tsp	fine sea salt	2 mL
½ tsp	sweet paprika	2 mL
½ tsp	dried thyme leaves (see Tip, left)	2 mL
¼ tsp	garlic powder	1 mL

1. In a large bowl, toss together bread, oil, salt, paprika, thyme and garlic powder, until bread is well coated.
2. Spread in a single layer on prepared baking sheet and bake in preheated oven for 8 to 10 minutes, or until golden brown and crisp. Remove from oven and set aside to cool. Use immediately or transfer to an airtight container and store at room temperature for up to 2 weeks.

Variation

Pesto Croutons: In a food processor fitted with the metal blade, combine 2 cups (500 mL) flat-leaf (Italian) parsley leaves, ¼ cup (60 mL) freshly squeezed lemon juice, ¼ cup (60 mL) extra virgin olive oil and ¼ cup (60 mL) sunflower seeds. Process until smooth. Toss with croutons in Step 1 and bake as directed. Serve over your favorite salad or tossed with pasta.

Gluten-Free Dried Bread Crumbs

To make dried bread crumbs, let Gluten-Free Croutons cool completely after baking. Transfer to a food processor fitted with the metal blade and process until no large pieces remain, stopping the motor to scrape down sides of work bowl as necessary. Transfer to an airtight container and store at room temperature for up to 1 week.

Whipped Non-dairy Butter

This is the perfect butter substitute. The recipe creates a classic firm butter that will melt on toast, can be used in baking and is perfect to slather over Buckwheat Coconut Pancakes (page 23) or Chocolate Hazelnut Waffles (page 25).

**MAKES
2 CUPS (500 ML)**

Tips

Substitute an equal amount of Hemp and Chia Milk (page 64) or Coconut Milk (page 62) for the cashew milk. Keep in mind that the coconut milk will give your butter a slightly stronger coconut flavor.

I like to use unpasteurized apple cider vinegar in this recipe for its superior flavor and nutritional benefits, but conventional apple cider vinegar will work as well.

Refined coconut oil does not have as much coconut flavor as unrefined. You can use extra virgin coconut oil, but the butter will taste like coconut.

Either sunflower or soy lecithin works well for this recipe. Just make sure it is organic, as most lecithins are extracted using chemical processes.

- Food processor
- Ramekin or soufflé dish, lined with plastic wrap, or silicone mold

½ cup	Cashew Milk (page 61; see Tips, left)	125 mL
2 tsp	raw (unpasteurized) apple cider vinegar (see Tips, left)	10 mL
¼ tsp	fine sea salt	1 mL
1¼ cups	melted refined coconut oil (see Tips, left)	300 mL
2 tbsp	grapeseed oil	30 mL
5 tsp	lecithin granules (see Tips, left)	25 mL
½ tsp	ground raw flax seeds	2 mL

1. In a bowl, whisk together cashew milk, vinegar and salt. Cover and set aside for about 20 minutes so milk can curdle.

2. In food processor fitted with the metal blade, combine milk mixture, coconut oil, grapeseed oil, lecithin and ground flax seeds. Process for about 5 minutes, stopping the motor to scrape down sides of work bowl as necessary, until mixture is slightly frothy and lecithin has completely dissolved.

3. Spread mixture evenly in prepared dish, cover tightly with plastic wrap and freeze for at least 3 hours or overnight.

4. Remove from freezer. Immerse dish in hot water to loosen butter and lift out. Transfer to an airtight container and refrigerate for up to 2 months.

Vegan Sour Cream

This sour cream is a staple in my kitchen. You can spread it on any wrap, dollop it on piping-hot soup or use it to garnish dishes such as Slow-Cooked Barbecued Jackfruit (page 369), Black Bean Santa Fe Wraps (page 188), Black Bean and Sweet Potato Chili (page 346) or Cheesy Quesadillas (page 166).

MAKES ABOUT 2 CUPS (500 ML)

Tips

You can use either whole raw cashews or cashew pieces for this recipe.

A citrus reamer is a hand-held tool used to extract the juice from lemons and limes. It is available in most kitchen supply stores and would be ideal to use for the lemon juice in this recipe.

I prefer to use raw (unpasteurized) apple cider vinegar for this recipe, for its superior flavor and nutritional benefits, but regular apple cider vinegar will work as well.

● **Food processor**

2 cups	raw cashews (see Tips, left)	500 mL
1/3 cup	freshly squeezed lemon juice (see Tips, left)	75 mL
1/3 cup	water	75 mL
2 tbsp	raw (unpasteurized) apple cider vinegar (see Tips, left)	30 mL
1 tsp	fine sea salt	5 mL

1. In a saucepan filled with water, bring cashews to a boil. Remove from heat and drain, discarding liquid. Set cashews aside to cool.
2. In food processor fitted with the metal blade, process cooled cashews, lemon juice, water, vinegar and salt until smooth. Serve immediately or transfer to an airtight container and refrigerate for up to 2 weeks.

Variations

Cheesy Chipotle Cream: In Step 2, increase the amount of lemon juice to 1/2 cup (125 mL). Omit the vinegar. Add 3 tbsp (45 mL) nutritional yeast and 1/4 cup (60 mL) chopped chipotle peppers in adobo sauce.

Herbed Sour Cream: To food processor in Step 2, add 1/2 cup (125 mL) chopped fresh flat-leaf (Italian) parsley, 1/4 cup (60 mL) chopped fresh cilantro leaves and 1 sprig fresh dill, chopped. Store refrigerated for up to 1 week.

Vegan Worcestershire Sauce

Use this healthy vegan alternative wherever Worcestershire sauce is called for. This tangy blend is perfect for marinades, brushing on grilled foods, and adding to salad dressings or salads for a boost of flavor, or as a low-sugar substitute for ketchup.

**MAKES
2¾ CUPS (675 ML)**

Tips

To soak the tamarind: Break off a 2-inch (5 cm) piece and place in a bowl with 2 cups (500 mL) hot water; set aside for 1 hour. Drain, discarding liquid. Transfer to a blender or food processor and add ½ cup (125 mL) warm water; process until smooth. Transfer to a fine-mesh sieve set over a bowl and, using the back of a spoon, press pulp through sieve (discard solids).

To remove the skin from fresh gingerroot with the least amount of waste, use the edge of a teaspoon. With a brushing motion, scrape off the skin to reveal the yellow root.

Wheat-free tamari is a gluten-free seasoning made from fermented soybeans. It can be found in most well-stocked supermarkets and natural food stores.

Blender

½ cup	soaked tamarind pulp (see Tips, left)	125 mL
1 tbsp	grapeseed oil	15 mL
¼ cup	chopped onion	60 mL
1 tbsp	minced peeled gingerroot (see Tips, left)	15 mL
2 to 3	cloves garlic, minced	2 to 3
1 cup	raw (unpasteurized) apple cider vinegar (see Tips, page 555)	250 mL
½ cup	freshly squeezed orange juice	125 mL
½ cup	wheat-free tamari (see Tips, left)	125 mL
½ cup	blackstrap molasses	125 mL
¼ cup	water	60 mL
½ tsp	ground cinnamon	2 mL
¼ tsp	ground allspice	1 mL
¼ tsp	ground cloves	1 mL
¼ tsp	fine sea salt	1 mL

1. In a saucepan over medium heat, heat oil. Add onion, ginger and garlic; cook, stirring constantly, until onion is softened and translucent, about 6 minutes. Add tamarind, vinegar, orange juice, tamari, molasses, water, cinnamon, allspice, cloves and salt. Stir to combine and bring mixture to a boil. Reduce heat to a simmer and cook for 25 to 30 minutes or until slightly thickened.

2. Transfer mixture to blender. Blend at high speed until smooth. The sauce will keep for up to 1 month in an airtight container in the refrigerator.

Curry Paste

An aromatic blend of spices and fresh tomato, this mixture can be used as a base for flavorful soups and stews or simply whisked into Basic Vinaigrette (page 548) for an exotic salad dressing variation. Use it instead of store-bought versions, which often contain unwanted additives.

**MAKES
1 CUP (250 ML)**

Tip

The quantity of garlic depends on the size of the cloves. If large, use the smaller number. If small, more may be required.

¼ cup	coconut oil	60 mL
2 tbsp	grapeseed oil	30 mL
½ cup	finely diced onion	125 mL
8 to 10	cloves garlic, minced	8 to 10
2 tbsp	minced gingerroot	30 mL
2 tbsp	ground cumin	30 mL
1 tbsp	ground coriander	15 mL
1 tsp	fennel seeds	5 mL
1 tsp	fenugreek seeds	5 mL
½ tsp	whole coriander seeds	2 mL
½ tsp	ground turmeric	2 mL
¼ tsp	cayenne pepper (optional)	1 mL
1 cup	chopped tomato	250 mL

1. In a saucepan over medium heat, melt together coconut oil and grapeseed oil. Add onion and cook until translucent, about 3 minutes. Add garlic and ginger; cook, stirring frequently, until fragrant (be careful not to burn the garlic), about 12 minutes.

2. Stir in cumin, coriander, fennel seeds, fenugreek seeds, coriander seeds, turmeric and cayenne (if using). Cook, stirring constantly, for 1 minute. Add tomato and cook, stirring constantly, until broken down and soft, 8 to 10 minutes. Remove from heat and set aside to cool. Transfer to an airtight container and refrigerate for up to 2 weeks.

Variations

For a creamier paste that can be used to thicken soups and stews, add ½ cup (125 mL) full-fat coconut milk with the tomatoes.

For a spicier paste, add ¼ cup (60 mL) chopped fresh chile pepper and cook it with the onion.

For a Thai twist, omit the tomato. Replace it with 2 tbsp (30 mL) chopped lemongrass, 2 lime leaves, ¼ cup (60 mL) lime juice, 2 tbsp (30 mL) organic coconut sugar and 2 tbsp (30 mL) wheat-free tamari.

Holiday Gravy

If rich, dark brown gravy is something you missed after becoming vegan, here is a perfect substitute. This recipe is a tasty addition to any holiday meal. I love to serve it alongside Creamy Mashed Potatoes (page 178) or Glazed Lentil Loaf (page 210), with a side of crispy green salad.

<table>
<tr><td colspan="3">MAKES
3 CUPS (750 ML)</td></tr>
</table>

Tips

Button or cremini mushrooms work well in this dish.

Wheat-free tamari is a gluten-free seasoning made from fermented soybeans. It can be found in most well-stocked supermarkets and natural food stores.

Most cornstarch is made from genetically modified corn. Purchase organic cornstarch to avoid GMOs.

Look for unpasteurized brown rice miso in the refrigerated section of your health food store or supermarket. It is gluten-free and, since it is not pasteurized, it has more health benefits than the shelf-stable varieties.

2 tbsp	grapeseed oil	30 mL
½ cup	finely diced onion	125 mL
3 cups	quartered mushrooms (see Tips, left)	750 mL
3	cloves garlic, minced	3
2 tbsp	dry white wine (optional)	30 mL
2 cups	water	500 mL
3 tbsp	wheat-free tamari (see Tips, left)	45 mL
1 tbsp	organic cornstarch (see Tips, left)	15 mL
1 tbsp	cold water	15 mL
1 tbsp	chopped fresh thyme leaves	15 mL
2 tbsp	brown rice miso (see Tips, left)	30 mL

1. In a saucepan over medium heat, heat oil. Add onion and cook until just golden, 7 to 8 minutes. Add mushrooms and cook, stirring occasionally, for 10 minutes or until softened and lightly golden. Stir in garlic and cook for 1 to 2 minutes or until fragrant.

2. Add wine (if using), stirring with a wooden spoon to pick up any brown bits from bottom of pan; cook until very little liquid remains, about 2 minutes. Add water and tamari and bring to a boil. Reduce heat and simmer for 5 minutes.

3. In a small bowl, whisk together cornstarch and cold water until no lumps remain. Add to mushroom mixture. Bring to a boil, reduce heat and simmer for 2 to 3 minutes.

4. Remove from heat and stir in thyme and miso. Serve immediately or cool, transfer to an airtight container and refrigerate for up to 2 weeks. To reheat, transfer to a saucepan and heat over medium heat, stirring frequently, until hot, about 5 minutes.

Vegetable Stock

Making your own stock is easy, and it's a simple way to create a flavorful base for soups and stews. Use it when cooking vegetables or rice to add flavor and nutrients.

Tips

To give your stock a deeper flavor, replace the raw onion with cooked. Cut 1 onion in half lengthwise. In a skillet over high heat, heat 1 tsp (5 mL) grapeseed oil. Add onion halves, cut side down, and cook until golden brown on the bottom, 10 to 12 minutes. Add to the pot with the other vegetables.

Substitute 2 fresh bay leaves for the dried bay leaf.

For additional flavor, you can also add 1 sprig fresh thyme, 8 to 10 sprigs fresh parsley and about 1 cup (250 mL) sliced mushrooms.

- Fine-mesh strainer

16 cups	water	4 L
2 cups	chopped carrots	500 mL
2 cups	chopped celery	500 mL
4 cups	chopped onions (see Tips, left)	1 L
1	medium tomato, halved	1
1	clove garlic, peeled	1
1	bay leaf (see Tips, left)	1
½ tsp	whole black peppercorns	2 mL

1. In a large pot, combine water, carrots, celery, onions, tomato, garlic, bay leaf and peppercorns. Bring to a boil, reduce heat and simmer for 45 minutes (broth will be lightly golden and have a delicious aroma). Remove from heat and pour through fine-mesh strainer, discarding solids. Use immediately or let cool, transfer to an airtight container and refrigerate for up to 2 weeks.

Variation

Dark Vegetable Stock: In a skillet over high heat, heat 1 tbsp (15 mL) grapeseed oil. Add the carrots and celery and cook until golden, about 6 minutes. Add to pot with other vegetables, along with 1 cup (250 mL) sliced portobello mushrooms and 2 tbsp (30 mL) wheat-free tamari. Continue with recipe as directed.

Chickpea Pizza Crust

This recipe is great to make ahead of time and have in the fridge, ready to go for a quick meal. I top my pizza with Classic Garlicky Tomato Sauce (page 110), pan-fried mushrooms, kalamata olives and greens sautéed with white wine and garlic.

MAKES 1 8-INCH (20 CM) CRUST

Tips

For additional flavor, season the flour with your favorite dried herbs. I like to add ½ tsp (2 mL) dried rosemary or dried thyme.

Nutritional yeast is an inactive yeast that is grown on beet molasses and then pasteurized. It provides a rich, cheesy flavor in sauces, stews, soups and dips. Look for it in most well-stocked supermarkets and natural food stores.

1 cup	chickpea flour (see Tips, left)	250 mL
1 tsp	nutritional yeast (see Tips, left)	5 mL
¼ tsp	fine sea salt	1 mL
½ cup	water	125 mL
1 tbsp	grapeseed oil	15 mL

1. In a bowl, whisk together chickpea flour, nutritional yeast and salt. Add water and whisk vigorously until batter is smooth and no lumps remain. Cover and set aside for 30 minutes to rest.

2. In a skillet over medium-high heat, heat oil. Spread batter evenly in pan — it should be about 8 inches (20 cm) in diameter and from ¼ to ⅜ inch (5 to 8 mm) thick. Cook until bubbles begin to form on top and bottom is golden brown, about 3 minutes. Flip and cook other side for 3 minutes, until golden brown.

3. Remove from heat. Use immediately or transfer to an airtight container and refrigerate for up to 5 days.

Variation

Cheesy Chickpea Pizza Crust: In Step 1, increase the amount of nutritional yeast to ¼ cup (60 mL). Add ½ cup (125 mL) Vegan Shredded Mozzarella (page 537) to the batter before cooking.

Vegan Pizza Three Ways

- Preheat oven to 350°F (180°C)

- Baking sheet, lined with parchment paper

Margherita Pizza: Spread cooked Chickpea Pizza Crust with ⅔ cup (150 mL) Classic Garlicky Tomato Sauce (page 110). Top with 8 Vegan Cheese Curds (page 538) and ¼ cup (60 mL) sliced fresh basil leaves. Place on prepared baking sheet and bake in preheated oven for 12 to 15 minutes.

Breakfast Pizza: Spread cooked crust with ⅔ cup (150 mL) Scrambled Tofu with Caramelized Onions, Mushrooms and Peppers (page 30). Top with ¼ cup (60 mL) chopped Tempeh Bacon (page 38) and 2 tsp (10 mL) nutritional yeast. Place on prepared baking sheet and bake in preheated oven for 12 to 15 minutes or until toppings are lightly golden brown.

Easy Cheesy Pizza: Spread cooked crust with ⅔ cup (150 mL) Classic Garlicky Tomato Sauce. Top with ½ cup (125 mL) Creamy Cashew Ricotta (page 532), ⅔ cup (150 mL) Vegan Shredded Mozzarella and 2 tsp (10 mL) nutritional yeast. Place on prepared baking sheet and bake in preheated oven for 15 minutes.

All-Purpose Gluten-Free Flour Blend

Premix this blend and keep it in your pantry so you can bake up your favorite gluten-free recipes any time. Many of the recipes in this book use this go-to blend.

MAKES ABOUT 4 CUPS (1 L)

Tips

This recipe can easily be doubled or tripled.

For a pleasant mouthfeel, the brown rice and sorghum flours should be finely milled. If you have any questions, ask your purveyor.

1½ cups	finely milled brown rice flour (see Tips, left)	375 mL
1½ cups	finely milled sorghum flour	375 mL
⅔ cup	tapioca flour	150 mL
⅔ cup	arrowroot starch	150 mL

1. In a bowl, whisk together rice flour, sorghum flour, tapioca flour and arrowroot. Transfer to an airtight container and store at room temperature, away from light, for up to 3 months or freeze for up to 1 year.

Vegan Piecrust

Use this flaky gluten-free recipe whenever a traditional piecrust is called for. It's perfect for fruit pies.

Tips

When working with any flour, particularly those that are gluten-free, whisk before measuring. This aerates the flour and ensures more accurate measuring. Be sure to use a dry measure (not a glass measuring cup) and to level off with the side of a knife.

Chilling the dough before rolling and baking cools the fat from the coconut oil and butter, which yields a flakier crust.

- **10-inch (25 cm) glass pie plate, lightly oiled**

1 cup	brown rice flour, plus extra for dusting	250 mL
½ cup	chickpea flour	125 mL
½ cup	buckwheat flour	125 mL
⅓ cup	arrowroot starch	75 mL
1 tbsp	potato starch	15 mL
3 tbsp	organic coconut sugar	45 mL
Pinch	fine sea salt	Pinch
½ cup	melted coconut oil	125 mL
⅓ cup	coconut butter	75 mL
¾ cup	water	175 mL

1. In a bowl, whisk together brown, chickpea and buckwheat flours, arrowroot, potato starch, coconut sugar and salt. Set aside.

2. In a small bowl, whisk together coconut oil and coconut butter (mixture should be thick and creamy). Add water and whisk vigorously to combine. Add to dry ingredients and stir well (dough should be slightly sticky, with no lumps). Turn out onto a lightly floured work surface and shape into a rough disk. Wrap in plastic wrap and refrigerate for about 30 minutes to rest.

Rolling out a Double Piecrust

3. Divide chilled dough in half. On a floured clean work surface, roll out one portion into a circle(see Tip, page 563). Roll pastry loosely around rolling pin, then unroll over pie plate. Press into pie plate, bringing it up the sides of the pan and just over the edges. Trim edges as necessary.

4. Fill pie with desired filling.

5. Roll out remaining dough as above. Roll pastry loosely around rolling pin, then unroll over filling, covering completely. Using the tines of a fork, push down gently around the edges to seal the crust. Trim excess dough as necessary. Using a knife, cut a few slits in the top of the pie to allow steam to escape.

Tip

The rolled-out dough should be about 2 inches (5 cm) bigger in diameter than the pie plate you are using. Check by laying the prepared pie plate upside down on top.

6. Brush top crust with a little non-dairy milk and bake according to recipe instructions.

Variation

Savory Piecrust: For a double piecrust suitable for a savory filling, omit the coconut sugar. Add 1 tbsp (15 mL) chopped fresh thyme leaves and 1 tbsp (15 mL) nutritional yeast. Increase the salt to $\frac{1}{4}$ tsp (1 mL).

Blind-Baking a Single Piecrust

To prepare a single piecrust: Replace the ingredients with $\frac{1}{2}$ cup (125 mL) brown rice flour, plus extra for dusting, $\frac{1}{4}$ cup (60 mL) chickpea flour, $\frac{1}{4}$ cup (60 mL) buckwheat flour, 3 tbsp (45 mL) arrowroot starch, 2 tsp (10 mL) potato starch, 2 tbsp (30 mL) organic coconut sugar, a pinch fine sea salt, $\frac{1}{4}$ cup (60 mL) melted coconut oil, $\frac{1}{4}$ cup (60 mL) coconut butter and $\frac{1}{3}$ cup (75 mL) water. Complete Steps 1 to 3 above.

3. Refrigerate crust for 15 minutes to rest.

4. Using the tines of a fork, poke holes in crust to allow steam to escape. Lay a piece of parchment paper on top of crust. Pour about $\frac{1}{4}$ cup (60 mL) dried beans onto parchment. Preheat oven to 425°F (220°C) and bake in preheated oven for 12 to 15 minutes or until crust is golden brown all over. Carefully remove parchment and beans.

Quinoa Tempura Batter

Batter and fry almost any vegetable with this light tempura coating for a flavorful crispy appetizer or snack. The trick to good tempura batter is to make sure the water you are using is cold.

Tips

Use either quinoa flour you have purchased or grind your own.

To grind quinoa flour: Place ¾ cup (175 mL) quinoa in a blender. Blend at high speed until flour-like in consistency.

Nutritional yeast is an inactive yeast that is grown on beet molasses and then pasteurized. It provides a rich, cheesy flavor in sauces, stews, soups and dips. Look for it in most well-stocked supermarkets and natural food stores.

This batter should be used the same day it is made. If making it ahead of time, use within a couple of hours. In that case, reduce the water to ¾ cup (175 mL) and add ¼ cup (60 mL) crushed ice cubes. Cover and refrigerate until ready to use (the ice cubes will melt slowly and keep the batter cold).

1 cup	quinoa flour (see Tips, left)	250 mL
1 cup	cold water (see Tips, left)	250 mL
2 tbsp	nutritional yeast (see Tips, left)	30 mL
½ tsp	fine sea salt	2 mL
¼ tsp	sweet paprika	1 mL
Pinch	cayenne pepper	Pinch

1. In a bowl, whisk together quinoa flour, cold water, nutritional yeast, salt, paprika and cayenne. Use immediately or transfer to an airtight container and refrigerate for up to 2 hours (see Tips, left).

Variation

Asian-Style Tempura Batter: Replace the nutritional yeast and paprika with 2 tbsp (30 mL) wheat-free tamari, 1 tbsp (15 mL) toasted sesame oil, 2 tsp (10 mL) wasabi powder and 1 tsp (5 mL) raw black sesame seeds.

How to Make Vegetable Tempura

1. Using a sharp knife, cut vegetables (such as red bell peppers, zucchini or sweet potatoes) into slices ¼ inch (0.5 cm) thick.

2. In a deep skillet over medium heat, heat grapeseed oil to 375°F (190°C) — use enough oil to cover the vegetables you are using. (Alternatively, use a deep-fryer if you have one.)

3. Toss vegetables in Quinoa Tempura Batter until well coated. Using metal tongs and working in batches, add vegetables to hot oil, standing back to avoid splatters. Be careful not to overcrowd the pan. Deep-fry for 2 to 3 minutes, until golden. Using a spider or slotted spoon, transfer to a plate lined with paper towels to absorb excess oil. Repeat with remaining vegetables, making sure oil temperature remains at 375°F (190°C). Serve immediately.

Whipped Coconut Cream

Being a vegan doesn't mean you can't enjoy luscious whipped cream. Use this light, fluffy cream anywhere whipped cream is called for. It's particularly good served with fresh summer berries and a sprinkling of ground cinnamon, or as a topping for Fresh Berry Sabayon (page 481) or a Hot Fudge Sundae (page 487).

Tips

Before using, place the can of coconut milk in the refrigerator for at least 30 minutes.

Substitute ½ tsp (2 mL) alcohol-free vanilla extract for the vanilla powder.

Substitute 1 tbsp (15 mL) agave nectar or coconut nectar for the maple syrup.

- Mixing bowl, chilled in the freezer
- Electric mixer

1	can (14 oz/398 mL) full-fat coconut milk, chilled (see Tips, left)	1
¼ tsp	organic vanilla powder (see Tips, left and page 7)	1 mL
2 tbsp	pure maple syrup (see Tips, left)	30 mL

1. Flip chilled can of coconut milk upside down and open can. Carefully scoop out solid cream that has separated out. (Reserve remaining liquid in an airtight container in the refrigerator for up to 3 days. Use in recipes that call for light coconut milk.)

2. In chilled mixing bowl, using electric mixer at high speed, whip coconut cream for 4 to 5 minutes, or until soft peaks begin to form. Add vanilla and maple syrup and whip for 1 to 2 minutes more, until stiff peaks form.

3. Serve immediately or transfer to an airtight container and refrigerate for up to 1 week.

Variations

Chocolate Whipped Cream: Add 2 tbsp (30 mL) raw cacao powder along with the vanilla. Increase maple syrup to 3 tbsp (45 mL).

Citrus Whipped Cream: Add 2 tsp (10 mL) finely grated lemon zest, 1 tsp (5 mL) finely grated lime zest and a dash of fresh lemon juice along with the vanilla and maple syrup.

Orange Espresso Whipped Cream: Add 1 tbsp (15 mL) finely grated orange zest, a dash of freshly squeezed orange juice and 1 tsp (5 mL) pure coffee extract along with the vanilla and maple syrup.

Index

A

Açai Superfood Bowl, 21
African-Spiced Tempeh Chili, 348
agar, 14
agave nectar, 8
All-Purpose Gluten-Free Flour Blend, 561
almonds and almond flour, 13–14. *See also* almond butter; almond milk; nuts
  Almond Milk, 61
  Chocolate Almond Biscotti, 438
  Cookie Dough Pudding, 507
  Fall Harvest Squash Milk, 69
  Holiday Milk, 70
  Lemon Vanilla Biscotti, 437
  Spicy Pumpkinseed Parmesan (variation), 539
  Teriyaki Almonds, 150
  Vanilla Almond Butter, 128
  Watermelon "Cake", 478
  Whoopie Pie Smoothie, 56
almond butter
  Almond Beurre Blanc, 127
  Almond Oat Apple Wedges, 145
  Apricot Almond Squares, 494
  Banana Goji Cookies, 430
  Chickpea Popcorn Mix, 149
  Grilled Portobellos with Sweet Potato Gratin and Sautéed Green Beans, 390
  Oat Clusters, 156
  Stuffed Medjool Dates, 146
almond milk. *See also* milk (non-dairy); smoothies
  Baked Onion Rings, 87
  Berry Oat Bars, 157
  Blueberry Cheesecake, 458
  Bread Pudding, Traditional, 508
  Buttermilk Biscuits, 464
  Chai Almond Milk, 66
  Cheddar and Chive Biscuits, 466
  Cheesy Fondue, 84
  Cheesy Grits with Spinach, 31
  Coconut-Crusted French Toast, 24
  Creamy Citrus Polenta, 231
  Creamy Vegan Pepper Jack, 534
  Grilled Portobellos with Sweet Potato Gratin and Sautéed Green Beans, 390
  Mushroom and Asparagus Bread Pudding, 473
  Mushroom and Spinach Lasagna, 274
  Peach Cinnamon Sherbet, 528
  Quinoa-Crusted Onion Rings, 236
  Slow-Cooked Apple Cinnamon Oatmeal, 20
  Smoky Corn Chowder, 331
  Strawberry Sherbet, 527
  Vegan Benedict, 32
  Vegan Cheese Curds, 538
amaranth, 10
  Amaranth and Millet Balls, 234
  Amaranth Oatmeal, 18

apples. *See also* applesauce
  Almond Oat Apple Wedges, 145
  Apple Crisp, 452
  Apple Pie, 454
  Apple Strudel Loaf, 448
  Coconut-Crusted Tempeh with Sweet Potato Mash, 408
  Double Detox Smoothie, 54
  Easy Apple Pie Smoothie, 55
  The Gardener's Juice, 44
  Hemp Apple Rings, 144
  Holiday Lentil Loaf with Quinoa, 382
  Island-Time Juice, 46
  Kick-Me-Up Juice, 48
  Kitchen Sink Smoothie, 53
  Lawnmower Juice, 42
  Morning Glory Muffins, 442
  Muddy Waters, 43
  Pink Sunset Juice, 45
  Pop-Tart Juice, 47
  Slow-Cooked Apple Cinnamon Oatmeal, 20
  Spiced Apple Buckwheat Granola, 153
  Spiced Apple Juice, 48
  Spiced Holiday Juice, 49
  Warming Apple Juice, 49
  Wild Rice Stuffing, 180
applesauce
  Banana Bread, 445
  Banana Goji Cookies, 430
  Blueberry Squares, 447
  Lemon Poppyseed Muffins, 440
Apricot Almond Squares, 494
arrowroot starch, 14
arugula
  Green Tomato Carpaccio with Balsamic Arugula, 105
  Grilled Pepper and Navy Bean Salad, 186
  Spanakopita Pie with Red Pepper Slaw and Lemon Dijon Arugula, 422
Asian-Style Adzuki Bean Salad, 185
Avgolemono Soup, 315
avocado
  Avocado and Cucumber Salad, 543
  Avocado Spinach Smoothie, 51
  Avocado Tempura, 97
  The Big Salad, 541
  Black Bean Santa Fe Wraps, 188
  Breakfast Club Sandwich, 27
  Easy Burritos, 189
  Grasshopper Pie, 504
  Guacamole, Perfect, 81
  Jerk Tofu, Avocado and Plantain Wraps, 360
  Layered Tortillas, 418
  Mini Soft Tacos, 92
  Roasted Cauliflower and Chickpea Tacos, 196
  Silky Chocolate Mousse (variation), 505
  Sushi Wraps, 94

B

bacon (tempeh)
  Breakfast Club Sandwich, 27
  Breakfast Pizza, 561
  Breakfast Wrap, 28
  Fettuccini Carbonara, 263
  Loaded Baked Potatoes with Ginger Broccoli, 370
  Mushroom Colcannon, 364
  Stuffed Sweet Potatoes with Garlic-Braised Greens, 366
Balsamic Vinaigrette, 548
bananas. *See also* smoothies
  Banana Bread, 445
  Banana Goji Cookies, 430
  Banana Tempura, 489
  Buckwheat Coconut Pancakes, 23
  Chai-Spiced Muffins, 439
  Chocolate Banana Cake, 503
  Chocolate Banana Parfaits, 488
  Coconut-Crusted French Toast, 24
  Dessert Pancakes, 491
  The Elvis Wrap, 29
  Grasshopper Pie, 504
  Slow-Cooked Apple Cinnamon Oatmeal, 20
  Watermelon "Cake" (variation), 478
bars and squares, 157–65, 444
Basil Lemon Ice Cream, 514
beans, 10. *See also* peas
  Asian-Style Adzuki Bean Salad, 185
  Basic Slow-Cooked Legumes, 182
  Black Bean and Sweet Potato Chili, 346
  Black Bean and Sweet Potato Chowder, 332
  Black Bean Burgers, 208
  Black Bean Santa Fe Wraps, 188
  Black Bean Tortilla Bake, 205
  Blueberry Cheesecake, 458
  Buddhist Noodle Bowl, 286
  Charred Cauliflower and White Bean Soup, 330
  Creamy Pinto Bean Salad, 184
  Deep Chocolate Brownies, 444
  Dirty Brown Rice with Black Beans, 222
  Edamame Hummus, 73
  Ginger Lime Edamame Stir-Fry, 300
  Grilled Pepper and Navy Bean Salad, 186
  Grilled Portobellos with Sweet Potato Gratin and Sautéed Green Beans, 390
  Italian-Style Red Bean Meatballs, 206
  Layered Tortillas, 418
  Lemon Parsley Lupini Beans, 200
  Macrobiotic Platter, 363
  Maple Baked Beans, 204
  Mediterranean Bean Salad, 187
  Mexican Pozole, Traditional, 242
  Mung Bean Daal, 199
  Mushroom, Black Bean and Sweet Potato Ragoût, 339

ginger (*continued*)
Island-Time Juice, 46
Lemon-Lime Fusion Juice, 40
Lemon Tamari Ginger Dip, 113
Liquid Chlorophyll Juice, 41
Loaded Baked Potatoes with
Ginger Broccoli, 370
Matcha Me Green Juice, 41
Muddy Waters, 43
Orange Ginger Sauce, 114
Sautéed Ginger Miso Tempeh, 297
Soba Noodles with Sesame Ginger
Tempeh, 284
Spicy Ginger Juice, 47
Squash and Ginger Tofu, 374
Stir-Fried Broccoli with Ginger and
Hoisin, 301
Strawberry Rhubarb Crumble
(variation), 451
Sweet Potato, Ginger and Coconut
Soup, 319
Triple Ginger Cookies, 428
Warming Apple Juice, 49
Gnocchi in Tomato Sauce, 253
goji berries. *See also* berries; fruit,
dried
Banana Goji Cookies, 430
Strawberry Goji Berry Ice Cream,
516
grains, 10–12. *See also specific grains*
grapefruit and grapefruit juice
Creamy Citrus Polenta, 231
Minted Grapefruit Granita, 509
Pink Sunset Juice, 45
grapes
Kick-Me-Up Juice, 48
Pop-Tart Juice, 47
Strawberry Kiwi Smoothie
(variation), 50
Grasshopper Pie, 504
Greek-Style Gyro Wraps, 362
Greek-Style Potatoes with Charred
Eggplant, 416
Greek-Style Vegetable Skewers, 98
Green Goddess Wraps, 192
Green Milk, 64
greens. *See also* arugula; kale; lettuce;
spinach
Beet Cakes with Braised Fennel
and Creamed Swiss Chard, 376
Classic Green Smoothie, 51
Collard-Wrapped Sushi Rolls, 95
Double Detox Smoothie, 54
Green Goddess Wraps, 192
Moroccan-Style Collard Greens,
335
Spicy Southern-Style Slow-Cooked
Collard Greens, 173
Stuffed Sweet Potatoes with Garlic-
Braised Greens, 366
green tea. *See* tea
Green Tomato Carpaccio with
Balsamic Arugula, 105

H

hazelnuts and hazelnut butter
Chocolate Hazelnut Butter, 137
Chocolate Hazelnut Waffles, 25
Fluffernutter Sandwich, 26
Pure Chocolate Hazelnut Milk, 68
Strawberry Hazelnut Milk, 65

hemp seeds. *See also* seeds
Best Stovetop Protein Popcorn, 149
Cucumber Protein Cups, 143
Date-Me Bars, 158
Earl Grey Smoothie, 54
Hemp Apple Rings, 144
Hibiscus Melon Smoothie, 52
Mini Soft Tacos, 92
Peanut Butter Hemp Power Bars,
163
Poached Tofu with Vegetables in
Cheesy Hemp Sauce, 402
Polenta Cakes with Olive, Tomato
and Spinach Ragoût, 406
Quinoa Maple Berry Porridge, 21
Scrambled Tofu with Caramelized
Onions, Mushrooms and Peppers
(variation), 30
Herbed Cashew and Kale Hummus,
74
Herbed Roasted Potatoes, 179
Herbed Rösti Bake, 168
Herbed Tofu Ricotta, 530
Herb Salt, 551
Hibiscus Melon Smoothie, 52
Holiday Gravy, 558
Holiday Lentil Loaf with Quinoa, 382
Holiday Milk, 70
Hollandaise Sauce, 122
Hot Chocolate, 67
Hot Fudge Sundae, 487
hummus, 72–75
The Big Salad, 541
Easy Burritos, 189
Green Goddess Wraps, 192
Grilled Veggie Wraps, 193
Hummus Wraps, 191
Mediterranean Wraps, 190
Middle Eastern Platter, 426

I

ice creams, 512–26
Indian-Spiced Date Squares, 492
Indonesian Black Rice Salad, 216
Irish Soda Bread, 472
Island-Time Juice, 46
Italian-Style Red Bean Meatballs, 206

J

jalapeño peppers. *See* peppers, chile
Jasmine Rice Salad, 214
Jerk Tempeh with Plantains and
Mango Salsa, 412
Jerk Tofu, Avocado and Plantain
Wraps, 360
juices, 40–49

K

kale. *See also* greens; vegetables
The Big Salad, 541
Detoxifier Juice, 42
Easy Cheesy Kale Chips, 147
The Gardener's Juice, 44
Green Milk, 64
Herbed Cashew and Kale
Hummus, 74
Kitchen Sink Smoothie, 53
Lawnmower Juice, 42
Liquid Chlorophyll Juice, 41

Matcha Me Green Juice, 41
Muddy Waters, 43
Mushroom Colcannon, 364
Poached Tofu with Vegetables in
Cheesy Hemp Sauce, 402
Shred-Me-Up Slaw, 544
Spicy Ginger Juice (variation), 47
Springtime Smoothie (variation),
52
Key Lime Pie Bars, 161
Kick-Me-Up Juice, 48
Kitchen Sink Smoothie, 53
Korean-Style Tofu Tacos, 392

L

Lawnmower Juice, 42
Layered Tortillas, 418
leeks
Leek, Potato and Lentil Soup, 320
Mushroom and Asparagus Bread
Pudding, 473
Mushroom Colcannon, 364
Tofu en Papillote, 396
legumes, 15–16. *See also* beans;
lentils; peas
Basic Slow-Cooked Legumes, 182
lemon
Basic Chickpea Hummus, 72
Basil Lemon Ice Cream, 514
Citrus Sorbet, 511
Creamy Citrus Polenta, 231
Creamy Pinto Bean Salad, 184
Curried Zucchini Hummus, 75
Easy Cheesy Pasta Sauce, 540
Fettuccini with Lemon Parsley
White Wine Sauce, 254
Herb Salt, 551
Lemonade Smoothie, 53
Lemon Dill Cucumber Dressing,
547
Lemon-Lime Fusion Juice, 40
Lemon Parsley Lupini Beans, 200
Lemon Poppyseed Muffins, 440
Lemon Tamari Ginger Dip, 113
Lemon Vanilla Biscotti, 437
Lemon Vanilla Cashew Yogurt, 18
Middle Eastern Platter, 426
Preserved Lemons, 552
Sautéed Olives with Lemon, Garlic
and Fresh Herbs, 290
Spaetzle in Lemon Garlic Sauce,
256
Spanakopita Pie with Red Pepper
Slaw and Lemon Dijon Arugula,
422
Spicy Ginger Juice, 47
Tofu Squash Ravioli in Lemon Sage
Cream Sauce, 272
Vanilla Chai Power Bars (variation),
159
Warming Apple Juice, 49
lemongrass
Coconut Green Curry Angel Hair,
282
Curry Paste (variation), 557
Lemongrass Ice Cream, 515
Tofu and Lemongrass Vegetable
Coconut Curry, 306
Tom Yum Soup, 324
Yellow Coconut Curry Sauce
(variation), 118

Library and Archives Canada Cataloguing in Publication

McNish, Douglas, author
   Vegan everyday : 500 delicious recipes / Douglas McNish.

Includes index.
ISBN 978-0-7788-0499-4 (pbk.)

   1. Vegan cooking. 2. Cookbooks. I. Title.

TX837.M294 2015   641.5'636   C2015-900157-9